Natural Gas Flaring & Energy Transition

Energy and Environmental Law and Policy Series

VOLUME 44

Editor

Introduction

Environmental protection and energy efficiency/security are important societal challenges. In order to tackle them, policy and legal frameworks are developed at national, regional and global level. Through study and best practices development, the challenges will prove to be solvable.

Contents/Subjects

Environment/Nature/Energy/Climate.

Objective

The aim of this series is to publish works of excellent quality that focus on the study of energy and environmental policy. Through this series the editors:

- contribute to the improvement of the quality of energy/environmental law and policy in general and environmental quality and energy efficiency in particular; increase the access to environmental and energy information for academics, non-governmental organizations, government institutions, and business; and
- facilitate cooperation between academic and non-academic communities in the field of energy and environmental law and policy throughout the world.

Readership

Academics and practitioners in environmental and energy matters.

The titles published in this series are listed at the end of this volume.

Natural Gas Flaring & Energy Transition

Laws, Policies and Regulations

Edited by

Eduardo G. Pereira
Magnus C. Abraham-Dukuma
Opeyemi Y. Omotuyi

Wolters Kluwer

Published by:
Kluwer Law International B.V.
PO Box 316
2400 AH Alphen aan den Rijn
The Netherlands
E-mail: lrs-sales@wolterskluwer.com
Website: www.wolterskluwer.com/en/solutions/kluwerlawinternational

Sold and distributed by:
Wolters Kluwer Legal & Regulatory U.S.
920 Links Avenue
Landisville, PA 17538
United States of America
E-mail: customer.service@wolterskluwer.com

ISBN 978-94-035-2617-1

e-Book: ISBN 978-94-035-2627-0
web-PDF: ISBN 978-94-035-2637-9

Editors

Eduardo G. Pereira is a worldwide recognized scholar specializing in Natural Resources and Energy Law. Prof. Pereira has been active in the natural resources and energy industry for more than 15 years and is an international expert on oil, gas and energy contracts and regulations. Prof. Pereira experience in this area – both academic and practical – is extensive. Prof. Pereira has practical experience in over 50 jurisdictions covering America, Europe, Africa and Asia. Prof. Pereira concluded his doctoral thesis on oil and gas joint ventures at the University of Aberdeen (Scotland). Prof. Pereira conducted postdoctoral research at the Oxford Institute for Energy Studies (University of Oxford, UK), the Scandinavian Institute of Maritime Law (University of Oslo, Norway), the Institute of Energy and Environment (University of São Paulo, Brazil), the Canadian Institute of Resources Law (University of Calgary, Canada) and more recently at the Naval War College (Brazilian Navy, Brazil). Prof. Pereira possesses positions as a full-time, part-time, honorary, adjunct, and/or visiting scholar at several leading academic institutions worldwide. Prof. Pereira is also a series editor for the Global South Series at the Journal of Sustainable Development Law and Policy and an associate editor of OGEL. Prof. Pereira is also the author and editor of several leading oil and gas textbooks. Further information about his profile can be found at www.eduardogpereira.com."

Magnus C. Abraham-Dukuma is a legal and policy researcher specializing in climate change mitigation, including reducing gas flaring and other emissions, just transitions, and preventing the tragedy of the commons in an energy- and post-energy transition world. He has published extensively in law, policy, and interdisciplinary journals. Magnus holds an LL B and BL (Nigeria), an LLM in Oil and Gas Law (Aberdeen, Scotland), and a PhD in International Energy and Climate Law (Waikato, New Zealand). A barrister and solicitor of the Supreme Court of Nigeria, he is also a Senior Fellow at the Just Transition Network, Jakarta, Indonesia.

Opeyemi Y. Omotuyi is a law lecturer at the Federal University Oye-Ekiti, Nigeria. As an academic, she has built a research niche for herself in the area of sustainable development. Her research expertise borders on the deployment of law as an instrument of social change particularly, the realization of the global sustainable development agenda. Some of her research output in the areas of climate change, energy transition, EHS management, and oil and gas decommissioning, among others, have been published as scholarly articles and book chapters in various reputable journals and textbooks. She holds an LLB (Nigeria), LLM (Cape Town), and PhD (Witwatersrand, Johannesburg).

Contributors

Timothy Affonso is a Deputy Dean at the Faculty of Law at the University of the West Indies, St. Augustine Campus. He is also a Tutor at the Hugh Wooding Law School where he teaches constitutional law and law and legal systems. He is an attorney-at-law with over 18 years' of experience. He is a national scholarship winner and a Chevening Scholar. He holds a Bachelors of Laws Degree from UWI, Cave Hill Campus, a Master of Laws Degree, with Distinction, from the University College London and a Doctor of Philosophy in Public International Law and International Human Rights Law from the UWI, Cave Hill Campus. He is a Director and co-chair of the Caribbean Centre for Human Rights and a founding member of the International Law Association (Caribbean Branch).

Oluwabunmi Temitope Akinleye is a Barrister and Solicitor of the Supreme Court of Nigeria and a Lecturer in the Department of Public and International Law, Faculty of Law, Federal University Oye-Ekiti Nigeria. She is a PhD research student in the Faculty of Law, Ekiti State University Ado-Ekiti with research interests in environmental law, climate change law, oil and gas law and natural resource law.

Mostapha Al-Masry is a PhD *(Cand.)* in Petroleum Contracts, Energy Law & International Maritime Law (IUL), LLM in Business Law (LU). Their academic journey has been marked by a fervent interest in Energy Law, Petroleum Contracts and Governance, and International Maritime Law fields. With a passion for legal scholarship in the field of Energy and Petroleum, Mostapha has authored numerous articles in both Arabic and English, contributing significantly to the discourse surrounding Sustainable Development and Energy Transition. Mostapha is an Energy Law Expert and Guest Speaker at international prestigious universities, bringing cutting-edge insights on Petroleum Contracts, Environmental Sustainability and Energy Transition to prestigious institutions worldwide. Mostapha is a Practicing Legal Advisory before Lebanese Companies as a Business Contracts Manager.

Catherine Banet is a Professor of law specializing in Energy Law, at the Department for Energy and Resources Law, of the University of Oslo, Norway. She is a member of the

Academic Advisory Group of the Section on Energy, Environment and Infrastructure Law of the International Bar Association, and Chair of the Board of the Norwegian Energy Law Association. She is the Academic co-Director at the Centre on Regulation in Europe (CERRE).

Nuno Monteiro Dente is a lawyer practicing in Portugal and Angola and was also an associate in the Lisbon office of the Brazilian law firm Xavier, Bernardes & Bragança. He holds a law degree from the Faculty of Law of the University of Coimbra, Portugal. He also has postgraduate qualifications in management and taxation. He specializes in public law and is a member of the Centre for Public Law Studies at the Law Faculty of Agostinho Neto University in Luanda, Angola. He is also a member of the International Energy Law Training and Research Company and the International Energy Law Advisory Group.

Lei Ding is a master's student majoring in law at the Law School of Ningxia University.

Colton Edwards is an Associate at Holland & Hart, LLP. He is a graduate of the University of Wyoming College of Law, where he was the Salt Creek Energy Excellence Scholar. During law school, he was the Occidental Teaching and Research Fellow. Colton's practice includes all forms of energy production, including oil and gas, renewable energy, and mining.

Scarlett Forrest graduated from Virginia Tech in 2016 with a BS in Environmental Science and had a five-year career at an environmental consulting and engineering firm before attending law school at the University of Wyoming. She received her JD from the University of Wyoming College of Law in May 2024 and received her license to practice law the following October. She currently works as a researcher at the University of Wyoming School of Energy Resources.

Reg Fowler is a senior legal consultant admitted to practice in England & Wales, presently working for clients in the voluntary carbon and recycling markets. He has more than 25 years' of experience working in-house with three oil majors, in the U.K., Russia, Kazakhstan and Denmark. His experience includes oil and gas trading, derivatives, joint-venture governance, and production-sharing agreements. He has written or contributed to books on joint operating agreements, contract stabilization, oil trading, investor-state contracts, ESG due diligence and investment agreements.

Juan Gerolis is an associate in the Corporate and M&A, Energy and Africa practices of Tauil e Chequer Advogados in association with Mayer Brown in the Rio de Janeiro office. He is a Lawyer with an LLB Degree in Law from the University of the State of Rio de Janeiro—UERJ. His practice focuses on the O&G sector, particularly in the upstream and midstream sectors. Juan has experience in various cross-border projects, including corporate reorganizations, international and domestic contracts, and complex regulatory issues. His work includes conducting due diligence, analyzing and drafting contracts and drafting memoranda on various legal and contractual issues.

Keith B. Hall is the Nesser Family Chair in Energy Law at Louisiana State University, where he serves as Director of both the Mineral Law Institute and LSU's John P. Laborde Energy Law Center. He teaches oil and gas law courses, other energy law courses, and property law. He is the co-author of three books on oil and gas law and is co-editor of another. Before joining the LSU faculty in 2012, Professor Hall practiced law in New Orleans for 16 years. He also has taught energy law classes at Baku State University, the University of Pittsburgh, and Loyola University.

Eti Best Herbert is a Barrister and Solicitor of the Supreme Court of Nigeria and a Research Fellow at the College of Law, Bowen University, Iwo. He obtained a Master of Laws Degree from the University of Ibadan with distinction and academic prizes. He has a voracious appetite for legal research, with a particular interest in Taxation Law, Energy Law, Environmental Law and International Investment Law. He also engages in private legal practice and research consultancy.

Allan Ingelson is a distinguished Professor in the Faculty of Law & the Haskayne School of Business at the University of Calgary. He has taught numerous Canadian and international oil and gas law and petroleum land management courses during the last three decades including in the Global Energy Executive MBA Program. Professor Ingelson is the Executive Director of the Canadian Institute of Resources Law and General Editor of the Canada Energy Law Service. He has published numerous scholarly energy and environmental law in journals including the *Journal of World Energy Law & Business* and the *Journal of Energy & Natural Resources Law*.

Vanna Jankiepersad is an Attorney-at-Law, admitted to practice in Trinidad and Tobago. She is the holder of a Master of Laws (Distinction), specializing in the area of Legislative Drafting; a Bachelor of Laws (Honours) and a Legal Education Certificate. She is also a National Scholar. Ms. Jankiepersad serves as Legal Counsel to the Minister in the Office of the Attorney General and Ministry of Legal Affairs, Trinidad and Tobago, and has worked on a plethora of legislation and on complex legal matters on a wide range of issues. Her recent contribution to the standardization of oil and gas and energy contracts has solidified her expertise in the field of oil and gas law.

Aaron E. Koenck is a hardworking and driven litigator dedicated to producing results for his clients. Early experience with two National-Tier-1-ranked firms provided a solid foundation for representing energy clients in high-profile, catastrophic petroleum releases and petrochemical accidents, including Mass Tort litigation. This early experience has given Aaron a firm foundation for handling complex matters in state and federal courts. That experience and a strong work ethic quickly earned him the title of one of Texas's Rising Stars in litigation. Aaron represents clients in complex, high-stakes commercial and personal injury disputes relating to oil and gas (upstream, midstream, and downstream), marine, and contract matters. As a litigator, Aaron brings the grit, endurance, and accountability he earned as a former collegiate athlete at one of the NCAA's most respected Division I Track & Field programs. Those qualities are key to his success in demanding and high-stakes litigation. Aaron credits his accomplishments to his public-school educator parents, who instilled the importance of curiosity and determination in their children, which may explain why all four became NCAA Division I honor-roll student-athletes.

Bárbara Leite is an associate in the Corporate and M&A, Energy and Africa practices of Tauil & Chequer Advogados in association with Mayer Brown in the Rio de Janeiro office. She is a Lawyer with an LLB Degree in Law from the University of the State of Rio de Janeiro—UERJ. Bárbara focuses her practice on advising national and foreign O&G companies, having experience in the upstream and midstream segments, including biofuels. Bárbara has experience in corporate restructuring, international contracts and typical contracts of the oil industry. She also works in regulatory consultancy and administrative demands with government entities.

Ricardo Nery partner at the Portuguese firm RSA with extensive experience as a commercial/corporate lawyer in Portugal, Angola and Mozambique, namely in: Legal advice in international/national operations with expertise in projects, infrastructure, property and construction transactions; Structuring and restructuring various business and investments (all involving foreign direct investment) in the fields of energy, construction, banking, hotels, transport, heavy industry and others; Negotiating/structuring loan financing with international financing institutions and ECA's; Advising international cross border operations like mergers and acquisitions, joint ventures, etc.; Corporate legal support in commercial, corporate law.

Areas of activity: International Commercial Contracts; Syndicated Loans and Banking Transactions; Oil & Gas Law; Foreign Investment; Corporate law, M&A, Aviation law and International transactions.

Waniss Almashri Otman is a petroleum economist and analyst, who specializes in the area of risk and uncertainty analysis. He holds a PhD in risk analysis of investment in the upstream oil and gas sector (Aberdeen University, Scotland, U.K.) in 2005, as well as related Degrees; MSc (Petroleum Engineering, U.K.), LLM (International Law and Diplomacy, U.K.), MSc (Petroleum Economics and Engineering, U.K.), and BSc (Petroleum Engineering, Libya). This perspective has strengthened his background in areas of risk and uncertainty analysis of the petroleum industry. He has practical experience in the oil and gas industry, in executive positions, as an advisor and as a consultant to NOCs and IOCs. During his career in the oil and gas industry, he has successfully dealt with a wide spectrum of legal, commercial, and operational challenges. In a world where the oil and gas sectors are experiencing transformative change, his career stands as a beacon of expertise, guiding companies toward an economically prosperous and environmentally responsible future. He has contributed immensely to the African petroleum industry through several published textbooks and numerous papers for professional journals as well as presentations in world forums and to regional institutions. He is also an associate editor of OGEL and Country Analyst for the PRIX Index on Political Risk and Oil Exports, PRIX—Oslo.

Anna Ovcharova is Vice President Legal and Compliance at Wintershalldea Russia (previously head of legal Russia Repsol). She has also served as Head of offshore projects legal support in major Russian oil and gas company Rosneft. She has a master's degree in law from Lomonosov's Moscow State University Russia in 2004, a master's degree in international and comparative law from Rijks Universtiteit Groningen, the Netherlands in 2008 and a PhD from the Russian Academy of Science in 2013. She deals with setting the oil and gas projects as well as their ongoing support, mergers and acquisitions, new ventures, and integration in diversified oil and gas projects, including large-scale international projects, transitional energy and CM&H matters. Anna Ovcharova is a member of AIPN and several professional societies in Russia.

Roland Pettersson is a Partner at D'Empaire in Caracas, with a transactional practice focusing on special situations, financing, restructuring, and distressed M&A, mainly in O&G. He is an INSOL Fellow and a member of the International Insolvency Institute, and the Association of International Energy Negotiators (AIEN). Law degree from UCAB (2006) and postgraduate degrees in Finance (UC California, Berkeley—Extension) and International Business (UNIMET).

Tara Righetti is the Occidental Chair of Energy and Environmental Policies and the co-director of the Nuclear Energy Research Center at the University of Wyoming. She holds appointments in the School of Energy Resources, and College of Law, and the Haub School of Environment and Natural Resources. Professor Righetti's research focuses on property law and administrative regulation of the energy and decarbonization sectors. She was recently appointed to the White House Federal Lands CCS Permitting Task Force and is a member of the U.S. Technical Advisory Group to the International Standardization Organization technical committee for CCUS. From 2021-2022 Professor Righetti served as a Fulbright Research Scholar at the Université de Lille, in France.

Henrique Rojas is an attorney who focuses his practice on the energy, oil & gas and infrastructure industries. With a strong international background, including over a decade at a top-tier international law firm, he advises domestic and foreign companies on complex corporate, regulatory, and contractual matters. Henrique holds a Master's degree (LLM) from the University of Chicago Law School, a Master of Business in Petroleum, and a Post-Graduate Degree in International Law. He is a partner at Costa Rodrigues Advogados—COSRO, a mentor and member at the Association of International Energy Negotiators (AIEN), and an author of several publications.

María Serna is an energy policy and regulatory consultant with over ten years of experience in the fields of energy and climate regulatory compliance, bid design and evaluation, contract negotiation, and policy and regulatory consulting. Her primary experience is in energy and environmental legislation and regulation, contractual frameworks, environmental impact assessments and land access. María was the Bidding Director of the Mexican National Hydrocarbons Commission, and Legal Advisor to the Agency for Safety, Energy and the Environment. In the private sector, María has been in charge of the design and implementation of regulatory compliance strategies of international energy companies in Mexico and the U.S. and has been part of top-tier energy legal firms. María is part of Voz Experta, A.C., a non-profit organization for women empowerment in the energy sector in Mexico. María holds an

LLM in Energy, Environment and Natural Resources from the University of Houston Law Center, an MSc. in Regulation and Regulatory Improvement from Universidad Autónoma de Nuevo León, Mexico and a Juris Doctorate from Escuela Libre de Derecho in Mexico.

Nima Nasrollahi Shahri is currently affiliated with Université Paris II, Panthéon-Assas as a contractual doctoral researcher, where he is doing a second PhD thesis. He teaches law courses at the Master and LLM levels in English and French, most notably in areas such as French corporate law, energy law, dispute resolution and international contracts as an adjunct lecturer at the Sorbonne Law School. He worked full-time as a law teaching and research fellow at Université Paris I Panthéon-Sorbonne in 2023. In Tehran, he was the director of the Department of Oil and Gas Law at the University of Science and Culture from 2019 to 2022. He also co-founded Elite Pars law firm, a Tehran-based firm specializing primarily in energy and arbitration. He has had extended experience in negotiation and drafting of upstream oil and gas contracts, often representing International Oil Companies against host states.

Shereece Smith is an attorney at law who was called to the bar in 2020. She is a graduate from the University of Wolverhampton in 2017 and 2019, where she honed her legal skills and knowledge, completing both her LLB and LPC courses. With a passion for green transitions, local content, and sustainability, she completed her LLM in Oil and Gas Law (with distinction) from the University of the West Indies in 2023. In 2023, she was awarded an OAS scholarship and in 2024, graduated with an Executive MBA from the Formato Educativo Business School in Madrid, Spain. Ms. Smith has a robust background in policy analysis, regulatory compliance, and business development. Shereece served within the Local Content Secretariat at the Ministry of Energy and Energy Industries, focusing on research, analysis and energy sector operators' compliance with the Local Content and Participation Policy and its related legislation. She uses her expertise to offer legal consultancy and research to governance policies that promote sustainable development as well as urban development.

Thomas Kojo Stephens is an Associate Professor at the University of Ghana School of Law and heads its Energy Programme as well as the Private Law Department. He is also a Senior Partner at Stobe Law, where he heads the Energy Practice. He has published extensively on the upstream petroleum industry in international journals of high repute, edited and written award-winning books and articles, serves as jurisdictional author as well as reviewer for a number of international publications, as well as editor of some annual reports in the energy industry. He is an advisory board member of the International Energy Law Advisory Group and a Specialist Trainer at the International Energy Law Training and Research Centre (IELTRC). He served from 2015-2020, on Ghana's Public Interest and Accountability Committee (PIAC)—a statutory body with oversight over the use of petroleum revenue by the government—ending his tenure as Vice-Chairman. He is a Notary Public of the Republic of Ghana and a member of the Ghana Bar Association as well as the Association of International Energy Negotiators (AIEN). He obtained his Bachelor of Arts degree in Political Science and Philosophy (*Highest Honours*) from Emory University, Atlanta, United States (Gates Scholar), graduating *Summa Cum Laude, Phi Beta Kappa.* He obtained his LLB from the University of Ghana, his QCL from the Ghana School of Law, and his LLM from Cornell University, New York, United States. He attended the University of Aberdeen (Commonwealth Scholar) and obtained a PhD in Petroleum Law, Policy and Regulation.

Michael Uche Ukponu is a Barrister and Solicitor of the Supreme Court of Nigeria. He specializes in energy regulation and environmental law. He obtained a Master of Energy and Resources Law degree from the University of Melbourne, Australia via the Australian Government's Australia Awards Scholarship 2018. Michael is currently a Teaching Fellow and Melbourne Research Scholar (Doctoral) at the University of Melbourne since 2022. He has presented research papers at seminars and conferences, including the Guest Forum at Max Planck Institute, Luxembourg (October 2023) and the EWIS Conference at Kadir Has University, Turkey (July 2024). He has (co-) authored several journal articles and book chapters on legal topics cutting across environmental law, energy/electricity law, mining, construction, and arbitration. He is a member of notable international professional associations, namely the Chartered Institute of Arbitrators (CIArb), U.K. and is affiliated with the Melbourne Centre for Law and the Environment (MCLE).

Hamis Ussif is an energy professional, chartered accountant, and former Banker, with over 20 years of diverse and progressive experience, in the energy sector (across policy, regulation and operations), international development, banking and finance as well as strategy. He is currently the Director for Market Surveillance and Development at the West African Gas Pipeline (WAGP) Authority based in Abuja—Nigeria, the regulator of the WAGP. The WAGP is a 678-kilometer transnational pipeline that transports natural gas from Nigeria through the Republics of Benin, Togo and Ghana. Prior to this, he managed the Gas Business operations of Ghana's national oil company, the Ghana National Petroleum Corporation (GNPC), where he led or was involved in all natural gas projects such as the Jubilee and TEN associated gas, the Sankofa Gye-Nyame non-associated gas and the Tema LNG projects. He chaired the Working Groups of the Energy Sector Recovery Programme (ESRP), the Cash Waterfall Mechanism (CWM) and the Natural Gas Clearinghouse (NGC) of the Government of Ghana. He previously worked as the Macroeconomist at the State Secretariat for Economic Affairs of Switzerland, Head of Strategy and Business Intelligence at Amalgamated Bank (now Bank of Africa—Ghana), and an accountant at Spacefon Ghana (now MTN Ghana). Hamis is a graduate of the London School of Economics and Political Science (MSc in Development Studies) and the University of Ghana Business School (BSc in Business Administration).

Felipe Villasuso is a Senior Compliance Officer at AIQ Artificial Intelligence (a joint venture between Abu Dhabi National Oil Company "ADNOC" and Presight AI), where he is responsible for ensuring compliance with Ethics and Compliance policies, assessment of new technologies and compliance with AI and Energy regulations. Before joining AIQ, Felipe was the governance lead at ADNOC Logistics & Services PLC in Abu Dhabi and Senior Manager at PwC Legal in Dubai and Qatar. Felipe is a PhD candidate at the London South Bank University.

Yuanyuan Zhang is a lecturer at the Law School of Ningxia University. She has obtained a PhD in Laws degree, an LLM degree and an LLB degree. Dr. Zhang's research field includes Chinese energy law and international economic law. She has published in journals including the Journal of Energy & Natural Resources Law, Journal of International Economic Law, Journal of World Trade, and Oil, Gas & Energy Law.

Summary of Contents

Table of Contents

Part I Introduction, Conceptual and Technical Framings

CHAPTER 1
Introduction

Eduardo G. Pereira, Magnus C. Abraham-Dukuma & Opeyemi Y. Omotuyi

The global energy landscape is undergoing a profound transformation, driven by the urgent need to address climate change and transition towards more sustainable energy systems. Within this context, natural gas occupies a unique and often contentious position.[1] On one hand, it is recognized as the cleanest and least polluting of all hydrocarbon energy sources, offering a potential bridge to a low-carbon future.[2] On the other hand, the practice of gas flaring continues to be a significant environmental and economic challenge in many oil and gas-producing countries.[3]

This book, *Natural Gas Flaring & Energy Transition: Laws, Policies and Regulations*, aims to provide a comprehensive and systematic analysis of the transformational implications of global energy transitions on natural gas markets, with a particular focus on the issue of gas flaring. By bringing together perspectives from various global natural gas hubs, this work introduces readers to the latest developments in law, policy, market regulations, contractual arrangements, and technological responses to tackle natural gas flaring in the context of ongoing global energy transitions.

The global energy transition is one of the most pressing challenges of our time, as countries work to reduce carbon emissions and meet climate change goals. In this context, natural gas has emerged as a crucial transition fuel. Its significance lies in its ability to serve as a bridge between high-carbon fossil fuels, such as coal and oil, and cleaner, renewable energy sources. This makes natural gas an important player in the move toward a more sustainable, low-carbon energy future.

1. Odunayo Adewunmi Adelekan et al., *Energy Transition Policies: A Global Review of Shifts Towards Renewable Sources*, 5 Engineering Science & Technology Journal 272-287 (2024) https://doi.org/10.51594/estj.v5i2.752.
2. Salman Masoudi Soltani et al., *A Parametric Study of CO2 Capture From Gas-Fired Power Plants Using Monoethanolamine (MEA)*, 63 International Journal for Greenhouse Gas Control 321-328 (2017) https://doi.org/10.1016/j.ijggc.2017.06.001.
3. International Energy Agency, *Gas Flaring*, IEA https://www.iea.org/energy-system/fossil-fuels/gas-flaring.

Natural gas is often referred to as a 'transition fuel' due to its potential to reduce the carbon intensity of energy systems while renewable technologies like wind and solar scale up.[4] Compared to other fossil fuels, it offers a cleaner alternative that can maintain energy reliability and security during this transition period.[5] Its flexibility, especially when paired with renewable energy sources, helps to balance energy supply and demand, making it an ideal partner in the global shift to a more sustainable energy system. The International Energy Agency (IEA) and other global energy bodies have consistently identified natural gas as playing a pivotal role in stabilizing energy markets while reducing dependence on more polluting fuels like coal.[6]

One of the key reasons for the growing reliance on natural gas is its significantly lower emissions profile compared to other hydrocarbons.[7] When burned, natural gas emits approximately 50% to 60% less carbon dioxide (CO_2) than coal and around 25% less than oil.[8] Studies have shown that modern natural gas technologies, such as combined-cycle natural gas-fired plants, contribute to this substantial reduction in emissions.[9] For instance, the Intergovernmental Panel on Climate Change (IPCC) has recommended the use of natural gas combined-cycle (NGCC) power plants as an effective means to reduce global greenhouse gas emissions by replacing more carbon-intensive coal-fired plants.[10] Furthermore, liquefied natural gas (LNG) is increasingly recognized as a key fuel to reduce sulfur emissions in industries like shipping, as advocated by the International Maritime Organization (IMO).[11]

Despite these advantages, the practice of natural gas flaring remains a significant challenge. Flaring contributes to greenhouse gas emissions and represents a waste of valuable resources from the revenues and developments it could generate.[12] Addressing this issue requires a multifaceted approach, encompassing legal, regulatory, economic, and technological solutions.

This book is structured in three main parts (A, B and C), offering readers a holistic view of the subject matter.

Part I provides a foundation by introducing key concepts and technical framing. It covers a range of critical topics, including:

(1) The relationship between climate change, natural gas, and sustainable development.

4. International Energy Agency (IEA), *The Role of Gas in Today's Energy Transitions*, 2019.
5. U.S. Energy Information Administration (EIA), *Natural Gas Explained: How Natural Gas Is Used*, 2020.
6. International Energy Agency (IEA), *World Energy Outlook 2020*, 2020.
7. U.S. Environmental Protection Agency (EPA), *Greenhouse Gas Emissions: Overview of Greenhouse Gases*, 2021.
8. U.S. Energy Information Administration (EIA), *Natural Gas Explained: Natural Gas and the Environment*, 2020.
9. International Energy Agency (IEA), *The Role of Gas in Today's Energy Transitions*, 2019.
10. Intergovernmental Panel on Climate Change (IPCC), *Special Report on Renewable Energy Sources and Climate Change Mitigation*, 2011.
11. International Maritime Organization (IMO), *IMO 2020: Cutting Sulphur Oxide Emissions*, 2020.
12. World Bank Group, *Global Flaring and Methane Reduction Partnership (GFMR)*, World Bank https://www.worldbank.org/en/programs/gasflaringreduction/gas-flaring-explained (accessed on 23 August 2024).

(2) Energy transition, energy security, and energy justice.
(3) Carbon capture, utilization, and storage.
(4) Fiscal aspects of natural gas.
(5) The technical and practical aspects of gas flaring.
(6) Natural gas utilization and commercialization.
(7) The role of law, regulation, and policy in addressing these issues.

The said section aims to equip readers with the necessary background to understand the complex interplay of factors influencing natural gas flaring and its role in the energy transition.

Part II forms the core of the book, presenting detailed case studies from key jurisdictions around the world. Each chapter in this section examines:

(1) The context of natural gas flaring in a specific country.
(2) The legal framework governing natural gas flaring.
(3) Current issues and challenges.
(4) Recommendations for improvement.

This comprehensive analysis covers major gas-producing nations across different continents, including Algeria, Angola, Australia, Brazil, Canada, China, Iran, Kazakhstan, Libya, Mexico, Nigeria, Norway, Qatar, Russia, the UAE, the USA, and Venezuela. By examining diverse regulatory approaches and market conditions, this section provides valuable insights into best practices and potential solutions that can be adapted to different contexts.

Part III looks to the future, exploring emerging trends and challenges. It addresses:

(1) Environmental, Social, and Governance (ESG) considerations in natural gas production and flaring.
(2) Forecasts of possible future scenarios for natural gas commercialization and flaring.
(3) Potential disputes arising from changing regulations and market conditions.
(4) Comprehensive recommendations for policymakers, industry stakeholders, and regulators.

This last section aims to prepare readers for the evolving landscape of natural gas markets and flaring regulations in the context of the global energy transition.

Throughout the book, the authors strive to balance technical rigour with accessibility, making complex issues understandable to a diverse readership. This work is intended for academics, students, and professionals in the fields of law, economics, commerce, international oil and gas, energy, and sustainable development. It combines essential information about natural gas flaring with analyses of upcoming trends and realistic approaches from a global perspective, making it valuable for both young and senior experts and scholars in this field across different regions around the globe.

By providing this comprehensive analysis, the book aims to fill a significant gap in the existing literature. While the importance of natural gas as a transition fuel has been increasingly recognized, a comparative analysis and evaluation of the business, legal, economic, and sustainability aspects of natural gas flaring across global energy markets has yet to receive a book-length, exhaustive, and rigorous exposition and analysis.

As the world grapples with the challenges of climate change and the need for sustainable energy systems, understanding the role of natural gas and addressing the issue of flaring becomes increasingly critical. This book seeks to contribute to this understanding by shedding new light on the often-neglected discourse on how natural gas markets can play crucial roles in the global energy transition. It examines the key opportunities and challenges to the sustainable development of natural gas, provides a comparative analysis of the natural gas industries and the role they play in flaring, and offers recommendations on the guiding principles of a sustainable and low-carbon approach to the design, application, and implementation of natural gas development and marketing.

In doing so, this work aims to provide a valuable resource for all those engaged in shaping the future of energy systems, from policymakers and regulators to industry professionals and academics. By fostering a deeper understanding of the complex issues surrounding natural gas flaring and its place in the energy transition, this book hopes to contribute to more informed decision-making and ultimately to more sustainable and equitable energy systems worldwide.

CHAPTER 2

Climate Change, Natural Gas and Sustainable Development

Eti Best Herbert & Oluwabunmi Temitope Akinleye

1 INTRODUCTION

Studies on the various patterns of the Earth's climate system throughout history have revealed that the climate constantly fluctuates, with unique oscillations occurring at varying intervals.[1] Incidentally, recent years have witnessed a different and significant acceleration in climate change, posing a global emergency, as a result of its potential catastrophic impact on humanity and the ecosystem.[2] Climate change has now become the greatest threat to human life on earth, surpassing other historical pandemics such as plagues, smallpox, HIV/AIDS and COVID-19.[3] Climate change is the alterations in climate patterns recognised by statistical analysis of changes in the means, value and unpredictable properties. This change, majorly caused by human activities, continues for a prolonged duration, spanning through decades.[4] It is characterised by prolonged changes in weather patterns, such as increased warmth, precipitation and dryness, spanning many decades. This long-term shift differentiates climate change from the ordinary natural fluctuations in the weather.[5]

1. M Nadal, M Margues and M Montse, 'Climate Change and Environmental Concentrations of POPs: A Review', (2015) 143 (Part A) Environmental Research 177, 178 https://doi.org/10.1016/j.envres.2015.10.012.
2. *Ibid.*
3. US Onoja, UME Dibua and AA Enete, 'Climate Change: Causes, Effects and Mitigation Measures: A Review Global', (2011) 17 (4) Journal of Pure and Applied Sciences 469, 470.
4. H Lee and J Romero (eds), *Summary for Policy Makers in Climate Change 2023: Synthesis Report* (Intergovernmental Panel on Climate Change, 2023) https://www.ipcc.ch/report/ar6/syr/downloads/report/IPCC_AR6_SYR_SPM.pdf, accessed 14 December 2023.
5. Climate Change Knowledge Portal, *What is Climate Change*, https://climateknowledgeportal.worldbank.org/overview, accessed 25 December 2023.

The impact of climate change is well documented. This global phenomenon already affects the well-being of the population in various ways, including air pollution, diseases, extreme weather events, forced migration, mental health strain and food scarcity in areas with difficulties in cultivation. Reports indicate that environmental factors annually claim the lives of approximately 13 million individuals due to alarming weather shifts that increase the spread of diseases leading to fatalities and putting the healthcare system under immense pressure.[6] Climate change not only has a detrimental impact on the environment but also places significant strain on the energy system. The rising temperatures of many States, such as the United States, Africa, the Arab Emirates and beyond, have led to an increased demand for cooling systems, resulting in a higher likelihood of power disruptions, blackouts and national grid breakdowns.[7]

The global concern which climate change raised stimulated the rise in global action to address the situation. This has culminated in the establishment of foremost international treaties, such as the United Nations Convention Framework on Climate Change (UNFCC); the Kyoto Protocol to UNFCC; and the Paris Convention targeted at phasing out the use of fossil fuel and ensuring energy transition to renewable or cleaner energy sources. Apart from being a mitigation strategy for climate change, resorting to renewable energy is considered to be a more sustainable energy consumption measure.

Despite the anticipated gains in energy transition, there are concerns about the dangers of abrupt energy transition, which would mean that states that are rich and wholly dependent on fossil fuel for their economic sustenance would sacrifice their right to development at the altar of climate preservation. There are also concerns about energy security and the sustainability of wholesome recourse to renewable energy. This, therefore, puts natural gas into perspective.

This chapter shall, therefore, examine the complex role of natural gas as a contributor to climate change and means towards the mitigation of the impact of global climate change. It shall situate natural gas in the energy transition scheme, while justifying the role of natural gas in guaranteeing sustainable development, with particular respect to energy security. It shall be argued that, at the moment, renewable sources such as solar, wind power, geothermal and wave energy are not robustly developed to attain efficiency, consistency and self-sufficiency. This would, therefore, suggest the continuous relevance of natural gas to meet energy demands, guarantee energy security and ensure just transition in line with the aspiration of numerous countries, particularly those of the global south.

2 EMERGENCE AND UNSUSTAINABLE EXPLORATION OF NATURAL GAS

Natural gas, also referred to as methane or simple gas, is a blend of naturally occurring gaseous hydrocarbons. Its primary constituent is methane, as well as minimal amounts

6. *Ibid.*
7. RK Pachuri and LA Meyer (eds), *Climate Change 2014: Synthesis Report,* (Intergovernmental Panel on Climate Change, 2014) 151, https://www.ipcc.ch/site/assets/uploads/2018/05/SYR_AR5_FINAL_full_wcover.pdf, accessed 13 December 2023.

of other higher alkanes and some trace gases such as Carbon dioxides (CO_2), hydrogen, nitrogen, sulphide and helium. Natural gas is a non-renewable resource formed from the decomposition of organic matter, mainly marine micro-organisms, that have been subjected to heat intensity and underground pressures for millions of years.[8] Although it was discovered several decades ago, it was predominantly used for religious rites in ancient Persian civilization, considering the significance of fire in their worship. It was not until 900 BC that natural gas gained recognition for its energy value in China. The earliest natural gas well was first drilled in 211 BC China, where bamboo stems were improvised as pipelines for gas transportation.[9]

Naturally occurring natural gas became known in America around 1626. While coal-generated natural gas was utilised as a fuel source in 1785, it was used to power streetlights in Baltimore and Maryland in 1816. Natural gas wells had already been dug since 1821 in America, while it only became known to Europe during the twentieth century, with Great Britain first commercialising it in 1959. World War II was another historical event that heralded rapid growth in natural gas usage, which can particularly be attributed to the development of modern gas pipeline grids and storage facilities.[10]

Presently, natural gas has become an increasingly significant source of energy worldwide, especially following the crude oil shortages of the 1970s. Natural gas accounts for about a quarter of global electricity generation, more than 23% of the global energy mix after petroleum at 30% and coal at about 27%.[11] Natural gas was primarily utilised as a source of light and its usage remained localised due to a lack of transportation infrastructure, making it so challenging to transport large amounts of natural gas over long distances. However, the invention of a leak-proof pipeline coupling in 1890 marked a significant turning point. However, it was not until the 1920s that the transportation of natural gas to distant customers became practicable due to technological advancement in pipeline technology. Liquefied natural gas (LNG) further boosted its use, as it can be shipped internationally in a more compact form. The mere fact that LNG can be liquefied and shipped when it cannot be delivered on land or through the pipeline is one of the significant features of natural gas efficiency.[12] For example, in Europe, Russia's invasion of Ukraine has prompted many European countries to diversify their gas sources, as the traditional delivery of natural gas by pipeline has been disrupted leading to many investments in LNG terminals that eventually made gas to be traded much the same way as oil is.

It is a common occurrence for natural gas to be discovered as an unwanted by-product in the course of crude oil exploration. Thus, most petroleum drilling

8. JR Levine, 'Coalification: The Evolution of Coal as Source Rock and Reservoir Rock for Oil and Gas', in BE Law and DD Rice (eds), *Hydrocarbons from Coal: American Association of Petroleum Geologists, Studies in Geology* (Vol. 38 Semantic Scholar, 1993) 9.
9. JG Speight, *Natural Gas: A Basic Handbook* (2nd edn, Gulf Professional Publishing, 2019).
10. GA Olah, 'Beyond Oil and Gas: The Methanol Economy', (2005) 44 (18) Angewandte Chemie 2636, 2636 https://doi.org/10.1002/anie.200462121.
11. International Energy Agency, *Natural Gas*, https://www.iea.org/energy-system/fossil-fuels/natural-gas, accessed 16 August 2024.
12. *Ibid.*

operations were discontinued once any gas in the reservoir was tapped during the drilling processes, thereby allowing the gas to freely discharge into thin air.[13] Regarding natural gas as a worthless by-product and burning it out in giant flame is an unsustainable means of petroleum exploration with severe environmental consequences. This is what is referred to as gas flaring, which is a major contributor to ozone layer depletion and climate change.

Russia is the country with the highest gas reserve in the world, while Nigeria has the highest gas reserve in Africa.[14] In 2021, Russia retained its record as the highest gas-flaring nation in the world, thereby surpassing its previous highest record of 2012.[15] In sequential order, the 2022 top nine countries responsible for 75% of gas flaring in the world are: Russia, Iraq, Iran, Algeria, Venezuela, United States of America, Mexica, Libya and Nigeria.[16] Nigeria used to be the top gas-flaring country in Africa. World Bank report of 2004 holds Nigeria responsible for about 70% of gas flaring in Africa.[17] As of 2009, the country had flared about 40% of its gas reserve.[18] It is reported that 289.6 billion Standard Cubic Feet of gas representing 11.47% of gas production for 2014 was flared in that year alone.[19] Nigeria's greenhouse gas (GHG) emission rate has steadily increased from its 1990 figure of 287.31 Mton CO2eq to 409.45 Mton CO2eq as of 2021.[20] A 2024 report indicates that there is hardly any significant reduction in Nigeria's gas flaring intensity.[21]

The pre-existing legal and policy framework of Nigeria must have been responsible for its unsustainable practice and awful record of gas flaring. The now-repealed Associated Gas Reinjected Act 1978 enabled sector operators to flare gas in the course of petroleum explorers, provided they get a flare permit from the minister of petroleum and pay a nominal fee. A World Bank Report released in 2023 credited Nigeria, Mexico

13. *Ibid.*
14. A David-West, *Nigerian Power Sector: Value Investment Opportunity or Value Trap?,* (CSL Power Sector In-depth Report, 2014), https://www.scribd.com/document/366757261/Power-Sector-IN-DEPTH-Report-part1-pdf, accessed 28 January 2024.
15. The World Bank, *Gas Flaring and Venting Regulations: Russian Federation* (2021) https://flaringventingregulations.worldbank.org/russian-federation, accessed 28 January, 2024.
16. The World Bank, *Global Gas Flaring Tracker Report* (2023) https://www.worldbank.org/en/topic/extractiveinductries/publication/2023-global-gas-flaring-tracker-report, accessed 28 January 2024.
17. F Gerner, B Svensson, and S Djumena, *Gas Flaring and Venting: A Regulatory Framework and Incentives for Gas Utilization: Viewpoint* (World Bank, 2004) https://openknowledge.worldbank.org/handle/10986/11253, accessed 17 January 2024.
18. ON Alphonsus, 'An Examination of the Challenges of Power Supply in Nigeria in Post-Privatization Era, 2013-2016', (2016) 3 (1) Asian Journal of Basic and Applied Sciences 34, 47.
19. Nigerian National Petroleum Corporation, *Annual Statistical Bulletin* (2014), https://s3.amazonaws.com/rgi-documents/d190c2401fb7cfce62a2cc9bd95853a066a2f861.pdf, accessed 23 January 2024.
20. NA Izoukumor, 'The Decline in Gas Flaring in Nigeria has not led to a Decrease in Greenhouse Gas Emissions' (2024) 8 (4) American Journal of Humanities and Social Sciences Research 1, 8.
21. The World Bank, *Global Gas Flaring Tracker Report June 2024* (World Bank, 2024) 15, https://thedocs.worldbank.org/en/doc/d01b4aebd8a10513c0e341de5e1f652e-0400072024/original/Global-Gas-Flaring-Tracker-Report-June-20-2024.pdf, accessed 7 August 2024.

and the United States of America for being instrumental to the highest decline in global gas flaring since the 2010 record.[22] This achievement for Nigeria may not be unconnected with the replacement of the retrogressive Associated Gas Reinjected Act 1978 with a more progressive Petroleum Industry Act in 2021.

Gas flaring raises the temperature of the environment to uninhabitable standards.[23] It has been reported that inhabitants of communities where gas is flared are susceptible to certain health risks such as respiratory illness, cough and fever.[24] Apart from the health and environmental hazards that are associated with gas flaring, the economic implication for the country is enormous. It depletes the gas reserves of the country. One is only left to imagine the amount of foreign exchange that would have accrued to the country had that gas been exported. It could also have been used to power the several generating plants that depend on gas for production of electricity. The implication of gas flaring on the environment, social and economic fortunes of a state is devastation. Being the three-cardinal point of measure of sustainability, the reasonable conclusion would necessarily be that gas flaring is an unsustainable approach to gas exploration and utilisation.

It has been reported that the climate is substantially changing as a result of unsustainable human activities leading GHGs emission.[25] This has resulted in surface temperature increase of 1.1°C above 1850-1900 in 2011-2020. The estimate of global temperature is between 0.95°C and 1.20°C, with a more significant increase above land at 34°C to 1.83°C more than the ocean's 0.68°C to 1.01°C. Without immediate action, global surface temperature increases could reach between 3.7°C and 4.8°C in 2010.[26] As of 2019, approximately 79% of global GHG emissions are attributed to various energy sectors, industries, transport sector and buildings, while 21% are traceable to agriculture, forestry (deforestation), urbanisation and other land use.[27] CO_2, emanating from fossil fuels incineration and industrial activities, followed by methane and nitro oxide accounts for the major contributions to GHGs emission.[28]

22. The World Bank, *Global Gas Flaring Tracker Report* (2023) https://www.worldbank.org/en/topic/extractiveinductries/publication/2023-global-gas-flaring-tracker-report, accessed 28 January 2024.
23. SO Oyedepo, AF Agbetuyi, and MK Odunfa, 'Transmission Network Enhancement with Renewable Energy', (2014) 5 (1) Journal of Fundamentals of Renewable Energy and Applications 1, 4 https://doi.org/10.4172/2090-4541.1000145.
24. O Alimi and J Gibson, *The Impact of Gas Flaring on Child Health in Nigeria* (World Bank Blogs, 2022) https://blogs.worldbank.org/developmenttalk/impact-gas-flaring-child-health-nigeria, accessed 28 January 2024.
25. *Ibid.*
26. U Shahzad, 'Global Warming: Causes, Effects and Solution', (2015) 1 (4) Durreesamin Journal, https://www.scribd.com/document/506891732/PDF-Global-Warming-Causes-Effects-and-Solutions-Umair-Shahzad-and-Durreesamin-Journal-Academia-edu, accessed 28 January 2024.
27. O Evseeva, S Evseeva and T Dudarenko, 'The Impact of Human Activity on the Global Warming', (2021) 284 E3S Web of Conferences 11017 https://doi.org/10.1051/e3sconf/202128411017.
28. *Ibid.*

3 THE PLACE OF NATURAL GAS IN CLIMATE CHANGE MITIGATION

The Intergovernmental Panel on Climate Change (IPCC) was jointly created by the United Nations Environmental Programme and the World Meteorological Organization. The panel confirmed that climate change and certain noxious gases arising from anthropogenic activities gave rise to increased atmospheric condition beyond the average temperatures of the planet.[29] The panel recommended a reduction in limiting the GHG concentrations as the way out. The United Nations Framework Convention on Climate Change (UNFCCC), adopted at the Earth Summit 1992, was a direct international response to the global challenge. The UNFCCC seeks to stabilise GHGs concentrations to such a point that enables the ecosystems' natural adaptation to climate change and guarantees food supply and sustainable economic growth.[30]

Meanwhile, Member States were expected to commence actions that could promote the development of various technologies in energy and other relevant sectors. Article 4(5) of the Convention gives significant responsibilities to developed states to apply measures to encourage, enable and finance the transfer of environmentally friendly technologies and technicalities to developing Member States towards implementation of the Convention. Although the Convention was established to guide every Member State, lack of enforcement and absence of speedy actions and mandatory obligations on the Member States have led to the criticism of the UNFCCC, as climate change still persists.[31] For instance, the aforesaid provision of the Convention did not stipulate the specific time for the achievement of the objectives. It is expressed in a manner that does not suggest urgency in implementation.

Unlike the UNFCCC, its Protocol, adopted in Kyoto in 1997, inserted legally binding obligation and targets for the reduction of GHG emission with specific timelines. There are legal obligations to achieve the objectives imposed on industrialised countries contained in Annex-I of the Protocol between the period from 2008 to 2012. It was subsequently updated in the Paris Agreement on Climate Change (PACC), adopted in 2015. Paris Agreement establishes long–term targets to guide Member States in reducing GHGs emissions with the goal of limiting the global temperature increase to well below 2 °C above the pre-industrial levels.[32] The treaty also encourages Member States to strive for loftier targets of limiting the increase to 1.5 °C. Under the PACC, Member States are obliged to prepare, communicate and mitigate against climate change and develop low GHG emission strategies for the long-term target.[33]

29. International Panel of Climate Change, *Overview and Policymaker Summaries and 1992 IPPC Supplement* (IPCC Assessment Report, 1992) https://www.ipcc.ch/site/assets/uploads/2018/05/ipcc_90_92_assessments_far_full_report.pdf, accessed 13 September 2023.
30. The United Nations Framework Convention on Climate Change 1992 (adopted 9 May 1992, entered into force on 21 March 1994), https://unfccc.int/process-and-meetings/the-convention/status-of-ratification-of-the-convention, accessed 20 October 2023.
31. J Gupta, 'Global Energy Governance in the Twenty First Century: Challenges and Opportunities', in MP Amenih and Y Guang (eds), *Secure Oil and Alternative Energy: The Geopolitics of Energy Paths of China and the European Union* (Brill, 2012) 427, 434.
32. Paris Agreement, Art. 2.
33. *Ibid.*, Art. 4.

Paris Agreement adopted the 'common but differentiated responsibilities' principle whereby individual states are allowed to stipulate and submit their nationally determined contribution (NDC) to climate change reduction. While it appears voluntary, states are encouraged to adopt ambitious mitigation goals. The NDC is subject to update each five-year interval, giving details of progressive strides towards the achievement of the state's NDC.[34] This is the basis for undertaking a comprehensive review of the collective advancement towards achieving the long-term temperature objective.

As countries work towards meeting their climate goals in the Paris Agreement, the demand for natural gas is on the increase. Nigeria, for instance, has set a target of achieving carbon neutrality by 2060, in line with its energy transition plan. Increased utilisation of natural gas in her energy mix has a prominent feature towards this end. Nigeria plans to ramp up its renewable energy capacity, primarily through solar power, before 2030, followed by the deployment of centralised renewable energy systems such as solar PV and hydrogen storage, starting from 2040.[35] Liquefied petroleum gas is expected to play a significant role by 2030, while biogas and electric cooking stoves will be prioritised after 2030 because of their carbon-neutral properties. To achieve this target, Nigeria is proposing support schemes and tax benefits to encourage investments in the natural gas sector and promote local participation. Also, education and awareness campaigns aimed at rural communities are considered crucial for encouraging the adoption of cleaner energy sources to alleviate the concerns about their effectiveness.[36]

Meanwhile, China's 14th five-year plan, which spans from 2021 to 2025, aims to improve national energy security and deal with the critical challenge of air pollution by expanding the natural gas utilisation proportion in its energy mix and transitioning coal-based systems in many households and industries to gas-fuelled ones. The country further commits to attain net-zero emissions/carbon neutrality by 2060 and pledged that its CO_2 emissions reduction would reach the peak before 2030. To meet these ambitious climate targets, China must accelerate its transition further away from fossil fuels, especially coal. Although natural gas is the core component of its national energy strategy, since demands exceed the current domestic production, it necessitates increased imports despite all the efforts to expand China's vast reserves. India is equally experiencing rapid industrial growth and has implemented policies to phase out the traditional biomass-based cooking in favour of cleaner sources like natural gas.

34. N Ole, 'The Paris Agreement 2015 as a Premier for Developing Nigerian Off-grid Solar Electricity', (2018) 26 (3) African Journal of International and Comparative Law 426, 431 https://doi.org/10.3366/ajicl.2018.0240.
35. Nigeria Energy Transition Plan, *Nigeria's Pathway to Achieve Carbon Neutrality by 2060* (Climate Change Laws of the World, 2022), https://energytransition.gov.ng/, accessed 25 November 2023.
36. OC Dike, *Framing Nigeria's Energy Transition Strategy: Imperative of an Overarching Policy Direction* (Nigeria Economic Summit Group, 2023), https://nesgroup.org/researchdocument/framing-nigeria%E2%80%99s-energy-transition-strategy--imperative-of-an-overarching-policy-direction, accessed 25 November 2023.

Regardless of all these efforts, coal still remains the primary energy source in these countries.[37]

4 APPLICATION OF SUSTAINABLE DEVELOPMENT IN GAS EXPLORATION AND UTILISATION

The industrial revolution emerged towards the end of the eighteenth century and early nineteenth century. It is a period which marked a shift from human labour-intensive production towards reliance on technology-driven labour, following the invention of weaving machine, coal, steam engines and other forms of industrial machines for production.[38] The technological change of this era, which transformed the manufacturing sector, became the epicentre of modern economic growth.[39] These inventions heralded massive industrial activities leading to increased productivity which transformed the economic and social fortunes of Europe and the world at large.[40]

The industrial revolution has occasioned vast development and urbanisation of the modern world. It is a period which was associated with industrial utilisation of natural resources on a massive scale. The shortfall with the attainment of industrialisation is that it heralded economic gains at the expense of the social and environmental well-being of mankind. The devastation associated with industrialisation gradually raised the consciousness to apply certain restraints in attaining developmental strides. This gave rise to the concept of sustainable development, which has eventually become a global policy on development.

Sustainable development essentially canvasses the three-pronged approach to development comprising economic, social and environmental objectives. The environmental dimension of this principle is that, in the utilisation of resources obtained from the environment, care is to be taken to ensure that irreparable damage is not visited on the environment.[41] The social consideration is that development should have a human-centric approach, in such a manner that bares the core objective of improvement of the quality of human lives.[42] The need to ensure responsible and conservative utilisation of natural resources forms the element of intergenerational equity.

In its 1987 report, the World Commission on Environment and Development canvassed the imperative for development to be sustainable, in that the needs of the

37. SD Olawuyi, 'Can MENA Extractive Industries Support the Global Transition? Current Opportunities and Future Directions', (2021) 8 (2) The Extractive Industries and Society 100685 https://doi.org/10.1016/j.exis.2020.02.003, accessed 25 January 2024.
38. RC Allen, 'The British Industrial Revolution in Global Perspective', (2010) 167 Proceedings of the British Academy 199, 199 https://doi.org/10.5871/bacad/9780197264775.003.0007.
39. M Kniivilä, 'Industrial Development and Economic Growth: Implications for Poverty Reduction and Income Inequality', in *Industrial Development for the 21st Century: Sustainable Development Perspectives* (United Nations, 2002) 295, 296.
40. JJ Spielvogel *Western Civilization; Since 1300 AP Edition* (9th edn Cengage Learning, 2015) 596.
41. SI Abumere, 'Some Thoughts on GIS Cartography and Sustainable Development', in IA lkhuoria (ed.), *Cartography and Geographic Information Systems for Sustainable Development* (Nigerian Cartographic Association, 1997) 1, 5-6.
42. W Ajai, 'Achieving Environmental Protection through the Vehicle of Human Rights: Some Conceptual, Legal and Third World Problems' (1995) 5 (1) University of Benin Law Journal 41.

present generation are satisfied without reducing the chances of the forthcoming generations attaining their own needs.[43] The United Nations General Assembly (UNGA) has further given global appeal to sustainable development by virtue of its resolution 42/187, wherein sustainable development was adopted as its fundamental guiding principle, which all States, corporations, organisations and enterprises should comply with.[44] The United Nations has gone on to categorise sustainable development into 17 goals, with various targets which embody the tripartite construct of sustainable development.

There is no doubt that the UN legal frameworks on sustainable development are within the realm of international soft law.[45] However, it has formed a philosophical underpinning based on which foremost international legal instruments have been founded.[46] It has also formed a basis for which several bilateral treaties have been established.[47] The decision of the International Court of Justice (ICJ) in the *Gabicikovo-Nagymaros Project (Hungary/Slovakia)*[48] has given a judicial stamp of approval on the sustainable development principle. In the said case, the ICJ pronounced the need for sustainability standards to be upheld by states in the course of developmental strides. This landmark decision of ICJ has the implication of giving sustainable development a higher significance in international law than as a mere soft law.

The global recognition of sustainable development implies that states must take cognisance of sustainability considerations while exploring their natural resources or undertaking development projects. Sustainable development has therefore rendered archaic the practice of petroleum exploration where natural gas is burnt out as an unwanted petroleum by-product. Thus, states must ensure that they adopt modern petroleum exploration techniques, where natural gas is captured and utilised as an energy source. Alternatively, unwanted natural gas could be re-injected into the soil as gas reserves pending such time when there is a need for it. Towards this extent, there is a need for states to also enact a legal framework which establishes legally entrenched petroleum exploration techniques that forestall gas flaring and establish consequences for non-compliance. Rather than flare gas, states' legal and policy drive should be directed towards the utilisation of gas as a power source for electricity generation and LNG for domestic and industrial use. Sustainability considerations would also implicate the construction of energy projects such as natural gas power stations.

43. Report of the World Commission on Environment and Development, GA Res. 42/187, UNGAOR, 42nd Sess., Supp. No. 49 (Vol. 1), UN Doc. A/42/ 49 (1987) 15.
44. The World Commission on Environment and Development, *Our Common Future-The Brundtland's Commission Report* (Oxford University Press, 1987).
45. United Nations General Assembly, Transforming Our World: The 2030 Agenda for Sustainable Development (UNGA Resolution A/RES/70/1, 21 October 2015).
46. Examples of these instruments include: the Montreal Protocol on Substances that Deplete the Ozone Layer 1987, United Nations Framework Convention on Climate Change (UNFCCC) 1994 and its Protocol, Paris Agreement, etc.
47. NC Ole, OY Omotuyi, EB Herbert and DE Omukoro, 'Environmental Laws and Enforcement: Prospects and Challenges', in R Fraszer-Williams, MB Ogundiran and EI Unuabonah (eds), *Environmental Pollution and Public Health: Case Studies on Air, Water and Soil from Interdisciplinary Perspective* (Elsevier Book, 2024) 305, 326.
48. Gabicikovo-Nagymaros Project (Hungary/Slovakia), 1997, https://www.icj-cij.org/case/92, accessed 9 January 2024.

5 RELEVANCE OF GAS UTILISATION IN ACHIEVING SUSTAINABLE DEVELOPMENT

Sustainable Development Goals (SDGs) is the 17-point agenda developed by the UNGA in 2015, which aims at achieving a global consensus for the next 15 years culminating in 2030. The SDGs have associated targets, follow-ups and audit protocols.[49] With 17 goals, SDGs addressed the world's most imminent challenges of social, economic and environmental dimensions, so as to promote social inclusion, environmental sustainability and economic development. These goals range from ending poverty (SDG 1) to partnership (SDG 17) and they are highly interconnected. This implies that progress in one area will likely affect progress in others; while achieving significant progress in one area may require progress in multiple areas.

Although all the goals are important, one of the most significant is SDG 7, which aims at ensuring that by the end of 2030, everybody should have access to cost-effective, dependable, sustainable and modern energy. This is in view of the status of energy as a crucial driver of economic growth. The gradual shift of the global economy towards electrification, with electric vehicles leading the way, would expectedly pave the way for higher demand for electric power. Without universal access to energy, it will be difficult for countries to achieve a prosperous future. In the same manner, it would be near impossible for a significant portion of the SDGs to be attained without the realisation of SDG 7.[50] An assessment of the SDG establishes an instrumental role for energy in the attainment of 125 over 169 of the specific SDG targets.[51]

Industrially developed countries, such as Germany, Canada, the United Kingdom, the United States of America, etc., have developed solid technology to satisfy their energy needs. Countries such as China, Indonesia, Brazil, etc., that are fast advancing out of the league of developing countries, would not have achieved such a result without the development of formidable energy access to boost their production and general economic growth. In summary, prioritising access to energy is indeed very important, but the key factor is to use clean, sustainable energy to achieve SDGs.[52] This sentiment has been re-echoed by Obama when he stated thus:

> Access to electricity is fundamental to opportunity in this age. It's the light that children study by; the energy that allows an idea to be transformed into a real

49. United Nation Department of Economic and Social Affairs, *Transforming our World: The 2020 Agenda for Sustainable Development* (2015) https://sdgs.un.org/publications/transforming-our-world-2030-agenda-sustainable-development-17981, accessed 19 January 2024.
50. OE Aksyutin, AG Ishkov, KV Romanov and VA Grachev, 'The Role of Natural Gas in Achieving Sustainable Development Goals', (2020) 10 (4) International Journal of Energy Economics and Policy 463 https://doi.org/10.32479/ijeep.9359.
51. International Bank for Reconstruction and Development, *State of Electricity Access Report* (2017), https://documents1.worldbank.org/curated/en/364571494517675149/pdf/114841-REVISED-JUNE12-FINAL-SEAR-web-REV-optimized.pdf, accessed 19 January 2024.
52. United Nation Department of Economic and Social Affairs, *supra* n. 49.

business. And it's the connection that's needed to plug Africa into the grid of the global economy. You've got to have power.[53]

Towards the attainment of SDG 7, states must explore and deploy all available energy sources at their disposal to ensure sufficient energy to meet the energy needs of their people. This is without prejudice to the need to utilise energy sources that meet the sustainability criteria or utilise it in a sustainable manner. Thus, it is desirable for states to phase out environmentally unfriendly energy sources and stimulate investments in renewable energy sources and technologies. However, this does not imply the irrelevance of natural gas towards addressing climate change concerns. Natural gas can still serve as a useful energy source, as it can be developed into a clean-burning natural gas which is not only environmentally friendly but can also open up pathways toward the realisation of SDG 7 and other SDGs by extension.[54]

It is recognised that replacing coal-based power plants with those fuelled by natural gas will not only mitigate climate change but also lead to the attainment of sustainable development.[55] While natural gas is technically a fossil fuel, among other hydrocarbon fuels, it is proven as the cleanest, contains minimal pollutants, and is richest in hydrogen content.[56] Advanced gas-turbine and combined-cycle natural gas-powered generation systems emit 50% to 60% less CO_2 than coal-fired plants.[57] LNG is also the recommended non-petroleum fuel for ships due to its tendency to reduce Sulphur emissions and address climate change on a global scale.[58] As global energy demand is anticipated to scale up to 50% by 2050 due to growth in advancing economies such as China, India and many others in Africa, the emphasis is on acquiring safe, secure sustainable and affordable energy through a diverse energy mix.[59]

States, particularly of the global south, have canvassed for a slow-paced, just energy transition. Thus, the pathway towards decarbonisation and energy transition should necessarily contemplate renewable energy development alongside the utilisation of transition fuel with low carbon properties. While renewable energy is developing, natural gas can efficiently supplement various wind and solar power energy generation facilities. This is because there is hardly any country which can boost 100% renewable energy source utilisation for its power sector. Indeed, renewable energy

53. This declaration was made by Barack Obama, former US President, during the launch of the US Government Power Africa Initiative in 2013. *See*, 'Obama in Africa: "Let's do business,"' *BBC News*, 2 July 2013, https://www.bbc.com/news/world-africa-23151152, accessed 19 January 2024.
54. MG De Leon and S Di-Sciio-Cimetta, 'The Role of Natural Gas in Today's Energy Transition', (2022) 89 (211) Universidad Nacional Colombia 92-94 https://doi.org/10.15446/dyna.v89n221.99347.
55. RK Pachauri and LA Meyer (eds), *Mitigation of Climate Change* (Intergovernmental Panel on Climate Change, 2014), https://www.ipcc.ch/report/ar5/wg3/, accessed 29 January 2024.
56. DS Olawuyi and EG Pereira, 'Introduction: Nature and Scope of the International Gas Market', in DS Olawuyi and EG Pereira (eds), *The Palgrave Handbook of Natural Gas and Global Energy Transitions* (Palgrave Macmillan, 2022) 3, 14.
57. *Ibid.*
58. International Maritime Organization Regulation 2020.
59. Pachauri and Meyer, *supra* n. 55.

only accounts for 0.4 electricity generation source across the globe.[60] Even though there is, natural gas can also be a viable energy source for dealing with the seasonal and demand instabilities associated with renewable energy. A 2022 report attributes over 20% of globally generated electricity to gas-fired energy source, behind coal.[61] The power generating potential of Nigeria is 80% dependent on thermal generation plants, which are powered by natural gas.[62] It accounts for 43% of power output in Russia.[63] Imagine the impending energy security doom should natural gas be abruptly taken out of the equation for these countries.

5.1 Natural Gas and Carbon Emission Reduction

Coal is widely considered the most harmful fossil fuel in the environment due to its significant release of GHGs. However, natural gas is a cleaner and less carbon-intensive energy source. It produces around 30% less CO_2 than oil, approximately 50% less CO_2 than coal and very few pollutants that contribute to climate change. The transition from coal fuel to natural gas in power generation and other energy sectors has a substantial impact on the environment, as demonstrated by the United States. From 2005 to 2019, the US decreased coal contribution to power production from 50% to 23%, while increasing natural gas usage from 19% to 38%, thereby resulting in a 32% decrease in CO_2 emission in the US electricity sector in 2019 as compared to its 2005 record.[64] Coal-to-gas switch has contributed to the reduction of CO_2 emissions by approximately 500 million tonnes from 2010 to 2018.[65]

It is reported that between 2011 and 2019, 103 of 121 coal-fired thermal plants in the US ceased operations and were replaced with natural gas-thermal plants, thereby decreasing coal power consumption by 315GW between 2000 and 2020, while increasing natural gas plants' capacity from 220GW to 483GW within the stated

60. Statista Research Department, *Distribution of Electricity Generation Worldwide in 2022, by Energy Source* (Statista, 2023) https://www.statista.com/statistics/269811/world-electricity-production-by-energy-source/#: ~ :text = Global%20electricity%20mix%202022%2C%20by%20energy%20source&text = Fossil%20fuels%20remain%20the%20greatest,with%20a%2022%20percent%20share, accessed 31 January 2024.
61. *Natural Gas*, https://www.iea.org/energy-system/fossil-fuels/natural-gas, accessed 30 January 2024.
62. EB Herbert, 'America or India: Identifying a Suitable Off-Grid Rural Electrification Model for Nigeria', (2022) 13 (1) The Journal of Sustainable Development, Law and Policy 36, 40 https://doi.org/10.4314/jsdlp.v13i1.2.
63. Statista Research Department, *Distribution of Electricity Generation in Russia in 2022, by Source* (Statista, 2023), https://www.statista.com/statistics/1237590/russia-distribution-of-electricity-production-by-source/#: ~ :text = Natural%20gas%20is%20the%20most,was%20sourced%20from%20fossil%20fuels, accessed 31 January 2024.
64. US Energy Information Admiration, *Electric Power Sector CO_2 Emissions Drops as Generation Mix Shifts from Coal to Natural Gas* (Today in Energy 2021), https://www.eia.gov/todayinenergy/detail.php?id = 48296, accessed 24 January 2024.
65. K Ranney and M Mukati 'The Role of Natural Gas in Energy Transition' *Sustainalytics* (2021) 5 https://doi.org/10.18235/0002868 https://connect.sustainalytics.com/hubfs/SFS/SFS%20-%20Transition%20Bonds/The%20Role%20of%20Natural%20Gas%20in%20the%20Energy%20Transition.pdf, accessed 24 January 2024.

period.[66] Similarly, China increased its natural gas capacity to about 6%, while decreasing its coal capacity from 67% to almost 62% between 2012 and 2016. Coal-to-gas policy/strategy has therefore decreased the carbon intensity, from 3.11tCO_2/toe in 2012 to around 2.95tCO_2/toe in 2016. In other words, the increase in the usage of natural gas well above the polluting carbon-intensive fuels has helped to reduce CO_2 emissions in the atmosphere and accumulated into the GHGs responsible for air degradation.[67]

Despite the potential benefits of a coal-to-gas switch, the process is yet to be fully actualised due to the easy availability and cheaper price of coal. This trend has, however, resulted in increased usage of coal for electricity generation, particularly in countries where natural gas prices are much higher and people cannot afford to buy the gas due to poverty. Furthermore, the gas-back-to-coal transition has also been driven by the decrease in the availability of domestic gas supply (especially during Russia's invasion of Ukraine). As a result, coal power emissions have risen again by 16% in the US and 20% in the EU in 2021.[68] Similarly, India, Vietnam and Indonesia have in recent times reduced their total reliance on natural gas as their primary energy source for power generation. Incidentally, this shift has led to an increase in carbon intensity, as the share of coal in the power sector has grown at the expense of natural gas. With coal's share in the global power mix reaching a high record, it has therefore become increasingly challenging to achieve the goals of the Paris Agreement.[69] Even though the rising cost of carbon emission could potentially increase demand for natural gas, carbon pricing policies will make coal and other carbon-intensive energy sources less viable. But, so far, the relatively low carbon price has not totally caused a significant shift away from coal towards gas.

A study found that exchanging existing coal-powered boilers for natural-gas-powered boilers has the potential of reducing CO_2 emissions by 52,000-57,000 tons each boiler per annum, which is a representation of 56%-59% emission reduction.[70] Natural gas is more environmentally efficient for electricity generation, as it emits less than half the quantity of CO_2 emission by coal, thereby making natural gas a more viable source of electricity.[71] Several measures have been formulated toward the utilisation of natural gas for commercial benefit instead of it being flared at the detriment of the environment. These measures include gas reinjection for reservoir pressure support; gas capture and storage; and conversion to compressed or liquified

66. US Energy Information Admiration, *EIA Projects Renewable Share of US Electricity Generation Mix Will Double by 2050* (2021) https://www.eia.gov/todayenergy/details.php?id=46676, accessed 10 December 2023.
67. *International Gas Union 2016 and 2018 Case Studies in Improving Urban Air Quality*, https://smartnet.niua.org/sites/default/files/resources/IGU_Urban%20Air%20Quality%20FINAL%20for%20web%20etc.pdf, accessed 24 January 2024.
68. International Energy Agency Coal-Fired Electricity September 2022 https://www.iea.org/reports/coal-fire-electricity, accessed 28 December 2023.
69. De Leon and Di-Sciio-Cimetta, *supra* n. 54.
70. *Leveraging Natural Gas to Reduce Greenhouse Gas Emissions* (Center for Climate and Energy Solutions, 2013) 58, https://www.c2es.org/wp-content/uploads/2013/06/leveraging-natural-gas-reduce-ghg-emissions.pdf, accessed 7 August 2024.
71. *Natural Gas: Emissions Reduction*, https://appea.com.au/wp-content/uploads/2020/06/Factsheet-Natural-Gas-Emissions-Reduction.pdf, accessed 7 August 2024.

gas.[72] These approaches will go a long way towards reducing carbon emissions into the atmosphere.

5.2 Natural Gas Contribution to Energy Security

To ensure adequate energy security on a long-term basis, it is very crucial to adopt diverse approaches towards energy sources. In some Arab countries, mostly oil-based economies, energy consumption and population increase at an annual rate of 5%-10%.[73] In the past four years, Qatar has experienced a 34% surge in electricity demand, while Saudi Arabia's highest electricity demand is projected to triple to 120,000 MW by 2023, against the 46,000 MW of 2010. Energy demand within the region is expected to be on a steady rise by 1.9% per annum until 2035, which will require significantly increased generation capacity to satisfy peak energy needs.[74] Natural gas will play a vital role in this regard. It would reduce over-reliance on traditional fossil fuels, and diversify energy sources, thereby promoting energy security. While renewable energy sources are often touted as climate-friendly, increasing domestic energy demand is a critical concern beyond its reach. Thus, gas provides a viable alternative to meet the growing energy needs.

5.3 Natural Gas and Energy Poverty Alleviation

Despite global efforts to provide sufficient electricity to all, over 700 million people across countries still lack access to this basic amenity. In Africa, the situation is particularly dire, with an astonishing 600 million people (43% of the population) living without electricity, despite access to 60% global solar resources and one of the largest gas reserves in the globe. Surprisingly, only 1% of electricity in Africa is generated through solar photovoltaic panels.[75] Lack of easy access to clean energy cooking methods has caused major reliance on traditional energy sources such as coal and biomass, making Africa constitute the majority of the 2.6 billion people living in energy poverty globally.[76]

72. International Energy Agency, *Emissions from Oil and Gas Operations in Net Zero Transitions: A World Energy Outlook Special Report on the Oil and Gas Industry and COP28 18* (2023) https://iea.blob.core.windows.net/assets/743af33c-b2f5-4a93-a925-1b08f6438e61/EmissionsfromOilandGasOperationinNetZeroTransitions.pdf, accessed 7 August 2024.
73. DS Olawuyi, 'The Role of Natural Gas in a Just and Equitable Energy Transition', in DS Olawuyi and EG Pereira (eds), *The Palgrave Handbook of Natural Gas and Global Energy Transitions* (Palgrave, 2022) 73, 78.
74. *Ibid.*
75. International Energy Agency, *African Energy Outlook Key 2022 Analysis* (2022) https://iea.blob.core.windows.net/assets/220b2862-33a6-47bd-81e9-00e586f4d384/AfricaEnergyOutlook2022.pdf, accessed 15 December, 2023.
76. World Bank, *Report: Universal Access to Sustainable Energy Will Remain Elusive Without Addressing Inequalities* (2021) https://www.worldbank.org/en/news/press-release/2021/06/07/report-universal-access-to-sustainable-energy-will-remain-elusive-without-addressing-inequalities, accessed 15 December 2023.

Basically, natural gas is an excellent alternative to alleviate energy poverty, because of its versatility, which can be readily used for electricity, clean cooking and heating.[77] It has helped to provide easy access to electricity for millions of people, replacing pollutant sources like coal and crude oil. Electricity demand is expected to double by 2040 due to pollution increase and urbanisation. Fortunately, Africa has significant gas reserves and increasing gas consumption will not significantly increase GHGs due to its low emission rate.[78] It is, therefore, a sheer lack of ingenuity to leave such energy resources unutilised.

5.4 Natural Gas Support for Renewable Energy

The world is phasing out fossil fuel-based energy and moving towards reliance on renewable energy. Between 2000 and 2040, global reliance on renewable energy is expected to increase from 6.5% to 17.5%. The ultimate goal is to see renewable energy become the primary energy source. Although there are significant advancements in energy storage and distribution, but to generate electricity and heat from wind, solar and water sources remains inconsistent.[79] Developments in processes of converting solar energy, water and carbon dioxide into usable chemicals and fuels are still in their early stages and may take some years to be economically viable.

However, natural gas serves beneficial purpose as a complementary energy source to renewable energy. Natural gas could easily adjust its output to match the fluctuations with the renewable energy supply, thereby ensuring a stable and reliable power supply.[80] In addition, gas-based power generation can easily be adjusted by periodic demand, thereby providing flexibility lacking in other energy sources. The flexibility of gas supply chain through its storage, LNG and the operational flexibility of gas pipelines has made natural gas an attractive alternative fuel source in diverse sectors.[81]

Moreover, as natural gas infrastructure appears to be a viable solution for reliable and flexible energy, it is equally important to consider the potential drawbacks of its progress towards meeting the net zero emission targets outlined in the PACC. It has been argued that the USD 132 billion invested in natural gas projects since 2016 would

77. New Africa, 'Why Is the Switch to Gas for Cooking Still so Slow in Africa?', *New African Magazine* (12 October 2020), https://newafricanmagazine.com/24602/, accessed 20 December 2023.
78. World Economic Forum, '12 Reasons Why Gas Should Not be Part of Africa's Clean Energy Future', *The World Economic Forum* (23 July 2020) https://www.weforum.org/agenda/2020/07/12-reasons-gas-africas-renewable-energy-future/, accessed 15 December 2023.
79. SA Hamdani, *The Role of Natural Gas in the Global Climate Agenda* (Gas Exporting Countries Forum, 2018) https://www.gecf.org/_resources/files/publications/gecf_role_natural_gas_global_climate_agenda.pdf, accessed 26 December 2023.
80. C Gursan and V de Gooyert, 'The Systemic Impact of a Transition Fuel: Does Natural Help or Hinder the Energy Transition?', (2021) 138 Renewable and Sustainable Energy Reviews 14, https://doi.org/10.1016/j.rser.2020.110552, accessed 29 December 2023.
81. F Ess, F Peter and F Klumpp, *Flexibility in Thermal Power Plants: With a Focus on Existing Coal-fired Power Plants* (Agora Energiewende, 2017) https://www.agora-energiewende.de/fileadmin/Projekte/2017/Flexibility_in_thermal_plants/115_flexibility-report-WEB.pdf, accessed 29 December 2023.

have far ensured renewable energy development. Notwithstanding the aforementioned, it must be noted that natural gas has great potential to provide a more reliable and flexible energy source than renewable energy technologies. It can be easily dispatched to meet the peak demand and act as a backup when the renewable energy supply is limited. To this end, there is the possibility of developing a hybrid renewable and natural gas-based technology that will emerge as future solutions.[82]

The viability and reliability of renewable energy as a sole energy source is still questionable, as it is still at the incubation stage for most countries. A total phase out of natural gas spells doom for most hydrocarbon-rich countries, particularly of the global south, in which economic subsistence is highly dependent on hydrocarbon. This can be said of countries such as Angola, Bahrain, Nigeria, Venezuela, Saudi Arabia, etc. The economic fortunes of these countries would be badly affected. It has been predicted that climate action has the capacity to make 40 fossil fuel-dependent countries lose up to 46% of their oil revenues in the coming 20 years.[83] The economic shock will be dire and unsustainable considering that economy is one of the cornerstones of sustainable development.

6 CONCLUSION

This chapter has examined the nexus between natural gas and climate change, on the one hand, and sustainable development, on the other hand. It has been shown that even though natural gas is classified as an energy source with a significant contribution to climate change, it has minimal emission content compared to other categories of fossil fuel. It is the unsustainable practice of petroleum exploration leading to gas flaring that portends grave danger to the environment and climate. Thus, resorting to modern hydrocarbon exploration techniques where the gas is captured or reinjected into the soil, can effectively address the challenges of gas flaring. While energy transition from fossil fuel consumption to renewable energy is a sure means of climate change mitigation, sole reliance on renewable energy to achieve that purpose is unrealistic at the moment. Therefore, natural gas is a viable option to supplement renewable energy pending such time when it has attained self-sufficiency as a sole energy source. Until such time, the relevance of gas towards achieving energy security, alleviating energy poverty, complementing renewable energy and attaining sustainable development cannot be over-emphasised.

82. C Kemfert F Priger, I Braunger, FM Hoffart and H Brauers, 'The Expansion of Natural Gas Infrastructures put Energy Transitions at Risk', (2022) 7 Nature Energy 582 https://doi.org/10.1038/s41560-022-01060-3, accessed 31 January 2024.
83. MJ Coren, *Climate Action is Poised to Punch a $9 Trillion Hole in Petrostates' Budgets* (Quartz, 2021) https://qz.com/1970294/economies-reliant-on-oil-will-lose-trillions-to-climate-action, accessed 31 January 2024.

CHAPTER 3

Energy Transition, Energy Security and Energy Justice

Eduardo G. Pereira, Magnus C. Abraham-Dukuma, Opeyemi Y. Omotuyi & Henrique Rojas

1 INTRODUCTION

Over the past years, especially after the Paris Agreement (in 2015),[1] the energy transition has become a central concern for policymakers, industry leaders, and communities worldwide. This can be noted by the increase in the energy transition investment, which has quadrupled in the last decade, according to BloombergNEF and grew 17% from 2022 to 2023.[2] However, recent events such as the COVID-19 pandemic, the conflict between Ukraine and Russia, the surge in energy prices in 2022 and the ongoing instability in the Middle East have shown that the path to a successful energy transition is neither simple nor linear.

The threat to energy supply has raised concerns about future energy security and energy justice, particularly the reliability of internal supply chains. One of the multiple dimensions of the reliability and affordability of energy is the intermittency, typical for renewable sources. As well exemplified by Jeff Colgan, et al.: '*the sun does not always shine, and the wind does not always blow, but heat and power typically can be generated from fossil fuels on demand*'.[3]

1. Paris Agreement to the United Nations Framework Convention on Climate Change, (adopted 12 December 2015, entered into force 4 November 2016) T.I.A.S. No. 16-1104 (Paris Agreement).
2. (BloombergNEF 2024) rep https://assets.bbhub.io/professional/sites/24/Energy-Transition-Investment-Trends-2024.pdf, accessed 16 September 2024.
3. Colgan J, Gard-Murray A and Hinthorn M, 'Quantifying the Value of Energy Security: How Russia's Invasion of Ukraine Exploded Europe's Fossil Fuel Costs' (2023) 103 Energy Research & Social Science 103201, https://www.sciencedirect.com/science/article/pii/S221462962300261X, accessed 13 September 2024 https://doi.org/10.1016/j.erss.2023.103201.

Those three opposing challenges (energy transition, energy security and energy justice) are frequently referred to as the 'energy trilemma', as further detailed below. This chapter aims to correlate natural gas and the energy trilemma, considering that, although natural gas is not a renewable source, it is less emissions-intensive than other fossil fuels, such as coal and oil. Thus, it is reasonable to conclude that the use of gas can lead to more achievable improvements in the near future until renewable energies become more widely available and affordable.

The purpose of this chapter is to analyse the role that the reduction of gas flaring can play in the balance between economic, security and environmental concerns in the energy industry, which also encompasses discussions regarding the role of natural gas in the energy transition. Additionally, this chapter also discusses possible mitigation measures to address gas flaring under a pragmatic approach.

2 ENERGY TRILEMMA

Most decisions on the world's energy future inevitably revolve around the complex interaction between economic, security, and environmental concerns. The World Energy Council's publication 'World Energy Trilemma' consists of the goals that governments face in securing competitive energy supplies while providing universal energy access and promoting environmental protection. The World Energy Council's definition of energy trilemma is based on three core dimensions: energy equity (generally associated with affordability aspects), security and the environmental sustainability of energy systems. For its part, the World Energy Council's Energy Trilemma Index ranks countries on their ability to provide sustainable energy through the three dimensions. According to the World Energy Council:[4]

> Balancing these three goals constitutes a 'Trilemma' and balanced systems enable prosperity and competitiveness of individual countries. The World Energy Trilemma Index has been prepared annually since 2010 by the World Energy Council. It presents a comparative ranking of 126 countries' energy systems. It provides an assessment of a country's energy system performance, reflecting balance and robustness in the three Trilemma dimensions.

This aims to find a sweet spot to guarantee a reliable and resilient energy supply and ensure energy access at reasonable costs, while also minimizing adverse environmental impacts through clean energy sources. The energy trilemma is often the subject of relentless discussions among consumers, policymakers and companies involved in the energy production sector, in the pursuit of an optimal balance between affordability, security and sustainability.

The affordability portion aims to ensure accessible energy costs for individuals and businesses, with the objective of fostering economic growth and enabling social

4. World Energy Council, 'Evolving with Resilience and Justice' (2024) https://trilemma.worldenergy.org/reports/main/2023/World%20Energy%20Trilemma%20Index%202024.pdf, accessed 13 February 2024.

development. It generally relates to the access to electricity, clean fuels and technologies, to the reliability, availability and abundance of energy, as well as to the affordability of fuel, electricity and gas. The top-ranked countries are predominantly developed, with a high Gross Domestic Product ('GDP'), and provided with abundant, reliable and affordable access to energy.[5] As the balance with the other two dimensions of the trilemma is sought, low prices may conflict with the high investments in cleaner technologies and necessary infrastructure upgrades. Achieving this balance often involves targeted assistance, market mechanisms that incentivize efficiency, and fostering competition within the energy sector.

In this context, the World Energy Council highlights and illustrates as follows:[6]

> Strong Energy Equity performance is directly correlated with strong socioeconomic metrics such as GDP per capita or UN Human Development Index, creating a virtuous cycle of improving economic prosperity and quality of life where abundant, reliable, affordable energy taken as given and energy policies and investment are aligned to maintain this expectation. In contrast, many of the poorest Energy Equity performers are also some of the least economically developed, creating a vicious cycle of underinvestment in energy infrastructure to boost even basic energy access requirements. The gap between top and bottom performers is widening, and those in the bottom are in danger of being left behind.
>
> The top ranked Energy Equity performers are all developed, higher GDP countries with universal access to abundant, reliable, affordable prosperity enabling energy at the flick of a switch
>
> (...)
>
> While the top energy equity performers have little room for improvement, further down the rankings some countries have made remarkable improvements through increasing energy access and affordability. The top 10 improvers since 2000 and over the past decade are dominated by a consistent group of developing sub-Saharan African and South East Asian countries whose energy policies have driven energy equity score improvements.[7]

On the security dimension, history shows that a reliable energy supply has been one of the foundations of national security and economic well-being. This also encompasses resilience against economic crises, natural disasters and geopolitical disruptions – as energy-secure communities will often respond more effectively to supply shocks and minimize disruption to their economic activities. Adopting a diverse energy mix that combines renewables with reliable sources like natural gas will generally address intermittence and other challenges while also reducing emissions.

The World Energy Council[8] makes the following consideration regarding energy security:

> For the top performing countries – all developed nations integrated into global energy markets where universal access to affordable, reliable energy at the flick of a switch is taken for granted – the threat of supply disruption is frightening and is resulting in a rewiring of global energy trade flows. Global energy trade will

5. *Ibid.*
6. *Ibid.*
7. *Ibid.*
8. *Ibid.*

> continue, and many countries will continue to rely on others for energy imports – but increasingly countries are looking to harness domestic generation potential where possible to improve energy security.
>
> For developing nations, Energy Security is perhaps more about increasing energy access, increasing energy supply and generation, and improving energy system reliability though investments in energy infrastructure. A significant share of new capacity is renewable energy, but also into gas for some, which will impact Sustainability scores.

The sustainability part relates to the ability to avoid environmental damage and mitigate climate change. High-sustainability countries are typically those who employ large-scale deployment of low-emission energy sources such as nuclear and renewables, with high levels of energy efficiency. Renewable energy sources offer a cleaner path forward, but their intermittent nature can pose challenges to grid stability and demand significant initial investments in infrastructure.

Addressing this sustainability part of the equation still requires advancements in energy storage, sufficient infrastructure, smart grids, and efficient integration of diverse energy sources, so that transitioning away from fossil fuels is properly balanced out with the affordability aspects. Besides, emerging markets and developing economies will likely require different approaches, strategies and timing:[9]

> Natural gas is expected to play a role in important aspects of energy transitions, including as a source of flexibility to ensure the integration of variable renewables into energy systems and to meet growing energy demand and industrialization needs in EMDEs. The context for the security of natural gas supply has also shifted dramatically in recent years as a result of Russia's cuts to pipeline deliveries to Europe, highlighting the importance of well-functioning liquefied natural gas (LNG) markets. Enhanced dialogue between producers and consumers, transparent information sharing, and reliable short- and medium-term analysis, taking into account risk factors, remains important for the stability of oil and gas markets. Gas reserve mechanisms and policy measures including joint procurement and flexible use of LNG storage tanks, tailored to each country's circumstances, could also contribute to global market stabilisation.

In line with the above, a number of countries have enacted new energy policies to mitigate those concerns and redesigned their energy frameworks to be more resilient and prepared to react to global supply constraints. The dimensions of the trilemma are undividable and must be considered in a broader context. It is fair to admit that achieving a global supply of energy that is affordable, secure and sustainable is essential but requires a careful and pragmatic approach to navigate its associated inherent complexities.[10]

One of the possible pragmatic approaches, as detailed below, is the use of natural gas to guarantee an energy transition balanced with the other pillars of the 'energy trilemma'. In this context, addressing gas flaring can contribute to the reduction of

9. (International Energy Agency) rep https://iea.blob.core.windows.net/assets/29875a66-aebe-49aa-a2b1-d0824db302c2/OvercomingtheEnergyTrilemma_SecureandInclusiveTransitions.pdf, accessed 16 September 2024.
10. (World Energy Council) rep https://www.worldenergy.org/assets/downloads/World_Energy_Trilemma_2024_Full_Report.pdf, accessed 13 February 2024.

greenhouse gas emissions (supporting the energy transition) and increase natural gas availability (energy security and energy justice), further collaborating to balance the energy trilemma.

3 FLARING

Natural gas is a natural hydrocarbon gas mixture containing predominantly methane. It may also include amounts of other components, such as alkanesethane, propane and butane, in addition to a small percentage of carbon dioxide (CO_2), nitrogen, and hydrogen sulfide. The formation of natural gas occurs when layers of decomposing plant and animal matter are exposed to intense heat and high pressure over thousands of years.[11] The energy originally obtained from the sun is stored in the form of chemical bonds in the gas. Natural gas can be 'associated' (typically located in oil fields), or 'non-associated' (specific natural gas fields), and is also found in coal beds.[12]

Gas flaring has been a common practice across the oil and gas industry, especially in remote areas where the infrastructure for gas transportation and processing is limited, or even where the gas itself is contaminated with other incombustible gases.[13] The procedure consists of burning off excess of associated natural gas extracted alongside crude oil in exploration and production, in onshore or offshore wells and platforms, as well as in landfills, oil refineries, chemical plants and natural gas processing plants. Typically, the flaring of gas aims to ensure that the gas is released into the atmosphere in a way that is less harmful to the environment compared to its original form.[14]

Historically, the practice of combusting unwanted gas associated with oil production served as a convenient disposal method. Natural gas was not originally considered a useful product, due to its transportation and storage challenges. Gas was simply burned off at the well or vented into the atmosphere, so that routine operations could continue, allegedly mitigating the risks of a gas explosion on the production site.

Flaring and venting natural gas also play a specific role at several stages of the oil and gas exploration and production processes – from providing information about the oil or gas composition during well testing to preventing fires or explosions by flaring or venting excess at gas-processing plants. As a brief overview of the most common applicability of gas flaring, we detail below its three main types: (i) routine flaring; (ii) non-routine flaring; and (iii) safety flaring.[15]

11. 'U.S. Energy Information Administration – EIA – Independent Statistics and Analysis' (*Natural gas explained – U.S. Energy Information Administration (EIA)*), https://www.eia.gov/energyexplained/natural-gas/, accessed 17 September 2024.
12. Ismail OS and Umukoro GE, 'Global Impact of Gas Flaring' (*SCIRP*, 25 June 2012) https://www.scirp.org/journal/paperinformation?paperid=20231, accessed 12 February 2024.
13. *Ibid.*
14. 'Methane: A Crucial Opportunity in the Climate Fight' (*Environmental Defense Fund*), https://www.edf.org/climate/methane-crucial-opportunity-climate-fight, accessed 17 September 2024.
15. 'What Is Gas Flaring? Definition, Types, Impact, and Alternatives' (*Blackridge Research and Consulting*), https://www.blackridgeresearch.com/blog/what-is-gas-flaring-definition-types-impact-alternatives-and-future-outlook, accessed 12 February 2024.

Routine flaring is the most usual type. It occurs when the gas withdrawn along with the oil is flared in the course of normal operations, typically because of the lack of appropriate infrastructure for its transportation and storage, which require massive investments that are not always commercially viable in a given economic, legal and political context similarly for natural gas reinjection to the reservoir which could help in the extraction of oil but might be an expensive endeavour. Nonetheless, it may also occur because of the lack of suitable geology, which may prevent the reinjection of the extracted gas into the reservoir.

For its part, non-routine flaring is an intermittent process, which may or may not be planned, and is typically of short time duration. Non-routine flaring is often necessary for operational stabilization when process parameters are outside permissible safety or operating limits. It might occur during the temporary failure of a gas equipment, in the event of preventive maintenance and inspections, or in the occasion of an initial plant startup before the process reaches normal operating conditions.[16]

The safety flare is a measure adopted on an ad hoc basis – lasting days or hours – at oil and gas production facilities to curb temporary interventions, depressurize equipment and manage large variations in pressure. It aims to prevent the escape or accumulation of flammable gases in the atmosphere, which can cause destructive and long-lasting accidents and fires, thus minimizing the risks to people, facilities and the environment.

While natural gas flaring involves the controlled combustion of gas, venting refers to the direct release of such gas into the atmosphere without burning it. In general, the concept of venting is used in the industry to refer to the controlled release of '*in natura*' gas streams, considered to be surplus or residual, which can originate from different processes or facilities in the exploration and production units.

Venting takes place at different stages of the process, such as the maintenance of pipelines, tanks and wells, as is the case when wells are completed. Gas is also vented during the unloading of liquids in low-pressure gas wells and routine emissions from pneumatic pumps driven by natural gas.

This 'in natura' release of natural gas, under which the gas is released without any flaring or treatment, results in large quantities of methane being added to the atmosphere. However, due to the high warming potential of methane gas, the adoption of flaring tends to be prioritized by operators.

3.1 Potential Consequences of Gas Flaring

The global emissions of CO_2 declined in 2020 as a result of the COVID-19 pandemic but returned strongly in 2021 and 2022.[17] Furthermore, the global demand for both coal

16. *Ibid.*
17. 'Global CO2 Emissions Rebound in 2021 after Temporary Reduction During Covid19 Lockdown' (*EU Science Hub*, 14 October 2022), https://joint-research-centre.ec.europa.eu/jrc-news-and-updates/global-co2-emissions-rebound-2021-after-temporary-reduction-during-covid19-lockdown-2022-10-14_en#:~:text=Global%20fossil%20CO2%20emissions%20increased,Environmental%20Assessment%20Agency%20(PBL), accessed 16 September 2024.

and oil – which are responsible for a substantial amount of CO_2 emissions – is still increasing. According to the IEA, *each of the three fossil fuels categories* [coal, petroleum and natural gas] *is now projected to reach a peak by 2030.*[18] This projection draws attention to the available data on greenhouse gases emissions in the fossil fuel sector, which also encompasses flaring activities.

Despite the recent decline in gas flaring, the relevant emissions still cause major environmental concerns worldwide as flaring directly contributes to climate change due to the emission of CO_2 and also because of the release of methane as a result of venting, which is estimated to have a global warming potential 28 times higher than CO_2 over one hundred years.[19] Reducing methane emissions is considered one of the most effective ways to mitigate the effects of climate change.

In addition to climate change implications, gas flaring is often claimed to be directly or indirectly related to the increase of acid rain, water, air and soil pollution, adverse effects on agriculture and further implications on human health, particularly resulting from the incomplete combustion of gas. According to a new study by researchers at the School of Public Health, the University of North Carolina at Chapel Hill Institute for the Environment, and the Environmental Defense Fund found that pollution from oil and gas venting and flaring resulted in USD 7.4 billion in health damages, approximately 700 premature deaths, and 73,000 asthma exacerbations among children annually. The researchers also noted that '*emissions are underreported and controlling emissions is not only profitable for operators, but can significantly improve public health in surrounding communities*'.[20]

In due course, in accordance with Tade Oyewunmi:[21]

> Flares are commonly used in oil and gas operations as a control device to provide pressure relief to prevent the risk of explosions and to avoid realizing methane and other air pollutants into the atmosphere. The pollution and externalities arising from flaring and venting operations create an energy policy and regulation trilemma because of the essential role gas production and utilization play in the energy value chain and as a resource for several industrial applications. There are best practices and technical, operational solutions to curb the negative externalities arising from flaring and venting. These practices include a range of approaches to monitor, eliminate, or minimize these emissions, which in many cases have the benefit of reducing multiple pollutants at once and recovering saleable product that also contributes to economic and energy supply security. Gas utilization in a carbon-constrained world is becoming more determined on the extent to which

18. IEA, 'World Energy Outlook 2023: Analysis' (*IEA*), https://www.iea.org/reports/world-energy-outlook-2023, accessed 21 February 2024.
19. IEA, 'Closing the Gap: Technology for a Net Zero North Sea' (2020), https://www.netzerotc.com/reports/closing-the-gap-technology-for-a-net-zero-north-sea/, accessed 16 February 2024.
20. 'Oil and Gas Flaring Linked to $7.4B in Health Damages' (*SPH Oil and Gas Flaring Linked to 74B in Health Damages Comments*, 13 March 2024), https://www.bu.edu/sph/news/articles/2024/oil-and-gas-flaring-linked-to-7-4-b-in-health-damages/, accessed 17 September 2024.
21. Oyewunmi T, 'The Energy Trilemma and Regulatory Complexities of Gas Flaring and Venting in the US' (SSRN Electronic Journal 2022), https://papers.ssrn.com/sol3/papers.cfm?abstract_id=4025433 accessed 16 September 2024 https://doi.org/10.2139/ssrn.4025433.

> relevant operators and institutions can work together to understand the energy policy complexities in this context and develop practical solutions that would be just and fair to all stakeholders and society at large.

In other words, the reduction in gas flaring and venting may not only reduce greenhouse gas emissions but also increase natural gas availability and facilitate its monetization, contingent upon certain enabling circumstances. As further detailed in the following sections, addressing gas flaring challenges with a pragmatic approach has the potential to achieve sustainable development goals and promote equitable access to cleaner energy while promoting economic growth and environmental responsibility through the rational use of natural gas to meet energy demand.

4 NATURAL GAS AND ENERGY TRANSITION

There is no doubt that a responsible transition from fossil fuels to renewable energy is a key step towards addressing environmental issues. Nonetheless, one should reasonably agree that using less emissions-intensive fuels such as natural gas will lead to more achievable improvements in the near future, up to the point where the different forms of renewable energies effectively become widely available and affordable to consumers. In this regard, a study by Ernest Young emphasized:[22]

> Even as electrification increases, hydrocarbons will remain part of the energy mix for longer than anticipated. Demand for gas will stay strong, partly because of its role as an interim fuel, but also because it powers so much existing infrastructure and is used as a feedstock in industrial applications. Transitioning from old to new assets will take time, and the impact of change will differ across the sector and global businesses. Upstream oil and liquefied natural gas (LNG) businesses will be driven by global trends that are less volatile and somewhat insulated from local policies. Downstream and midstream oil and gas assets, highly exposed to local market dynamics such as EV adoption, will have to adapt much more quickly.

As an example of such improvement, the United States has reduced its energy-related CO_2 emissions by approximately 18% since 2005. The switch from coal to natural gas is responsible for a significant portion of such decline, resulting in the reduction of approximately 532 million metric tons in CO_2 emissions over this period.[23]

To the extent electrification of energy demand is in the spotlight of energy transition efforts, energy security matters become of utmost importance. Although the global gas demand growth is expected to slow down in the near term, from an average

22. (Earnest Young) rep https://www.ey.com/content/dam/ey-unified-site/ey-com/en-gl/insights/energy-resources/documents/ey-energy-and-resources-transition-acceleration-report-v4.pdf, accessed 17 January 2025.
23. Brick J, Dediu D and Noffsinger J, 'The Role of Natural Gas in the Move to Cleaner, More Reliable Power' (*McKinsey & Company*, 1 September 2023) https://www.mckinsey.com/industries/electric-power-and-natural-gas/our-insights/the-role-of-natural-gas-in-the-move-to-cleaner-more-reliable-power, accessed 15 January 2024.

rate of 2.5% per year during 2017-2021 to 1.6% during 2022-2026,[24] the demand for gas is expected to be higher on peak demands as a result of intermittent renewables.

In general, a higher electricity demand should be met with a clean power supply – typically by means of an increase in the participation of renewables in the grid, such as solar, wind, hydroelectric power or nuclear. In this context, the desired decarbonization of power supply towards a more sustainable energy will naturally have to overcome the intermittency challenges posed by the different types of new energies available to consumers.

Reliability challenges and other obstacles relating to renewable energies will vary across different countries, as a result of climate, existing infrastructure, land availability (typically much more land is required for solar generation compared to gas), logistic constraints and legal framework. In virtually all scenarios, however, it is true that gas-fired power generation can provide an affordable and reliable power supply to balance intermittency challenges while also reducing emissions.

Many countries have the opportunity to explore the potential of natural gas as part of their energy transition process alongside viable renewable supplies, by implementing carbon capture and storage solutions, blue hydrogen production from natural gas, coal-to-gas switching in existing plants and other alternative solutions.

5 POSSIBLE MITIGATION MEASURES TO ADDRESS GAS FLARING

Clean energy investments are directed to few markets and face serious challenges in most emerging markets and developing economies. According to a report issued by the IEA, USD 770 billion is invested each year in those economies, being more than three-quarters of the investments divided between China, India and Brazil.[25]

As an example, Africa is the target of less than 2% of investments in clean energy, although it represents 20% of the world's population. By 2030, African countries will require more than two-fold the level of investments currently made to meet their climate goals. Nonetheless, one must not lose sight of energy affordability and security when addressing those critical sustainability demands.

This is why the oil and gas industry has the utmost relevance to energy transition. A study on the role of the oil and gas industry indicates that around 30% of the energy consumed in 2050 in a decarbonized energy system results from technologies that could benefit from such industry's skills and resources. These technologies include hydrogen and hydrogen-based fuels, carbon capture, utilization and storage (CCUS), offshore wind, liquid biofuels, biomethane, and geothermal energy.[26]

24. IEA, 'Medium-Term GasReport 2023', https://iea.blob.core.windows.net/assets/f2cf36a9-fd9b-44e6-8659-c342027ff9ac/Medium-TermGasReport2023-IncludingtheGasMarketReportQ4-2023.pdf, accessed 15 January 2024.
25. IEA, 'Overcoming the Energy Trilemma: Secure and Inclusive Transitions' (2023), https://www.iea.org/reports/overcoming-the-energy-trilemma-secure-and-inclusive-transitions, accessed 12 February 2024.
26. IEA, 'The Oil and Gas Industry in Net Zero Transitions', https://iea.blob.core.windows.net/assets/7a4b0c4e-d78c-4a8e-998c-6cde10a4e49b/TheOilandGasIndustryinNetZeroTransitions.pdf, accessed 16 February 2024.

From a practical perspective, oil and gas companies already have a large stake in the planned hydrogen projects that use CCUS and electrolysis. The study indicates that *'[t]he oil and gas industry is involved in 90% of CCUS capacity in operation around the world*, being *CCUS and direct air capture* [...] *important technologies for achieving net zero emissions, especially to tackle or offset emissions in hard-to-abate sectors'*.[27]

Particularly regarding investments to mitigate flaring and methane emissions, the IEA estimates that a joint effort in that regard would make approximately 35 bcm available to markets. The IEA reinforces the possibility of avoiding 80% of methane emissions from oil and gas operations in Africa and roughly 95% of flared volumes. Reducing flaring and venting activities seems to be a rapid low-cost opportunity for emissions reduction, thus slowing the near-term accumulation of greenhouse gases as well as reducing the risk of crossing climatic tipping points.[28]

Gas flaring mitigation measures can be categorized into several key areas. Regulatory measures play a crucial role, as exemplified by Norway's 1971 policy which banned routine flaring and required gas utilization plans before field development. In Norway, these policies induced companies to invest in the construction of new pipelines to transport the associated gas, which ultimately resulted in the reduction of gas flaring.[29]

Other regulatory approaches include improving, monitoring and reporting systems, setting limits on flaring exempt from authorization, and prohibiting the flaring of non-associated gas except for safety or emergency reasons. These regulatory efforts are often complemented by infrastructure development initiatives, such as the construction of new pipelines for gas transportation. A prime example of this is Brazil's Route 1, which significantly contributed to reducing gas flaring in the country. In Brazil, the first regulation on flaring was issued by the National Agency of Petroleum, Natural Gas and Biofuels ('ANP') in 2000, which limited flaring of associated gas exempt of authorization and prohibited the flaring of non-associated gas, except for safety or emergency reasons. Nevertheless, there was an increase in gas flaring, reaching a record level in 2009, when almost 3.5 billion m^3 were flared.[30]

The results started to improve when restrictive ANP's policies were combined with more specific measures to address the effects of flaring, in addition to the development of infrastructure to take the gas somewhere else, such as the so-called

27. *Ibid.*
28. Calel R and Mahdavi P, 'The Unintended Consequences of Antiflaring Policies: And Measures for Mitigation | Proceedings of the National Academy of Sciences' (*National Library of Medicine*, 20 May 2020), https://www.pnas.org/doi/10.1073/pnas.2006774117, accessed 16 February 2024.
29. IEA, 'Closing the Gap: Technology for a Net Zero North Sea' (2020), https://www.netzerotc.com/reports/closing-the-gap-technology-for-a-net-zero-north-sea/, accessed 16 February 2024.
30. Costa Junior, Nonato, 'As políticas regulatórias da ANP voltadas para a redução das perdas e queimas de gás natural' (2018), https://repositorio.fgv.br/items/73fe22bd-4d3e-4550-8687-0196a3a89d2e, accessed 19 February 2024.

Route 1,[31] operating since 2011. The combined measures led to a 27.4% gas flaring reduction in the country between 2010 and 2011.[32]

Limiting flaring may also have the unintended consequence of driving companies to vent instead. While flares are highly visible both to the naked eye and remote sensing instruments, vented gas is invisible and most existing instruments are not capable of identifying specific venting sites. According to a study on the unintended consequences of anti-flaring policies, *[t]he result is a 'multitask problem', in which a firm substitutes from the easily observed task (in this case, flaring) to the other (venting) to avoid punishment.*[33]

International experience shows that there is no one-size-fits-all approach when it comes to regulation, given that standalone prohibitive measures seem not to be enough to promptly solve the problem. Along with the required updates in the applicable legislation with a focus on effectiveness and enforceability to gradually reduce routine flaring activities, additional measures must be taken to provide an economically viable destination for the associated gas produced. Improving the associated infrastructure and general business environment, ensuring legal certainty, reducing the cost of capital, fostering competition, as well as developing appropriate market mechanisms and incentives are key to unlocking the full potential of natural gas.

Operational alternatives offer practical solutions to reduce flaring. These include using natural gas for on-site power generation, reinjecting gas into the reservoir for pressure maintenance and enhanced oil recovery, implementing offshore gas compression or liquefaction, converting gas to synthetic fuels (Gas-to-Liquid) or methanol (Gas-to-Methanol), and utilizing gas in Gas-to-Wire projects. Each of these alternatives provides a way to make productive use of gas that might otherwise be flared.[34]

Among the possible alternatives is the offshore compression or liquefaction of natural gas, which can eliminate the need for gas pipelines for transportation and also reduce the amount of pollutants released into the environment as a result of gas flaring.[35] Both can be used for the exportation of natural gas, although the LNG should be in the spotlight within the coming years, as its demand is expected to rise by more than 50% by 2040.[36]

Technological solutions focus on improving the efficiency of necessary flaring and reducing emissions. These include replacing flare burners to optimize fuel-air

31. In 2011, the first pre-sal offloading pipeline (Route 1) began its operations. It is 369 km long and has the capacity to transport up to 10 million m^3 of natural gas.
32. ANP, 'Anuário Estatístico Brasileiro do Petróleo, Gás Natural e Biocombustíveis' (2012), https://www.gov.br/anp/pt-br/centrais-de-conteudo/publicacoes/anuario-estatistico/arquivos-anuario-estatistico-2012/anuario-estatistico-2012.pdf, accessed 23 February 2024.
33. Calel R and Mahdavi P, 'The Unintended Consequences of Antiflaring Policies: And Measures for Mitigation | Proceedings of the National Academy of Sciences' (*National Library of Medicine*, 20 May 2020), https://www.pnas.org/doi/10.1073/pnas.2006774117, accessed 16 February 2024.
34. (IBP) rep https://www.ibp.org.br/personalizado/uploads/2022/08/relatorio-ibp-cenergia-coppe.pdf, accessed 20 February 2024.
35. Aregbe A, 'Natural Gas Flaring: Alternative Solutions' (2017) 5 World Journal of Engineering and Technology 139, https://www.researchgate.net/publication/307967387_Natural_Gas_Flaring_-_Alternative_Solutions https://doi.org/10.4236/wjet.2017.51012.
36. 'LNG Outlook 2024' (*Shell Global*), https://www.shell.com/what-we-do/oil-and-natural-gas/liquefied-natural-gas-lng/lng-outlook-2024.html, accessed 19 February 2024.

mixture, installing ignition systems to light flares only when needed, and implementing Flare Gas Recovery Systems (closed flare). These technologies can significantly increase flaring efficiency and reduce methane emissions.

Different from routine flaring, the prompt reduction or discontinuance of safety flaring will be challenging. To mitigate greenhouse gas emissions in those cases, certain technology-driven alternatives have been made available to increase flaring efficiency, including: (i) the replacement of flare burners to allow adequate mixtures of fuel and air; (ii) the installation of ignition systems to enable the flame to be lit only when needed; and (iii) the implementation of a Flare Gas Recovery System (closed flare) to allow the gases usually directed to the flare to be captured, processed and destined for a useful purpose instead of being flared.[37] According to the United Nations Economic Commission for Europe (UNECE), by combining measures (i) and (ii), flaring efficiency can be increased by 99.8%, which corresponds to a significant reduction in methane emissions.[38]

Economic and market-based measures are critical for fostering a climate conducive to flare reduction. This includes enhancing the overall business climate, guaranteeing legal stability, lowering capital costs, encouraging competition, and creating suitable market processes and incentives. These strategies provide economic incentives for businesses to invest in flare-reduction technology and practices.

International collaboration is critical, especially in resolving escalating difficulties in rising markets and developing economies. This includes expanding renewable energy investments in these regions and overcoming investment impediments such as high loan rates and ineffective legislative frameworks. Furthermore, harnessing the oil and gas industry's experience in energy transition technologies such as CCUS and hydrogen generation can help to reduce total emissions.

Effective solutions frequently include a combination of these measures, adapted to the unique situation of each country or area. It is also said that caution must be exercised to avoid unforeseen outcomes, such as increased venting in reaction to stringent flaring limits. The key to successful flaring reduction is a multifaceted strategy that tackles the economic, technological, and regulatory components of the problem while maintaining energy affordability and security.

6 CONCLUSION

One can say that the oil and gas industry, especially through natural gas production, has the utmost relevancy to guarantee an energy transition balanced with the other pillars of the 'energy trilemma'. This is because the use of less emissions-intensive fuels (such as natural gas) will lead to more achievable improvements in the near future, while there are not several sources of renewable energy widely available and affordable.

37. *Ibid.*
38. 'Best Practice Guidance for Effective Methane Management in the Oil and Gas Sector' (*UNECE*), https://unece.org/sustainable-energymethane-management/best-practice-guidance-effective-methane-management-oil-and, accessed 16 September 2024.

To further reduce the emissions intensity associated with natural gas production, it is crucial to address the issue of gas flaring. The reduction of gas flaring and venting offers multiple benefits, including a decrease in greenhouse gas emissions and an increase in the availability of natural gas, which facilitates its economic monetization. Effectively managing and mitigating gas flaring can significantly contribute to achieving sustainable development goals. This strategy not only promotes equitable access to cleaner energy sources but also supports economic growth and enhances environmental responsibility. By optimizing the use of natural gas to meet energy demands, this approach advances both economic and environmental objectives, contributing to a more sustainable and responsible energy framework.

Addressing the challenges associated with gas flaring requires a multifaceted approach, as international experience demonstrates that a one-size-fits-all regulatory approach is insufficient for resolving this issue effectively. Evidence suggests that prohibitive measures alone are inadequate for promptly tackling the problem of gas flaring. Therefore, it is advisable to implement a combination of regulatory and supplementary measures to fully materialize the potential of natural gas. These measures include, but are definitely not limited to, the development of infrastructure, enhancement of the business environment, assurance of legal certainty, reduction of capital costs, and promotion of competition.

Also, operationally driven approaches have the potential to promote the use of natural gas as an alternative to flaring. For instance, it is possible to: (i) use the natural gas to generate energy at the production unit itself; (ii) carry out the compression or liquefaction of the natural gas offshore, facilitating its transportation; (iii) convert the natural gas into synthetic fuels or methanol; (iv) flare the gas for Gas-to-Wire projects, among others. It is important to note that reducing safety flaring presents a greater challenge compared to the reduction of routine flaring. To address this, various technology-driven alternatives have been developed to enhance the efficiency of gas flaring and, according to UNECE, some of these technological solutions have the potential to increase flaring efficiency by up to 99.8%.

Therefore, despite the great potential for the reduction of natural gas flaring to contribute to a balanced energy transition, there is no panacea to address such challenges. Overcoming these challenges will require the implementation of policies that foster competition and attract investments, combined with additional incentives for the development of new technologies to promote the use of natural gas and enhance the efficiency of gas flaring activities.

CHAPTER 4

Natural Gas Flaring and Energy Transition: The Role of Carbon Capture, Utilization and Storage

Opeyemi Y. Omotuyi, Magnus C. Abraham-Dukuma & Eduardo G. Pereira

1 INTRODUCTION

Natural gas flaring is a persistent challenge in the oil and gas industry globally having been practised since the beginning of oil exploration over 16 decades ago till date.[1] Gas flaring refers to the burning of associated natural gas from oil exploration and production.[2] Historically, the option to release natural gas to the atmosphere either by flaring or venting was a common practice in oil industries because of the volume of natural gas associated with oil production. The global agitation towards addressing the undesirable environmental challenges associated with venting led to the widespread adoption of flaring as a better option for the disposal of associated natural gas by oil industries.[3]

Gas flaring has however become one of the most pressing challenges facing the world in the twenty-first century especially because of the adverse impacts it poses to various aspects of sustainable development. The impacts of gas flaring are multidimensional with significant effects on various aspects of sustainable development especially environmental protection, economic development, and human health and well-being. Although these effects are more apparent in developing countries, they

1. The World Bank, 'Gas Flaring Explained', https://www.worldbank.org/en/programs/gasflaringreduction/gas-flaring-explained [accessed 15 January 2024].
2. Earthworks, 'Flaring and Venting', https://earthworks.org/issues/flaring_and_venting/ [accessed 15 January 2024].
3. F.A. Akeredolu & J.A. Sonibare, 'A Review of the Usefulness of Gas Flares in Air Pollution Control' (2004) 15(6) *Management of Environmental Quality* 574-583 https://doi.org/10.1108/14777830410560674.

however remain issues of global concern because sustainable development issues have global implications. For instance, gas flaring causes the emission of substantial volumes of greenhouse gases (GHGs) such as methane, nitrous oxide, black soot, etc., into the atmosphere thereby contributing to the global climate change.[4] According to the International Energy Agency (IEA), about 140 billion cubic meters of natural gas is flared annually around the world.[5] The carbon emissions from this volume of gas account for about 5% of GHG emissions from the oil and gas industry which is estimated at about 265 million metric tons of carbon emissions in 2020 alone.[6] This estimated volume excludes invisible, unburned methane resulting from an incomplete combustion during gas flaring causing the emission of black soot and other particulate matter.[7] In 2021 alone, 144 billion cubic meters of gas was flared during upstream oil and gas operations globally resulting in an estimated 400 million tons of carbon equivalent emissions.[8] These emissions are environmental stressors that not only adversely affect the quality of the environment but also pose some negative effects on society particularly, with regard to public health and well-being.[9]

Beyond its adverse environmental and social impacts, gas flaring is perceived as a waste of natural resource particularly because of the economic value of natural gas as a source of energy and a business opportunity.[10] According to the World Bank, the total volume of gas flared in 2022 alone could provide about 750 billion kWh of electricity and more than the annual electricity consumption on the African continent as a whole.[11] Likewise, it is estimated that the 144 billion cubic meters of natural gas flared in 2021 alone is sufficient to power the entire Sub-Saharan Africa for that year.[12] These imply that the utilization of natural gas could play a significant role in the enhancement of energy security and accessibility.

4. International Energy Agency, 'Gas Flaring', https://www.iea.org/energy-system/fossil-fuels/gas-flaring [accessed 15 January 2024]; S.O. Ismail & E.G. Umukoro, 'Global Impact of Gas Flaring' (2012) 4 *Energy and Power Engineering* 290-302 https://doi.org/10.4236/epe.2012.44039.
5. *Ibid.*
6. *Ibid.*
7. *Ibid.*; D. Pomerantz & M. Bulova, 'Oil Field Flaring: Why It Happens and What Is Being Done to Minimize the Impact', https://www.slb.com/resource-library/insights-articles/oilfield-flaring-why-it-happens-and-whats-being-done-to-minimize-the-impact [accessed 15 January 2024].
8. The World Bank, '2022 Global Gas Flaring Tracker Report', https://thedocs.worldbank.org/en/doc/1692f2ba2bd6408db82db9eb3894a789-0400072022/original/2022-Global-Gas-Flaring-Tracker-Report.pdf [accessed 15 January 2024].
9. G.C. Ndinwa, S.A. Akpafun & C.O. Chukumah, 'Perceived Environmental and Health Impacts of Gas Flaring on Residents in Kwale Communities, Southern Nigeria' (2020) 4(1) *Asian Journal of Energy Transformation and Conservation* 1-21; W. Blundell & A. Kokoza, 'Natural Gas Flaring, Respiratory Health and Distributional Effects' (2022) 208 *Journal of Public Economics* 104601 https://doi.org/10.1016/j.jpubeco.2022.104601; J. Motte et al., 'Quantification of the Global and Regional Impacts of Gas Flaring on Human Health via Spatial Differentiation' (2021) 291 *Environmental Pollution* 118213 https://doi.org/10.1016/j.envpol.2021.118213; J. Argo, 'Unhealthy Effects of Upstream Oil and Gas Flaring', A Report Prepared for Save Our Seas and Shores (SOSS) (Canada, 18 January 2002), https://www.osti.gov/etdeweb/biblio/20291224 [accessed 15 January 2024].
10. The World Bank, 'Gas Flaring Explained', *supra* n. 1.
11. The World Bank, 'Gas Flaring Reduction', https://www.worldbank.org/en/topic/gas-flaring-reduction [accessed 17 January 2024].
12. Pomerantz & Bulova, *supra* n. 7.

Hence, even though the agitation against gas flaring was traditionally attributable to the numerous adverse impacts it poses on sustainable development, the agitation has been further propelled by the contemporary energy transition agenda. The energy transition agenda implies an integrated transformation of global energy production and consumption systems across various levels including fuel switching, development and deployment of advanced sustainable energy technologies, among others.[13] The role of natural gas in the transition to low and/or zero-carbon energy systems is evolving and varies from region to region. In the surge towards transition to clean energy sources, natural gas has been identified as capable of playing a key role in fuel switching and serving as a complement to variable renewable energy.[14] This is because natural gas is globally perceived as a cleaner fossil fuel that may be utilized as a transition fuel in order to ensure a just energy transition.[15]

However, notwithstanding that natural gas may play significant roles in the realization of sustainable development and energy transition agendas, the continued exploration of natural gas in a 'business-as-usual' manner may be ironical to the objectives of these global agendas. This portends the need for the adoption of viable and sustainable strategies for natural gas development including the development and deployment of relevant technologies that ensure the achievement of negligible carbon emissions from natural gas development.[16] Carbon capture, utilization and storage (CCUS) is attracting increasing global momentum as a significant aspect of such decarbonization technologies.

Subsequent sections of this chapter are as follows: section 2 examines the energy transition agenda and the role that natural gas development plays in this agenda. Section 3 elaborates on the concept of CCUS, and the role it plays in enhancing sustainable natural gas development. Section 4 highlights relevant factors that enable and barriers that hinder the development of natural gas and CCUS. Section 5 concludes the chapter with the relevant findings and recommendations.

2 NATURAL GAS AND THE ENERGY TRANSITION AGENDA

Energy transition, which describes a shift from fossil-based systems of energy production and consumption to renewable energy sources, constitutes one of the global agendas to achieve climate neutrality as aimed by the Paris Agreement.[17] According to the International Renewable Energy Agency (IRENA), the success of the energy

13. A. Abanades, 'Natural Gas Decarbonization as Tool for Greenhouse Gases Emission Control' (2018) 6 *Frontiers in Energy Research* 1 https://doi.org/10.3389/fenrg.2018.00047.
14. The Atlantic Council Global Energy Centre, 'The Role of Natural Gas in a Decarbonized World' (2021), https://www.atlanticcouncil.org/event/role-of-natural-gas-in-a-decarbonized-world/ [accessed 17 January 2024].
15. International Energy Agency, 'The Role of Gas in Today's Energy Transitions', World Energy Outlook Special Report (July 2019), https://www.iea.org/reports/the-role-of-gas-in-todays-energy-transitions#: ~ :text = Natural%20gas%20is%20one%20of,of%20today's%20key%20 energy%20markets [accessed 17 January 2024].
16. Abanades, *supra* n. 13.
17. United Nations, 'Theme Report on Energy Transition: Towards the Achievement of SDG 7 and Net-Zero Emissions' (United Nations, 2021).

transition agenda depends partially on a reduction of energy-related carbon emissions so as to mitigate climate change and limit global temperature to well below 2°C of pre-industrial levels.[18] While the need to address climate change is the major driver of the energy transition agenda, there is however the challenge posed with regard to energy security which connotes an accessible and affordable energy system in accordance with the sustainable development goals. Many countries around the globe benefit from fossil fuel energy and as such, fossil fuels may continue to play a significant role in the energy security of such countries in the short and medium term.[19] Likewise, there is the dilemma with regard to the choice between climate change mitigation and the adverse socio-economic impacts of transitioning to a low-emissions future that is driven by renewable energy technologies. The fossil fuel sector contributes immensely to the economic development of many nations ranging from gross domestic product (GDP) growth to job creation and energy supply, among others.[20] Thus, it is not enough to achieve an energy transition that supports climate action, but the transition must be just and equitable and must leave no one behind.[21] The energy transition agenda therefore requires long-term strategies that enhance the creation of cleaner and sustainable energy options through an energy mix that reduces carbon emissions, as well as the adoption of other decarbonization strategies.

Natural gas, being the cleanest of all fossil fuels, is capable of playing a significant role in this regard. As captured by the IEA, natural gas is one of the mainstays of the global energy transition as it replaces more polluting fuels, and limits emissions of carbon dioxide.[22] Therefore, unlike other fossil fuels, gas will experience growing demand until the mid-2030s.[23] This is because, in a 1.5°C climate pathway scenario, natural gas will be more resilient than other fossil fuels, and will be the last to be replaced as part of the energy transition.[24]

Another significance of a shift from other fossil fuels to natural gas is the low cost of gas in key markets across the world. The cost of gas in key markets, especially North America, has decreased more than that of other fossil fuels over the last decade thus, promoting the competitiveness of natural gas.[25] Moreover, natural gas plays a very important role in society as a raw material for a variety of industrial processes, while also useful in a number of ways from electricity generation to cooking, transportation,

18. International Renewable Energy Agency, 'World Energy Transitions Outlook 2023', https://www.irena.org/Digital-Report/World-Energy-Transitions-Outlook-2023 [accessed 14 January 2025].
19. United Nations Economic Commission for Europe, 'Carbon Capture, Use and Storage (CCUS)', https://unece.org/sustainable-energy/cleaner-electricity-systems/carbon-capture-use-and-storage-ccus [accessed 12 February 2024].
20. *Ibid.*
21. D. Ogunbiyi 'A Global Energy Transition Must Be a Just Energy Transition' (2021), https://www.seforall.org/news/damilola-ogunbiyi-a-global-energy-transition-must-be-a-just-energy-transition [accessed 12 February 2024].
22. International Energy Agency, 'The Role of Gas in Today's Energy Transitions', *supra* n. 15.
23. A. Agosta et al., 'The Impact of Decarbonization on the Gas and LNG Industry' (McKinsey & Company, 30 June 2021), https://www.mckinsey.com/industries/oil-and-gas/our-insights/the-impact-of-decarbonization-on-the-gas-and-lng-industry [accessed 17 January 2024].
24. *Ibid.*
25. *Ibid.*

and heating system for houses.[26] This versatility of natural gas makes it a good complement to renewable sources of energy such as solar and wind, with output depending on the weather rather than tracking demand. In other words, on a still, grey day with an absence of wind or sunlight, backup power will be needed and this may be provided by natural gas. Natural gas could supply low-carbon electricity with the help of CCUS.[27] Thus, the share of natural gas in the global energy mix may increase or remain significant while the energy transition continues.

3 CCUS AND SUSTAINABLE NATURAL GAS DEVELOPMENT

3.1 The Concept of CCUS

With the growing global climate and energy transition agenda, the prevention of carbon from being released into the atmosphere is a significant approach to cutting down global emissions.[28] CCUS has received heightened global interest in this regard over the last decade. CCUS describes a set of methods deployed to prevent carbon from being released into the atmosphere or remove carbon already released into the atmosphere. It refers to the capture of carbon from large point sources or industrial facilities, and the utilization or storage of carbon. In other words, CCUS encompasses different phases including, carbon capture, carbon transportation, carbon utilization, and carbon storage. Carbon capture involves the separation of carbon from other gases emitted during industrial operations. Such captured carbon is either utilized directly on-site in other applications such as enhanced oil recovery (EOR), or compressed and transported to be used in a range of other industrial applications such as power generation and low-carbon hydrogen production, among others. Where captured carbon remains unutilized, it is injected into deep geological formations for storage.[29] Where captured carbon is not utilized but stored permanently in deep geological formations, the process is generally described as carbon capture and storage (CCS). Carbon capture may also entail the removal of carbon directly from the atmosphere in order to balance emissions that are unavoidable or technically difficult to abate.[30] This process of direct carbon removal from the atmosphere is generally referred to as direct air capture (DAC). Thus, CCUS, CCS and DAC are related carbon capture processes generally aimed at a reduction in atmospheric carbon concentrations and the enhancement of the achievement of the global climate goals.

CCUS consists of several technologies that are capable of playing significant and diverse roles in the achievement of the global energy transition agenda. First, CCUS can contribute to the clean-up of stubborn emissions especially in hard-to-abate industrial

26. *Ibid.*
27. The CCUS Hub, 'CCUS Basics: Understanding CCUS', https://ccushub.ogci.com/ccus-basics/understanding-ccus/ [accessed 24 January 2024].
28. International Energy Forum, 'What Is CCUS and Why Is It Necessary' (20 July 2021), https://www.ief.org/news/what-is-ccus-and-why-is-it-necessary [accessed 24 January 2024].
29. International Energy Agency, 'Carbon Capture, Utilisation and Storage', https://www.iea.org/energy-system/carbon-capture-utilisation-and-storage [accessed 19 January 2024].
30. *Ibid.*

sectors such as oil and gas. Second, it can provide power support to ensure energy security and a just energy transition. Moreover, emissions reduction alone may be inadequate to meet the global climate goals. In addition to emissions reduction, there may be a need to remove carbon dioxide already in the atmosphere so as to balance atmospheric carbon concentrations. DAC provides a viable technology for such carbon removal.[31] In other words, the deployment of various CCUS technologies plays a significant role in bridging the gap between energy security and just energy transition on one hand, and carbon neutrality on the other.

Aside from the potential positive contribution to the realization of the global climate goals and energy transition agenda, CCUS also possesses some inherent business value. For instance, fitting new industrial plants and retrofitting existing industrial plants with CCUS technologies may allow for the continued operation of such plants albeit with significant emissions reduction. This may contribute to preserving employment and other economic opportunities presented by such industries, particularly in countries and regions that depend on emission-intensive industries for economic prosperity.[32] Within the oil and gas industry specifically, the deployment of CCUS technologies may significantly improve corporate environmental, social and governance (ESG) performance. Besides the potential maximum economic output from oil and gas operations through EOR, CCUS poses positive value to the environment and society by reducing the carbon footprint of oil and gas operations and enhancing affordable and reliable energy sources.[33]

3.2 CCUS and Natural Gas Development

As already stated, the development and utilization of natural gas as against gas flaring provides a beneficial opportunity for the global energy transition agenda. Particularly, it ensures a just energy transition through the enhancement of energy accessibility and security. In the bid to meet the climate targets, many countries around the world are increasingly exploiting natural gas as a complement to renewable sources of energy in order to ensure energy security within their jurisdictions. In 2023, natural gas constituted the second most utilized energy source, accounting for 23 % of the global energy mix.[34] Within this period, natural gas turbines with a combined power capacity of more than 2.02 terawatts are installed worldwide, and global gas power generation increased to about 6,635 terawatt hours, the highest-ever volume recorded.[35] More prominent is the exploitation of natural gas in various gas-to-power projects; for instance, the United

31. The CCUS Hub, *supra* n. 27.
32. International Energy Agency, 'Special Report on Carbon Capture Utilisation and Storage: CCUS in Clean Energy Transitions' (2020), https://iea.blob.core.windows.net/assets/181b48b4-323f-454d-96fb-0bb1889d96a9/CCUS_in_clean_energy_transitions.pdf [accessed 15 February 2024].
33. *Ibid.*
34. 'Global Electricity Mix 2023, By Energy Source' (Statista Research Department, 28 June 2024), https://www.statista.com/statistics/269811/world-electricity-production-by-energy-source/ [accessed 27 August 2024].
35. 'Global Gas Power Capacity 2000-2023' (Statista Research Department, 7 August 2024), https://www.statista.com/statistics/1304427/global-gas-power-capacity/ [accessed 27 August 2024].

States, which was the largest consumer of natural gas in 2023, has the electric power sector as one of the highest consumer sectors of natural gas in the country.[36]

It is noteworthy that in spite of the role and relevance of natural gas in the global energy transition agenda, natural gas is not without its shortcomings. The extraction, processing, transportation, and use of natural gas emit GHGs into the atmosphere in various concentrations. Natural gas, in addition to other fossil fuels, constitutes the largest single source of GHGs emissions globally as a result of the carbon they produce.[37] In addition, methane leaks from the extraction and transportation of natural gas further exacerbate global climate change. Methane, which is the primary component of natural gas, poses a more severe threat to global warming than carbon dioxide over the long term.[38] Also, natural gas reservoirs can contain impurities including carbon dioxide which must be separated before natural gas can be processed. The need to prevent emissions completely across the board will therefore affect all fossil fuels, including natural gas. Moreover, the reduction of fugitive methane emissions and prevention of routine gas flaring are significant aspects of natural gas production.[39] Hence, a just energy transition will require the decarbonization of the natural gas sector through a reduction of gas flaring, as well as the adoption of specific strategies for the decarbonization of natural gas production.

Hence, as countries around the world strive to reduce emissions from the energy sector generally, different forms of decarbonization strategies including CCUS are deployed to capture GHGs from energy production.[40] Even though the potential of CCUS to enhance emissions reduction has been recognized for decades, the relevance of CCUS in the energy sector has been further emphasized by the IEA. Based on a hypothetical net-zero scenario, the IEA predicts about 1.7 billion tonnes of carbon captured by 2030 and more than 7.6 billion tonnes of carbon captured, transported and used or stored across the global energy system by 2050.[41] This posits CCUS as a significant decarbonization strategy to be adopted by countries and sectors wishing to achieve the net zero target.

With regard to natural gas production, carbon capture is either deployed during the pre-combustion or post-combustion process. During pre-combustion, carbon may be captured by removing the carbon from the fuel source before conventional combustion is completed. Post-combustion capture involves the pulling of carbon out of flue gases from the combustion exhaust or a process stream.[42] Over the past decades,

36. 'Global Natural Gas Consumption by Country 2023' (Statista Research Department, 8 July 2024), https://www.statista.com/statistics/265407/world-natural-gas-consumption-by-country/ [accessed 27 August 2024].
37. The CCUS Hub, *supra* n. 27.
38. Centre for Climate and Energy Solutions, 'Natural Gas', https://www.c2es.org/content/natural-gas/ [accessed 24 January 2024].
39. World Bank, 'Decarbonizing Natural Gas through Carbon Capture, Utilization and Storage (CCUS)' (International Bank for Reconstruction and Development/The World Bank, 2023) 59.
40. The CCUS Hub, *supra* n. 27.
41. International Energy Agency, 'Net Zero by 2050: A Roadmap for the Global Energy Sector' (International Energy Agency, 2021).
42. M. McGrath, 'Decarbonizing Through Carbon Capture' (American Gas Association True Blue Blog, 4 October 2023), https://www.aga.org/decarbonizing-through-carbon-capture/ [accessed 15 February 2024].

CCUS has increasingly emerged as a major technology for placing natural gas development, particularly on a sustainable trajectory. This may be a result of several factors that enhance the viability of CCUS as a strategy for addressing emissions associated with gas production and processing. For instance, the deployment of CCUS technologies may currently constitute the most economically viable strategy for decarbonising natural gas production. The application of CCUS technology in natural gas production and processing is estimated to cost about USD 15 to USD 20 per tonnes of captured carbon. Hence, CCUS is perceived as a mature and cost-effective technology that supports affordable and near-term emissions reduction in natural gas production and processing.[43] This is because the concentrated stream of carbon resulting from the separation of carbon from natural gas is generally easy to transport and store thus, making natural gas processing one of the easiest and cheapest applications of CCUS.[44] In fact, until the second millennium, almost all the captured carbon from large-scale facilities globally was from gas processing. Likewise, about 70% of existing large-scale CCUS facilities operating around the world are associated with natural gas plants.[45]

Also, the viability of natural gas as a transition fuel presents near-term opportunities for fuel-switching, thereby enhancing the transition from coal and oil as energy sources to natural gas. Such fuel-switching could enhance the elimination of gas flaring in the oil industry; by promoting the capturing and re-injection of gas that would otherwise be flared, or the utilization of such captured gas for power generation and in other sustainable programmes. This is capable of reducing the use of coal and oil by about 15% and carbon emissions by about 5% by 2030,[46] thereby enhancing the objectives of the energy transition agenda. In addition to such fuel-switching, the application of CCUS to natural gas production could capture between 50 and 180 million tonnes of carbon per annum by 2050 depending on the carbon content of various gas fields, and also occasion reduced emissions by 90% to 95%.[47]

4 CCUS: ENABLING FACTORS AND BARRIERS

In spite of the potential of CCUS in the energy transitions, its impact has been limited because its development and deployment have been slow across the globe.[48] However, the urgent need to reduce emissions across all sectors, coupled with strengthened national climate targets and commitment to a just energy transition, portends the need for a radical shift from other fossil fuels to natural gas over the next decades. With the need to ensure sustainable natural gas development, CCUS is attracting growing

43. World Bank, 'Decarbonizing Natural Gas through Carbon Capture, Utilization and Storage (CCUS)', *supra* n. 39, 13, 59.
44. *Ibid. See also* Global CCS Institute, 'CCS: Applications and Opportunities for the Oil and Gas Industry' (2020), https://www.globalccsinstitute.com/wp-content/uploads/2020/05/Brief-_CCS-in-OAG-3.pdf [accessed 15 February 2024].
45. World Bank, 'Decarbonizing Natural Gas through Carbon Capture, Utilization and Storage (CCUS)', *supra* n. 39, 59.
46. *Ibid.*
47. *Ibid.*, 63.
48. International Energy Agency, 'Special Report on Carbon Capture Utilisation and Storage: CCUS in Clean Energy Transitions', *supra* n. 32.

momentum globally as a valuable enabler of the global climate and energy transition agendas. There are various CCUS projects in operation or under development in over 25 countries across the world.[49] Currently, about 51 commercial CCUS facilities are in operation, about 44 CCUS projects are under construction, and an additional 744 projects are being planned globally.[50] This brings to the fore the potential of global carbon capture capacity quadrupling by 2030.[51] The multiplier effect of this is the need for a rapid scale-up of investment and accelerated innovation in CCUS development and deployment. Countries must therefore be attuned to relevant factors that either drive or hinder the development of CCUS, so as to enhance sustainable natural gas development within their jurisdictions.

While the deployment of CCUS is paramount for ensuring reduced carbon emissions, the potential adverse effects of carbon storage including the risk of carbon leakage and impacts of CCUS installations on groundwater resources among others, has been a source of public concern.[52] Likewise, the storage of large volumes of carbon is perceived as capable of affecting the physical and chemical properties of a reservoir's rocks, thereby posing adverse impacts on the local ecosystems. In addition, the transportation and storage of carbon may pose significant risks to public health where not adequately managed.[53] Thus, the potential adverse impacts of CCUS constitute one of the major factors that may hinder the successful scaling up of CCUS deployment globally. Some other factors include regulatory uncertainty, long-term liability for carbon storage sites, limited commercial incentives to deploy CCUS, and limited public acceptance of CCUS, among others.[54] These factors must be adequately addressed in order to ensure the efficacy of CCUS as a viable technology for sustainable natural gas development. This calls for strategic actions to be taken by relevant stakeholders including governments, industries, financial institutions, and the public.

Addressing the potential adverse impacts of CCUS requires strategic actions on the part of developers such as conducting risk assessments prior to the implementation of CCUS projects, analysing geological properties of proposed carbon storage sites, and detecting potential leakage pathways, among others.[55] Furthermore, there is the need to select storage sites that are geologically stable and secure with a low risk of leakage,

49. S. McCulloch, 'Scaling CCUS to meet Net-Zero Goals', in The Oxford Institute for Energy Studies, 'Carbon Capture, Utilization and Storage (CCUS): Barriers, Enabling Frameworks and Prospects for Climate Change Mitigation' (2022) 130 *Oxford Energy Forum* 7-10.
50. International Energy Agency, 'CCUS Projects Database' (2024), https://www.iea.org/data-and-statistics/data-product/ccus-projects-database.
51. McCulloch, *supra* n. 49.
52. H. Eldardiry & E. Habib, 'Carbon Capture and Sequestration in Power Generation: Review of Impacts and Opportunities for Water Sustainability' (2018) 8 *Energy, Sustainability and Society* 1-15 https://doi.org/10.1186/s13705-018-0146-3.
53. M.D. Aminu, 'A Review of Developments in Carbon Dioxide Storage' (2017) 208 *Applied Energy* 1389-1419 https://doi.org/10.1016/j.apenergy.2017.09.015.
54. World Bank, 'Decarbonizing Natural Gas through Carbon Capture, Utilization, and Storage (CCUS)', *supra* n. 39, 85-86; S. Chen et al., 'A Critical Review on Deployment Planning and Risk Analysis of Carbon Capture, Utilization, and Storage (CCUS) Toward Carbon Neutrality' (2022) 167 *Renewable and Sustainable Energy Reviews* 112537 https://doi.org/10.1016/j.rser.2022.112537.
55. S. Yasemi et al., 'Carbon Capture and Storage: Application in the Oil and Gas Industry' (2023) 15 *Sustainability* 14486 https://doi.org/10.3390/su151914486.

implement a system of regular post-injection monitoring of carbon storage sites to ensure early detection and remediation of leakages, and implementation of emergency response plans to ensure a prompt and effective response in the event of a leak.[56]

With regard to regulatory uncertainty, it is noteworthy that a successful deployment of CCUS on a large scale will significantly depend on the existence of policy frameworks, as well as robust legal and regulatory regimes that enable such development.[57] As highlighted by the United Nations (UN) in its sustainable development agenda, requisite climate actions include the integration of preventive and mitigating measures into national policies, strategies and planning.[58] In other words, the growing acknowledgement of the value of CCUS needs to be complemented by an increased political and policy support for CCUS, without which a scale-up of the technology may not be feasible.[59] Such regulatory and policy support may take the form of government regulation through the command and control approach, market-based regulation or economic approach, or principles-based approach. Thus, countries may either implement formal regulations requiring the adoption of CCUS technologies or formulate market-based policies that disincentivize carbon emissions. These regulatory approaches have received considerable attention in a subsequent chapter of this text. An example of a formal regulation is the final 'Greenhouse Gas Standards and Guidelines for Fossil Fuel Fired Power Plants' recently announced by the United States Environmental Protection Agency under the Clean Air Act. The guidelines require the fitting of carbon capture technology into new and existing power plants so as to lower carbon emissions from such plants.[60] The European Union's Emissions Trading System (ETS), which requires large carbon emitters to reduce their emissions or purchase carbon credits, is an example of a market-based policy for CCUS. Such a system of prescribing a cost on carbon emissions drives businesses to cut emissions by deploying low or zero-carbon technologies such as CCUS.[61]

A robust CCUS regime serves several objectives including ensuring safe, secure and permanent storage of carbon; ensuring environmental and public health protection; clarification of the rights and obligations of different CCUS stakeholders, and provision of a legal basis for the development, operation and long-term management of

56. A. Shahbazi & B.R. Nasab, 'Carbon Capture and Storage (CCS) and its Impacts on Climate Change and Global Warming' (2016) 7(4) *Journal of Petroleum & Environmental Biotechnology* 291 https://doi.org/10.4172/2157-7463.1000291.
57. International Energy Agency, *Legal and Regulatory Frameworks for CCUS: An IEA CCUS Handbook* (IEA Publications, 2022) 7.
58. United Nations, 'Sustainable Development Goals', Goal 13.
59. Juho Lipponen et al., 'The Politics of Large-Scale CCS Deployment' (2017) 114 *Energy Procedia* 7581-7595 https://doi.org/10.1016/j.egypro.2017.03.1890.
60. *See* 'EPA Finalizes Greenhouse Gas Emission Limits for Fossil Fuel Power Plants' (26 April 2024) https://www.whitecase.com/insight-alert/epa-finalizes-greenhouse-gas-emission-limits-fossil-fuel-power-plants#:~:text=EPA%20finalizes%20greenhouse%20gas%20emission%20limits%20for%20fossil%20fuel%20power%20plants,-Alert&text=EPA%20requires%20existing%20coal%2Dfired,in%20GHG%20emissions%20by%202032. [accessed 5 September 2024].
61. N. Heesh, 'Low Carbon Policy and Market Mechanisms to Enable Carbon Capture and Storage and Decarbonisation in Australia' (2021) 105 *International Journal of Greenhouse Gas Control* 103236 https://doi.org/10.1016/j.ijggc.2020.103236.

carbon storage facilities.[62] For instance, the Canadian Province of Alberta implemented a framework of regulatory support for CCUS through amendments made to the existing provincial oil and gas laws such as the Mines and Minerals Act, as well as the implementation of the Carbon Sequestration Tenure Regulations (CSTR), and the Carbon Capture and Storage Funding Act. The revised Mines and Minerals Act empowers the government to enter into an agreement with a lessee, pursuant to which the lessee is granted the right to inject captured carbon into a subsurface reservoir for sequestration.[63] Addressing the issue of the long-term liability for carbon storage sites, the government of Alberta assumes the long-term liability of licensed carbon sequestration projects in Alberta. Upon assumption of liability, the government becomes the owner of any captured carbon and assumes all obligations of the lessee. The government also indemnifies a lessee against liability for damages attributable to such licensed carbon sequestration projects.[64] The assumption of liability and the indemnification of lessees by the government of Alberta provides an incentive and instils investment confidence in the CCUS industry, thus capable of promoting a rapid scale-up of the industry in Alberta. The CSTR establishes a Post-closure Stewardship Fund to be expended for ongoing monitoring of CCUS operations and any required maintenance and remediation of leased areas.[65] The Carbon Capture and Storage Funding Act encourages and expedites the design, construction and operation of CCUS projects in Alberta.[66]

Aside from the scaling up of the development and deployment of CCUS, a robust regulatory regime also enhances public confidence in, and acceptance of CCUS technologies.[67] This is more so because public perception about the benefits and risks of CCUS plays a crucial role in the effective implementation of a CCUS regime. Thus, mechanisms for stakeholder engagement that communicate clearly and transparently the benefits and risks associated with CCUS should be incorporated into CCUS regimes in order to improve public acceptance of the technology.[68] Such stakeholder engagement mechanisms may also allow for engagement in CCUS project design and implementation while creating an effective system of communication that addresses public concerns and feedback on CCUS development.[69] Stakeholders to be engaged may include local communities and other interested parties, and engagement should typically be had early in the developmental phase of a CCUS project.

62. International Energy Agency, *Legal and Regulatory Frameworks for CCUS: An IEA CCUS Handbook*, *supra* n. 57.
63. Mines and Minerals Act, Revised Statutes of Alberta 2000, Chapter M-17, section 116(1).
64. *Ibid.*, section 121.
65. Carbon Sequestration Tenure Regulation, Alberta Regulation 68/2011, section 20.
66. Carbon Capture and Storage Funding Act, Statutes of Alberta 2009, Chapter C-25.
67. *Ibid.*
68. *Ibid.*; F. Mulyasari et al., 'Potentials of the Public Engagement Strategy for Public Acceptance and Social License to Operate: Case Study of Carbon Capture, Utilisation, and Storage *Gundih* Pilot Project in Indonesia' (2021) 108 *International Journal of Greenhouse Gas Control* 103312 https://doi.org/10.1016/j.ijggc.2021.103312.
69. *Ibid.*

Although CCUS is cost-effective in the long term, it may be quite cost-intensive in the short to medium term.[70] Just like any other developmental project, this cost is more regarding financing the development of CCUS infrastructures and capacity. There may however be willing investors who will only invest on the guarantee that their investment is protected, including sufficient return on investment, availability of adequate capital procurement, and availability of a highly dynamic natural gas market, among others.[71]

Likewise, even though the capturing and re-injection or utilization of associated gas may contribute to the elimination of gas flaring, the current underdevelopment of gas markets and infrastructure particularly in developing economies may constitute a barrier to this opportunity.[72] This is more so when there are limited financial incentives to exploit associated gas. To maximize the opportunities presented by gas capturing and re-injection or utilization for reduced gas flaring, therefore, these challenges must be addressed. First, gas markets need an end-use application, and the most common end-use of gas is power generation.[73] This calls for the formulation of policies that promote the building of electricity grids and fuelling of power plants with associated gas from oil production.[74] Beyond this, governments could implement policies that allow developers to recover the costs of procuring gas and running gas-fired power plants from consumers.[75] This may be achieved through the implementation of a feed-in-tariff policy (FIT), for instance. Although a FIT is a globally acceptable strategy for the development of renewable energy, it is capable of adjustment to align with the features of the energy market, infrastructure and technological conditions of countries.[76] In addition, a subsidy reform which makes a switch from fuel subsidies to investments in sustainable energy and development may play a significant role in this regard.[77] In other words, rather than subsidize the price of crude oil and coal, for instance, governments can make a switch to subsidizing other energy efficient sources such as natural gas and renewables. This may influence consumers' behavioural changes and energy preferences, thus reducing gas flaring and promoting natural gas development instead.

---

70. S. Budinis et al., 'An Assessment of CCS Costs, Barriers and Potential' (2018) 22 *Energy Strategy Reviews* 61-81 https://doi.org/10.1016/j.esr.2018.08.003.
71. Asia-Pacific Economic Cooperation, 'Investments in Natural Gas Supply Chain under the Low Price Environment' APEC Oil and Gas Security Studies, Series 12 (2018) 3-4.
72. M. Thurber, 'Gas Flaring: Why Does It Happen and What Can Stop It?' (Energy for Growth Hub, 4 February 2019), https://www.energyforgrowth.org/memo/gas-flaring-why-does-it-happen-and-what-can-stop-it/ [accessed 20 February 2024].
73. *Ibid.*
74. J. Gnana, 'Iraq Could Save $5.2bn in Four Years from Flared Gas Reduction, Says Siemens' (The National, 14 February 2018).
75. M.C. Thurber & J. Chang, 'The Policy Tightrope in Gas-Producing Countries: Stimulating Domestic Demand Without Discouraging Supply' (National Bureau of Asian Research Paper for Pacific Energy Summit, Jakarta, Indonesia, 21-23 February 2011).
76. 'Low Carbon Green Growth Roadmap for Asia and the Pacific: Fact Sheet: Feed-In Tariff', https://www.unescap.org/sites/default/files/26.%20FS-Feed-In-Tariff.pdf [accessed 20 February 2024].
77. V. Bassetti & K. Landau, 'Seizing Opportunities for Fuel Subsidy Reform' (Brookings, 25 February 2021), https://www.brookings.edu/blog/up-front/2021/02/25/seizing-opportunities-for-fuel-subsidy-reform/ [accessed 20 February 2024].

Moreover, the scaling up of investment in CCUS and natural gas development will require the creation of a value mechanism for decarbonization. The mechanism may be regulatory-driven or enabled by a market incentive such as a green premium on decarbonized products or services.[78] Such a value system is in practice in countries such as the United States and Canada which have implemented regulatory provisions on enhanced tax credits for CCUS investments, research and development funding, as well as loans and permitting support for CCUS projects.[79] Such a value system is also reflected in the European Union's carbon pricing system whereby carbon is traded through the ETS. These create valuable incentives that can enhance a scale-up of CCUS deployment and natural gas development.

Additionally, sustainable finance has a key role to play in delivering a scalable CCUS and natural gas industry. It does this by channelling financial resources from the financial sector into the transition to a climate-neutral, climate-resilient, resource-efficient and fair economy, as a complement to public finance.[80] To ensure this, governments must implement and promote sustainable finance policies in the energy sector. Such policies may promote divestment from other fossil fuel sources, and increase investment by financial institutions in natural gas development. To this end, governments must also ensure that incentives are shifted so that investments in such sustainable development are financially attractive to investors.

5 CONCLUSION

This chapter examines the significance of natural gas development against flaring in the energy transition agenda, as well as the relevance of CCUS in such development. It finds that natural gas is a viable complement to renewable energy in the surge towards a just energy transition. This is based on the premise that the exploitation of natural gas as an energy source enhances energy efficiency and energy security. This is because, unlike other fossil fuels, natural gas is perceived as a cleaner source of energy. Thus, the development and utilization of natural gas as an energy source contribute to the realization of the objectives of energy transition by encouraging fuel-switching from other fossil fuels to natural gas. In addition, unlike renewable energy which depends on weather conditions for sustenance, natural gas constitutes a constant source of energy.

The chapter however highlights that in order to enhance the potential posed by the development and utilization of natural gas, it is essential to place such development

78. A. Belani & D. Gerard, 'Carbon Capture and Sequestration: The Business', in The Oxford Institute for Energy Studies, Carbon Capture, Utilization and Storage (CCUS): Barriers, Enabling Frameworks and Prospects for Climate Change Mitigation, *supra* n. 49, 12.
79. *See* the Inflation Reduction Act of 2022, H.R.5376, 117th Congress (2021-2022), https://www.congress.gov/bill/117th-congress/house-bill/5376 [accessed 20 February 2024]; Infrastructure Investment and Jobs Act, H.R.3684, 117th Cong. (2021-2022), Title III – Fuels and Technology Infrastructure Investments, https://www.congress.gov/bill/117th-congress/house-bill/3684/text [accessed 20 February 2024]; the Government of Canada Budget 2022, https://www.budget.canada.ca/2022/report-rapport/toc-tdm-en.html [accessed 20 February 2024].
80. The European Commission, 'Overview of Sustainable Finance', https://ec.europa.eu/info/business-economy-euro/banking-and-finance/sustainable-finance/overview-sustainable-finance_en [accessed 20 February 2024].

on a sustainable trajectory. The chapter identifies CCUS as a viable technology that is capable of bridging the gap between energy efficiency and security on one hand, and net-zero goals on the other. In other words, to ensure sustainable natural gas development, it is essential to accelerate the development and deployment of CCUS technologies in jurisdictions across the world. To this end, the chapter examines the value of CCUS to natural gas development and the energy transition agenda. In so doing, it finds that aside from sustainable natural gas development, CCUS with natural gas presents near-term opportunities for fuel-switching, while also enhancing corporate ESG performance. The chapter further highlights some of the factors that may enable or hinder the successful deployment of CCUS and natural gas development including, regulatory uncertainty, inadequate commercial incentives, and public acceptance, among others.

In conclusion, national governments and policymakers must accelerate the development and deployment of CCUS within their jurisdictions so as to ensure sustainable natural gas development. Going by the enabling and inhibiting factors highlighted in this chapter, it is deducible that governments and policymakers may take actions across two major phases of CCUS development including, planning and scale-up. The planning phase may involve taking actions such as identification and characterization of potential carbon storage sites; conducting technical, economic and other relevant assessments; development of the legal and regulatory framework for CCUS; etc. These are preparatory actions required to ensure that CCUS is developed and deployed cost-effectively and efficiently. The scale-up phase may typically involve the commissioning and development of large-scale CCUS projects by governments, as well as the implementation of various mechanisms to incentivize investments in CCUS projects by the private sector.

CHAPTER 5

Natural Gas Fiscal Aspects

Thomas Kojo Stephens & Hamis Ussif

1 INTRODUCTION

> With natural gas prices at historic highs, gas flaring is an extraordinary waste of money in addition to its negative impacts on climate change and human health. Bringing this gas to market could offer relief to very tight gas markets and, in many cases, could do so faster and cheaper than investing in new supply.[1]

Natural gas plays a significant role in the energy mix of many countries. Globally, natural gas contributed 22.5% of electricity generation in 2023.[2] Yet, for decades, natural gas flaring has remained a major challenge in many oil and gas-producing nations. Natural gas flaring is the burning of natural gas associated with oil extraction.

Gas flaring is not only detrimental to the environment but it may also be a waste of an economically useful product. Environmentally, gas flared directly releases carbon dioxide as well as black carbon into the environment, which is a major contributor to Green House Gas (GHG) emissions.

The World Bank notes that 148 billion cubic meters (bcm) of associated gas was flared at upstream oil and gas facilities and liquefied natural gas (LNG) liquefaction plants in 2023.[3] The World Bank notes further that the largest increases in flaring in 2023 occurred in four of the top nine flaring countries – the Islamic Republic of Iran,

1. International Energy Agency, *Gas Flaring* (IEA, 2024), https://www.iea.org/energy-system/fossil-fuels/gas-flaring accessed 31 July 2024.
2. Energy Institute, *Statistical Review of World Energy 2023*, p. 54.
3. World Bank Group, *Global Flaring and Methane Reduction Partnership (GFMR)* (World Bank, 2024), https://www.worldbank.org/en/programs/gasflaringreduction/global-flaring-data accessed 31 July 2024.

Russia, the United States, and Libya – which together accounted for 9 bcm of additional gas flaring.[4]

Per computations of the World Bank, the 2020 gas flare by energy companies around the world (about 142 bcm), which released the equivalent of about 400 million tons of carbon dioxide into the atmosphere, was enough to provide electricity to the whole of Sub-Saharan Africa.[5] Natural gas flares of between 1 MMscfd and 10 MMscfd constitute 58 % of associated gas wastefully burnt each year.[6] Flare volumes within this range are complicated to manage because investments required are not as low as could be easily incorporated in field development programmes, yet the volumes are also not large enough to attract major investment programmes such as Carbon Capture Storage and Utilisation (CCSU).

2 NATURAL GAS IN THE ENERGY MIX OF DEVELOPING COUNTRIES: CASE – GHANA

> The Ghana National Energy Transition Framework aims at achieving economy-wide decarbonization, energy security and access, and energy efficiency by 2070. These would be achieved through the development and utilization of diversified energy sources including renewables (such as solar and wind), nuclear energy, natural gas … and low-carbon solutions such as Carbon Capture Utilization and Storage.[7]

The Republic of Ghana made two large-scale commercial discoveries of petroleum in its Deepwater Tano (DWT) and the West Cape Three Points (WCTP) blocks, which were developed, under a unitization arrangement, as the Jubilee Field. Commercial production commenced in 2010 and the area held 368 million tonnes of oil and associated gas. At the time of production and immediately after, Ghana did not yet have the infrastructure to utilize the gas. Thus, the Operator of the field, Tullow Ghana Limited, reinjected the gas into the reservoir to maintain and increase the reservoir pressure. However, reinjecting beyond the technical limit would damage the reservoir so the gas was flared, which was not only environmentally harmful but also a waste of a resource which could be utilized as a source of energy for the nation, as well as a source of further revenue.

4. World Bank, *Global Gas Flaring Tracker Report* 12 (World Bank, 2024), https://thedocs.worldbank.org/en/doc/d01b4aebd8a10513c0e341de5e1f652e-0400072024/original/Global-Gas-Flaring-Tracker-Report-June-20-2024.pdf accessed 29 July 2024.
5. Lorenzato, Gianni et al., *Financing Solutions to Reduce Natural Gas Flaring and Methane Emissions. International Development in Focus* (Washington, DC: World Bank 2022).
6. World Bank Group, *Financing Solutions to Reduce Natural Gas Flaring and Methane Emissions* (World Bank Group, 2022), https://www.worldbank.org/en/programs/gasflaringreduction/publication/financing-solutions-to-reduce-natural-gas-flaring-and-methane-emissions accessed 29 July 2024.
7. Public Interest and Accountability Committee 2023 Annual Report on Management and Use of Petroleum Revenue 21.

Flowing from all this, Ghana made a concerted effort to put infrastructure in place so as to utilize the gas. To pre-empt flaring, the government developed a strategic plan to make use of the gas and inaugurated the National Gas Development Taskforce in February 2011 to review and make recommendations for the speedy realization of a national gas commercial infrastructure system.[8] The Taskforce submitted its report in 2011, recommending the evacuation and processing of associated gas from the Jubilee Field.[9] In line with the recommendations of the Taskforce, the government approved the establishment of an indigenous company – the Ghana National Gas Company (GNGC) – as a limited liability company in July 2011. GNGC started commercial operations in 2014 with the responsibility to build, own and operate the infrastructure required for the gathering, processing, transporting and marketing of natural gas resources in the country.[10]

In furtherance of this, the Atuabo Gas Processing Plant (GPP) was constructed in the Western Region of Ghana. The GPP receives raw gas from upstream producers, converts it into lean gas, condensates and liquified petroleum gas and delivers the lean gas to power and industrial users.[11]

The Jubilee Field, which started commercial operations in 2010 is primarily an oil field, but with significant associated gas – registering a gas to oil ratio (GOR) of about 2,668 standard cubic feet scf per stock tank barrel (scf/stb) as of July 2024. In August 2016, Ghana's second field, the Tweneboah-Enyennra-Ntomme (TEN), commenced commercial production. Like Jubilee, TEN is primarily an oil field with associated gas – with current GOR of about 8,739 scf/stb. In May 2017, commercial production started from the Sankofa-Gye Nyame (SGN) Field, which is a non-associated gas field.

All three producing fields in Ghana are flaring gas but usually for technical reasons. In 2021, for instance, greenhouse gas (GHG) emissions by Tullow (the operator of both the Jubilee and TEN fields) increased, which it attributed to gas flaring. Though Tullow aims to eliminate its routine flaring by 2025,[12] it continues to flare as of 2024. The Petroleum Agreement (PA)[13] and the Plan of Development and Operation (PDO) give priority to oil production and export over gas utilization. Therefore, at any time that oil production is negatively impacted by gas handling, the International Oil Company (IOC) will choose oil over gas.

Tullow's position is that its oil production is being negatively affected by the challenges in gas handling. The decisions of the IOCs are based on sound commercial principles. The TEN gas is being sold to Ghana at approximately USD 0.60 per MMBtu, while crude oil price of around USD 80 per barrel on the international market is equivalent to about USD 13.79 per MMBtu. The situation is similar with the Jubilee gas,

8. *Ibid.*, 81.
9. *Ibid.*
10. *Ibid.*
11. *Ibid.*
12. Energy Voice, *Tullow Emissions Rise on Ghanaian Flaring* (Energy Voice, 2022), https://www.energyvoice.com/oilandgas/africa/rigs-vessels-africa/398834/ghana-tullow-emissions-flaring/ accessed 20 July 2024.
13. Article 15.5.

where since Ghana exhausted the 200 billion cubic feet of free gas, there has not been an agreement on gas price between Ghana National Petroleum Corporation (GNPC) and its Jubilee partners. Tullow and the other Jubilee gas sellers maintain that even if the issue is fixed for which it is flaring, it would rather reinject the gas unless a reasonable gas price is agreed with GNPC.

Ghana has maintained a zero flaring or venting of natural gas policy since 2010 when oil production began.[14] Ghana's *Petroleum (Exploration and Production) Act*, 2016 (Act 919) provides for no flaring of gas except for operational safety and under exceptional circumstances. Section 33 of the *Petroleum Act*– titled *Restrictions on Flaring* – states:

> (1) A person shall not flare or vent petroleum unless that person is authorized under subsection (2) or (3).
> (2) The Commission shall after consultation with the Environmental Protection Agency authorize a person to flare or vent petroleum, where:
> (a) it is necessary in the interests of normal operational safety of the petroleum activities;
> (b) it is necessary in order to comply with a requirement imposed under any Act; or
> (c) it is warranted by exceptional circumstances.
> (3) In case of an emergency, and where there is insufficient time to request an authorization from the [Petroleum] Commission, a contractor may flare or vent petroleum without the approval of the Commission under subsection (2), but shall ensure that the flaring or venting is done in accordance with the prescribed procedure and kept at the lowest level possible … .

Regulation 49 of the *Petroleum (Exploration and Production) General Regulations*, 2018 (L.I.2359)[15] stipulates that where a Contractor applies for permission to flare or vent petroleum, the Petroleum Commission – the regulator of the industry – shall grant permission where the flaring or venting was foreseen in the long-term production schedule included in the approved Plan of Development and Operation,[16] or where relevant new information warrants the permission to flare or vent.[17]

The Regulations further stipulate that where the NOC or a person other than the Contractor seeks to utilize gas that would otherwise be flared or vented, the Contractor must make available the gas to the NOC or a third party on terms to be agreed to between the parties.[18] Where a person flares or vents petroleum, that person must measure and report the venting or flaring in the same manner as for the production of petroleum.[19] A person must not inject petroleum underground unless the injection is

14. Toledano, Perrine and Vivian Xiangyi Xu, *Ghana: Associated Gas Utilization Study* 6 (Columbia Center on Sustainable Development, 2015), https://ccsi.columbia.edu/sites/default/files/content/docs/our%20focus/Ghana-APG-utilization-study-September-2015-CCSI.pdf accessed 27 July 2024.
15. Regulation 49 – *Restrictions on Flaring, Venting and Injection of Petroleum.*
16. Regulation 49(1)(a).
17. Regulation 49(1)(b).
18. Regulation 49(2).
19. Regulation 49(6).

for the purpose of production of petroleum pursuant to the authorization in the Plan for Development and Operation.[20]

In Ghana, about two-thirds of electricity is generated using natural gas. Ghana's *Petroleum (Exploration and Production) (Measurement) Regulations*, 2016 (L.I. 2246) refers to 'flare gas' as 'a natural gas burnt off or vented to the atmosphere'.[21] Ghana's Ministry of Energy and Environmental Protection Agency do approve flaring in the fields if it is in the interest of the economy.[22] In 2023, with respect to the Jubilee field, a total of 13,472.43 MMscf was flared, while 9,642.66 MMscf was flared from the TEN field and 5,331.00 MMscf from the SGN Field.[23]

In May 2024, the African Petroleum Producers Organization (APPO) completed its roundtable on gas flaring and fugitive methane emissions in Accra, Ghana, under the theme 'Towards Zero Routine Gas Flaring and Lower Methane Emissions in APPO Member Countries'. The discussions focused on the latest strategies and developments to minimize routine gas flaring and methane emissions, practices that significantly contribute to climate change and economic losses due to wasted resources. In an eleven-point communique, APPO acknowledged among others, the significant environmental damage and economic losses due to routine gas flaring and methane emissions.[24] APPO further emphasized the importance of utilizing all available natural gas resources to enhance energy availability and accessibility on the continent, so as to spur development and growth.[25]

2.1 Natural Gas Production in Ghana

Ghana's natural gas production has been on a steady increase over the years until a recent decline. It started from under 20,000,000 MMBtu in around 2013, reaching a peak of 120,000,000 MMBtu in 2022 and then declining slightly thereafter. In 2014, Natural gas produced was 2,156,782.5 MMBtu rising to 27,904,269.5 MMBtu in 2015 and rising over the years to a high of 118,396,139.3 MMBtu in 2022, before declining in 2023 to 114,866,867.9 MMBtu.[26]

20. Regulation 49(7).
21. Regulation 41 – *Interpretation.*
    In respect of Natural Gas, Ghana has in place the Natural Gas Distribution and Sale (Technical and Operational) Rules, 2007 (LI 1911), Natural Gas Distribution and Sale (Standard of Performance) Regulations, 2007 (LI 1912), Natural Gas Transmission Utility (Technical and Operational) Rules, 2007 (LI 1913) and Natural Gas Transmission Utility (Standards of Performance) Regulations, 2008 (LI 1936).
22. Toledano, *supra* n. 14, 6.
23. PIAC, *supra* n. 7, 27-28.
24. Ghanaweb, *APPO Vows to End Gas Flaring, Reduce Methane Emissions in Africa's Oil and Gas Industry* (Ghanaweb, 2024), https://www.ghanaweb.com/GhanaHomePage/business/APPO-vows-to-end-gas-flaring-reduce-methane-emissions-in-Africa-s-oil-and-gas-industry-1933469 accessed 27 July 2024.
25. *Ibid.*
26. Ghana Energy Commission, *Ghana Energy Database System*, http://gheatoolkit.energycom.gov.gh/Analysis/EnergySupply accessed 22 July 2024.

Table 5.1 Natural Gas Production in Ghana's Petroleum Industry

Year	*Natural Gas Production (MMBtu)*
2013	0
2014	2,156,782.5
2015	27,904,269.5
2016	24,818,628.2
2017	35,683,773.5
2018	41,312,740.7
2019	58,492,676.3
2020	95,591,554.8
2021	108,315,791.2
2022	118,396,139.3
2023	114,866,867.9

Culled from Energy Commission.[27]

2.2 Ghana's Energy Mix

Ghana's major sources of energy in 2023 were oil (37.7%), Natural Gas (26.4%), biomass (29.8%), hydro (6%) and solar energy accounting for less than 1% of the total energy supply.[28] Ghana's energy mix over the last twenty years is depicted below.

Table 5.2 Ghana's Energy Mix

Year	*Oil %*	*Natural Gas %*	*Hydro %*	*Solar %*	*Biomass %*	*Total Ktoe*
2003	38.6	–	5.5	–	55.9	6,079
2004	35.9	–	7.8	–	56.3	5,824
2005	36.5	–	8.4	–	55.1	5,766
2006	42.6	–	7.1	–	50.4	6,830
2007	45.3	–	4.7	–	50.0	6,811
2008	42.5	–	7.9	–	49.6	6,738
2009	37.8	0.1	9.4	–	52.7	6,316

27. *Ibid.*
28. Ghana Energy Commission, *2024 National Energy Statistical Bulletin* 3 (Ghana Energy Commission 2024), https://energycom.gov.gh/index.php/planning/energy-statistics, accessed 18 July 2024.

Year	*Oil %*	*Natural Gas %*	*Hydro %*	*Solar %*	*Biomass %*	*Total Ktoe*
2010	39.1	6	8.6	–	46.3	6,988
2011	38.1	11	8.5	–	42.8	7,614
2012	42.9	5	8.7	–	43.2	7,965
2013	46.7	3	7.9	0.3	41.9	8,927
2014	43.5	7	7.8	0.3	41.6	9,217
2015	41.3	13	5.2	0.3	40.6	9,663
2016	46.1	8	4.9	2	41.5	9,694
2017	40.1	12	4.9	2	42.6	9,801
2018	42	15	4.7	3	38.0	10,942
2019	39.4	19	5.5	4	36.5	11,286
2020	36.2	25	5.2	5	33.5	12,030
2021	37.3	27	5.5	11	30.1	11,822
2022	33.6	28	5.7	14	32.4	12,342
2023	37.7	26	6	12.8	29.8	13,218

Culled from the Energy Commission.

The Energy Commission – with the mandate to regulate and manage the utilization of energy resources in the Republic[29] – notes; 'In 2024, natural gas will remain the predominant fuel for thermal power facilities.'[30] The total volume of raw gas received from the Jubilee and TEN fields for processing at the GPP was 35,690.20 MMscf in 2023.[31]

Globally, approximately one-fifth of the world's energy use today comes from natural gas and it plays a central role in the global economy.[32] 'Rawat and Garg note that, natural gas is considered as the fuel for the 21st century and is expected to play an important role in developing countries' energy mix because it is cleaner fuel, with less damage to the environment.'[33]

29. *Energy Commission Act*, 1997 (Act 541); section 2 – *Object and Functions of the Commission.*
30. Ghana Energy Commission, *2024 National Energy Statistical Bulletin* (Energy Commission 2024), https://www.energycom.gov.gh/index.php/licensing/energy-efficiency-guidelines?download=88:the-success-story-of-the-energy-efficient-refrigerator-project accessed 28 July 2024.
31. PIAC, *supra* n. 7, 82.
32. Stoppard, Michael, *The Role of Gas in the Energy Transition* (S& P Global 2024), https://www.spglobal.com/en/research-insights/special-reports/look-forward/the-role-of-gas-in-the-energy-transition accessed 26 July 2024.
33. Rawat, Atul and Chandra Prakash Garg, *Assessment of the Barriers of Natural Gas Development and Implementation: A Case of Developing Country*, Energy Policy, Volume 152 May 2021 https://doi.org/10.1016/j.enpol.2021.112195.

3 NATURAL GAS FLARING IN THE CONTEXT OF ENERGY TRANSITION

As noted earlier, around 140 bcm of natural gas is flared globally each year. This is 'a major source of CO_2 emissions, methane and black soot, and is damaging to health …'[34] Further, it is the case that, 'In the Net Zero Emissions by 2050 (NZE) Scenario [of the International Energy Agency], all non-emergency flaring is [expected to be] eliminated globally by 2030, resulting in a 95% reduction in flared volumes and avoiding 365 Mt CO_2-eq.'[35] Gas flaring is defined under Ghana's National Energy Transition Framework (2022-2070) as 'combustion of natural gas produced during oil production or industrial activity'.[36] GHGs refer to 'gases that trap heat in the atmosphere'.[37] The framework underscores Ghana's commitment to tread the path of decarbonization and achieve a net-zero emissions target by 2070, with intermediate milestones to be met in 2030 and 2050. To achieve these targets, appropriate measures need to be taken to curb natural gas flare.

As the Columbia Center on Sustainable Development aptly notes, 'Flaring became an issue in Ghana only when Jubilee's first oil came online in 2010. At the Jubilee field, with government authorization, 0.048 BCM of gas was flared between June and September 2014.'[38] That authorization ended in 2014. The Atuabo GPP processes gas that is not needed for the internal power needs of the Floating Production Storage and Offloading (FPSO) vessel or oil recovery enhancements and the processed gas is used domestically.[39]

Oil and gas production in Ghana in 2010 and 2017 significantly increased emissions in the energy sector due to increased gas flaring in these years.[40] In Ghana, in the past three decades, the carbon dioxide emissions from the energy sector 'increased elevenfold from 2.5 Mt to 26.4 Mt at an 8.9% annual growth rate …'[41] The growth is attributed to the increasing proportion of thermal electricity generation since 2010, gas flaring and fossil fuel use in the transport industry.[42]

In 2023, a total of 13,472.43 MMscf was flared from the Jubilee field,[43] 9,642.66 MMscf from the TEN field[44] and 5,331.00 MMscf from the SGN field.[45] Ghana has a 'no flare policy' but flaring is permitted when the exigencies of the situation necessitate it and flaring still takes place in the Jubilee and TEN Fields, operated by Tullow, though

34. IEA, *supra* n. 1.
35. *Ibid.*
36. Ghana Ministry of Energy, *Ghana's National Energy Transition Framework* xv *(2022-2070)* (Ministry of Energy 2022), https://www.energymin.gov.gh/sites/default/files/2023-09/FINAL%20GHANA%27S%20NATIONAL%20ENERGY%20TRANSITION%20FRAMEWORK_2023_compressed%20%281%29_compressed%20%282%29.pdf accessed 10 July 2024.
37. *Ibid.*
38. Toledano, *supra* n. 14, 4.
39. *Ibid.*, 2.
40. Ghana Ministry of Energy, *supra* n. 36, 40.
41. *Ibid.*
42. *Ibid.*
43. PIAC, *supra* n. 7, 27.
44. *Ibid.*, 28.
45. *Ibid.*

there is a concerted effort to reduce that. The Petroleum Commission notes in its 2024 outlook report that, 'TGL [Tullow Ghana Limited] will continue to run the three Low Pressure Gas Compressors (LPGC) on the FPSO JEAM [John Evans Attah Mills] to help reduce flare rates. In addition, TGL will continue with the maintenance and asset integrity initiatives of the FPSO JEAM in 2024.'[46] In respect of the SGN Field, the FPSO John Agyekum Kufuor saw a high flare rate in February, June and October to December 2024.[47] This was attributed to various compression challenges faced by the operator on the field.[48]

In Ghana's *National Energy Transition Framework* (2022-2070), it is noted that Ghana recognizes that the energy sector is a key area in reducing emissions. As such, steps must be taken to transition that sector towards a net-zero-emissions future and to attain this, Ghana 'must transition to the production and utilization of clean energy and the implementation of measures to mitigate any emissions that occur in the process'.[49] Natural gas can provide significant near-term emissions reductions through fuel substitution and flare reduction. Low-carbon gases can further reduce emissions in the longer term.

The immediate push of natural gas can help achieve fast decarbonization. A focus on developing low-carbon gases can achieve deep decarbonization, providing a further cut in emissions and a pathway to net zero.[50]

The UN's annual climate change conference (COP28), held in the United Arab Emirates in 2023, concluded with a call to transition away from fossil fuels. However, any concerted action to reduce GHG emissions is likely to mean efforts to reduce oil and coal consumption as soon and as much as reasonably possible.[51] For natural gas – the fossil fuel with the lowest GHG footprint – the arguments are more complex. The option exists to transition away from either coal or oil toward natural gas.[52] This brings quick and significant near-term benefits in reduced emissions but does not reach the desired goal of net zero.[53]

4 THE FISCAL IMPLICATIONS OF NATURAL GAS FLARING

The Public Interest and Accountability Committee (PIAC) reports that a total of 255,171.97 MMscf of raw gas was produced in 2023 from the three fields compared to the 2022 volume of 253,555.05 MMscf.[54] In 2018, the Jubilee field generated USD

46. Ghana Petroleum Commission, *Upstream Petroleum Business Outlook Report 2024* 24 (Petroleum Commission, 2024), https://petrocom.gov.gh/wp-content/uploads/2024/04/2024-Ghana-Upstream-Petroleum-Business-Outlook-Report-pdf.io_.pdf accessed 15 July 2024.
47. *Ibid.*, 14.
48. *Ibid.*
49. Ghana Ministry of Energy, *supra* n. 36, 42.
50. Stoppard, *supra* n. 32.
51. *Ibid.*
52. *Ibid.*
53. *Ibid.*
54. PIAC, *supra* n. 7, 25 notes that 'A total of 255,171.97 MMSCF of raw gas (Associated Gas [AG] and Non-Associated Gas [NAG]) was produced in 2023 from the three Fields compared to the 2022 volume of 253,555.05 MMSCF.'

59,420,952.81, the TEN field, USD 25,793,872.52 and the SGN field, USD 48,815,874.82.[55] In 2023, a total of 26,525.10 MMscf of raw gas worth USD 144,927,344.80, was delivered to GNGC in 2023.[56] PIAC notes that, 'The total volume of lean gas sold by [GNGC] was 117,956,609.71 MMBtu in 2023 relative to 118,799,496.14 MMBtu in 2022. This is equivalent to a downturn of 0.7 percent. On the other hand, the monetary value of the lean gas sales increased by 9.4 percent to US$284,302,438.91 in 2023 from US$259,968,833.64 in 2022.'[57]

However, PIAC notes that despite the generation of this revenue, except for 2015 and 2016, there were no payments in respect of gas revenues from raw gas supplied by the NOC, GNPC,[58] into the Petroleum Holding Fund, the designated account where petroleum revenues belonging to the State are required by law to be deposited. This is due to the non-payment for gas use by the power sector.

In order to maximize the potential revenue from this sector, it is aptly noted that 'significant investments in the gas sector are required to convert flared gas to economic value'.[59] It is noted that 'between 2019 and 2021, about 47 bcf of gas was flared, equivalent to about USD 300 million in value'.[60] Ghana needs investments to unlock the gas; once produced, it needs to be processed, transported and distributed to end-users. Non-associated gas needs less processing capacity because the processing is often done upstream as part of the production operations. The government does not have enough capacity to construct another processing plant. Once Ghana has the capacity constraint, then the IOCs may be forced to flare.[61]

Flaring of the gas is a challenge fiscally in the sense that such gas could have been utilized domestically to bring revenue to the country. Nasir Alfa Mohammed, the former Vice-Chair of the PIAC – a statutory body with oversight over the utilization of petroleum revenue by the government – noted that 'the flaring of gas keeps occurring due to inadequate investment and lack of facilities to store and utilize the commodity'.[62]

The Atuabo GPP, with name-plate capacity of 150 MMscfd, does not have enough capacity to process all the gas and even though there has been a plan on the drawing board to expand the GPP, this has still not been done.[63]

55. Public Interest and Accountability Committee 2018 Annual Report on Management and Use of Petroleum Revenue, Ghana 49, 50.
56. PIAC, *supra* n. 7, 42.
57. *Ibid.*
58. *Ibid.*
59. Africa Centre for Energy Policy, *The State of the Energy and Extractive Sectors of Ghana: Critical Reforms Required for Sustainable Economic Recovery* 2 (ACEP 2022), https://acep.africa/the-state-of-the-energy-and-extractive-sectors-of-ghana-critical-reforms-required-for-sustainable-economic-recovery/ accessed 20 July 2024.
60. *Ibid.*
61. Modern Ghana, *More Investment Needed in Oil Sector to Stop Flaring of Gas-ACEP* (Modern Ghana 2023), https://www.modernghana.com/news/1230092/more-investment-needed-in-oil-sector-to-stop-flari.html accessed 17 July 2024.
62. Mohammed, Issah, *Ghana flares $169 worth of Natural Gas* (Ghana News Agency, 2023), https://gna.org.gh/23/05/ghana-flares-169m-worth-of-natural-gas/ accessed 13 July 2024.
63. ACEP, *supra* n. 59, 7.

This expansion was to receive additional gas not only from the Jubilee and TEN fields but also from other discoveries.[64] However, since the capacity has not yet been expanded, gas that could have been utilized for industrial use and power generation is being flared or reinjected because the Atuabo GPP cannot process the additional gas from the fields.[65] As Africa Centre for Energy Policy (ACEP) notes, 'About 246 bcf of gas was either flared or reinjected between 2019 and 2021. Out of this quantity, about 46.8 bcf was flared while 199.8 bcf was reinjected. Additional processing capacity would increase the production of propane and butane (Liquified Petroleum Gas), and reduce the import bill on this product. The flared gas from Jubilee and TEN fields could account for a daily supply of about 50 mmscfd if the GPP were expanded as scheduled.'[66] ACEP further notes that:

> In addition, the cumulative volume from reinjected and flared gas could provide an additional volume of over 100 MMscfd from the Jubilee and TEN fields, enough to meet Ghana's medium-term gas needs. Again, gas delivered from the expanded GPP to power plants and non-power users could be another revenue-generating source for the upstream gas sector. The total flared volume of 47 bcf accounts for a forgone gross revenue of about $300 million in addition to the allied benefits as indicated above.[67]

ACEP aptly notes that '[t]he decision to import gas has implications for how much investment Ghana can attract for domestic production and the ability of the country to optimise existing infrastructure, which is contrary to the communicated capacity of domestic sources by the operators, Tullow Ghana and Eni.'[68] In its 2021 Annual Report, Tullow highlighted its investment in upstream gas infrastructure and expressed confidence in its ability to meet growing domestic gas demand.[69]

The fiscal challenges Ghana is facing would be alleviated if it was able to fully utilize its domestic gas discoveries, thereby reducing imports of natural gas and petroleum products. There have been other discoveries awaiting appraisal such as the Afina and Akoma discoveries, which have the potential to meet Ghana's gas demand.[70] ACEP thus notes that 'therefore, the government's focus must be to optimise those resources rather than imports. Thus, optimising domestic gas utilization would provide a wide range of fiscal and non-fiscal benefits to the state. These include job provision, local content development, technology development, and increased government revenue from corporate taxes, PAYE, tax on services, etc.'[71]

Despite the promise of significant fiscal benefit from the use of domestic gas, however, the viability or sustainability of the gas sector is threatened by the power

64. *Ibid.*, 17.
65. *Ibid.*
66. *Ibid.*
67. *Ibid.*
68. *Ibid.*
69. *Ibid.*
70. *Ibid.*
71. *Ibid.*, 16-17.

sector's inability to pay for gas used domestically. The electricity distribution utility company grapples with technical and commercial losses as well as irregular payments by government agencies, making it unable to pay for gas used for power generation. This has created a huge disincentive for investment in the gas sector. Once there is no commercial avenue to use gas, the host state cannot compel the IOC not to flare gas for operational reasons.

5 HARNESSING FLARED NATURAL GAS FOR INDUSTRIALIZATION

The flared gas could be harnessed for industrial use. Ghana's recurrent power crisis has had a significant toll on its industrialization drive. Economic use of the flared gas would therefore alleviate the power deficits and ensure security of supply for industrialization. The Energy Commission notes that 'Ghana has experienced several periods of power inadequacies since 1984. The most recent stretched over several years, from 2012 to 2015, with its attendant incessant load shedding.'[72] The Energy Commission also notes that another major cause of the power outages is 'the increase in demand without a commensurate generation capacity expansion'.[73]

Further, as noted by the Columbia Center for Sustainable Development, thermal and hydro have been two major sources of energy supply in Ghana[74] with output from both the Akosombo Hydro Power Station and the Kpong Hydro Power Station affected by changes in rainfall pattern and climate change. The Energy Commission notes that 'the power shortfalls had been attributed to the natural phenomenon of prolonged draught at the upper course of the Volta River which affected water inflow into the Akosombo dam'.[75] It is expected that thermal generation will be the leader in the generation mix in the next decade.[76] Thus, 'the Atuabo project plays an important role and associated gas naturally fits into the plan'.[77]

The Atuabo GPP has proved very useful, serving as a source of supply of Liquefied Petroleum Gas (LPG) for domestic use. The GPP has also been supplying gas to industrial customers such as Keda (Twyford), Wangkang and MarcoPolo for the production of sanitary ware. In November 2023, it commenced supply to the Sentuo oil refinery.[78] Increasing availability of affordable natural gas for industrial users, through the commercialization of flared gas, would increase the competitiveness of Ghana's industries.

72. Ghana Energy Commission, *The Success Story of the Ghana Refrigerator Efficiency Project Implemented by the Energy Commission* 1 (Ghana Energy Commission 2016), https://www.energycom.gov.gh/files/The%20Success%20story%20of%20the%20Energy%20Efficient%20Refrigerator%20Project.pdf accessed 12 July 2024.
73. Notice, is the increase in demand without a commensurate generation capacity expansion.
74. Toledano, *supra* n. 14.
75. Ghana Energy Commission, *supra* n. 72, 1.
76. Toledano, *supra* n. 14.
77. *Ibid.*
78. PIAC, *supra* n. 7, 22.

6 USING THE PETROLEUM FISCAL SYSTEMS TO INCENTIVIZE COMMERCIALIZATION OF FLARED GAS

The petroleum fiscal regime or system of a country 'encompass taxation, contractual framework, state participation and bonus payments'.[79] Typically, government take in respect of upstream oil production tends to be higher than that of a non-associated gas production.

It must be highlighted that the upstream oil and gas sector tends to have a unique fiscal regime compared to other sectors, as well as midstream and downstream segments of the sector. Different countries have different fiscal regimes/policies and some countries have had different regimes/policies at different times. The main thrust of a petroleum fiscal regime/policy is about risk allocation and reward attribution between the host country (owner of the resource) and the private investor – normally a foreign IOC. The fiscal terms in any country may be legislated (in whole or in part), or subject to negotiations between the State (or its National Oil Company (NOC)) and the IOC.

An effective fiscal regime should seek to achieve a number of objectives, including encouraging investments by ensuring an appropriate balance between risk and reward, a high degree of beneficiation through, among other policies, appropriate level of revenue sharing, local content and local participation, optimal exploitation of the hydrocarbon resources, efficient administration of the fiscal terms and promotion of transparency. States and their NOCs, being the resource owners, will always want to capture the economic rent from the exploitation of the resource in addition to all the other non-fiscal benefits they seek. Yet, in all individual exploration and production contracts, the agreed fiscal terms will inevitably represent a trade-off between the interests of the state and those of the oil companies.

Basically, countries with highly prospective, or mature basins, have been able to appropriate a higher State share of oil and gas produced. Conversely, frontier provinces and countries with hard-to-find or hard-to-market hydrocarbons have had to allocate a greater share of the oil and gas produced to private investors to entice them to invest. Another dynamic affecting oil and gas fiscal regimes is the global decarbonization agenda. With the threat to divest from fossil fuels, countries are having to lower their state share expectations in order to attract uninterested investors.

We do recognize that the natural gas fiscal regimes differ between the upstream and the downstream segments of the value chain. However, for the purpose of this analysis, we deal simultaneously with the fiscal aspects of natural gas across both upstream and midstream segments and how the design or implementation of the petroleum fiscal system could help or hinder the commercialization of flared gas. We take this approach because managing gas flaring could be either integrated in the upstream or a downstream activity or be a stand-alone activity. An integrated approach of this sort would allow Governments to have a holistic view of the sector and direct incentives to the segment most willing or capable of managing the gas flare challenges.

79. International Monetary Fund, *The Taxation of Petroleum and Minerals Principles, Problems and Practice* 4 (IMF, 2010).

In this regard, we review below the key fiscal terms typically used by oil and gas-producing nations and highlight design issues that should be considered by a government as tools to incentivize investment in gas flare management.

6.1 Royalty

It must be noted that 'Royalty can be a per-unit tax, which is a uniform fixed charge levied on a specified level of volume of production or an ad-valorem tax, which is a fixed charge levied on the value of the output (gross revenues).'[80] Royalty usually applies to upstream operations and so the analysis below reflects situations where the effort to manage the flaring is carried out by an upstream operator.

In economic terms, royalties are deemed regressive because they do not exact more reward to the state from more profitable projects. Hence royalties have a higher propensity to deter investments in marginal projects that are barely profitable. Though royalty rates for natural gas are historically lower than those for oil for discoveries in the same basin and water depth, additional efforts may be needed to minimize this regressive impact of royalties on natural gas investments. In developing countries, since much of the flared gas would be used domestically for power generation or industrial feedstock, a (near) zero-royalty rate on captured gas that would otherwise be flared should be encouraged. Nigeria already incentivizes domestic gas utilization with a lower royalty rate of 2.5% as opposed to 5% for export gas. For countries with significant gas flare challenges, imposing lower royalty rates for flare gas would provide additional incentive to increase utilization of flared gas.

Table 5.3 below illustrates the differences in royalty rates between crude oil and natural gas in Ghana's existing PAs.

Table 5.3 Royalty Rates in Ghana's Upstream Petroleum Industry

Year	*Agreement*	*Royalty Rate*
2004	West Cape Three Points (Tullow, Kosmos, Anadarko, PetroSA Ghana, GNPC)	7.5% - Crude Royalty with API* gravity less than twenty shall be 5% 5% - Natural Gas
2006	Deepwater Tano (Tullow, Anadarko, Kosmos, PetroSA Ghana Ltd. GNPC)	5% - Crude 3% - Natural Gas
2006	Deepwater Tano/Cape Three Points (Aker, Lukoil, FT Exploration and Production, GNPC)	4% on crude 3% on Natural Gas

80. *Ibid.*

Year	*Agreement*	*Royalty Rate*
2008	Offshore Cape Three Points (ENI, Vitol, GNPC)	10% on Crude 5% for Natural Gas
2013	East Cape Three Points (Medea, Cola, GNPC)	10% - Crude 5% - Natural Gas (Destined for the domestic market) 10% - Natural Gas to be exported as LNG
2014	Central Tano Block (Amni International, GNPC)	12.5% on Crude 5% on Natural Gas (Destined for Domestic Market) 10% on Natural Gas to be exported as LNG
2014	South Deepwater Tano (AGM, GNPC, GNPC Explorco)	10% - Crude 6% - Natural Gas
2014	South West Saltpond (Brittania-U Ghana Limited, Hills Oil Marketing Company Ltd., GNPC)	10% - Crude 6% - Natural Gas (for domestic gas projects) 7.5% - Natural gas to be exported
2014	Shallow Water Cape Three Points (Sahara Energy, GNPC, Sapholda E & P Limited)	12.5% - Crude Natural Gas - 6%
2014	Offshore Cape Three Points South (UB Resources, Royalgate Ghana Limited, Houston Drilling Management Gh. Limited, GNPC)	12.5% - Crude 5% - Natural Gas (Destined for the domestic market) 10% - Natural Gas (To be exported as LNG)
2015	Deepwater Cape Three Points West Offshore Eco Atlantic, A-Z Petroleum Products, Petrogulf, GNPC Explorco, GNPC	12.5% - Crude 10% - Natural Gas
2015	East Keta Block (GNPC Operating Services Company Limited -GOSCO, Heritage, Blue Star Exploration, GNPC Explorco)	10% - Crude 6% - Natural Gas (Destined for the domestic market) 10% - Natural Gas to be exported as LNG
2015	Expanded Shallow Water Tano (Erin, GNPC Explorco, Base, GNPC)	12.5% - Crude 7.5% - Natural Gas
2015	Expanded Shallow Water Tano Block (Erin, GNPC, Base Energy, GNPC)	12.5% - Crude 7.5% - Natural Gas

Year	*Agreement*	*Royalty Rate*
2015	Offshore South-West Tano Block (GNPC Offshore Operating Services Company Ltd - GOSCO, Heritage, Blue Star, GNPC Explorco)	12.5% - Crude 10% - Natural Gas (Destined for the domestic market) 10% - Natural Gas to be exported as LNG
2016	Cape Three Points Block 4 (ENI, Vitol, Woodfields, GNPC, Explorco)	10% on Crude 7.5% on Natural Gas
2016	Onshore/Offshore Keta Delta Block (Swiss African Oil Company, Pet Volta Investments Limited, GNPC)	13% - Crude (Onshore Production) 12.5% (Offshore production) 6% - Natural Gas (Destined for the domestic market) 7.5% - Natural Gas (To be exported as LNG)
2018	Deepwater Cape Three Points (ExxonMobil, Goil Offshore, GNPC)	10% - Crude 5% - Natural Gas (Destined for the domestic market) 5% - Natural Gas (to be exported as LNG)

Source: Ghana Petroleum Register.

*API stands for American Petroleum Institute

To mitigate the regressive tendency of royalties, Governments may consider linking the royalty to the value of the flare gas or its derivatives to the investing company. This way, the Government would not miss out on profitable gas flare projects, nor would the investors be subjected to excessive royalty on marginal projects.

In Nigeria, for example, the Petroleum Industry Act (PIA) of 2021 Schedule 7, Part III, Clause 8(3) states that:

> Royalties applicable to natural gas shall be based on the fiscal gas price determined for the field at the measurement point under applicable regulations or guidelines and this price shall be determined by the Commission, taking into consideration submissions by the lessees, and shall be based on the netback value at the measurement point based on the composition of the natural gas in terms of marketable natural gas, ethane, propane, butane, pentanes and other natural gas liquids ... .

The PIA further stipulates that the netback approach would take into consideration: the target market for the natural gas - whether export or domestic, conditioning costs, processing costs and transportation costs as well as the value of the liquids in the natural gas.

6.2 Corporate Income Tax Rate

Corporate income tax (CIT) is a key element of the fiscal terms of any oil and gas-producing nation and applies to all segments of the value chain. For the upstream sector, CIT is usually more important where the country uses service contracts because other instruments of state reward such as carried interest for the NOC do not usually exist. In many countries, the tax rate is typically between 25% and 35%.[81]

To facilitate the development of required infrastructure to commercialize flared gas, governments should consider incentivizing oil and gas companies or other prospective investors with reduced tax liabilities through such measures as lower tax rate and extended income tax holidays. These would free up cash flow for expansion, speed up the payback period of the investments and increase the attractiveness of the country's oil and gas sector.

6.3 Capital Allowance

Another instrument countries may use to incentivize companies to invest in gas flaring management projects is capital allowance. Capital allowance is an allowed deduction of portions of capital expenditure from earnings for tax purposes. A high rate of capital allowance will give investors an accelerated recovery of capital expenditure. Depending on the cost structure, a capital allowance period of three to five years should be considered for investments related to flaring management. This would reduce the payback for the investment. This is common in the upstream segment but may be extended to any entity that invests in gas flaring management.

6.4 Ring-Fencing

Also, integrated companies - those that engage in both upstream and downstream - should be allowed to consolidate costs for the purpose of taxation. Section 272(1) of the Nigerian PIA provides this incentive to attract upstream investments. In a similar vein, countries that have ring-fencing rules may consider relaxing those rules for gas flare management companies that have multiple projects.

6.5 Flare Gas Price

The interplay between the flare gas price and the fiscal terms can also be an effective policy tool to incentivize investment in gas flaring through the distribution of the value chain's rent among the Government, upstream players and downstream participants. Typically, Government take is higher if the distribution of the rent is skewed towards the upstream because by the design of the upstream fiscal terms - which includes royalty, and carried interest of NOC among others, the Government gets more. Thus, if

81. IMF, *supra* n. 79.

gas flare management is not to be handled upstream, the Government may, by policy, require a low flare gas transfer price from the upstream producers to the midstream investor, to attract midstream investment in gas flare management. If upstream players are to manage the gas flare, the transfer price may need to be high enough to dampen the impact of Government take.

6.6 Flare Penalty

The fiscal system of a country can also be used to impose a flare penalty to disincentivize flaring and encourage investment in monetizing the natural gas that would otherwise be flared. The Nigerian Upstream Petroleum Regulatory Commission, for instance, imposes fines of USD 3.5 per 1,000 scf of gas flared by licensees, lessees and producers of gas. Additionally, if the company fails to provide accurate, timely and adequate data, which includes flare or vent data, the company is liable to an administrative charge of USD 10,000.[82] This was increased in 2023 from a penalty of USD 2 per 1,000 scf of gas flared, imposed in 2018, for companies producing more than 10,000 barrels per day (bpd), and USD 0.5 for those producing less than 10,000 bpd.[83]

The question however is one of enforcement, given that Nigerian laws had proscribed gas flaring without written permission from the Minister of Petroleum Resources since 1984. Prior to the recent increase in the penalties in 2023, the penalty for gas flaring generated revenues of USD 341 million in the 10 months between January and October 2022. If enforced and deployed properly, proceeds from the penalty could support investment in flare management and/or finance mitigation interventions in the affected communities.

7 DEVELOPING REGIONAL MARKET FOR NATURAL GAS IN WEST AFRICA

The West African sub-region has one of the lowest rates of electrification in the world, with only 52% of its people having access to electricity according to the World Bank. The region registers electric shortages of up to 80 hours per month on average, and charges some of the highest electricity tariffs in the world, at USD 0.25 per kilowatt-hour, which is more than twice the global average.[84]

Natural gas has a critical role to play in the efforts to increase access to affordable electricity for about 48% of the population of the sub-region. Contribution of natural

82. Nigerian Upstream Regulatory Authority, *Nigerian Gas Flaring Regulations* (Nigerian Upstream Regulatory Authority 2023), https://www.nuprc.gov.ng/wp-content/uploads/2023/07/GAS-FLARING-REGULATIONS.pdf accessed 31 July 2024.
83. Ngiwe, Chinedu, *Gas flaring penalties hit $341m in 10 months* (Businessday NG 2022), https://businessday.ng/energy/oilandgas/article/gas-flaring-penalties-hit-341m-in-10-months/accessed 31 July 2024.
84. World Bank, *Regional Power Trade in West Africa Offers Promise of Affordable, Reliable Electricity* (World Bank 2018), https://www.worldbank.org/en/news/feature/2018/04/20/regional-power-trade-west-africa-offers-promise-affordable-reliable-electricity accessed 31 July 2024.

gas to electricity generation in the Ecowas region has been steadily growing, reaching 42% in 2021 as shown below.

Figure 5.1 Contribution of Natural Gas to Electricity Generation

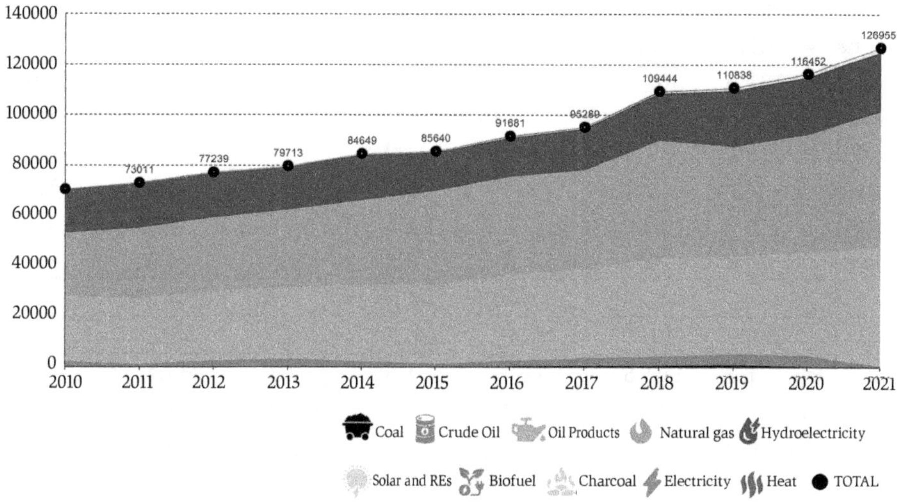

Source: Culled from ECOWAS Key Energy Facts and figures, 2023.

But only a few countries of the region – mainly Nigeria, Ghana, Cote d'Ivoire, Senegal and Niger – have natural gas resource endowments. And even among the fewer producers, only Nigeria currently has a surplus to export. But if harnessed well, Nigeria's gas reserves can supply the rest of the ECOWAS region. Senegal is expected to begin export of natural gas through its LNG projects currently under development. Table 5.4 below provides details of natural gas production, consumption and surplus/ deficit among selected countries.

Table 5.4 Natural Gas Producing Countries: Production, Consumption and Balance (in bcf)

	Production						
	2016	*2017*	*2018*	*2019*	*2020*	*2021*	*2022*
Nigeria	1,474.8	1,570.8	1,609.3	1,635.0	1,644.5	1,529.1	1,410.9
Ghana	22.5	32.3	37.4	52.9	91.1	103.1	112.7
Cote d'Ivoire	81.6	81.6	75.4	80.5	82.6	88.1	93.0
Benin	0.0	0.0	0.0	0.0	0.0	0.0	0.0
Senegal	2.1	2.1	2.1	2.1	2.3	2.2	1.9

Niger	0.0	0.0	1.2	1.4	1.4	1.0	1.0
Togo	0.0	0.0	0.0	0.0	0.0	0.0	0.0
				Consumption			
	2016	*2017*	*2018*	*2019*	*2020*	*2021*	*2022*
Nigeria	653.0	609.3	654.5	663.5	677.1	689.7	731.7
Ghana	26.3	43.5	62.3	75.7	114.4	121.0	138.2
Cote d'Ivoire	81.6	81.6	70.4	75.1	77.2	82.0	93.0
Benin	0.1	1.4	0.7	2.0	5.8	6.4	6.4
Senegal	2.1	2.1	2.1	2.1	2.3	2.2	1.9
Niger	0.0	0.0	1.2	1.3	1.3	1.0	1.1
Togo	0.4	1.4	1.6	3.5	3.5	4.6	4.6
				Surplus/Deficit			
	2016	*2017*	*2018*	*2019*	*2020*	*2021*	*2022*
Nigeria	821.8	961.5	954.9	971.5	967.3	839.4	679.2
Ghana	-3.8	-11.2	-24.9	-22.8	-23.3	-17.9	-25.4
Cote d'Ivoire	0.0	0.0	5.0	5.4	5.4	6.1	0.0
Benin	-0.1	-1.4	-0.7	-2.0	-5.8	-6.4	-6.4
Senegal	0.0	0.0	0.0	0.0	0.0	0.0	0.0
Niger	0.0	0.0	0.0	0.0	0.0	0.0	0.0
Togo	-0.4	-1.4	-1.6	-3.5	-3.5	-4.6	-4.6

Source: Authors' computation from United States Energy Information Administration database.[85]

This provides the opportunity for trade among the countries. The West African Gas Pipeline (WAGP) has, since its inception in 2011, provided an efficient means of transporting natural gas from Nigeria to Benin Republic, Togo and Ghana. It is also used to transport gas from the western coast of Ghana to the eastern coast. From inception to mid-2024, gas delivered through the WAGP totalled 245 million MMBtu to Ghana, 33 million MMBtu to Togo and 35 million MMBtu to the Benin Republic.

The availability of natural gas through the WAGP has significantly contributed to energy security and cost savings for the three buying countries of the WAGP – Benin, Togo and Ghana as shown in Table 5.5 below.

85. U.S. Energy Information Administration 'Electricity' (U.S. Energy Information Administration 2024), https://www.eia.gov/international/data/world/natural-gas/dry-natural-gas-production?pd=2&p=0000000000000000000000000000a00000000000000000000000000000008&u=1&f=A&v=mapbubble&a=-&i=none&vo=value&&t=R&g=none&l=2-00060001000000001b0000000800400c0000000048004&s=1451606400000&e=1640995200000&ev=false accessed 24 July 2024.

Table 5.5 Share of Natural Gas for WAGP Buyers

		Total Electricity Generation; Share of Natural Gas for WAGP Buyer Countries						
		2016	2017	2018	2019	2020	2021	2022
Benin	Total Generation (MWh)	276,000	330,500	201,800	529,200	988,700	1,127,100	1,128,123
	Share of NG (%)	*2.5*	*42.3*	*31.1*	*59.6*	*75.8*	*79.1*	*79.0*
Ghana	Total Generation (MWh)	13,166,000	13,292,200	14,906,900	17,297,800	19,734,000	22,070,700	22,498,875
	Share of NG (%)	*30.4*	*30.0*	*34.3*	*41.6*	*58.7*	*62.5*	*63.2*
Togo	Total Generation (MWh)	945,700	804,700	588,000	718,200	698,100	847,700	887,270
	Share of NG (%)	*3.3*	*15.7*	*35.7*	*63.5*	*68.7*	*65.7*	*66.4*

Concerted efforts should be made to co-invest in regional projects to harness flare gas and improve gas supply to the region. What the WAGP and other regional projects such as the West African Power Pool (WAPP) have shown is that even in the face of limited investment capital, nations can have a joint or concerted approach to financing the investment in, and operation of, critical infrastructure, and share the benefits therefrom.

8 CONCLUSION

For decades, especially in the twentieth century, oil and gas-producing countries/ companies treated natural gas as an unwelcome byproduct of oil because its market was limited due to limited infrastructure to transport and use in distant locations. This, coupled with loose regulation around GHG emissions created a situation where most companies found it convenient to flare or vent associated natural gas or plug-in and leave undeveloped, most non-associated gas discoveries.

Today, however, natural gas is more valuable with an increasingly liquid market due to the rapid development of technologies for liquefaction, transportation and regasification. In addition, global awareness of the effect of gas flare on GHG emissions has galvanized concerted efforts to curb the practice.

Natural gas is critical for many countries – both developed and developing – in their quest to attain energy security. Besides legislation and other efforts to manage natural gas flaring, we have explored how oil and gas-producing countries may use the fiscal petroleum fiscal systems to provide incentives for investment in the management of gas flare. The core theme is to use the fiscal tools to redistribute the rents accruing across the value chain to the segments that have the capacity and interest to invest in gas flare.

CHAPTER 6

Natural Gas Flaring and Other Oil and Gas Emissions: The Technicality and Practice

Magnus C. Abraham-Dukuma & Michael Uche Ukponu

1 INTRODUCTION

The very nature of gas flaring in the oil and gas industry does not easily lend itself to the simple comprehension of all and sundry. Although not an intrinsically abstruse phenomenon beyond reach, there is a chance that most non-specialists would merely construe flaring as a generic air pollutant without a good sense of why and how it occurs. The thrust of this chapter is to discuss the very nature of gas flaring. Within this broad envelope, the authors will discuss how flaring occurs across the various streams of the oil and gas industry, and then delve into some mitigation techniques as well as the key challenges limiting the mass-scale deployment of technical interventions to abate or totally stop gas flaring globally.

Due to the nature of these matters, some of the themes and concepts get technical almost immediately. Nonetheless, a measurable understanding of gas flaring is essential to the design of legal, regulatory, and policy interventions that work. Thus, this chapter, as part of its discussion, will consider the direct and indirect emissions from oil and gas industry operations, including but not limited to the following: exploration, production, refining and transportation/distribution-related emissions; and fugitive and asset integrity-related emissions.

The production of oil and gas is generally classified as either conventional or unconventional (production using techniques other than the conventional oil well method).[1] Shale gas, tight gas, coal bed methane, light tight oil, extra heavy oil, oil/tar

1. Cesar A. Poveda, *Sustainability Assessment: A Rating System Framework for Best Practices* (Ringgold Inc. 2017) 192.

sands and oil shale are the notorious unconventional oil and gas resources. Conventional and unconventional oil and gas production techniques all result in gas flaring and venting needing effective regulatory interventions.

The rest of the chapter is divided into four key sections. The next section (section 2) provides a quick overview of the oil and gas industry to aid an appreciation of the very nature of the industry which this entire text focuses on. Section 3 discusses gas flaring particularly and other emissions associated with the production of oil and gas resources. In section 4, the authors delve into proven mitigation techniques for abating gas flaring and some of the challenges inhibiting the mass-scale deployment of known interventions to reduce gas flaring and industry emissions more broadly. Conclusions are presented in section 5.

2 OVERVIEW OF THE OIL AND GAS INDUSTRY

The oil and gas industry is multi-streamed and consists primarily of the upstream, midstream, and downstream sectors.[2] The upstream sector covers exploration activities and eventual production of oil and gas in their crude forms.[3] Oil and gas are sometimes found together in oil and gas fields and are formed by a similar geological process. However, oil and gas require different processing schemes due to their different physical states.[4] While oil is refined after production, gas is treated and compressed for distribution.[5] Some fields or wells produce just gas, which can be directly treated or compressed through industrial processes; but most wells more often produce a mixture of oil and gas, water and numerous contaminants, which all pass through separation processes.[6]

The midstream sector includes processing and transportation of produced petroleum products to refineries (for crude oil) and gas plants for treatment, processing, gasification and compression (for gas) and further technical processes.[7] The downstream sector involves refining of the produced crude oil into derivatives (heating oil, kerosene, liquefied petroleum gas (LPG), aviation fuel, diesel, asphalt base, gasoline and fuel oils) and marketing/supply to end consumers.[8] The key aim of the refining phase is to provide a range of products in line with conventional industry specifications.[9] This is done through crude distillation to derive gases; light gasoline (technically called light strain naphtha); heavy gasoline (military jet fuel); kerosene (also called

2. Joseph Hilyard, *The Oil and Gas Industry: A Nontechnical Guide* (PennWell Corporation 2012) 226.
3. *Ibid.*
4. US EPA Oil, *Exploration, Production, Transport and Natural Gas* (US EPA 2010) 4.
5. *Ibid.*
6. Hâvard Davold, *Oil and Gas Production Handbook: An Introduction to Oil and Gas Production, Transport, Refining and Petrochemical Industry* (Edition 3.0 Oslo, ISBN 978-82-997886-3-2 August 2013) 14.
7. *Ibid.*, at 16.
8. Mohamed Al Fahim, Taher Al-Sahhaf & Amal Elkilani *Fundamentals of Petroleum Refining* (Elsevier 2010) 1.
9. Davold, *supra* n. 6, at 18.

light distillate); diesel (technically called middle distillates or light gas oil); and heavy distillates (also called atmospheric gas oil or heavy gas oil).[10]

Other important derivatives in the refining process are petrochemicals. Petrochemicals are derived from the petroleum and natural gas value chain, and are in three primary classifications, namely: olefins (ethylene, propylene, and butadiene), aromatics (benzene, toluene, and xylenes) and synthesis gas (syngas).[11] These three broad classifications constitute raw materials to produce plastics, synthetic detergents, dyes, ammonia, fertilizer, and methanol in the petrochemical industry.[12]

Particularly, flaring, and more broadly, greenhouse gas (GHG) emissions occur in these three streams traversing extraction, processing, transportation, refining and distribution operations.[13] All these operations are energy intensive, requiring large amounts of heat or electricity, as necessity demands. The details of how these emissions occur are expanded in later sections of this chapter. The International Petroleum Industry Environmental Conservation Association (IPIECA), the American Petroleum Institute (API) and the International Association of Oil & Gas Producers (IOGP) all agree that virtually all companies within the oil and gas industry immensely contribute to the emission of a wide range of GHGs – carbon dioxide (CO_2), methane (CH_4), nitrous oxide (N_2O), hydrofluorocarbons (HFCs), perfluorocarbons (PFCs) and sulphur hexafluoride (SF_6).[14] These all have global warming potentials (GWPs) and thereby pose grave adverse risk to the climate.[15]

There are a few classifications for broadly grouping the GHG emissions emanating from oil and gas industry operations, all of which cover flaring and venting of gas. The API specifically recognises that different segments of exploration, production, gas processing; transportation; refining and treatment; and marketing and distribution are the direct operational sources of GHG emissions – predominantly CO_2, CH_4 and N_2O, among others.[16] This does not however disregard other indirect emission sources and factors in the entire industry chain.[17] The API classifies GHG emissions in the industry into three main sources, namely: combustion sources (combustion of GHG-containing fuels in either stationary or mobile equipment), vented sources (releases in the course of operations) and fugitive sources (unintentional releases from equipment leakage).[18]

According to the Greenhouse Gas Protocol (GGP), introduced by the World Business Council for Sustainable Development (WBCSD) and the World Resources Institute (WRI), GHG emissions from industries in general typically occur directly,

10. Fahim, Al-Sahhaf & Elkilani, *supra* n. 8, at 69.
11. Davold, *supra* n. 6, at 19.
12. *Ibid.*
13. Giovanni Di Lullo, Hao Zhang & Amit Kumar, 'Evaluation of Uncertainty in the Well-to-Tank and Combustion Greenhouse Gas Emissions of Various Transportation Fuels' (2016) 184 Applied Energy 413, 414 https://doi.org/10.1016/j.apenergy.2016.10.027.
14. IPIECA, API & OGP, *Petroleum Industry Guidelines for Reporting Greenhouse Gas Emissions* (2nd edn IPIECA, API and OGP 2011) 5-1.
15. *Ibid.*
16. API, *Compendium of Greenhouse Gas Emissions Methodologies for the Oil and Natural Gas Industry* (3rd edn API 2009) 2-4.
17. *Ibid.*
18. *Ibid.*, at 3-2.

indirectly and in three scopes.[19] Scope one emissions occur from direct sources under the immediate ownership and control of the company, for example, generation of electricity, heat or steam, physical and chemical processing, transportation of raw materials and fugitive emissions.[20] Scope two emissions occur indirectly from the generation of electricity used by the company, while Scope three emissions occur outside the immediate control of the company, but are indirectly linked to its operations and activities.[21]

The IPIECA Joint Industry Tax Force on Greenhouse Gas[22] relies on the GGP three-scope approach[23] but with an oil and gas industry-specific context.[24] Accordingly, Scope one GHG emissions come from combustion in stationary sources; combustion in flares, incinerators and mobile sources (motor vehicles, tank trucks and oil tankers); process emissions; venting emissions; fugitive emissions; and non-routine vents, especially occurring during planned asset maintenance and unplanned events.[25] Scope two GHG emissions are generally energy-related indirect emissions such as purchased electricity, steam, heating and cooling systems in the industry.[26] Scope three GHG emissions are a different category of indirect emissions, which do not come under scope two but occur in the life cycle and are necessarily incidental to the company's operations and activities.[27] Examples include raw materials necessary for operations, transportation, use and disposal of products.[28]

The Intergovernmental Panel on Climate Change (IPCC) classifies the GHG emission sources for the energy industry into two, namely: fuel combustion activities and fugitive emissions.[29] This classification by the IPCC echoes aspects of other classifications above but without regard for distinguishing direct and indirect emission sources. On the contrary, it views all fuel combustion-related releases in the value chain of the energy extraction and production industry as fuel combustion sources;[30] and fugitive emissions as 'intentional or unintentional releases, which can ordinarily occur from production, processing, transmission, storage and use of fuels'.[31] Another classification strand is a quadruple recognition of upstream (covering extraction to transportation to refinery), refinery (covering oil refining and gas process), distribution (covering products supply and marketing) and combustion emissions.[32] All the

19. WBCSD & WRI, *The Greenhouse Gas Protocol: A Corporate Reporting Standards* (2nd edn WBCSD & WRI 2004) 25.
20. *Ibid.*, at 27.
21. *Ibid.*
22. This task force comprises the IPIECA, the API and the IOGP.
23. WBCSD & WRI, *supra* n. 19.
24. IPIECA, API & OGP, *supra* n. 14, at 3-14.
25. *Ibid.*
26. *Ibid.*, at 3-15.
27. *Ibid.*, at 3-17.
28. *Ibid.*
29. IPCC, *Guidelines for National Greenhouse Gas Inventories* (IPCC 2006), 1.5.
30. *Ibid.*, 1.3.
31. *Ibid.*, 1.6.
32. Christian Moretti & Others, 'Analysis of Standard and Innovative Methods for Allocating Upstream and Refinery GHG Emissions to Oil Products' (2017) 206 Applied Energy 372 at 374 and 375 https://doi.org/10.1016/j.apenergy.2017.08.183.

classifications considered in the foregoing paragraphs are relevant to this chapter and the entire book, as they all help in forming an appreciable understanding of emission sources of the industry, and situate gas flaring within the broad envelope of GHG emissions in the oil and gas industry.

3 UPSTREAM PROCESSES AND EMISSIONS

GHG emissions in the petroleum industry could be grouped into four broad categories, namely: upstream emissions, midstream emissions, downstream emissions, and fugitive emissions. This taxonomy is consistent with the classifications of the multi-streams that characterise the industry. It helps to understand the broad spectrum of emissions associated with the entire industry value chain. But the discussion in this chapter has focused more on upstream gas flaring as it aligns more with the scope of this book. It also touched on fugitive emissions, although their contribution to the industry's emissions profile is little, compared to flaring volumes.

3.1 Flaring and Other Emissions

The upstream sector is characterised by five core phases, namely exploration (searching for oil and gas), appraisal (feasibility study of the well/field and commercial viability of production), development planning, production and decommissioning (field abandonment/closure).[33] Apart from the diversity, complexity and cost implications of these phases,[34] the time interval for navigating through them varies from one oilfield to another, depending on the peculiarities and characteristics of different fields.[35] Irrespective of these likely variations, the projected timing for the phases usually ranges between 1 to 5 years for exploration, 4 to 10 for appraisal, 4 to 10 for development, 20 to 50 for production and 2 to 10 for decommissioning.[36] Although the exploration and production processes and procedures may vary across different jurisdictions because of characteristic differences in oilfields, geological peculiarities and resource diversity,[37] various conventional petroleum industry activities and processes generate considerable volumes of GHGs in the core upstream phases,[38] except the appraisal phase, which is just a feasibility study of the oilfield or well.[39] In

33. Frank Jahn, Mark Cook & Mark Graham, *Developments in Petroleum Science, vol. 55: Hydrocarbon Exploration and Production* (2nd edn Elsevier 2008) 2-6.
34. Nadine Bret-Rouzaut & Jean-Pierre Favennec, *Oil and Gas Exploration and Production: Reserves, Costs, Contracts* (3rd edn Editions Technip 2011) 2.
35. Robert Clews, *Project Finance for the International Petroleum Industry* (Elsevier 2016) 102.
36. Emily Darko, *Short Guide Summarising the Oil and Gas Industry Lifecycle for a Non-Technical Audience* (Overseas Development Institute October 2014), www.assets.publishing.service.gov.uk.
37. Angela Zahniser, *Characterization of Greenhouse Gas Emissions Involved in Oil and Gas Exploration and Production Operations* (8 November 2013), Wrapair www.wrapair.org.
38. *Ibid.*
39. Jan Petter Morten & Others, 'Field Appraisal and Accurate Resource Estimation from 3D Quantitative Interpretation of Seismic and CSEM Data' (2012) 31:4 The Leading Edge 447, 448 https://doi.org/10.1190/tle31040447.1.

fact, emissions occur in the different processes of exploration, well construction and drilling, well completion and during continuous production activities (from production pads, consisting of wellheads, separation units and storage tanks), even up until decommissioning.[40]

The exploration phase is the first stage of the upstream sector and is characterised by the search for oil and gas resources by the international oil company (IOC) to provide geological data for appraisal of the field and to enable optimal resource management.[41] It requires initial, geological and geophysical evaluation of data generated from seismic activities.[42] Seismic surveys apply to both onshore and offshore exploration and usually involve the use of sound waves.[43] The process usually involves use of vibroseis and explosives, especially for onshore exploration with waves of energy similar to an earthquake.[44] Apart from the scientific evidence of the sonic and structural effects of onshore and offshore seismic activities on human and aquatic creatures,[45] there are also carbon and methane emissions from heavy-duty trucks, vibroseis and the use of explosive devices.[46] In this respect, the dominant GHG associated with the exploration phase is CO_2, which ordinarily occurs as a direct consequence of combustion from vehicles, stationary engines and other heavy-duty equipment.[47]

The second phase of the upstream sector is well/field development. It is an important phase because of the corresponding investment decisions, which hinge on its outcome.[48] It requires a field development plan, which establishes the number of wells to drill, recovery techniques, type/cost of installations and environmental concerns.[49] It practically encompasses all activities necessary to prepare the site (beyond the infrastructure already put in place at the exploration phase) for production,[50] and climaxes with the production of the first oil (an exploratory well bearing the first-discovered reservoir of oil and gas, also called discovery well).[51]

40. Halley L. Brantley, 'Assessment of Methane Emissions from Oil and Gas Production Pads using Mobile Measurements' (2014) 48 Environmental Science and Technology 14508 https://doi.org/10.1021/es503070q.
41. Oil & Gas Portal, *Petroleum Exploration* (August 2018), Oil and Gas Portal www.oil-gasportal.com.
42. *Ibid.*
43. OGP, *An Overview of Marine Seismic Operations*, Report No. 488 April 2011, www.norskoljeoggass.no.
44. Mahmoud Sroor, *Geology and Geophysics in Oil Exploration* (2010), www.fac.ksu.edu.sa.
45. API, *Seismic Surveying 101: Seismic Survey Fact Sheet* (API 2014) DM2014-229/12.16, www.api.org.
46. Zahniser, *supra* n. 37, at 2.
47. *Ibid.*
48. Majid Shakhsi-Niaei, Seyed Hossein Iranmanesh & Seyed Ali Torabi, 'Optimal Planning of Oil and Gas Development Projects Considering Long-Term Production and Transmission' (2014) 65 Computers and Chemical Engineering 67, 79 https://doi.org/10.1016/j.compchemeng.2014.03.002.
49. IFP School, *What Are the Main Steps of an Oil or Gas Field Development Project?* (IFP School October 2014), www.ifp-school.com.
50. Darko, *supra* n. 36, at 2.
51. Norman J. Hyne, *Dictionary of Petroleum Exploration, Drilling and Production* (2nd edn PennWell Corporation 2014) 138.

The fundamental goal of this phase is the efficient drilling of target wells, as a test case for production in commercial quantity.[52] Key activities of the phase include: clearing the well pad area, construction of access roads, rigging up (setting up the rig for drilling), drill-bit lubrication with drilling fluids, casing, well completion and testing.[53] Virtually all these activities contribute to the emission of GHGs due to their energy requirement and application.[54] Clearing of the well pad and access road construction requires the use of trucks and other heavy-duty equipment. The combustion of fuels for equipment operation is the primary source of emission in these activities.[55] It applies also to rigging up. Lubricating the drill bit with spray drilling fluids is another source of CO_2 and CH_4 emissions through flaring or venting of vapours from the drilling fluids. Fracturing, flaring, venting, compressor engines and tube installation are technical processes, which characterise the well completion and testing stage of well development. These various activities are also considerable sources of CO_2 and CH_4 emissions because of fuel injection machinery, combustion fuel input (diesel or natural gas) for compressor engines, combustion requirement for equipment installation, and flaring during production test (production of first oil).[56] Similarly, offshore platforms are also very energy-intensive systems in need of energy efficiency.[57] Thus, there are also similar emissions from offshore operations due to emissions from ships, Floating Production Storage and Offloading (FPSO) vessels, fuel combustion and energy requirements for power generation, waste heat recovery, constructing and setting up oil rigs, drilling platforms, which all contribute to the exergy cost of offshore petroleum production.[58]

The extraction or recover phase is the third and core phase of the upstream sector and involves extensive extraction or recovery of oil and gas to the surface after satisfactory testing of the discovery well (first oil),[59] with the primary objective of delivering the resources at required rate/volume and quality.[60] CO_2, CH_4, and volatile organic compounds (VOCs) from flaring account for vast amounts of GHG emissions in the upstream sector and contribute immensely to the greenhouse footprint of the oil and gas industry.[61] The volume of global gas flaring associated with this core production phase has hovered around 140+ billion cubic meters (bcm) over the last

52. Deutsche Bank, *Oil and Gas for Beginners: A Guide to the Oil and Gas Industry* (Deutsche Bank, London 2013) 72.
53. Zahniser, *supra* n. 37.
54. *Ibid.*
55. *Ibid.*
56. *Ibid.*
57. Tuong-Van Nguyen & Others, 'Energy Efficiency Measures for Offshore Oil and Gas Platforms' (2016) 117 Energy 325 https://doi.org/10.1016/j.energy.2016.03.061.
58. Julio A.M. da Silva & S. de Oliveira Junior 'Unit Exergy Cost and CO2 Emissions of Offshore Petroleum Production' (2018) 147 Energy 757 https://doi.org/10.1016/j.energy.2018.01.100.
59. Darko, *supra* n. 36.
60. Jahn, Cook & Graham, *supra* n. 33, at 312.
61. David T. Allen & Others, 'Carbon Dioxide, Methane and Black Carbon Emissions from Upstream Oil and Gas Flaring in the United States' (2016) 13 Current Opinion in Chemical Engineering 119, 121 https://doi.org/10.1016/j.coche.2016.08.014.

decade and plateaued at approximately 144 bcm in 2021.[62] In 2022, global gas flaring volumes fell by 3% related to the volume flared in the previous year, but flaring still accounted for 500 metric tonnes of CO_2 equivalent annual GHG emissions.[63]

Gas flaring volumes vary between jurisdictions and oilfields, depending on production practices and reservoir qualities.[64] Despite jurisdictional variations, the actual extraction phase involves conventional processes (crude oil separation, natural gas conditioning, wastewater disposal, routine well site visits) and the use of certain equipment (compressor engines, dehydrator, stations, rigging pumps, gas lift valves, separator, and other site facilities).[65] These processes and equipment are energy-intensive and account for vast emissions of CO_2, CH_4, N_2O and other VOCs[66] due to the combustion of fossil fuels for process energy and the flaring and venting of gas.[67]

Associated gas (AG) is found and extracted alongside crude oil in most reservoirs. It is dissolved in crude oil, mixed with water and condensates, and used interchangeably as solution gas in some jurisdictions.[68] It is a byproduct of oil in most reservoirs,[69] which leads to its inextricable extraction or production with oil.[70] Usually, during production, due to increased reservoir pressure and temperature changes, the solution gas becomes free gas, which can be utilised for wellhead platform operations, re-injected or flared into the atmosphere; while the water component is re-injected into the reservoir of origin.[71]

The AG volume usually ranges between 5 to 1,000 m^3 per ton of oil[72] and has concentrations of hydrogen, methane, ethane, propane, butane, isobutene and other

62. World Bank, *2022 Global Gas Flaring Tracker Report* (World Bank Global Gas Flaring Reduction Partnership, 5 May 2022) at 15.
63. International Energy Agency Flaring Emissions Tracker, https://www.iea.org/energy-system/fossil-fuels/gas-flaring accessed 21 October 2023.
64. Hassan M. El-Houjeiri, Adam R. Brandt & James E. Duffy 'Open-Source Tool for Estimating Greenhouse Gas Emissions from Crude Oil Production Using Field Characteristics' (2013) 47 Environmental Science and Technology 5998, 6002 https://doi.org/10.1021/es304570m.
65. Zahniser, *supra* n. 37, at 8 and 9.
66. *Ibid.*
67. Hsien H. Khoo & Reginald B.H. Tan 'Environmental Impact Evaluation of Conventional Fossil Fuel Production: Oil and Natural Gas and Enhanced Resource Recovery with Potential CO_2 Sequestration' (2006) 20 Energy and Fuels 1914, 1918 https://doi.org/10.1021/ef060075+.
68. Cutler Cleveland & Christopher Morris (eds), *Dictionary of Energy* (2nd edn Elsevier 2015) at 1086; David M. Carson & Jan W. Henderson (eds), *Our Petroleum Challenge* (7th edn Canadian Centre for Energy Information 2004) 82.
69. Cheryl L. Weyant & Others, 'Black Carbon from Associated Natural Gas Flaring' (2016) 50 Environmental Science and Technology 2075 https://doi.org/10.1021/acs.est.5b04712.
70. Vladimir A. Kirillov & Others 'Experimental and Theoretical Study of Associated Petroleum Gas Processing into Normalized Gas by Soft Steam Reforming' (2017) 51:1 Theoretical Foundations of Chemical Engineering 12. https://doi.org/10.1134/s0040579517010110.
71. Michael R. Johnson, Larry W. Kostiuk & James L. Spangelo, 'A Characterization of Solution Gas Flaring in Alberta' (2001) 51 Journal of the Air and Waste Management Association 1167 at 1168 https://doi.org/10.1080/10473289.2001.10464348; Petropedia, *Solution Gas*, www.petropedia.com.
72. Alexey A. Solov'yanov, 'Associated Petroleum Gas Flaring: Environmental Issues' (2011) 81:12 Russian Journal of General Chemistry 2531 https://doi.org/10.1134/s1070363211120218.

hydrocarbons with potential greenhouse implications.[73] It is a common industry practice in the various oil and gas jurisdictions of the world to flare excess flammable gas,[74] especially when it is difficult to achieve total re-injection of the AG produced alongside oil.[75]

Optimal gas re-injection reduces flaring, but there is usually a very high emission rate when all the produced AG is flared.[76] Purges, leakages and emergency releases are other industry gas flaring processes, apart from mainstream production.[77] In addition to CO_2 and VOCs, flaring also creates particulate matter (other hazardous pollutants in the form of black carbon or soot),[78] which all interact directly and indirectly, with negative effects on the earth's climatic processes.[79] The World Bank Global Gas Flaring Reduction (GGFR) Partnership categorises gas flaring into three: routine flaring (occurring during normal oil and gas production from oil and gas separators and process units); safety flaring (occurring as a safety mechanism through gas stemming, blow-down, etc.); and non-routine flaring (every other flaring, for example, through equipment failure, process upsets, reservoir or well maintenance).[80]

3.2 Fugitive Emissions

Fugitive emissions from both oil and natural gas operations constitute direct and indirect sources of GHG emissions across the whole industry chain in many oil and gas jurisdictions of the world.[81] The IPCC defines fugitive emissions as 'all intentional and unintentional emissions from the extraction, processing, storage and transport of fuel to the point of final use'.[82] The United States Environmental Protection Agency (USEPA) argues that the IPPC's definition is not intuitive since the word 'fugitive' in

73. Irina Burenina, 'Associated Petroleum Gas: Problems, Prospects, Ways to Increase its Effective Use' (2017) 8:7 Journal of Environmental Management and Tourism 1399, 1400 https://doi.org/10.14505//jemt.v8.7(23).09.
74. World Bank, *Global Gas Flaring Reduction Partnership*, www.worldbank.org.
75. Matthew R. Johnson & Adam R. Coderre, 'An Analysis of Flaring and Venting Activity in the Alberta Upstream Oil and Gas Industry' (2011) 61:2 Journal of the Air and Waste Management Association 190 https://doi.org/10.3155/1047-3289.61.2.190.
76. Pernille Seljom & Eva Rosenberg 'A Study of Oil and Natural Gas Resources and Production' (2011) 5:1 International Journal of Energy Sector Management 101, 103 https://doi.org/10.1108/17506221111120929.
77. James D.N. McEwen & Matthew R. Johnson, 'Technical Paper: Black Carbon Particulate Emission Factors for Buoyancy-Driven Associated Gas Flares' (2012) 62:3 Journal of the Air and Waste Management Association 307 https://doi.org/10.1080/10473289.2011.650040.
78. *Ibid.*
79. Olusegun G. Fawole, Xiaoming M. Cai & Alistair R. MacKenie 'Gas Flaring and Resultant Air Pollution: A Review Focusing on Black Carbon' (2016) 216 Environmental Pollution 182 https://doi.org/10.1016/j.envpol.2016.05.075.
80. World Bank, *Global Gas Flaring Reduction Partnership Gas Flaring Definitions* (GGFR June 29 2016), World Bank www.worldbank.org.
81. David Picard, *Energy, Transportation and Fugitive Emissions: Fugitive Emissions from Oil and Natural Gas Activities* (25 February 2003) IPPC, www.ipcc-nggip.iges.or.jp.
82. IPCC, *2006 IPPC Guidance for National Greenhouse Gas Inventories* (IPCC 2006), www.ipcc-nggip.iges.or.jp.

itself means unintentional.[83] So, it strictly views fugitive emissions as 'equipment leaks' - those emissions which could not reasonably pass through a stack, chimney, vent or other functionally equivalent opening; while vented emissions are intentional or designed releases of CH_4 or CO_2 containing natural gas or hydrocarbon gas (not including stationary combustion flue gas).[84]

This chapter does not attempt a critical analysis of differing or nuanced definitions of fugitive emissions. In any case, these (fugitive emissions) occur in virtually all the streams, primarily from equipment component leaks; process venting; evaporation losses; disposal of waste gas streams (e.g., by venting or flaring), wastewater treatment, air conditioning/refrigeration, accidents and equipment failures because of infrastructure type, quality and integrity, quantum of waste generated and absence of (or inadequate) waste control incentives.[85] These releases occur generally through valves, seals and flanges of equipment related to oil and gas operations.[86]

Additionally, gas migration (GM) - methane leakage from oil and gas wells traversing well cement sheath and casing to the surface - is a recurring source of fugitive emissions from oil and gas wells.[87] Extraction type, whether conventional or unconventional, can have varied potential impacts on the likelihood of GM, especially where cyclic steam injection (CSI) - oil recovery method by steam injection into the well - is a technique during extraction of bitumen or heavy crude.[88] This raises well integrity concerns, generally known in the industry as loss of internal integrity,[89] and this is a globally recognised cardinal operational safety consideration in petroleum engineering parlance.[90]

Considerable volumes of CH_4 disperse into the atmosphere during gas distribution because of leak-prone distribution infrastructure,[91] which presents an explosion risk, apart from the climate change implication.[92] Apart from the methane migration, which occurs from wells at the upstream production phase, there are also fugitive emissions percolating from most decommissioned oil and gas wells onto groundwater

83. USEPA, *Greenhouse Gas Emissions Reporting from Petroleum and Natural Gas Industry: Background Technical Support Document* (4 December 2012), US EPA www.epa.gov at 7.
84. *Ibid.*
85. Picard, *supra* n. 81, at 53, 105 and 106.
86. API, *Compendium, supra* n. 16, at 2-12 and 6-1.
87. Stefan Bachu 'Analysis of Gas Leakage Occurrence Along Wells in Alberta, Canada, from a GHG Perspective: Gas Migration Outside Well Casing' (2017) 61 International Journal of Greenhouse Gas Control 146 at 147 https://doi.org/10.1016/j.ijggc.2017.04.003.
88. *Ibid.*, at 149.
89. A.K. Wojtanowicz, 'Environmental Control of Well Integrity', in Stefan Orszulik (ed.), *Environmental Technology in the Oil Industry* (3rd edn Springer, 2016) at 61.
90. Liane Smith & Dragan Zivko Milanovic 'The Total Control of Well Integrity Management' (SPE-117121-MS) Abu Dhabi International Petroleum Exhibition and Conference, 3-6 November 2008, Abu Dhabi, UAE.
91. Margaret F. Hendrick & Others 'Fugitive Methane Emissions from Leak-Prone Natural Gas Distribution Infrastructure in Urban Environments' (2016) 213 Environmental Pollution 710 at 711 https://doi.org/10.1016/j.envpol.2016.01.094.
92. *Ibid.*, at 714.

and to the surface and dispersing into the atmosphere.[93] Different studies[94] reveal emissions from three broad categories of well integrity factors: chemical (reactions arising from the use of chemicals for well activities), mechanical (geo-mechanical stresses on the well), and physical (failure of integrity barriers such as casing and cement).

Fugitive emissions occurring particularly from leaks raise asset integrity questions in the oil and gas industry and the need to avoid such leaks by ensuring the integrity or reliability of installations and facilities in the entire industry chain.[95] Similar to the issue of asset integrity as an emission factor, another issue of concern is ageing infrastructure. Masnadii and Brandt[96] argue that the age of an oilfield can significantly increase the climate impacts of oil and gas production. In a study of GHG emission intensity from oilfields, applying the Oil Production Greenhouse Gas Emissions Estimator formulae,[97] they examined 25 global oilfields over a production span of 66 years (1949-2015). The study found that the intensity of GHG emissions from the examined oilfields increased to greater proportions as the oilfields got older. This discovery led them to the conclusion that 'the GHG intensities of both average and marginal petroleum resources will probably increase over time'.[98]

4 MITIGATION TECHNIQUES AND CHALLENGES

Gas flaring, venting, and the emitting of GHGs more broadly in the oil and gas industry are not occurrences that are irredeemably beyond solution. There are proven technological and policy interventions to abate flaring and other emissions. But there are also challenges associated with the large-scale implementation or execution of the interventions, hence the current difficulty in totally eradicating the egregious volume of gas flared annually from oil and gas production worldwide. This section of the chapter provides a summary discussion of some of the approaches and key challenges.

93. Ian Malcolm Boothroyd & Others, 'Fugitive Emissions of Methane from Abandoned, Decommissioned Oil and Gas Wells' (2016) 547 Science of the Total Environment 461 at 462, 467 and 468 https://doi.org/10.1016/j.scitotenv.2015.12.096.
94. Richard J. Davies & Others, 'Oil and Gas Wells and their Integrity: Implications for Shale and Unconventional Resource Exploitation' (2014) 56 Marine and Petroleum Geology 239 at 241-245 https://doi.org/10.1016/j.marpetgeo.2014.03.001; Raj Kiran & Others, 'Identification and Evaluation of Well Integrity and Causes of Failure of Well Integrity Barriers' (A Review) (2017) 45 Journal of Natural Gas Science and Engineering 511 at 516 https://doi.org/10.1016/j.jngse.2017.05.009.
95. Testo, *Flue Gas Analysis in Industry* (Testo 2004) 18.
96. Mohammad S. Masnadi & Adam R. Brandt 'Climate Impacts of Oil Extraction Increase Significantly With Oilfield Age' (2017) 7 Nature Climate Change at 551 https://doi.org/10.1038/nclimate3347.
97. Hassan M. El-Houjeiri & Others, *Oil Production Greenhouse Gas Emissions Estimator: User Guide and Technical Documentation* (Stanford University, 5 June 2017), www.pangea.stanford.edu/.
98. Masnadi & Brandt, *supra* n. 96, at 554.

4.1 Mitigation Measures

4.1.1 Efficiency Measures

To maximise energy efficiency and reduce flaring and venting emissions, oil and gas companies can integrate Advanced Process Control (APC) systems into their gas production processes. APCs are innovative technology which simultaneously leverages computer software and mathematical algorithms to enhance petroleum production.[99] APCs can be applied in refineries as well as petrochemical and power plants. Apart from energy efficiency and reduced emissions, APCs are beneficial for stabilising operations by reducing variability and managing disturbances leading to maximal operational reliability and consistent production outcomes.[100] In addition, it is beneficial for enhancing gas throughput and ensuring that production meets specific quality standards and reduces waste of petroleum feedstock and refined products.[101]

There is also the flare-to-production ratio (FPR) which is an efficiency metric for measuring the efficiency of gas utilisation and the volume of flared/vented gas in petroleum processing. FPR for determining flare efficiency is calculated by dividing the volume of gas flared by the total volume of gas produced.[102] FPR calculations determine the volume of flared gas against the volume of captured gas and how effectively it has been utilised.[103] The FPR procedure involves data collection of gas flared against captured gas, monitoring and reporting gas flaring activities pursuant to legal and regulatory mandates, as well as ensuring that current FPR data outperforms previous plant FPR data or prevailing industry standards.[104] A high FPR indicates that a substantial volume of gas is being wasted through flaring which contributes to GHG emissions, while a lower FPR is reflective of an effective utilisation of gas which would have been flared as a matter of ensuring energy efficiency in gas production.[105] FPR metrics help oil and gas companies plan for and enhance technical measures to reduce emissions in line with their corporate responsibility toward climate action.

4.1.2 Re-injection and Direct Air Capture

Re-injection (or sequestration) at source is an effective gas flaring mitigation technique which entails capturing gas at the oil well which would have otherwise been flared and re-injecting it back into the oil well or a designated subterranean formation elsewhere

99. Magesh John, 'Overview of Advanced Process Control' (*LinkedIn*, 8 October 2023) [2], https://www.linkedin.com/pulse/overview-advanced-process-control-apc-magesh-john accessed 8 August 2024; ABB, *Advanced Process Control: The Proven Way to Process Optimization* (Brochure, 2012) 2, https://library.e.abb.com/public/fa34b897958489a9c1257ad7005753d5/Brochure_APC_low.pdf accessed 11 August 2024.
100. John, *supra* n. 99, at [1]; ABB, *supra* n. 99, at 2.
101. John, *supra* n. 99, at [15]; ABB, *supra* n. 99, at 2.
102. Christopher D Elvidge et al., 'A Fifteen Year Record of Global Natural Gas Flaring Derived from Satellite Data' (2009) 2 Energies 595, 616 https://doi.org/10.3390/en20300595.
103. *Ibid.*
104. *Ibid.*, 597-599 and 619-620.
105. *Ibid.*, 616.

for storage.[106] Re-injection reduces the need to flare gas and aids oil and gas companies to comply with regulatory and corporate obligations to lower GHG emissions.[107] The carbon capture and storage (CCS) procedure, which is a subset of the wider Carbon Capture, Utilisation and Storage (CCUS) procedure, is used to capture gas during oil extraction after which the gas is compressed and transported via pipelines for re-injection into underground formations.[108] Notably, as gas is captured and stored back in the well or other underground formations, this measure helps to conserve gas that could be later extracted and utilised for energy or other multi-sectoral purposes.[109] However, the challenges of implementation include the capital-intensiveness of constructing and operating CCS for re-injection or sequestration purposes which leads to increased energy consumption.[110] Also critical is the need to ensure proper management of underground formations to prevent groundwater contamination and possible CO_2 leakages after re-injection/sequestration is achieved.[111] Post-re-injection CO_2 leakages pose, in a new form, the same emissions challenge which would have otherwise occurred through gas flaring/venting or other fugitive means.

Direct Air Capture (DAC) is a technology used to capture CO_2 directly from the atmosphere.[112] This technology uses either solvent-based (liquid) or sorbent-based (solid) systems to capture air from the atmosphere.[113] Solvent-based DAC systems capture CO_2-laden air and pass it through chemicals that distil CO_2 from the captured air, and then return the treated air with less CO_2 back into the atmosphere.[114] Sorbent-based systems absorb CO_2-laden air with physical filters, and distil, capture, transport, and sequestrate in underground formations CO_2 in a concentrated form.[115] As with CCUS, the captured and concentrated CO_2 through DAC reduces the need for gas flaring and can also be commercialised by creating new or expanding existing markets for the captured gas such as in industrial and energy sectors.[116] DAC technology, compared with CCUS, removes rather than captures CO_2 – CCUS captures

106. Ibinye E. Sampson, Julius E. Akpabio & Charles I. Anyadiagwu, 'Economic Analysis of Gas Reinjection for Enhanced Oil Recovery: A Case Study of the Niger Delta' (2020) 17(1) Journal of Engineering Research and Reports 48, 50 https://doi.org/10.9734/jerr/2020/v17i117181.
107. Organization of Petroleum Exporting Countries (OPEC), 'Carbon Capture and Storage, CO2 for Enhanced Oil Recovery, and Gas Flaring Reduction' (*OPEC*, 2004) https://www.opec.org/opec_web/en/905.htm accessed 11 August 2024.
108. Chioma Vivian Basil & Michael Uche Ukponu, 'Carbon Capture and Storage (CCS) Technology Development in Australia: Economics, Policy and Regulation' (2022) 20(4) OGEL 1, 9.
109. *Ibid.*
110. *Ibid.*, 13.
111. Eylem Kaya & Sadiq J. Zarrouk, 'Reinjection of Greenhouse Gases into Geothermal Reservoirs' (2017) 67 International Journal of Greenhouse Gas Control 111, 112 https://doi.org/10.1016/j.ijggc.2017.10.015.
112. Abayomi A. Okesola et al., 'Direct Air Capture: A Review of Carbon Dioxide Capture from the Air' (2018) 413 IOP Conference Series: Materials Science and Engineering 1, 1-2, https://iopscience.iop.org/article/10.1088/1757-899X/413/1/012077/pdf accessed 14 August 2024 https://doi.org/10.1088/1757-899x/413/1/012077.
113. US Department of Energy, 'DOE Explains ... Direct Air Capture' (*DOE*) https://www.energy.gov/science/doe-explainsdirect-air-capture#: ~ :text = Sorbent%2Dbased%20direct%20air%20capture,in%20geologic%20formations%20or%20used accessed 14 August 2024.
114. *Ibid.*
115. *Ibid.*
116. *Ibid.*

CO_2 at the source of the emissions activity while DAC removes CO_2 that is already in the atmosphere.[117] However, while DAC is a capital- and energy-intensive technology[118] and may not be a direct mitigation solution for gas flaring such as CCUS, it is a valuable complementary technology in the broader strategy to reduce GHG emissions from gas flaring.

4.1.3 Fugitive Emissions Interventions

Leak Detection and Repair (LDAR) programmes help to curb fugitive emissions, which is another cause of CH_4, emissions, by identifying and effectively containing CH_4 leaks from gas production equipment and pipelines used for transporting gas.[119] LDAR detection equipment includes infrared cameras, ultrasonic detectors, and gas analysers.[120] Any detected leak is documented and reported, and the leak information is used to prioritise repairs based on its severity and impact. After repairs, the gas production and transport systems usually undergo technical re-assessment to ensure that the leaks have been effectively contained. It is essential that detected leaks are promptly contained because this will reduce the high volume of fugitive emissions and improve the efficiency of gas production and transport systems.

There is the 'Smart LDAR' which is an upgraded version of the 'Traditional LDAR'. It uses real-time data collection and analytic mechanisms, including artificial intelligence, wireless sensors, Internet of Things (IoT) devices, and machine learning algorithms, as a proactive measure to predict and prevent fugitive methane emissions or leaks from petroleum and allied infrastructure.[121] The difference between the Traditional and Smart LDAR is that the former is executed using handheld, analogue devices to detect leaks which are prone to human errors; while the latter leverages modern, digital and virtual technology to analyse large volumes of data to identify patterns, predict potential leaks, and enhance leak detection accuracy, frequency, and

117. US Department of Energy, *Carbon Dioxide Removal*, 1, https://www.energy.gov/sites/default/files/2023-05/2023CDRfactsheet.pdf.pdf accessed 14 August 2024.
118. *Ibid.*
119. Chengliang Zhang et al., 'Reduction of Fugitive VOC Emissions Using Leak Detection and Repair (LDAR) In A Petroleum Refinery of Pearl River Delta, China' (2022) 324 Applied Energy 1, 2 https://doi.org/10.1016/j.apenergy.2022.119701; A.P. Ravikumar et al., 'Repeated Leak Detection and Repair Surveys Reduce Methane Emissions Over Scale of Years' (2020) 15 Environmental Research Letters 1, 2 https://doi.org/10.1088/1748-9326/ab6ae1.
120. Sensemore, 'What Is Leak Detection and Repair (LDAR)?' (*Sensemore*, 13 May 2024), https://sensemore.io/what-is-ldar/ accessed 11 August 2024; Klinger Australia, 'Find and Reduce Methane Emission Leaks' (*Klinger Australia*), https://www.klinger.com.au/reduce-methane-emissions-leaks/ accessed 11 August 2024.
121. Aditya S. Jadhav et al., 'Assessing Emission and Reduction Strategies for Volatile Organic Compounds (VOCs) in Refinery' (2023) 43(3) Journal of Indian Association for Environmental Management 10, 13; Nasr Alkadi et al., 'Ubiquitous Sensing Network for Continuous Monitoring and Quantification of Methane Emissions' (Proceedings Paper, Society of Petroleum Engineers Offshore Europe Conference and Exhibition, Aberdeen, UK, 3-6 September 2019), https://doi.org/10.2118/195703-MS accessed 11 August 2024.

efficiency.[122] Smart LDAR models can retrieve historical data and coupled with analysing environmental factors for better informed inspections and maintenance programmes, leading to more efficient leak detection.[123] In upstream oil and gas operations where equipment is often spread across large, remote areas, especially at offshore locations, Smart LDAR systems provide enhanced monitoring capabilities that are otherwise difficult to achieve with manual, traditional LDAR inspections.[124] When a potential leak is detected, the system can automatically notify operators via alerts, enabling immediate response and reducing the leak duration.[125] This minimises the need for flaring or venting as a safety measure to burn off excess gas.

Another flaring mitigation technique, Optical Gas Imaging (OGI) is an advanced technique that uses infrared camera technology to make invisible gases, such as methane, visible to the naked eye.[126] OGI cameras operate in the infrared spectrum, where gases like methane absorb infrared light. When these cameras are focused on an area of interest, they can detect the gas as it absorbs and re-emits infrared radiation, thereby creating a visual image of the gas leak in real time.[127] This capability makes OGI a powerful tool for detecting leaks, thereby helping to reduce the overall environmental impact of oil and gas production. OGI is often used in conjunction with LDAR to enhance leak detection capabilities.[128]

Apart from Smart LDAR, there are emissions detection technology known as Methane Detection Satellites (MDS). These are cutting-edge remote sensing technologies used to detect and monitor flared gas and fugitive methane emissions and leaks from outer space.[129] EdMDS is equipped with remote sensors which use spectrometers to measure the specific wavelengths of light absorbed by methane, allowing for precise detection of methane plumes from outer space.[130] The data collected by these satellites is analysed to produce detailed maps of methane emissions.[131] These maps can be relied upon to identify specific sources of emissions, including gas flaring sites, and

122. Prompt Engineering and Trading Services Co. W.L.L., 'Smart LDAR and OGI Cameras: Revolutionizing Leak Detection and Repair in Industrial Facilities' (*LinkedIn*, 3 August 2023) [1], https://www.linkedin.com/pulse/smart-ldar-ogi-cameras-revolutionizing/ accessed 17 August 2024.
123. *Ibid.*, [2], [6], [7] and [13].
124. *Ibid.*, [9].
125. *Ibid.*, [8].
126. Torgrim Log, Wegar Bjerkeli Pedersen & Heike Moumets, 'Optical Gas Imaging (OGI) as a Moderator for Interdisciplinary Cooperation, Reduced Emissions and Increased Safety' (2019) 12 Energies 1 https://doi.org/10.3390/en12081454.
127. A.P. Ravikumar, J. Wang & A.R. Brandt, 'Are Optical Gas Imaging Technologies Effective For Methane Leak Detection?' (2017) 51(1) Environmental Science and Technology 718, 719 https://doi.org/10.1021/acs.est.6b03906.
128. Log, Pedersen & Moumets, *supra* n. 126, 3; Ravikumar, Wang & Brandt, *supra* n. 127, 718.
129. Bertrand Rouet-Leduc & Claudia Hulbert, 'Automatic Detection of Methane Emissions In Multispectral Satellite Imagery Using A Vision Transformer' (2024) 15 Natures Communications 1 https://doi.org/10.1038/s41467-024-47754-y; Frances Reuland & Sasha Bylsma, 'Methane-Detecting Satellites 101: The Completeness Quotient' (*RMI*, 8 February 2023), https://rmi.org/clean-energy-101-methane-detecting-satellites/ accessed 17 August 2024.
130. Yuhan Jiang et al., 'Methane Retrieval Algorithms Based on Satellite: A Review' (2024) 15 Atmosphere 449, 453-467 https://doi.org/10.3390/atmos15040449.
131. Michael Buchwitz et al., 'Satellite-Derived Methane Hotspot Emission Estimates Using a Fast Data-Driven Method' (2017) 17 Atmospheric Chemistry and Physics 5751.

provide insights into the scale and frequency of emissions.[132] The data from MDS is often made publicly available, thereby increasing transparency and enabling government, civil society, non-governmental organisations, and investor stakeholders to hold companies accountable for their methane emissions.[133] This public visibility encourages better practices and more aggressive emissions reduction actions. The UN Environment's Methane Alert and Response Satellite (MARS), Environmental Defense Fund-led MethaneSAT programme and the European Union's TROPOMI are notable running MDS facilities.[134]

4.1.4 Commercialisation

Another efficiency measure is the aspect of utilisation in CCUS. Here, gas which would otherwise have been flared is captured and used to manufacture valuable products relevant to other economic sectors such as petrochemicals for industrial/mechanical use; cement, steel, and concrete for the built economy; plastics for domestic purposes or micro-enterprises; and biomass for electricity generation.[135] Utilisation of captured gas is also highly tenable in the process of enhancing oil recovery (EOR) where CO_2 is re-injected into wells to optimise oil and gas extraction processes.[136] By using captured gas for EOR and manufacturing purposes, oil and gas companies will be contributing immensely to mitigating GHG adverse environmental impacts and enhancing the efficiency and sustainability of resource production processes. Gas utilisation and commercialisation will also help to expand the commercial value chain of the oil and gas industry and promote an interdependent effect between it and other economic sectors such as manufacturing, construction, and gas-powered electricity in line with the promotion of low-carbon fuels for the energy transition.

4.2 Key Challenges

4.2.1 Lack of Optimal Pipeline Networks

Most jurisdictions do not have the requisite pipeline network for optimal gas utilisation.

The lack of optimal pipeline networks is a significant challenge to gas flaring mitigation, particularly in resource-rich developing countries. For such countries,

132. *Ibid.*
133. International Energy Association, 'Global Methane Tracker 2023' (*IEA*, 2023), https://www.iea.org/reports/global-methane-tracker-2023 accessed 19 August 2024.
134. UN Environment Programme, 'What Is The Methane Alert and Response System (MARS)?', (*Brochure*, 2022), https://unenvironment.widen.net/s/7pmjgcdgkz/mars-infographic-1 accessed 20 August 2024; Environmental Defense Fund, 'How MethaneSAT Is Different From Other Satellites' (*Environmental Defense Fund*), https://www.edf.org/methanesat/how-this-satellite-different accessed 20 August 2024; 'TROPOMI' (*TROPOMI*) https://www.tropomi.eu/ accessed 20 August 2024.
135. Basil & Ukponu, *supra* n. 108, 12-13.
136. *Ibid.*, 12.

pipeline infrastructure development linking remote or offshore wells to available gas markets can be capital-intensive. In addition, it is an economic disincentive to develop pipeline infrastructure in jurisdictions where gas resources or prices are low.[137] The dearth of pipeline infrastructure increases the likelihood of flaring or venting as gas often cannot be efficiently transported for utilisation and commercialisation purposes in relevant manufacturing industries and retail markets.[138]

Furthermore, without adequate pipeline assets for transportation, large volumes of natural gas will remain economically stranded at the extraction site — such gas is called 'stranded gas'.[139] Stranded gas is susceptible to the risk of being flared because the cost of developing pipelines to transport gas from remote sites to gas markets may be prohibitive.[140] Even where stranded gas could be utilised, the cost of developing the necessary gas transport infrastructure may outweigh any economic benefits resulting in a resort to gas flaring as the alternative action to avoid economic losses to the detriment of the environment.[141] Apart from sourcing adequate financing for pipeline infrastructure procurement, harnessing stranded gas to fuel on-site power, and re-injection for EOR or sequestration purposes, stranded gas could be liquified (e.g., methane to methanol) for ease of transport through other means than pipelines.[142]

4.2.2 Investment Cost and Return on Investment Considerations

Gas monetisation/commercialisation is intrinsically an expensive venture. This capital-intensive angle will always be viewed against the profit motive, i.e., preference for quicker Return on Investment (ROI) through more viable commercial investments (drilling and production to meet immediate demand and derive profits). Implementing gas flaring mitigation technologies, such as CCUS, pipeline networks, gas-to-liquid (GTL) plants, LDAR programmes, MDS and Continuous Emissions Monitoring Systems (CEMS) requires substantial investment and maintenance capital which could be prohibitive for resource-rich developing countries or smaller companies or companies

137. Katerina Roumeliotis, 'The Effect of Plummeting Oil Prices in the Energy Industry: A Study on Exploration, Drilling and Pipeline Projects' (SSRN Research Paper, 2016) 5-7, https://ssrn.com/abstract=2951870 or http://dx.doi.org/10.2139/ssrn.2951870 accessed 20 August 2024.
138. Katherine A. Willyard, 'A License to Pollute? Opportunities, Incentives, And Influences on Oil and Gas Venting and Flaring in Texas' (2020) 62 Energy Research and Social Science 1,2 https://doi.org/10.1016/j.erss.2019.101381; Matthew R. Johnson & Andrew R. Coderre, 'An Analysis of Flaring and Venting Activity in the Alberta Upstream Oil and Gas Industry' (2011) 61(2) Journal of the Air and Waste Management Association 190, 191 https://doi.org/10.3155/1047-3289.61.2.190.
139. Stranded gas cannot be delivered to a commercial market due to its poor quality, or the reserve volume is not commercially profitable, or there are no pipeline facilities to transport it to required gas markets: *See* Rachel Henderson & Robert Fickes, 'Oilfield Flare Gas Electricity Systems (OFFGASES) Project' (US Department of Energy Final Technical Progress Report, 2008) 1 and 3, https://www.osti.gov/servlets/purl/936728 accessed 20 August 2024.
140. Jerome Rajnauth, Kehinde Ayeni & Maria Barrufet, 'Gas Transportation: Present and Future' (Conference Paper, CIPC/SPE Gas Technology Symposium 2008 Joint Conference held in Calgary, Alberta, Canada, 16-19 June 2008) 1 https://doi.org/10.2118/114935-MS accessed 20 August 2024; Henderson & Fickes, *supra* n. 139, 1-3.
141. Willyard, *supra* n. 138.
142. Henderson & Fickes, *supra* n. 139, 1; Rajnauth, Ayeni & Barrufet, *supra* n. 140, 1 and 4-16.

operating in locations with lower profit margins. For example, there are recurring controversies and criticisms about the high monetary costs of construction and operation as well as the unreliability of CCUS projects.

The Gorgon Carbon Dioxide Re-injection Project in Western Australia is often cited by critics for managing to achieve only 30% of its emissions storage capabilities and emitting around 10 million tonnes of CO_2 into the atmosphere despite a huge construction cost of AUD 54 billion.[143] But these monetary costs do not outweigh the multi-sectoral and environmental benefits of the CCUS technology as research and development activities are underway to further improve CCUS operational outcomes, with recent studies positing that the price of cutting CO_2 emissions per tonne is incrementally reducing.[144]

ROIs with respect to gas flaring mitigation is highly dependent on market conditions such as the price of natural gas and the availability of markets for captured gas. In regions where gas prices are low or there is limited demand, the financial returns from selling captured gas may not justify the initial investment. Also, the payback period for gas flaring mitigation investments is usually extensive, especially in regions with high initial costs and limited infrastructure. This long wait time before receiving ROI is a major investment deterrent, particularly for companies with short-term financial goals.

4.2.3 Risk Aversion

Regulatory and policy risks and uncertainties are another challenge that deters high capital investment in gas flaring mitigation infrastructures. In some jurisdictions, gas flaring regulations are weak or inconsistently enforced. This regulatory uncertainty can discourage companies from substantially investing in gas flaring mitigation as the ROI is heavily influenced by the strength or weakness of the regulatory environment.[145] On the policy side, some host governments' interventions such as tax breaks, investment subsidies, and other incentives to oil and gas companies to reduce gas flaring have oftentimes proven to be insufficient to offset high costs of investment and operation, thereby impacting competitiveness and fiscal imbalances among oil and gas companies.[146]

Apart from regulatory, market, and investment risks, gas flaring mitigation also faces technology risks. Implementing new or unproven technologies for flaring mitigation can be risky. Recalling the Gorgon CCS example,[147] companies may begin to fear that flare mitigation-related technologies could fail to perform as expected, leading to

143. Basil & Ukponu, *supra* n. 108, 12.
144. *Ibid.*, 13.
145. Mohammad Soltanieh et al., 'A Review of Global Gas Flaring and Venting and Impact on the Environment: Case Study of Iran' (2016) 49 International Journal of Greenhouse Gas Control 488, 507 https://doi.org/10.1016/j.ijggc.2016.02.010.
146. Jun Erik Rentschler & Morgan Bazilian, 'Reforming Fossil Fuel Subsidies: Drivers, Barriers and the State of Progress' (2017) 17(7) Climate Policy 891, 896 https://doi.org/10.1080/14693062.2016.1169393.
147. Basil & Ukponu, *supra* n. 108, 12.

further financial losses. The fear of technological capital-intensiveness and failure to meet operational expectations often results in a preference by oil and gas companies for maintaining the status quo of flaring and venting rather than adopting innovative solutions to mitigate gas flaring.[148] Thus, integrating new flaring mitigation technologies into existing operations can pose risks of operational disruptions, which could affect overall gas production efficiency and profitability.

The potential for disruptions makes companies more cautious in adopting flaring mitigation measures because failure of implementation portends reputational risks for their corporate profile. Companies may even become uncertain about the long-term strategic value of investing in flaring mitigation, especially in the wake of renewable energy technologies which could render flaring mitigation investments to be surpluses to future energy requirements. This strategic uncertainty can contribute to a more cautious approach to flaring mitigation investment to the detriment of the environment.

5 CONCLUSIONS

The discussion in this chapter evinces the fact that gas flaring is an egregious occurrence in the entire chains of the oil and gas industry, alongside other emissions. The scientific literature referred to in this chapter brings the major emitting stream of the industry to sharp focus – the upstream sub-sector where primary resource recovery happens – accounting for over 75% of the GHG emissions profile of the oil and gas production process. As highlighted above, AG is usually found and extracted alongside crude oil in most reservoirs, as a by-product. While venting of gas occurs in a controlled environment, fugitive methane emissions also occur mostly because of leaks from pipelines and assets that have lost their integrity, including from decommissioned oil and gas wells and infrastructure. All these forms and sources of emissions need regulatory and policy interventions in petroleum-producing jurisdictions.

As the discussions in the jurisdictional chapters will show in this text, the prevalence of gas flaring is not necessarily a function of a lack of legal and regulatory measures, but partly because of the ineffectiveness of regulatory measures and the lack of political will for ambitious climate measures due to the economy-environment tension that often plays out across multiple countries. Having said that, there are proven mitigation measures that could be adopted and scaled to achieve significant reduction in flaring, venting, and other industry-related emissions. Some of such measures discussed in this chapter include efficiency measures, re-injection and direct capture, fugitive emissions interventions, and commercialisation. However, lack of optimal pipeline infrastructure, investment needs, and risk aversion are some of the clear and present challenges that stymie the successful deployment of technical interventions to abate flaring. Thus, there is not only a place for law and policy to

148. Ryan Gunderson, Diana Stuart & Brian Pedersen, 'The Fossil Fuel Industry's Framing of Carbon Capture and Storage: Faith in Innovation, Value Instrumentalization, and Status Quo Maintenance' (2020) 252 Journal of Cleaner Production 1, 4 https://doi.org/10.1016/j.jclepro.2019.119767.

ensure the existence of a legal and governance architecture that enables the deployment of technological interventions that work but also to incentivise best practices across the entire chain of the oil and gas industry.

CHAPTER 7

Natural Gas Utilization and Commercialization

Vanna Jankiepersad

1 INTRODUCTION

Gas flaring has been a common practice exercised by oil field operators in the production of oil, a practice which has done irreversible harm to the environment over the past few decades. It has increased by 7% in 2023, reversing a decline in 2022,[1] and it contributes to the release of large amounts of environmental pollutants such as carbon dioxide (CO_2), sulfur oxide (SO_x), nitrogen oxide (NO_x) and hydrocarbons as well as other adverse human and environmental effects. It has been a controversial practice amounting to grave environmental and legislative concerns. With jurisdictions moving closer to energy transition by removing carbon footprints, the management of natural gas produced alongside crude oil along with its safe and environmentally friendly practices is now on the front burner. Gas flaring has been so controversial in recent times that Guyana has assimilated measures to combat gas flaring into its licensing regime and its production-sharing agreement. The revised Environmental Permit to the Liza Phase One modified terms and conditions and timelines for flaring events. It also imposed an obligation on ExxonMobil Guyana to pay for the emission of CO_2 as a result of flaring in excess of those timelines.[2]

1. According to satellite data released by the World Bank, gas flaring increased by 7% in 2023, reversing a decline in 2022. The rise resulted in extra planet-warming emissions equivalent to 23 million tonnes of carbon dioxide, Clogue, Daisy 'Gas flaring back on the rise, fuelling calls for stronger regulation', dated 20 June 2024, https://www.climatechangenews.com/2024/06/20/gas-flaring-back-on-the-rise-fuelling-calls-for-stronger-regulation/ accessed on 2 October 2024.
2. OilNow, Guyana receives GYD 1.7 B in payments for flaring from ExxonMobil, dated 29 May 2022, https://oilnow.gy/featured/guyana-receives-gy1-7b-in-payments-for-flaring-from-exxonmobil/ accessed on 10 October 2024.

In addition, in light of the environmental impact, resource wastage and economic loss which gas flaring has placed on oil-producing countries, countries have gone as far as adopting more sustainable energy practices and creating stronger policy and legislative frameworks to ensure that international commitments are fulfilled and that corporate social responsibility is factored into its regulatory compliance expectations. For instance, petroleum agreements have now been tailored to stimulate the utilization and commercialization of its natural gas resources, both being alternatives to flaring.[3] Albeit flaring has been practised in jurisdictions which lack the necessary infrastructure to capture or utilize excess gas, the economic implications for oil and gas companies far outweigh its short-term operational flexibility.

This chapter will first begin by explaining the reasons (why and how) for gas flaring. The alternatives to gas flaring will then be briefly explained. The key challenges of gas flaring will also be highlighted in this chapter as a precursor to the solutions that would later be proposed so as to address or cure the defects posed by those challenges of gas flaring in the oil and gas industry. The solutions and a path forward, including the legal and policy measures, market-based measures and any other measures will be explained. The main focus of the chapter will be on what are the alternatives to avoid flaring and finally, it will cover the contractual terms that are needed in the sales agreements to dispose of the gas.

2 WHY AND HOW GAS FLARING HAPPENS

As mentioned before, flaring occurs when oil reserves have been discovered together with associated gas.[4] It occurs where excess natural gas is burned off rather than captured and utilized. The natural gas which is burned off is found dissolved in crude oil reservoirs along with oil. This is called 'associated gas'. Therefore, some oil and gas experts may refer to 'gas flaring' as 'associated gas flaring'.[5] Notwithstanding there being an absence of a legal definition of what constitutes gas flaring, it has been recognized as 'burning gas byproducts from its petroleum activities'.[6]

From a scientific backdrop, associated gas occurs when natural gas is left dormant in oil reservoirs and it expands rapidly. Thereafter, gas is emitted from a wellbore and a small fraction of the natural gas condenses into liquid. One author has

3. For instance, Art. 12.1(b) of the Petroleum Agreement between the Government of the Cooperative Republic of Guyana and Esso Exploration and Production Guyana Limited. CNOOC Nexen Petroleum Guyana Limited and HESS Guyana Exploration Limited dated 2016 which states that 'Based on the principle of full utilization of the Associated Gas, and with no impediment to normal production of Crude Oil, a plan of utilization of the Associated Gas shall be included in the Development Plan of each Oil Field ...', https://petroleum.gov.gy/documents/petroleum-agreement-stabroek-block accessed on 2 October 2024.
4. Associated Gas is gas found in a reservoir along with crude oil. Flaring does not arise in the case of Non Associated Gas (gas without oil reserves) as limited reserves simply means the whole field development is uneconomic.
5. Indep. Evaluation Grp., World Bank, Climate Change and the World Bank Group: Phase I: An Evaluation of World Bank Win-Win Energy Policy Reforms 81 (2009).
6. Creighton P (University of Western Australia & SPC RRRT), Secretariat of the Pacific Community (SPC), 2013, Pacific Human Rights Law Digest – Volume 4.

used the analogy of champagne to explain the process of how flaring works, that is, flaring being akin to the result of opening a bottle of champagne. Where the natural gas is dissolved in the reservoir, it drops to atmospheric pressure and consequently, the associated gas bubbles out of the crude oil. To capture this excess associated gas, it would involve the oil producer needing to have the necessary infrastructure in place to capture, transport, process and sell the gas.

In some cases, the gas reserves may be very small and/or the discovery location may be remote from potential markets for natural gas. Although the development of oil may be economic, the gas reserves may be too small to develop and transport to market. This is mainly because gas is much less dense than oil and the energy content of 1 m^3 of oil is around 13 times as great as that of natural gas.[7] As a result, transport costs for gas per millijoule (mj) are much higher than for oil. In the past in these circumstances, when field development occurred, the gas was simply burnt off or 'flared' in order to dispose of it and to facilitate oil production.

A total of 139 billion cubic meters (bcm) of natural gas was flared worldwide in 2022, equivalent to around 3.4% of world gas production. Owing to the steep cost factor involved, oil producers are interested in taking the most economically viable route, that is, by disposing of the gas. This means that they ignite and burn the gas for disposal.[8] Flaring is damaging both to humans and the environment. Oil producers can only 'vent' the gas, meaning they release it directly into the atmosphere – much like uncorking a bottle of champagne and letting the bubbles escape, as highlighted in the previous analogy.The gas released from venting is hydrogen sulfide. This substance is a lot more toxic to human health than the substance released from flaring, sulfur dioxide.[9]

Gas flaring was a practice which originated as early as 1859 in jurisdictions such as the United States since the inception of oil production.[10] What made this environmental hazard persist was the delay of legislators to impose fines and penalties on oil producers who engaged in flaring. It can be argued that notwithstanding the passage of laws in certain jurisdictions to penalize the act of flaring by oil producers, the effectiveness of such laws has proven to be futile on account of political will and lack of enforcement.

In countries like Guyana, while it is acknowledged that some degree of gas flaring is inevitable in oil and gas production – such as the presence of a safety, background, or pilot flare – this does not mean it is equivalent to flaring tonnes of gas … Therefore,

---

7. CETINER ENGINEERING CORPORATION – Engineering Conversion Tables, https://www.cetinerengineering.com/conversiontables.html. I m^3 of oil contains around 35,170MJ but 1 m^3 of gas at compressed to 70 bar has around 2681 MJ accessed on 13 October 2024.
8. Robert D. Bott, Flaring: Questions & Answers 1 (Michael Brown et al. eds, 2nd ed. 2007), available at http://siteresources.worldbank.org/EXTGGFR/Resources/578068-1258067586081/FlaringQA.pdf.
9. World Bank Group, Global Flaring and Methane Reduction Partnership (GFMR) https://www.worldbank.org/en/programs/gasflaringreduction/gas-flaring-explained accessed on 7 October 2024.
10. Mohammed Soltanieh and others, A Review of Global Gas Flaring and Venting and Impact on the Environment: Case Study of Iran, 49 International Journal of Greenhouse Gas Control, 488-509 (June 2016) https://doi.org/10.1016/j.ijggc.2016.02.010.

if oil companies exceed the prescribed amount in flaring, they will have to seek approval.[11]

Owing to regulatory requirements, there is a limit on the amount of gas that can be flared via pilot flaring. Companies involved in exploration, if found to be flaring gas in excess of the regulations, would be penalized. Accordingly, it stands to reason that gas flaring is inevitable and the burden falls squarely on the Government's shoulders to adopt more sustainable practices by virtue of technological advancements or by increasing regulatory compliance as encapsulated in its legislative framework.

3 ALTERNATIVES TO FLARING: UTILIZATION AND COMMERCIALIZATION UTILIZATION

In a world where we have all become very conscious of the need to minimize and ultimately avoid CO_2 emissions, it is highly undesirable to burn gas with no benefit in terms of providing heat or energy to consumers. Not only does flaring emit CO_2 but it also emits methane (CH4) and other greenhouse gases (GHGs) which contribute significantly to global warming. This represents a breach of States' commitments to the Kyoto Protocol and even the Polluter Pays Principle. Notwithstanding the Kyoto Protocol not expressly mentioning gas flaring, provisions concerning emission reduction obligations,[12] duties to report and monitor;[13] sustainable development;[14] and joint implementation and clean development mechanism all, by implication, speak to a State's obligation in combating climate change in conjunction with the commitment to reduce gas flaring. Quite apart from the release of CO_2 during flaring, there are other adverse environmental impacts. Flaring also results in the release of substantial volumes of other potent GHGs,[15] including methane, black soot and nitrous oxide. Venting of unburned methane[16] causes even worse environmental damage than flaring.

Two alternatives to natural gas flaring are natural gas utilization and commercialization. Utilization involves various techniques or methods in which natural gas is

11. Oil Now 'Guyana receives GY$1.7B in payments for flaring from ExxonMobil' dated 29 May 2022, https://oilnow.gy/featured/guyana-receives-gy1-7b-in-payments-for-flaring-from-exxon mobil/.
12. Article 2, para. 1 (a)(iii), Kyoto Protocol to the United Nations Framework Convention on Climate Change, 1998, which states that each Party, in achieving its quantified emission limitation and reduction commitments, in order to promote sustainable development, shall, *inter alia*, 'Implement and/or further elaborate policies and measures in accordance with its national circumstances, such as: (iii) Protection and enhancement of sinks and reservoirs of greenhouse gases not controlled by the Montreal Protocol, taking into account its commitments under relevant international environmental agreements … .'
13. Article 3, para. 3, Kyoto Protocol to the United Nations Framework Convention on Climate Change, 1998.
14. Article 2, Kyoto Protocol to the United Nations Framework Convention on Climate Change, 1998.
15. GHG means Greenhouse Gases.
16. Venting means the release of unburnt Methane to the atmosphere. Methane, which is the principal component of Natural gas, is 28 times as powerful as a GHG as CO_2. Source https://www.epa.gov/gmi/importance-.

captured and used for energy processes in lieu of being flared or vented. It can include power generation, heating, transportation, Gas to Liquids (GTL) and Combined Heat and Power (CHP).

Commercialization, however, involves those processes and strategies to extract, process, transport and sell natural gas efficiently, thereby making it a valuable commodity in the energy market. In brief, it refers to the methods by which natural gas is used and brought to the market for consumption.

4 KEY CHALLENGES TO UTILIZATION AND COMMERCIALIZATION

- **Solutions and a Path Forward:** Challenges which hinder utilization and commercialization vary from jurisdiction to jurisdiction but mostly involve infrastructural issues, regulatory and environmental issues, geopolitical issues and economic viability issues. The political will of the jurisdiction is the primary challenge of most jurisdictions as it is the legislators and policymakers who determine the fate of natural gas utilization and commercialization and whether it would fit into the mould of the applicable jurisdiction's regulatory framework by virtue of the passage of laws which makes provision of energy utilization and commercialization; investment and funding through the use of allocations of public funds to bolster infrastructure development and research; regulatory and environmental policies; and long term energy planning.
- **Investment and funding – Infrastructural issues:** The cost and complexity of building the requisite pipeline infrastructure to facilitate the transport of natural gas can be a major hurdle, especially for underdeveloped countries. Gas flaring systems are usually installed on onshore and offshore platform production fields, on transport ships and in port facilities. One instance of where infrastructural issues are prominent is in Nigeria. With this country having one of the highest quantities of gases flared, the Government sought to establish a liquefied natural gas (LNG) plant in order to transport gas via pipeline to some neighbouring countries.[17] The movement of natural gas from its source to the markets is dependent on the transportation infrastructure of the oil and gas-producing country. In 2007 Nigeria produced 1,204 bcf of natural gas while consuming only 456 bcf. Evidently, if such gas were to be transported, stored, and exported then this would have bode well for the economy of Nigeria in 2007. Many of Nigeria's oil fields lack the infrastructure to produce and market associated natural gas, and as such, natural gas is often flared, according to the National Oceanic and Atmospheric Administration (NOAA). Moreover, jurisdictions have mandated that proper metering be installed in order to measure the volume of gas being flared. The installations of meters onto the pipelines leading to the flare form an essential component

17. Eboh, Camillus, 'Nigeria Licenses First Floating LNG Plant for Export and Domestic Use', dated 6 September, 2024, Available at: https://www.reuters.com/business/energy/nigeria-licenses-first-floating-lng-plant-export-domestic-use-2024-09-06/, Accessed on 17 February 2025.

of the infrastructure needed to regulate the amount of gas flared and moreover, allow for oil companies to be properly monitored.[18]

- **Regulatory and environmental issues:** Regulatory and environmental issues are pertinent to the State's economic benefit. If no obligation is conferred on oil companies to minimize the environmental impact of gas flaring, which in turn contributes to GHG emissions, then companies would not be persuaded to adhere to environmental standards which promote accountability and transparency. In addition, by imposing fines for excessive flaring, oil companies can adopt more efficient practices. On the face of it, certain countries such as Nigeria and Guyana have developed robust legislative and regulatory frameworks to address gas flaring. However, political will has been the underlying cause of such frameworks being efficient on account of the weak enforcement mechanisms and failure of the Government, from a policy level. For instance, the Gas Flaring and Venting (Prevention of Waste and Pollution) Regulations, 2022 of Nigeria seeks to fulfil the objectives of, *inter alia,* reducing the environmental and social impact caused by flaring and venting of natural gas, protecting the environment; enhancing energy transition; and creating social and economic benefits from gas flaring and venting capture.[19] Moreover, Nigeria has passed a plethora of legislation which sought to address gas flaring in the Niger Delta communities. This included the Petroleum Act (Drilling and Production) Regulations made pursuant to the Petroleum Decree of 1969 (now the Petroleum Act, which has been superseded by the Petroleum Industry Act, 2021).
- **Geopolitical issues:** In jurisdictions where communities are situated near oil extraction sites where gas flaring occurs, citizens may respond to such problems through social unrest and conflict.[20] Citizens may resort to vandalism, for instance, in response to the exploitation by oil companies and environmental degradation. Specifically, between 1998 and 2003, Nigerians committed an estimated 400 vandalizations at facilities owned by multinational corporations, which resulted in losses amounting to USD 1 billion annually. The vandalizations were attributable to the multinational corporation's practices which harmed the environment and left local citizens without any of the benefits of oil production.

18. Regulation 20, Gas Flaring and Venting (Prevention of Waste and Pollution) Regulations, 2022: 20(1) The metering equipment used for measuring natural gas flared and vented shall be manufactured, operated, calibrated and inspected in conformity to the Metering and Data Collection Standards issued by the Commission. 20(2) The metering equipment used for measuring natural gas flared and vented shall have an accuracy in conformity to the Metering and Data Collection Standards issued by the Commission.
19. Regulation 1, Gas Flaring and Venting (Prevention of Waste and Pollution) Regulations, 2022.
20. The Nigerian government's failure to address economic disparity and environmental pollution has resulted in community uprisings for decades. In 1997, a movement started to end the ecological devastation. This continued in 1998 with over 500 communities declaring that they were tired of, *inter alia,* gas flaring. Robert D. Bott, Flaring: Questions & Answers 1 (Michael Brown et al. eds, 2nd ed. 2007), available at http:// siteresources.worldbank.org/EXTGGFR/ Resources/578068-1258067586081/FlaringQA.pdf accessed on 3 October 2024.

- **Economic viability issues:** Market volatility is also an influential factor which underlies geopolitical issues. Where the price of oil is low it may be more economically viable for companies to flare gas rather than store it.[21]

5 LEGAL AND POLICY MEASURES

In order to put an eminent stop to gas flaring the Government of every jurisdiction must accept accountability despite the acts of flaring being carried out by private entities. The Government indirectly owes a duty of care to act reasonably and take steps to prevent harm to the citizens of its country. It follows that the Government, through its Legislature, must create and implement legal and policy measures to combat the issue of flaring. A comparative analysis of the legal and policy measures undertaken in other jurisdictions is considered below:

- Norway was one of the first countries to introduce regulations requiring operators to meter gas and tax flaring-related CO_2 emissions. In 1971, the country, through legislative measures, banned routine burning. This resulted in an increase in oil production and the simultaneous reduction in gas flaring. Thereafter, in 1991, Norway introduced several measures one of which was stated in section 4-4 of the Petroleum Act (Act of 29 November 1996 No. 72 relating to petroleum activities)[22] which speaks to the stipulation of production schedules. It states that 'flaring in excess of the quantities needed for normal operational safety shall not be allowed unless approved by the Ministry'. Associated gas utilization mandated approval from the authority by virtue of a Plan for Development and Operation which imposed a carbon tax. In 2016, Norway was the first country to indicate its intention to further initiatives to end routine gas flaring by 2030.[23] In terms of policy measures undertaken, shortly after the introduction of regulations in 1971, the Government bolstered its efforts in combating flaring subsequent to its research finding that global warming was a consequence of such. The policy introduced combined direct regulation with environmental schemes. Moreover, oil and gas developers are required to come to terms with gas utilization plans prior to carrying out any field development operators, and the responsibility of reporting and monitoring rests on their shoulders.[24]
- Colombia cut its flaring intensity by around half between 2015 and 2021 and has reduced flared volumes by 70% since 2012. This stems from the country's focus on emission reductions, creation and empowerment of the National Hydrocarbon Agency (Agencia National de Hidrocarburos [ANH]), Ecopetrol

21. Michael J. Watts, Righteous Oil? Human Rights, the Oil Complex and Corporate Social Responsibility, 30 Ann. Rev. Env't Res. 373, 400 (2005) https://doi.org/10.1146/annurev.energy.30.050504.144456.
22. Petroleum Act (Act of 29 November 1996 No. 72 relating to petroleum activities) of Norway.
23. Pursuant to the World Bank Initiative.
24. Olfat Kamel, NORWEGIAN Lesson in Gas Flare Elimination, Egypt Oil and Gas Group, dated 4 May 2016, https://egyptoil-gas.com/features/norwegian-lesson-in-gas-flare-elimination/ accessed on 9 October 2024.

has made progress on emission reductions and overall redirection of gas volumes towards the domestic market. Legislative-wise, *Law 10/1961* was the first legislative attempt of Colombia to prohibit gas flaring in fields. Colombia was one of the first countries to introduce specific subsidiary legislation, the MME *Resolution 40066/2022,* which speaks to specific measures to be adopted to monitor fugitive methane emissions, as well as venting and flaring. To date, the Ministry of Mines and Energy (MinEnergía) published a resolution on 10 August 2021 regarding the prohibition of natural gas flaring.[25]

- In the United States, while further regulation and more stringent enforcement across more producer states is needed, regulators in Colorado and New Mexico have joined Alaska in introducing a ban on routine flaring. Around one-fifth of US oil production now occurs in states with a routine flaring ban. In January 2024, the U.S. Environmental Protection Agency (EPA) set out new rules to curb methane emissions from the oil and gas industry in line with the Biden-Harris administration's Inflation Reduction Act (IRA), which prioritized clean energy deployment, taking steps to incentivize adoption of industry best practices that reduce pollution.[26] In 2022, the European Union, the United States and 11 countries launched the Global Methane Pledge (GMP) Energy Pathway to catalyse methane emissions reductions in the oil and gas sector, advancing both climate progress and energy security. To limit warming to 1.5°C and avoid near-term tipping points, the world must rapidly reduce methane emissions, in addition to decarbonizing the global energy sector. Consequently, the United States, the European Union, and more than 100 countries have launched the GMP at COP26 to reduce anthropogenic methane emissions by at least 30% by 2030 from 2020 levels. With the recent additions of Egypt, Kosovo, Moldova, Oman, Qatar, Saint Lucia, Trinidad and Tobago, and Uzbekistan, 120 countries have now endorsed the Pledge, representing half of global methane emissions and nearly three-quarters of the global economy.
- In 2023, the EU struck a deal that will force the fossil fuel industry to rein in dangerous methane pollution. Under the proposed law, the first of its kind, coal, oil and gas companies would be required to report their methane emissions and take steps to avoid them. The measures include finding and fixing leaks and limiting wasteful practices such as venting and flaring gas by 2027.
- In the UK, the OGA Strategy[27] came into force in February 2021 and incorporates a range of new net zero obligations for the UK oil and gas industry. The Central Obligation of the OGA Strategy requires, among other things, that

25. Colombia to prohibit natural gas flaring, Hydrocarbons Colombia, hydrocarbonscolombia.com accessed on 2 October 2024.
26. EU-US Joint Press Release on the Global Methane Pledge Energy Pathway, https://ec.europa.eu/commission/presscorner/detail/en/ip_22_3793 accessed on 1 October 2024.
27. North Sea Transition Authority, https://www.nstauthority.co.uk/regulatory-information/licensing-and-consents/consents/flaring-and-venting accessed on 30 August 2024.

relevant persons, in securing that the maximum value of economically recoverable petroleum is recovered from the strata beneath relevant UK waters, take appropriate steps to assist the Secretary of State in meeting the net zero target including by reducing, as far as reasonable in the circumstances, GHG emissions from sources such as flaring and venting.

- Nigeria has had a long history of gas flaring.[28] Its gas reserves tend to be in the form of associated gas linked to oil production and are often relatively small and hard to develop economically. However, the Government is now trying hard to reduce flaring levels. The Government approved the Nigerian Gas Flare Commercialization Programme in 2018. This was launched by the Minister of State for Petroleum Resources on 13 December 2016. The Programme will offer flare gas for sale by the Federal Government of Nigeria through a transparent and competitive bidding process. A structure has been devised to provide project bankability for the Flare Gas Buyers.

6 MARKET-BASED MEASURES

Market-based measures adopted by jurisdictions include but are not limited to, cap-and-trade systems, carbon pricing and incentives for gas utilization. Cap-and-trade systems impose a threshold or ceiling on the amount of emissions companies are allowed. Through this, companies are encouraged to develop and implement technologies and practices to reduce flaring. In Quebec, Canada, the Government has instituted the Order in Council 1126-2017 which stipulates the emission units that are granted by the Minister of Sustainable Development, the Environment and the Fight Against Climate Change for each year for the period 2021 to 2023. The permittable emission units for 2024 is 51.55 million emission units.[29]

Carbon pricing serves to minimize flaring by virtue of imposing a cost to carbon emissions. The aim is to adhere to both national and international climate change commitments through emissions reporting. Norway has implemented a CO_2 tax on offshore and oil and gas operations which includes provisions on gas flaring. In 2021, explicit carbon prices in Norway consist of emissions trading system (ETS) permit prices and carbon taxes, which cover 80.8% of GHG emissions in CO_2. In total, 82.9% of GHG emissions in Norway are subject to a positive Net Effective Carbon Rate (ECR) in 2021, down from 83.5% in 2018. Fuel excise taxes, an implicit form of carbon pricing, cover 26.5% of emissions in 2021, unchanged since 2018[30]

28. Nigerian Gas Flare Commercialisation Programme, IEA 50, 23 December 2020 https://www.iea.org/policies/8680-nigerian-gas-flare-commercialisation-programme accessed on 5 October 2024.
29. Government du Quebec, O.C. 1126-207, 22 November 2018, Gazette Officielle Du Quebec, 29 November 2017, Vol. 149, No. 48, https://www.publicationsduquebec.gouv.qc.ca/fileadmin/gazette/pdf_encrypte/lois_reglements/2017A/103198.pdf accessed on 8 October 2024.
30. OECD, Pricing Greenhouse Gas Emissions, Country Notes, Carbon pricing in Norway, https://www.oecd.org/content/dam/oecd/en/topics/policy-sub-issues/carbon-pricing-and-energy-taxes/carbon-pricing-norway.pdf accessed on 3 October 2024.

Moreover, incentives for gas utilization vary from jurisdiction to jurisdiction, however, the central aim is to encourage the capture and use of associated gas rather than flaring it. The United States has introduced tax credits for companies to capture and utilize natural gas, while Nigeria has adopted a different approach by incorporating in its policy document, the Gas Master Plan, incentives for investments in gas infrastructure which include tax holidays, import duty exemptions and other fiscal incentives.

7 COMMERCIAL ALTERNATIVES TO FLARING

It is not easy to identify commercial alternatives to flaring. By definition, flaring would only be considered by oil companies in instances where commercial alternatives to flaring are not economically viable. Set out below is an outline of some possible alternative uses. These are shown in ascending order of feasibility. In each case the net economic revenue, that is the revenue from additional sales, less than the costs involved, is likely to be negative. In these circumstances, such an alternative may still be acceptable to the field developer in order to secure official permission to develop the oil reserves. However, the increased costs cannot reduce the rate of return on the entire project below the economic threshold[31] for the investors, or the entire project will be uneconomic. Hopefully, in most cases there will still be an alternative use for the gas, which will enable the project to meet the hurdle rate for the project. Potential alternatives to gas flaring, in ascending order of probability, are:

- **Hydrogen Production:** One possible option for the use of surplus gas is to create blue hydrogen. Blue hydrogen is when natural gas is split into hydrogen and CO_2, either by Steam Methane Reforming (SMR) or AutoThermal Reforming (ATR), but the CO_2 is captured and then stored. As the GHGs are captured, this mitigates the environmental impacts on the planet. The 'capturing' is done through Carbon Capture Usage and Storage (CCUS).[32] There are many problems with implementing a blue hydrogen project, not least the capital cost, estimated to be USD 770/kWh in 2021.[33] For a 300 MW plant, this would mean an additional capex of around GBP 230 Million. Also, the plant would probably need a guaranteed gas supply of up to 0.4 bcm/year for 15-20 years. This may not be possible in oil fields with small gas reserves. Finally, if the field is remote then the cost of transporting hydrogen to customers may also be

31. Oil and gas companies typically rank projects on an internal rate of return basis. This compares the yearly levels of revenue with the capital and operating costs in each year of the project's life, the next cash flow. The internal rate of return or 'IRR' is the discount rate required to reduce the value of the net cash flows to zero over the project lifetime. The higher the IRR the better. Companies will generally have a target rate of return below which they will not invest. This target IRR is not constant and will be higher in areas with higher political and geological risk.
32. Petrofac, The Difference Between Green Hydrogen and Blue Hydrogen, https://www.petrofac.com/media/stories-and-opinion/the-difference-between-green-hydrogen-and-blue-hydrogen/ accessed on 3 October 2024.
33. Blue Hydrogen, April 2021, https://www.globalccsinstitute.com/wp-content/uploads/2021/04/Circular-Carbon-Economy-series-Blue-Hydrogen.pdf accessed on 10 October 2024.

prohibitive. Although it cannot be ruled out at the present time, it seems unlikely that building a blue hydrogen plant would be a viable means of avoiding gas flaring. However, this could change in future if the technology evolves, and capital costs decline.

- **Other Petrochemical Production:** Although it is not widely used as a petrochemical feedstock, natural gas does have some applications here, notably in the production of fertilizer/ammonia. However, the problems here are similar to those for blue hydrogen: High additional capital cost, uncertainty over the level of long-term gas production and high cost of transportation to markets. Again, this seems an unlikely alternative to flaring and this position, unlike blue hydrogen, is less likely to change in future. Fertilizer/ammonia production is a relatively mature technology and costs are unlikely to improve significantly.
- **Selling gas to end users:** Although the sale of gas to end-user markets may initially seem to be uneconomic, field developers may be required to consider this if flaring is to be avoided and permits for field development are to be secured. The economics of such gas sales will depend on three main factors:
  (i) Quantity of gas reserves. The bigger the reserves, the greater the level of gas production and the lower the transport cost per MJ.
  (ii) Gas composition – If the gas contains a high proportion of natural gas liquids such as butane /propane and condensate, then the value of the gas will be higher, and production is more likely to be economic.
  (iii) Distance to market – The gas will have to be piped to end-user markets. Gas pipeline costs are generally determined by the requisite distance from the source to the end user. So, if the market is relatively close, gas sales are more likely to be economic than if the distance involved is substantial.
  (iv) The type of market may also be important. If associated gas is produced, it is essentially a byproduct of oil production; and most of the value to the producer will be determined based on oil sales, not based on the sale of gas. Therefore, oil production is always given priority in such a field and gas will only flow when oil is being produced. In these circumstances, it is difficult to sell associated gas to a single customer such as a power station or a petrochemical plant. These customers may need a guaranteed continuous flow of gas, which an associated gas producer will be unable to provide. However, if there is a relatively mature developed gas market in the country, albeit in a different region, then these difficulties can be overcome. Such a market will have multiple sources of gas and many thousand, or even millions of customers. There is no longer a need to match the profile of supply with that of demand from individual customers and the variations in the level of associated gas production can be more easily accommodated. Making gas sales does not necessarily have to be economic in its own right but the additional costs must not be so great as to reduce the rate of return on the combined oil and gas project below the hurdle rate for the investors.

- **Gas Reinjection.** Although associated gas is often produced along with crude oil, it can also be reinjected back into the reservoir after production. This process is known as cycling and in some reservoirs, it can have the advantage of increasing oil production in the short and medium term. The anticline petroleum trap figure[34] below shows a generic example of how this can work. Oil and gas reservoirs often form in geological anticlines, rather like an upturned saucer in shape. Within the anticline, the fluids tend to get sorted out in layers, according to their weight with the lightest, gas on top, then oil and finally, if water is present, it will be at the bottom. The gas will generally be under considerable pressure, possibly at hundreds of bars. When wells are drilled for production, the high gas pressure acts as a driver to push oil to the surface for production. However, over time as gas is produced, the gas pressure in the reservoir will drop and the driving force will reduce, and oil production will start to decline.

Figure 7.1 The Image Shows a Structural Trap

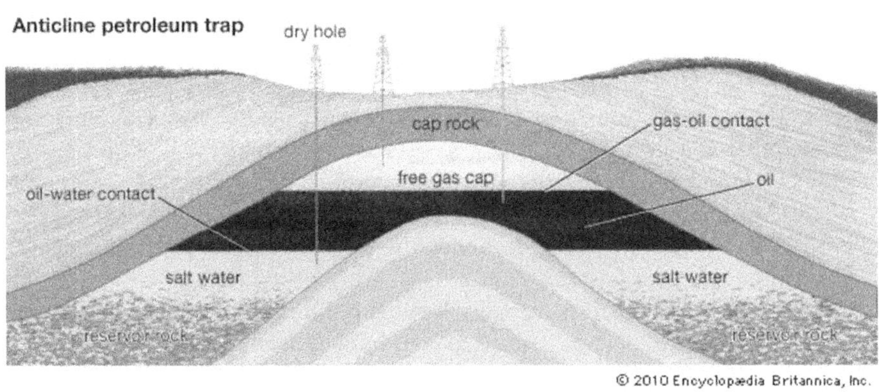

This process of decline can be arrested if gas is reinjected back into the reservoir after production. This maintains the reservoir pressure and keeps up the level of oil production. This process of 'gas cycling' cannot continue indefinitely but can often go on for a number of years after the start of oil production. Thereafter, the field will move into the 'blow down' phase, when gas production commences, and a market for gas sales has to be found. This process is not without its cost. After a year or so of cycling it may be necessary to install compression to re-inject the gas and additional wells may be required for gas injection. This can significantly increase the capital cost of field development.

34. Encyclopaedia Britannica Gas Reservoir, https://www.britannica.com/science/gas-reservoir accessed on 2 October 2024.

The advantage of Cycling of gas is twofold for the following reasons: (i) Increased oil production in the short and medium term, with consequent improvements in project economics; and (ii) the decision on what to do with gas can thus be postponed for a number of years, during which time alternative solutions may emerge, which allow the avoidance of flaring. For example, in the interim period, other gas discoveries may be made in the same area. The increase in gas availability may mean lower transport costs to market per MJ and hence sales of gas may then become economic. It is noteworthy to mention that cycling may not be technically feasible on all reservoirs:

- Electricity Generation: Electricity is a higher value product than gas.[35] This is illustrated in the Eurostat table below which shows prices of gas and electricity to Households in the EU, 2008 to 2023 in EUR/100kWh. Over this period electricity is around 2.5 times more valuable than gas.

Figure 7.2 The Table Shows Consumers' Electricity and Gas Prices for the Period 2008 to 2023

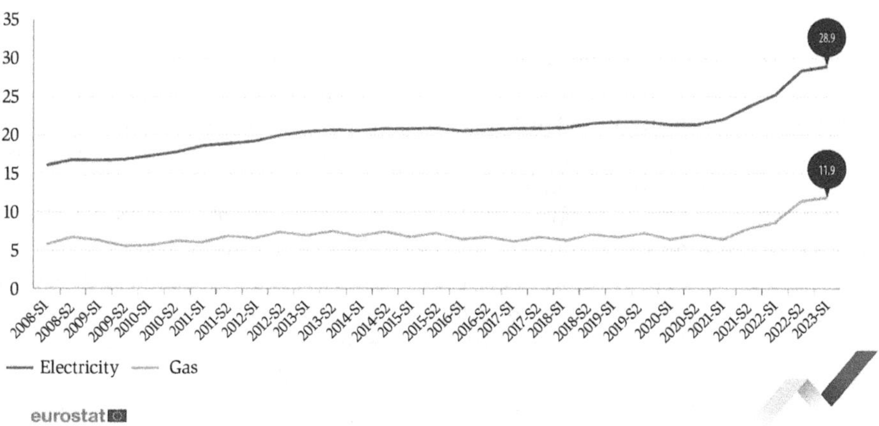

The greater value of electricity opens up another possibility for the avoidance of flaring. This involves the installation of a small gas-fired generation set at the oil production site to generate electricity. This offers a number of advantages which are listed below:

- The generator can be used to generate power for the production facilities themselves, to avoid having to buy electricity from outside sources. The generator can be sized to exactly meet the availability of fuel from the field. Accordingly, oil production levels can be maintained without restrictions

35. Eurostate, Evolution of Household Consumers' Electricity and Gas Prices in the EU, 2008-2023, https://ec.europa.eu/eurostat/documents/4187653/16179947/vis1-Electricity-and-gas-261023.png/722092b0-9465-b280-47cf-85307ae86c3a?t=1698302182681 accessed on 2 October 2024.

imposed by customers for the gas. This will enable the project rate of return to be optimized. If, as seems likely, the quantity of electricity that can be generated is greater than the onsite requirements for the field, it can be sold in local markets. In the Western world virtually, every household is an electricity consumer so the distance to local markets is likely to be less than that it is to gas markets and hence the cost of transportation may well be less.

- The use of onsite electricity generation from gas is quite common in small onshore fields in the UK. In the small Kirby Misperton, Malton, Marishes and Pickering fields in North Yorkshire, operated by Third Energy, the gas is gathered and sent to a central generating facility. This is a 50 MW gas turbine and all electricity generated is sold to customers. Egdon Resources planned to use gas engine generation and export to utilize gas from its Wressel field in Lincolnshire. Unfortunately, this plan had to be dropped because of a lack of grid capacity locally to receive the power, a common problem for renewables projects. Gas will now be treated, compressed and exported to the LDC. Microturbines remain in use for onsite power demand. Star Energy exports electricity and gas from its Albury field and plans to generate electricity from Bletchingly in Surrey.

8 CONTRACTUAL ISSUES

In the past, many oil producers were focused entirely on oil and regarded gas as a nuisance to be disposed of. Even though other uses for gas may well have been feasible, this required some effort and imagination to investigate, which oil producers were often reluctant to do. Now, the pressure is on to avoid flaring and the alternatives are being taken more seriously. However, many of the alternative uses set out above may not necessarily be economic in their own right. That is, the additional cost of implementation may be less than the additional revenue generated. Despite this, such uses may well be viable, as they enable the project to avoid flaring and so gain permits for development. The only constraint is that the overall economics of the project, including the cost of gas sales, must be sufficiently attractive to meet the investors' hurdle rate of return.

Key contract terms for alternative solutions. Even if a successful gas sale is made, oil will still remain the dominant revenue stream and vital to the success of the project. Therefore, contracts for the sale of gas will have to recognize that oil production is paramount and must be maintained whether possible. Gas production will inevitably have to take second place. This will drive a lot of the key contract terms set out below. Some of the key issues surrounding contracts for the sale of associated gas in order to avoid flaring are:

- sales on this basis will be much easier to make if they are made to a gas utility or gas marketing company rather than to an isolated large customer such as a petrochemical plant or a power station;

- a gas utility/marketer will have many customers and many sources of gas. It can therefore tolerate some rigidity in the delivery obligations on the part of the gas producer; and
- a single isolated large customer will have specific requirements for gas quantities and time of delivery, which would be very difficult for single inflexible source of gas, such as that of associated gas from an oil field, to meet.

The key terms in a gas sales contract for associated gas, designed to avoid flaring, are as follows:

- Contractual Rights and Obligations

Most gas sales contracts in non-traded markets[36] are on a 'Buyers Option' basis., that is, the Buyer has the right to nominate the quantities of gas to be supplied on each day, within defined limits, and the Seller is obliged to deliver such volumes. The alternative is a Seller's Option contract in which the Seller has the right to nominate the quantities of gas to be supplied on each day, within defined limits, and the Buyer is obliged to accept such volumes. This loss of control means a Seller's option contract is less valuable to the Buyer and this in turn will have implication for the value of the gas and hence the price. Clearly, a Seller's Option basis is more suitable for gas sold from an associated gas field.

- Start Date

All gas contracts will specify a date by which nominations for and deliveries of gas must commence (the 'Start Date'). There may well be some uncertainty when oil production and hence gas production will commence. The Seller will wish to ensure that the Buyer is ready to receive its gas whenever field production starts but it will wish to avoid any obligation to deliver before this period. Therefore, the ideal provision is for the Seller to have the right to nominate the Start Date. However sudden arrival of gas unexpectedly may be hard for a Buyer to accommodate, so the best approach is to use the Start Date Window approach.

The Seller has the right to nominate the Start Date within a window of say three months, which will be set out in the gas sales contract. The Seller must then nominate a one-month window for the Start Date by a defined date, but this one-month period must be within the previous window. Finally, the Seller will nominate the Start Date by a later defined date, but the Start Date must be within the one-month window.

By this, it means that the start of gas deliveries can be tailored to the start of gas production in a manner acceptable to the gas Buyer.

- Contract Period

The Contract Period will set out the term of the agreement during which the Seller is obliged to sell gas and the Buyer is obliged to accept. This is normally a fixed period of

36. A traded gas market is one in which most gas purchasing and many sales to larger customers are done on the basis of traded prices for gas; such as NBP in the UK, TTF in the Netherlands, HH in the USA and THE in Germany. A non-traded market is one in which gas is sold on a more traditional basis, without reference to traded prices.

time linked to the start date; for example, the contract period will end say 10 or 15 years after the Start Date. This gives the developer, and also any bank which is financing the project, the confidence that their gas will be accepted and paid for over a period of time. However, there may well be some variants of this basic term:

(i) As oil is the dominant product for the Project the Seller may seek a right of earlier termination if oil production ceases and the field is to be abandoned. This would normally involve a significant period of notice to the Buyer perhaps of 6 or 12 months.

(ii) There will also be standard rights of termination for either party if the other party: Fails to pay invoices due. Goes into administration. Is guilty of a breach of material obligation, such as the obligation to take gas. Suffers from a prolonged period of force majeure.

(iii) If the Seller is concerned about what will happen after the end of the contract period, it may also be possible, although relatively unusual, for it to have an option to extend the contract period for a defined additional period, on giving a specified period of notice to the Buyer.

- Force Majeure/Default

All gas contracts will contain a provision for liquidated damages if a Seller fails to deliver nominated volumes on a day. Normally no charge will be made if the Seller can demonstrate it was relieved by force majeure. This is less of an issue on Seller's option contracts, as the Seller is responsible for nominating daily quantities. If it has problems with gas availability, it can simply nominate zero. However, nominations have to be done in advance of each day and problems could arise after the nomination window has closed. In these circumstances, it is advisable for the Seller to include a provision to ensure that problems with oil production and hence with gas production, will qualify as force majeure under the gas contract. However, the normal qualifications for claiming force majeure will still apply; that is the Seller must have acted as a reasonable and prudent operator.

- Applicable Law

All contracts will define the legal system which governs the contract. It may be possible to use local law from the country in which the project is located but if the project is debt-financed, lenders may press the field developer to use an international standard such as English Law or New York law.

- Price

Finally, it will have become apparent from the description of contract terms in this section that, while many of them are very attractive from a Seller's perspective, they are relatively unattractive to a Buyer, especially the lack of control over daily gas volumes and the timing of the contract period and the start date. As a result, a Seller's option contract is less valuable to a Buyer than a conventional Buyer's Option agreement. This will inevitably have to be reflected in the price and a Seller's Option deal will normally have a discount compared with the price in a Buyer's Option contract, perhaps between 10% and 20%.

9 CONCLUSION

Conclusively, gas flaring has posed significant challenges within the last few decades given the economic, environmental, legal and policy factors. Fundamental to reducing emissions and regulating gas flaring in the oil and gas industry is the creation and implementation of solutions, policy, legal and market-based measures, in order to ensure that sustainable practices align with global climate goals. The reduction of gas flaring is not only a regulatory obligation but it is also a stepping stone for energy transition. Therefore, Governments must ensure that there are proper management and robust frameworks in place to maximize the value of their gas resources while ensuring that such solutions redound to the benefit of the citizens.

CHAPTER 8

The Place of Law and Regulation for abating Gas Flaring

Magnus C. Abraham-Dukuma, Opeyemi Y. Omotuyi & Eduardo G. Pereira

1 INTRODUCTION

As seen in Chapter 6 of this text, gas flaring occurs due to multifaceted challenges, including lack of optimal pipeline networks, high investment cost for commercialization, and risk aversion, thus making flaring a cheaper option in most cases. Amidst this complex situation, petroleum host states need functional and effective regulatory regimes to abate flaring. In furtherance of the focus of this text, the current chapter discusses the function of law and regulation in mitigating flaring, particularly, and emissions more broadly in the oil and gas industry. For this discussion, it is important to make useful connections with the general nature of law and the theory of regulation. This is not an exhaustive examination of both concepts. The intention here is to draw on existing bodies of thought to provide a theoretical context for the subject matter addressed in this book, and to build on the state-of-the-art regarding the governance of gas flaring and other petroleum-related emissions.

The chapter also adopts a regulatory lens to understand what the regulation of gas flaring and other emissions in various countries may be ideally seeking to accomplish. While some relationships between these concepts – law and regulation – and upstream emissions may show in this chapter, connections that are more direct will show in subsequent chapters covering national regimes to regulate gas flaring and other emissions emanating or traceable to the oil and gas industry.

A theoretical understanding of regulation at a generic level serves as a good foundation for a later examination of ideal regulatory approach/approaches for abating petroleum emissions broadly. This theoretical discussion focuses on the meaning, elements, and kinds of regulation; and makes connections to the objective of regulating upstream emissions. It is also possible to observe certain regulatory theories that are more useful to the research inquiry.

The rest of the chapter is divided into four sections. Section 2 discusses the theory of law, the concept of regulation, and the key elements of the two concepts as they apply to the subject matter of the present inquiry. Section 3 extrapolates four key forms of regulation from the various regulatory theories in literature. This is with a view to appreciate regulatory forms that might be or are already applied in many jurisdictions to address gas flaring. Section 4 discusses the application of regulation to the control of gas flaring more directly, while section 5 concludes the chapter.

2 LAW AND REGULATION

2.1 Theory of Law

The inquiry into the meaning of the theory of 'law' has remained the subject of cogitation to legal jurists, theorists, and thinkers across many epochs.[1] Here, the authors draw from the literature on jurisprudence and legal thought. From this jurisprudential dimension, Hart construes law as an instrument for social control.[2] Law, in this sense, can either be descriptive or prescriptive in nature.[3] Laws that seek to achieve a reduction in gas flaring and other emissions can be either descriptive or prescriptive. Positivist scholars such as John Austin, Jeremy Bentham, and Hans Kelsen construed law in this respect as the command of the sovereign backed with sanctions for noncompliance. This command creates an obligation to obey or defer to rules and norms, which eventually control human conducts in society at both personal, institutional and international spheres.[4] There are jurisdictions that may stipulate prescriptive requirements for reducing gas flaring and punitive measures for non-compliance. Law in this sense becomes a body of rules or norms, which prescribe a course of conduct, and indicate what should happen in default. This is the normative character or force of law.[5] This normative character will show in this text and particularly in the context of the different regimes of petroleum-producing jurisdictions.

The normative nature of law embodies a control function, which creates a legal order for different spheres of society.[6] This phenomenon manifests in civil relationships, constitutional matters, contracts, and the administration of states. It also features in the governance of natural resources and their associated environmental

1. H.L.A. Hart, *The Concept of Law* (2nd edn OUP 1994) 1.
2. *Ibid.*, at 6-12. *See also* Jeffrie G. Murphy & Jules L. Coleman, *Philosophy of Law: An Introduction to Jurisprudence* (Westview Press 1990) at 6-7.
3. Murphy & Coleman, *Philosophy of Law: An Introduction to Jurisprudence, supra* n. 2, at 7.
4. Phillip Soper, *The Ethics of Deference: Learning from Law's Morals* (Cambridge University Press 2002) at 79, 91, 159 and 168.
5. *Ibid.*
6. Larry D. Barnett, *The Place of Law: The Role and Limits of Law in Society* (Routledge 2011) at 4, 50 and 198. *See also* Ralph A. Newman & Clarice H. Newman, *Role of Law in Society: Readings and Materials* (Lerner Law Book Co. 1958) at 9, 16, 50, 63, and 69.

externalities. This explains why there are different laws to govern different areas and issues of life. For example, there are laws to create a legal order in matrimonial relationships, trade, politics, environmental governance, climate change, and resource extraction. In the absence of this legal order, humanity would be in a state of disarray and lawlessness.

Recognizing the normative character of law is not a denial of the independent existence of natural laws, such as the law of gravity, the law of motion, and the law of light and matter. Rather, the normative character here is in relation to human laws that guide civil, socio-political, economic, and legal existence in the world. According to Thomas Hobbes, human life in the state of nature was solitary, poor, nasty, brutish, and short.[7] In Jeremy Bentham's view, 'the more we are watched, the better we behave'.[8] This control function also applies to the relationship that exists between sovereign states in the realm of international law. It is what creates an international legal order.[9]

There are often legal instruments to further the ends of law in the society. Some common examples are legislation and regulation.[10] This explains the prevalence of different legislative and regulatory instruments for the governance of different issues and activities. Beyond this general understanding, there can also be regulatory regimes or laws to achieve different specific objectives.[11] For present purposes, the focus is on instruments that apply specifically to gas flaring and other emissions related to oil and gas production. As the discussion in the jurisdictional chapters of this book will show, there are primarily relevant legislation and regulations on the issue. There are also policy instruments and regulations at the national level that touch on gas flaring. Thus, apart from understanding the general theory of law, it is also important to devote attention to appreciating the theory of regulation.

2.2 Theory and Elements of Regulation

The theory of regulation has been broadly defined as a set of propositions or hypotheses about *why* regulation emerges, '*which actors* contribute to that emergence and the typical *patterns of interaction* between regulatory actors'.[12] This complex

7. Thomas Hobbes, *Leviathan* (Online Edition, Lerner Publishing 2018) at 115. *See also* David Dyzenhaus & Thomas Poole (eds), *Hobbes and the Law* (Cambridge University Press 2012) for detailed exposition on Hobbes' jurisprudence.
8. Jeremy Bentham, unpublished. Cited in *Christopher Hood and Others Regulation Inside Government: Waste-Watchers, Quality Police, and Sleazebusters* (OUP 1999) at 1.
9. Herbert W. Briggs, 'International Law: World Government and the Role of Law' (1947) 33:7 American Bar Association Journal 680-683. *See also,* Myres S. McDougal, 'The Role of Law in World Politics' (1948-1949) 20 Mississippi Law Journal 253.
10. John Burrows, 'Legislation: Primary, Secondary and Tertiary' (2011) Victoria University of Wellington Law Review 65 https://doi.org/10.26686/vuwlr.v42i1.5408. *See also* Ross Carter, *Regulations and Other Subordinate Legislative Instruments: Drafting, Publication, Interpretation and Disallowance* (New Zealand Centre for Public Law, Victoria University of Wellington, Occasional Paper No. 20 December 2010).
11. Anthony Ogus, *Regulation: Legal Forms and Economic Theory* (Hart Publishing 1994) at 180.
12. Bronwen Morgan & Karen Yeung, *An Introduction to Law and Regulation: Texts and Materials* (Cambridge University Press 2007) at 16.

phenomenon has received scholarly attention across various disciplines crisscrossing law, economics, politics, and sociology;[13] and the regulation of specific areas such as energy and natural resources, and their environmental implications.[14]

Conceptual inquiries into the theory of regulation are yet to yield a straitjacketed interpretation of the term. A multiplicity of meanings could be construed as producing varied outcomes – at worst, an obfuscation in man's attempt to decipher the concept (e.g., reflexive regulation which is an essentially slippery thing); and at best, a fortuitous pervasive growth of the concept. An appreciation of the postulations of different theorists is expedient for current purposes, so we begin.

Daintith offers a generic definition of regulation as 'all acts of controlling, directing or governing according to a rule, principle or system'.[15] This generic definition comprises three key elements – rules/standards, monitoring/compliance, and enforcement mechanisms. But it inadvertently excludes other key features such as decision-making on rules/standards and the workings of specialist agencies. For instance, there are legal and regulatory arrangements that vest discretionary powers in ministers and agencies in different countries to require the performance or non-performance of an act. Beyond the generic definition, Daintith also offers three distinctive insights on the possible meanings of regulation – as opposition to markets, as systematic control, and as a policy instrument.[16]

From a more legalistic and specific standpoint, Prosser describes regulation as 'the legal rules and other measures which express such command-and-control arrangements, contrasted with other forms of law such as criminal and contract law'.[17] This framing construes regulation to be rules that are promulgated through statutory instruments to address various problems in society, including environmental externalities such as gas flaring.

These two divides – general and specific notions of regulation – do not solve the complexity of defining regulation. Baldwin, Cave and Lodge demonstrate this difficulty by analysing several definitions of the theory: as a deliberate state influence, as a specific set of commands, and as all forms of social control.[18] They go on to argue that these definitions suffer from 'under- and over-inclusiveness'. Prosser says regulation consists of public interventions which affect the operation of markets through command and control, though one should be aware of the fact that command and control

13. Some examples include Robert Baldwin, Colin Scott & Christopher Hood (eds), *A Reader on Regulation* (OUP 1998); Robert Baldwin & Martin Cave, *Understanding Regulation: Theory, Strategy, and Practice* (OUP 1999); Colin Scott (ed.), *Regulation* (Ashgate 2003); Robert Baldwin, Martin Cave & Martin Lodge (eds), *The Oxford Handbook of Regulation* (OUP 2010); David Levi-Faur (ed.), *Handbook on the Politics of Regulation* (Edward Elgar Publishing 2011).
14. Barry Barton et al. (eds), *Regulating Energy and Natural Resources* (OUP 2006); Chih-kuo Kao, *Environmental Regulation of Oil and Gas* (Kluwer Law International 1998); Aileen McHarg (ed.), *Property and the Law in Energy and Natural Resources* (OUP 2010).
15. Terrence Daintith, 'Regulation, State and Economy: Some Preliminary Considerations' in Richard Buxbaum and Ferenc Mádl (eds), *International Encyclopaedia of Comparative Law. Vol. XVII* (Tübingen: Mohr Siebeck 1997) at 3.
16. *Ibid.*, at 15-21.
17. Tony Prosser, *Law and The Regulators* (Clarendon Press Oxford 1997) at 4.
18. Robert Baldwin, Martin Cave & Martin Lodge (eds), *The Oxford Handbook of Regulation* (OUP 2010) at 12.

may be regulated through the use of self-regulation.[19] Selznick describes the concept as sustained and focused control exercised by a public agency over activities that are valued by a community.[20] Re-echoing Prosser's legalistic perspective to construing regulation, Lange defines the concept as the images of space and interactions.[21] Lange's postulation may seem abstract for achieving clarity of meaning. But she also refers to Scott who defines regulation as 'any process or set of processes by which norms are established, ... monitored or fed back into the regime, and for which there are mechanisms for holding the behaviour of regulated actors within the acceptable limits of the regime (whether by enforcement action or by some other mechanism)'.[22]

There are also scholarly examples that refer to Julia Black's work as a good illustration of the difficulty in defining regulation[23] and as a good example of a more wide-ranging definition of the concept.[24] Perhaps it might be profitable to learn of Black's theorization on the concept of regulation. Black construes regulation as 'the sustained and focused attempt to alter the behaviour of others according to defined standards or purposes with the intention of producing a broadly identified outcome or outcomes, which may involve mechanisms of standard-setting, information-gathering and behaviour-modification'.[25]

From the quick review of various scholarly attempts to define the theory of regulation, the theory is conceived in varied forms by various scholars. But, for present purposes, we could draw insights from the different theories of regulation. Undertaking *an explication de texte* on the variety of definitions of the concept could crystalize multiple elements, but we think there are five striking elements that come to sharp focus. The first element is behaviour/conduct alteration/modification - could be facilitative or restrictive. It is facilitative if it facilitates the performance of an act. It is restrictive if it restricts the performance of an act. Within the context of the core of this book, the objective of regulation would be to modify the behaviour or practice of entities with an abatement in gas flaring as a result. The second element is standard-setting and entails the stipulation of suitable standards or rules - for our purposes, it could be prescriptions to control gas flaring and other oil and gas emissions. The third element is decision-making, which captures the powers of the relevant minister or government official to approve or reject applications related to petroleum production activities. An application to flare or vent gas is a direct example within the context of

19. Prosser, *supra* n. 17.
20. Philip Selznick, 'Focusing Organizational Research on Regulation' in Roger G. Noll (ed.), *Regulatory Policy and the Social Sciences* (University of California Press 1985) 363.
21. Bettina Lange, 'Regulatory Spaces and Interactions: An Introduction' (2003) 12:3 Social and Legal Studies 411 https://doi.org/10.1177/0964663903012004001.
22. Colin Scott, 'Analysing Regulatory Space: Fragmented Resources and Institutional Design' (2001) 53 Public Law 329 at 331.
23. Barry Barton, 'The Theoretical Context of Regulation' in Barry Barton, Lila K. Barrera-Hernandez and Alastair R. Lucas & Anita Ronne (eds), *Regulating Energy and Natural Resources* (OUP 2006) 11 at 13.
24. Tony Prosser, *The Regulatory Enterprise: Government, Regulation, and Legitimacy* (OUP 2010) at 2.
25. Julia Black, 'Critical Reflections on Regulation' (2002) Australian Journal of Legal Philosophy 1 at 26 https://doi.org/10.4324/9781351126816-2; Julia Black, 'Regulatory Conversations' (2002) 29:2 Journal of Law and Society 163 at 170 https://doi.org/10.1111/1467-6478.00215.

this book. The fourth element is the workings of a specialist agency, which usually shows in two forms - either as a specialist organization such as the industry-driven Oil and Gas Climate Initiative (OGCI) or as a specialist state agency such as the United States Environmental Protection Agency whose rules also cover oil and gas industry operations generally and gas flaring specifically. The fifth element is a mix of enforcement and monitoring and entails the adoption of various mechanisms to monitor the compliance of the regulated entities and the use of sanctions for non-compliance. These elements and some others would be evident in the jurisdictional chapters that cover what happens in various countries, but it is also good to get a sense of how regulation could be grouped into various types or forms from a theoretical standpoint.

3 FORMS OF REGULATION

The authors' objective here is to highlight some regulatory trends and practices, and their predominant characters, with an intent to distil the common forms or classification of regulation. As we will show, the taxonomy of regulation is varied among different scholars. For instance, Morgan and Yeung[26] classify regulation into public interest, institutional interest, and private interest types. They construe public interest regulation as welfare economics approaches, procedural political approaches, and substantive political approaches; while private interest regulation relates to political private interest approaches and economic private interest approaches; and institutionalist regulation comprising tripartism, regulatory space and systems theory.

Ogus splits regulatory typology into two broad categories - forms of economic regulation and forms of social regulation.[27] The economic categories include public ownership; price controls; and public franchise allocation. The social categories include information regulation; general and specific standards; prior approval; economic instruments; and private regulation. A few aspects of these categories may be relevant to the thesis of this book. For example, specific rules and standards for abating gas flaring and other emissions, regulatory approval for such emissions, and private regulatory interventions of non-state actors as we shall address later in this chapter.

According to Prosser, there are four regulatory models, which include regulation to protect rights, regulation for social solidarity, regulation as deliberation, and regulation for economic efficiency and consumer choice.[28] This sort of formulation is problematic due to its circumscribed range of activities, which may not apply to the subject matter of our inquiry. But turning to Baldwin, Cave, and Lodge, we see seven regulatory forms,[29] some of which are relevant to the focus of this book. These are incentives, market-harnessing controls, command and control, direct action and

26. Morgan & Yeung, *supra* n. 12.
27. Anthony I. Ogus, *Regulation: Legal Form and Economic Theory* (Hart Publishing 1994).
28. Tony Prosser, *The Regulatory Enterprise: Government, Regulation, and Legitimacy* (OUP 2010) at 18.
29. Robert Baldwin, Martin Cave & Martin Lodge, *Understanding Regulation: Theory, Strategy, and Practice* (2nd edn OUP 2012) 106.

design solutions, disclosure, public compensation/social insurance, and rights and liabilities laws.[30] They also point to a conventional practice where the machinery of government utilizes 'nudge' as an alternative to command and control.[31]

The classifications by various scholars are divergent, but one thing is clear – they overlap. But the prevalent forms of regulation are conventional regulation and market-based alternatives. Authors also recognize that regulation percolates different society's strata and structures and does not sit exclusively within the powers of any state. This understanding underpins the rationale behind decentred regulation and the application of hybrid regulatory forms towards the governance of many issues in society. We turn to these specific forms below.

3.1 Conventional Regulation

Rules-based and principles-based approaches are the common forms of conventional regulation. These two broad forms will show in the jurisdictional chapters in the context of how various countries apply divergent regulatory forms and approaches to mitigate gas flaring and other sources of emissions in the petroleum industry. Rules-based regulation specifies definite rules or prescriptions on the regulated issue. It prescribes specific processes/actions and/or proscribes acts. It is also known as command and control or prescriptive regulation because of its prescriptive character.

Prescriptive regulation is usually suitable for governing highly risky, complex, contested, delicate, or unfamiliar matters.[32] Its key merits are transparency, certainty, and predictability, while its major drawback is a lack of responsiveness or slowness in responding to unforeseen circumstances.[33] For addressing gas flaring and other petroleum emissions, rules-based regulation would provide prescriptions and rules for the compliance of operators. The jurisdictional chapters of this book will look at specific examples of the prescriptions prevalent in various countries.

The principles-based variant of conventional regulation establishes policy goals or principles and allows the regulated entities to decide the best approaches to achieve the set goals. It is also known as result-oriented, goals-based, or policy-based regulation. The regulation would usually set standards or tests to satisfy compliance. The primary merit of this approach is its flexibility, which lends it handy for regulating

30. *Ibid.*, at 134-136.
31. Robert Baldwin, 'From Regulation to Behaviour Change: Giving Nudge the Third Degree' (2014) 77:6 The Modern Law Review 831 at 837 https://doi.org/10.1111/1468-2230.12094.
32. Beatrice Junquera & Jesús Ángel Del Brío, 'Preventive Command and Control Regulation: A Case Analysis' (2016) 8 Sustainability 99 https://doi.org/10.3390/su8010099; Elen Stokes, 'Demand for Command: Responding to Technological Risks and Scientific Uncertainties' (2013) 21 Medical Law Review 11 https://doi.org/10.1093/medlaw/fws042.
33. David Seall, 'Over-Prescriptive Regulations Stifle Innovation' (2004) 1 Electronics Weekly 2160; Productivity Commission, Australian Government, *Review of the Regulatory Burden on the Upstream Petroleum (Oil and Gas) Sector* (Productivity Commission Research Report, April 2009); Sue Taylor, Anthony Asher & Julie Anne Tarr, 'Accountability in Regulatory Reform: Australia's Superannuation Industry Paradox' (2017) 45 Federal Law Review 257 at 278 https://doi.org/10.1177/0067205x1704500205.

fast-paced and innovative industries.[34] For the present inquiry, principles-based regulations would establish goals for abating gas flaring and other emissions with the discretion to implement measures for achieving the goals.

3.2 Market-Based Instruments

Several legal scholars have explored the history and adoption of market-based instruments (MBIs) as alternatives to conventional command and control regulatory approaches.[35] These alternatives generally include invisible market forces and economic instruments. They operate in the form of carbon prices (taxes, prices, charges); subsidies, tradeable emissions rights, and eco-labelling. In addition to these common MBIs, Ogus observes the potential of two specific instruments – the 'nudging tax' and 'rectificatory tax' – to induce behavioural change as alternatives to conventional regulatory approaches.[36]

Proponents of MBIs argue that these alternatives overcome the deficiencies of traditional command and control regulation.[37] There is also a common discussion on the use of MBIs to address environmental concerns, both generally,[38] and in the energy transition from fossil fuels to a low-carbon economy.[39] These instruments generally occur in the regulatory frameworks for abating gas flaring in various petroleum jurisdictions, as would be seen in the jurisdictional chapters of this collection.

3.3 Decentred Understandings

Julia Black introduced the terms 'decentring regulation' and 'decentred regulation' into the regulation literature to convey the idea that the state does not have a monopoly

34. Christopher Decker, *Goals-Based and Rules-Based Approaches to Regulation* (The United Kingdom Department for Business, Energy and Industrial Strategy Research Paper Number 8, May 2018) at 6, 17, 21. *See also* Julia Black, Martin Hopper & Christa Band, 'Making a Success of Principles-Based Regulation' (2007) 1:3 Law and Financial Markets Review 191 https://doi.org/10.1080/17521440.2007.11427879; Julia Black, 'Forms and Paradoxes of Principles-Based Regulation' (2008) 3 Capital Markets Law Journal 425-457 https://doi.org/10.1093/cmlj/kmn026.
35. Baldwin, Cave & Lodge, *supra* n. 29, at 169 and 203; Ogus, *supra* n. 27, at 245-259.
36. Anthony Ogus, 'Nudging and Rectifying: The Use of Fiscal Instruments for Regulatory Purposes' (1999) 19:2 Legal Studies 245 https://doi.org/10.1111/j.1748-121x.1999.tb00094.x.
37. Ogus, *supra* n. 27, at 246. For detailed discussion of this, *see* earlier works: Richard B. Stewart, 'Regulation, Innovation and Administrative Law: A Conceptual Framework' (1981) 69:5 California Law Review 1263-1377 https://doi.org/10.2307/3480247; Donald N. Dewees (ed.), *The Regulation of Quality: Products, Services, Workplaces, and the Environment* (Butterworths 1983) at 36-40.
38. Andrew Jordan, Rudiger K.W. Wurzel & Anthony R. Rito (eds), *New Instruments of Environmental Governance? National Experiences and Prospects*' (Routledge 2003); George Rock Pring & Rick A. Feger, *Alternatives to Conventional Regulation in United States Environmental Law* (OUP 2006) at 335-354.
39. Catherine Banet, 'The Use of Market-Based Instruments in the Transition from a Carbon-Based Economy' in Donald N. Zilman and Others (eds), *Beyond the Carbon Economy: Energy Law in Transition* (OUP 2008) 207.

over regulatory powers.[40] Several regulatory relationships occur among various societal strata and entities. For instance, rules for technical committees, professional organizations, and companies are manifestations of regulation occurring outside the confines of state power.[41] Sometimes also, wealth, technical capacity, information, and organizational capacity could be examples of sources of power, apart from the established legal authority.

For gas flaring and other petroleum-related emissions, decentred understandings can include technical industry rules, information, and procedures for mitigating upstream emissions. Specialized industry-driven frameworks such as the OGCI and other forms of self-regulation also form part of the decentred understanding of regulation. Responsive regulation and reflexive regulation are common forms of a decentred understanding of regulation.

3.3.1 Responsive Regulation

Nonet and Selznick set the foundation for responsive regulation through their exposition on the concept of responsive law,[42] which entails dynamic legal development, purposive law, openness and flexibility, citizen participation, and the design of competent legal institutions. Responsive law presupposes that a legal system should be more responsive to the needs of society, more like Rosco Pound's social interest theory.

Drawing on the responsive law concept, Ayres and Braithwaite canvass a responsive theory of regulation.[43] The focal point of their theorization is that governments should be responsive to the conduct of those they seek to regulate in deciding whether a more or less interventionist response is needed.[44] They suggest that regulation should be responsive to industry structure in that different degrees and forms of regulation may be appropriate or suitable to different industry structures. This also applies to the measure of response for regulatory infraction.

Within the purview of Ayres and Braithwaite's responsive regulation theory, there are two pyramids for governmental response in terms of regulatory strategies and punishments for infraction. For regulatory strategies, there should be a system that graduates from self-regulation to enforced self-regulation, to command regulation with discretionary punishment, and to command regulation with nondiscretionary punishment.[45] For punishments, they suggest persuasion, warning letter, civil penalty,

40. Julia Black, 'Decentring Regulation: Understanding the Role of Regulation and Self-Regulation in a "Post-Regulatory" World' (2001) 54 Current Legal Problems 102 https://doi.org/10.1093/clp/54.1.103.
41. *Ibid.*
42. Philipe Nonet & Philip Selznick, *Law and Society in Transition: Toward Responsive Law* (Harper and Row 1978).
43. Ian Ayres & John Braithwaite, *Responsive Regulation: Transcending the Deregulation Debate* (OUP 1992).
44. *Ibid. See also* John Braithwaite, *Restorative Justice and Responsive Regulation* (OUP 2002) at 29.
45. Ayres & Braithwaite, *supra* n. 43, at 39.

criminal penalty, licence suspension, and licence revocation in ascending order depending on the gravity of regulatory infraction.[46]

Authors are of the view that responsive regulation as conceptualized by Ayres and Braithwaite may not be an effective regulatory strategy to curb gas flaring. Since petroleum companies consider flaring as a cheaper option for the disposal of their associated gas, they may be unwilling to self-regulate against such practice in an effective and strict manner. Thus, state regulation might be a better option. In practice, a hybrid of regulatory strategies is the norm, wherein state regulation exists amidst self-regulation and external entities such as non-governmental organizations and other civil society actors. These various entities all play a significant role in enhancing an understanding and the effectiveness of decentred regulations.

3.3.2 Reflexive Regulation

Reflexive regulation originated from socio-legal studies, as developed by Gunther Teubner, who built on the theory of autopoiesis (self-organization and self-creation) propounded by Humberto Maturana, Heinz von Foerster and Niklas Luhmann.[47] Autopoiesis resonates in domains such as biology of cognition and living systems and systems theory. It presupposes that a system or living organism can autonomously self-create and self-organize without recourse to external intervention.[48]

Drawing on autopoiesis, Teubner propounds reflexive regulation as a self-referential system through self-regulation and openness to natural forces which systems can adapt to for survival.[49] He suggests the likelihood of regulatory trilemma in circumstances where law acts as an external intervention that unsettles the internal dynamics of self-referential structures. These include: (a) incongruence of law, politics, and society; (b) possible over-regulation of society; and (c) over-socialization of law.[50] Braithwaite captures this trilemma in the context of law-corporate interaction as follows:

> [A] law that goes against the grain of business culture risks irrelevance; a law that crushes normative systems that naturally emerge in business can destroy virtue; a law that lets business norms take it over can destroy its own virtues.[51]

46. *Ibid.*, at 35. In addition, John Braithwaite discusses five types of responsive regulation – pyramidal responsiveness; micro-responsiveness; networked, nodal responsiveness; meta-regulatory responsiveness; socialist responsiveness. *See* John Braithwaite, 'Types of Responsiveness' in Peter Drahos (ed.), *Regulatory Theory: Foundations and Applications* (ANU Press 2017) 117-130.
47. Gunther Teubner, *Law as an Autopoietic System* (Blackwell 1993).
48. Humberto R. Maturana & Francisco J. Varela, *Autopoiesis and Cognition: The Realisation of the Living* (Dordrecht, Holland; Boston: D. Reidel Publishing Company 1980).
49. Teubner, *supra* n. 47, 13-99. *See also* Gunther Teubner, 'Substantive and Reflexive Elements in Modern Law' (1983) 17:2 Law and Society Review 239-286 https://doi.org/10.2307/3053348.
50. Gunther Teubner, 'After Legal Instrumentalism? Strategic Models of Post-Regulatory Law' in Gunther Teubner (ed.), *Dilemmas of Law in the Welfare State* (De Gruyter 1985) 299 at 309.
51. John Braithwaite, 'Responsive Regulation and Developing Economies' (2006) 34 World Development 844 at 885 https://doi.org/10.1016/j.worlddev.2005.04.021.

Other proponents of reflexive law share Teubner's views. Habermas construes the incongruence between law and the supposed intrinsic internal dynamics of systems to be a *legitimation crisis*; and suggests the avoidance of overburdening social systems through excessive legal intervention.[52] Gunningham advocates a regulatory reform that transcends conventional command and control.[53] Some reflexive options he identifies are process-based and meta-regulation, information regulation, ecological modernization, smart regulation and a new form of environmental governance.[54] These align with another school of thought which posits that addressing complex problems requires a smart mix of multiple policy instruments, and not just the adoption of options such as command and control regulation and market instruments.[55] Schutter and Lenoble extensively discuss suitable applications of this regulatory approach to governance, market structures, state institutions, corporate governance, and social rights.[56]

There are also nuanced perspectives on reflexivity. Two notions present good examples. One is a moderate assessment of reflexivity and some advice on achieving efficient reflexive regulation. The other clearly opposes reflexivity in praxis. On the moderate spectrum, Vincent-Jones cautions that the success of reflexive frameworks would largely depend on the tightness of the law and its manner of interpretation, implementation and enforcement, considering the problem of the regulatory trilemma.[57] He argues for regulatory oversight to ensure that systems under reflexive regulation perform their assigned roles in an efficient, effective and socially accountable manner.[58] On the contrary, Picciotto argues that regulatory reality deflects reflexivity.[59] According to him, legal rules actually constitute the order of things, such as businesses and markets. This specifically applies to the establishment of corporate forms that determine the order and approaches to issues. In this sense, reflexivity becomes an adaptation to established legal rules.[60]

The ideas from responsive and reflexive regulation may seem abstract and of little use to the present inquiry, but there are some specific consequences of decentred understandings of regulation that are helpful. They include self-regulation, co-regulation, voluntary measures, third-party regulation, enforcement measures, and

52. Jürgen Habermas, *The Theory of Communicative Action* (Cambridge, England: Polity Press 1989); Andrew Edgar, *The Philosophy of Habermas* (Routledge 2005) at 138, 156-158.
53. Neil Gunningham, 'Regulatory Reform and Reflexive Regulation' in Bernd Siebenhüner, Tom Dedeurwaerdere, and Éric Brousseau (eds), *Reflexive Governance for Global Public Goods* (MIT Press 2012) 85.
54. *Ibid.*, at 88-97.
55. Neil Gunningham & Peter Grabosky, *Smart Regulation: Designing Environmental Policy* (Clarendon Press 1998) at 15, 37-91.
56. Oliver de Schutter & Jacques Lenoble (eds), *Reflexive Governance: Redefining the Public Interest in a Pluralistic World* (Hart Publishing 2010).
57. Peter Vincent-Jones, 'Competition and Contracting in the Transition from CCT to Best Value: Towards a More Reflexive Regulation' (1999) 77:2 Public Administration 273 https://doi.org/10.1111/1467-9299.00154.
58. *Ibid.*, at 284.
59. Sol Picciotto, 'Regulation: Managing the Antinomies of Economic Vice and Virtue' (2017) 26:6 Social and Legal Studies 676 at 692 https://doi.org/10.1177/0964663917729873.
60. *Ibid.*; Sol Picciotto, 'Introduction: Reconceptualising Regulation in the Era of Globalization' (2002) 29 Journal of Law and Society 1.

environmental management and audit systems.[61] More specifically, voluntary measures, self-regulation, and environmental management initiatives of petroleum organizations and companies help in understanding the import of decentred understandings of regulation.

3.4 Regulatory Hybridity

Leaving the idealistic world of theorizing and conceptualizing and coming to practice, we find the rarity of a regime that purely implements only one regulatory approach.[62] An amalgam of different approaches is the conventional pattern.[63] Different scholars have also explored hybridity for regulating different issues. Riaz has examined a hybrid of state-regulation and self-regulation for remuneration in Australia.[64] Lantz has analysed a combination of revenue capping and incentive regulation to control the profit level of monopolistic firms.[65] Alexius and Furusten have explored hybridity for governing large multifaceted organizations.[66] Ewert and Maggetti have also investigated hybridization in transnational environmental governance.[67]

However, hybridity is not a guarantee for successful regulation.[68] There may be external and remote factors for the achievement of regulatory objectives. Sometimes regulatory failure can result because of improper controls, low monitoring, and enforcement.[69] It is also probable to see instances of regulatory trilemma, as Teubner and Braithwaite argue.[70] A lot depends on a system's design, as much as on its implementation.[71]

It is possible to optimize hybridity. But a successful implementation of any hybrid governance model would depend on an optimal design and the key elements that characterize the system. This point would become evident in the subsequent chapters

61. Barto, *supra* n. 23, at 28-31.
62. Decker, *supra* n. 34, at 5 and 42.
63. David Levi-Faur (ed.), *Handbook on the Politics of Regulation* (Edward Elgar 2011) at 10 and 11; Larry Blank & John W. Mayo, 'Endogenous Regulatory Constraints and the Emergence of Hybrid Regulation' (2009) 35 Review of Industrial Organization 233 at 235-238 https://doi.org/10.1007/s11151-009-9227-y.
64. Zahid Riaz, 'A Hybrid of State Regulation and Self-Regulation for Remuneration Governance in Australia' (2016) 16:3 Corporate Governance 539-563 https://doi.org/10.1108/cg-10-2015-0133.
65. Björn Lantz, 'Hybrid Revenue Caps and Incentive Regulation' (2008) 30 Energy Economics 688-695 https://doi.org/10.1016/j.eneco.2006.09.003.
66. Susanna Alexius & Staffan Furusten (eds), *Managing Hybrid Organisations: Governance, Professionalism and Regulation* (Palgrave Macmillan 2019).
67. Christian Ewert & Martino Maggetti, 'Regulating Side by Side: The Role of Hybrid Organisations in Transnational Environmental Sustainability' (2016) 35 Policy and Society 91-102 https://doi.org/10.1016/j.polsoc.2015.12.004.
68. Bärbel R. Dorbeck-Jung & Others, 'Contested Hybridization of Regulation: Failure of the Dutch Regulatory System to Protect Minors from Harmful Media' (2010) 4 Regulation and Governance 154.
69. *Ibid.*, at 156-158.
70. *Supra* nn 46 and 47.
71. Michiel A. Heldeweg, 'Hybrid Regulation as a Legal Design Challenge' in A.L.B. Colombi Ciacchi & Others (eds), *Law and Governance: Beyond the Public-Private Law Divide* (Eleven International Publishing 2013) 107 at 136-138.

that come in this text, and more especially in the jurisdictional chapters that discuss the specific regulatory settings of various countries.

4 APPLICATION TO FLARING AND OTHER EMISSIONS

Our intention here is to provide a broad and more direct application of law and regulatory theories to gas flaring and other petroleum-related emissions. The application is direct as we are now narrowing our focus on specific measures through which the theories come alive. It is broad as we intend to present an overview of the matter here while the jurisdictional chapters would provide in-depth discussion of a more direct nature. We will also narrow the discussion to three broad themes – prescriptive application, principles-based application, and market-based application. This taxonomy is with a view to providing a broad range of commonplace approaches that could exist distinctively or conjunctively in various regulatory regimes. The authors would like to clarify here that these broad themes occur predominantly in state regulatory approaches, depending on the choices of regulators in various jurisdictions. However, they could also manifest in other decentred regulatory approaches, especially the principles-based and market-based applications.

4.1 Prescriptive Application

While mindful of the drawbacks of prescription, as discussed above, a measure of specificity may be necessary for regulating gas flaring and other emissions. In some jurisdictions such as the United States of America and Canada, there has been a shift from decades-long implementation of resource conservation legislation to a more specific and prescriptive (rules-based) regulatory setting for abating gas flaring and other petroleum-related emissions.[72]

Prescriptive regulations usually stipulate the compulsory implementation of specific measures for decarbonization of oil and gas operations more broadly, and for addressing gas flaring and venting more specifically. For example, operation optimization (through asset integrity, energy efficiency and flaring/venting elimination) and sustainable design (through efficient resource recovery and optimal gas monetization) are some ascertainable decarbonization levers for the petroleum upstream sector.[73] We will now turn to distilling and providing a summary discussion of a selected number of prescriptive measures just to give a flavour of how prescriptive regulations work in practice. The discussion below is not exhaustive but only indicative and demonstrative.

---

72. Allan Ingelson, 'Plugging the Holes: New Canadian and US Regulations to Reduce Upstream Methane Emissions' (2019) Journal of World Energy Law and Business 1-20 https://doi.org/10.1093/jwelb/jwz014.
73. Paul Gargett, Stephen Hall & Jayanti Kar, 'Toward a Net-Zero Future: Decarbonizing Upstream Oil and Gas Operations' (McKinsey & Company 6 December 2019) available at www.mckinsey.com.

4.1.1 *Optimal Gas Utilization/Monetization*

The reference to optimal gas utilization/monetization here means ensuring that oil and gas operators endeavour to utilize the highest quantity of gas to reduce gas flaring during production activities. In North Dakota, for example, there is a regulatory requirement for operators to utilize at least 75% of associated natural gas to avoid flaring.[74] If regulators in more jurisdictions stipulate far-reaching or ambitious ratios of gas utilization, that might positively impact the volume of gas flared globally. For example, if regulations required operators of any producing field to utilize about 80%-90% of the associated natural gas produced during oil recovery operations, production-related gas flaring could reduce significantly.

Nevertheless, the barriers to gas utilization are evident as discussed in Chapter 6 and several other chapters of this text - lack of large gas markets, lack of the necessary infrastructure, and the high-cost implication of commercialization. These barriers, however, present an opportunity for regulators in petroleum-producing jurisdictions to implement innovative incentives to attract more investments for expanding gas infrastructure. They could also leverage public-private partnerships to fund the large-scale monetization of gas as a transition fuel. These and other possible levers could be transitioning pathways for an eventual cessation of gas flaring.

4.1.2 *Monitoring and Data Collection*

Emissions monitoring and data collection are two good regulatory prescriptions practised in some jurisdictions, for example, in the United States, Norway, Nigeria, and Canada. In Nigeria, a metering system requires oil and gas licensees to install metering equipment to quantify the volume of flared gas and ensure that operators comply with flaring limits. In the United States, Canada, and Norway, there are also regulatory arrangements such as lead detection and repair (LDAR) programmes, especially for fugitive emissions (methane leaks).

Authors acknowledge that different jurisdictions would have unique circumstances that inhibit the successful implementation of approaches from other jurisdictions. But it would be useful for countries' regulatory regimes to ensure a form of emissions monitoring, data collection and an obligation to address sources of emissions during oil and gas operations.

4.1.3 *Strict Moratorium on Gas Flaring*

Some countries have a history of stipulating futuristic dates to end gas flaring but only end up with multiple extensions. Most other oil and gas producing countries merely maintain a permit regime - that is, flaring based on permission by the regulator and with payment of necessary penalties. Such permissive penalty regimes would further

74. North Dakota Century Code, Control of Gas and Oil Resources Chapter 38-08, Effective 1 April 2010; amended 1 April 2013, sections 38-08-03, 38-08-04, 38-08-06.4.

encourage the continuity of gas flaring. While implementing other prescriptive measures, it is also important to work with a strict legally binding date for eventually putting an end to gas flaring.

Most countries have signed up for the 2030 Zero Flaring partnership as part of international industry-centric initiatives to end gas flaring. This also complements the Global Gas Flaring Reduction partnership facilitated by the World Bank. These are all plausible measures to address gas flaring. However, petroleum-producing countries would need to further work on more concrete regulatory regimes, incremental steps, policy milestones and strategies for achieving zero flaring. Such steps could be on annual flaring reduction targets leading up to 2030 or any other future date(s). To avoid unending extensions of such a date, regulators can also use the expertise of modelling experts to properly ascertain feasible flare reduction targets based on available technologies, technical expertise, and incentives. This would help to set well-informed realistic goals within the stipulated moratorium.

4.1.4 Energy Efficiency Improvements

Energy efficiency is a useful tool for planning long-term climate policies more broadly.[75] But it is equally relevant for energy-specific emissions abatement in the oil and gas industry.[76] It could trickle down to more granular applications to gas flaring, venting, and other emissions sources in the industry.

Our reference to energy efficiency here relates to the production of oil and gas resources with the use of less process energy to reduce emissions. Regulatory and policy measures such as carbon taxes and emissions trading all seek to incentivize energy efficiency, among other objectives, in energy-intensive industries such as manufacturing, mining, agriculture, oil and gas. Modelling by the International Energy Agency suggests that there could be a 12% decline in energy-related emissions by 2040, representing about 40% of the emissions abatement requirement of the Paris Agreement.[77]

75. Vaibhav Chaturvedi & Priyadarshi R. Shukla, 'Role of Energy Efficiency in Climate Change Mitigation Policy for India: Assessment of Co-Benefits and Opportunities within an Integrated Assessment Modelling Framework' (2014) 123 Climatic Change 597 at 606 https://doi.org/10.1007/s10584-013-0898-x; Robert D. Marchand, S.C. Lenny Koh & Jonathan C. Morris, 'Delivering Energy Efficiency and Carbon Reduction Schemes in England: Lessons from Green Deal Pioneer Places' (2015) 84 Energy Policy 96 at 97 https://doi.org/10.1016/j.enpol.2015.04.035.
76. Saahil Parekh & Siddharth Singh, *Towards an Energy Efficient Oil and Gas Sector* (The Energy and Resources Institute Policy Brief 2015); Birgit Fais, Nagore Sabio & Neil Strachan, 'The Critical Role of the Industrial Sector in Reaching Long-Term Emission Reduction, Energy Efficiency and Renewable Targets' (2016) 162 Applied Energy 699-712 https://doi.org/10.1016/j.apenergy.2015.10.112; Jun Yan & others, 'Creating and Energy Analysis Concept for Oil and Gas Companies: The Case of the Yakutiya Company in Russia' (2019) 12 Energies 268 https://doi.org/10.1016/j.apenergy.2015.10.112; Alejandro M. Arriola-Meddellin & others, 'Energy Efficiency to Increase Production and Quality of Products in Industrial Processes: Case Study Oil and Gas Processing Centre' (2019) 12 Energy Efficiency 1619-1634 https://doi.org/10.1007/s12053-019-09803-0.
77. IEA, *Energy Technology Perspectives 2014* (IEA 2014) at 48.

Different studies[78] suggest that 'energy efficiency improvements' in different economic sectors can further influence emissions reduction, even though there is uncertainty regarding the precise quantitative volume of emissions reduction. However, the impact of energy efficiency (or energy efficiency improvements), among other things, will depend on the scale of implementation.[79] Larger-scale 'energy efficiency improvements' would potentially culminate into larger-scale emissions reduction.

From the prescriptive perspective of our current discussion, two propositions may be useful. First, regulators could set efficiency performance indicators for various upstream petroleum processes. These indicators should profit from robust technical consultations with independent experts for determining ascertainable benchmarks for reducing flaring and other emissions where possible through energy efficiency. These can also be harmonious with set emissions reduction targets for the industry. The second, and probably more important, proposition is for regulators to strictly monitor and assess the energy efficiency performance of operators periodically or annually. There can be incentives and punitive measures to both encourage and compel compliance. One benefit of the periodic or annual assessment is to understand the efficacy or inefficacy of the prescribed efficiency performance indicators amidst other complementary policy measures.

4.2 Principles-Based Application

As discussed above, principles-based, or results-based regulation stipulates goals and allows the regulated entities to decide suitable approaches and modalities for achieving the goals. A traditional principles-based regulation targeting gas flaring and other petroleum-related emissions could establish the regulatory goal for industry operators to work towards decarbonising oil and gas operations. This could potentially circumvent the drawbacks associated with rules-based regulation – slowness/rigidity to respond to new unforeseen problems and barriers to innovation. This would also avail the oil and gas industry the opportunity to further research into possible innovation options for abating gas flaring, rather than circumscribing mitigation efforts only to prescriptive regulatory stipulations. The ultimate result would possibly be the availability of numerous technological approaches and practices for solving the problem of flaring and other emissions.

78. Sandra Backlund & Others, 'Extending the Energy Efficiency Gap' (2012) 51 Energy Policy 392-396 https://doi.org/10.1016/j.enpol.2012.08.042; Hongbo Duan & Others, 'Role of Endogenous Energy Efficiency Improvement in Global Climate Change Mitigation' (2017) 10 Energy Efficiency 459-473 https://doi.org/10.1007/s12053-016-9468-1; WRI, *Long-Term Low Greenhouse Gas Emission Development Strategies: Input Document of the G20 Climate Sustainability Working Group* (World Resources Institute Working Paper 2018) at 24; IEA, *Material Efficiency in Clean Energy Transitions* (IEA 2019) at 29.
79. Nicola Labanca & Paolo Bertoldi, 'Beyond Energy Efficiency and Individual Behaviours: Policy Insights from Social Practice Theories' (2018) 115 Energy Policy 494 at 496 https://doi.org/10.1016/j.enpol.2018.01.027.

It would also allow industry operators across different jurisdictions to adopt and implement efficacious emerging technologies introduced by international industry-centric initiatives such as the OGCI. For example, the OGCI has a suite of portfolios that help to detect, monitor, control and reduce methane emissions during the production, delivery, and usage of petroleum resources.[80] Some of these portfolios may offer useful support to specific measures prescribed by regulation, but that is possible if the regulatory regime allows oil and gas companies the liberty to explore other useful technologies on a complementary basis.

4.3 Market-Based Application

Carbon pricing schemes such as emissions taxes and emissions trading are useful complementary climate policy measures. They are also prevalent in many jurisdictions as we would see in the jurisdictional chapters. But the success of these instruments largely depends on the extent to which they cover gas flaring and other oil and gas emissions, as well as the strength of their price signals.

Oil and gas regulators would need to ensure that carbon pricing schemes capture upstream oil and gas operations to a significant extent, with strong price signals that compel serious modifications in industry operations. For what amounts to a significant coverage, it sounds logical to focus more on oil and gas industry operations that account for larger emissions in the oil and gas industry. For what amounts to a compelling price signal, a lot depends on appropriate design and modelling. The Intergovernmental Panel on Climate Change (IPCC) estimates a 50%-66% probability of keeping peak temperature below 1.5°C range from USD 135–6,050/tCO2e in 2030, USD 245–14,300/tCO2e in 2050, USD 420–19,300/tCO2e in 2070, and USD 690–30,100/tCO2e in 2100.[81] None of the carbon pricing schemes currently existing globally measures with the IPCC estimates. Therefore, petroleum-producing countries would have to adopt more stringent carbon pricing regimes to cover flaring and other emissions associated with petroleum operations with strong signals that are capable of really influencing a large-scale abatement in emissions.

5 CONCLUSION

To bring the curtain down on this chapter, authors would like to reiterate the timeless dictum of the naturalist legal philosopher, Thomas Hobbes – in humanity's pristine existence (the state of nature), life was short, solitary, poor, nasty, and brutish. It was the reign of might over right. Humanity has evolved beyond that pristine barbarism

80. OGCI, *What OGCI Climate Investments is Doing* (OGCI 2020) available at www.oilandgasclimate initiative.com.
81. IPCC, *Global Warming of 1.5°C, an IPCC Special Report on the Impacts of Global Warming of 1.5°C above Pre-industrial Levels and Related Global Greenhouse Gas Emission Pathways, in the Context of Strengthening the Global Response to the Threat of Climate Change, Sustainable Development, and Efforts to Eradicate Poverty*, report available at https://www.ipcc.ch/sr15/, at 152.

after many centuries, yet a scintilla of that very nature resides in the bosom of man. So, according to Jeremy Bentham, the more we are watched, the better we behave. This is the control function of law. It is also the normative function of law that percolates various spheres of human existence in the form of rules and regulations. Absent this legal order, life and human activities would be chaotic, and social cohesion would be an illusory phenomenon.

In this chapter, we have established that regulation is one of the instruments employed to further the ends of law in society, in addition to legislation/statutes. From the various theoretical attempts to conceptualize the meaning of regulation, we distilled some cardinal elements such as behaviour/conduct alteration/modification, standard-setting, decision-making, the workings of a specialist agency, and enforcement mechanisms (comprising compliance monitoring and sanctions for noncompliance). We also narrowed the numerous forms that characterize the typology of regulation to three broad classes - conventional command and control regulation, MBIs, and decentred regulation. All these elements and categories also apply to the regulation of gas flaring and other emissions associated with oil and gas production particularly, and the oil and gas industry more broadly.

While we have attempted to summarize the application of regulatory typology and its fundamental ingredients to gas flaring and other petroleum-related emissions in this chapter, there would be a more exhaustive discussion of the connections in the jurisdiction chapters of this book. It is the authors' hope that the exposition on law and regulation in this chapter will set the scene for the discussion in the remaining parts of this book. Of particular interest would be an interrogation of how legal and regulatory theories and elements play out in countries' regimes to address gas flaring and other petroleum-related emissions.

Part II Jurisdictional Practices

CHAPTER 9
Jurisdictional Focus: Algeria

Waniss Almashri Otman

1 INTRODUCTION

Within the context of the energy transition, and the enhancement of its national economy, Algeria, like other oil and gas-producing countries, seeks to eliminate natural gas flaring to consolidate its energy security. This can be achieved by providing additional quantities of gas to the domestic market or facilitating export. This chapter therefore provides a critical overview of the current legal and policy framework related to these issues.

2 OVERVIEW OF THE ALGERIAN UPSTREAM OIL AND GAS SECTOR

Algeria depends on oil and gas exports for more than 90% of its foreign (US Dollar) revenues[1] and this sector has been the backbone of the Algerian economy for decades. This will remain the dominant position for many years to come, thanks to its vast oil and gas reserves, favorable geological structures, and promising new opportunities for both conventional and unconventional resources.

– Oil and Gas Reserves and Production

As of January 1, 2023, Algeria possessed 12.2 billion barrels of proven oil reserves, positioning the country as the third largest holder of oil reserves in Africa, after Libya and Nigeria respectively.[2] According to the last British Petroleum (BP) Statistical

1. Energy world, January 4, 2022. Energy firm Sonatrach to invest USD 40 billion in five years: CEO. Available at: https://energy.economictimes.indiatimes.com/news/oil-and-gas/atf-price-hiked-by-2-75-lpg-cut-by-rs-102-5/88656712.
2. OPEC Annual Statistical Bulletin 2023, 58th edition. Available at: www.opec.org.

Review, in 2022, oil production in Algeria reached 1.474 million barrels per day (b/d), an increase compared to the previous year's production of 1.353 million b/d. But between 2012 and 2020, figures decreased from 1.537 to 1.332 million b/d, respectively.[3]

Algeria holds the world's tenth-largest and Africa's second-largest proved natural gas reserves, with approximately 4,504 billion cubic meters (bcm).[4] The country is the major natural gas producer in Africa and holds the world's tenth producer position in 2021 at around 105 bcm.[5] Algeria is a key hydrocarbon provider to Southern Europe; on completion of the liquefied natural gas (LNG) plant at Arzew in 1964, Algeria became the world's leading producer of LNG and still leads African LNG exports to European markets. These amount in 2021 to 15.4 bcm and in 2021 Algeria was Europe's third-largest natural gas supplier by pipeline, with 34.1 bcm, after Russia and Norway, respectively.[6]

Gas production in Algeria has increased remarkably over the last five decades, from around 2.6 bcm in 1970 to the current level at the end of 2021 of 105 bcm, ranking it as the leading producer in Africa with 37% of the continent's total gas production.[7]

Despite the considerable rapid growth of its domestic market, Algeria continues to be Africa's largest gas exporter. In 2021, Algeria exported approximately 55 bcm, or approximately 45% of the continent's gas trade. This is unsurprising, given its geographical proximity, particularly to southern Europe; almost 90% of this gas amounting to 49.5 bcm found its way to European markets.[8]

Algeria is also Africa's second-largest gas consumer after Egypt. In 2022, the total local demand was recorded at 51.4 bcm, or around 32% of the continent's total consumption.[9]

– *Regulatory Structure*

The oil and gas industry in Algeria is currently regulated by Hydrocarbons Law No. 19-13 of December 11, 2019,[10] and amendments, which cover all matters related to oil and gas exploration and production (E&P), including abandonment, flaring and environmental impacts.

In institutional terms, the Algerian Ministry of Energy and Mines (MEM), established in 1962, is the leading organization regulating the oil and gas industry. It is responsible for implementing hydrocarbon policy, developing the country's hydrocarbon resources, ensuring coordination and rationalization of hydrocarbon production, granting all mining titles, approval procedure for oil and gas contracts and their amendments, and permissions for exploitation.

3. British Petroleum (BP) Statistical Review of World Energy June 2022, 71st ed. London, UK, 2022.
4. OPEC 2023, *supra* n. 2.
5. *Ibid.*
6. BP 2022, *supra* n. 3.
7. OPEC Annual Statistical Bulletin 2022, 57th edition. Available at: www.opec.org.
8. BP 2022, *supra* n. 3.
9. OPEC 2023, *supra* n. 2.
10. Replaces Hydrocarbons Law No. 05-07 of 2005. Since the issuing of Law No. 19-13, within a period of three years (2020-2023), dozens of decrees passed by the competent authority dealt with many aspects of the O and G industry.

In 2005, aiming for the liberalization of the O and G industry, a reform policy established to avoid permanent conflicts of interest, a new Hydrocarbons Law (Law No. 05-07) made fundamental changes through the creation of two new public entities replacing Sonatrach.[11] Its previous mandate was replaced by two new institutions, the National Agency for the Valorization of Hydrocarbon Resources (ALNAFT) and the Hydrocarbon Regulatory Authority (ARH). With two new bodies in play, Sonatrach[12] was significantly strengthened in its crucial task as the industry regulator. In line with Article 22 of the 2005 Hydrocarbon Law, both bodies enjoy legal and financial independence. Before 2005, Sonatrach was the regulator as well as the state national oil company, a situation leading to frequent disputes and conflicts of interest.

– *Legal Framework*

Although the hydrocarbon sector was regulated early in Algeria's colonial period, for reasons of word economy the author shall concentrate on an analysis of the current phase, 2019-2023.

– *The 2019 Hydrocarbons Law*

Law No. 19-13 tackles fundamental weakness provisions of the former 2005 hydrocarbons law and associated tax regimes. The preceding law placed a substantial burden of taxes and duties rates on E&P activities as well as complex and ambiguous production sharing contract (PSCs) terms with Sonatrach. Despite a few key amendments introduced to the 2005 law (in 2006 and 2013) aiming at attracting IOCs participation in the E&P oil and gas sector, it became apparent through the four bid rounds after the 2005 law that these amendments had not worked.

However, Law No. 19-13 improved the regulatory framework by introducing a stable legal, institutional and fiscal environment as well as positing an attractive, clear and simple legislation.

The new law reorganizes the roles dedicated to each of the state institutions involved in the oil and gas industry, namely the MEM, ALNAFT, and ARH, as well as Sonatrach as the state body. Among other significant reforms brought about by the new law is a decrease in the use of Minister's approvals, clearly highlighting the independence of the two agencies and reinforcing their regulatory and supervisory powers. Additionally, it is also worth mentioning that the new law grants both agencies the right to terminate a contract entered into with a foreign or national partner, in case the latter fails to comply with the contract clauses, without requiring the MEM approval.

A new change is that ALNAFT will no longer take part in E&P contracts. As such, ALNAFT will confer on Sonatrach and its IOCs partners the right to carry out E&P activities within the framework of the contract execution. However, ALNAFT is

11. A state-owned entity in the oil and gas E&P activities. It now owns around 80% of the country's total oil and gas production and has evolved into the chosen instrument of national petroleum policy.
12. After independence, Sonatrach was created in December 31, 1963 and emerged as a colossal integrated corporation absorbing the rapidly expanding oil and gas industry from the previous French colonial interests. Since then, it has rapidly expanded, jealously guarding its control over the country's hydrocarbon resources, both upstream and downstream.

permitted to conclude prospection service contracts for offshore explorations (this can be done in conformity with Article 46 of the new law).

Law No. 19-13 replaces Law No. 05-07. It should be noted that contracts concluded under previous laws, especially Law Nos. 14-86 and 07-05, remain valid in accordance with their provisions, but may not be extended or renewed beyond the initial contract period. However, the requirements of Law No. 19-13 relating to health, security and environmental issues, as well as the provisions related to the dismantling and restoration of oil production sites, will apply to previously signed contracts.

Thus, the law emphasizes the necessity of conducting and securing the approval of an environmental impact assessment (EIA) in order to request a license to operate oil and gas development projects, subject to the approval of the competent authority (ALNAFT and ARH). ARH is also charged with implementing an assessment and reporting system regarding greenhouse gas emissions (GHG emissions) in the oil and gas sector.

3 GAS FLARING: A PERMANENT DILEMMA?

As touched on later, Algeria has always ranked among the world's top 10 gas-flaring nations, a rank held over for many years. Applying a practical solution to reduce these wasteful resources can help to boost gas exports. For the year 2021, the total GHG emissions stood at 221.7 mtCO2e, where the GHG emissions grew 1.3 mtCO2 from 2020, in which energy-related GHG emissions represented 64.4% of the total.[13] In 2022, Algeria's share of global natural gas flaring recorded 5.8% of the total.[14]

In the period from 2012 to 2022, a total of 95 bcm of natural gas were flared in Algeria. In the period under review, the country registered the highest levels of natural gas flaring in 2016 and 2019 at 9.7 bcm, and the flaring intensity for the last decade remained high after peaking in 2013 at over 8.8 bcm. Over the same period, oil production dropped by a quarter. Among the countries covered, Algeria's flaring intensity in 2022 was the highest in Africa with 18.5% of the total.[15] There were 177 flare sites in the last flare count, conducted in 2019.[16]

Sonatrach produces approximately 80% of its oil and gas needs, mostly from older oil fields, and as a result, is responsible for most of its gas flaring.[17] It owns in full most of the major oil fields in the country that produce oil and flare-associated gas, while Sonatrach, in partnership with foreign companies, operates fields that produce free gas and condensate, in which the flaring process is very limited.

13. The World Bank, APRIL 14, 2022, Algeria's Economic Update, April 2022. Available at: https://www.worldbank.org/en/country/algeria/publication/economic-update-april-2022 (accessed on October 20, 2022).
14. British Petroleum (BP) Statistical Review of World Energy June 2023,72nd ed. London, UK, 2023.
15. *Ibid.*
16. World Bank Group, September 2021, Algeria/Policy and Targets: Background and the Role of Reductions in Meeting Environmental and Economic Objectives. Available at: https://flaringventingregulations.worldbank.org/algeria (accessed on October 10, 2022).
17. The World Bank Group. Algeria: Global Flaring and Venting Regulations. Available at: https://flaringventingregulations.worldbank.org/node/5.

Algeria's recent rate of natural gas flaring comes from around 200 discretely resolvable flaring sites across the country. The top 11 assets are: owned by Sonatrach (Hassi Messaoud, Alrar, Hassi R'Mel, Amassak, Rhourde Nouss, Rhourde Chegga); owned by Sonatrach and IOCs (TFT, In Amenas, Bir Seba, Bir Berkine Nord).[18]

Table 9.1 Natural Gas Flaring in Algeria Compared to Oil-Producing African Countries, 2012-2022 (bcm)

Country	*2012*	*2013*	*2014*	*2015*	*2016*	*2017*	*2018*	*2019*	*2020*	*2021*	*2022*
Algeria	3.4	8.8	9.2	9.6	9.7	9.2	9.4	9.7	9.3	8.1	8.5
Egypt	0.4	2.6	3.0	3.0	3.0	2.5	2.4	2.5	2.5	2.3	2.2
Libya	3.8	4.1	2.9	2.7	2.4	4.0	4.7	5.1	2.5	5.9	5.4
Nigeria	12.9	9.2	8.3	7.5	7.2	7.5	7.3	7.8	7.0	6.5	5.3
Other African	12.1	9.3	9.7	10.4	10.4	9.4	8.5	8.2	7.8	7.4	7.9

Source: BP Statistical Review of World Energy 2023, p. 13.

Note: As can be seen from the table for the last decade (2013-2022), Algeria was the top gas-flaring country in the African continent. Its average flared gas of about 9.15 bcm[19] or the equivalent of 18% of its last year's domestic gas consumption.[20]

One of the main reasons for the continued flaring of gas in some producing countries is the lack or inadequacy of policies and strategies to reduce gas flaring. There is often a lack of coordination or integration between energy policies and environmental policies that address gas emissions, and more specifically gas flaring. This may explain why some Nationally Determined Contributions (NDCs) submitted by Arab producers include general measures to reduce gas flaring or do not include any measures at all. It must be emphasized that this problem also exists in other oil and gas-producing countries.[21]

Therefore, the lack of appropriate policies and strategies translates into the absence of effective frameworks to regulate gas flaring. A very limited number of Arab oil and gas producers have regulations that adequately cover the reduction/elimination of gas flaring. If a regulatory framework is in place but it is not properly implemented, or if too many exceptions are called to allow gas flaring to continue, the framework becomes ineffective. It should be noted that some Arab producers who do not have

18. Capterio, November 4, 2020. Eliminating flaring and accelerating the transition: a practical roadmap for Algeria. Available at: www.capterio.com.
19. BP Statistical Review 2023, *supra* n. 14.
20. OPEC 2023, *supra* n. 2.
21. UN-ESCWA 2019, Reducing Gas Flaring in Arab Countries A Sustainable Development Necessity. United Nations publication issued by ESCWA, United Nations House, Beirut, Lebanon, p. 12. Available at: https://www.unescwa.org/sites/default/files/pubs/pdf/reducing-gas-flaring-arab-countries-english.pdf.

clear regulations to limit gas flaring have been able to significantly reduce gas flaring through financial grants, government commitments and initiatives.[22]

4 LAWS AND REGULATIONS APPLICABLE TO GAS FLARING AND VENTING

The new Law No. 19-13 maintains the prohibition on flaring and venting without specific exceptions, mentioning that there may be special exceptions to this. As in the previous law, where a specific exception is granted, a non-deductible flaring tax applies unless the activity falls under exempt status. The penalty was raised to 12,000 Algerian dinars per thousand cubic meters, taking into account an annual review based on the Algerian consumer price index.

With regard to methane, there are no specific emission restrictions and reporting requirements.

Similar to the previous Hydrocarbons Law No. 05-07, as amended, the new Law No. 19-13 continues to establish more stringent controls to limit gas flaring.

Again, among the requirements of the Law related to environmental, health and security issues, along with provisions related to decommissioning and restoration of oil and gas facilities, as briefly stated above, these shall apply to all E&P contracts signed under previous petroleum legislation.

Article (10) of the Law No. 19-13 provided that: "In addition to the provisions stipulated in the regulations and legislation in force, hydrocarbon activities must be conducted in a manner that protects against all risks related to them. The practice of this activities requires respect for obligations relating to: the security and health of people; hygiene and public health; the basic features of the surrounding land or marine environment; the protection of biological resources, the protection of the environment; industrial security and the use of chemicals, the rational use of natural resources and energy; the protection of groundwater resources; protection of archaeological heritage."

The ARH authority is empowered to coordinate with the institutions and administrations concerned with all aspects related to environmental protection and industrial safety. In this regard, Article (43) of the new law regarding the functions of the ARH in this aspect referred to the following two points: Regulation in the field of health, industrial security, environment, prevention and management of major risks, especially in the field of atmospheric emissions, as well as in the field of protection of groundwater and aquifers containing water during the exercise of the activities subject to this law, by resorting to all legal means, including That is the referral to the competent judicial authorities. The second, implementation of technical rules that ensure the safety of production and injection wells, prevention of risks to the health and safety of people, protection and management of the environment, as well as protection of layers containing water during the stages of well drilling, exploitation and abandonment. These technical rules are determined by the regulations.

22. *Ibid.*

Article (45) of the new Law No. 19-13 empowered the ARH with full supervision over aspects related to environmental protection, people's health and safety, and industrial security of facilities and structures related to hydrocarbon activities, in coordination with the concerned authorities and departments.

With regard to the environment, Article (151) of the new Law No. 19-13 stipulates that every person working in hydrocarbon activities is obligated to respect best practices in order to prevent any risks or damages that may affect people, property, facilities or the environment. Without prejudice to the legislation and regulations in force, any damage to the environment as a result of the practice of hydrocarbon activities, and whoever caused it is obligated to implement the necessary operations to protect the environment and restore the sites to their original condition, and in the absence of this, to pay financial compensation.

Article (155) of the new Law No. 19-13, stipulates that research activities are subject to the obligation to submit a study on risks to health, safety and the environment, including plans to manage these risks. This study is subject to the approval of ARH.

It's worth mentioning that, in September 2015, Algeria submitted its first NDC to the UN Framework Convention on Climate Change (UNFCCC).[23] The NDC has an unconditional target of reducing greenhouse gas emissions by 7% by 2030 from a business-as-usual scenario and a conditional reduction target of 22%. One of the planned actions is to reduce the flared gas volumes to less than 1% by 2030, likely of the total associated gas volume (and not of total natural gas) produced. Algeria's NDC and Sonatrach have adopted a target of less than 1% of total associated gas to be flared by 2030. This assured by Sonatrach in its 2017 annual report, stated its target of reducing flaring to less than 1% of associated gas by 2021. Sonatrach is accountable for most of the flaring. It produces around 80% of oil and gas, mainly from matured oil fields. In 2018, Sonatrach, affirmed the World Bank's Zero Routine Flaring by 2030 initiative.[24]

Back then, a few years after independence, in 1966 for the first time Algeria prohibited gas flaring produced from the oil and gas fields. Since then, the prohibition on flaring become a national policy governed by national regulators. Since its creation in 2005, the ARH is also authorized to prepare and deliver environmental regulations, including emissions resulting from hydrocarbon operations.

Law No. 05-07, 2005, clearly defined the prohibition and authorized new Algeria's regulatory agencies ARH and ALNAFT to determine and implement flaring and venting restrictions. The latest hydrocarbon Law No. 19-13, 2019, prohibits routine

23. Ratified in June 1993. The country submitted two national reports, it was drafted with the assistance of UNDP on measures taken to implement the UNFCCC.

    Kyoto Protocol ratified in 1997 and on February 16, 2005, ratified again (As an extension of the UNFCCC, the Kyoto Protocol seeks to achieve the goal of reducing GHG emissions).

    Paris Agreement on Climate ratified October 20, 2016. The treaty requires each country to communicate a NDC, represent goals and actions for the post-2020 period.
24. World Bank Group, September 2021, Algeria/Policy and Targets: Background and the Role of Reductions in Meeting Environmental and Economic Objectives. Available at: https://flaringventingregulations.worldbank.org/algeria (accessed on October 10, 2022).

flaring and venting of natural gas, sets taxes on flared or vented volumes, and outlines the responsibilities of the two regulatory agencies. However, the recent Law, except for flaring and venting under certain conditions does not specify any targets or limits. Implementing regulations for the law had not been yet published by the competent authority ARH.[25]

It is worth citing that, in 2008 the government passed Executive Decree No. 08-312, which specifics the conditions of EIAs in the oil and gas sector and the ARH's role in monitoring and implementing compliance with EIAs. EIAs have to include measures to remove, decrease, or compensate for environmental impacts from flaring or venting. The Decree also requests and illustrates the process for the ARH to consult with other ministries and provincial governments during the approval of EIAs. This approach has been affirmed by the recent legislation, the ARH will consult with other ministries and provincial authorities before approving EIAs conducted at oil and gas facilities (Article 44 of Law No. 19-13).

The new hydrocarbon Law No. 19-13 (Articles 210-213) introduced a tax on the quantities of flared gas. For instance, for each 1,000 cubic meters, the imposed tax rate is DZD 12,000 (approximately USD 85 as of October 19, 2022). This tax is nondeductible for the purposes of calculating other payments under the E&P fiscal regime. ALNAFT can modify this tax at the start of each year based on the national inflation index. This tax rate is subject to increase by 50% if IOCs as an operator flare gas without obtaining permission from the competent authorities[26] or flare gas greater than the volume allowed in the consent license,[27] excluding the volume of gas flares for safety purposes (as defined in Article 159 of the law).

This tax is not due during the exploration activities or well testing as well throughout the start-up phase, this period is to be determined by one of the regulators ALNAFT or ARH. Also, due to a lack of capacity for gas recovery or pipeline infrastructure. Finally, at oil and gas facilities or plants constructed before 2005 (Article 215).

Nonmonetary Penalties: According to Article (226) of the 2019 Act, allows ALNAFT to suspend or cancel authorizations for upstream prospecting or concessions if a licensee violates any provision of this Act.

Monetary Penalties: According to Article (127) of the Law No. 19-13, allows the ARH to assess a daily penalty of 100,000 Algerian dinars for noncompliance with the new Act or its implementing regulations.

Article (160) of the Law No. 19-13 stipulates that ALNAFT and ARH monitor gas flaring operations and quantities flared.

25. The Law does not mention the estimation of flaring and venting volumes, but the ARH is in charge for developing technical regulations following international best practices.
26. Authorized Flaring or Venting: according Art. (158) of the 2019 Hydrocarbon Law, prohibits flaring and venting. Flaring is allowed under specific conditions, for instance throughout well testing or in the absence of enough takeaway pipeline or processing capacity.
27. Upstream flares require authorization from ALNAFT; midstream or downstream flares require authorization from the ARH.

Key executive decisions related to the environment and natural gas flaring:[28]

- Executive Decree No. 21-330 of August 25, 2021.
- Executive Decree No. 08-312 of October 5, 2008.
- Executive Decree No. 2007-145 of May 19, 2007.

5 AMBITIOUS NON-FLARING POLICY: ECONOMIC AND ENVIRONMENTAL CONSIDERATIONS

Algeria is one of the few hydrocarbon producers in the world with regulations that impose penalties or taxes on associated gas flaring. Gas flaring was first prohibited in 1966. Since then, Algeria, through Sonatrach, has invested heavily in more than 30 projects that have significantly reduced associated gas flaring and allowed the monetization of recovered gas and valuable liquefied petroleum gas (LPG). However, significant efforts, especially investments, are needed to reach zero routine gas flaring by 2030.[29]

According to Sonatrach, associated gas flaring has decreased significantly from about 75% in 1975 to 8% in 2017.[30]

On January 6, 2023, a Middle East Economic Survey (MEES) interview with Sonatrach CEO Tawfik Hakar concerning his company's plans for 2023 and beyond with increasing gas production high on the agenda asked him what Sonatrach was doing to cut gas flaring.

He answered "I would like to remind you that Sonatrach has always invested in the recovery of flared gas, through several projects of associated gas recovery and facility revamps, particularly in major production sites such as Hassi Messaoud, which has enabled us to reduce the flaring rate to 2%. Today, we have registered a number of projects to recover flared gases at the relevant production sites and LNG complexes. These projects will enable us in the medium term to achieve our goals that consist of reducing gas flaring to less than 1% and eliminating routine flaring."[31]

28. - https://documents1.worldbank.org/curated/en/099040224142516462/pdf/P1596901b43cdb00b1a2b91c58afc12f6f3.pdf.
    - https://www.iea.org/policies/15723-executive-decree-no-08-312-2008.
    - https://www.iea.org/policies/15964-executive-decree-no-2007-145-of-2-joumada-el-oula-1428-corresponding-to-19-may-2007-determining-the-scope-content-and-approval-procedures-for-environmental-impact-studies-and-notices.
29. Dahlab Fazia (Director of Climate Change, Algeria Ministry of Environment and Renewable Energy), Project Fact Sheet (Project Title: Recovering Associated Gas Flaring in Area of In Amenas Algeria). United Nations Economic and Social Commission for Western Asia (ESCWA). Towards COP27: Arab Regional Forum on Climate Initiatives to Finance Climate Action and the SDGs, UN House, Beirut, Lebanon, September 2022. Available at: https://www.unescwa.org/sites/default/files/event/materials/Mitigation_Algeria_Project_Fact_Sheet_Algeria_Gas%20Flaring_In%20Amenas%20%2813Sept22%29_web.pdf (accessed October 13, 2023).
30. Sonatrach Annual Report 2017. Available at: Rapport-Annuel_2017.pdf (sonatrach.com).
31. Middle East Economic Survey (MEES), January 6, 2023, Issue: 66/1, by Aydin Calik. Algeria's Sonatrach Targets "Rapid New Output": Exclusive MEES Interview with CEO Toufik Hakkar.

Sonatrach has now begun implementing a project to eliminate gas flaring, which will take four years (implementation period 2023-2027). The project aims to recover 532,000 cm/d of flared (associated) gas from two crude (petroleum) production fields, namely the "Tiqentourin" field with a capacity of 450,000 cm/d and the "La Reculée" field with a capacity of 70,000 cm/d per day in the In Amenas region.[32]

The global context of the project fulfills Algeria's obligations regarding environmental protection and promotion of environmental goods and services and is in line with the UNFCCC and the Paris Climate Agreement. The benefits of reducing and ultimately eliminating gas flaring are largely linked to Sustainable Development Goal (SDG) 13 on climate action. Moreover, gas flaring affects not only humans but also the entire ecosystem. The benefits are linked to several SDGs, including: SDG 3 (good health and well-being); SDG 8 (decent work and economic growth); SDG 9 (industry, innovation and infrastructure); SDG 15 (life on land); SDG 12 (responsible consumption and production) in addition to SDG 7 (clean and affordable energy). Furthermore, Algeria's NDC gas flaring mitigation and routine zero flaring targets include reducing gas flaring to 1% by 2030, and Sonatrach has mandated zero routine gas flaring by 2030.[33]

In summary, the In Amenas project is in line with the SDGs and the Paris Agreement because it will enable the following to be achieved:[34]

- Recovering the flared gas and using it as a cleaner fuel (compared to other polluting fuels) for generating electricity will ensure or improve access to energy.
- The monetization of recovered gas to create projects that consume natural gas and/or LPG extracted from associated gas will create economic growth and employment opportunities.
- Reducing or ending gas flaring will have a significant impact on land and ecosystems close to flaring sites. This could also be relevant to SDG 6, as gas flaring could affect water supplies through acid rain.

In this connection, the International Energy Agency in June 2022 published an excellent study entitled "The energy security case for tackling gas flaring and methane leaks." The study highlights key African oil and gas-producing countries and identifies their possible gas savings from current and potential exports to the European Union from reducing flaring and methane emissions.

Available at: https://www.mees.com/2023/1/6/corporate/algerias-sonatrach-targets-rapid-new-output-exclusive-mees-interview-with-ceo-toufik-hakkar/55e111f0-8dc3-11ed-b111-630c86e3be0d (accessed October 13, 2023).

32. Dahlab Fazia, *supra* n. 29.
33. *Ibid.*
34. *Ibid.*

Table 9.2 Possible Gas Savings from Current and Potential Exporters to the European Union from Reducing Flaring and Methane Emissions (bcm)

Country	*Reducing Flaring*	*Reducing Methane*	*Total*	*Difference Between 2022 Export Capacity and 2021 Exports*	*Additional Gas Available*
Algeria	8	2	10	10	10
Nigeria	6	2	8	7	7
Libya	5	2	7	7	7
Angola	2	0.4	2	2	2
Equatorial Guinea	0.2	0.2	0.4	0.4	0.4
Egypt	2	1	3	7	3
Total	22.2	7.6	30.4	33.4	29.4

Source: International Energy Agency (IEA): The energy security case for tackling gas flaring and methane leaks, p. 10, June 2022. Available at: www.iea.org.

It is certain that over the next few decades, gas markets in southern Europe will remain dependent on Algerian gas supplies. For example, the following table shows contract renewals during the period for future time periods.

Table 9.3 Algeria: Sonatrach's Renewed Gas Export Contracts

Company	*Renewal Date*	*Duration (Year)*	*Volume (bcm/year)*	*Export Via*
Enel (Italy)	October 26, 2019	8 to 10	3	Pipeline
Galp Energia (Portugal)	June 11, 2019	10	2.5	Pipeline
Eni (Italy)	May 16, 2019	8 to 10	9	Pipeline
Botas (Turkey)	September 4, 2018	5	4.4	LNG
Naturgy (Spain)	June 14, 2018	9	9	Pipeline
Total			27.9	

Sources: Ouki Mostefa. Algerian Gas in Transition: Domestic transformation and changing gas export potential.

Oxford Institute for Energy Studies (OIES PAPER: NG 151), 2019. Available at: www.jstor.org/stable/resrep30955.11.

Proposed Gas Flaring Elimination Master Plan

Since Algeria currently holds the unenviable position of being, in Africa, the major gas flarer over the past decade, the country's decision-makers must now develop an effective Master Plan to overcome this dilemma. These steps should include:

> First, all fields in which associated gas is burned must be identified to evaluate their technical/ geological attributes in terms of reserves, production, quantities burned both daily and annually, and their locations within the country's oil infrastructure.
> Second, the preparation of a comprehensive economic study that will include the ownership of these fields, whether by Sonatrach or in partnership with foreign companies, to determine the financial commitments and technology necessary to install the equipment and facilities required to eliminate gas flaring.
> The third and final step, derived from the data collected from the previous two steps, is to re-evaluate current legislation and contractual terms. This process will determine the necessary legal amendments required to incentivize current partners with Sonatrach, or potentially, open the way for the participation of experienced third parties, via service contracts, to share best practices in eliminating gas flaring.

Underpinning these initiatives is of course the absolute necessity for the implementation of existent legal sanctions for gas flaring. Since the 2019 Hydrocarbons Law, the legal position has been abundantly clear: gas flaring is prohibited unless the regulatory body, ALNAFT, grants a specific exemption for a specified period of time, otherwise, penalties will be imposed.[35]

6 ALGERIA: THE CASE FOR A NEW ENERGY TRANSITION POLICY

In Algeria, gas prices in the local market are heavily subsidized, and this is one of the reasons that has led to an increase in local demand for gas over the past decades. For example, during recent years, demand has increased from about 44.4 bcm in 2018 to about 51.4 bcm in 2022, driven largely by subsidized pricing.[36] The government is pursuing a gasification strategy. There are programs to convert light vehicles to LPG and buses and trucks to compressed natural gas (CNG) to reduce the consumption of petroleum products. However, most of the demand growth reflects increased power

35. Article 227 of Hydrocarbon *Law No. 19-13, 2019,* allows the ARH to assess a daily penalty of 100,000 Algerian dinars (about USD 739.634 as of November 8, 2023) for noncompliance with *the law or* its implementing regulations. The penalty starts at least the month after the offending party is notified of the violation. This delay is to allow for remediation or elimination of the violation.
36. OPEC Annual Statistical Bulletin 2023, 58th edition.

generation and distribution in cities. The phasing out of energy subsidies is seen as necessary to avoid an imbalance between supply and demand and encourage further development of non-associated gas fields.[37]

Therefore, the rapid increase in natural gas consumption in recent decades, which has reached nearly half of the gas produced, has put the Algerian government to the corner, with the necessity of finding a way out of this situation, either by increasing gas production through participation with IOCs in the field of E&P, or eliminating associated gas flaring, or exploiting unconventional gas resources, or finally using renewable energies (REs), as potential solutions to this situation.

In 2022, the GoA formed a High Energy Council, chaired by the Algerian President, which defines the national strategy of the energy sector, its funding, the energy transition, RE and scientific research.

In order to diversify energy sources, reduce dependence on fuel, and confront increasing domestic consumption, the GoA has announced a national plan to develop REs,[38] with the aim of reaching a volume of 15,000 MW generated by RE by 2035.[39] Also important among the proposed strategies the green hydrogen[40] industrial sector from renewable electrical energy is another effective way of effecting a successful energy transition.

In an interview with *Der Spiegel* magazine in 2021, Algerian President Abdelmadjid Tebboune noted that the country has "a great deal of potential in the field of renewable energies," noting that "with Germany's help, Algeria can supply Europe with solar energy." Regarding the country's green energy potential at a time when Algeria is beginning to suffer the catastrophic effects of climate change.[41]

Sonatrach has placed reducing the carbon footprint at the heart of its strategy and has ambitions to be an effective player in the REs value chain. The following table briefly summarizes these developments in the energy transition.

---

37. The World Bank Group. Global Gas Flaring Reduction Partnership (GGFR). Global Flaring and Venting Regulations: Algeria, September 2021. Available at: https://flaringventingregulations.worldbank.org/algeria.
38. National Programme for the Development of Renewable Energies 2020 (it was approved in 2011 and amended in 2015 and 2020).
    Also, the GoA adopted Law No. 04-09 of August 14, 2004 relating to the promotion of RE within the framework of sustainable development.
39. On February 17, 2022, the tender relevant requirements were issued. This project aims to start the first phase of electricity generation capacity of 15,000 MW.
40. Within the framework of the Algerian energy transition policy, a national plan for green hydrogen is currently being prepared.
41. Chibani Achref, August 24, 2022. pressures and openings that affect energy transition in a country with large hydrocarbon reserves.
    Available at: https://timep.org/2022/08/24/algerias-green-energy-transition-an-energy-transition-diverted-by-oil-and-gas-profits/.

Table 9.4 Algeria via Sonatrach: Energy Transition Policy 2022

Type	*Framework*	*Achievements*
Photovoltaic power station	Pursue the implementation of low carbon policy and production of clean energy	Launching of first construction works of a new photovoltaic solar power station "BRN2" jointly with ENI.
Biofuels	Discussion on feasibility of transforming a refinery for the production of biofuels.	Signing an agreement with the partner ENI in order to develop pilot projects for green hydrogen and biofuels.
Solar Lab	First Solar Lab inaugurated	Solar Lab inaugurated with the aim to evaluate the photovoltaic technologies and measuring the environmental data with intelligent systems. This lab is open to universities for research purposes
Green hydrogen	Feasibility study of a pilot project of green hydrogen on one of Sonatrach sites.	Signing of an MoU with the German company VNG AG for the development of green hydrogen and ammonia.

Source: Sonatrach Achievements in 2022—Preliminary Results. Energy Transition, p. 27.

The climate issue is at the core of Sonatrach's strategy.[42] Several projects are planned to enable Sonatrach to reach in the long term its goals of reducing flared gas to less than 1% and eliminating routine flaring by the year 2030.[43] In this regard, Sonatrach has achieved these goals:

- In 2018, Sonatrach supported the World Bank's "Zero Routine Flaring by 2030" (ZRF) initiative.[44]
- Sonatrach confirms in its latest annual report that as a result of operating new units to recover flared gas in a number of production areas, especially Hassi Messaoud (GOSP separation project) and Ohant, together representing a total reduction in the flaring of associated gases by more than 20% when compared with 2017.[45] For example, recently Sonatrach operating several gas flaring reduction projects, in particular in the Hassi Messaoud area, such as the GOSP

42. Algerian National Climate Plan (NCP) commenced on 2019, for the period from 2020 to 2030.
43. According to Sonatrach latest Annual Report (2022, p. 71), the company aims in the medium term to achieve the goals of reducing gas flaring to less than 1% and stopping routine gas flaring by 2030.
44. The World Bank Group. Algeria: Global Flaring and Venting Regulations. Available at: https://flaringventingregulations.worldbank.org/node/5.
45. Sonatrach Annual Report 2022, p. 71.

separation project in Hassi Katar allowed the recovery of about 3 million cm/d of associated gases, and a compressor at the center of the Burkin CPF well. This allowed the recovery of 170 thousand cm/d of associated gas. These efforts have allowed the rate of gas flaring to be reduced from 4.45% in 2021 to 3.68% in 2022. A project was also completed to develop a method to estimate the volume of flared gas used in satellites in cooperation with the Algerian Space Agency.[46]

- Global downward trend registered for the second consecutive year with a reduction of more than 20% from 2017 to 2022. And less than 9% flared gas versus 2021.
- Thanks to the coming on stream of new flare gas recovery units in several production regions, notably in Hassi Messaoud and Ohanet.
- Defining the methodology of assessment of flared gas volumes via the satellite instrument in partnership with the Algerian Spatial Agency (ASAL).
- Completion of a pilot project in Rhourd Nouss (RNS) and Bir Rabaa North (BRN) for the implementation of a device of Measure, Reporting and Verification (MRV) of emissions and actions for reducing GHG emissions.
- Organization of workshops to examine the opportunities for technological sequestration of carbon.

7 FINAL REMARKS

The process of recovering flared associated gas poses technological challenges, and the need for significant amounts of capital to install the necessary facilities. Still, eliminating or reducing gas flaring is certainly worth the effort, as the recovered associated gas can be monetized either locally or injected into pipelines linked to the Southern European market.

In macroeconomic terms, the current Algerian government is imposing strict restrictions on the general budget, as a result of the post-COVID crisis. The government has had to make tough economic decisions to determine the amount of funds allocated to state institutions and ministries, of which Sonatrach is the major one. In this challenging economic scenario, the government cannot provide the level of capital required to construct projects to prevent gas flaring, of which there are potentially dozens if not hundreds.

To address these issues, the Algerian oil and gas policymakers urgently need to reconsider the current contractual terms. These will require comprehensive reforms and incentives, aimed at encouraging IOCs, as second-party investors in conjunction with Sonatrach in current producing fields, to overcome this dilemma. The writer believes that this can be achieved by implementing a series of steps in a well-structured master plan.

46. *Ibid.*

CHAPTER 10

Angola

Ricardo Nery & Nuno Monteiro Dente

1 INTRODUCTION

Angola has proven natural gas reserves of 1.6 trillion cubic feet and highly probable reserves of 10.5 trillion cubic feet (297 billion cubic metres).[1] However, despite the fact that, according to the law, the use of natural gas is mandatory and the flaring of gas is expressly forbidden,[2] until recently,[3] most of the natural gas produced in Angola (around 85%) was flared,[4] the remainder being reinjected to aid in the recovery of crude oil, and only a small part processed to produce liquefied gas.[5] This significant

1. The data are provided by ALBINA FARIA ASSIS PEREIRA AFRICANO in her master's thesis, which was published by the Getúlio Vargas Foundation in January 2007 (ASSIS, Albina, *Gestão Sustentável do Petróleo Angolano, Estudo Comparativo Angola/Noruega*, Fundação Getúlio Vargas, 2007, p. 86).
2. Article 73°, No. 1, of Law No. 10/04 of 12 November, also known as the Petroleum Activities Law (hereinafter, Petroleum Law), states that the use of natural gas produced in any oil field is mandatory and flaring is expressly prohibited, except for a short period and when necessary for testing or operational reasons'.
3. According to the World Bank, historically, most of the natural gas extracted has been re-injected in oil fields to enhance oil recovery or flared. In 2011, re-injection and flaring still accounted for 91% of all the natural gas produced in the country, https://flaringventingregulations.worldbank.org/angola#section2, last access 23 October 2024.
4. ASSIS, *supra* n. 1, p. 86.
5. Reinjection of natural gas is a technique used to increase oil production. In reservoirs where both hydrocarbons – natural gas and oil – are present, it is common to produce natural gas and then reinject it to maintain well pressure, which affects the movement of fluids in the reservoir and allows more oil to be produced. Reinjection is currently one of the most important tools for adding value to oil and gas exploration and production projects, especially in the pre-salt layer. In fact, according to some studies, reinjection can increase the recoverable volume of oil in the field by 25%-30% compared to managing the field with water injection alone. However, some fields are only viable with reinjection, https://www.alemdasuperficie.org/setor/gas-natural/reinjecao-de-gas-natural-como-funciona-e-quais-beneficios, last access 23 October 2024.

percentage of associated gas flaring,[6] in addition to the significant environmental impact of CO_2 and greenhouse gas emissions, was/is a huge waste of a valuable energy resource.

In order to bring an end to this situation, the Angolan government approved the Angola liquefied natural gas (LNG) Project in 2007.[7] The project's objective was to exploit, transport, treat and process a range of natural gases and other hydrocarbons, including associated natural gas and non-associated natural gas, LNG, dry gas, condensates and liquids extracted from natural gas.[8] The initial objective was to exploit the associated natural gas, condensates and natural gas liquids present within the oil concessions.[9] From its outset, the Angola LNG Project has been predicated on the reduction, or even the complete cessation, of flaring and the utilisation of associated gas. Indeed, the preamble to Decree-Law (DL) 10/07 is notably assertive in its proclamation that the utilisation of Angola's natural gas potential, along with the elimination of associated flaring, are principles of Angolan oil legislation that the government is committed to implementing in the near future. The Angola LNG Project marked the beginning of the Angolan government's efforts to reduce gas flaring, establish zero-flaring wells,[10] and commercialise gas from offshore oil blocks.[11] This gas was transported to facilities in the onshore area of Soyo, which were designed to have a capacity of 750 million cubic feet per day of LNG.[12]

6. In accordance with the provisions of Art. 2, No. 1.20, of Decree-Law No. 10/07, of 3 October, which approves the implementation of the Angola LNG Project and defines its legal regime (hereinafter, DL 10/07), associated gas means 'gas in solution with crude oil, including what is commonly known as gascap gas, covering and in contact with crude oil, in particular gas produced from condensate reservoirs, which exists only in the gaseous state under reservoir conditions and from which liquid hydrocarbons can be recovered in surface installations'.
7. The Angola LNG Project was initiated through the implementation of DL 10/07, with the commencement of the respective studies occurring in 2001. This was formalised through the publication of Council of Ministers Resolution No. 17/01, of 12 October, which, in light of the significance of the project for the Republic of Angola, namely 'by taking advantage of a natural resource that is either burnt or not properly exploited and by the economic, social and environmental benefits that are inherent to its implementation', approved the fundamental premise of the Angola LNG Project.
8. Article 2(1.4), of DL 10/07 defines the Angola LNG Project as follows: 'the activities and facilities and all extensions and additions thereto, with a view to receiving and processing gas in Angola, producing LNG and NGL in Angola and commercialising the same, which include i) receiving gas from offshore blocks in Angola ii) evaluating, developing and producing Non-Associated Gas from offshore blocks in Angola, iii) processing, storing and transporting gas in Angola, including the supply of domestic gas and butane, and development and production of Non-Associated Gas from offshore blocks in Angola, iii) the processing, storage and transport of gas in Angola, including the supply of domestic gas and butane, iv) the export, transport and processing of LNG and NGL, v) the sale of LNG and NGL, vi) the construction, operation and maintenance of facilities, vii) the operation and maintenance of the Associated Gas Pipeline Network'.
9. Article 9(1) of Decree-Law 11/07 of 5 October, granted Sociedade Nacional de Combustíveis de Angola – Empresa Pública (SONANGOL – EP), the mining rights to evaluate, develop and produce natural gas, condensates and liquids extracted from natural gas (hereinafter, DL 11/07).
10. The initial zero-burn wells were the Nemba and Lomba wells, followed by the Kuito well (ASSIS, *supra* n. 1, p. 86).
11. From blocks 1, 2, 3, 4, 15, 16, 17 and 18 (ASSIS, *supra* n. 1, p. 85).
12. The first LNG cargo was exported in 2013, exports remained low until 2017 but increased nearly tenfold by 2020.

In 2015, Angola endorsed the World Bank's Zero Routine Flaring by 2030 initiative.[13] This initiative, which brings together governments, oil companies and development institutions, acknowledges that gas flaring is unsustainable from both a resource management and an environmental perspective. It aims to foster cooperation in order to eliminate routine flaring by 2030. Governments that endorse the initiative provide the legal, regulatory, investment and operational environmental conditions that are conducive to upstream investments and to the development of viable markets for the utilisation of gas and the infrastructure necessary to deliver the gas to these markets. It will be incumbent upon governments to stipulate in their new prospect offers that field development plans for new oil fields incorporate sustainable utilisation or conservation of the field's associated gas without routine flaring. Moreover, it is incumbent upon governments to ensure that routine flaring at existing oil fields is brought to a swift and definitive end, with a view to achieving this objective by 2030 at the latest.[14]

Nevertheless, the aforementioned commitments did not promptly result in the enactment of the requisite legal and regulatory instruments to achieve the aforementioned goals, which, as will be demonstrated subsequently, are currently being drafted. As a consequence, and as will be demonstrated in section 4 of this chapter, the Angolan regulatory framework is currently incomplete. The Angolan Executive, through the National Oil and Gas Agency,[15] is currently engaged in the process of drafting the requisite legal and regulatory instruments with a view to pursuing the objectives of the Zero Routine Flaring Initiative. Moreover, in mid-2021, Angola submitted an updated Nationally Determined Contribution (NDC) to the United Nations Framework Convention on Climate Change and committed to an unconditional reduction in greenhouse gas emissions from the business-as-usual scenario of up to 14% by 2025.[16]

Notwithstanding the aforementioned actions and initiatives, the results obtained thus far remain distant from the objectives initially set forth by the Angolan Executive. Indeed, as evidenced by the World Bank figures for December 2023,[17] the volume of gas flared in Angola increased from 3.2 billion cubic meters (bcm) in 2012 to 4.5 bcm in 2016 before falling to 1.7 bcm in 2022 (*see* Figure 10.1 below). The flaring intensity was 21% lower in 2022 than in 2012. And still, there are 53 individual flare sites in the most recent flare count conducted in 2022. The volume of gas flared in Angola increased from 3.2 billion cubic meters (bcm) in 2012 to 4.5 bcm in 2016 before falling to 1.7 bcm in 2022 (Figure 10.1). Oil production increased slightly in 2015, but has been declining steadily since then. The flaring intensity was 21% lower in 2022 than in 2012. There were 53 individual flare sites in the most recent flare count conducted in 2022.[18]

13. www.worldbank.org/zeroroutineflaring, last access 23 October 2024.
14. www.worldbank.org/zeroroutineflaring, last access 23 October 2024.
15. Hereinafter ANPG.
16. https://flaringventingregulations.worldbank.org/angola#section2, last access 23 October 2024.
17. https://flaringventingregulations.worldbank.org/angola#section2, last access 23 October 2024.
18. https://flaringventingregulations.worldbank.org/angola#section2, last access 23 October 2024.

Figure 10.1 Gas Flaring Volume and Intensity in Angola, 2012-22[19]

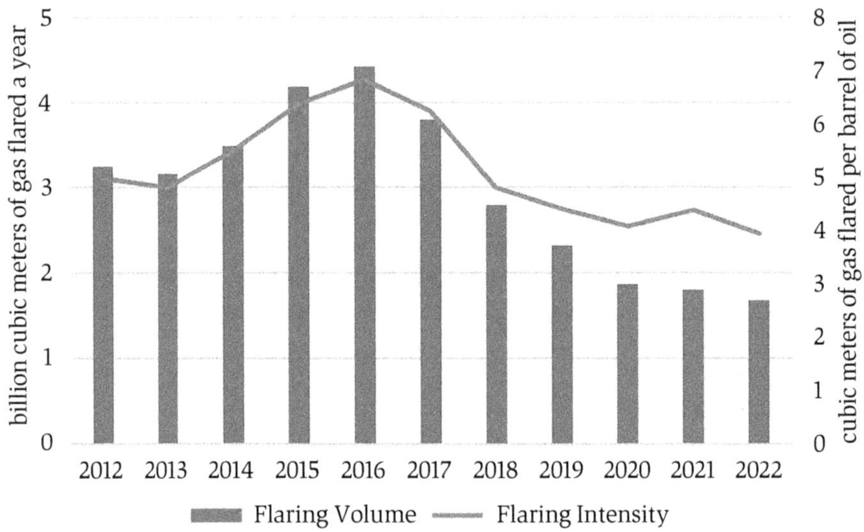

The following section 2 will examine the legal stipulations pertaining to the authorisation of gas flaring. Despite the fact that this violation is characterised as an offence, it is noteworthy that no sanctions or fines are imposed in such instances.[20] This section will also examine the mandatory legal content of the General Development and Production Plan, the Annual Production Plans and the Deposit Utilisation and Recovery Reports, as well as the requirements for measuring gas. The third section (section 3) will address the regulatory framework currently in force in Angola, providing an overview of the legislation that is in effect, with a particular emphasis on the Angola LNG Project. Section 4 addresses the regulatory projects currently underway, which will provide Angola with a comprehensive legal framework aligned with its international obligations, notably the Zero Routine Flaring Initiative. The chapter concludes with a section (section 5) devoted to the drawing of conclusions.

19. https://flaringventingregulations.worldbank.org/angola#section2, last access 23 October 2024.
20. According to Art. 88(1)(f) of the Petroleum Law, failure to comply with the provisions of Arts 69 to 73 of the same Law, i.e., failure to comply with the natural gas obligations provided for in Art. 73 of the Petroleum Law, constitutes, *inter alia,* an offence under the Petroleum Law. According to the same Art. 88 of the Petroleum Law, the fines corresponding to the offences provided for in this Article shall be established by decree. This provision in a separate law, specifically with regard to the violation of the natural gas obligations set out in Art. 73 of the Petroleum Law, has not yet been made, so it remains an offence without sanction.

2 CONTEXT ABOUT NATURAL GAS FLARING IN ANGOLA

2.1 Gas Flaring Is Permitted as an Exceptional Measure, Contingent Upon the Issuance of Special Administrative Authorisation

Angolan legislation currently in force establishes the general principle of prohibiting the flaring of associated gas. This principle is closely linked with, and a consequence of, the principle of the obligation to utilise natural gas. This obligation falls to the Angolan Executive, for the benefit of Angola and its citizens.

Article 73(1) of the Petroleum Law states that the utilisation of natural gas produced in any oil field is mandatory and that flaring is expressly prohibited, except for a limited period of time and when necessary for testing or operational reasons. In such instances, authorisation must be obtained. Furthermore, the legislation stipulates that oil field development plans must be designed in a manner that ensures the utilisation, conservation or commercial exploitation of the associated gas.[21] Therefore, in Angola, the legislation in force stipulates, as a general principle, that the associated natural gas must be utilised in the production of oil, either through its reinjection into the well to stimulate production and conserve it for future use, or through commercial exploitation.[22] The flaring of associated natural gas is prohibited, as a rule, and is only possible in the cases provided for by law and following express authorisation to do so.

Accordingly, the authorisation of gas flaring is contingent upon the fulfilment of the following criteria, as stipulated in the relevant legislation:

(a) in the event of a limited duration, when imperative for the purpose of testing or other operational considerations (Article 73(1) of the Petroleum Law);
(b) in the case of marginal or minor deposits, when indispensable for the viability of their exploitation (Article 73(3) of the Petroleum Law).

The application for authorisation to flare gas is addressed to the Minister of Petroleum and must be accompanied by a duly substantiated technical-economic study and an environmental impact assessment study. These studies must demonstrate that the use or conservation of natural gas is unfeasible. In the event that gas flaring is authorised, the Minister of Petroleum is empowered to determine the applicable duty,

21. Article 73°, No. 2 of the Petroleum Law.
22. In accordance with the provisions of clause 30 of the Model Production Sharing Contract currently in force, the contractor group is entitled to utilise the associated natural gas produced in the course of petroleum operations free of charge (No. 3). Any surplus gas that the contractor group is unable or unwilling to utilise or sell must be made available free of charge to the National Concessionaire at the delivery point determined by the latter (No. 4). The financial burden of constructing the gas infrastructure shall be borne by the Contractor Group. This cost can be fully recovered through Cost Recovery Crude Oil and is deductible for the purposes of calculating the Internal Rate of Return. Furthermore, this cost shall not have a negative impact on the development and Petroleum Operations of Crude Oil, https://anpg.co.ao/wp-content/uploads/2023/07/30.Modelo_Contrato_Partilha_de_Producao.pdf, last access 23 October 2024.

taking into account the quantity and quality of the gas in question, as well as its location.[23]

As already mentioned in the Introduction (section 1), it is important to note that while Article 88(1)(f) of the Petroleum Law states that failure to comply with the provisions of Article 73 of the same Petroleum Law - which includes unauthorised flaring - constitutes an offence punishable by a fine, there is no provision in the law for a fine to be imposed for this offence. Article 88(2) of the Petroleum Law stipulates that the penalties for the infringements it enumerates must be established by decree-law. However, Decree 1/09 of 27 January, which approved the Petroleum Operations Regulation (hereinafter, Decree 1/09), and which provides for infractions and fines in Articles 50 and 51, is devoid of any mention of the applicable fine for the infraction of unauthorised gas flaring. In accordance with the extant legal framework, the unauthorised flaring of gas, or flaring in contravention of the terms of authorisation, is therefore or appears to be, an offence devoid of a prescribed fine or penalty.

2.2 General Development and Production Plan, Annual Production Plans and Deposit Utilisation and Recovery Reports

Article 73(2) of the Petroleum Law, states that the development plans for petroleum deposits should always be formulated in such a way as to allow for the use, preservation, or commercial exploitation of associated gas. In accordance with Article 22(1) of Decree 1/09, the General Development and Production Plan for a concession must comprise, *inter alia*, the following elements:

(i) a development work programme with a description of the drilling, production and injection facilities and equipment, including the number and type of wells to be drilled (Article 22(1)(e) of Decree 1/09);
(ii) an environmental impact study highlighting technical solutions to prevent, minimise and combat pollution (Article 22(1)(j) of Decree 1/09);
(iii) a plan for using the associated natural gas (Article 22(1)(l) of Decree 1/09).

Conversely, in accordance with Article 23 of Decree 1/09, Annual Production Plans must be submitted on an annual basis. These plans must include, in addition to forecasts for oil and natural gas production, the following:

(a) a forecast for flaring and loss of natural gas (Article 23(1)(a) of Decree 1/09);
(b) a forecast for the injection of special fluids into deposits for the purpose of enhanced recovery (Article 23(1)(b) of Decree 1/09).

23. According to Art. 73(6) of the Petroleum Law, 'whenever gas flaring is authorised, the Minister may determine the application of the corresponding fee depending on the quantity and quality of the gas flared and its location'. However, despite this legal provision, the criteria for applying the flaring tax can't be found in the regulations. It is not known whether this tax has ever been applied and under what conditions.

In accordance with Article 24 of Decree 1/09, the National Concessionaire is obliged to submit a report containing the forecast production of crude oil and natural gas by 30 December of each year. This report must include, among other elements, the accumulated injection of natural gas (Article 24(2)(e) of Decree 1/09).

2.3 Measuring of Gas[24]

Metering and recording practices must adhere to established methodologies and utilise instruments that have been certified in accordance with the prevailing legal and technical standards. In accordance with Article 34 of Decree 1/09, operators are obliged to propose to the Minister of Oil the measurement system, equipment, and procedures for measuring oil and gas production and sales. Article 39 of the aforementioned Decree 1/09 enumerates the components of the gas measurement system, while Article 40 of the same decree delineates the requirements for measurement facilities.

In accordance with Article 44 of Decree 1/09, a report on the systems employed for the measurement, testing, and calibration of the equipment must be submitted to the Ministry of Oil on a quarterly basis. The reports must include data pertaining to daily production and the associated shipments. In accordance with the stipulations set forth in Production Sharing Agreements, contractors are obliged to document the monthly quantities of crude oil, natural gas, and water produced from each designated development area. The aforementioned data must be transmitted to the concessionaire within 30 days of the conclusion of the month in question.

3 NATURAL GAS FLARING LEGAL FRAMEWORK

3.1 The Constitution

As pointed out by CARLOS FEIJÓ and N'GUNU TINY,[25] any analysis of the legal regime governing the exploitation of natural gas in Angola must take into account the constitutional framework that underpins it. Indeed, the Constitution of the Republic of Angola (hereinafter Constitution) clearly states that all natural resources located on Angolan land or sea (in the soil and subsoil, internal waters, territorial sea and continental shelf) and in the corresponding exclusive economic zone are the property of the State. This means that natural resources, including oil and gas deposits, are part of the assets of the Angolan State, part of the public domain.

Gas Natural is a natural resource, property of the State and subject to the public domain. Gas flaring of associated natural gas is, therefore, also a constitutional issue, as this practice conflicts with the use of natural gas. In this sense, the establishment of

24. https://flaringventingregulations.worldbank.org/angola#section2, last access 23 October 2024.
25. FEIJÓ, Carlos and TINY, N'Gunu, *A Regulação do Gás Natural em Angola, Estudos e Pareceres*, Almedina, 2009, p. 14.

his regime must be in accordance with the Constitution, namely through the procedures provided for in the Constitution – an Act of the National Assembly and/or an authorised Presidential Decree.

3.2 The Petroleum Law

The Petroleum Law, approved by the National Assembly in accordance with the constitutional mandate, establishes part of the legal regime governing access to and the exercise of petroleum activities in the national territory and its exclusive economic zone.

As pointed out by CARLOS FEIJÓ and N'GUNU TINY, although the Petroleum Law refers in all its articles to oil and not to natural gas, it applies in the same way to petroleum activities involving natural gas. In fact, according to the definition of petroleum in Article 2.15 of the Petroleum Law, petroleum for the purposes of the Law is 'crude oil, natural gas and all other hydrocarbon substances that may be found and extracted or otherwise obtained and collected from the area of a petroleum concession'. Thus, the Petroleum Law applies in the same way to natural gas, i.e., to petroleum activities whose object is natural gas. The Petroleum Law regulates upstream petroleum activities, while other petroleum activities are expressly excluded, namely the storage, transport, distribution and commercialisation of oil and natural gas.[26] The basic principles governing the organisation and performance of petroleum activities are therefore applicable to the exploration, exploitation, development and production of natural gas, namely the principle of concessionaire exclusivity,[27] the performance of petroleum activities exclusively based on a prospecting licence or a petroleum concession,[28] and the principle of mandatory affiliation in the form set out by law,[29] among others.

It is the Petroleum Law, as already mentioned, which, in its Article 73, establishes the principle that the use of associated natural gas is mandatory, as well as the principle that the flaring of associated natural gas is prohibited, except in the cases provided for by law and always with the prior authorisation of the Ministry. Related to the obligation to exploit associated gas and the principle of prohibiting gas flaring is the regime for the exploitation and recovery of deposits, according to which the exploitation rights granted under the Petroleum Law correspond to the obligations to explore for and produce oil and natural gas in a rational manner, in accordance with the most appropriate technical and scientific rules used in international petroleum practice and in accordance with the national interest,[30] as well as the environmental protection regime, which stipulates that, in carrying out their activities, the National Concessionaire and its associates must take the necessary precautions to protect the environment in order to guarantee its preservation, particularly with regard to health, water, soil and

26. Article 2(2) of the Petroleum Law.
27. Article 4 of the Petroleum Law.
28. Article 6 of the Petroleum Law.
29. Article 13 of the Petroleum Law.
30. Article 21° of the Petroleum Law.

subsoil, air, the preservation of biodiversity, flora and fauna, ecosystems, landscape, atmosphere and cultural, archaeological and aesthetic values.[31]

3.3 DL 10/07, Which Created the Angola LNG Project

DL 10/07 approved the implementation of the Angola LNG Project and defined its legal regime.[32] As is evident from the preamble to DL 10/07, one of the objectives of the publication and implementation of the Angola LNG Project is, in addition to the utilisation of natural gas (both associated and non-associated), the elimination of the flaring of associated natural gas. This decree-law and the Angola LNG Project aim to create the conditions for the realisation of these objectives. In fact, in Angola, the flaring of associated natural gas has been addressed through the Angola LNG project, which is why the same scheme is included here.

Furthermore, the preamble to DL 10/07 revealed that the feasibility studies conducted at the inception of the Angola LNG Project necessitate the establishment of a supportive framework encompassing tax, exchange, and customs incentives. This is to ensure that the project's proponents are able to secure a reasonable return on their investment and compensation for the inherent risks while safeguarding the legitimate interests of the state. Consequently of the aforementioned circumstances, the Angolan government was impelled to devise and establish its own legal and contractual framework for the exploration and production of natural gas, which came to be known as the Angola LNG Project. The Angola LNG Project was thus established and constituted through the enactment of the following legislative instruments and contractual agreements:[33]

(1) National Assembly Resolution 17/07 of 25 April, which authorised the government to legislate on tax matters, as well as on other legal aspects not regulated or developed by oil legislation.
(2) DL 10/07, which:
    (i) approved the Angola LNG Project;
    (ii) defined its legal regime and the conditions of the 1st phase of the project;
    (iii) defined its own tax, customs and exchange rules; and
    (iv) approved the Investment Agreement signed between the Angolan Government, Sonangol E.P., Angola LNG Limited, Cabinda Golf Oil

31. Article 24° of the Petroleum Law.
32. DL 10/07, currently in force, has been amended on two occasions. The first amendment was made by Presidential Legislative Decree 4/12 of 10 May, while the second was made by Presidential Legislative Decree 6/22 of 23 July (hereinafter DLP 6/22). The preamble to DLP 6/22 posits that the rationale for this legislation is the necessity to facilitate the development of new natural gas projects, necessitating adjustments to the existing regulatory structure to provide additional incentives for prospecting, research, evaluation, development, production, and sale of natural gas.
33. FEIJÓ and TINY, *supra* n. 25, pp. 17, 18, 19.

Company, Sonangol Gás Natural Limitada, BP Exploration Angola and Total LNG Angola.

(3) The Investment Agreement signed between the Angolan Government, Sonangol E.P., Angola LNG Limited, Cabinda Golf Oil Company, Sonangol Gás Natural Limitada, BP Exploration Angola and Total LNG Angola.

(4) DL 11/07, which granted Sonangol, E.P., as concessionaire, the mining rights for the evaluation, development and production of natural gas in the concession areas.

(5) The service provision agreement with risk, signed between Sonangol and Angola LNG Limited, for the evaluation, development and production of non-associated gas.

In regard to the utilisation of associated gas – thus addressing gas flaring – DL 10/07 stipulates, namely, the following:

(a) the Angola LNG Project is founded upon the principle of unity, with the primary support derived from the supply of associated gas produced from oil concessions, complemented by non-associated gas;[34]

(b) operating expenses incurred in relation to the Gas Pipeline Network, namely any costs incurred in coordinating, designing, constructing and insuring said network, as well as any maintenance or repair work that may be carried out, and also any payments made in relation to the use of the Associated Gas Pipeline Network under the terms of the Gas Transport Contract, are considered necessary for the purpose of obtaining income or gains subject to taxation and maintaining the productive source, and, in this sense, costs and losses deductible for tax purposes and without limitation;[35]

(c) in accordance with the stipulations set forth in the Investment Contract, the remuneration for the utilisation of the Associated Gas Pipeline Network is deemed a fully deductible expense for tax purposes;[36]

(d) the capital expenditure incurred by Angola LNG Limited with respect to the maritime facilities and any capital expenditure incurred by Angola LNG Limited with respect to the transportation of associated gas to the aforementioned facilities is fully reinstated at a constant rate of 25%, effective from the year in which the expenditure occurs or the year in which the date of commercial production occurs, whichever is later;[37]

(e) the income generated by Sonangol in relation to the remuneration for the utilisation of the associated gas pipeline network provided by Angola LNG Limited in accordance with the terms of the Investment Agreement is exempt from any and all taxes, fees, obligations, duties, contributions or charges, regardless of their designation, nature or description. Angola LNG Limited is

34. Article 6(1) of DL 10/07.
35. Article 12(2)(a) of DL 10/07.
36. Article 12(2)(i) of DL 10/07.
37. Article 13(b) of DL 10/07.

not obliged to make any withholding taxes on the aforementioned payments to Sonangol.[38]

3.4 Presidential Legislative Decree 7/18 of 18 May

Presidential Legislative Decree No. 7/18, of 18 May (DLP 7/18), establishes the fiscal legal regime applicable to the prospecting, research, evaluation, development, production and sale of natural gas in Angola.

As explicitly stated in Article 2, this legislation pertains to oil investment companies that have entered into a contractual agreement with the National Concessionaire for the exploration, appraisal, development and production of oil, and that produce associated natural gas and surplus natural gas within the context of this agreement.

In accordance with the stipulations set forth in this legislation, these oil investment companies are entitled to:

(a) engage in the prospecting, research, evaluation, development and sale of natural gas on both the national and international markets;[39]
(b) use freely and free of charge the natural gas produced in the oil operations themselves and for their realisation, i.e., to use the associated gas freely to stimulate production (re-injection);[40]
(c) freely sell surplus gas, i.e., associated gas produced in petroleum operations that exceeds the need for the concession's operations.[41]

In the event that the oil investment company has no intention of utilising or selling the surplus gas, it is obliged to make that gas available to the National Concessionaire free of charge at the delivery point that the National Concessionaire determines.[42]

The DLP 7/18 is to be understood as a derogation from certain provisions of Law 13/04 of 24 December, which sets out the tax regime for petroleum activities (Law 13/04). Consequently, the regime established by Law 13/04 remains applicable to the oil investment companies referred to in DLP 7/18, subject to the adaptations and derogations provided for in that regime by DLP 7/18.[43] In accordance with Article 8 of DLP 7/18, oil investment companies that engage in activities falling within the scope of the aforementioned DLP 7/18 are exempt from the oil transaction tax set forth in Law 13/04. The tax rate applicable to oil production for these companies is 5%, while the tax rate on oil income is 15%.[44] In addition, with respect to associated gas and surplus

38. Article 26° of DL 10/07.
39. Article 4(1) of DLP 7/18.
40. Article 4(2) of DLP 7/18.
41. Article 4(3) of DLP 7/18.
42. Article 4(3) of DLP 7/18.
43. Article 7 of DLP 7/18.
44. Article 9 of DLP 7/18.

gas, the costs incurred in the development and production of associated gas, including the costs of making available and delivering surplus associated gas to the point determined by the National Concessionaire, including the construction of the respective pipeline, are recoverable and deductible for the purposes of the tax due on the income from crude oil obtained in the concessions in which this associated gas is extracted.[45]

3.5 Decree 1/09 ('Petroleum Operations Regulation')

As previously stated, Decree 1/09 defines and establishes the conditions and modalities to be observed in petroleum operations.[46] The decree stipulates that the General Development and Production Plan must include, among other elements, a plan for the utilisation of associated gas, which is to be authorised by the Minister of Petroleum.[47] Furthermore, the aforementioned decree stipulates that annual plans must be submitted, which should include forecasts for the flaring and loss of natural gas, as well as the injection of special fluids into the fields[48,49]

4 CURRENT ISSUES AND RECOMMENDATIONS

As can be observed from the aforementioned analysis, the extant legal regime governing gas flaring and the utilisation of associated natural gas exhibits a number of deficiencies at the current regulatory stage. These shortcomings have already been identified and acknowledged by the Angolan Executive, as evidenced by Presidential Decree No. 282/20 of 27 October (Approves Angola's Hydrocarbon Exploration Strategy 2020-2025) (hereinafter, DP 282/20) and Presidential Decree No. 125/24, of 14

45. Article 10(1) of DLP 7/18.
46. Article 1 of Decree 1/09.
47. Article 22(1)(l) of Decree 1/09.
48. Article 23(1)(a) of Decree 1/09.
49. Other relevant legislation may include:
    - (a) Law No. 13/04, of 24 December, or Law on the Taxation of Petroleum Activities, as amended by Law No. 6/19, of 18 April.
    - (b) Law No. 2/12, of 13 January ('Angolan Foreign Exchange Law on Oil and Gas for the Oil Industry').
    - (c) Presidential Decree No. 91/18, of 10 April (establishes the framework for the abandonment and decommissioning of wells).
    - (d) Presidential Legislative Decree 6/18, of 18 May, rectified by rectification 13/18, of 31 July, which establishes the framework applicable to the development of marginal fields.
    - (e) Law No. 26/12, of 22 August ('Oil and Gas Transport and Storage Law').
    - (f) Presidential Decree No. 52/19, of 18 February (Approves the Petroleum Concession Allocation Strategy for the period 2019-2025).
    - (g) Presidential Decree No. 282/20, of 27 October (Approves Angola's Hydrocarbon Exploration Strategy 2020-2025).
    - (h) Presidential Decree No. 125/24, of 14 July (Approves the Activity Plan and Budget of the National Oil and Gas and Biofuels Agency).

July (Approves the Activity Plan and Budget of the National Oil and Gas and Biofuels Agency) (ANPG) (hereinafter DP 125/24).

Also, as already mentioned, in 2015, Angola endorsed the World Bank's Zero Routine Flaring by 2030 initiative. And in mid-2021, it submitted an updated NDC to the United Nations Framework Convention on Climate Change and committed to an unconditional reduction in greenhouse gas emissions from the business-as-usual scenario of up to 14% by 2025.

In light of the aforementioned regulatory shortcomings and international commitments, the Angolan Executive published DP 125/24, which approves a regulatory agenda comprising initiatives to monitor and implement actions pertaining to the entirety of the upstream oil and gas and biofuels sector value chain.

It is anticipated that 14 regulatory initiatives will be developed in various sectors of the ANPG, including:

(a) Flaring and Gas Loss Technical Regulations.
(b) Technical Regulations for Natural Gas Processing Units.

Conversely, the ANPG is directed in DP 125/24 to present an Expansion Plan for the gas pipeline network, including access to infrastructure, in light of the Executive's determination that the existing infrastructure is inadequate to meet future demands associated with ongoing gas projects. Furthermore, DP 125/24 stipulates the formulation and implementation of decarbonisation strategies in existing operations and new oil projects, with the objective of reducing gas emissions on an annual basis.

In light of the aforementioned considerations, DP 125/24 thus provides for the following actions to be taken and implemented:

(1) in collaboration with operators, the implementation of measures aimed at reducing gas flaring, improving the efficiency of compression systems in older concessions and maximising LNG production;
(2) the promotion of the utilisation of new gas collection equipment in new installations, as well as the adoption of hybrid energy in oil installations;
(3) the formulation of a Decarbonisation Strategy for the oil and gas sector;
(4) the promotion of the development of carbon capture and storage projects;
(5) the design of studies for the implementation of renewable energy projects.

The actions set forth in DP 12/24 remain merely objectives at this time. The implementation of these measures will require a certain amount of time. Nevertheless, upon implementation, they could furnish Angola with a comprehensive legal and regulatory framework. Nevertheless, the precise content of these measures remains to be seen. It is recommended that these regulations be adopted as expeditiously as possible, with the objective of providing Angola with comprehensive regulations governing the utilisation of associated natural gas, with the ultimate goal of achieving zero flaring by 2030.

5 CONCLUSION

The utilisation of mineral resources, with specific reference to natural gas and associated gas, is a legal obligation, foreseen in the Petroleum Law, that requires the Executive to implement the requisite measures. In light of these considerations, the practice of gas flaring, which represents a waste of a valuable mineral resource and causes environmental damage, constitutes a violation of the law.

In Angola, the flaring of natural gas is therefore prohibited, except in specific cases expressly provided for by law. As has been demonstrated, the Angola LNG Project was also initiated with the objective of utilising associated natural gas, with the aim of promoting the production of LNG with surplus gas. It is evident that the extant legislation and regulations do not encompass all activities pertaining to gas flaring. This leaves certain aspects unregulated.

Conversely, despite the illegality of gas flaring, as evidenced by the World Bank data referenced above, the volume of gas flared in Angola increased from 3.2 billion cubic meters (bcm) in 2012 to 4.5 bcm in 2016 before falling to 1.7 bcm in 2022. The flaring intensity was 21 % lower in 2022 than in 2012.[50] As a result, the letter of the law is far removed from reality and has been overtaken by it. Aware of this reality, the Angolan Executive has initiated a process of regulatory reform, with the objective of implementing new regulatory actions and publishing regulatory instruments that will provide Angola with a comprehensive legal and regulatory framework. As the relevant projects have yet to be made available for public consultation, it is only possible to await further developments. The extent and depth of the actions provided for in DP 125/24 can only be described as a positive indication of forthcoming developments.

50. https://flaringventingregulations.worldbank.org/angola#section2, last access 23 October 2024.

CHAPTER 11
Australia

Michael Uche Ukponu[*]

1 INTRODUCTION

Australia is a significant player in the global gas supply industry and is endowed with large reserves of natural (conventional) gas and unconventional gases such as shale, coal seam, and tight gases.[1] Australia, alongside the United States of America and Qatar, is currently among the top three leading exporters of liquefied natural gas (LNG) globally;[2] and has the world's top twenty largest gas reserves of at least 800 trillion cubic feet as of 2020.[3] Australia's energy sector is fundamental to its economic prosperity as it heavily supports electricity supply, industry, transportation, employment, and government export revenue to fund infrastructure, welfare, and other government programmes.[4]

* Special thanks to Dr Agatha Ojimelukwe, Yusuf Sulayman, and Onyeka Nwaigbo for their helpful comments. Any errors or omissions are mine.

1. 'Gas' (*Geosciences Australia*) https://www.ga.gov.au/digital-publication/aecr2022/gas accessed 8 July 2024.
2. 'New Leader In World's Top Three LNG Exporters' (*Global Energy*, 15 September 2023) https://globalenergyprize.org/en/2023/09/15/new-leader-in-worlds-top-three-lng-exporters/ accessed 8 July 2024; R Rapier, 'How The U.S. Became The World's Top LNG Exporter' (*Forbes*, 5 January 2024) https://www.forbes.com/sites/rrapier/2024/01/05/how-the-us-became-the-worlds-top-lng-exporter/?sh = 78a6498f786d accessed 8 July 2024; R Liao, 'US Becomes Top LNG Exporter After Overtaking Australia and Qatar' (*Bloomberg Law*, 3 January 2024) https://news.bloomberglaw.com/international-trade/us-becomes-top-lng-exporter-after-overtaking-australia-qatar accessed 8 July 2024.
3. T Swann, 'Weapons of Gas Destruction: Lifting The Lid On Greenhouse Gas Emissions from Australian Fossil Gas Projects and Resources' (*The Australia Institute Research Report*, September 2020) 16 and 26, https://australiainstitute.org.au/wp-content/uploads/2020/12/Weapons-of-Gas-Destruction-WEB.pdf accessed 8 January 2024.
4. 'Australian Energy Facts' (*Geosciences Australia*) https://www.ga.gov.au/education/minerals-energy/australian-energy-facts accessed 11 July 2024; R Cheema, '20 Countries With The Largest

Australia's energy sector is largely driven by natural gas and other fossil fuels.[5] The Australian Government, in its tracking and reporting of greenhouse gas (GHG) emissions from several sources or sectors, classifies GHG emissions from gas flaring and venting as part of 'fugitive emissions'.[6] As of December 2023, fugitive emissions, including gas flaring and venting, stood at 9.5% or 4.1 Mt CO_2-e above 2005 levels,[7] a decrease from 14.1% or 6.1 Mt CO_2-e above 2005 levels as of December 2022.[8] The Australian Government attributes these marginal improvements to a 3.5% decrease in oil and gas production, a 0.3% reduction in gas flaring and venting, and a 0.9% decrease in coal fugitive emissions throughout 2023.[9] On a global level, Australia ranks as the sixth highest carbon emitter globally from gas flaring alone, accounting for 13 Mt CO_2 as of 2022.[10] Australia had ranked the same global position for gas flaring-linked carbon emissions in 2020 and 2021 respectively, albeit with a marginally steady reduction recorded in Mt CO_2 for these two preceding years.[11] However, the Australian Government's burgeoning facilitation of greenfield gas projects[12] may erode this marginal gain in the global carbon emissions reduction race if emissions abatement measures for both greenfield and brownfield[13] gas projects are not mandated and substantially enforced.

The Renewable Energy Target (RET), Australia's long-standing renewable energy transition plan, was initiated in 2001 as the Mandatory RET to develop a greener grid for Australia by 2020, largely through hydro, solar and wind energies.[14] The implementation of the RET is also responsible for at least 50% of Australia's GHG abatement.[15] Despite this laudable feat, the RET is being statutorily wound down by 2030[16]

Natural Gas Reserves in 2023' (*Yahoo Finance*, 16 November 2023) https://finance.yahoo.com/news/20-countries-largest-natural-gas-170518933.html accessed 8 July 2024.

5. Australian Gas Industry Trust (AGIT), 'The Australian Natural Gas Industry: Monitoring, Reporting, and Reducing Methane Emissions' (2021) AGIT Report, 9 https://agit.org.au/wp-content/uploads/2021/11/AGIT-Methane-Emissions-Report-2021.pdf accessed 8 January 2024.
6. *See* generally 'National Green House Gas Inventory: Quarterly Updates March 2009 – December 2023' (*Department of Climate Change, Energy, the Environment, and Water (DCCEEW)*) https://www.dcceew.gov.au/climate-change/publications/national-greenhouse-gas-inventory-quarterly-updates accessed 8 July 2024.
7. Mt CO_2-e means million tonnes of carbon or equivalent. *See* 'Quarterly Update of Australia's National Greenhouse Gas Inventory: December 2023' (*DCCEEW*, December 2023) 11 https://www.dcceew.gov.au/sites/default/files/documents/nggi-quarterly-update-dec-2023.pdf accessed 8 July 2024.
8. 'Quarterly Update of Australia's National Greenhouse Gas Inventory: December 2022' (*DCCEEW*, December 2022) 10 https://www.dcceew.gov.au/sites/default/files/documents/nggi-quarterly-update-dec-2022.pdf accessed 8 July 2024.
9. 'Quarterly Update of Australia's National Greenhouse Gas Inventory: December 2023' (*DCCEEW*) 18 https://www.dcceew.gov.au/sites/default/files/documents/nggi-quarterly-update-dec-2023.pdf accessed 8 July 2024.
10. Mt CO_2 means million tonnes of carbon. *See* 'Gas Flaring (Mt CO_2)' (*Global Carbon Atlas*) https://globalcarbonatlas.org/emissions/carbon-emissions/ accessed 8 July 2024.
11. 15 Mt CO_2 (2020) and 13 Mt CO_2 (2021): 'Gas Flaring (Mt CO2)', *supra* n. 10.
12. Swann, *supra* n. 3. A greenfield gas project means a newly developed gas facilities on an undeveloped gas field.
13. A brownfield gas project is an existing gas field that is being re-developed or expanded.
14. 'Renewable Energy Target' (*Clean Energy Regulator*) http://www.cleanenergyregulator.gov.au/RET accessed 8 July 2024; 'Renewable Energy Target Scheme' (*Australian Government*

as the Australian Government (under the erstwhile Morrison-led Liberal-National Coalition administration) decided to focus on a 'gas-fired recovery' from the adverse socio-economic impacts of the 2020 global pandemic.[17] There have been calls for not only the extension of the RET beyond 2030[18] but also the expansion of the RET to include clean energy technologies deployed alongside fossil fuel energies as a stop-gap measure in the emissions reduction drive.[19]

However, the current Albanese-led Labour Government spearheaded the enactment of the Climate Change Act (Cth) which statutorily increased Australia's Paris Agreement-inspired emissions reduction target from 26%-28% below 2005 levels to 43% below 2005 levels.[20] As a fulfilment of its election manifesto, the current government is promoting an energy transition plan to achieve 82% renewable energy penetration by 2030 by, *inter alia,* deploying carbon capture and storage (CCS) technology for existing coal and gas-powered plants.[21] Ironically, Australia seems to be simultaneously upscaling investment opportunities in new natural gas and other unconventional gas fields without express mandatory provisions for CCS/abatement technologies in these projects.[22] It appears that the main objective of Australia's current policy drive to upscale greenfield natural gas developments is to meet growing local energy demand and export revenue expectations. Nevertheless, the development and utilization of greenfield natural gas in addition to brownfield ones continue to raise concerns about the socio-economic and socio-environmental impacts of (un)regulated flared gas during natural gas processing on Australians.

Gas flaring is the non-emergency burning of associated or non-associated natural gas during oil and gas production, leading to the by-production and emission of GHGs

---

Department of Climate Change, Energy, the Environment and Water) https://www.dcceew.gov.au/energy/renewable/target-scheme accessed 8 July 2024.

15. T Nelson, J Gilmore and T Nolan, 'RET Is Still The Best: Why It's Time to Renew Australia's Renewable Energy Policy' (*Renew Economy*, 19 October 2023) https://reneweconomy.com.au/ret-is-still-the-best-why-its-time-to-renew-australias-renewable-energy-policy/ accessed 8 July 2024.
16. Renewable Energy (Electricity) Amendment Act 2015 (Cth), Schedule 1(2); Australia HR Deb 18 September 2018, 9325 https://parlinfo.aph.gov.au/parlInfo/download/chamber/hansardr/85002e7c-56d5-4875-be11-147ed4bea861/toc_pdf/House%20of%20Representatives_2018_09_18_6568_Official.pdf;fileType=application%2Fpdf, accessed 8 July 2024.
17. Swann, *supra* n. 3, iv and 1.
18. CV Basil and MU Ukponu, 'Carbon Capture and Storage (CCS) Technology Development in Australia: Economics, Policy and Regulation' (2022) 20(4) OGEL 1, 20.
19. *Ibid.*, 18-22.
20. Climate Change Act 2022 (Cth), section 10.
21. Department of Industry, Science and Resources, 'Future Gas Strategy' (*Policy Document*, 2024) 6, 22-24 and 55 https://www.industry.gov.au/sites/default/files/2024-05/future-gas-strategy.pdf accessed 8 July 2024.
22. S Long, 'How Labor Out-Loved The Coalition in Its Embrace of Big Oil and Gas' (*The Australia Institute*, 14 November 2023) https://australiainstitute.org.au/post/how-labor-out-loved-the-coalition-in-its-embrace-of-big-oil-and-gas/ accessed 8 July 2024; R Campbell, M Ogge and P Verstegan, 'New Fossil Fuel Projects in Australia 2023: Potential Emissions from New Major Coal and Gas Projects' (*The Australia Institute Report*, March 2023) 26 https://australiainstitute.org.au/wp-content/uploads/2023/03/P1359-New-fossil-fuel-projects-on-major-projects-list-and-emissions-WEB.pdf accessed 8 July 2024; K Kouchakji, 'Gas in Australia: The Elephant in the Room' (*Energy Monitor*, 14 December 2022) https://www.energymonitor.ai/policy/gas-in-australia-the-elephant-in-the-room/ accessed 8 July 2024.

(e.g., carbon, methane, etc.) into the atmosphere.[23] There is another similar emissions activity known as gas venting through which natural gases are emitted into the atmosphere without burning them.[24] GHGs are also released into the atmosphere through fugitive leaks from wellheads, mines, pipelines, or storage facilities.[25] Of known GHGs, methane is the dirtiest, most toxic, and highest emitted gas after carbon; a significant volume of which is emitted from natural gas facilities through flaring and fugitive leaks.[26] Australian federal and state/territories governments have respectively legislated on the development, transportation, utilization, and commercialization of natural gas in order to mitigate these impacts while shoring up government revenue and meeting local and foreign energy demands. This is based on its policy position to leverage natural gas as a 'transition fuel' and cleaner alternative to coal pending the full and durable deployment of renewable energy; a policy position which is disapproved by environmental scientists, think tanks, and peak bodies for undermining Australia's climate change mitigation commitments.[27]

2 NATURAL GAS FLARING IN AUSTRALIA: AN INTERPLAY OF ECONOMIC AND ENVIRONMENTAL CONSIDERATIONS

As of 2021, methane emissions from the oil and gas industry accounted for 1.74% of Australia's annual GHG emissions.[28] With the continuous operation of existing fossil fuel-powered plants and the upscaled development of new natural gas reserves, the risk of higher volumes of emissions in Australia's natural gas industry is rife, whether by fugitive methane leakages from LNG pipelines and transportation facilities and gas flaring or venting during processing.

Proponents of natural gas argue that it is a more reliable and less environmentally noxious alternative energy source to other fossil fuels.[29] It is claimed that coal and diesel-fired power plants respectively emit at least 25% and almost 50% more carbon than natural gas.[30] Nevertheless, the International Energy Agency (IEA) emphasizes that this claim should not detract from the point that natural gas is also a fossil fuel and remains a source of GHG emissions in the future if greenfield gas projects continue to be developed without efficient abatement measures.[31] This claim by natural gas proponents did not take into account the emissions that come from gas flaring or

23. 'Gas Flaring' (*International Energy Agency*) https://www.iea.org/energy-system/fossil-fuels/gas-flaring accessed 8 July 2024.
24. *Ibid.*
25. Swann, *supra* n. 3, iv.
26. *Ibid.*, iv-v.
27. *Ibid.*, 44-49.
28. AGIT, *supra* n. 5, 6.
29. ENEA Consulting, '2030 Emission Reduction Opportunities for Gas Networks' (*Final Report*, 2022) 11 https://www.energynetworks.com.au/miscellaneous/2030-emission-reduction-opportunities-for-gas-networks-by-enea-consulting-2022/.
30. *Ibid.*, 4.
31. International Energy Agency (IEA), 'The Role of Gas in Today's Energy Transitions' (*Report*, 2019) 2 and 71 https://iea.blob.core.windows.net/assets/cc35f20f-7a94-44dc-a750-41c117517e93/TheRoleofGas.pdf accessed 8 July 2024. *See also* Swann, *supra* n. 3, 44-46 and 50.

venting, extraction, transportation, and fugitive leakages, and the fact that an inefficient gas plant can emit as much carbon as an efficient coal plant, especially on a whole-of-life basis.[32]

On the international front, Australia is mandated to report GHG emissions in line with its obligations as an Annex 1 Party under the United Nations Framework Convention on Climate Change.[33] In addition, major international oil and gas companies individually publish their emissions reduction programmes in Australia. These international corporate petroleum resource players also co-founded an initiative known as the Oil and Gas Climate Initiative whose main objective is to lead an industry action towards mitigating climate change in Australia by addressing gas flaring intensity.[34] They pledged AUD 1 billion investment in technologies and innovative firms for the purpose of significantly cutting GHG emissions and commercializing gas that would have been otherwise flared.[35] However, while outcomes of this private sector-conceived initiative are yet to be felt, it is expected that these investments in emissions mitigation technologies will continue to be made towards improving energy operations efficiency by reducing gas flaring through plant equipment upgrades and operational safety changes.

Consequent to the critical intensity of LNG plants' activities, the petroleum industry union – Australian Petroleum Production and Exploration Association (APPEA) – has been monitoring the activities of major LNG operations towards reducing GHG emissions from gas flaring and other means. These LNG operations include the Ichthys LNG Project (Darwin, Northern Territory (NT)), the Shell Australia QGC's LNG Facility (Curtis Island, Queensland), and the Prelude Floating LNG Project (Browse Basin, Commonwealth Exclusive Economic Zone).[36] Most of the industry action to reduce gas flaring involves the deployment of technological advancements and innovative methods such as capturing waste heat from gas turbine exhausts to provide process heat; boil-off gas compressors to recover boil-off gas during routine ship loading; commitment to zero non-safe routine flaring by installing flare gas recovery systems which recover otherwise unused flare gas and channel it to fuel gas systems; the use of a chemical compound known as activated-methyldiethanolamine (aMDEA) for the removal of reservoir carbon; and air or water cooling.[37]

Where flaring cannot be entirely avoided, whether for testing or safety concerns, LNG plant operators should endeavour to ensure that appropriate design and control mechanisms are deployed to upscale energy efficiency and preclude adverse economic

32. A Morton and G Readfearn, 'How The Australian Gas Industry's Audacious Net Zero Claims Stack Up: Explainer' (*The Guardian*, Australia, 22 May 2023) https://www.theguardian.com/australia-news/2023/may/22/how-the-australian-gas-industrys-audacious-net-zero-claims-stack-up-explainer accessed 8 July 2024.
33. 'Australia' (*United Nations Climate Change*) https://unfccc.int/process/parties-non-party-stakeholders/parties-convention-and-observer-states.
34. AGIT, *supra* n. 5, 44; Australia Petroleum Production and Exploration Association (APPEA), 'Industry Action on Emissions Reduction' (*Report*, 2020) 6 https://www.appea.com.au/wp-content/uploads/2020/06/Industry-Action-on-Emissions-Reduction.pdf accessed 8 July 2024.
35. AGIT, *supra* n. 5, 45.
36. APPEA, *supra* n. 34, 8-9.
37. *Ibid.*

and environmental impacts.[38] Woodside Energy installed Advanced Process Control (APC) systems[39] which enable its LNG facilities to operate closer to their design limits, the result of which may be higher gas throughput and/or reduced energy use. An APC installed at Woodside's Pluto LNG Facility (Western Australia (WA)) reportedly reduced gas flaring by 10,000 tonnes of GHGs annually.[40]

There is another gas project imbued with CCS capabilities known as the Gorgon Carbon Dioxide Reinjection Project (Barrow Island, WA). This is the largest pioneer GHG emissions mitigation project in Australia and globally.[41] However, there are criticisms about the unreliability of the Gorgon CCS technology for failing to reach its five-year target of an average of 80% carbon capture after Chevron's investment of AUD 54 billion.[42] It could only achieve 30% of its emissions reduction while emitting a staggering 10 million tonnes of carbon.[43] Critics have also decried the additional 55% capital costs of CCS operations, increasing fossil fuel consumption by 40% in an era where the Australian Government is interested in the deployment of technology to lower electricity prices.[44] The energy consumers, being the last stakeholder group in the energy supply chain, will ultimately bear the brunt of these additional costs. Nevertheless, the Gorgon experience is a valuable lesson for improving CCS in other important gas projects.

Santos' Moomba Carbon Capture Project (Cooper Basin, South Australia) proposes to capture 1.7 million tonnes of GHGs, as well as compress, dehydrate, transport, and reinject GHGs into targeted geological formations that have contained oil and gas for centuries.[45] Other CCS arrangements are being made by Santos in the Cooper Basin to power oil well pumps with solar energy costing over AUD 16 million, as well as its facilities at Port Bonython, South Australia.[46] Santos is investing in an innovative energy storage battery project at its Darwin LNG Battery Project (NT) which it hopes would cut emissions by 20%.[47]

On global comparative terms, data released in 2022 implies that flared gas has marginally dropped to 0.7 billion cubic meters in Australia compared to other major

38. Additionally, leak detection and repair (LDAR) programs and continuous monitoring and/or regular testing, inspection and maintenance of wells and process piping and equipment are executed: *Ibid.*, 10.
39. An APC system leverages computer software and mathematical algorithms to simultaneously enhance petroleum production and reduce energy consumption. *See* M John, 'Overview of Advanced Process Control' (*LinkedIn*, 8 October 2023) https://www.linkedin.com/pulse/overview-advanced-process-control-apc-magesh-john accessed 8 July 2024.
40. APPEA, *supra* n. 34, 12.
41. *Ibid.*, 15.
42. R Prka, 'Chevron Misses Gorgon LNG Carbon Capture and Storage Project Target' (*The Market Online*, 20 July 2021) https://themarketonline.com.au/chevron-misses-gorgon-lng-carbon-capture-and-storage-project-target-2021-07-20/ accessed 8 July 2024.
43. N Kilvert, 'Carbon Capture and Storage: Does It Work And Does It Mean We Can Keep Burning Fossil Fuels?' (*ABC*, 5 November 2021) https://www.abc.net.au/news/science/2021-11-06/carbon-capture-storage-coal-gas-fossil-fuels/100585034 accessed 8 July 2024.
44. W Kuckshinricks and S Vögele, 'Economic Analysis of Carbon Capture in the Energy Sector' in W Kuckshinrichs and J-F Hake (eds), *Carbon Capture, Storage and Use* (Springer, 2015) 153.
45. APPEA, *supra* n. 34, 16.
46. *Ibid.*
47. *Ibid.*, 17.

LNG producers like Qatar which increased to 1.0 billion cubic meters.[48] A combination of factors are responsible for this marginal decline, namely improved operational performance in the form of reduction in flaring intensity (reduced gas flares) as well as reduction in oil and gas production.[49] However, with the winding down of the RET and the upscaling of new gas projects, this marginal reduction will very likely be eroded in the coming years if regulatory abatement measures and technical solutions (such as CCS technology) are not deployed at scale by federal and state/territory governments. The ways to reduce gas flaring-linked emissions are to limit flaring to only emergency situations and deploy CCS technology to capture gas which otherwise would have been flared. It is estimated that if Australia and other LNG producers like Egypt and Malaysia were to radically execute these measures, they could together account for an additional 8 billion cubic meters of LNG to the global market without even tapping from new gas reserves.[50]

3 NATURAL GAS FLARING IN AUSTRALIA: COOPERATIVE FEDERALISM, POLICIES AND REGULATIONS

3.1 Natural Gas Governance and Cooperative Federalism

Australia's gas market is divided into the eastern, western, and northern markets.[51] The eastern market is the largest and most interconnected market covering Queensland (QLD), New South Wales (NSW), Australian Capital Territory (ACT), Victoria (VIC), South Australia (SA), and Tasmania (TAS).[52] The western market, which serves WA, has the largest gas production outcomes which are largely channelled for exportation, but with a mandate that 15% of gas produced in WA is reserved for domestic use.[53] The northern market, Australia's smallest gas market in size and output, covers the NT.[54]

Australia practices a federal system of government where the ownership and governance of resources are shared between the Commonwealth (central unit/federal government) and the states and territories (component units/subnational governments) for the public good. This arrangement entails that the states and territories have jurisdiction over gas and other resources found in onshore locations and offshore

48. Capterio, 'Gas Flaring Shows Modest Improvement: But Not in the Countries That Matter Most' (*Flare Intel*, 13 April 2023) https://flareintel.com/insights/gas-flaring-shows-modest-improvement-but-not-in-the-countries-that-matter-most accessed 8 July 2024.
49. *Ibid.*
50. IEA, 'The Energy Security Case for Tackling Gas Flaring and Methane Leaks' (*Report*, June 2022) 4 and 10 https://iea.blob.core.windows.net/assets/9414ec9a-bbba-4592-b005-4af05c894bdc/Theenergysecuritycasefortacklinggasflaringandmethaneleaks.pdf accessed 8 July 2024.
51. 'Gas Markets' (*AEMC*) https://www.aemc.gov.au/energy-system/gas/gas-markets accessed 8 July 2024.
52. *Ibid.*
53. *Ibid.*
54. *Ibid.*

locations up to three nautical miles, while the Commonwealth has jurisdiction over offshore gas and other resources from three nautical miles into the continental shelf.[55]

Consequently, natural gas flaring is regulated by various federal and state laws and administered by the Commonwealth and states and territories at varying levels and mandates with the tendency for regulatory overlap. Notably, Australia upholds the governance principle of cooperative federalism to preclude regulatory overlap between national and subnational laws and policies as much as possible.[56] As a political solution to economic and legal issues arising from regulatory conflicts and overlaps, the Commonwealth and state(s) and/or territory(ies) which are involved usually execute an intergovernmental agreement. In the case of natural gas governance, the Australian Energy Market Agreement (AEM Agreement) was executed in 2004 to collaboratively increase the penetration of natural gas to boost electric power supply and reduce GHG emissions.[57]

With respect to promoting cooperative governance and managing regulatory conflicts and overlaps in environmental governance, the Council of Australian Governments (predecessor to the National Cabinet) consisting of federal, state, territory, and local governments signed the Inter-Governmental Agreement on the Environment in 1992.[58] This agreement obligates the above parties to, *inter alia,* collaborate in common areas related to certainty in environmental impact assessment procedures for public and private projects,[59] developing and applying national environment protection measures,[60] and combatting greenhouse-enhance climate change.[61] Also, there is the opportunity for executing specific assessment bilateral agreements to collaboratively assess the impact of projects on matters of national environmental significance (MNES), including gas flaring and emissions reduction installations. For example, the Commonwealth and Queensland Governments executed an Assessment Bilateral Agreement in 2009 (with its latest amendment in 2014) for the purpose of achieving government-to-government coordination in environmental impact assessment processes for projects bordering on MNES which overlap their respective jurisdictions.[62] This bilateral agreement generally allows for the application of Queensland state law,

55. Constitutional Powers (Coastal Waters) Act 1979 (Cth), Schedule 1 section 4. This Act derives its basis from the Constitution: Commonwealth of Australia Constitution Act, section 51 (xxxviii). *See also*: Attorney-General's Department, 'Offshore Constitutional Settlement: A Milestone in Constitutional Federalism' (*Policy Paper*, 1980) 6 and 7 https://www.ag.gov.au/international-relations/publications/offshore-constitutional-settlement-milestone-cooperative-federalism accessed 8 July 2024.
56. Attorney-Generals' Department, *supra* n. 55, 17.
57. Australian Energy Market Agreement ('AEM Agreement'), Art. 2(b)(v) https://assets.nationbuilder.com/nice/pages/21/attachments/original/1675801804/AustralianEnergyMarketAgreement_2004.pdf?1675801804 accessed 8 July 2024. Amended in 2013: https://policy.asiapacificenergy.org/node/3068 accessed 8 July 2024.
58. Intergovernmental Agreement on the Environment 1992 https://faolex.fao.org/docs/pdf/aus13006.pdf accessed 8 July 2024.
59. *Ibid.*, Schedule 3.
60. *Ibid.*, Schedule 4.
61. *Ibid.*, Schedule 5.
62. A Bilateral Agreement Between the Commonwealth and the State of Queensland Under section 45 of the Environment Protection and Biodiversity Conservation Act 1999 Relating to Environmental Assessment (Amending Agreement No. 4) 2014 https://www.dcceew.gov.au/sites/

rather than Commonwealth law, to regulate environmental impact assessment of controlled actions (projects bearing on MNES usually falling under the Commonwealth's exclusive subject matter jurisdiction) which overlap Commonwealth and Queensland jurisdictions.[63] Gas-related projects with flare or abatement capabilities, whether offshore or onshore, are examples of controlled actions of which the environmental impact assessment process for such projects may be covered by an assessment bilateral agreement.

3.2 Commonwealth Regulation of Natural Gas Flaring

The National Gas Law (NGL)[64] and the National Gas Rules (NGR)[65] are the primary laws governing Australia's gas markets. The NGL applies in all states and territories except WA where a modified version of the NGL known as the National Gas Access (WA) Act is applicable.[66] As enshrined in the NGL, one of the national gas objectives and principles is to ensure the quality and safety of natural gas supply and reduction of Australia's GHG emissions.[67] In a supportive vein, the NGR governs the gas market in relation to gas pipelines and transportation of gas.[68] The regulation of gas pipelines and transportation is essential due to the risk of fugitive emissions from gas supply and transport infrastructures and associated safety issues.

The Australian Energy Market Commission (AEMC), the Australian Energy Regulator (AER), and the Australian Energy Market Operator Ltd. (AEMO) are the main AEM institutions established for the governance of Australia's gas markets.[69] In the context of natural gas, the AEMC is responsible for rule-making and market development functions in respect of the natural gas wholesale markets, distribution and transmission networks as regulated by the NGL, including undertaking changes to the NGR and initiating gas market reviews and rule changes of a minor administrative nature.[70] The AER is responsible for economic regulation and ensuring compliance with the NGL and NGR as they relate to natural gas industries and pipelines at a national level except in WA.[71] The AEMO is responsible for the day-to-day operation and administration of gas wholesale and retail markets in all jurisdictions except WA.[72]

Another key legislation related to natural gas flaring and venting in the Commonwealth jurisdiction is the Offshore Petroleum and Greenhouse Gas Storage Act

default/files/env/pages/b44206bc-d8e5-450b-a05e-4d7c26d8afa1/files/qld-bliateral-agreement-assessment-2014.pdf accessed 8 July 2024.

63. *Ibid.*, Arts 1, 3, 5, 8, 12, 12.1, 12.2 and 12.4. *See also* Environmental Protection and Biodiversity Conservation 1999 (EPBC) (Cth), section 45 and Part 8 sections 80-105.
64. NGL is contained in the Schedule to the National Gas (South Australia) Act 2008 (SA).
65. NGR 2023 (Version 71). The NGR is made by the AEMC under NGL, sections 74-77.
66. National Gas Access (WA) Act 2009 (WA).
67. NGL, section 23.
68. 'Natural Gas Rules' (*AEMC*) https://www.aemc.gov.au/regulation/energy-rules/national-gas-rules accessed 8 July 2024.
69. AEM Agreement, Art. 5.
70. *Ibid.*, Art. 5.1(a).
71. *Ibid.*, Art. 5.1(b).
72. *Ibid.*, Art. 5.1(c). AEMO was formerly National Electricity Market Management Company Ltd. (NEMMCO).

(OPGGSA).[73] The Act establishes the National Offshore Petroleum Safety and Environmental Management Authority (NOPSEMA) to administer environmental management provisions of the Act[74] – which naturally includes matters relating to gas flaring and venting. The Act regulates the construction and operation of infrastructure facilities relating to petroleum or GHGs.[75] This omnibus (less specific) term, 'infrastructure facilities relating to petroleum or GHGs', can be interpreted to include gas flaring and venting facilities because a 'secondary line' associated with a facility for the recovery, processing, storage, or offloading of petroleum, or the combination of these activities is deemed to be a facility.[76] Petroleum processing involves gas flaring and venting and a secondary line is statutorily defined as a pipe or system of pipes for conveying petroleum that is to be flared or vented.[77] In addition, the Offshore Petroleum and Greenhouse Gas Storage (Resource Management and Administration) Regulations,[78] a subsidiary legislation, require petroleum licence holders to report the amount of flared GHG on a monthly and annual basis.[79]

Other key laws include the Environmental Protection and Biodiversity Act 1999 (Cth) (EPBC) which mandates the conduct of environmental impact assessments for proposed projects that are likely to impact MNES.[80] Petroleum production/processing facilities with secondary pipes for gas flaring and venting are examples of projects that will likely impact the environment and climate because of carbon, methane, and other GHG emissions as an objective of the proposed project. Ironically, even proposed abatement projects like CCS facilities meant to reduce carbon emissions are subject to this law. This is because of likely environmental and public health externalities associated with the increased scale of carbon sequestration and transportation via pipelines, emissions storage procedures and leakages, and what they portend for terrestrial/agricultural land and freshwater eco-toxicity.[81] Furthermore, the National Greenhouse and Energy Reporting Act (NGER Act) mandates the Clean Energy Regulator to report GHG emissions and GHG emissions projects in order to assist public policy formulation with current data, inform the general Australian public, meet international reporting commitments, and preclude potential GHG statistical duplication by state and territory governments.[82] The NGER Act applies throughout the Commonwealth to the exclusion of and with supremacy over any other state or territory law for similar purposes.[83]

The 'Safeguard Mechanism' is the Commonwealth tool for implementing emissions reduction laws and policies in specified GHG-intensive industries, including

73. Offshore Petroleum and Greenhouse Gas Storage Act 2006 (OPGGSA) (Cth).
74. *Ibid.*, Part 6.9.
75. *Ibid.*, section 4(c).
76. *Ibid.*, section 15(2)(b) and (e) and Schedule 3 section 4(1)(b)(i) and 4(c).
77. *Ibid.*, section 7.
78. Offshore Petroleum and Greenhouse Gas Storage (Resource Management and Administration) Regulations 2011 (Cth).
79. *Ibid.*, rr 3.08(1)i and 7.19(2)(b)(iv).
80. EPBC, Part 3 division 1.
81. Basil and Ukponu, *supra* n. 18, 11-12.
82. NGER Act (Cth) section 3(1) and (2).
83. *Ibid.*, sections 4 and 5.

natural gas plants.[84] The Safeguard Mechanism is governed by several regulatory instruments.[85] In order to meet net-zero targets, the Safeguard Mechanism sets statutory limits ('baselines') for GHG emissions from gas facilities which fall annually (starting from 1 July 2023) at 4.9% on a trajectory determined by the Clean Energy Regulator.[86] Here, gas facilities should not emit more than 100 million tonnes of GHGs by 1 July 2029 and zero tonnes of GHGs after 30 June 2050.[87] The Safeguard Mechanism applies to both existing and new gas facilities,[88] with international best practices to be applied to new facilities (and new installations within existing facilities emitting less than 100 million tonnes of GHGs) so that they can deploy the latest abatement technologies.[89] There are government incentives given to businesses which key into the Australian Carbon Credit Units (ACCUs) scheme and whose facilities perform better than the stipulated emission baselines.[90]

Australia's target to achieve net-zero emissions by 2050 is focused on strategic government plans which prioritize leveraging technologies to cut down emissions while creating jobs and growing the economy. In the Long-Term Emissions Reduction Plan, the Australian Government set five core principles for reaching its 2030 and 2050 emissions targets. These principles entail that the Australian Government will (1) encourage deployment of technology and not raise energy costs or taxes for households and businesses with the expectation that the technology will eventually drive down energy costs; and in doing so, (2) prioritize choices over mandates, thereby allowing its emissions strategy to be driven largely by private sector investments in clean energy technology and the government creating an enabling environment.[91] To achieve low energy costs for households and industries, (3) there must be an economy-wide deployment of such technology and a reduction in the cost of deploying such technology.[92] However, the attraction of private sector investment in this regard will be balanced with (4) protecting Australian livelihoods as well as enhancing the competitiveness of local businesses and industries.[93] The implementation of these four core principles will be underpinned by (5) transparency and accountability in accordance with international best practices and standards.[94]

84. DCCEEW, 'Safeguard Mechanism Reforms' (*Media Release*, May 2023) 1-2 https://www.dcceew.gov.au/sites/default/files/documents/safeguard-mechanism-reforms-factsheet-2023.pdf accessed 21 July 2024.
85. Safeguard Mechanism (Crediting) Amendment Act 2023 (Cth); NGER Act (Cth); NGER (Safeguard Mechanism) Rules 2015 (Cth) – read together with NGER (Safeguard Mechanism) Amendment (Production Variables Update) Rules 2023 (Cth); Carbon Credits (Carbon Farming Initiative) Act 2011 (Cth); Carbon Credits (Carbon Farming Initiative) Rules 2015 (Cth).
86. DCCEEW, 'Safeguard Mechanism Reforms', *supra* n. 84, 1-2.
87. NGER Act (Cth) section 3(2)(c)(i)-(ii).
88. DCCEEW, 'Safeguard Mechanism Reforms', *supra* n. 84, 2.
89. *Ibid.*, 3.
90. *Ibid.*, 1.
91. Australian Government, 'Australia's Long-Term Emissions Reduction Plan: A Whole-Of-Economy Plan to Achieve Net Zero Emissions by 2050' (*Policy Document*, 2021) 27 https://www.dcceew.gov.au/sites/default/files/documents/australias-long-term-emissions-reduction-plan.pdf accessed 8 July 2024.
92. *Ibid.*
93. *Ibid.*
94. *Ibid.*

At the COP28 Summit held in Dubai in December 2023, the Australian Government reaffirmed its commitment to reduce carbon emissions by 43 % below 2005 levels by 2030.[95] This 43 % target has received legislative imprimatur vide the Climate Change Act.[96] While the Australian Government is yet to release an updated Nationally Determined Contribution (NDC) for COP28, its statement on a 43 % reduction is in tandem with Australia's 2021 NDC for COP26.[97] However, the Australian Government in a brief release titled 'National Statement – COP28' made a commitment to transit from coal, oil and gas, but admitted that fossil fuel consumption will 'peak in the near term'.[98] Perhaps, this represents the reason behind Australia's facilitation of new gas investments at scale because it deems natural gas as the transition fuel towards net-zero emissions. Nonetheless, it is still refreshing that Australia aims to phase out fossil fuels in line with 1.5 degrees pathways.[99]

3.3 Subnational Regulation of Natural Gas Flaring

Australian states and territories also exercise regulatory competence over gas flaring and venting on natural gas production/processing facilities within their constitutional territorial jurisdiction, which is from onshore to three nautical miles offshore.[100] Queensland's Petroleum and Gas (Protection and Safety) Act prohibits natural gas flaring without express authority; which is only given under the strict conditions that the use of flared gas would not be commercially or technically feasible, or the flaring activity is associated with an approved activity pursuant to a petroleum and gas-related license under the QLD Act.[101] In addition, the QLD Environmental Protection Act requires that project contractors seek approval called an Environmental Authority from the state's environmental regulator before an 'environmentally relevant activity' can commence.[102] Gas flaring and venting are clearly environmentally relevant activities due to their proven adverse environmental impacts.

South Australia's Petroleum and Geothermal Energy Act is not as express as QLD's. The SA Act provides for the regulation of 'associated activities license[s]' for the establishment and operation of 'associated facilit[ies]' and any type of 'associated regulated activity' (e.g., a processing plant or other infrastructure) by a primary licence

95. The Hon Chris Bowen MP (Minister for Climate Change and Energy), 'National Statement: COP28' (*Web Page*, 9 December 2023) https://minister.dcceew.gov.au/bowen/speeches/national-statement-cop28.
96. Climate Change Act 2022 (Cth), section 10.
97. Australian Government, 'Australia's Nationally Determined Contribution' (*Communication*, 2021) 3 https://www4.unfccc.int/sites/ndcstaging/PublishedDocuments/Australia%20First/Australia%20Nationally%20Determined%20Contribution%20Update%20October%202021%20WEB.pdf.
98. Bowen, *supra* n. 95.
99. *Ibid.*
100. Constitutional Powers (Coastal Waters) Act 1979 (Cth), Schedule 1 section 4.
101. Petroleum and Gas (Protection and Safety) Act (Qld), sections 72 and 151. Similar prohibitions and exceptions also apply to gas venting.
102. Environmental Protection Act 1994 (Qld), division 5.

(e.g., exploration, production, pipeline, etc.) holder.[103] The Act also establishes 'special facilities license[s]' for certain purposes including the production/processing of petroleum and other incidental activities.[104] These provisions imply that natural gas flaring and venting are associated regulated activities and associated facilities under associated licences, and perhaps, activities under special facilities licences. Natural gas flaring or venting is not a primary activity but an ancillary activity of primary activities such as petroleum production/processing.

The Victorian OPGGSA[105] largely adopted the less-than-specific provisions of the Commonwealth's OPGGSA (Cth) on gas flaring, with the regulation of infrastructure facilities[106] and secondary lines[107] which impliedly refer to gas flaring and venting. It established 'infrastructure license[s]' as authority for the construction and operation of gas flaring and other infrastructure facilities.[108] However, there is slightly better clarity for regulating gas flaring and venting provided in the Third Schedule to the OPGGSA (Vic) where the Act expressly outlined the matters for regulation under the Act. These include the prevention of the waste of natural resources (petroleum or otherwise) from secondary lines and infrastructure facilities;[109] construction and operation of pipelines, secondary lines, GHG facility lines, and GHG infrastructure lines;[110] construction, erection, maintenance, and operation of installations, structures, equipment, or facilities;[111] and controlling the discharge or preventing the escape of GHGs.[112]

In Western Australia, express natural gas flaring and venting regulation can be found in environmental protection-related legislation than in petroleum governance legislation. The Environmental Protection Act (WA) generally criminalizes the act of discharging any matter, including gaseous chemical substances or waste or fuels, into the environment and prescribes conditions for the discharge of such matter into the environment.[113] It defines waste as including liquid, solid, gaseous, or radioactive matter, whether useful or otherwise, and any other matter so prescribed to be waste.[114] The discharge of waste or other matter must be approved under a works approval or licence.[115] Furthermore, gas flaring and venting are prohibited during a total fire ban (TFB) unless the Minister in charge of fire and emergency services and/or the local government permits under strict conditions, including the duty to prevent the discharge of soot or other hot substances capable of igniting a fire.[116] New South Wales

103. Petroleum and Geothermal Energy Act 2000 (SA), section 56.
104. Petroleum and Geothermal Energy Act 2000 (SA), sections 59A-59B.
105. Offshore Petroleum and Greenhouse Gas Storage Act 2010 (Vic).
106. *Ibid.*, section 17.
107. *Ibid.*, section 6 and Schedule 3 section 6(1)(b)(i), (2) and (4)(c).
108. *Ibid.*, sections 187-202.
109. *Ibid.*, Schedule 4 sections 5 and 15.
110. *Ibid.*, Schedule 4 section 8.
111. *Ibid.*, Schedule 4 section 9.
112. *Ibid.*, Schedule 4 section 10.
113. Environmental Protection Act 1986 (WA), sections 49, 50, 73, and Schedule 2 sections 4, 9, 10, 11, 14, 16, 17, 19 and 20.
114. *Ibid.*, section 3.
115. *Ibid.*, section 53.
116. Bush Fires Act 1954 (WA), section 25 and 25A; Bush Fires Regulations 1954 (WA), rr 24v-24w; Western Australian Government's Department of Fire and Emergency Services, 'Gas Flaring:

also follows this model of using environmental legislation to regulate gas flaring. The Protection of the Environment Operations Act (NSW) requires gas flaring facilities which can cause air pollution to operate in a proper and efficient manner in accordance with statutory and license conditions.[117] Gas flaring is prohibited during TFBs except where it is permitted by the Minister for Fire and Emergencies under the *Rural Fires Act*.[118]

4 CURRENT ISSUES AND CHALLENGES

4.1 Statutory Explicitness and Specificity

It can be deduced from the above analysis that the various Australian state legislations which have been highlighted in this chapter appear to contain more explicit wordings and provisions with relation to regulating natural gas flaring within their respective jurisdictions compared to the relevant Commonwealth laws. In other words, Commonwealth laws on natural gas flaring are omnibus-like or less specific than state laws under review. On one hand, the dearth of explicitness and specificity could create lacunæ which enable the abdication of obligations and liabilities. On the other hand, omnibus provisions, as far as they are not practically ambiguous, have the advantage of covering the field to include all forms of resource extraction facilities and activities beyond natural gas flaring (e.g., GHG sequestration, capture, and utilization). Nonetheless, it is important to note that insufficient specificity or explicitness of Commonwealth laws on natural gas flaring does not necessarily give rise to ambiguity, but it is desirable that the provisions of the law are expressly constructed for the avoidance of doubt and regulatory clarity.

4.2 Investor Choices and Voluntary Actions Towards Decarbonization

The Long-Term Emissions Reduction Plan laudably encourages the deployment of technology with the expectation that it will eventually drive down energy costs. The principle of 'choices over mandates', which allows investors to choose which and how to deploy clean energy and abatement technologies in their fossil fuel projects[119] is a delicate issue. This policy is also linked to the statutorily-backed ACCU scheme to support investments in emissions reduction projects, but investor participation in the scheme is voluntary.[120] It is a delicate issue because, for economic reasons, it prefers to

Prescribed Activity and Conditions' (*Media Release*) https://publications.dfes.wa.gov.au/publications/prescribed-activity-and-conditions-gas-flaring accessed 8 July 2024.

117. Protection of the Environment Operations Act (NSW), sections 124-128.
118. Rural Fires Act 1997 (NSW), sections 86 and 99.
119. Australia's Long-term Emissions Reduction Plan, *supra* n. 91, 3, 11 and 27.
120. 'Eligible Voluntary Action': *See* Carbon Credits (Carbon Farming Initiative) Act 2011 (Cth), sections 5 and 138.

allow investors to choose which and how to deploy technology in reducing emissions, fearing an over-regulated environmental regime may discourage or disincentivize investments.[121] Allowing private investors to 'drive' climate change mitigation strategies by choosing what technology and how it could be deployed could impact meeting prescribed standards and outcomes within timelines. Naturally, private investors are profit-oriented, and to preserve long-term economic projections, there is a potential risk to the government where the road to net-zero emissions is driven by the private sector at 'its own speed'.

To address this issue, while allowing deployment of technology as investors may choose, there are statutorily stipulated baseline outcomes for carbon-intensive industries under the Safeguard Mechanism.[122] Thus, no matter the technology choices that investors make, they must abide by set legal mandates for GHG-intensive facilities such as LNG plants to reduce emissions of stipulated GHG volumes by 2050. Compliance with the Safeguard Mechanism is enforced through civil penalties which are channelled to government-funded abatement projects.[123] This is a fair balancing by the Australian Government of the need to reap socio-economic benefits from gas resources within the context of climate change mitigation. Notwithstanding, the confidence that this balanced strategy will direct Australia towards meeting its emissions reduction targets within set timelines is not very strong, but there is room for further study and better adjustment of the existing policy and legal frameworks to boost confidence in the plausibility of achieving a net-zero economy by set timelines.

4.3 Unauthorized Gas Flaring, Environmental Law, and Criminal Culpability

It is observed that while the environmental laws of a few States establish criminal culpability for infringement of gas flaring regulations,[124] the EPBC, the principal Commonwealth environmental law, appears to exclude criminal liability for breach of gas flaring provisions. The EPBC defines an 'action' as a project, development, undertaking, or activity or series of activities, including those that may have significant impact on MNES.[125] Considering the significant impact on MNES, gas flaring activities and facilities naturally fall under these categorizations. However, after establishing criminal culpability for unpermitted actions, the Act proceeds to exclude certain acts pursuant to the OPGGSA (Cth), such as gas flaring, from categorization as actions

121. A Dechezleprêtre and M Sato, 'The Impacts of Environmental Regulations on Competitiveness' (2017) 11(2) Review of Environmental Economics and Policy 183, 200-201 https://doi.org/10.1093/reep/rex013.
122. For example, NGER (Safeguard Mechanism) Rules 2015 (Cth).
123. DCCEEW, 'Safeguard Mechanism Reforms', *supra* n. 84, 8.
124. *See* Environmental Protection Act 1986 (WA), sections 49, 50, 73, and Schedule 2 sections 4, 9, 10, 11, 14, 16, 17, 19 and 20; Petroleum and Gas (Protection and Safety) Act 2004 (Qld), sections 816 and 837(8)(a)(iii).
125. EPBC, sections 12-25A and 523.

under the Act.[126] It is a probable justification that this exclusion of certain actions under the OPGGSA (Cth) is necessary to encourage competitiveness and maintain investor confidence even in the event of environmental degradation arising from petroleum resource development.[127]

Again, several petroleum projects cut across respective jurisdictions of the Commonwealth and states and territories, requiring the contemporaneous application of Commonwealth and states and territories' laws to a project or different aspects of a project. For example, petroleum extraction may occur in Commonwealth waters, but for commercial and technical reasons, petroleum extracted from Commonwealth waters would have to be transported in pipelines through VIC waters and lands to NSW lands for processing. While this scenario represents the federal governance structure of Australia, it potentially creates problems of bureaucracies, double regulation, and even the abdication of obligations in environmental governance and compliance. A state or territory law may require a separate 'associated activities license' to operate an 'associated facility' for an 'associated regulated activity' such as gas flaring activities which are not ordinarily granted except there is a 'primary license' for primary activities such as petroleum production.[128] It would amount to an unauthorized gas flaring and possible criminal culpability without the prerequisite license.

The implication of these regulatory lacunæ is that while unauthorized gas flaring[129] in some states and territories would be an environmental crime, it will at best only incur civil penalties or even mere warnings at the federal level which may not effectively disincentivize unauthorized gas flare recidivism. The erring company may even regard civil penalties for unauthorized gas flaring as part of investment costs which would be easily recovered from windfall profits that are a usual occurrence in resource development ventures. On criminal culpability and environmental governance in the context of unauthorized gas flaring, there is the need for far-reaching regulatory reform in terms of harmonizing Commonwealth and subnational laws guided by the laudable principle of cooperative federalism.

126. EPBC, section 524(f).

127. MA Cohen, 'Environmental Crime and Punishment: Legal/Economic Theory and Empirical Evidence on Enforcement of Federal Environmental Statutes' (1992) 82(4) The Journal of Criminal Law and Criminology 1054, 1102-1104 https://doi.org/10.2307/1143716; N Gunningham and J Norberry, 'Introduction' in N Gunningham, J Norberry and S McKillop (eds), *Environmental Crime: Proceedings Of A Conference Held 1-3 September 1993, Hobart* (Australian Institute of Criminology, 1995) 49, 53; N Mabey and R McNalley, 'Foreign Direct Investment and the Environment: From Pollution Havens to Sustainable Development' (*Report*, World Wildlife Fund for Nature, August 1999) 3 http://assets.wwf.org.uk/downloads/fdi.pdf accessed 21 July 2024.

128. For example, *see* Petroleum and Geothermal Energy Act 2000 (SA), section 56. However, this regulatory gap may have been addressed through the 'special facilities license' regime: Petroleum and Geothermal Energy Act 2000 (SA), section 59A-59B.

129. This chapter simply defines 'unauthorized gas flaring' as the flaring of gas without authorization/license, or below prescribed standards, or in breach of stipulated procedures and conditions.

4.4 Between Implementing Climate Change Mitigation Policies and Peaking Greenfield Natural Gas Investments

Whereas Australia committed to ambitious 43% emissions reduction targets by 2030, 82% RETs by 2030, and net-zero targets by 2050,[130] it continues to facilitate investments in new gas reserves at scale.[131] The global climate change mitigation goal is behind schedule and in order to reach net-zero targets, Australia must desist from developing greenfield fossil fuel potentials and start winding down brownfield ones.[132] In the alternative, greenfield gas developments must be accompanied by CCS capabilities,[133] and the more CCS capabilities are developed, the faster it would be to achieve net-zero targets.[134] However, the global scale of CCS facilities development for both new and existing gas facilities is slow considering the exigency of the global climate crisis and global net-zero economy by 2050.[135]

The Australian Government's decision to encourage investments in new gas fields potentially undermines national and global efforts in climate change mitigation if it does not mandate CCS development and other abatement measures at scale. Having chosen to develop new gas reserves rather than keep them in the ground, Australia currently faces an energy trilemma – reducing emissions and facilitating clean technology deployment in natural gas development, balancing investors' interests in long-term natural gas investments, and ensuring energy security for Australians. Finding a fine balance among these competing needs is essential to achieving net-zero targets by set deadlines. As there is no singular solution for climate change mitigation,[136] it would also require a simultaneous deployment of 'multiple approaches, policies, and technologies', including renewable energy.[137] Rather than wind down the RET, it would have been desirable for Australia to build on the massive gains of the policy and find a way to link it with natural gas, GHG emissions, and abatement technologies policies for a holistic, synchronized climate change mitigation and energy security strategy.

130. Climate Change Act 2022 (Cth), section 10; 'Powering Australia' (*DCCEEW*) https://www.dcceew.gov.au/energy/strategies-and-frameworks/powering-australia accessed 8 July 2024; Australia's Long-term Emissions Reduction Plan, *supra* n. 91; Bowen, *supra* n. 95.
131. Swann, *supra* n. 3, iv and 14.
132. *Ibid.*, 45.
133. T Satherley, 'Coal, Gas and Decarbonization: Challenges and Policy Choices' (*Parliament of Australia*) https:// https://www.aph.gov.au/About_Parliament/Parliamentary_departments/Parliamentary_Library/Research/Issues_and_Insights_Articles/47th_Parliament/CoalGasDecarbonisation, accessed 8 July 2024.
134. IEA, 'Energy Technology Perspectives 2020: Special Report on Carbon Capture Utilization and Storage: CCUS in Clean Energy Transitions' (*Report*, 2020) 150-167.
135. Satherley, *supra* n. 133.
136. IEA, *supra* n. 31, 24.
137. *Ibid.*

5 CONCLUSION

5.1 Natural Gas Flaring and the Energy Transition: Lessons from Australia

The first lesson from Australia's routine gas flaring and GHG emissions reduction drive is that the utilization of natural gas as a transition fuel appears to be based not only on the 'energy transition' movement but also on the concept of 'energy progression'. Energy transition is the shift from high-carbon fossil energy sources to zero-carbon energy sources for the purpose of mitigating climate change, upscaling renewable energy and energy efficiency, and phasing out carbon-intensive energy sources by 2050.[138] Rather, energy progression is the improvement in the utilization of carbon energies in a manner that balances the need to meet energy demand, address energy poverty, and protect the environment as a short-to-mid-term pathway towards energy transition and net-zero carbon energy by 2050.[139] Energy transition is largely associated with developed economies like Australia, while energy progression is a better alternative for developing countries to meet rising energy demands and reduce energy poverty for their teeming populations.[140] Australia is a developed economy but faces rising energy demands due to certain factors including increasing population and the impact of the 2020 global pandemic,[141] hence generating more revenue from gas resources is necessary to fund infrastructure to cater for this population increase. The upscaling of natural gas energy development and utilization as a transition fuel is a hallmark of energy progression but with an emphatic twist in the Australian context – the deployment of abatement technology such as CCS to satisfy environmental activist concerns about the adverse effects of natural gas flaring and venting while simultaneously advancing the currently impressive penetration of its renewable energy credentials in accordance with its climate change mitigation commitments. This multi-strategic approach to energy transition is worthy of note.

Australia's emissions tracking and reporting every quarter of the year is worthy of commendation. Apart from the fact that this is part of its national and international climate laws and commitments, it is also necessary to track successes and areas for improvement in the global emissions reduction race and a way of showing accountability to Australians about the activities of the government in managing their commonwealth. This is very encouraging as it positively reflects the Australian Government's commitment to transpose international climate commitments into local climate action. Australia's cooperative federalism is structured in a manner that promotes national and subnational ownership of natural resources and this close

138. VR Nalule, 'How to Respond to Energy Transitions in Africa: Introducing the Energy Progression Dialogue' in VR Nalule (ed.), *Energy Transitions and the Future of the African Energy Sector: Law, Policy and Governance* (Palgrave Macmillan, 2021) 1, 17-19.
139. *Ibid.*, 20-23.
140. *Ibid.*, 14.
141. DCCEEW, 'Australian Energy Update 2023' (*Report*, September 2023) 24 https://www.energy.gov.au/sites/default/files/Australian%20Energy%20Update%202023_0.pdf accessed 21 July 2024.

periodic tracking helps to achieve effective macro-economic planning and coordination of resource management, climate, and emissions policies among the federating units and the central government. This is a lesson for other federally structured natural gas-rich countries like Nigeria whose mineral ownership is solely vested in the central government.

The Australian Government is happy to incentivize private sector efforts to reduce their own emissions by setting incremental emissions baselines under the Safeguard Mechanism and rewarding those private sector players who perform better than set baselines with carbon credit units.[142] This carrot-and-stick mechanism would likely avert the adverse effects of a strictly 'stick' approach favouring environmental fundamentalism and potentially scaring away private investment finance from the gas sub-sector. Australia realizes the socio-economic benefits which accrue from increased gas investments, including creating jobs for Australians, increasing government export revenue, and driving down energy prices through competition among private sector players in the gas sub-sector, hence the need to strike a balance between climate change mitigation and socio-economic benefits.

5.2 Recommendations

Natural gas flaring and emissions reduction continue to be topical issues in Australia's energy governance space due to surrounding economic, legal, and sustainability issues as discussed throughout this chapter. The current focus of the Australian Government is centered around the promotion of abatement technology to reduce GHG emissions which has been a recurring decimal in Australia's energy sector. Australia's climate change mitigation plans and energy security measures, especially as they relate to natural gas, are clear. However, in the light of increased investments in greenfield natural gas projects and the voluntary nature of the CCS and ACCU provisions, it is difficult to appreciate how Australia's interim and long-term emissions reduction targets would be met by 2050 if left to be largely driven at the speed of private sector players.

It is encouraged that Australia's natural gas flaring provisions are made express in petroleum and fossil fuel-related laws, rather than implied provisions which could allow for abdication of regulatory and investor obligations, particularly at the federal level. It is also recommended that the laudable principle of cooperative federalism be applied beyond civil environmental law (e.g., assessment bilateral agreements). While QLD took the commendable initiative to criminalize unauthorized flaring and venting, cooperative federalism should be leveraged as the driver for the harmonization of federal and subnational laws to create criminal culpability for unauthorized gas flaring or venting. This is because civil penalties may be insufficient to ensure deterrence and disincentivize gas flare recidivism. Having decided to promote new gas investments and allow investors' choices among available emissions reduction technologies, the Australian Government is encouraged to strictly enforce the Safeguard Mechanism

142. DCCEEW, 'Safeguard Mechanism Reforms', *supra* n. 84, 1.

baselines for critical GHG-intensive industries such as gas plants to meet national emissions reduction targets.

It is understandable that the Australian Government, for energy security and revenue reasons, may prefer not to 'overregulate' the fossil fuel industry with strict environmental laws which could slow investor capital and discourage increased competitiveness. However, recent studies reveal that strict environmental laws in energy and other emissions-intensive sectors marginally impair productivity and prices in the short term, an externality that can be substantially addressed by purposeful government policy.[143] Germany's *Energiewende*[144] experience reminds us of short-term high energy prices occasioned by the deployment of renewable/clean energy technologies; of which the price curve begins to dip in the long run with government subsidy policy partly responsible.[145] Thus, statutory abatement technology mandates in the form of the Safeguard Mechanism are necessary for both greenfield and brownfield gas projects to achieve climate change mitigation targets by set timelines even if energy prices are high in the interim.

143. Dechezleprêtre and Sato, *supra* n. 121.
144. Germany's energy transition plan for a low-carbon, environmentally sustainable, reliable, and affordable energy supply where renewable energy sources will account for 80% of the country's electricity by 2050. *See* Federal Foreign Office, 'The German Energiewende: Transforming Germany's Energy System' (*Policy Document*, 2010) https://www.auswaertiges-amt.de/blob/610620/5d9bfec0ab35695b9db548d10c94e57d/the-german-energiewende-data.pdf accessed 8 July 2024.
145. MU Ukponu and K Oyibo, 'Harnessing Stand-alone Bio-energies in Nigeria: Some Policy and Regulatory Considerations' (2021) 19 (1) OGEL Intelligence 1, 15.

CHAPTER 12
Brazil

Eduardo G. Pereira, Bárbara Leite & Juan Gerolis

1 INTRODUCTION

Over the past decade, Brazil has demonstrated its commitment to increasing its oil and natural gas production, while simultaneously reducing the flaring of natural gas. This progress is not merely the product of regulatory framework improvements on natural gas flaring but also the positive outcome of using technologies and alternatives towards the economic feasibility of using the produced associated gas.

The entire petroleum chain is composed of different activities that are potential sources of fugitive emissions of greenhouse gases (GHGs).[1] In the production stage, the main sources are the natural gas flaring and venting. While in oil refining and natural gas processing, the emission can also result from Hydrogen Generation Units (UGH) and Fluid Catalytic Cracking Units (FCCU). In transport, emissions can occur from leaks in joints, seals and rotating surfaces, as well as pipeline depressurization and cleaning processes (pigging).[2]

With regard to GHG emissions in the production phase, flaring is considered the controlled burning of natural gas, while venting is the direct release of natural gas into the atmosphere without burning or destroying combustible elements that are harmful to the environment. The decision on whether the residual gas should be flared or vented takes into account several different factors, ranging from the technical specifications of the natural gas to environmental and safety aspects.[3]

1. Mainly CO_2, CH_4 and N_2O.
2. Dias AN, "As emissões fugitivas de gases do efeito estufa da indústria de petróleo e gás natural no Brasil: inventário, cenários e propostas de mitigação" [2015] UFRJ 11-12.
3. Machado L, "Metodologias para estimativa de emissões de gases de efeito estufa na produção de óleo e gás" [2013] UFRJ.

In this sense, venting of natural gas can be broadly understood as the controlled release of gases into the atmosphere, which can take place during the exploration and production, refining and transportation activities. Since venting involves natural gas emission instead of natural gas burning (like flare), this process is not visible and, therefore, it can be quite challenging to identify and quantify the whole process.

Meanwhile, flaring consists of burning off excess of associated natural gas extracted alongside crude oil in the exploration and production phase, in onshore or offshore wells and platforms, as well as in oil refineries, chemical plants and natural gas processing plants.[4] It is a practice to avoid the direct release of natural gas in the atmosphere, as the natural gas "in natura" contains methane, which is 80 times more harmful than the CO_2 released with flaring.[5]

Gas flaring can be classified into three primary categories based on its application: routine flaring, non-routine flaring, and safety flaring. Routine flaring is the most usual type, in which the gas withdrawn along with the oil is flared because of: (i) the lack of appropriate facilities for its transport and storage, given that these are structures that require massive investments, which is not always commercially viable; or (ii) the lack of adequate geological and operational conditions, which prevents the practice of reinjecting the natural gas into the reservoir. Therefore, burning off the extra gas before releasing it into the environment is the most appropriate and safe course of action.

Non-routine flaring, however, is the intermittent flaring, of short time duration, which may or may not have been planned. Sometimes, it is necessary to ensure compliance with stabilization and safety parameters. Similarly, safety flaring is a measure adopted in emergency situations at O&G production facilities to prevent the escape or accumulation of flammable gases in the atmosphere, which can cause destructive and long-lasting accidents and fires, thus minimizing the risks to people, facilities and the environment.

Although safety flaring and non-routine flaring are indispensable alternatives in urgent cases, gas flaring, especially routine flaring, must be avoided because of its environmental damage. This is why the World Bank has created the Zero Routine Flaring by 2030 (ZRF) Initiative, which brings together oil companies and governments to develop solutions to reduce routine flaring. The initiative is continuously monitored and progress is reported annually.

According to the most recent World Bank Report,[6] gas flaring at upstream oil and gas facilities increased by 9 billion cubic meters (bcm) last year. It went from accounting for 139 bcm in 2022 to 148 bcm in 2023, an increase of 7%. A 1% increase in oil output coincided with a 5% rise in the average flaring intensity worldwide, or the

4. "What Is Gas Flaring? Definition, Types, Impact, and Alternatives" (*Blackridge Research*, 2022) https://www.blackridgeresearch.com/blog/what-is-gas-flaring-definition-types-impact-alternatives-and-future-outlook accessed January 25, 2024.
5. "What's the Deal with Methane?" [2022] UNEP https://www.blackridgeresearch.com/blog/what-is-gas-flaring-definition-types-impact-alternatives-and-future-outlook accessed June 23, 2024.
6. "Global Gas Flaring Tracker Report" (*The World Bank Group and GFMR*, 2024) https://thedocs.worldbank.org/en/doc/d01b4aebd8a10513c0e341de5e1f652e-0400072024/original/Global-Gas-Flaring-Tracker-Report-June-20-2024.pdf accessed January 25, 2024.

quantity of gas flared for every barrel of oil produced. The total volume of gas flared in 2023 may have had a market value of between USD 9 billion and USD 48 billion at the present price of gas. At least 381 million tons of CO_2 equivalent emissions would not be discharged into the environment annually if gas flaring were eliminated.

The reduction of gas flaring is essential to minimize the environmental impact of energy production and support improvements in energy transition in the near future, while there are not several sources of renewable energy widely available and affordable, in practice. This paper has the objective of providing a direct overview of the Brazilian scenario in natural gas flaring, its regulatory framework, current challenges and bottlenecks, as well as possible regulatory and practical solutions based on the Brazilian perspective and experience.

2 NATURAL GAS FLARING LEGAL FRAMEWORK

2.1 General Overview

The subject of natural gas flaring is broadly mentioned under Law No. 9.478/1997 ("Petroleum Law")[7] when addressing the payment of royalties, as translated below:

> Art. 47. Royalties will be paid monthly, in national currency, from the start date of commercial production in each field, in an amount corresponding to ten percent of oil or natural gas production.
>
> (...)
>
> § 3 The burning of gas in flares, to the detriment of its commercialization, and the loss of product occurring under the responsibility of the concessionaire will be included in the total volume of production to be computed to calculate the royalties due.

Natural gas flaring is not further mentioned in the Petroleum Law, which is limited to appointing the National Agency of Petroleum, Natural Gas and Biofuels ("ANP") as responsible for ensuring that the industry agents comply with the good practices for conservation and rational use of petroleum, natural gas, its byproducts and biofuels and the preservation of the environment.[8] This makes ANP the main entity in charge of regulating the flaring of natural gas in the country.

Pursuant to the Petroleum Law, the purpose of the ANP is to promote the regulation, contracting and inspection of the economic activities of the oil industry, and it is responsible for "enforcing good practices of conservation and rational use of oil, natural gas, its derivatives and biofuels and preservation of the environment."

7. Brazil, *Law No. 9.478, of August 6th, 1997. Establishes the national energy policy, activities related to the oil monopoly, establishes the National Energy Policy Council and the National Agency of Petroleum, and makes other provisions*—Federal Official Gazette, Brasília, DF, August 7, 1997, https://www.planalto.gov.br/CCivil_03/leis/L9478.htm accessed June 21, 2024.
8. The Brazilian Constitution guarantees right to an ecologically balanced environment as a fundamental right and establish that the protection of the environment is one of the principles that govern the Brazilian economic order.

Ordinance No. 265/2020[9] ("Statute of the ANP") divides the attributions related to the flaring of natural gas between various internal departments, as follows: (i) the Superintendence of Exploration ("SEP") is responsible for authorizing the volumes of associated natural gas flaring during the Exploration Phase; (ii) the Superintendence of Development and Production ("SDP") is responsible for approving and authorizing the validation of extraordinary natural gas flaring; and (iii) the Oil and Natural Gas Production Measurement Inspection Center is responsible for inspecting the levels of natural gas flaring in accordance with the authorized limits. The power to authorize extraordinary gas flaring was, at first, held by the ANP's Board of Directors, but was delegated to the SDP by means of Ordinance No. 452/2016[10] and, subsequently, incorporated into the ANP's Internal Regulations, as set out in Ordinance No. 265/2020.

2.2 First Regulations and Measures in Brazil

The first regulation issued by ANP on the subject of gas flaring was ANP Ordinance No. 249/2000[11] ("Ordinance 249/2000"), which was enacted only a few years after the creation of the Agency itself in 1998. This regulation established the guidelines and limits for flaring and wasting exempt from authorization (such as the flared volume being equal to or less than 3 % of the field's monthly production of associated natural gas is exempt from prior authorization), as well as the volumes of flaring and wasting not subject to the payment of government takes. As a general rule, the flaring and losses of oil and natural gas subject to prior authorization are due to operational limitations; scheduled maintenance; construction in progress; contamination; and economics.

In addition to the hypothesis of exemption from authorization for flaring in a volume equal to or less than 3 % of the monthly production of associated natural gas, the following are also exempt from prior authorization, but on a cumulative basis: (i) flaring during well tests, during the exploratory phase, with a flow period, continuous or not, of 72 hours or less per test; (ii) flaring for safety reasons, limited to a volume of

9. Brazil, *ANP Ordinance No. 265 of September 10th, 2020. Establishes the Internal Regulations of the National Agency of Petroleum, Natural Gas and Biofuels—ANP*—Federal Official Gazette, Brasília, DF, September 11, 2020 https://atosoficiais.com.br/anp/portaria-anp-n-265-2020-estabelece-o-regimento-interno-da-agencia-nacional-do-petroleo-gas-natural-e-biocombustiveis-anp#: ~ :text = Estabelece%20o%20Regimento%20Interno%20da,Regimento%20Interno%20e%20pelo%20 art accessed June 19, 2024.
10. Brazil, *ANP Ordinance No. 452, of December 19th, 2016. Delegates competences of the Superintendence of Development and Production of the National Agency of Petroleum, Natural Gas and Biofuels—ANP*—Federal Official Gazette, Brasília, DF, December 20, 2016 https://atosoficiais.com.br/anp/portaria-anp-n-452-2016-estabelece-o-regimento-interno-da-agencia-nacional-do-petroleo-gas-natural-e-biocombustiveis-anp accessed June 21, 2024.
11. Brazil, *ANP Ordinance No. 249, of November 1st, 2000. Approves the Technical Regulation on Oil and Natural Gas Flaring and Losses, which deals with issues related to flaring and natural gas losses*—Federal Official Gazette, Brasília, DF, November 3, 2000, https://atosoficiais.com.br/anp/portaria-tecnica-n-249-2000-aprova-o-regulamento-tecnico-de-queimas-e-perdas-de-petroleo-e-gas-natural-que-dispoe-sobre-as-questoes-relacionadas-com-as-queimas-em-flares-e-as-perdas-de-gas-natural?origin = instituicao accessed June 21, 2024.

15,000 m^3 for pilot equipment flares, 30,000 m^3 for those on land installations and 60,000 m^3 for those on marine installations; (iii) flaring and losses due to low production; (iv) flaring or losses in land tanks or storage ships, and (v) flaring and losses for emergency reasons (such as emergency shutdowns or uncontrolled well).

Additionally, per month, flaring could not exceed 15% in relation to the level of flaring forecasted for that month in the current Annual Production Program, and could not exceed 10% per year. Pursuant to such ordinance, flaring of non-associated gas was not permitted, except for safety or emergency reasons or well tests.

Also in 2000, with the possibility of a crisis in Brazil's energy sector, Petrobras and ANP intensified their control over gas flaring in the Campos Basin, resulting in the creation of the Program for Optimizing the Use of Natural Gas in the Campos Basin ("POAG"). This program consisted of 93 actions aimed at increasing the use of associated natural gas on 24 platforms. The actions included the installation and upgrading of gas compressors, the construction of new gas pipelines and the optimization of natural gas processing plants, corresponding to an investment of USD 200 million and a potential gain in the natural gas use of 4.2 million m^3/day.[12]

Notwithstanding the enactment of Ordinance 249/2000, there was an increase in gas flaring, reaching a record level in 2009, when almost 3.5 billion m^3 were flared, which can be explained by the oil discoveries in the pre-salt of Campos Basin.[13] As a result, in addition to applying Ordinance 249/2000, ANP began to demand greater investments in order to increase the use of the natural gas produced.[14] In addition, ANP also began to limit the volumes of flaring to be carried out during Long Duration Tests, to authorize such tests for a shorter period of time and to prohibit early flaring in pilot production projects located in areas with an offloading infrastructure already in place.[15]

Although not directly related to regulatory improvements towards the reduction of natural gas flaring, it is worth praising the initiative of the Brazilian Institute of Environment and Renewable Natural Resources (IBAMA) on compensatory measures through reforestation in view of the GHGs emissions resulting from Long Duration Tests. The first of these cases was in the environmental licensing of the Tupi Long Term Test, by Petrobras, in the pre-salt of Santos Basin. The factors that led to the need to mitigate emissions were, essentially: (i) the forecast of extraordinary flaring of the natural gas produced in the order of 500,000 m^3 per day; (ii) the production of around 8% of associated CO_2, which would be vented directly into the atmosphere; and (iii) other fugitive emissions, resulting from inefficiency in flare burning and gas leaks from valves, agreed at 2% of the project's total emissions. The Technical Opinion CGPEG/DILIC/IBAMA No. 540/08 requested Petrobras to propose compensatory measures in view of the emission of GHGs resulting from the Tupi Long Term Test. In response, Petrobras proposed the execution of a reforestation program "Projeto de Restauração Florestal no Parque Estadual da Pedra Branca—Setor Piraquara/Rio de

12. Dias, *supra* n. 2, 22-23.
13. Nonato, *infra* n. 35.
14. *Ibid.*
15. *Ibid.*

Janeiro—RJ," that aimed to offset around 10% of the GHGs emissions through the reforestation of 204 hectares.

After the Tupi Long Term Test, other Petrobras' Long Term Tests were carried out afterward in the Santos Basin pre-salt area—Tupi NE and Iracema (Block BM-S-11) and Guará and Carioca NE (Block BM-S-9)—with similar characteristics: extraordinary flaring of the produced natural gas produced amounting to approximately 500,000 m^3 daily and a high percentage of associated CO_2.

These Long-Term Tests were also subject to compensation for GHG emissions, through which Petrobras was required to enter into two Terms of Commitment[16] with ANP, with the objective of reducing the flaring and venting of natural gas in its operations. The first agreement was executed back in 2002 and was in force until 2004, and the second was in force between 2010 and 2014 and aimed to control the burning of associated gas in the 20 main producing fields in the Campos Basin.[17] Another action by the Brazilian Government to try to reduce GHG emissions was the creation, in 2009, of the National Policy on Climate Change ("PNMC"). The PNMC aimed to encourage the development and improvement of mitigation actions in the country, collaborating with the global effort to reduce GHG emissions, as well as creating internal conditions to deal with the impacts of global climate change.[18]

It was also in 2009 when Law No. 12,187 was enacted, establishing the National Plan on Climate Change, and was later further regulated by means of Decree No. 7,390/2010, which, in turn, created the PNMC, as mentioned above. The PNMC formalized Brazil's voluntary commitment presented to the United Nations Framework Convention on Climate Change ("UNFCCC") to reduce GHG emissions between 36.1% and 38.9% of projected emissions by 2020, and the Decree No. 7,390/2010 estimated the baseline of GHG emissions for 2020 at 3.236 $GtCO_2eq$. Thus, the corresponding absolute reduction was established between 1.168 $GtCO_2eq$ and 1.259 $GtCO_2eq$. To meet this voluntary commitment, the Decree also established the elaboration of Sector Plans aimed at the different sectors of the economy e.g., Action Plan for the Prevention and Control of Deforestation in the Legal Amazon—PPCDAm; Ten-Year Energy Expansion Plan—PDE; Plan for the Consolidation of a Low Carbon Emission Economy in Agriculture.

In addition to the above measures, together with the second Term of Commitment, the Adjustment Program to Reduce Gas Flaring in the Campos Basin (PARQ) was launched, setting targets for the use of natural gas by 2014 and an action plan to support compliance. Since then, the authorized volumes of extraordinary natural gas flaring have also been restricted by the ANP, which has led to increasingly better results.[19]

16. The term of commitment is a legal instrument that formalizes the agreement of wills between two or more parties, where one or both commit to fulfilling certain obligations or responsibilities.
17. *Ibid.*
18. Fernandes ODP et al., "Emissões dos Gases de Efeito Estufa Provenientes do Segmento de Exploração e Produção do Setor de Petróleo e Gás," apresentado no 9° Congresso Brasileiro de P&D em Petróleo e Gás, Maceió, 2017.
19. Dias, *supra* n. 2, 23.

2.3 Adaptations to the New Global Concerns

As a result of the growing concern to reduce carbon emissions, as well as to make better use of the country's natural resources, the National Energy Policy Council ("CNPE")[20] defined, as one of the guidelines for the E&P policy, the promotion of the Brazilian natural gas production in the supply of the national market. The resolution also expressly stated that reducing the gas flaring in E&P activities was encompassed under this objective.[21]

Driven by the guideline brought by CNPE,[22] ANP initiated the Public Consultation No. 22/2019,[23] in order to revise Ordinance 249/2020. The revision of the aforementioned ordinance was necessary for a number of reasons, starting with its long time in force (almost 20 years).[24] During this period, there were several technological advances and the valorization of the Pre-salt reservoirs with large amounts of oil and natural gas, which also ratified the need to update the regulation.[25]

The use of natural gas to generate electricity also became important after 2013, when there were successive periods without enough rainfall to maintain the potential of the reservoirs at hydroelectric plants. Finally, the environmental importance of reducing GHGs is increasingly recognized, especially with the guidelines given by Law No. 12.187/2009[26]—PNMC and the Paris Agreement—United Nations Treaty on Climate Change.[27]

All these factors contributed to the process which resulted in the revocation of ANP Ordinance 249/2000 by the newly issued ANP Resolution No. 806/2020 ("RANP

20. The CNPE was created by Law No. 9.478/97, based on the now extinct National Council of Petroleum. CNPE is a joint ministerial entity presided by the Minister of MME and formed by representatives of other Ministries and relevant entities such as the Energy Research Office (EPE). CNPE's has mere suggestive attributions, its meetings result in propositions to be considered by the President. Recently, its importance has been increased, encompassing, such as, the attribution to propose to the President the national policies for the definition of Pre-Salt blocks to be offered in bid rounds.
21. As established under CNPE Resolution No. 17/2018 Art. 1, item III.
22. The revision of Ordinance 249/2000 was already on the 2015/2016 Agenda, but the public consultation only began in 2019.
23. ANP, *Public Consultation No. 22/2019* (ANP) https://www.gov.br/anp/pt-br/assuntos/consultas-e-audiencias-publicas/consulta-audiencia-publica/2019/consulta-e-audiencia-publicas-no-22-2019 accessed June 21, 2024.
24. Back in 2017, ANP's regulations were in force for an average of seven years, according to Nota Técnica SDP.
25. ANP, *Technical Note No. 041/2019/SDP* (ANP) https://www.gov.br/anp/pt-br/assuntos/consultas-e-audiencias-publicas/consulta-audiencia-publica/2019/arquivos/cp-22-2019/cp22-2019_nota-tecnica-041.pdf accessed January 15, 2024, p. 6.
26. Brazil, *Law No. 12.187, of 29 December 2009. Establishes the National Policy on Climate Change—PNMC and makes other provisions*—Federal Official Gazette, Brasília, DF, December 30, 2009 https://www.planalto.gov.br/ccivil_03/_ato2007-2010/2009/lei/l12187.htm?trk=article-ssr-frontend-pulse_little-text-block accessed June 21, 2024.
27. ANP, *Technical Note No. 041/2019/SDP* (ANP), https://www.gov.br/anp/pt-br/assuntos/consultas-e-audiencias-publicas/consulta-audiencia-publica/2019/arquivos/cp-22-2019/cp22-2019_nota-tecnica-041.pdf accessed January 15, 2024, p. 6.

806/2020"),[28] with the purpose of governing the applicable procedures for controlling the flaring and loss of oil and natural gas.

2.4 ANP Resolution No. 806/2020

Ordinance 249/2000 did not expressly address a number of issues that had to be later addressed in alternative ways by the ANP to implement the necessary measures to reduce gas flaring even before the publication of RANP 806/2020. The "new" resolution had the purpose of complementing and updating the previous rules with rules and concepts that have already been applied, including, for example, the definition of "IUGA" and "IUGAmov" (as detailed below) and relocation of flaring.[29]

However, RANP 806/2020 also brought in rules that did not exist in the previous regulation. These include: (i) evaluation of flaring based on the Associated Gas Utilization Index ("IUGA"); (ii) evaluation of flaring per SPU for offshore fields; (iii) different treatment for old and new SPUs; (iv) different treatment for SPUs that handle a significant volume of associated gas in addition to that produced directly from the wells connected to them; and (v) mandatory use of individual wells with a minimum production of 1,500 m^3/day.[30]

Initially, RANP 806/2020 defines "associated gas" as the natural gas produced from deposits where it is dissolved in oil or in contact with oil saturated with gas. This definition is important to understand another concept used to determine the amount of gas that can be flared: the Associated Gas Utilization Index ("IUGA"), which consists of the percentage of the volume of associated gas used in relation to the total volume of associated gas produced.

RANP 806/2020 establishes that the ANP will annually approve the forecasts of flaring and losses of associated natural gas together with the approvals of the Annual Production Programs ("PAP") and will define the volumes that will not be subject to the payment of royalties. It then makes it clear that the volume of flaring or loss of natural gas in each month cannot be more than 15% higher than the IUGA forecast for the same month in the approved PAP.

Such volumes are calculated per production unit in the case of offshore fields and, in the case of onshore fields, the volumes are calculated per field. In addition, no royalties will be due for the flaring of associated gas, provided that the activity is duly authorized by the ANP and there are safety reasons or proven operational needs.

The "non-associated gas," however, is defined as the natural gas produced from a dry gas field or a gas and condensate field. This resolution prohibits the flaring or loss

28. Brazil, *ANP Resolution No. 806, of January 17th, 2020. Regulates the procedures for controlling flaring and loss of oil and natural gas*—Federal Official Gazette, Brasília, DF, January 20, 2020 https://atosoficiais.com.br/anp/resolucao-n-806-2020 accessed June 21, 2024.
29. ANP, *Summary of the Public Hearing No. 22/2019* (ANP) https://www.gov.br/anp/pt-br/assuntos/consultas-e-audiencias-publicas/consulta-audiencia-publica/2019/arquivos/cp-22-2019/sei-anp-0556249-sumula-ap.pdf accessed January 15, 2024, 2.
30. Brazil, *ANP Resolution No. 806, of January 17th, 2020. Regulates the Procedures for Controlling Flaring and Loss of Oil and Natural Gas*—Federal Official Gazette, Brasília, DF, January 20, 2020, https://atosoficiais.com.br/anp/resolucao-n-806-2020, accessed June 21, 2024.

of non-associated gas, as well as the flaring of oil, which may only be authorized exceptionally for safety, emergency, testing or well cleaning reasons. Ordinary flares, which are not subject to prior authorization, may occur in the following cases:

(1) Flaring and associated gas losses corresponding to a volume equal to or less than:
  (a) 3% (IUGA greater than or equal to 97%) of the monthly production of associated natural gas, not cumulative to any other reason for flaring or loss, carried out in an offshore production unit that is already in production or whose production begins within five years of the publication of this Resolution.
  (b) 2% (IUGA greater than or equal to 98%) of the monthly production of natural gas associated with no other reason for flaring or loss, carried out in an offshore production unit whose production begins at least five years after the publication of this Resolution.
  (c) 1.5% (IUGA handled greater than or equal to 98.5%) of the monthly movement of natural gas, not cumulative to any other reason for flaring or loss, carried out in an offshore production unit that circulates gas for oil lifting or receives gas from other units in volumes equal to or greater than 50% of the volume of gas handled.
  (d) 3% (IUGA greater than or equal to 97%) of the monthly production of associated natural gas per onshore field, not cumulative to any other reason for flaring or loss.
(2) Flaring volumes greater than those approved, when the new IUGA or IUGA handled, as the case may be, is equal to or greater than that considered when authorizing such flaring.
(3) The flaring of the volume of oil and the flaring or loss of the volume of natural gas produced in the well test provided for in the Annual Work and Budget Program (PAT), with a total free flow time of up to 72 hours per tested interval.
(4) Flaring and associated losses of natural gas in fields that produce, per month, a total volume equal to or less than that corresponding to an average flow rate of 5,000m^3/day, except for fields with wells with an average flow rate of more than 1,500m^3/day, for which a project must be proposed to make use of it.
(5) Flaring and losses of the volume of associated natural gas produced in onshore fields or offshore production units with a gas/oil ratio equal to or less than 20m^3/m^3, measured under basic conditions.
(6) Flaring for safety reasons, limited to a monthly volume of up to 1,000m^3/day for each flare pilot in onshore production units and up to 2,000m^3/day for each flare pilot in offshore production units, provided that these pilots are operational.

In circumstances other than the cases of evident necessity (explained above), the flaring must be an exception and will require prior approval from ANP, under penalty of a sanction for each month in which the infraction occurred. The administrative sanctions arising from non-compliance with the rules of the O&G sector are mainly consolidated in Law No. 9,847/1999.[31] However, since such law purports to address several subjects (most related to fuel supply) the topic of prohibited natural gas flaring is not expressly addressed in any of its articles. Upon analysis of administrative proceedings before the ANP, the infractions involving flaring have been classified by the Agency under Article 3, IX of the aforementioned law:

> Art. 3. The fine penalty will be applied in the event of infractions and within the following limits:
>
> (...)
>
> IX—build or operate facilities and equipment needed to carry out the activities covered by this Law in disagreement with the applicable legislation: Fine—from BRL 5,000.00 (five thousand reais) to BRL 2,000,000.00 (two million reais).

Law No. 9,847/1999 does not set forth a fixed amount, but rather an amount that can vary from BRL 5,000.00 to BRL 2,000,000.00, observing the following four factors: (i) the severity of the infraction; (ii) the advantage obtained from the infraction by the agent; (iii) the financial condition of the agent; and (iv) prior convictions. Moreover, depending on how many times the agent commits the same infraction, such an agent may also be subject to a total or partial suspension of the unit's operation, pursuant to Law No. 9,847/1999.

3 CHALLENGES

Brazil has successfully increased its oil and gas production in the past 10 years while reducing the amount of natural gas flaring. Between 2012 and 2022, there was a 47% increase in national gas production, while in the same period, the country managed to reduce gas flaring by 45%. This included Brazil[32] in the top ten countries that evidenced the greatest decrease in such a period of time.[33] In 2022, only 2.5% of the

31. Brazil, *Law No. 9.847 of October 26th, 1999. Provides for the inspection of activities related to the national supply of fuels, dealt with in Law No. 9.478, of August 6, 1997, establishes administrative sanctions and makes other provisions*—Federal Official Gazette, Brasília, DF, October 27, 1999 https://www.planalto.gov.br/ccivil_03/leis/l9847.htm accessed June 21, 2024.
32. Rio de Janeiro is the Brazilian state in which the largest amount of gas is flared in Brazil, corresponding to more than 1 billion cubic meters, i.e., approximately 80% of all gas flared in Brazil. The second state with the highest gas flaring in Brazil is Amazonas, with 76.1 million cubic meters being flared in 2022. (ANP., *Anuário Estatístico Brasileiro do Petróleo, Gás Natural e Biocombustíveis 2023*. Available at: (ANP) https://www.gov.br/anp/pt-br/centrais-de-conteudo/publicacoes/anuario-estatistico/arquivos-anuario-estatistico-2023/anuario-2023.pdf accessed January 26, 2024, p. 84).
33. Canadian Energy Centre. *International*, "International Comparisons of Gas Flaring Among Top Oil *Producers*. Producers" (CEC Fact Sheet #98/, October 2023). Available at: https://www.canadianenergycentre.ca/wp-content/uploads/2023/10/CEC-Fact-Sheet-98-V2-Sept-29-2023.pdf accessed January 29, 2024.

country's gas production was flared or lost and 49.6% was reinjected into the wells, resulting in a usage percentage of 47.9%.[34]

The fact that over 50% of the production is not commercialized is mainly due to the associated natural gas being produced in pre-salt fields, which require a complex set of technical and economic challenges to make the production offloading feasible, such as the distance between the coastline and the offshore fields.[35] In spite of such bottlenecks, the Brazilian regulation is proving to be efficient since natural gas flaring remains low and the surplus is usually reinjected.

Brazil is not currently tackling any major challenges to reduce the flaring of natural gas flaring, the reason why only 2.5% of the country's gas production was flared or lost back in 2022.[36] However, the main reason why players still resort to the flaring of natural gas is the lack of infrastructure, especially the underdeveloped and incipient systems to offload the production predominantly located in offshore basins, in spite of a growing demand to supply the national market. The insufficient infrastructure hampers the complete process of making the Brazilian natural gas sector more competitive, which could play a major role in further reducing the flaring percentage.

Given the above scenario, the regulatory measures adopted by the Government with the purpose of fostering private investment in infrastructure and technology have been key to overcoming the infrastructure problems. For instance, Brazil's natural gas legislation experienced a major adjustment in 2021, when Law No. 14,134/2021[37] ("New Gas Law" or just "Gas Law") was enacted. Significant changes were made to speed up the development of the sector and protect free competition, such as the adoption of the authorization regime for the transportation of natural gas. Also in 2021, Decree No. 10,712/2021[38] ("Gas Decree") was issued, to regulate the Gas Law, providing guidelines for ANP regulations.[39]

34. ANP, *Anuário Estatístico Brasileiro do Petróleo, Gás Natural e Biocombustíveis 2023* (ANP), https://www.gov.br/anp/pt-br/centrais-de-conteudo/publicacoes/anuario-estatistico/arquivos-anuario-estatistico-2023/anuario-2023.pdf accessed June 23, 2024, p. 84.
35. For example, 230 km in the case of the Lula field and 290 km in the case of the Sapinhoá field, pursuant to COSTA JUNIOR, to Nonato CJ, "As políticas regulatórias daPolíticas Regulatórias Da ANP voltadas paraVoltadas Para a redução das perdasRedução Das Perdas e queimasQueimas de gás natural.Gás Natural" [2018] FGV. 2018. Available at: https://repositorio.fgv.br/items/73fe22bd-4d3e-4550-8687-0196a3a89d2e accessed January 25, 2024, p. 7.
36. ANP, *Anuário Estatístico Brasileiro do Petróleo, Gás Natural e Biocombustíveis 2023* (ANP) https://www.gov.br/anp/pt-br/centrais-de-conteudo/publicacoes/anuario-estatistico/arquivos-anuario-estatistico-2023/anuario-2023.pdf accessed June 23, 2024.
37. Brazil, *Law No. 14.134 of April 8th, 2021. Provides for the inspection of activities related to the national supply of fuels, dealt with in Law No. 9.478, of August 6, 1997, establishes administrative sanctions and makes other provisions*—Federal Official Gazette, Brasília, DF, April 9, 2021, https://www.planalto.gov.br/ccivil_03/_ato2019-2022/2021/lei/l14134.htm accessed June 21, 2024.
38. Brazil, *Decree No. 10.712 of June 2nd, 2021. Regulates Law No. 14,134, of April 8, 2021, which provides for activities related to the transportation of natural gas, referred to in Article 177 of the Constitution, and on the activities of flow, treatment, processing, underground storage, packaging, liquefaction, regasification and marketing of natural gas*—Federal Official Gazette, Brasília, DF, June 4, 2021 https://www.planalto.gov.br/ccivil_03/_ato2019-2022/2021/decreto/D10712.htm accessed June 21, 2024.
39. Benevenuto T de F, "Reflexões Iniciais Sobre a Nova Lei Do Gás e Decreto N° 10.172/2021" [2021] RDPE 76.

In a complementary manner, the Federal Court of Auditors ("TCU") established a series of measures to be taken after the legislative changes mentioned in order to enable greater growth in the national natural gas industry.[40] TCU even classified RANP 806/2020 as a measure to foster competition in the natural gas sector.

These changes were stimulated by the signing and ratification of the Paris Agreement by almost 150 countries, including Brazil. Through the Agreement, the signatories committed themselves to reducing GHG emissions in order to limit the average increase in global temperature to 2°C compared to pre-industrial levels. Although it is also a hydrocarbon, natural gas emits fewer GHGs than oil and coal and allows the safe entry of renewable sources into the various sectors, as it ensures the supply of electricity in times of intermittency.[41]

All these measures are in line with the Brazilian Government's practices over the last decade. In spite of this bottleneck (which was once greater than now), the Brazilian legal framework has proved to be quite efficient in view of the 45% reduction in natural gas flaring between 2012 and 2022. Such percentage becomes even more remarkable when one verifies that during this same 10-year period, Brazil increased its production by 47%.

The current Brazilian scenario and future perspectives indicate a great potential for the use of techniques to further reduce the flaring of natural gas in the country. Petrobras, for instance, has implemented[42] a system to recover flared gases (the so-called FGRU) in three of its platforms: P-66 (Tupi), P-70 (Atapu) and P-77 (Búzios). The company expects to reduce around 80,000 tons of CO_2 equivalent per year, and also to apply the FGRU system and other eight platforms located in the Santos and Campos basins.[43]

4 REGULATORY AND PRACTICAL SOLUTIONS

Brazil has been committed to addressing and regulating flaring activities and developed a specific regulation on the subject in 2000 (Ordinance 249/2000). The country recently revisited such regulation and updated its provisions by enacting RANP 806/2020, as mentioned above.

40. TCU, *Decision 2301/2021* (Plenary, September 29, 2021) https://pesquisa.apps.tcu.gov.br/documento/acordao-completo/*/NUMACORDAO%253A2301%2520ANOACORDAO%253A2021/DTRELEVANCIA%2520desc%252C%2520NUMACORDAOINT%2520desc/0/%2520 accessed July 18, 2024.
41. Santos EM dos "Oportunidades e Desafios Do Gás Natural e Do Gás Natural Liquefeito No Brasil" [2020] Letra Capital 29.
42. Back in 2019 Petrobras also planned on investing USD 850 million by 2024 in decarbonization measures for its oil and natural gas production, which included the use of closed flare systems. ([2019] "Os planos de descarbonização da Petrobras e o desafio global para eliminar o flaring" https://epbr.com.br/os-planos-de-descarbonizacao-da-petrobras-e-o-desafio-global-para-eliminar-o-flaring/ accessed July 18, 2024).
43. Petronotícias, "Petrobras Inaugura Sistema de Recuperação de Gás para reduzir suas emissões" [*Petronotícias*, 2022] https://petronoticias.com.br/petrobras-inaugura-sistema-de-recuperacao-de-gas-para-reduzir-suas-emissoes/#: ~ :text=Antes%2C%20esse%20energ%C3%A9tico%20era%20queimado,e%20Campos%20ainda%20neste%20ano accessed June 23, 2024.

Some issues, however, must still be tackled in order to maximize the efficiency of regulatory measures when addressing natural gas flaring. An interesting pathway that could be followed is expanding (and regulating) the use of compensatory measures to offset the GHGs emission resulting from natural gas flaring.[44] For such purpose, it would be necessary to properly consolidate the use of compensatory measures under a regulatory instrument, addressing at a minimum address the general parameters to require carbon offsetting in environmental licensing (e.g., which cases require carbon offsetting and which is the applicable proportion of the required offsetting).

A more thorough and detailed regulation could have better results if associated with additional measures to provide an economically feasible destination for the associated gas produced. This lesson can be extracted from Brazil's experience, when analyzing the results obtained in the last two decades, which were more expressive when ANP's restrictive policies were combined with infrastructure and technological developments, such as the Route 1 (the first Pre-Salt offloading pipeline), operating since 2011, with the capacity of transport up to 10 million m^3/d of natural gas.[45] The combined measures led to a 27.4% natural gas flaring reduction in the country between the years of 2010 and 2011.[46]

Other operationally driven approaches also have the potential to promote the use of natural gas as an alternative to flaring. Common options are: (i) the use of natural gas to generate energy at the production unit itself; and (ii) the reinjection of the gas in the reservoir to maintain the pressure and enhance oil recovery, although its feasibility depends on appropriate geological and operational conditions.

When there is no pipeline to offload the production, another common alternative is the offshore compression or liquefaction of natural gas, which can eliminate the need for gas pipelines for transportation and also reduce the amount of pollutants released into the environment as a result of gas flaring.[47] The natural gas may also be converted into synthetic fuels (Gas-to-Liquid or GTL) or gas to methanol (Gas-to-Methanol) offshore, and the relevant byproducts may be transported by ship.

There are also some technology-driven alternatives to increase flaring efficiency. In accordance with the United Nations Economic Commission for Europe (UNECE), the two main measures are the improvement of combustion efficiency by changing the flare tip and the installation of flare ignition systems. When combined, the above measures have the potential to increase the combustion efficiency up to 99.8%.[48]

44. Please refer to footnote 21 for further information on the use of compensatory measures by the Brazilian Institute of Environment and Renewable Natural Resources (IBAMA), in relation to Long Term Tests carried out by Petrobras.
45. IBP, "Ciclo de Debates sobre Petróleo e Economia" [2017] IBP https://www.ibp.org.br/personalizado/uploads/2017/02/5-Mauro-Yuji-Petrobras-Gas-do-Pr%C3%A9-sal-Ciclo-de-Debates-17-03-2017.pdf accessed June 23, 2024.
46. ANP, *Anuário Estatístico Brasileiro 2012* (ANP) https://www.gov.br/anp/pt-br/centrais-de-conteudo/publicacoes/anuario-estatistico/arquivos-anuario-estatistico-2012/anuario-estatistico-2012.pdf accessed February 23, 2024.
47. Aregbe AG, "Natural Gas Flaring: Alternative Solutions" [2017] World Journal of Engineering and Technology 139.
48. UNECE, "*Best Practice Guidance for Effective Methane Management in the Oil and Gas Sector: Monitoring, Reporting and Verification (MRV) and Mitigation,*" United Nations Economic Commission for Europe. Energy Series, No. 65, 2019.

Another interesting example of the use of technological solutions to reduce the impacts of flaring of natural gas is the *Gas Flare Recovery System* (FGRU), employed by Petrobras in its FPSO P-58, located in Espírito Santo. This system allows for the reduction of GHGs emission from natural gas flaring, which is in line with Petrobras' goal of stopping flaring *(queima zero)* by 2030. The company claims that the Gas Flare Recovery System is fundamental to achieving such a goal. The use of system on P-58 was a project pilot and, in addition to reducing the emission of GHGs, also had another positive outcome: an increase in revenue, since the recovered gas can be exported and sold.

5 CONCLUSION

The growing concern of players in the oil and gas industry to meet, not only legal requirements but also their internal policy goals toward the reduction of GHGs emissions is widely known. This concern has contributed to the improvement of projects, the production of relevant information and the conservation of natural environments where companies' activities are carried out, including the use of new technologies.

Specifically in Brazil, the notable decrease in gas flaring is much more than statistics, as it reflects a profound commitment to environmental protection, management of natural resources and promotion of less emissions-intensive fuels (such as natural gas). The legal and regulatory framework was crucial in this regard but has been even more effective due to its association with the development of infrastructure and the use of new technologies.

At a global level, Brazil is aligning itself with international efforts to mitigate climate change and promote energy efficiency. Its strategy to reduce gas flaring resonates with the global directives outlined in the Paris Agreement, which aims at reducing GHGs emissions and promoting a sustainable future. Brazil's achievements, marked by a 45% reduction in flaring while increasing gas production by 47% over a decade, provide a model for other countries addressing similar issues and prove that significant environmental and economic benefits are within reach through concerted efforts and cooperation.

The implications of Brazil's efforts extend beyond national borders, influencing the wider narrative of the global energy transition. As the petroleum industry moves towards sustainable energy solutions, the efficient management of resources becomes increasingly crucial to meet energy transition goals. By promoting the use of natural gas and reducing flaring, the country may, in the upcoming years, reduce the environmental impacts of energy production while simultaneously ensuring energy security.

This journey, however, is far from over. Brazil continues to face challenges such as the technical and economic complexities of offshore pre-salt production and the need for ongoing infrastructure enhancement. Overcoming these hurdles will require consistent effort and investment from both the public and private sectors. The innovative technologies being created and applied by E&P companies are pivotal in achieving further reductions in natural gas flaring in the near future.

CHAPTER 13
Canada

Allan Ingelson

1 INTRODUCTION

Methane, a potent greenhouse gas ("*GHG*"), has a global warming potential of more than 70 times that of carbon dioxide ("CO_2"), over a 20-year period.[1] As methane is a significant component of natural gas,[2] Environment and Climate Change Canada ("*ECCC*") monitors the level of national GHG emissions, and provincial governments monitor the level of methane emissions from their individual provinces. ECCC reported that the Canadian oil and gas sector (the "*Industry*") was responsible for releasing 25% of the nation's GHG emissions during the period 1990 to 2012, with trends indicating a continuous increase in the volume of methane emissions. In 2017, ECCC reported that 44% of Canada's methane emissions were from Industry.[3] Most of the Canadian oil and gas production is from four of ten provinces: Alberta, Saskatchewan, British Columbia, and Newfoundland.

1. Environment and Climate Change Canada, "Canada's methane regulations for upstream oil and gas," (ECCC, April 2018), online: https://www.canada.ca/en/environment-climate-change/services/canadian-environmental-protection-act-registry/proposed-methane-regulations-additional-information.html; *see also* ECCC, "Canada finalizes major commitment to reduce carbon pollution," (Ottawa, April 26, 2018), online: https://www.canada.ca/en/environment-climate-change/news/2018/04/canada-finalizes-major-commitment-to-reduce-carbon-pollution.htm.
2. American Geosciences Institute, "Methane Emissions in the Oil and Gas Industry," (June 1, 2018), online: www.americangeosciences.org/critical-issues/factsheet/pe/methane-emissions-oil-gas-industry.
3. ECCC, "General factsheet regarding the release of methane and certain volatile organic compounds," (ECCC, January 2020), online: https://www.canada.ca/en/environment-climate-change/services/canadian-environmental-protection-act-registry/factsheet-general-information-regulations-reduction-methane.html.

In light of Canada's commitments under the Paris Agreement,[4] on June 29, 2016, Prime Minister Justin Trudeau announced that by 2025, the federal government would reduce national methane emissions from the Industry to 40%-45% below the 2012 levels. The federal government has promoted the Pan-Canadian Framework on Clean Growth and Climate Change, a national plan directed toward reducing the effects of climate change, under which more stringent emission standards have been recommended.[5] In April 2018, pursuant to section 332(1) of the *Canadian Environmental Protection Act* ("*CEPA*"),[6] the ECCC published "Regulations Respecting Reduction in the Release of Methane and Certain Volatile Organic Compounds (Upstream Oil and Gas Sector)" ("*Federal Methane Regulations*"), in Part II of the *Canada Gazette*.[7] These Federal Methane Regulations apply to methane emissions from various upstream facilities, such as gathering and transmission pipelines; natural gas gathering, boosting and transmission compression stations; and natural gas processing plants. The Federal Methane Regulations largely focus on the extraction, primary processing, transportation, and storage of hydrocarbons.[8] The Federal Methane Regulations, currently being phased in, are designed to establish uniform, national requirements, to further significantly reduce methane emissions from upstream offshore and onshore operations.

Further, the Government of Canada introduced a federal carbon pollution pricing system, under the *Greenhouse Gas Pollution Pricing Act* ("*GGPPA*"), which received royal assent on June 21, 2018.[9] The GGPPA is composed of two parts: Part 1, which applies a fuel charge to certain fuel types and combustible waste, and Part 2, which is the output-based pricing system for industrial facilities.[10] It is well-established and recognized that carbon pricing is one of the most effective, transparent, and efficient approaches to reduce GHG emissions. Providing an incentive for emissions reduction has the added benefit of stimulating investment in clean innovation and encourages a competitive and prosperous economy.[11] The GGPPA sets out minimum national stringency standards that all provincial carbon pricing systems must meet. If a provincial or territorial system does not meet this backstop, then the federal carbon pollution pricing system will apply in that province or territory.

---

4. United Nations, "Climate Change," entered into force November 4, 2016, online: https://unfccc.int/process/the-paris-agreement/status-of-ratification.
5. Government of Canada, Environment and Climate Change Canada, "Pan-Canadian Framework on Clean Growth and Climate Change: Canada's Plan to Address Climate Change and Grow the Economy," (Gatineau, Quebec: Environment and Climate Change Canada, 2016).
6. Canadian Environmental Protection Act, SC 1999, Chapter 33.
7. Regulations Respecting Reduction in the Release of Methane and Certain Volatile Organic Compounds (Upstream Oil and Gas Sector), SOR 2018-66, P.C. 2018-3296 2018-04-03; online: https://laws-lois.justice.gc.ca/eng/regulations/SOR-2018-66/FullText.html ["*Federal Methane Regulations*"].
8. *Ibid.*
9. Government of Canada, "Carbon Pollution Pricing," (April 8, 2024), online: https://www.canada.ca/en/services/environment/weather/climatechange/climate-action/pricing-carbon-pollution.html.
10. *Ibid.*
11. Government of Canada, "Greenhouse Gas Pollution Pricing Act: Annual Report for 2020," online: https://www.canada.ca/en/environment-climate-change/services/climate-change/pricing-pollution-how-it-will-work/greenhouse-gas-annual-report-2020.html.

This chapter will explore the legislative framework underpinning methane and volatile organic compound (*"VOC"*) emissions reduction regulations, starting with the historical and policy reasons for regulating methane emissions and the cooperative approach between federal and provincial governments under CEPA. The following discussion will delve into the Federal Methane Regulations, highlighting their scope, objectives, and specific provisions targeting equipment leaks, venting, and new oil and gas wells. This includes a detailed look at the design of the regulations to reduce immediate and long-term harmful effects of methane emissions and the associated VOCs. Additionally, the impact of these regulations on operational practices within the oil and gas industry will be discussed, along with the commitments made by the Canadian government under the Paris Agreement. The role of federal/provincial equivalency agreements will be examined, focusing on the regulatory frameworks in Alberta, British Columbia, and Saskatchewan, and comparing their standards to the federal requirements. The chapter will analyze how these provinces implement their methane reduction strategies through specific regulations and directives, and the conditions under which provincial regulations can replace federal ones. Further, the major sources of methane emissions, such as equipment leaks and venting, and the approaches in the federal and provincial methane regulations for mitigating these emissions will be investigated. This includes the implementation of leak detection and repair (LDAR) programs, the establishment of venting limits, and the requirements for HF and well completions. The technological advancements and innovations aimed at improving methane detection and reduction will also be discussed. Enforcement mechanisms and the effectiveness of the regulations will be assessed, with a review of compliance and non-compliance cases in different provinces. This section will cover the roles of provincial and federal regulators, the methods used for inspections, and the penalties for non-compliance. The discussion will conclude with an evaluation of the overall impact of these regulations on reducing methane emissions and Canada's commitments under international agreements such as the Paris Agreement. The ongoing challenges and future directions for methane and VOC regulations in Canada will be examined.

2 CONSTITUTIONAL FRAMEWORK FOR FEDERAL & PROVINCIAL METHANE & VOC EMISSIONS REGULATIONS

The *Constitution Act, 1867* provides both the federal and provincial governments with legislative authority to restrict and manage the level of methane and VOC emissions to protect the environment, air quality, and the health of residents. The volume of methane emitted from upstream operations from the Industry has been regulated for decades by both levels of government for several policy reasons—minimizing the waste of finite oil and gas resources, protecting residents from the negative health and safety effects from methane releases into the environment, and most recently responding to climate change to reduce the level anthropogenic GHG emissions contributing to global warming. In light of the range of different energy resources, some with lower methane emissions, individual provincial governments can negotiate agreements with the federal government for different approaches to reducing the level of provincial methane emissions under CEPA,[12] as long as the national level of methane emissions stipulated by the national government pursuant to CEPA is achieved. If provincial governments clearly demonstrate that their emission reductions are equivalent to the federal regulations, then they can create and apply their provincial regulations. The GGPPA acts as a "backstop" if a province does not have an equivalency agreement.[13]

ECCC reported that facility equipment leaks account for 34% of upstream emissions, and venting accounts for 23%.[14] Canada's Federal Methane Regulations have prompted oil and gas operators to adopt operational practices to significantly reduce the volume of methane intentionally released or vented from Industry facilities, which along with equipment leaks, represent two major sources of upstream methane emissions.[15]

2.1 Federal Regulations

The Federal Methane Regulations apply to upstream oil and gas facilities that extract, process, and transport hydrocarbon gas.[16] Section 1 indicates that the Federal Methane Regulations are designed to reduce the immediate or long-term harmful effects of methane emissions and the associated *VOCs*,[17] which can include negative health effects, such as cardiovascular and respiratory morbidity, heart and asthma attacks, and premature adult mortality.[18] In 2020, ECCC reported that the upstream Industry emits 34% of the nation's VOCs.[19] The Federal Methane Regulations focus on reducing methane emissions from the largest and emerging sources in Canada's upstream Industry: equipment leaks, venting and new oil and gas wells.[20] ECCC estimates that the regulatory requirements to further reduce the volume of emissions by prompting the installation of new equipment should, by 2025, result in an emissions reduction

12. CEPA, section 10.
13. Government of Canada, "Greenhouse Gas Pollution Pricing Act: Annual Report for 2020," online: https://www.canada.ca/en/environment-climate-change/services/climate-change/pricing-pollution-how-it-will-work/greenhouse-gas-annual-report-2020.html.
14. Government of Canada, "Greenhouse Gas Sources and Sinks in Canada: Executive Summary 2023," online: https://www.canada.ca/en/environment-climate-change/services/climate-change/greenhouse-gas-emissions/sources-sinks-executive-summary-2023.html.
15. Government of Canada, "Federal Regulations to Reduce Methane Emissions in the Oil and Gas Sector," online: https://www.canada.ca/en/environment-climate-change/services/canadian-environmental-protection-act-registry/proposed-methane-regulations-additional-information.html.
16. Government of Canada, "Review of Canada's Methane Regulations for the Upstream Oil and Gas Sector," online: https://www.canada.ca/en/environment-climate-change/services/canadian-environmental-protection-act-registry/review-methane-regulations-upstream-oil-gas-sector.html#toc5.
17. *Supra* n. 1.
18. EPA, "Overview of Final Amendment to Air Regulations for the Oil and Natural Gas Industry," online: https://www.epa.gov/sites/default/files/2016-09/documents/natural_gas_transmission_fact_sheet_2012.pdf, accessed January 14, 2019.
19. Environment and Climate Change Canada, "Canada's Air Pollutant Emissions Inventory Reports 2020: Chapter 2.4," (Ottawa, ECCC, March 2020), online: https://publications.gc.ca/collections/collection_2020/eccc/En81-30-2018-eng.pdf.
20. *Supra* n. 1.

equivalent to 232 million tonnes of CO_2 by 2025.[21] Further, in October 2021, the Minister of ECCC announced a commitment to reduce methane emissions from Industry by at least 75% below 2012 levels by 2030.[22] Doing so is consistent with Canada's commitments under the Paris Agreement.

2.2 Equivalency Agreements and Provincial Methane Regulations

The largest volume of GHG emissions in Canada is from upstream operations on provincial lands, where regional governments have restricted the volume of emissions for decades under oil and gas conservation ("*OGC*") legislation and regulations. As most of the Canadian onshore oil and gas development has occurred on provincial lands in the western provinces of Alberta, British Columbia, and Saskatchewan, provincial regulators have more experience than federal regulators in restricting the volume of GHG emissions, and more comprehensive provincial frameworks exist that provide a foundation for the federal government to further reduce GHG emissions. The Minister of Environment can enter into an equivalency agreement for methane regulations with a province, territory, or Aboriginal government pursuant to section 10 of CEPA. Equivalency agreements must be agreed upon in writing that they are in force with provisions equivalent to a regulation made under CEPA or provisions similar to sections 17 to 20 of CEPA allowing for citizens to request investigation of alleged offenses.[23] Where an agreement has been made, the Governor in Council may make an order declaring that the CEPA Regulations, subject to the equivalency agreement, do not apply in the jurisdiction of that government. As of 2020, the provinces of Alberta, British Columbia, and Saskatchewan had finalized equivalency agreements, meaning the provincial regulations replaced the Federal Methane Regulations for up to five years.[24]

In the province of Alberta, the provincial energy regulator, the Alberta Energy Regulator ("*AER*"), employs the *Environmental Protection and Enhancement Act* ("*EPEA*"),[25] *Oil and Gas Conservation Act*,[26] *Oil and Gas Conservation Rules*,[27] and *Directive 060: Upstream Petroleum Industry Flaring, Incinerating, and Venting*,[28]

21. Regulations Respecting Reduction in the Release of Methane and Certain Volatile Organic Compounds (Upstream oil and Gas Sector) (2018) 152(1) C Gaz 11 62 (Regulatory Impact Analysis Statement), online: http://gazette.gc.ca/rp-pr/p2/2018/2018-04-26-x1/html/sordors6 6-eng.html accessed May 27, 2019.
22. Environment and Climate Change Canada, "Review of Canada's Methane Regulations for the Upstream Oil and Gas Sector," (Ottawa: ECCC, December 2021), online: https://www.canada.ca/en/environment-climate-change/services/canadian-environmental-protection-act-registry/review-methane-regulations-upstream-oil-gas-sector.html.
23. *Ibid.*
24. *Ibid.*
25. Environmental Protection and Enhancement Act, RSA 2000, c E-12.
26. RSA 2000, c 0-6.
27. Alta Reg 15/1971.
28. *Directive 060: Upstream Petroleum Industry Flaring, Incinerating, and Venting*, https://www.aer.ca/regulating-development/rules-and-directives/directives/directive-060.

Directive 017: Measurement Requirements for Oil and Gas Operations,[29] and *Directive 084: Requirements for Hydrocarbon Emission Controls and Gas Conservation in the Peace River Area*[30] in order to limit methane emissions. These requirements are incorporated by reference in the *Methane Emission Reductions Regulation* (the "*Alberta Regulation*"), which sets out the requirements and directives that upstream oil and gas facilities must follow regarding methane emissions. On November 11, 2020, an Order-in-Council was published that the Federal Methane Regulations do not apply in Alberta for the next five years, as per the equivalency agreement. The *Order Declaring that the Provisions of the Regulations Respecting Reduction in the Release of Methane and Certain Volatile Organic Compounds (Upstream Oil and Gas Sector) Do Not Apply in Alberta,*[31] set out that the Minister and the Government of Alberta have entered into a written agreement to the effect that there are in force by or under the laws of Alberta:

(a) provisions that are equivalent to the provisions of the *Regulations Respecting Reduction in the Release of Methane and Certain Volatile Organic Compounds (Upstream Oil and Gas Sector),* made under subsection 93(1) of the Act; and
(b) provisions that are similar to sections 17 to 20 of that Act for the investigation of alleged offenses under the environmental legislation of Alberta.

With (a) coming into force with the publication of the Order-in-Council in 2020 and (b) coming into force on January 1, 2023. Compared to the Federal Methane Regulations, the Alberta Regulations are more stringent for new facilities since 2022, contain more stringent requirements for pneumatic controllers, have specific requirements for glycol dehydrators, allow a lower leak detection frequency at some facilities, and contain less stringent routine venting and pneumatic pump requirements.[32]

In the province of British Columbia, the provincial government regulates much of the current shale oil and gas development and limits methane emissions through the BC *Environmental Management Act,*[33] *Climate Change Accountability Act,*[34] *Drilling and Production Regulation* ("*B.C. Regulation*"),[35] and the *Oil and Gas Processing Facility Regulation.*[36] In 2020, an Order-in-Council was published that the Federal Methane Regulations do not apply in British Columbia for the next five years, per the equivalency agreement—the B.C. Regulation was approved in 2018 as an equivalent to the Federal Methane Regulations. Compared to the Federal Methane Regulations, the B.C. Regulations contain regulatory standards for the same sources with additional standards for glycol dehydrators, have more stringent control measures for new

29. *Directive 017, Measurement Requirements for Oil and Gas Operations,* https://www.aer.ca/regulating-development/rules-and-directives/directives/directive-017.
30. *Directive 084: Requirements for Hydrocarbon Emission Controls and Gas Conservation in the Peace River Area,* https://www.aer.ca/regulating-development/rules-and-directives/directives/directive-084.
31. SOR/2020-2333.
32. *Supra* n. 19.
33. SBC 2003, c 53.
34. SBC 2007, c 42.
35. BC Reg 282/2010.
36. BC Reg 48/2021.

facilities, require a lower leak detection frequency at some facility types, and have less stringent routine venting requirements.[37]

In the province of Saskatchewan, regulations for methane emissions include the *Oil and Gas Emissions Management Regulations*,[38] *Directive PNG036*: *Venting and Flaring Regulations*,[39] *Directive PNG017: Measurement Requirements for Oil and Gas Operations*,[40] and the *Methane Action Plan*.[41] In November 2020, an Order-in-Council was published that the Federal Methane Regulations do not apply in Saskatchewan as per the equivalency agreement that will end on December 31, 2024.[42]

3 SOURCES OF METHANE EMISSIONS

3.1 Equipment Leaks

According to a peer-reviewed 2024 report, "Canada's oil and gas industry emitted 2.6 million tonnes of methane into the atmosphere in 2021," more than 2% of the total gas produced with approximately 90% from production sites (leaks from equipment at oil wells and tanks or from intentional venting.[43] In section 2 of the Federal Methane Regulations, "fugitive emissions" refers to natural gas leaks from equipment and is defined as "the emission of hydrocarbon gas from an upstream oil and gas facility in an unintentional manner."[44] The Federal Methane Regulations focus on reducing these emissions from larger facilities—those that receive more than 60,000 standard m^3 of hydrocarbon gas during a 12-month period.[45] These larger facilities are responsible for approximately 75% of Canada's vented emissions.[46] Addressing a smaller number of larger sources of emissions (facilities) reflects a high-leverage approach. To reduce emissions, section 29 of the Federal Methane Regulations requires operators to carry out "*LDAR*" programs as follows:

37. BC Reg 282/2010.
38. *Oil and Gas Emissions Management Regulations*, RRS c O-2 Reg 7.
39. Directive PNG036*: Venting and Flaring Regulations,* https://publications.saskatchewan.ca/api/v1/products/103751/formats/115120/download/.
40. *Directive PNG017: Measurement Requirements for Oil and Gas Operations, revision 5.0,* https://www.saskatchewan.ca/business/agriculture-natural-resources-and-industry/oil-and-gas/oil-and-gas-licensing-operations-and-requirements/oil-and-gas-drilling-and-operations/measurement-requirements.
41. PNG017: Measurement Requirements for Oil and Gas Operations, and the Methane Action Plan, https://www.saskatchewan.ca/business/agriculture-natural-resources-and-industry/oil-and-gas/oil-and-gas-licensing-operations-and-requirements/oil-and-gas-drilling-and-operations/measurement-requirements.
42. *Supra* n. 19.
43. Environmental Defense Fund, "New Study Provides Comprehensive Estimates of Methane Emissions for Canada's Oil & Gas Industry Based on Direct Measurements," (August 6, 2024) online: https://www.edf.org/media/new-study-provides-comprehensive-estimates-methane-emissions-canadas-oil-and-gas-industry.
44. Federal Methane Regulations, *supra* n. 7.
45. *Ibid*, sections 26-45.
46. Government of Canada, "Technical Backgrounder: Proposed federal methane regulations for the oil and gas sector," (Ottawa, August, 2018), online: https://www.canada.ca/en/services/environment/weather/climatechange/climate-action/technical-backgrounder-proposed-federal-methane-regulations-oil-gas-sector.html.

> Operators of a facility must ... establish and carry out at the facility a) a regulatory [LDAR] that satisfies sections 30- 33; or b) an alternative leak detection and repair program referred to in subsection 35(1) that results in at most the same quantity of those fugitive emissions as would result from a regulatory program referred to in paragraph a).[47]

As far as the types of LDAR options available to facility operators, section 35(1) of the Federal Methane Regulations provides flexibility in regard to the types of leak repair programs employed on the condition that the repair provides the same required reduction in emissions. Section 32 of the Federal Methane Regulations provides that in most cases a leak must be repaired within 30 days of it being detected:

A leak from an equipment component that is detected, whether as a result of an inspection or otherwise, must be repaired (a) if the repair can be carried out while the equipment component is operating, within 30 days after the day on which it was detected; and (b) in any other case, the equipment component must be repaired within the period before the end of the next planned shutdown unless that period is extended under section 33.[48]

In regard to facility inspections, the Federal Methane Regulations provide that:

> An equipment component at an upstream oil and gas facility must be inspected... on or before the later of May 1, 2020 and the day that occurs 60 days after the day on which production at the facility first began; and ... at least 3 times/year and at least 60 days after a previous inspection.[49]

The Federal Methane Regulations mandate three annual inspections and specify the types of technologies that will be used during inspections such as infrared cameras, sniffers, drones, and satellite systems, to avoid arguments and disputes that could arise regarding whether there have been emissions that exceed the level permitted under the Federal Methane Regulations.[50]

The federal requirements convey the increased emphasis that ECCC is placing on operators to take action to prevent, detect, and repair equipment leaks in a timely manner to further significantly reduce the volume of emissions from larger oil and gas facilities. The fact that time periods are specified in the Federal Methane Regulations by which operators must complete equipment repairs should prompt facility operators to pay closer attention to the current volume of emissions from equipment leaks. In addition to the general provisions in the Federal Methane Regulations that govern equipment leaks, there are specific provisions that apply to different types of equipment.

It is estimated that 20% of methane emissions from the industry are from pneumatic device leaks.[51] A variety of automated instruments called pneumatic devices are employed throughout the Industry that employ natural gas to pump liquids and for other purposes. Some of these devices release methane. As with other types of

47. Federal Methane Regulations, *supra* n. 7, section 29.
48. *Ibid.*, section 32.
49. *Ibid.*, section 30(1)-(3).
50. *Ibid.*
51. *Supra* n. 16.

Industry equipment, the Federal Methane Regulations prescribe operating efficiency standards for pneumatic controllers and pumps.[52] The Federal Methane Regulations require operators to replace certain types of high-bleed pneumatic controllers that produce a larger volume of emissions with low-bleed or no-bleed controllers that release a smaller volume of emissions. As with the other types of equipment, the repairs and equipment replacements must be completed within the time specified in the Federal Methane Regulations. In order to provide facility operators with reasonable notice to budget for the upgrade or purchase new equipment to replace existing equipment, the provisions that apply to pneumatic devices, as with other types of equipment, came into force in 2023.[53]

Provincial regulatory systems rely heavily on voluntary Industry guidelines developed by the Canadian Association of Petroleum Producers ("*CAPP*"), a national Industry association that represents most Canadian oil companies.[54] The CAPP guidelines provide valuable technical information on where the most common sources of methane leaks are in upstream facilities, recommend early equipment LDARs, and provide information on how to economically manage emissions by focusing on larger leaks. Unlike the Federal Methane Regulations, the provincial regulations do not prescribe specific timelines for repairs, nor time deadlines by which inspections are to be carried out to verify that equipment leaks have been repaired.

The OGC systems were not originally designed to reduce the volume of emissions from equipment leaks and venting, albeit now required by the Canadian government to satisfy its GHG emissions reduction commitments under the Paris Agreement.[55] Provincial regulators rely heavily on voluntary Industry guidelines and practices for the frequency of equipment inspections, extent of repairs, and venting practices. The federal government has concluded that less stringent provincial methane emissions standards result in a higher volume of emissions than is necessary from facility equipment leaks and venting and therefore adopted the Federal Methane Regulations.[56]

The province of Alberta and the Federal government have the "Canada-Alberta equivalency agreement respecting the release of methane from the oil and gas sector,"[57] which states that the Alberta Regulation has equivalent provisions to the Federal Methane Regulations. Specifically, the AER's *Directive 084* sets out, among others, the requirements that a licensee must use reliable and appropriate leak

52. *Ibid*, sections 37(1), 37(2), 39(1).
53. *Ibid.*
54. CAPP, "Best Management Practice: Management of Fugitive Emissions at Upstream Oil and Gas Facilities," (2007) 9.
55. *Ibid.*
56. The AER in 2018 and 2019 has revised *Directive 060*, created *Directives 084* and *017*, and is currently in the process of better aligning the Alberta provincial emissions reduction requirements with the Federal Methane Regulations.
57. CEPA "Canada-Alberta Equivalency Agreement Respecting the Release of Methane from the Oil and Gas Sector," https://www.canada.ca/en/environment-climate-change/services/canadian-environmental-protection-act-registry/agreements/equivalency/canada-alberta-methane-oil-gas.html.

detection equipment and must address the leak immediately upon detection.[58] *Directive 084* further sets out that a licensee must develop, document, and implement plans to accurately identify leaking components.

Under the Alberta Regulation, the following definitions have been set out which help provide clarity to project proponents:

(a) "fugitive emissions" means the unintentional release of hydrocarbons, including methane, into the atmosphere and includes, but is not limited to, unintentional releases of hydrocarbons as a result of:
  (i) worn, broken or loose components;
  (ii) surface casing vent flows and gas migration; and
  (iii) equipment emitting in excess of design or normal operating conditions.
(b) "fugitive emissions management program" means a program to track, manage or
  repair a release of fugitive emissions;
(c) "methane" means, in addition to its normal scientific meaning, a mixture mainly of methane that ordinarily may contain some ethane, nitrogen, helium or CO_2;
(d) "operator" means an operator as defined in the Oil and Gas Conservation Act;
(e) "regulator" means the AER;
(f) "upstream oil and gas facility" means:
  (i) a scheme or operation approved under section 10 of the Oil Sands Conservation Act;
  (ii) an installation as defined in the Pipeline Act; or
  (iii) a well or facility as defined in the Oil and Gas Conservation Act.
(g) "vent gas" means uncombusted gas that is released into the atmosphere at an upstream oil and gas facility and includes, but is not limited to:
  (i) waste gas;
  (ii) gas used to operate pneumatic devices;
  (iii) gas from compressor seals, starters and blowdowns;
  (iv) gas from facility upsets and emergency shutdowns;
  (v) gas from dehydrator still columns;
  (vi) gas from production tanks other than methanol or chemical tanks;
  (vii) gas released during pigging operations;
  (viii) gas produced during well completions;
  (ix) gas produced during well unloading volumes; and
  (x) blanket gas;

but does not include fugitive emissions.[59]

Further, the volume of gas produced, received, vented, and destroyed at an upstream oil and gas facility must be determined in accordance with the methods set out in *Directive 017*. With regards to fugitive emissions, a duty holder must follow the

58. *Directive 084*, section 6.2.3, 6.2.5.
59. MERR, section 4.

emission management requirements set out in *Directive 060* in section 8.10 to 8.10.6.[60] An annual report must also be submitted in accordance with section 8.2 of *Directive 060*, including the information in section 8.4.1, 8.6.1.2, 8.6.2.4, 8.6.3.3 and 8.10.5, as well as any other information requested by the director. The director can also request additional reports, and the duty holder must retain the annual report for the facility, the fugitive emissions management program and the records, information, and data on which the latter two are based for four years from the date they were created.[61]

Leaks are often detected using hand-held optical gas imaging cameras that cost CAD 130,000 and require the user to be close to each site, making testing under the Federal Methane Regulations difficult and expensive. At half the cost of a gas imaging camera, a team from the University of Calgary has developed a new technology called PoMELO, which uses equipment mounted on the roof rack of a pickup truck. PoMELO allows the user to drive by and get data to see what is emitting and how much.[62]

3.2 Venting and Flaring

Venting is a common industry practice that releases methane directly into the atmosphere, which accounts for 23% of Industry methane emissions.[63] As natural gas is used to control pressurized equipment including pumps in multiple Industry operations, methane is intentionally released from equipment in processing facilities through vents. The Federal Methane Regulations are designed to reduce by 95% the volume of methane that is intentionally vented from larger oil and gas facilities. To achieve this objective, section 26 of the Federal Methane Regulations creates an annual venting limit for an upstream oil and gas facility of not more than 15,000 m^3 of hydrocarbon gas. One exception to the maximum emissions limit in the Federal Methane Regulations that provides flexibility to facility operators allows them to apply for approval to vent methane for safety reasons in exceptional cases when there is an emergency, such as an emergency depressurization or plant maintenance upset at a larger gas processing facility.[64]

As an alternative to venting gas in non-emergency situations, the Federal Methane Regulations require operators to capture and use at least 95% of the methane in facilities for one of three stipulated beneficial purposes rather than wasting the gas. Section 5 requires a minimum equipment operating efficiency as follows: "[h]ydrocarbon gas conservation equipment that is used at an upstream oil and gas facility must be operated in such a manner that at least 95% of the hydrocarbon gas is captured and conserved."[65] Section 7 stipulates that gas must be captured and conserved in one of the three following methods:

---

60. MERR, section 5.
61. MERR, sections 7-8.
62. Doug Fergusson, "University of Calgary Research Team Meets Methane Leak Detection Challenge," online: https://ucalgary.ca/news/university-calgary-research-team-meets-methane-leak-detection-challenge.
63. *Supra* n. 16.
64. *Ibid.*
65. Federal Methane Regulations, *supra* n. 7.

(a) used at the facility as fuel in a combustion device that releases at most 5% of the combusted hydrocarbon gas into the atmosphere as hydrocarbon gas;
(b) delivered; or
(c) injected into an underground geological deposit for a purpose other than to dispose of the gas as waste.[66]

Regarding the first option, no more than 5% of the gas can be released. The second option, "delivered," refers to piping the gas to be sold and used. The third option, subsurface injection (also referred to as enhanced recovery), requires natural gas to be reinjected into an oil and gas reservoir to avoid the release of methane into the atmosphere.

Another type of equipment compressors, accounts for approximately 9% of Canada's methane emissions. These are mechanical devices used to increase the pressure in pipelines to move natural gas from production sites to consumers.[67] Different types of compressors emit different levels of emissions, and the Federal Methane Regulations contain special provisions that limit the volume of emissions that can be vented from different types of compressors.[68] To reduce the volume of emissions from each type of compressor, there is a requirement that Industry operators complete annual measurements to ensure that the emission limits stipulated in the Federal Methane Regulations are satisfied. Section 14(a) requires measurement of gas flow volumes as the first step toward further reducing the volume of emissions. Section 16(3) requires that operators take initial and subsequent gas flow measurements during specific time periods, as follows:

> The flow rate must be initially measured on January 1, 2021, if the compressor is installed at the facility before January 1, 2020, and the 365th day after the day on which the compressor was installed at the facility in any other case; and subsequently, the period that ends on the 365th day after the day on which a previous measurement was taken.

Section 14 provides for optimal equipment performance that takes into account the different types of compressors used at different sites, and the Federal Methane Regulations focus on optimal equipment maintenance and efficiency to minimize the level of emissions.[69] As with other types of equipment, compressor operators are required to conserve or destroy methane and meet the relevant gas release limits tailored to the type of compressor. Corrective action is required if emissions exceed the limit applicable to the compressor, which depends on the installation date, the type of compressor, and its rated brake power.[70] Timelines of 30 days and 90 days are specified in the Federal Methane Regulations to complete the required work on compressors to reduce methane emissions.[71]

66. *Ibid.*
67. *Supra* n. 1.
68. Federal Methane Regulations, *supra* n. 7, sections 14(b), 16(3).
69. *Ibid.*, section 18(2), 18(3).
70. *Ibid.*, section 14.
71. *Ibid.*

The Federal Methane Regulations implemented several new requirements starting on January 1, 2023, regarding venting. Venting from compressors requires annual measurements of natural gas emissions from compressor vents and corrective action when emissions exceed the applicable limit. Further, the requirements from venting from well completions involving hydraulic fracturing ("*HF*") include no venting and conservation of natural gas for re-use on-site or for sale, or flaring/clean incineration of natural gas.

The Alberta Regulations, similar to the Federal Methane Regulations, have measures to reduce venting emissions from the upstream Industry.[72] Section 8.3 to 8.632.2 of *Directive 060* sets out the requirements operators must follow with regard to venting in Alberta for specific equipment, including pneumatic devices, compressor seals, and glycol dehydrators. Certain regulations came into force in January 2020, including the overall vent gas limit, while the defined vent gas limit and specific limits came in January 2022. Lastly, in January 2023, the last set of requirements came into force surrounding vent gas limits for pneumatic devices. *Directive 060* has applications under three general categories: (1) temporary and well test flaring and incinerating permits; (2) pipeline flaring, incinerating and venting permits; and (3) requests pertaining to upstream facilities. The Alberta Regulation sets out under section 3(2) that "if a duty holder engages in flaring or incineration for the purpose of meeting the requirements of subsection (1), the duty holder shall also comply with each requirement of section 3.6 and 7 to 7.12.5 of Directive 060."[73] Section 3.6 sets out the site-specific requirements related to well flaring and incineration, and section 7 sets out the design and operation requirements.

3.3 HF and Completion of Oil & Gas Wells

Another potential source of methane emissions addressed in the Federal Methane Regulations is HF operations and well completions at newly drilled oil and gas wells. HF refers to the process used to create cracks or fractures in rock that allow oil and gas to move more freely to the well surface. It is an essential process at most shale oil and gas wells today for there to be economic hydrocarbon production.[74] Fluids that contain methane in solution flow back to the well site surface and can release the gas into the atmosphere if not properly managed. Recently, technology has been refined to detect and monitor methane releases from oil and gas wells. Employing satellite data, atmospheric methane emission trends in North America have been analyzed and compared before and after unconventional shale gas development. It has been reported that the concentration of fugitive emissions has increased in areas with shale oil and gas development.[75] Compared to conventional wells, it is estimated that in some areas,

72. *Supra* n. 19.
73. MERR, section 3(2).
74. Canadian Centre for Energy Information, "Our Petroleum Challenge," 8th ed. at 140.
75. Oliver Scheising et al., "Remote Sensing of Fugitive Methane Emissions from Oil and Gas Production in North America Tight Geologic Formations," (2014) 2(10) Earth's Future 548 https://doi.org/10.1002/2014ef000265.

HF of shale oil and gas wells releases 40 to 60% more methane into the atmosphere, where more than 8% to 12% of the methane escapes through equipment leaks and venting.[76]

To prevent methane emissions from new oil and gas wells drilled throughout Canada, section 11(2) of the Federal Methane Regulations entitled "No Venting" prohibits venting at new well sites and requires the capture and use of natural gas for a beneficial purpose or combustion/destruction of the gas. The section provides that "hydrocarbon gas associated with flowback at a well … must not be vented during flowback but must instead be captured and routed to hydrocarbon gas conservation equipment or hydrocarbon gas destruction equipment."[77] The prohibition on venting gas at new oil and gas wells will prevent an increase in methane emissions from these wells.

In regard to existing provincial standards in British Columbia and Alberta that limit emissions from HF of oil and gas wells, section 13 of the Federal Methane Regulations entitled "Non-application—British Columbia and Alberta" provides:

Sections 11 and 12 do not apply in respect of an upstream oil and gas facility that is located in:

(a) British Columbia, if the facility is subject to the requirements with respect to well completion involving HF that are set out in the guideline entitled *Flaring and Venting Reduction Guideline,* published by the Oil and Gas Commission of British Columbia in June 2016.
(b) Alberta, if the facility is subject to the requirements with respect to well completion involving HF that are set out in the directive entitled *Directive 060: Upstream Petroleum Industry Flaring, Incinerating, and Venting,* published by the AER on March 22, 2016.[78]

Section 13 of the Federal Regulations provides that operators which satisfy the current provincial requirements in British Columbia[79] and Alberta[80] do not have to comply with the new standards in the Federal Methane Regulations as well, as the federal government concluded that the 2016 provincial requirements that apply to emissions from HF and completion of new wells were adequate.[81] However, in contrast to British Columbia and Alberta, operators engaged in HF and well-completion

76. Robert Howarth et al., "Natural Gas: Should Fracking Stop?," (2011) 477(7364) Nature 271 https://doi.org/10.1038/477271a; Robert Howarth et al., "Methane and the Greenhouse-Gas Footprint of Natural Gas from Shale Formations" (2011) 106(679) Climate Change 679 https://doi.org/10.1007/s10584-011-0061-5.
77. Federal Methane Regulations, *supra* n. 7, section 11(2).
78. Federal Methane Regulations, *supra* n. 7.
79. BC Oil and Gas Commission, "Flaring and Venting Reduction Guideline," online: https://www.bcogc.ca/node/5916/download.
80. Alberta Energy Regulator, "Upstream Petroleum Industry Flaring, Incinerating and Venting, AER Directive 060," online: www.aer.ca/documents/directives/Directive060.pdf.
81. Federal Methane Regulations, *supra* n. 7, sections 11, 12.

operations in other provinces, such as Saskatchewan and the territories, must satisfy the federal requirements to avoid prosecution.[82]

In 2018 and 2019, the AER revised *Directive 060*[83] and created *Directives 084*[84] and *017,*[85] further contributing to Alberta's ongoing efforts to create provincial emissions reduction requirements that better align with the Federal Methane Regulations. The methane reduction requirements in *Directive 017* went into effect in December 2018 whereas the requirements in *Directive 060* went into effect in January 2020. Both *Directives* had revisions released in May 2020.[86] In response to the federal and provincial regulatory reforms discussed above, the CanadaWest Foundation noted in October 2022, that during the previous five years, methane emissions from the Western Canadian upstream oil and gas industry were reduced by approximately 44 %, resulting in both environmental and economic benefits.[87]

4 ENFORCEMENT

Since its adoption in 2018, there have been no reported decisions on a completed enforcement action under the Federal Methane Regulations.[88] Conversely, there have been reported cases of noncompliance within the provinces. In 2020, regulators in Alberta reported that nearly 30 % of operators in the province were out of compliance with the province's pollution standards, yet there have been no penalties.[89] The following year in Alberta, 850 methane inspections were conducted, with 224 of these resulting in notices of noncompliance.[90] As a result, the operations at only one facility were suspended for exceeding the venting limits and is expected to develop, implement, and submit a plan to address the noncompliance and prevent future occurrences.[91] Except for this one case, there were no other orders or penalties of convictions related to the enforcement of the Alberta Regulations in 2021.[92] Since then, in 2024, the AER fined Tallahassee Exploration Inc. CAD 191,885 for failing to meet its methane

82. *Ibid.*
83. *Supra* n. 25.
84. Alberta Energy Regulator, "Requirements for Hydrocarbon Emission Controls and Gas Conservation in the Peace River Area, AER Directive 084," online: https://www.aer.ca/documents/directives/Directive084.pdf.
85. Alberta Energy Regulator, "Measurement Requirements for Oil and Gas Operations, AER Directive 017," online: https://www.aer.ca/documents/directives/Directive017.pdf.
86. Methane Reduction, "Alberta Energy Regulator," online: https://www.aer.ca/protecting-what-matters/protecting-the-environment/methane-reduction.
87. Marla Orenstein & Nayantara Sudhakar, Canada West Foundation, "Methane Emissions and Canada's Oil and Gas Sector: The Start of a Good News Story," (October 20, 2022): online: https://cwf.ca/research/publications/methane-emissions-and-canadas-oil-and-gas-sector/.
88. Federal Methane Regulations, *supra* n. 7.
89. How to meet Canada's methane reduction goals, Environmental Defense Fund, available online at: https://www.edf.org/sites/default/files/documents/CanadaFactSheet2023.pdf.
90. 2021 Methane emissions management from the upstream oil and gas sector in Alberta, Alberta Government, available online at: https://open.alberta.ca/dataset/7e41d270-075f-498c-9b3d-7b822c930760/resource/f4fe807e-0763-43e7-9c96-f107b3fbf8ab/download/epa-methane-emissions-management-upstream-oil-and-gas-sector-2021.pdf.
91. *Ibid.*
92. *Ibid.*

emission reporting requirements under the Alberta *Methane Emission Reduction Regulation (MERR)* and failing to conduct fugitive emission surveys at any of its facilities in 2021.[93] The *MERR* requires compliance with *Directive 060: Upstream Petroleum Industry Flaring, Incinerating, and Venting,* which directs companies to submit annual methane emission reports for all facilities to inform the AER of the methane emissions a facility emits from vent gas sources.[94] Additionally, fugitive emission surveys are required annually to identify the source of a fugitive emission and repair it. Repairs are required within 30 days of identification, or within 24 hours if there are odors, flare, or potential safety issues. In failing to conduct these surveys, Tallahassee lacks information on the quantity of any methane emitted, reducing the ability to monitor and reduce harmful methane emissions. The company was also found to contravene the *EPEA* by providing false or misleading information by resubmitting information from the 2020 reporting period and representing it as data from the 2021 reporting period.[95]

5 VOLATILE ORGANIC COMPOUNDS

Canada produced 1.4 million metric tons of VOC emissions in 2021, with the oil and gas industry being the largest contributor, accounting for 32% of emissions. VOCs are regulated to reduce their impact on air quality and human health. The key regulations include the National Pollutant Release Inventory (NPRI) and various provincial regulations.[96]

The "Reduction in the Release of Volatile Organic Compounds Regulations (Petroleum Sector)" is administered by ECCC to mitigate the environmental and health impacts of VOCs emitted from the petroleum sector.[97] VOCs contribute to the development of ground-level ozone and particulates, both of which are components of smog. The regulations target various phases of oil production, including extraction, processing, and storage, for more comprehensive coverage of sources of emissions. The regulations address VOC releases during the HF process, specifically during flowback, which is the period when fluids, water, and hydrocarbons flow back to the surface after fracking. Facilities must implement technologies and practices to capture VOCs during flowback, such as closed-loop systems and other emission control technologies to minimize releases. Fugitive emissions refer to unintentional releases of VOCs from equipment, valves, connectors, pumps, and compressors. Facilities are required to implement LDAR programs to identify and fix leaks. The regulations specify inspection frequency, acceptable detection methods (e.g., infrared cameras, sniffers), and repair timelines. Inspections must be conducted regularly, and any detected leaks

93. Alberta Energy Regulator, News Release, "The AER Penalizes Tallahassee for Failing to Report Methane Emissions," (May 7, 2024).
94. Alberta Energy Regulator, "Directive 060: Upstream Petroleum Industry Flaring, Incinerating, and Venting," (April 6, 2022).
95. *Supra* n. 25.
96. Canada's Air Pollutant Emissions Inventory Report, En81-30-2022-eng.pdf (publications.gc.ca).
97. *Reduction in the Release of Volatile Organic Compounds Regulations (Petroleum Sector),* SOR/2020-231.

must be repaired promptly, usually within 30 days. The regulations that specify limits on VOC emissions require the use of best available control technologies (BACT) to minimize emissions and meet these limits. Operators are to use vapor recovery units and other equipment designed to capture and control VOCs.

The regulations may allow for time extensions under specific circumstances to prevent facility explosions, but the emphasis is on timely repairs to reduce emissions. Venting may occur during equipment maintenance, pressure relief, or other operational activities for safety reasons, however, the regulations impose strict limits on venting activities. Operators are required to minimize venting by employing alternative natural gas management methods such as flaring (controlled burning) or capturing and reusing the gas. Venting is only allowed under specific circumstances when it is necessary for safety or operational reasons. Facilities must monitor and report venting activities to ECCC, including documenting the volume of gas vented and the reasons for venting. Regular reporting provides for increased transparency and assists in tracking VOC emission reduction progress. U.S. EPA Method 21 developed in the United States is also employed in Canada to implement the LDAR program. The method describes procedures for detecting VOC leaks from equipment using portable instruments. Facilities must use instruments that meet the performance criteria outlined in EPA Method 21, to ensure reliable and accurate VOC detection. The method specifies the steps to calibrate instruments, techniques for monitoring different types of equipment, and the criteria for determining a leak. Compliance with EPA Method 21 ensures a standard approach to leak detection, contributing to the overall effectiveness of the LDAR programs in reducing VOC emissions.

The regulations also provide clear timelines for compliance, providing facilities with a reasonable amount of time to upgrade equipment and industry practices. The phased approach has provided for a smoother transition and allows for adjustments based on technological progress and industry. Non-compliance with the regulations can result in significant penalties, including fines and potential shutdown of facilities. ECCC provides support and guidance to facilities to assist with compliance, including technical assistance, training programs, and informational resources that describe best industry practices and emerging technologies for VOC reduction. The regulations promote technological innovation and the adoption of cleaner technologies to reduce VOCs.[98]

The "Order Declaring that the Provisions of the Reduction in the Release of Volatile Organic Compounds Regulations (Petroleum Sector) Do Not Apply" in Alberta (SOR/2020-233),[99] Saskatchewan (SOR/2020-234),[100] and British Columbia

98. Reduction in the Release of Volatile Organic Compounds Regulations (Petroleum Sector), Reduction in the Release of Volatile Organic Compounds Regulations (Petroleum Sector) (justice.gc.ca)
99. Order Declaring that the Provisions of the Reduction in the Release of Volatile Organic Compounds Regulations (Petroleum Sector) Do Not Apply in Alberta (SOR/2020-233), Order Declaring that the Provisions of the Regulations Respecting Reduction in the Release of Methane and Certain Volatile Organic Compounds (Upstream Oil and Gas Sector) Do Not Apply in Alberta (justice.gc.ca).
100. Order Declaring that the Provisions of the Reduction in the Release of Volatile Organic Compounds Regulations (Petroleum Sector) Do Not Apply in Saskatchewan (SOR/2020-234),

(SOR/2020-60)[101] exempts these provinces from certain parts of the Federal VOC Regulations, recognizing the provincial regulations provide equivalent VOC emission reduction. Alberta's regulatory framework, enforced by the AER, includes strict controls on emissions during HF, detailed measures for managing flowback emissions, and comprehensive LDAR programs. The provincial equivalents also mandate more regular inspections, use of advanced detection technologies, and prompt repairs of equipment leaks. The AER enforces regulations that require operators on provincial lands to minimize venting and to utilize flaring or gas capture systems, to reduce VOC emissions.

Saskatchewan's regulations, administered by the Ministry of Energy and Resources, include rigorous emission control measures during HF and flowback, utilizing technologies like vapor recovery units. Saskatchewan also implements extensive LDAR programs with frequent inspections and advanced leak detection methods, ensuring timely repairs of detected leaks. The province's venting regulations are stringent, requiring operators to report venting activities comprehensively and minimize venting through the use of flaring or capture systems.

British Columbia's regulatory framework, managed by the BC Oil and Gas Commission (BCOGC) and guided by the Environmental Management Act, mandates the use of BACT for managing hydrocarbon emissions during various stages of petroleum extraction, processing, storage, and transportation. British Columbia's regulations include detailed measures for controlling flowback emissions during HF, requiring vapor recovery units and other effective technologies. The province's LDAR programs involve regular inspections, use of approved detection methods, and prompt repairs, while stringent venting regulations ensure minimal release of VOCs through comprehensive reporting and the use of flaring or gas capture systems.

The provincial regulations in Alberta, Saskatchewan, and British Columbia ensure effective management of VOC emissions, demonstrating a commitment to maintaining high environmental standards. The comprehensive and stringent measures in place across these provinces justify their exemptions from certain federal VOC regulations, recognizing the strength and efficacy of their respective regulatory frameworks.

The federal "Volatile Organic Compound Concentration Limits for Certain Product Regulations" (SOR/2021-268) also establish maximum allowable concentrations of VOCs in specified consumer and commercial products to reduce emissions and protect human health. These regulations target products including petrochemicals, paints, coatings, adhesives, sealants, and cleaning products, that can be significant sources of VOC emissions. By creating stringent concentration limits, the regulations are designed

Order Declaring that the Provisions of the Regulations Respecting Reduction in the Release of Methane and Certain Volatile Organic Compounds (Upstream Oil and Gas Sector) Do Not Apply in Saskatchewan (justice.gc.ca).

101. Order Declaring that the Provisions of the Reduction in the Release of Volatile Organic Compounds Regulations (Petroleum Sector) Do Not Apply in British Columbia (SOR/2020-60), Order Declaring that the Provisions of the Regulations Respecting Reduction in the Release of Methane and Certain Volatile Organic Compounds (Upstream Oil and Gas Sector) Do Not Apply in British Columbia (justice.gc.ca).

to reduce the volume of VOCs released into the atmosphere, decrease ground-level ozone and smog, improve air quality, and reduce the health risks from exposure to VOCs.

6 CONCLUSION

The Federal Methane Regulations are further reducing the volume of methane that is released into the atmosphere from equipment leaks, venting at facilities and from recently drilled oil and gas wells. Similarly, in the case of VOCs, the Reduction in the Release of Volatile Organic Compoounds Regulations (Petroleum Sector) are designed to reduce the volume of VOC emissions.

Since January 1, 2020, facility operators have implemented LDAR programs to reduce emissions from equipment leaks and venting. The Federal Methane Regulations require timely implementation of LDAR programs within a specified time period at facilities, along with three annual equipment inspections. Other provisions are being phased in to allow facility operators to budget for equipment upgrades and replacement to prevent methane emissions. The Federal Methane Regulations create a cap on the volume of emissions that can be vented from facilities. There is a maximum venting limit from larger oil and gas facilities of 250 m^3 of methane per month, or a cumulative annual total of 3,000 m^3. ECCC now has the technical capability to detect and measure the volume of emissions from facilities to enforce new venting limits. To comply with the venting limits, operators have two basic options. The preferred option is to capture and use otherwise wasted methane for beneficial purposes, such as facility heating or generating electricity. A second, less desirable option is more efficient combustion (flaring) of natural gas that results in a smaller volume of emissions than venting. The Federal Methane Regulations prohibit venting at newly drilled oil and gas well sites. The natural gas is to be captured and used for a beneficial purpose such as electricity generation or facility heating.

As the federal government has concluded that Alberta and British Columbia have adopted equivalent MERRs, oil and gas operators in those provinces do not have to satisfy the federal regulations as well. However, in the other significant, western Canadian hydrocarbon-producing province of Saskatchewan, operators must satisfy the Federal Methane regulations, as there is no equivalency agreement. In the most recent AER enforcement action in 2024, Tallahassee was fined CAD 191,855 by the AER for failing to report methane emissions. As discussed above, the stricter Federal and Alberta regulations to reduce equipment methane leaks and the volume of vented methane combined with more frequent site inspections and enforcement actions have resulted in a significant reduction in methane emissions. The reformed regulations are based on a sound environmental and economic foundation.

CHAPTER 14

China

Yuanyuan Zhang & Lei Ding

1 INTRODUCTION

Natural gas flaring primarily occurs during the extraction process in oil and natural gas fields, where associated natural gas that is not efficiently captured is flared or vented into the atmosphere due to inadequate facilities, outdated technology, or economic considerations. It not only causes energy waste but also releases large quantities of greenhouse gases such as methane and carbon dioxide which contribute to global climate change. Furthermore, the combustion of natural gas can release hazardous substances such as sulfides and particulate matter, further deteriorating air quality and posing threats to public health.

According to the World Bank's Global Gas Flaring Tracker, China, as a major energy consumer and producer, ranked 11th in the world in terms of gas flaring volume and intensity in 2023. It is worth noting that China's gas flaring volume and intensity have declined for three consecutive years since 2021.[1] However, more efforts are still needed to achieve the ultimate goal of eliminating gas flaring. Therefore, effective management of gas flaring is crucial to strengthening China's environmental protection and energy efficiency and mitigating global climate change.

Against this backdrop, the chapter delves into the issue of natural gas flaring in China, aiming to examine the applicable legal framework scattered in various statutes, regulations, policy documents, and technological standards. The objective is to scrutinize the extent to which this fragmented legal landscape addresses the gravity of the problem. This chapter is structured as follows. Section 2 provides a detailed overview of the current state of natural gas flaring in China, highlighting key data and trends. It also introduces key actors pertinent to natural gas flaring issues, including

1. "Global Gas Flaring Data" (*World Bank*) https://www.worldbank.org/en/programs/gasflaringreduction/global-flaring-data accessed September 9, 2024.

both oil and gas producers and regulatory agencies. In section 3, the chapter draws a comprehensive picture of the current legal framework applicable to natural gas flaring in China, which is composed of legal documents of different levels of authority and in different fields. Afterward, section 4 points out several key issues, namely, the major regulatory challenges related to natural gas flaring in China, and section 5 comes up with recommendations to address these challenges. Furthermore, section 6 lists the lessons that can be taken from China's practice, and section 7 includes conclusions.

2 NATURAL GAS FLARING IN CHINA

2.1 Natural Gas Flaring as an Ongoing Problem in China

China possesses abundant oil and gas resources with immense development potential. According to the *China Mineral Resources Report (2023)* released by the Ministry of Natural Resources, China's oil reserves amounted to 3.806 billion tons and natural gas reserves amounted to 6,569.012 billion cubic meters as of the end of 2022.[2] To enhance supply security, China has been intensifying its exploration and development efforts, which inevitably raises concerns related to natural gas flaring. In 2023, China's crude oil production reached 208 million tons, an increase of more than 3 million tons compared to last year. Meanwhile, China's natural gas production reached 230 billion cubic meters, marking a 4% year-on-year growth and sustaining the upward trend of a 10 billion cubic meter increment in production for the seventh consecutive year.[3]

At present, oil and gas production is inevitably accompanied by natural gas flaring. Harsh natural environmental conditions, remote geographical locations, and imperfect infrastructure may exacerbate the severity of natural gas flaring.[4] As of 2023, China's natural gas flaring intensity is 1.6 cubic meters per barrel (m^3/bbl), and the flaring volume is 2.4 billion cubic meters (bcm). In addition, natural gas flaring is concentrated in the Tarim Basin and Junggar Basin in western China, as well as oil and gas fields in Xinjiang, Inner Mongolia, Sichuan, and Northeast China.[5]

Meanwhile, China is actively exploring effective solutions to the problem of natural gas flaring in major oilfields. Enterprises such as the Changqing Oilfield Sulig Natural Gas Processing Plant and Qinghai Oilfield are making significant progress in optimizing natural gas flaring and venting technologies.[6] A prominent example is the

2. "China's Natural Gas Production Has Increased by over 10 billion Cubic Meters for Six Consecutive Years" (*China Petroleum Enterprises Association*, November 6, 2023) http://www.zgsyqx.com/list.asp?id=11738 accessed September 9, 2024.
3. "China's Oil and Gas Production Equivalent to Exceed 390 Million Tonnes by 2023" (*Xinhua News Agency*, January 9, 2024) https://www.gov.cn/lianbo/bumen/202401/content_6925077.htm accessed September 9, 2024.
4. "How Far Is the Road to Ending Natural Gas 'Venting and Flaring'?" (*China Petroleum News*, November 27, 2019) https://www.in-en.com/article/html/energy-2283704.shtml accessed September 9, 2024.
5. "Global Gas Flaring Data" (*World Bank*) https://www.worldbank.org/en/programs/gasflaringreduction/global-flaring-data accessed September 9, 2024.
6. Bai Hua, Xiao Yaxi and Xiao Xin, "Prospects for Eliminating Global Natural Gas Flaring Removal are Promising" (2021) 1 *Sinopec* 69-72.

Changqing Oilfield, which produces 6,098,500 tons of oil and gas equivalent annually.[7] Changqing Oil Extraction Plant No. 2 has established an integrated process flow from wellhead to light hydrocarbon recovery, realizing the systematic pathway of "gas collection at the wellhead under fixed pressure, oil and gas distribution at transfer stations, three-phase separation at joint stations, light hydrocarbon recovery and treatment, and gas power generation."[8] Simultaneously, Oil Production Plant No. 4 has developed a gas supply pipeline network characterized by "inter-station cascading and regional interoperability," achieving a 30% associated gas recycling rate and reducing carbon dioxide emissions by 260,000 tons annually.[9] Additionally, the Ninth Oil Production Plant has increased the associated gas recovery rate to 97% through an advanced gas gathering and supply technology system.[10] The Twelfth Oil Extraction Plant has implemented digital monitoring throughout the entire process of "production, treatment, and sales" by establishing a comprehensive utilization platform for associated gas, achieving a 100% comprehensive utilization rate. Annually, it treats 150 million cubic meters of associated gas, reducing carbon dioxide emissions by over 300,000 tons.[11]

Moreover, the associated gas treatment station of Xinjiang Oilfield, which is the largest one in Northwest China, processes 2 million cubic meters of natural gas per day.[12] Concurrently, researchers at Xinjiang Oilfield have discovered that a hydrothermal cracking reaction can occur between crude oil and water, producing carbon dioxide, methane, and other associated gases. The higher the temperature, the greater the production of associated gas. This marks the first instance in the history of China's ultra-thick oil development where substantial amounts of natural gas and carbon dioxide have been identified in the associated gas resources of ultra-thick oil.[13]

7. "Just Now! Good News from China's No. 1 Oil and Gas Field!" (*China Petroleum News,* December 1, 2023) https://baijiahao.baidu.com/s?id=1784012401409662594&wfr=spider&for=pc accessed September 9, 2024.
8. "Changqing Oilfield Companion Gas 'Waste to Treasure' Promotes Circular Economy and Guards Blue Water and Blue Sky" (*China News,* August 23, 2019) https://baijiahao.baidu.com/s?id=1642635770089117305&wfr=spider& for=pc accessed September 9, 2024.
9. "Changqing Oilfield Oil Extraction Plant No. 4: Comprehensive Utilization of Petroleum Associated Gas Lets Circular Economy 'Turn' Up" (*Northwest Information News,* April 7, 2023) https://m.163.com/dy/article/I1NASLJ50550A3NK.html accessed September 9, 2024.
10. "Changqing Oilfield Oil Extraction Plant No. 9 Companion Gas 'Waste to Treasure' Boosts Green Circular Economy Development" (*Shaanxi China,* June 29, 2023) https://www.shx.chinanews.com.cn/news/2023/0629/92677.html accessed September 9, 2024.
11. "Changqing Oilfield Oil Extraction Twelve Plant Comprehensive Utilization of Associated Gas Steps into a New Stage of High-Quality Development" (*Shaanxi Sunshine,* January 24, 2024) https://baijiahao.baidu.com/s?id=1788937178538681251&wfr=spider&for=pc accessed September 9, 2024.
12. "Northwest's Largest Associated Gas Treatment Station Runs at Full Capacity to Safeguard Industrial Production in Northern Xinjiang" (*Xinjiang Net,* November 17, 2023) https://finance.sina.com.cn/jjxw/2023-11-18/doc-imzuyake5321106.shtml accessed September 9, 2024.
13. "China's First Integrated Resource Utilization Project of Associated Gas from Ultra-Thick Oil Mining Successfully Put into Production" (*China News,* December 20, 2023) https://m.chinanews.com/wap/detail/chs/zw/5826380hcvzuxudf.shtml accessed September 9, 2024.

2.2 Oil and Gas Producers

China's national oil companies (NOCs) are the country's leading producers of natural gas. Among them, China National Petroleum Corporation (CNPC) is the largest oil and gas producer in China, responsible for more than 52% of China's oil and more than 60% of its natural gas production.[14] China National Offshore Oil Corporation (CNOOC) is China's largest offshore crude oil and natural gas producer,[15] and China Petroleum & Chemical Corporation (Sinopec) is the largest supplier of refined oil products and petrochemicals and the second largest oil and gas producer in China.[16] According to the satellite statistics by the U.S. Environmental Protection Agency in 2021, CNPC had a very low flaring intensity of 1%, which was one of the lowest flaring intensities of any NOC, thanks to its significant investment in the onshore transmission infrastructure that delivers associated gas, thereby eliminating the need for routine flaring. In contrast, CNOOC faced a much greater challenge in utilizing associated gas with a flaring intensity of 17%.[17]

In addition, these NOCs have taken collective actions to address natural gas flaring, such as forming the China Oil & Gas Methane Control and Emission Control Alliance. The Alliance was jointly initiated by PetroChina, Sinopec and CNOOC, together with PipeChina, Beijing Gas, China Resources Gas, and ENN Energy. It is dedicated to the control and reduction of methane emissions across the entire industrial chain, covering oil and gas production, storage and distribution. In particular, the Alliance draws attention to strengthening the recycling and utilization of vented gas during exploration and exploitation.[18]

Additionally, a pivotal alteration regarding the qualification criteria for oil and gas producers stemmed from the issuance of the *Opinions on Several Matters Concerning Promoting the Reform of Mineral Resource Management (Trial)* by the Ministry of Natural Resources in December 2019, which was replaced by the *Opinions on Several Matters Concerning Deepening the Reform of Mineral Resource Management* issued in July 2023. The two Opinions represent a fresh era of complete liberalization in China's oil and gas exploration and exploitation sector. Specifically, they qualify both domestic private and foreign energy companies registered in China, with a minimum net asset of RMB 300 million, to acquire oil and gas mining rights. Furthermore, these companies

14. "Petroleum Practices for a Stable and Secure Energy Bowl" (*China Petroleum News*, July 19, 2023) https://baijiahao.baidu.com/s?id=1771837089110494231&wfr=spider&for=pc accessed September 9, 2024.
15. "China National Offshore Oil Corporation" (*State-owned Assets Supervision and Administration Commission of State Council*, October 20, 2016) https://www.yidaiyilu.gov.cn/p/1932.html accessed September 9, 2024.
16. "Company Profile" (*China Petroleum & Chemical Corporation*) http://www.sinopecgroup.com/group/000/000/041/41703.shtml accessed September 9, 2024.
17. "How to Solve the Natural Gas Flaring Problem?" (*Environmental Defense Fund*) https://business.edf.org/wp-content/blogs.dir/90/files/How-to-Fix-Flaring_CN.pdf accessed September 9, 2024.
18. "China Oil and Gas Methane Alliance Was Inaugurated" (*CNPC*) https://www.cnpc.com.cn/en/nr2021/202105/98242b1b731e48a5bdd21ca711243fa7.shtml.

must adhere to safety and environmental protection standards and possess the requisite technical expertise. In essence, NOCs are no longer the sole participants in oil and gas production responsible for addressing natural gas flaring. It is yet to be observed how the involvement of private and foreign energy companies will shape the enforcement of regulations and policies pertaining to natural gas flaring.

3 LEGAL FRAMEWORK

3.1 Legislation

3.1.1 Legislation on Environmental Protection

The *Air Pollution Prevention and Control Law*, first enacted in 1987 and revised four times, most recently in 2018, serves as a cornerstone in safeguarding the atmospheric environment in China. This comprehensive legislation outlines standards for atmospheric environment quality, air pollutant emissions, and total control indicators. It also lays out specific requirements for formulating prevention and control plans, ensuring a thorough approach to tackling air pollution. The Law clarifies the supervisory and managerial roles of governments at all levels and their environmental protection departments, alongside the responsibilities and obligations of enterprises, institutions, and other production operators. It introduces prevention and control measures, tailored to address air pollution issues across various sectors. Additionally, the Law outlines measures for collaborative prevention and control in key areas, together with a mechanism for resolving air pollution disputes across administrative regions. Lastly, it stipulates requirements for early warning, emergency response, and post-event assessment of heavily polluted weather, and clarifies legal responsibilities and penalties for violations of relevant legal provisions.

The *Atmospheric Pollution Prevention and Control Law* primarily focuses on regulating the emission of pollutants such as particulate matter, sulfur dioxide, nitrogen oxides, volatile organic compounds, and ammonia. However, it also addresses natural gas flaring as part of its industrial pollution prevention and control framework. Article 49 specifically stipulates that combustible gases generated from industrial processes, garbage landfills, or other activities must be recycled or, if not feasible, be treated for pollution prevention and control. Moreover, if the recycling devices malfunction, they must be repaired or replaced promptly. In exceptional cases where it is necessary to discharge combustible gas due to equipment malfunction, the discharged combustible gas shall be fully burned or other measures for control over the discharge of atmospheric pollutants shall be taken. In addition, the situation shall be reported to the local competent department of ecology and environment, and the devices shall be repaired or updated as required within the prescribed time. In case of violating these requirements, the competent department of ecology and environment of the people's government at or above the county level shall order the operator to make a correction, impose a fine of not less than CNY 20,000 but not more than CNY 200,000, and, if it refuses to make a correction, order it to stop production for rectifications.[19]

3.1.2 Energy Law

The *Energy Law of the People's Republic of China,* currently in its drafting phase, stands as a comprehensive, fundamental, and overarching legal framework in the energy sector. Commencing its legislative journey in 2006, the Energy Law has progressed with the initial draft released for comment in December 2007 and a subsequent iteration in 2020.[20] On April 23, 2024, the Ninth Meeting of the Standing Committee of the 14th National People's Congress reviewed the Draft of Energy Law and announced it to the public for comment from April 26 to May 25.

This Draft encompasses nine chapters and sixty-nine articles, aiming to enhance the energy planning system, optimize the energy development and utilization framework, bolster the energy market system, strengthen energy reserve and emergency response mechanisms, foster energy science and technology innovation, and intensify oversight and administration. Specifically, Article 25 mandates the government to adopt diverse measures to intensify the exploration and exploitation of oil and natural gas resources, bolster reserves, and increase production in order to enhance domestic supply security for oil and natural gas. Article 31, however, stipulates that all parties involved in energy development and utilization must adhere to laws and regulations pertaining to environmental protection, production safety, and occupational health, minimizing pollutant and greenhouse gas emissions, safeguarding the environment, and preventing and mitigating production safety incidents and occupational hazards.

3.2 Policy Documents

The *Plan for Modern Energy System during the 14th Five-year Period* was jointly issued and implemented by the National Development and Reform Commission (NDRC) and the National Energy Administration (NEA) in March 2022. The *Plan for Modern Energy System during the 14th Five-year Period* was compiled based on the *Outline of the 14th Five-Year Plan (2021-2025) for National Economic and Social Development and Vision 2035 of the People's Republic of China.* It outlines the country's energy development policy, key objectives, and task measures, serving as the overarching blueprint and action plan for accelerating the construction of a modern energy system and fostering high-quality energy development during this five-year period. Notably, the Plan underscores the green and low-carbon transformation of the energy industry. To

19. *See Atmospheric Pollution Prevention and Control Law,* Art. 108.
20. Qin Yu, Du Lijing and Li Yunhan, "A Brief Comment on the Exposure Draft of the Energy Law" (*Junhe,* May 12, 2020) https://www.junhe.com/law-reviews/1196 accessed September 9, 2024.

reduce the carbon footprint of this sector, there is a specific focus on promoting carbon emission reductions in the development and production of fossil energy, including enhancing the recovery and utilization of methane in oil and gas fields.[21]

In November 2023, the Ministry of Ecology and Environment, alongside other authorities, released the *Action Plan for Methane Emission Control*, which is a department working document. This plan is vital to advancing China's high-quality development and fostering a harmonious approach to pollution and carbon reduction. It signifies China's autonomous initiative to actively tackle climate change and contribute positively to global climate governance.[22] One pivotal task outlined in the Action Plan is to control methane emissions in the energy sector, including the gradual reduction of traditional flaring practice in oil and gas systems. Specifically, it calls for optimizing the construction and management of ground projects in oil and gas fields, aiming to minimize the amount of natural gas burned in flaring systems. Furthermore, newly established oil and gas operational projects must undergo scientific planning and design, with a focus on gradually phasing out traditional flaring practice while ensuring workplace safety.[23]

The *Catalogue for Guiding Industry Restructuring (2024 Version)*, which is a department regulation, was formulated by NDRC in conjunction with relevant authorities and came into force in February 2024. It consists of three categories, namely, encouragement, restriction, and elimination. The encouragement category highlights basic, strategic, and forward-looking key fields, prioritizing areas which the market mechanism struggles to effectively address, require the government to play a guiding role, and hold significant influence on industrial development. Encouraged investment projects are to be reviewed, approved, or registered in accordance with the state's investment administration regulations. Financial institutions are encouraged to extend credit support to these projects, adhering to market-oriented principles. Additionally, other preferential policies for encouraged investments shall be implemented in line with the relevant regulations issued by the state.[24] The encouraged areas within the oil and gas sector include comprehensive utilization of associated resources, as well as the development and application of technology and equipment for automated monitoring and recovery of volatilized or vented oil and natural gas.[25]

21. *See Plan for Modern Energy System during the 14th Five-year Period,* Art. 4.11.
22. "The Person in Charge of the Department of Climate Change Response of the Ministry of Ecology and Environment Answered Reporters' Questions on Issues Related to the Action Programme for Methane Emission Control" (*Ministry of Ecology and Environment,* November 9, 2023) https://www.mee.gov.cn/ywdt/zbft/202311/t20231109_1055600.shtml accessed September 9, 2024.
23. "Action Plan for Methane Emission Control" (*Ministry of Ecology and Environment,* November 7, 2023) https://www.gov.cn/zhengce/zhengceku/202311/content_6914109.htm accessed September 9, 2024.
24. "Catalogue for Guiding Industry Restructuring (2024 Version)" (*Development and Reform Commission,* December 27, 2023) https://www.gov.cn/zhengce/202401/content_6924187.htm accessed September 9, 2024.
25. *Ibid.*, pp. 20-1.

3.3 Standards

The *Technical Policy for Pollution Prevention and Control in Oil and Gas Extraction Industry* issued by the Ministry of Ecology and Environment in 2012 belongs to ecological and environmental standards.[26] It is a guidance document applicable to onshore oil and gas extraction industries, serving as a reference for relevant units in management, design, construction, production, scientific research, etc. According to it, during the development process, it is imperative to recycle associated gas to minimize greenhouse gas emissions, aiming for a recovery and utilization rate of over 80%. And in the absence of recycling capabilities, the gas must be completely combusted. Similarly, natural gas vented from stations must undergo thorough combustion. Moreover, it is crucial that combustion and venting facilities are located in areas that do not intersect with bird migration routes.[27]

The *Emission Standard for Air Pollutants for Onshore Oil and Gas Exploitation and Production Industry* (GB39728-2020),[28] jointly issued by the Ministry of Ecology and Environment and the State Administration for Market Regulation, is China's first air pollution emission standard for the oil and gas industry, classified as a mandatory national standard.[29] Newly built enterprises were required to comply with this standard for air pollutant emission control from January 2021, while existing enterprises were required to do so from January 2023. The standard stipulates the requirements for controlling, monitoring, managing and supervising air pollutant emissions from onshore oil and gas extraction industries, and proposes requirements for the coordinated control of methane emissions. It also refers to natural gas flaring:

> 5.7.3 Vented natural gas in oil and gas fields shall be recovered as much as possible. For natural gas that cannot be recovered or is difficult to recover, it shall be treated by combustion before being vented; if combustion is not possible, it needs to be filed with the ecological and environmental authorities.
>
> 5.7.4 The flare system of oil and gas centralized processing stations and natural gas processing plants shall comply with the following regulations:
> a) Take measures to recover the liquid discharged into the flare system;
> b) VOCs and natural gas entering the flare should be able to be ignited in time and fully burned;
> c) Continuously monitor the working status of the torch and its ignition facilities (flare gas flow, torch flame temperature, fire gas flow, fire temperature, etc.), prepare monitoring records and keep them for at least 3 years.

26. Available at: https://www.mee.gov.cn/ywgz/fgbz/bz/bzwb/wrfzjszc/201203/t20120319_224789.shtml accessed September 9, 2024.
27. *Technical Policy for Pollution Prevention and Control in Oil and Gas Extraction Industry*, Art. 3.4.
28. Available at: https://www.mee.gov.cn/ywgz/fgbz/bz/bzwb/dqhjbh/dqgdwrywrwpfbz/202012/W020201225551948738018.pdf accessed September 9, 2024.
29. "Emission Standards for Air Pollutants from Onshore Oil Extraction Released" (*China Industry Newspaper Digital Newspaper*, February 2, 2021) http://dzb.cinn.cn/shtml/zggyb/20210202/104647.shtml accessed September 9, 2024.

4 KEY ISSUES

In China, the issue of natural gas flaring is addressed through a combination of regulations on environmental protection, energy development and industrial policy, with the first one playing a leading role. However, there exist significant shortcomings in addressing the issue effectively under the present legal framework. The latest Draft of China's Energy Law, for instance, only briefly mentions minimizing greenhouse gas emissions in energy development and utilization, without explicitly targeting natural gas flaring. Similarly, the *Plan for Modern Energy System during the 14th Five-Year Plan Period* emphasizes enhancing the recovery and utilization of methane in oil and gas fields, but it does not set specific targets or requirements for reducing flaring practice. China's industrial policy, outlined in the *Catalogue for Guiding Industry Restructuring (2024 Version)*, supports the development of relevant industrial areas, such as the comprehensive utilization of associated resources in the oil and gas sector, but it lacks direct measures to reduce the flaring practice.

In contrast, environmental regulations pertaining to pollution prevention and control offer a more holistic approach to regulating natural gas flaring. However, there are still significant areas for refinement. Primarily, there is a lack of a definitive timeline for the elimination of natural gas flaring. Instead, the practice remains permissible if recycling is deemed infeasible according to the *Atmospheric Pollution Prevention and Control Law*. Additionally, oil and gas producers are only mandated to promote the incremental reduction of traditional flaring practice under the *Action Plan for Methane Emission Control*. Furthermore, while the two standards outlined in section III.C of the chapter provide more detailed rules, the *Technical Policy for Pollution Prevention and Control in the Oil and Gas Extraction Industry* merely serves as a reference. The targeted recovery and utilization rate of associated gas, though exceeding 80%, still falls short of the goal of complete elimination. Simultaneously, the *Emission Standard for Air Pollutants for Onshore Oil and Gas Exploitation and Production Industry* fails to address the issue of recovery and utilization rates. It simply requires the maximum possible recovery of vented natural gas and the combustion of gas that cannot be recovered or is difficult to recover.

5 RECOMMENDATIONS

To effectively address gas flaring and emissions, primary legislation should clearly provide for the management of associated gas to eliminate flaring. Subordinate legal documents should clearly authorize regulators to enforce the elimination of gas flaring through technical standards, regular records, reports, and on-site inspections. In particular, China should develop and enforce stricter pollution prevention and control standards for the oil and gas industry, set specific targets for the recovery and utilization of associated gas, and impose severe penalties on oil and gas producers that fail to meet the targets. In addition, preferential policies, including financial incentives, should be provided to develop the utilization of associated gas. In addition, China must set specific timetables and deadlines to phase out gas flaring, making the elimination of flaring a mandatory task in the coming years.

It is also essential for the government to clearly define the roles and responsibilities of regulatory bodies to avoid overlapping or conflicting mandates. When regulatory functions are distributed among different authorities—such as oil and gas, environment, and finance—processes should be established to ensure cooperation in cross-cutting areas like flaring permit issuance or oil field development approvals. The regulatory framework must consider the capabilities and resources of enforcement agencies, ensuring they are sufficiently staffed and funded to perform effective monitoring and enforcement. Enhancing training programs and capacity-building initiatives to improve the professional skills of regulatory personnel is also crucial. Additionally, creating an inter-agency information-sharing platform can promote better collaboration and consistency in policy implementation.[30]

At last, Chinese NOCs should consider joining the Zero Routine Flaring by 2030 (ZRF) Initiative to make commitments on phrasing out natural gas flaring by 2030 and taking the initiative to release data and reports on its natural gas faring practice.

6 LESSONS TO BE LEARNT FROM CHINA

China is committed to reducing greenhouse gas emissions and has made initial achievements in terms of controlling natural gas flaring. In the process, NOCs have played a leading role. Taking the CNOOC's practice at offshore oil fields on Weizhou Island as an example, a notable practice is the implementation of advanced waste gas treatment technologies, such as the first offshore membrane decarbonization demonstration project. This project processes associated gas for use as fuel while sequestering separated carbon dioxide through pressurized injection into geological formations, significantly reducing carbon emissions and preventing resource wastage. Additionally, the construction of extensive pipeline networks, like the 70-kilometer underwater pipeline linking the Weizhou terminal to Beihai, facilitates the transport of associated gas to onshore facilities for utilization in power generation and heating, thereby minimizing the need for flaring. In addition, CNOOC has also proposed to completely eliminate flares above 10,000 cubic meters per day by 2025, and promote the gradual realization of "zero flaring," demonstrating CNOOC's determination to effectively solve the problem of natural gas flaring.[31]

30. "How to Solve the Natural Gas Flaring Problem?" (*Environmental Defense Fund*) https://business.edf.org/wp-content/blogs.dir/90/files/How-to-Fix-Flaring_CN.pdf accessed September 9, 2024.
31. "What Is the Weizhou Island Netflame Torch? It's a Global Phenomenon of Associated Gas Venting and Burning" (*Jiu Pai News*, August 31, 2023) https://baijiahao.baidu.com/s?id=1775701162926102722&wfr=spider&for=pc accessed September 9, 2024.

7 CONCLUSIONS

As China liberalizes its oil and gas exploration and exploitation sector and strives to enhance domestic oil and gas supply, addressing the challenge of natural gas flaring becomes increasingly complex and urgent. While NOCs have made considerable efforts in reducing natural gas flaring, achieving complete elimination remains a distant goal. At the regulatory level, although China is committed to controlling methane emissions, the current legal framework lacks specific requirements for eliminating natural gas flaring. Instead, it mandates the recovery of associated natural gas in oil and gas fields to the greatest extent possible and a gradual phasing out of flaring, indicating a less stringent approach. Given the gravity of the issue, it is imperative for China to take urgent and decisive actions to formulate precise plans for the elimination of natural gas flaring. This will require a combination of stronger regulatory measures, technological advancements, sustained commitment from all stakeholders, and participation in international collaboration to achieve the desired results. A comprehensive approach that integrates legal reform, enhanced enforcement, technological innovation, effective incentives, and robust data transparency is essential for achieving sustainable and environmentally responsible management of natural gas resources.[32]

32. "China's Natural Gas Development Situation and Outlook" (*Oil Business News,* March 16, 2023) http://center.cnpc.com.cn/sysb/system/2023/03/15/030095721.shtml accessed September 9, 2024.

CHAPTER 15
Guyana

Shereece Smith

1 INTRODUCTION

The practice of oil and gas flaring in Guyana has evolved significantly from its rudimentary beginnings to the complexities of modern regulatory frameworks. Historically, flaring was often viewed as an inevitable byproduct of oil extraction, with little regard for its environmental consequences. Early industrial activities in Guyana were characterized by a lack of technological sophistication and regulatory oversight, resulting in extensive flaring as companies prioritized production over environmental stewardship. This historical context set the stage for contemporary challenges faced by the nation as it seeks to balance economic growth with environmental protection.

In recent years, Guyana has emerged as a significant player in the global energy sector following substantial offshore oil discoveries. The current landscape is marked by heightened scrutiny regarding environmental practices, particularly concerning flaring, which poses serious risks to air quality and contributes to greenhouse gas emissions. The government has begun implementing stricter regulations aimed at minimizing flaring volumes while promoting responsible resource management. However, these efforts are complicated by the rapid pace of development and investment from multinational corporations eager to exploit Guyana's resources.

The growing petroleum production industry in Guyana has had a positive impact on the country's economic outlook, but it is also expected to lead to an increase in greenhouse gas emissions. Analysis of the greenhouse gas emissions from Guyana's emerging petroleum sector indicates that fugitive emissions, primarily from flaring and venting during well testing and conventional petroleum production, are the largest contributors. Projections show that annual greenhouse gas emissions from petroleum production are estimated to reach 9,034, 13,397, and 20,516 kilotons of carbon dioxide equivalent (CO2e) by 2025, 2027, and 2030, respectively.[1]

When considering emissions from oil and gas production alongside potential scenarios for growth in Guyana's energy sector, total annual greenhouse gas emissions could range from 4,445 kilotons of CO2e in 2025 to a peak of 24,888 kilotons of CO2e in 2030 across different conditions. In addition, the highest total greenhouse gas emissions for 2025 are projected to be 11,015 kilotons of CO2e, with a sequestration rate of 154,060 kilotons of CO_2 (7%).[2]

Concerns about routine gas flaring during oil extraction have been raised, with Exxon Mobil accused of surpassing allowable limits and inadequately utilizing the gas, leading to wasted resources and increased greenhouse gas emissions. There have been challenges in enforcing regulations, with criticisms that the initial contract with Exxon Mobil was too lenient on flaring, potentially undermining Guyana's environmental sustainability efforts. It is recommended that Guyana reviews, updates, and implements policies to mitigate greenhouse gas emissions and counterbalance unavoidable ones in alignment with its commitments to the UNFCCC[3] and the Paris Accord, while simultaneously enhancing the societal and economic well-being of its populace.

2 CONTEXT OF NATURAL GAS FLARING REGULATION IN GUYANA

"Flaring" denotes emissions from all continuous and emergency flare systems. Fugitive emissions encompass both deliberate and accidental releases during the extraction, processing, storage, and transportation of fuel until its eventual consumption. They arise from activities such as extracting, converting, and moving primary energy sources, like leaks in natural gas systems and methane emissions when flaring during oil and gas operations. Key contributors to fugitive emissions in oil and gas operations include equipment leaks, evaporative losses, venting, flaring, incineration, and unintended discharges.

The government of Guyana has recognized the need to regulate natural gas flaring in order to minimize environmental impacts and ensure that the country's natural resources are utilized in a sustainable manner. Furthermore, Guyana is a signatory to the Paris Agreement and has committed to reducing its greenhouse gas emissions, making it important for the country to monitor and control flaring activities.

In Guyana, oil and gas flaring is regulated by the Environmental Protection Agency (EPA) under the Environmental Protection Act. The EPA sets limits on the amount of gas that can be flared during oil and gas production activities. Operators are required to submit flare management plans and report regularly on their flaring activities to ensure compliance with these regulations. Additionally, the government of

1. Bynoe P, Wood S, Simmons D. Greenhouse Gas Emissions from Petroleum Production in Guyana: An Examination of the Implications for the Country's Net Carbon Sink Status. *Science Progress*. 2024, 107(1) https://doi.org/10.1177/00368504231218609.
2. *Ibid.*, 1.
3. United Nations Framework Convention on Climate Change 2021, COP26 Speeches and Statements, Glasgow.

Guyana has adopted the World Bank's guidelines on gas flaring reduction, which aim to minimize the environmental impact of flaring and encourage the reinjection of gas back into the reservoir or its utilization for energy production. Penalties can be imposed on operators who do not comply with these regulations.

The EPA modifies environmental permits to include more specific flare management conditions. For example, the EPA modified the Liza Phase 1 Permit to address flaring and bring it in line with the Payara Permit:

- *Flaring fees*
  The EPA charges a fee for flaring above background levels. For example, the EPA increased the fee from USD 50 per ton of carbon emitted.
- *Start-up flaring*
  The EPA has a 60-day allowance for flaring at start-up, which is stricter than international benchmarks.
- *Partnership with operators*
  The EPA works with operators to ensure zero-routine flaring
  Additionally, Guyana enforces a policy that sets limits on the flaring of natural gas aboard its Floating Production Storage and Offloading (FPSO) vessels. Flaring, which involves burning off excess natural gas to prevent potential explosions, is a common practice in the oil and gas sector. However, Guyana implements specific measures to minimize flaring:
  - Green State Development Strategy (GSDS): The GSDS highlights the importance of establishing mechanisms such as the Natural Resource Fund Act and adopting a medium-term expenditure framework to ensure that oil revenues are managed strategically, transparently, and effectively. This will help to avoid the pitfalls of resource mismanagement and ensure that the benefits of oil revenues are maximized for the long-term sustainable development of the country.
  - Furthermore, the Strategy emphasizes the transition towards lower-cost, renewable, and reliable energy sources to support business operations and address energy access and security concerns. This shift will not only contribute to mitigating the impacts of climate change but also promote sustainable economic growth in Guyana.
  - Additionally, the Strategy calls for more effective and coordinated management of natural resources, including the promotion of sustainable land use practices and the protection of biodiversity. This approach will help to safeguard the environment and ensure the long-term viability of natural resources for future generations.
  - Furthermore, the Strategy underscores the importance of diversifying Guyana's economic base and moving towards higher value-added products to create decent jobs for all. This will help to reduce the country's reliance on a single commodity and build a more resilient and inclusive economy.
  - Lastly, the Strategy emphasizes the need to invest in people, communities, and health and education to ensure that all citizens have access to the

best opportunities to prosper, prepare, and participate in emerging economic opportunities. By prioritizing investments in human capital, the Strategy aims to build a skilled workforce, promote social inclusion, and enhance the overall well-being of the population.
- Natural Resource Fund Act: This legislation was put in place to enhance the transparent and efficient management of oil revenues.

Guyana perused extensive expert studies and national consultations to address climate change challenges and formulated a Low Carbon Development Strategy (LCDS). The LCDS outlines plans for building climate resilience through adaptation actions while striving to reach net zero emissions by 2050 in line with the Paris Agreement. It also includes a Climate Resilience Strategy and Adaptation Plan (CRSAP) as the implementation plan for the climate resilience component. Despite financial constraints, these strategies prioritize actions in key sectors like energy, coastal infrastructure, agriculture, health, and water. The LCDS was originally developed by the People's Progressive Party government but faced interruptions due to a change in government. A new document, the "GSDS," was established in 2019 to continue Guyana's journey towards a low-carbon, climate-resilient path. Both strategies aim to steer Guyana towards sustainable development amidst the urgency of global climate change adaptation and mitigation efforts outlined in the Paris Agreement.

The GSDS outlines key actions aligned with green economy models, focusing on:

- Establishing the Natural Resource Fund Act and adopting a medium-term expenditure framework for transparent management of oil revenues.
- Transitioning to affordable renewable energy sources to enhance energy security and support business activities.
- Improving the coordinated management of natural resources.
- Diversifying Guyana's economy towards higher value-added products to create quality jobs.
- Investing in education, healthcare, and communities to empower citizens for economic participation and prosperity.

It was anticipated that reinvesting a portion of the oil wealth into sustainable policies that directly impact livelihoods would be cost-effective in the long term and align with the Green State Development priorities of social inclusivity and quality job creation. To fully benefit from these efforts, it was argued that investments in legal and regulatory frameworks were also necessary.

After the change in government in 2020, the LCDS was reintroduced and revised as the LCDS 2030. This updated version was officially endorsed by the government as the guiding strategy for Guyana's journey towards low-carbon, climate-resilient growth. The government has already begun implementation of certain aspects of the program.

Despite the widespread agreement on the necessity of a global carbon pricing system, efforts to advance such a system at the international level have been insufficient. The Government of Guyana advocated for the global community, under the guidance of organizations like the UNFCCC, to expedite the development and implementation of this pricing system. Additionally, Guyana supports the idea of discontinuing subsidies for fossil fuel production, particularly in OECD nations where these subsidies are most distorting. By implementing these measures, the aim is to eliminate the least economically rational and most carbon-intensive oil and gas products from the market, paving the way for a transition to more sustainable and efficient energy sources. To further reduce carbon emissions and align with the goals of the Paris Climate Agreement, Guyana introduced additional domestic policies such as imposing taxes on gas flaring.

Globally, gas flaring leads to the emission of over 300 million tonnes of CO2e annually. If this gas was utilized for energy production instead, it could generate enough electricity to meet the entire current annual demand of the African continent. Upon assuming office in 2020, the current Government found a lack of regulations to discourage or prohibit gas flaring. Simultaneously, the industry's initial floating production, storage, and offloading vessel (FPSO) was flaring excessively due to a malfunctioning gas compression system. The Government has taken steps to rectify the past issues concerning the absence of proper regulations and the resulting lack of incentives to prevent excessive flaring. Concurrently, measures have been implemented to discourage all future instances of excessive flaring from new FPSOs.

Several policies have been implemented to restrict routine gas flaring in oil and gas operations, except for essential flare streams needed for safety purposes (e.g., pilot flares). Limited instances of non-routine flaring are allowed only with the approval of the competent authority, the EPA, for specific situations such as well testing, emergencies, maintenance, and restarts.

In addition to these measures, the Government has introduced a unique tax on approved flaring, making it one of the few countries globally to do so. Flaring that has been authorized is now subject to an environmental tax, the amount of which is determined by the Government. As of mid-2022, the tax stands at USD 50 per tonne of carbon, in addition to payments for the actual lost gas.

Guyana has now established one of the strictest anti-flaring policy frameworks worldwide with the implementation of these regulations in 2021 and 2022. In an effort to share Guyana's experiences with other oil-producing nations and to learn from the experiences of others, Guyana will be joining the World Bank's Zero Routine Flaring by 2030 (ZRF) initiative. The ZRF initiative is described by the World Bank as a global coalition showcasing strong environmental stewardship and effective natural resource management. All oil and gas operators in Guyana will be encouraged to support this initiative, recognizing that Guyana's domestic policies and strategies exceed the ZRF's minimum requirements.

3 NATURAL GAS FLARING: THE LEGAL FRAMEWORK IN GUYANA

As a new player in the oil and gas industry, Guyana faces challenges in establishing the necessary policy, legal, and regulatory frameworks to maximize the benefits of oil revenues while minimizing associated risks. The sector has far-reaching effects on the economy, future generations, the environment, and local communities. Poor management of oil resources can result in economic and social costs, hindering sustainable growth and prosperity.

However, by looking at successful examples from resource-rich countries like Australia, Canada, Norway, and others, Guyana can implement good governance practices, invest in public and private institutions, enhance skills and technology, improve revenue management, and adopt sound macroeconomic policies to achieve overall poverty reduction and economic diversification.

The Government of Guyana is committed to following these examples and is focused on building capacity to manage oil and gas resources effectively. They are working towards developing a green economy and knowledge-driven growth industries through the GSDS Vision 2040. This long-term strategy will be supported by a comprehensive implementation plan with clear indicators and targets for accountability.

Technical assistance will play a vital role in achieving the objectives of the GSDS, including sound fiscal and monetary policies, sustainable resource management, and good governance. By enhancing legal and regulatory frameworks, mobilizing international expertise, and strengthening institutions, Guyana aims to lay the foundations for a successful oil and gas sector that contributes to overall growth and prosperity in the country.

Guyana's Zero Flare Policy represents a significant commitment to environmental sustainability and climate change mitigation. This policy aligns with the global initiative known as ZRF, launched by the World Bank, which aims to eliminate routine flaring of natural gas in oil production processes The policy is particularly relevant for Guyana, given its burgeoning oil industry and the potential environmental impacts associated with hydrocarbon extraction. By committing to zero routine flaring, Guyana seeks to minimize greenhouse gas emissions and promote a more sustainable energy landscape.

The implementation of this policy is integral to Guyana's broader LCDS for 2030, which emphasizes economic growth while prioritizing environmental protection. The strategy outlines measures that not only focus on reducing carbon emissions but also aim at harnessing renewable energy sources. By adhering to the Zero Flare Policy, Guyana positions itself as a leader in sustainable development within the Caribbean region and sets an example for other nations grappling with similar challenges. The successful execution of this policy will require collaboration among various stakeholders including government agencies, oil companies, and civil society organizations. Continuous monitoring and transparent reporting mechanisms will be essential in ensuring compliance and assessing the effectiveness of the Zero Flare Policy over time.

The Guyana LCDS outlines the nation's commitment to achieving net zero emissions:

> Guyana will act strategically and responsibly as the sector develops, supporting global energy security while diversifying and decarbonising Guyana's domestic economy and investing in development priorities for all Guyanese, including health, education and low-carbon opportunities. At the same time, the Government will advocate internationally for a strong global carbon price and the removal

of subsidies on fossil fuel—to incentivise the lowest carbon, most cost-effective oil and gas in the global marketplace in line with the goals of the Paris Climate Agreement under which there will be demand for decades to come. In parallel, Guyana will advance a "no flaring" policy, and mandate the use of best technology in the Oil and Gas sector to limit its environmental impact.

The LCDS has outlined a detailed plan for Guyana to transition to clean energy, which includes the early implementation of a natural gas generation facility to replace the current system. This facility will help meet part of Guyana's energy needs as the country works towards a zero-carbon status in the energy sector. The use of natural gas will provide the necessary firm capacity at a lower cost compared to other renewable energy options available in Guyana.

The LCDS aims to increase energy use by five-fold while keeping greenhouse gas emissions relatively stable, which is one of the highest levels of decoupling of economic growth and fossil fuel use in the world. Without changes, consumer costs are likely to remain high, and greenhouse gas emissions are projected to triple by 2027 and continue to rise.

The current government is focusing on decoupling economic growth from fossil fuel dependence by developing low-carbon energy sources such as solar, hydro, wind, biomass, and natural gas. The LCDS outlines a three-phase plan to achieve this goal:

- From 2022 to 2027, electricity demand will triple, primarily met by natural gas and the Amaila Falls Hydropower plant combined with solar power expansion on rural networks.
- From 2027 to 2032, further increases in electricity demand will be met by replacing HFO, expanding wind and solar power, and commissioning a second hydro plant.
- After 2032, new capacity increases will likely come from advanced battery technology enabling solar and wind plants to provide most of the energy while driving down electricity prices.

Therefore, the LCDS developed a comprehensive energy transformation plan that aims to significantly increase energy use while keeping greenhouse gas emissions at a constant level. This plan is not only ambitious but also groundbreaking, as it represents one of the world's highest levels of decoupling economic growth from fossil fuel use for energy.

The plan acknowledges that if the current electricity supply mix remains unchanged, consumer costs will not see a significant reduction. In fact, it is expected that greenhouse gas emissions will triple by 2027 and continue to increase steadily thereafter, posing a significant threat to the environment and long-term sustainability.

In response, the LCDS's energy transformation plan presents a sustainable solution that not only promotes economic growth but also ensures the protection of the environment. By implementing innovative strategies and investing in renewable energy sources, the plan aims to create a more efficient and cost-effective energy system that will benefit both consumers and the planet. With its forward-thinking approach, the LCDS is paving the way toward a more sustainable and prosperous future for all.

In Guyana, the imposition of fines for unauthorized flaring associated gas during oil production is primarily governed by the Environmental Protection Act of 1996. This legislation embodies the Polluter Pays Principle (PPP),[4] which mandates that companies responsible for environmental degradation must bear the costs associated with their actions (Ahamad & Chabrol, 2024).[5] ExxonMobil, operating as Esso Exploration and Production Guyana Limited (EEPGL), has faced significant penalties due to its flaring activities at the Liza Phase One operation in the Stabroek Block. As of December 2021, ExxonMobil had paid approximately USD 930 million in fines for these infractions, with a current penalty rate set at USD 45 per tonne of flared gas.

The regulatory framework governing these fines has evolved to reflect increasing environmental concerns and international best practices. In May 2022, it was announced that EEPGL would face a heightened fine of USD 50 per tonne for carbon monoxide emissions if it continued to breach established flaring limits under its renewed permit. This adjustment signifies Guyana's commitment to stricter enforcement measures aimed at reducing greenhouse gas emissions from oil operations. It was highlighted that adherence to such regulations is crucial not only for compliance but also for safeguarding Guyana's pristine environment from irreversible damage caused by excessive flaring.[6]

Ultimately, while financial penalties serve as a deterrent against non-compliance with environmental standards, they may not fully compensate for the ecological harm inflicted by flaring activities.[7] The effectiveness of these fines hinges on robust enforcement mechanisms and a commitment from oil companies like ExxonMobil to adopt more sustainable operational practices that minimize gas flaring and protect Guyana's natural resources. Moreover, the EPA in Guyana is actively working to enhance monitoring capabilities and ensure compliance through regular inspections and technological advancements that facilitate real-time tracking of flaring activities. To further bolster these efforts, Guyana's government is exploring collaborations with international environmental organizations to enhance regulatory frameworks and share best practices for sustainable resource management.

4 NATURAL GAS FLARING: ISSUES AND CHALLENGES IN GUYANA

One of the main concerns in Guyana's oil and gas industry is the common practice of gas flaring, While this practice is allowed under certain circumstances, Exxon Mobil

---

4. Environmental Protection Act 1996, Part 2, section 4(4)(a) The "polluter pays" principle: the polluter should bear the cost of measures to reduce pollution decided upon by public authorities, to ensure that the environment is in an acceptable state, and should compensate citizens for the harm they suffer from pollution.
5. Ahamad R. ExxonMobil Pays Guyana $930M for Flaring of Gas. 2021, Retrieved from https://guyanachronicle.com/2021/12/24/exxonmobil-pays-guyana-930m-for-flaring-of-gas/.
6. *Ibid.*, 5.
7. Govt. "penalises" Exxon on flaring but country ultimately has to pay—Kaieteur News (kaieteurnewsonline.com).

has been accused of going over the permitted limits and failing to use technologies to capture and utilize the gas. Not only does this waste a valuable resource but it also adds to greenhouse gas emissions and goes against Guyana's efforts towards environmental sustainability.

The EPA of Guyana has faced challenges in enforcing regulations due to concerns that the initial contract with Exxon Mobil was too lenient on flaring. The World Wildlife Fund (WWF)[8] has also raised alarms about routine flaring and its impact on Guyana's environment, noting that Exxon Mobil Guyana Limited (EMGL) has not followed through on its commitment to reducing flaring levels since 2016. The Executives of WWF Guyana[9] have called for accountability, stating that the continued use of flaring disregards the health of the planet and the well-being of the people of Guyana. In response to Exxon's flaring, the EPA imposed fines on the company based on the amount of carbon dioxide emitted, with fines later increasing to USD 50 per ton. In 2022, Exxon paid fines for approximately 279,537.33[10] tonnes of CO2e that were flared.

– Environmental Impacts

Flaring natural gas releases carbon dioxide, black carbon, and other emissions that contribute to global warming and climate change. Since December 2019, ExxonMobil's subsidiary, Esso Exploration and Production Guyana Ltd, has flared over 12 billion cubic feet of "associated gas" from the Liza 1 offshore oil field in Guyana. Despite violating the Liza 1 Environmental Permit, Esso continues to flare up to 18 million cubic feet of gas per day as of March 2021. This amount of gas being flared is more than a day's consumption of natural gas in Germany, a country with a population 107 times larger than Guyana's.

The carbon dioxide emissions from the flaring are equivalent to what Guyana's entire population generates in three months. With 90% of Guyana's population living on the coast, the destruction of reefs and increased global warming could lead to more flooding and damage to the sea defense against rising tides.

The energy wasted from the flared gas is equivalent to the electricity consumption of Guyana for a year. Incomplete flaring of natural gas produces methane, a gas that is 84 times more potent than carbon dioxide in causing climate change. This could result in hotter weather in Guyana and increased overtopping of the seawall protecting the low-lying capital city, coastal villages, and agricultural areas.

– Economic Interests

Some say that the government's focus on oil development is a key part of the country's development plan and that the country needs to produce oil to invest in other sectors. However, others say that the government's rules for flaring favor ExxonMobil at the expense of Guyana's fiscal outlook. Over the long term, continued gas flaring will likely

8. ExxonMobil's continued flaring undercuts Guyana's Low-Carbon interests. (n.d.). WWF. https://www.wwf.org.co/en/?365808/ExxonMobils-Continued-Flaring-Undercuts-Guyanas-Low-Carbon-Interests.
9. *Ibid.*, 8.
10. *Ibid.*

have a severe economic impact on Guyana and neighboring countries. As an example, annual economic losses related to gas flaring are estimated to be more than USD 5 billion in Russia and USD 11 billion in Nigeria.

– Flaring Fines

Some say that the government's fines for flaring are too low and that ExxonMobil has been able to make flaring a cost of doing business. Flaring fines in Guyana, while intended to mitigate environmental damage caused by oil extraction activities, are insufficient in addressing the broader issues surrounding flaring practices. The EPA of Guyana has implemented a fine of USD 30 per tonne of CO_2 equivalent emitted, which is consistent with carbon pricing benchmarks found in developed nations. However, this monetary penalty is grossly inadequate when juxtaposed with the potential social cost of carbon pollution. For instance, estimates from the United States place this cost at approximately USD 51 per tonne.[11] Such discrepancies suggest that the current fines do not reflect the true environmental and societal costs associated with flaring.

Moreover, the cumulative payments made by ExxonMobil for its flaring activities—amounting to around USD 4.5 million—indicate that these penalties do not serve as a significant deterrent against ongoing non-compliance.[12] Given that these fines represent only a fraction of ExxonMobil's operational budget and profit margins, they may be perceived as an acceptable cost of doing business rather than a genuine punitive measure. This situation leads to concerns about whether such fines effectively enforce compliance or inadvertently grant companies like ExxonMobil a "license to pollute"[13] While implementing fines for flaring represents an effort on the part of the EPA to deter and hold companies accountable for their environmental impact, these financial penalties remain insufficient. They fail to align with global standards regarding carbon emissions and do not impose meaningful consequences for environmentally detrimental practices. Consequently, without more stringent regulations and higher penalties reflective of true societal costs, flaring will likely continue unabated in Guyana.

– Zero routine flaring

Guyana's projects are designed to have zero routine flaring, but the government has allowed flaring in emergency situations and during commissioning. Other challenges related to natural gas production include:

11. Wilburg K. Flaring Penalty so Low Guyana Effectively Grants Exxon a Licence to Pollute—CIEL President. https://www.kaieteurnewsonline.com/2021/05/16/flaring-penalty-so-low-guyana-effectively-grants-exxon-a-licence-to-pollute-ciel-president/, May 18, 2021 and https://www.kaieteurnewsonline.com/2021/05/16/flaring-penalty-so-low-guyana-effectively-grants-exxon-a-licence-to-pollute-ciel-president/.
12. "Local Participation in ExxonMobil's Operations Increases by 1,000 This Year" (*Guyana Chronicle*, 2021) https://guyanachronicle.com/2021/12/24/local-participation-in-exxonmobils-operations-increases-by-1000-this-year/ accessed October 25, 2024.
13. *Ibid.*, 11.

- *Air pollution*: Well drilling can produce air pollution.
- *Water contamination:* Natural gas production can produce large amounts of contaminated water.
- *Land clearing*: Laying pipelines to transport natural gas requires clearing land.

One of the main challenges in addressing natural gas flaring in Guyana is the lack of regulation and enforcement. While the government has set targets to reduce flaring, there is a lack of clear guidelines and penalties for companies that continue to flare gas. This has allowed some companies to prioritize oil production over gas conservation, leading to high levels of flaring.

The debate surrounding flaring in Guyana is emblematic of the broader conversation about the country's rapid oil development and its implications for sustainable growth. Proponents argue that the government's focus on oil production is essential for financing other sectors, such as infrastructure, education, and healthcare. The influx of revenue from oil can provide the necessary capital to invest in these critical areas, thereby fostering comprehensive economic development.[14] This perspective posits that without a robust oil sector, Guyana may struggle to diversify its economy effectively.

Conversely, critics contend that the current regulatory framework governing flaring disproportionately benefits ExxonMobil at the expense of Guyana's fiscal health. The lax rules surrounding gas flaring can result in significant environmental degradation and financial loss for the nation. For instance, annual economic losses related to gas flaring have been substantial in other countries; Russia experiences over USD 5 billion in losses annually due to similar practices.[15] Such figures raise concerns about whether Guyana's short-term gains from oil extraction will translate into long-term economic stability or sustainability.

Moreover, continued gas flaring poses severe risks not only to Guyana but also to neighboring countries through shared environmental impacts. As evidenced by Nigeria's staggering USD 11 billion annual losses from gas flaring,[16] unchecked practices can lead to detrimental effects on public health and local economies. Therefore, while oil development may be integral to the current strategy, it is crucial that policymakers prioritize regulatory reforms that mitigate flaring and ensure equitable benefits for all stakeholders involved.

5 RECOMMENDATIONS

A major distress associated with gas flaring is the release of greenhouse gas emissions, particularly carbon dioxide and methane, which contribute to climate change and other environmental issues. The method of deep water oil exploration being used off the Atlantic Coast of Guyana poses significant environmental risks, including potential

14. International Monetary Fund. Guyana: 2022 Article IV Consultation-Press Release; Staff Report; and Statement by the Executive Director for Guyana. 2022, IMF Staff Country Reports 2022/317, International Monetary Fund.
15. *Ibid.*, 8.
16. *Ibid.*

spills that can harm marine life and require extensive cleanup efforts. Proper management of waste generated from the extraction process, such as produced water and excess gas, is crucial to prevent environmental contamination. Given the complexity and range of environmental impacts from oil and gas extraction, careful regulation and management are essential to minimize harm to the environment and public health.

Addressing gaps and creating stricter legal/regulatory frameworks to ensure compliance with environmental standards is crucial in tackling the issue of flaring in Guyana. This involves setting clear guidelines and regulations for oil companies to follow, as well as implementing penalties for non-compliance. By rigorously monitoring and evaluating the activities of these companies, the government can hold them accountable for their environmental impact. Performing independent audits of the operations of oil companies is essential in gaining a comprehensive understanding of their environmental impact. By making this data publicly available, it allows for ongoing analysis and transparency in the industry. This information can also be used to identify areas for improvement and inform policy decisions.

Requiring oil companies to conduct environmental impact assessments and meet corporate social responsibility mandates is vital for ensuring the health and safety of communities and the environment. This includes assessing the potential impacts of their operations, implementing measures to mitigate any negative effects, and engaging with local stakeholders to address their concerns. Focusing on Social and Economic Impact Assessment (SEIA) for sustainable development is key in ensuring that extractive projects benefit the local communities and economy. This involves evaluating the social and economic impacts of these projects and implementing measures to maximize the benefits and minimize any negative consequences.

Creating a systematic, ongoing plan for monitoring and evaluating the impacts of oil and gas operations is necessary for ensuring environmental protection. This can be done by the Guyana EPA through regular inspections and audits. Additionally, implementing rules for carbon emissions and requiring an environmental bond to be paid by oil companies can help incentivize compliance with environmental standards. The World Bank[17] has urged oil and gas companies to speed up efforts to reduce global flare volumes to end routine flaring by 2030. A recent report revealed that global gas flaring has dropped to its lowest level since 2010.

Despite this progress, Guyana continues to struggle with flaring issues, prompting calls from environmentalists for ExxonMobil and the government to take action to reduce pollution. Offshore flaring in Guyana reached a peak of 71.88 Million Standard Cubic Feet in January 2023.[18]

The Global Gas Flaring Tracker Report[19] shows that global gas flaring decreased by 3 % to 139 bcm in 2022 from 144 bcm in 2021. Oil production increased by 5 % to 80

17. World Bank. A Pivotal Moment for Guyana: Realizing the Opportunities: Systematic Country Diagnostic Report.
18. Global Gas Flaring Tracker Report 2023, GGFR available at 2023-Global-Gas-Flaring-Tracker-Report.pdf (worldbank.org) accessed October 25, 2024.
19. *Ibid.*, 18.

million barrels per day in 2022. The report emphasized the importance of countries like Nigeria, Mexico, and the United States in reducing global gas flaring. However, countries like Russia, Iraq, and Nigeria remain the top contributors to flare volumes and global oil production. ExxonMobil faced scrutiny for paying USD 9 million to the EPA for flaring excess gas in Guyana's Stabroek Block. The company has faced fines for rampant offshore flaring and has made efforts to address these issues and continue efforts to reduce methane emissions and sustain flare reductions globally to achieve the goal of ending routine flaring by 2030.

The report highlighted the need for greater efforts to reduce methane emissions and sustain flare reductions globally. It stressed the importance of effective regulation, enforcement, political will, and infrastructure to achieve significant progress in reducing flaring. Despite facing numerous challenges, Guyana serves as a crucial carbon sink for the global community. The country's expansive forests absorb more carbon than its human activities produce. With over 99.5% of its 18 million hectares of forest remaining intact, Guyana boasts the world's second-highest percentage of forest cover. Additionally, the country has one of the lowest deforestation rates worldwide and is one of only four nations (and one of just two in the Amazon Basin) certified as maintaining a High Forest Low Deforestation (HFLD) state. Through collaboration with international partners, Guyana aims to preserve its forests while transitioning to a low-carbon, eco-system economy. This shift can facilitate economic growth, support sustainable practices, mitigate climate change impacts on the coast and hinterlands, and stimulate economic prosperity within the country. Ultimately, Guyana's development of an eco-system economy has the potential to serve as a blueprint for similar initiatives globally (Government of Guyana, 2021).

In their efforts to achieve Net Zero emissions by 2050, the implementation of a carbon price regime and the removal of subsidies for fossil fuel production is highly recommended. These policies are crucial in driving the transition towards a low-carbon economy, incentivizing investments in renewable energy and sustainable practices while phasing out high-carbon fossil fuels.

By supporting global initiatives for a carbon price regime, Guyana can effectively internalize the cost of carbon emissions and encourage businesses to make environmentally-friendly choices. This market-based approach will not only help reduce greenhouse gas emissions but also spur innovation and investment in clean technologies. Additionally, the removal of fossil fuel subsidies will help level the playing field and provide a more accurate reflection of the true cost of energy production, thus paving the way for a more sustainable energy future. Guyana's commitment to implementing a tax on flaring and promoting responsible energy practices in the oil industry is commendable. By cracking down on excessive flaring and investing in technologies for lower carbon oil production, Guyana is setting a positive example for other countries to follow. Furthermore, initiatives like the "Zero Routine Flaring by 2030" program highlight Guyana's dedication to sustainable resource management and environmental protection.

As highlighted,[20] this initiative aims to promote responsible energy practices while ensuring that excess flaring—an environmentally detrimental practice—is curtailed. By adopting stringent policies against excessive flaring and investing in innovative technologies for lower-carbon oil production, Guyana aspires to establish itself as a leader in environmental stewardship. Such commitments not only align with global climate goals but also enhance the country's reputation as an environmentally conscious oil producer. The combination of global carbon pricing, the elimination of fossil fuel subsidies, and domestic initiatives like taxing flaring are essential steps in achieving net zero emissions by 2050. Domestically, Guyana is taking significant steps to reduce carbon emissions through measures such as implementing a tax on gas flaring in its oil industry.

In light of these strategies, it is recommended that Guyana continues to advocate for international cooperation on carbon pricing mechanisms and actively works towards eliminating fossil fuel subsidies. Joining initiatives like "Zero Routine Flaring by 2030" further underscores its commitment to sustainable resource management (Orozco et al., 2023).[21] By doing so, Guyana can effectively balance economic growth with environmental sustainability while contributing significantly to global efforts in combating climate change.

6 CONCLUSION

The evolution of oil and gas flaring in Guyana from basic practices to modern regulatory frameworks reflects a historical lack of environmental concern. With growing petroleum production, Guyana faces challenges balancing economic growth and environmental protection due to significant greenhouse gas emissions. Enforcement of stricter regulations and policy updates are recommended to mitigate emissions in alignment with international commitments such as the United Nations Framework Convention on Climate Change (UNFCCC) and the Paris Accord.

Flaring in Guyana is regulated by the EPA under the Environmental Protection Act, with fines imposed for exceeding flaring limits. The government collaborates with operators to minimize routine flaring, emphasizing sustainable resource management and environmental protection. Guyana enforces policies to reduce routine flaring aboard FPSO vessels and sets fees for excessive flaring above background levels. Guyana's commitment to reducing carbon emissions is evident through the Zero Flare Policy, aligning with global initiatives to eliminate routine flaring by 2030. Challenges include air pollution, water contamination, and limited enforcement, emphasizing the need for stringent regulations and penalties. Recommendations include enhancing regulatory frameworks, monitoring flaring activities, and ensuring compliance to mitigate environmental damage.

20. "On the Intersection of Energy Development and the Environment in Guyana." (*The Guyana Business Journal Magazine*, 2023).
21. Eriksson M. Afforestation and Avoided Deforestation in a Multi-Regional Integrated Assessment Model. 2020, Ecological Economics, 169, 106452.

Addressing gaps in regulations and creating stricter frameworks are crucial to tackling greenhouse gas emissions from flaring in Guyana. Independent audits, environmental impact assessments, corporate social responsibility mandates, and social and economic impact assessments are recommended for sustainable development. Implementing ongoing monitoring plans, regulating carbon emissions, and requiring environmental bonds can incentivize compliance and protect the environment. Collaborating with oil companies to end routine flaring by 2030, prioritizing sustainability, and global environmental stewardship is essential for Guyana's long-term growth and well-being.

Guyana faces challenges with flaring issues, leading to calls for action from ExxonMobil and the government to reduce pollution. Global gas flaring decreased by 3% in 2022, with Nigeria, Mexico, and the United States playing key roles. However, countries like Russia, Iraq, and Nigeria are major contributors to flare volumes. ExxonMobil paid fines for offshore flaring in Guyana and is working towards reducing methane emissions globally by 2030 through efforts to sustain flare reductions and improve regulations and infrastructure.

Despite challenges, Guyana acts as a vital carbon sink, with its vast forests absorbing more carbon than human activities produce. With over 99.5% of its forest intact, Guyana has the world's second-highest forest cover percentage and maintains a High Forest Low Deforestation status. Collaborating with international partners, the country aims to preserve its forests while transitioning to a low-carbon economy. This shift can drive economic growth, support sustainable practices, combat climate change impacts, and boost economic prosperity nationally, serving as a global initiative blueprint.

Guyana is navigating the complexities of economic development and environmental protection amid its offshore oil boom. The implementation of stricter regulations, such as the Zero Flare Policy, and the focus on sustainable development through initiatives like the LCDS 2030, showcase the country's commitment to balancing economic growth with environmental stewardship. The emphasis on independent audits and SEIA indicates a proactive approach to ensuring that oil companies operate responsibly and engage with local communities. Guyana's efforts to combat flaring and preserve its forests while transitioning to a sustainable, low-carbon economy position it as a sustainability leader. By working towards reducing methane emissions and sustaining forest cover, Guyana can set a precedent for other nations to follow in achieving environmental and economic progress simultaneously.

CHAPTER 16

Gas Flaring in Iran: A Legal Perspective

Nima Nasrollahi Shahri

1 BACKGROUND AND INTRODUCTION

Iran holds significant oil and gas resources and has in the past several decades always assumed a top ranking in oil production and exports. Its economy is very much dominated by its oil and gas revenues. In recent years, international and unilateral sanctions, primarily imposed by the U.S. in the wake of the U.S. withdrawal from the Joint Comprehensive Plan of Action (JCPOA), have taken a serious toll on its economy. Iran has been faced with serious internal and regional challenges in the past few years as well. This appears to markedly constrain the country's regulatory power especially when it comes to environmental policy. Having said this, policies to curb gas flaring have always featured in Iran's legislations even though, in most instances, the set goals have not been achieved.

Evidently, burning flared gases has broad economic, social, and environmental implications. In recent years, increased awareness of these adverse effects has prompted many countries and international organizations to enact laws, establish guidelines, reform natural gas markets, provide financial incentives to operating companies, and adopt punitive measures against gas flaring. Despite the implementation of various legal obligations and plans, a significant amount of flared gas, totaling 437.18 billion cubic meters in the year 2021 (Gregorian calendar), indicates an ongoing challenge even though Iran has expanded its equipment for collection of associated gas after 2018.[1] An analysis of Iran's flaring situation across various sectors reveals that, in

1. Mizan news agency; September 15, 2023, 45 million cubic meters of flares burnt daily in Iran, https://tinyurl.com/32kjsjr8.

recent years, there has been a notable increase in flaring at gas processing plants, unlike in the upstream segment. Additionally, the amount of flaring in oil refineries has risen over the past decade compared to the 2000s. Consequently, flaring in the downstream sector has become as significant as in the upstream sector in recent years.[2]

During the Sixth Development Plan of Iran, covering the period from 2016 to 2022, efforts resulted in the collection of a modest 1.43 million cubic meters of flared gas per day through auctions and sales. Gas processing plants achieved a daily reduction of 0.61 million cubic meters, reflecting an overall efficiency of approximately 5%.[3] In 2021, Iran ranked 8th globally in crude oil production and third in natural gas production, producing 3 million barrels of crude oil daily and over 250 billion cubic meters of natural gas annually. However, Iran became the second-largest country in gas flaring, trailing only Russia, with a flaring intensity over three times the global average (0.0318 cubic meters per barrel compared to the world average of 0.0111).[4] The below two figures, extracted from Global Gas Flaring Tracker Report (2024) demonstrate Iran's volume of gas flaring (Figure 16.1) and intensity of gas flaring (Figure 16.2) among the top 30 countries globally.

Figure 16.1 Flare Volumes in the Top 30 Flaring Countries

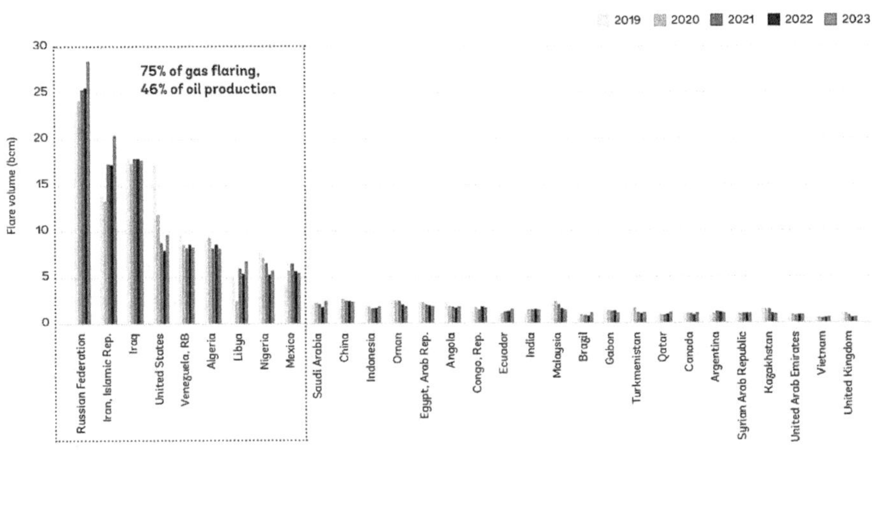

2. Amirhossein Khalili-Garakani, Mona Iravaninia & Mahya Nezhadfard, "A Review on the Potentials of Flare Gas Recovery Applications in Iran" (2021) 279 *Journal of Cleaner Production* 123345 https://doi.org/10.1016/j.jclepro.2020.123345.
3. Research Center of the Islamic Consultative Assembly. (2023). Strategic Issues in the Energy Sector in the Seventh Development Plan (No. 19288). Tehran: Research Center of the Islamic Consultative Assembly., https://rc.majlis.ir/fa/report/show/1783269.
4. *Ibid.*

Figure 16.2 Flaring Intensity in the Top 30 Flaring Countries

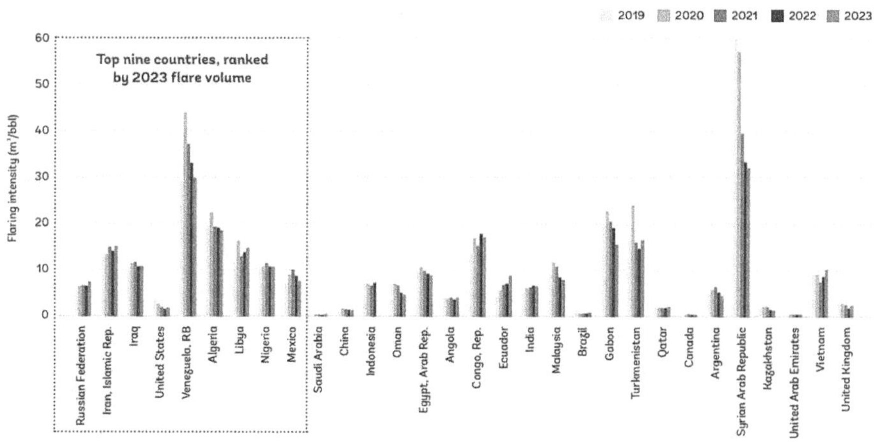

A report produced by the Parliament Research Center published in 2023 and cited many times in this article underscores the need for attention in future legislations. Analyzing gas flaring trends globally highlights the significant impact of legislation in reducing flaring levels. For instance, Nigeria experienced a more than 70% reduction in gas flaring volume and a two-thirds reduction in flaring intensity from 1975 to 2021 after implementing flaring control laws.[5] Many countries worldwide control gas flaring through dedicated laws, while others rely on overarching environmental or energy resource management laws to manage and organize flaring. These examples illustrate the crucial role of legislative measures in addressing and mitigating global environmental and energy-related challenges associated with gas flaring.

Gas flaring is a wasteful and polluting practice and while, considering the existing circumstances, the government of Iran may seem less concerned with its environmental effects, the economic effects of this wasteful practice are being increasingly noticed especially in light of the fly rocketing domestic gas and electricity consumption curve in Iran and little prospect for a significant increase in production.

Iran has had legislations concerning gas flares since 1989 when it started legislating its first Development Plan to introduce its ambitious reconstruction projects in the wake of the eight-year war with neighboring Iraq. All development Plans, so far sixth with a seventh recently enacted, have addressed the collection of associated gas and reduction of flares. In the same vein, throughout the years, Iran has adopted different policies, ranging from state ownership and control in the early days to encouragement of private investment in more recent years to cut down on flares. Despite all this, it is far from resolving the issue of gas flaring. The country has consistently ranked among the top three countries in terms of gas flaring volume and

5. Younes Khodaparast Pirsarayi, "Comparative Analysis of the Situation of Our Country in Collecting Associated Gases (Flare Gas)" (2022) 10(7-8) *Economic Security*.

is, along with Iraq, the worst oil-producing country in the world in terms of gas flaring intensity.[6] The figure below shows that gas flaring volume and intensity in Iran has not improved in the last few years.

Figure 16.3 Flaring Volume and Flaring Intensity in Iran

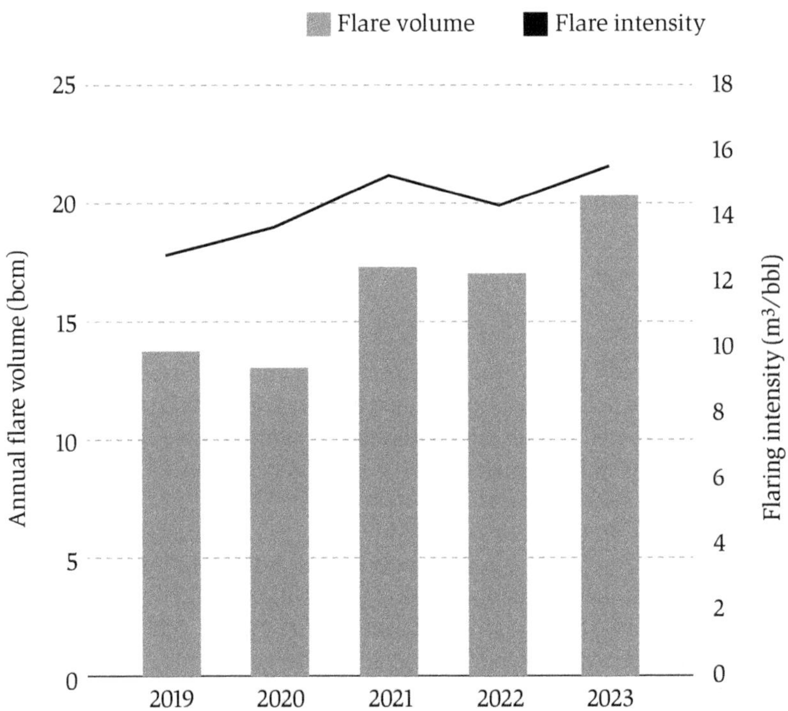

It appears that government projects to engage domestic and foreign investors to alleviate gas flares have not been attractive thus far. However, with new enactments, especially in the Seventh Development Plan and imposition of more serious penalties and fines on entities responsible for gas flaring, the situation could be expected to improve in the next few years.

In this chapter, gas flaring practice is viewed from two different prisms, namely an environmental perspective and an economic viewpoint. These two areas are the main driving forces behind new legislation intended to curb flares. Drawing on information available from international entities and that made public by state organs and agencies, the chapter attempts to offer a chronological summary of the legal developments within the last three decades, highlighting how such developments reflect the political and economic realities on the ground.

6. 2023 Global Gas Flaring Tracker Report, World Bank.

This article will start off by studying the environmental and economic impacts of gas flaring. Subsequently, it will review, through a historical prism, legislative efforts made thus far and plans to move forward, which reveals how different policies adopted thus far have failed to prove effective and why we could retain optimism about the new policies adopted.

2 GAS FLARING IN IRAN: AN ENVIRONMENTAL PERSPECTIVE

Iran is faced with a serious environmental crisis. This has created dissent and dissatisfaction within its domestic population. Environmental mismanagement has resulted in widespread migration within Iran[7] to the less affected northern areas, disserting central and southern Iran. It is not surprising then that most oil fields lie in the southern parts of the country and the oil-rich province of Khuzestan assumes a top rank in outgoing migration[8] within Iran due to pollution and climate change.

The difficulties which ensue from flare gases are significantly hazardous and irreparable not only for humans but also for flora and fauna and soil. Overall, flare gases released in the environment comprise several harmful substances, including volatile organic compounds (VOCs) such as aromatic and aliphatic hydrocarbons,[9] sulfur-containing compounds (SOx and H_2S), nitrogen oxides (NOx), carbon dioxide (CO_2),[10] carbon monoxide, and mercury-containing compounds (El-Feky et al., 2018). This is aggravated by releasing particulate matter (PM) and smoke. Other problems caused by burning flare gases include rising surrounding environment temperature and creating noise pollution.[11] The destructive effects of flaring on human health have been investigated and quantified in numerous studies. Via health risk assessment, some studies have reported the "noticeable effects of flaring-induced emission of benzene, toluene, ethylbenzene, and xylenes (BTEX) in industrial areas of Asaluyeh, Iran and cities nearby."[12]

"Air pollution caused by flaring is a long-lasting problem in the oil-rich regions of Iran, while traces of heavy metals have been found in the Zagros ecosystems in the soil and tree leaves." The pollution caused by flaring blurs the sight of motorists on Ahwaz road; the rate of cancer in areas surrounding flares is significantly higher than in other parts of the country and breathing problems in Assaluyeh are taking a serious toll.[13]

7. M.H. Moradi, "The Status of Climatic Migration in Iran; a Response to Environmental Crisis" (March 27, 2024) *Eco Iran* https://tinyurl.com/34tr44rj accessed August 8, 2024.
8. Mounting Environmental Crisis in Iran; the beginning of Reverse Migration, June 8, 2022, available online at: https://tinyurl.com/yuneensk.
9. N. Hadjizadeh Zaker, "Aliphatic and Aromatic Hydrocarbons in the Coastal Sediments of the Kharg Island in the Persian Gulf" (2022) 8(2) *Pollution* 705.
10. M. Heidari, A. Ataei & M.H. Rahdar, "Development and Analysis of Two Novel Methods for Power Generation from Flare Gas" (2016) 104 *Applied Thermal Engineering* 687 https://doi.org/10.1016/j.applthermaleng.2016.05.099.
11. L.U. Okoye et al., "Effect of Gas Flaring, Oil Rent and Fossil Fuel on Economic Performance: The Case of Nigeria" (2022) 77 *Resources Policy* 102677 https://doi.org/10.1016/j.resourpol.2022.102677.
12. M.A. Mirrezaei & A.A. Orkomi, "Gas Flares Contribution in Total Health Risk Assessment of BTEX in Asalouyeh, Iran" (2020) 137 *Process Safety and Environmental Protection* 223 https://doi.org/10.1016/j.psep.2020.02.034.
13. Radio Farhang, October 10, 2023, Islamic Assembly Parliament Discussions Coverage.

Certainly, the act of flaring essentially involves releasing waste gases, such as CO_2, CO, hydrocarbons, and acid gases (specifically nitric oxide, NO, and NOx, NO_2, collectively referred to as NOx, as well as sulfur oxides, predominantly identified as SO_2 with minimal amounts of SO_3), into the environment. This release can occur either as part of regular operations or in emergency situations. Typically, this practice is employed when the retrieval of valuable compounds is deemed impractical. However, advancements in relevant technologies heightened environmental concerns, and economic motivations have facilitated the recovery of gases from flaring.[14]

Burning flare gases is a significant source of CO_2 emissions in Iran. The huge quantity of gas flares partly contributes to the fact that Iran has not been able to live up to its international environmental obligations.[15] Some research indicates that it may account for up to 19 % of the country's total CO_2 emissions, although this figure might be overestimated. Other studies propose a lower but still substantial contribution. The graph below indicates the share of flares in CO_2 emissions in Iran between 2012 and 2019.

Figure 16.4 Iran's Flare Shares from Its Total CO_2 Emissions

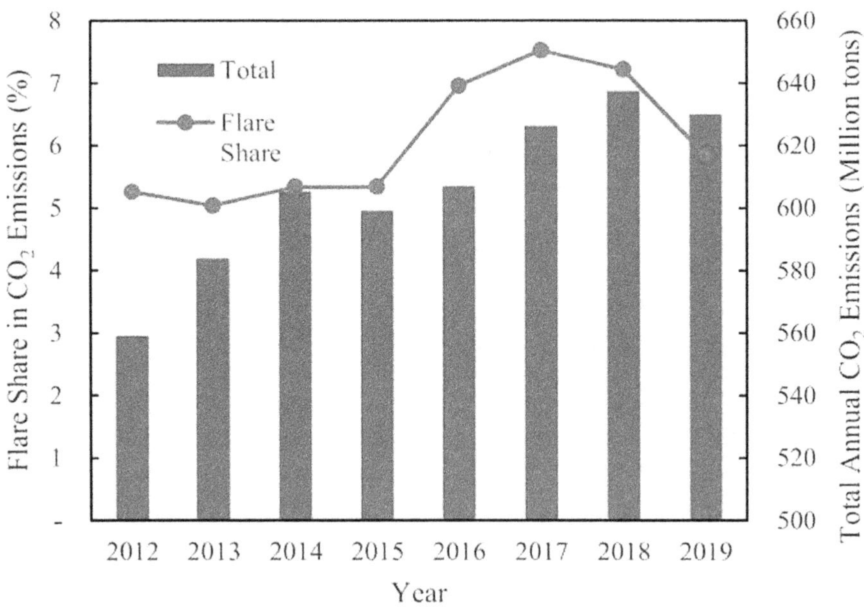

Source (World Bank, 2023)

14. Mohammad Shahab-Deljoo et al., "A Techno-Economic Review of Gas Flaring in Iran and Its Human and Environmental Impacts" (2023) 173 *Process Safety and Environmental Protection* 642 https://doi.org/10.1016/j.psep.2023.03.051.
15. Wahabpour Amir, Shojai Seyyed Mohammad, Tahmasbi Mohammad & Rasouli Fatemeh, "Investigating the Environmental Effects of Flare Gas in Iran and Its Importance in the Context of the Country's Commitments in the Paris Agreement" (2018) 8(27) *Strategic Studies in Public Policy (Globalization Strategic Studies)* 133.

Gas Flaring; An Economic Perspective

As the problem of gas shortage becomes more serious in Iran, it makes more economic sense to collect associated gas. With an increasing domestic gas consumption curve, shortage of electricity in peak hours and increasing restrictions on export of petroleum products from Iran, Iran needs to economize by taking advantage of resources saved by cutting down on flares, which are estimated to be around 45 million square meters.[16] The annual gas flares of Iran amount to the total gas exports of the country.[17] Thus, it has been suggested that gas flaring is annually causing about 6 billion dollars of economic damage.[18]

Gas storage capacity is also relatively low in Iran compared to many other petroleum-producing countries, standing at around 1.5% of total gas consumption in the country.[19] This compared to the world average of 11%,[20] could explain little interest in the collection of associated gas in the past.

Given the growth in gas consumption in the country and the lack of a significant increase in gas production in the future due to the completion of phases in the South Pars development and Iran's low share in the global gas market, the collection of flared gases can serve as a new source to meet domestic gas consumption and increase gas exports, thereby enhancing the country's energy and economic security. In this regard, government support for investments in the collection of flared gases, providing legal frameworks to attract private sector and foreign company participation, and establishing a supervisory body to monitor the volume of gases being burned in flares are essential.[21]

However, natural gas consumption, especially in household, commercial, power generation, and industrial sectors, is growing significantly, approximately 7% annually. The continuation of this trend, coupled with a decrease in production, means that the country's gas balance in the future (production minus consumption) will see a significant decrease. According to the text of the gas balance document,[22] by the year 2031, considering the current trend of production and consumption, the country will need to import 512 million cubic meters of gas per day.[23]

Projects to increase gas production and supply are time-consuming, focusing on one aspect and requiring substantial financial support. Implementing policies such as the collection of associated gases becomes crucial to avoid shortages. There are other capacities in the collection of flared gases that can contribute to the enhancement of the

16. Mizan news agency; September 15, 2023, 45 million cubic meters of flares burnt daily in Iran, https://tinyurl.com/32kjsjr8.
17. IRNA News Agency; October 23, 2023, Optimization of Consumption: The Most Important Energy Axis in the Seventh Plan/Burning 18 Billion Cubic Meters of Associated Gas Annually.
18. Radio Farhang, October 10, 2023, Islamic Assembly Parliament Discussions Coverage.
19. Research Center of the Islamic Consultative Assembly. (2023). Strategic Issues in the Energy Sector in the Seventh Development Plan (No. 19288).
20. IRNA News Agency; October 23, 2023, Optimization of Consumption: The Most Important Energy Axis in the Seventh Plan/Burning 18 Billion Cubic Meters of Associated Gas Annually.
21. Research Center of the Islamic Consultative Assembly. (2023). Strategic Issues in the Energy Sector in the Seventh Development Plan (No. 19288).
22. *Ibid.*
23. *Ibid.*

country's economic security, including increasing gas export capacity. Despite having the world's second-largest gas reserves, Iran has a very small share in the gas trade, mainly due to high domestic consumption. Therefore, by collecting a portion of flared gases (which constitute about 141% of the country's current gas export volume), it becomes possible to increase gas exports.

Considering that gas sanctions are not feasible, and Iran's gas exports were not sanctioned in previous rounds of sanctions, increasing gas exports can provide a stable income unaffected by sanctions. This enhances the economic security of the country. Additionally, with gas exports through pipelines, Iran's economic interests become intertwined with importing countries, increasing the costs of sanctions against Iran. Moreover, current oil fields in the country require gas injection for enhanced oil recovery, making the collection of flared gases crucial for these activities.[24]

What can be inferred from the above figures highlights the importance of collecting these gases. If these gases are collected, organized, and directed towards export (after processing and sweetening), the country's natural gas export volume can be doubled without increasing production. Additionally, comparing the volume of flaring with the consumption of gas in major industries in the country emphasizes the significant waste of this divine blessing. As seen in Figure 16.5 below, the country's flaring is higher than the consumption of gas by all major industries (except petrochemicals).[25]

Figure 16.5 Comparison of Gas Flaring Volume and Gas Consumption in Major Industries, Iran

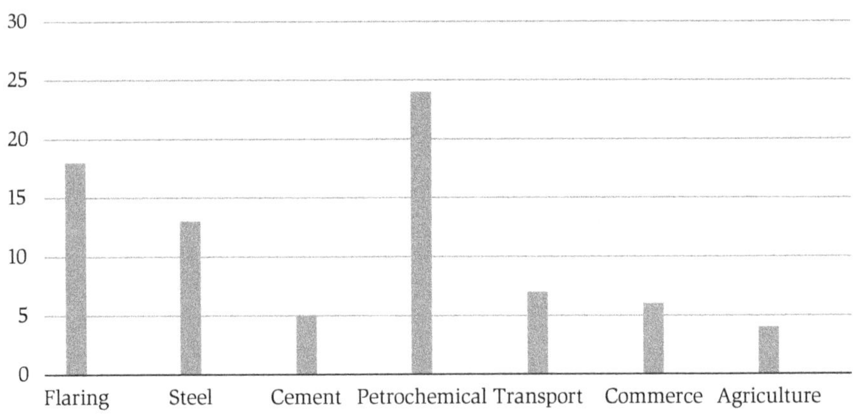

Source: Research Center of the Islamic Consultative Assembly. (2023).

24. Younes Khodaparast Pirsarayi, "Comparative Analysis of the Situation of Our Country in Collecting Associated Gases (Flare Gas)" (2022) 10(7-8) *Economic Security*.
25. Radio Farhang, October 10, 2023, Islamic Assembly Parliament Discussions Coverage.

Although the relatively low price of natural gas compared to oil and its other products has made investing in other oil and gas industry projects more advantageous, calculations show that collecting and organizing flaring gases not only prevents energy waste and pollution but also has considerable economic value. To better assess the economic aspect of this issue, the lack of benefit from flaring in terms of exports is shown in the following chart. Figure 16.6 plots the loss of profits resulting from flaring based on gas exports, assuming the flaring gases are processed, sweetened, and then exported based on the price of gas exports in the years under review.

Figure 16.6 Loss of Profit Resulting from Flares (10 years, Iran)

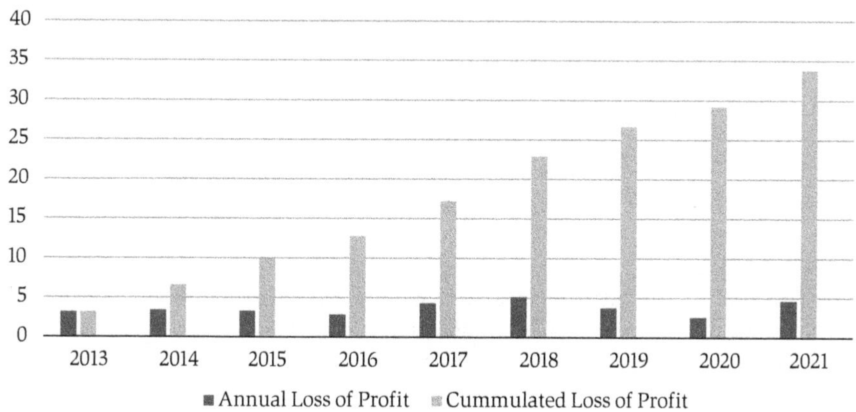

Source: Research Center of the Islamic Consultative Assembly. (2023).

The information presented in the above figure indicates that the failure to collect and use flaring gases, assuming natural gas exports, has deprived the country of approximately USD 4.6 billion in the past year and USD 33 billion in the past decade. Therefore, considering the economic dimensions of this issue, collecting flaring gases and preventing their burning seems highly essential.

"The flare gases recovery and usage are promising in economic terms" based on numerous studies.[26] As a case in point, Iran, with its abundant oil and gas reservoirs as well as diverse facilities in the upstream, intermediate, and downstream sections, still converts huge amounts of flare gases with high economic potential into harmful and

26. Mohammad Heidari, Abtin Ataei and Mohammad Hoseini Rahdar, "Development and Analysis of Two Novel Methods for Power Generation from Flare Gas" (2016) 104 Applied Thermal Engineering 687 https://doi.org/10.1016/j.applthermaleng.2016.05.099 accessed August 26, 2024.

E. Barekat-Rezaei et al., "Thermo-Economical Evaluation of Producing Liquefied Natural Gas and Natural Gas Liquids from Flare Gases" (2018) 11(7) *Energies* 1 https://doi.org/10.3390/en11071868 accessed August 26, 2024.

E. Romsom & K. McPhail, *Capturing Economic and Social Value from Hydrocarbon Gas Flaring and Venting: Solutions and Actions* (WIDER Working Paper 2021/6, UNU-WIDER 2021) https://doi.org/10.35188/UNU-WIDER/2021/940-2 accessed August 26, 2024.

detrimental emissions. Unfortunately, flare gas recovery in Iran is still at its primitive stage due to the high expense of recovery infrastructures, technical difficulties, and the lack of appropriate policies and regulatory frameworks ahead of such economic ventures.[27]

The proximity of Iran's giant petrochemical complexes to the major associated and non-associated gas flaring sites and the feasibility of their utilization as the feedstock signal favorable changes and is a positive outcome of this research. The expected rate of return (ROR) for feedstock production is between 120% and 250% and payback period (PB) is between 0.4 and 1.2 years. Due to massive inflation and difficulties in foreign financing and technology transfer, we recommend more straightforward recovery methods despite lower profit. In this regard, apart from feedstock utilization of associated gas, we recommend electricity generation from flare gases for smaller amounts of flaring since the technology is more available and the country is always in shortage of the product (electricity). The ROR and PB for electricity generation are reported to be between 15% and 40% and 2.5-6.5 years, respectively.[28]

The Legal Framework Applicable to Gas Flaring in Iran

In the past several decades, there has been abundant legislation aiming to decrease gas flares. Turning off gas flares at the National Iranian Oil Company (NIOC) goes back to 1970 when the National Iranian Gas Company (NIGC) was established.[29] The legislation put in place in 2015 was envisaged to decrease the gas flares by 90% by 2023. This goal has obviously not been met. At the same time, new legislation has been finalized in the Parliament, which is expected to be more effective.

Government obligations and policy-making are most observable in the Five-Year Development Plan Acts[30] and also present in annual Budget Acts. Five Year Development Plan Acts have contained provisions on collection of associated gas since their inception in 1989. Annual Budget Acts have also consistently contained relevant provisions since 2003. To better grasp the existing legal framework, this chapter attempts to offer a brief historical overview pinpointing the laws and regulations that have led to the existing framework.

Historically, it has been suggested that three different phases could be identified when studying the response of the Iranian state to the challenge of collecting associated

27. M.F. Farina, *Flare Gas Reduction: Recent Global Trends and Policy Considerations* (GE Energy Global Strategy and Planning 2010).
28. Mohammad Shahab-Deljoo et al., "A Techno-Economic Review of Gas Flaring in Iran and Its Human and Environmental Impacts" (2023) 173 *Process Safety and Environmental Protection* 642-665.
29. Shana Petro-energy Information Network, *Iran Determined in Zero-Flaring Projects*, July 25, 2021, https://en.shana.ir/news/318895/Iran-Determined-in-Zero-Flaring-Projects.
30. Five Year Development Plan Acts are laws enacted every five years with the aim of drawing up the development perspective of the country for five years and setting goals that different organs need to strive to meet. The tradition of five year-plans which existed before the revolution were resumed for the first time, after the 1979 revolution, once the government planned economic reconstruction after the eight-year war with Iraq in late 1980s.

gas in the last thirty years.[31] Such solutions are found in the laws and regulations enacted after the 1979 revolution. The three phases, thus far implemented, include Establishment and ownership of government units (2.1), Transfer of NGL to investors from the private sector (2.2) attracting private sector investment in the entire oil value chain (2.3).

2.1 Establishment and Ownership of Government Units (NGL)

This approach was predominant post the 1979 revolution until 2013. After the revolution, any investment or private ownership in the oil and gas industry became prohibited. That is mainly why, based on the legal obligations set during this period, the NIOC, as the main producer of associated gases and flaring, was put directly in charge of any investment, and construction of NGL units. Indeed, in the same vein, when plans were defined for the collection of associated gases from oil in the early 2000s, there was no plan for the participation of private sector investors. Therefore, potential limitations that private companies could face in investment were not taken into account.

The first five Year Development Plan mandated "Promoting economic growth by increasing the per capita production, generating employment, and reducing economic dependency, with an emphasis on the production of strategic goods and controlling inflation through the priority of collecting associated gases from various oil fields, particularly in the flat continental areas."[32]

Therefore, the Law did little more than put emphasis on the need to collect associated gas, highlighting the role iky=t could play in engendering economic growth.

The Second Five Year Development Plan went a little further and in effect authorized the Ministry of Oil to implement executable projects, including collection of associated gas and up to a maximum of USD 6,500,000,000 using Buyback and up to USD 3,500,000,000 using finance.[33] This means that the law granted the Ministry of Oil permission to use foreign finance to implement by itself collection schemes.

The Budget Act of 2002 followed suit and granted the NIOC permission to execute projects aimed at completely preventing the flaring of associated gases and renovating oil facilities through the utilization of external resources (financing). This initiative was to be coordinated with the Central Bank of the Islamic Republic of Iran, and the resulting commitments, up to a maximum of USD 2,000,000,000 were to be repaid from the proceeds of the sales of the implemented projects' produced products (excluding crude oil)[34]

31. Research Center of the Islamic Consultative Assembly. (2023). Strategic Issues in the Energy Sector in the Seventh Development Plan (No. 19288). Tehran: Research Center of the Islamic Consultative Assembly., https://rc.majlis.ir/fa/report/show/1783269.
32. First Five Year Development Plan, Art. 46(4)b.
33. First Five Year Development Plan, Note 22(m), Table 13.
34. Budget Act, Note 21(l).

The Fourth Development Plan Act authorized the NIOC to undertake the collection of associated gases, gas injection, renovation and optimization of oil facilities, conversion of natural gas into liquid products such as LNG, GTL, DME, etc., refining facilities, and optimization of fuel consumption. According to this Act, the repayment of the incurred commitments would be made from the additional income generated by such projects (NIOC's domestic resources).[35] These laws were never meaningfully effective in bringing about any reduction to annual gas flares.

2.2 Transfer of NGL to Private Sector Investors

In the wake of the 2013 presidential election, in which moderate Hassan Rouhani was elected, radical change was made to the general legal framework applicable to oil and gas contracts and projects. It was in 2014 that the Iranian Petroleum Contract (IPC) model was introduced and replaced buyback For the first time, in an attempt to curb gas flares, the government considered transferring NGL to the private sector. This short-lived approach kicked off with the enactment of the Budget Act of 2014 when the NIOC considered transferring NGL units to private sector investors. This approach lasted only for one year and the government soon introduced a more progressive plan that will be discussed below.

Based on this approach, NGL units 3,200 and 3,100 were respectively transferred to Petrochemical Companies of Bandar Imam and the Investment Fund of Petroleum Industry, and the Engineering and Construction Company of the Petroleum Industry in accordance with the related documents and regulations during the specified period. According to this approach, private sector investors were only required to invest in the construction and operation of NGL units, while the development of upstream sectors (development of oil and gas fields) to supply feedstock for NGL units remained the responsibility of the NIOC. The Ministry of Oil in Iran, through its state-owned entities, was granted the authority to execute oil and gas projects, emphasizing increasing crude oil and gas production capacities, refining capabilities, and promoting the export of oil products. The initiative, aligned with constitutional policies, encouraged investment from private and public sectors using methods like Build-Operate-Transfer (BOT). The Ministry was allowed to enter contracts, prioritize domestic equipment, and seek approvals based on technical, economic, and environmental justifications. The government committed to repaying project investments, utilizing savings from fuel exports, and affiliated companies were allowed to engage with non-governmental investors. Project approvals were made subject to a government commitment ceiling, and exceeding such limits required additional approvals from the Minister of Oil and the Economic Council.[36]

---

35. Article 14(d).
36. According to the Budget Act:

> The Ministry of Oil, through its affiliated state-owned companies, is authorized to implement oil and gas projects, including increasing the production capacity of crude oil and gas, with priority given to shared reservoirs. This includes increasing the refining capacity of crude oil, gas condensates, and petrochemical products, promoting

2.3 Authorization and Encouragement of Private Sector Investment in the Entire Oil Value Chain

The government went on to encourage private sector participation by introducing a new approach in 2015, allowing for more marked participation of the private sector. Accordingly, private sector companies interested in investing in an NGL unit to supply feedstock to that unit must engage in upstream projects, such as the development of oil fields or gas reservoirs. Notable projects under this approach include NGL 1,700, 1,800, and 2,300.

This approach was kicked off by virtue of the General Policies of the Sixth Development Plan enacted in 2015 providing for delegation of the projects of gathering, restraining, controlling, and exploiting associated gases produced in all oil fields and petroleum industry installations to the public.[37] In the same year, the Law on Removing Production Barriers, Enhancing Competitiveness, and Improving the Country's Financial System created an obligation in its Article 12 for the government to prioritize preventing the burning of associated gases in oil and gas production, as well as minimizing the flaring and venting of domestic and imported natural gas, along with related petroleum products and all relevant projects that lead to increased efficiency in the consumption of crude oil, gas flaring, and gas and petroleum product emissions. The executive by law of this Act provided that "entities subject to Article 12 of the law may, for the purpose of saving on resource consumption, reducing waste, losses, and expenses, increasing the production of goods and services, and in line with the provisions of Article 12 of the law, which do not result in increased revenue or

the export of oil products, preventing the flaring of associated gas, and replacing domestic or imported gas with oil products, up to a ceiling of one hundred billion (100,000,000,000) dollars or its equivalent in foreign or domestic currency. This is in accordance with the provisions of Article 44 of the Constitution, to attract mutual investment, construct, operate, and deliver projects through the Build-Operate-Transfer (BOT) method or other methods specified in Article 214 of the Fifth Five-Year Development Plan of the Islamic Republic of Iran, with guaranteed purchase of products and permission for long-term (minimum ten years) domestic sales or exports.

Furthermore, the Ministry of Oil is granted permission to enter into contracts, in compliance with the law on the execution of general policies outlined in Article 44 of the Constitution, with private and public sector applicants and investors, prioritizing the use of domestically manufactured equipment. Technical, economic, environmental justifications, implementation schedules, repayment terms, and the government's commitment ceiling for each project will be submitted by the Ministry of Oil for approval by the Economic Council. The government's commitment to repay the principal of the investments under this provision is the responsibility of the government, and the National Iranian Oil Company will settle the savings resulting from fuel exports (equivalent to crude oil) in each project after the Ministry of Oil's declaration in the years of maturity, simultaneously crediting the government's account (National Treasury).

Affiliated and dependent companies of the Ministry of Oil are allowed to participate with non-governmental investors, respecting the law on the execution of general policies outlined in Article 44 of the Constitution. Projects under this provision are approved by the Minister of Oil up to the government's commitment limit of five hundred million (500,000,000) dollars or its equivalent in domestic currency. Projects exceeding this limit require the approval of the Minister of Oil and further confirmation by the Economic Council.

37. Sixth Economic Development Plan Act (2016-2021), Art. 48.

decreased expenses, within the framework of domestic and international legal entities, and placing the necessary approved contracts in the context of laws and regulations with natural and legal persons, domestically and internationally, in the priority of the private sector, enter into cooperative agreements. They should refrain from taking action or transferring, in accordance with paragraph '2' of the mentioned article, unless it is solely for the repayment of the additional income or savings created."

The Sixth Development Act set an ambitious goal of lowering gas flares by 90%. Article 48 of this law provided that all projects related to the collection, containment, control, and utilization of associated gases produced and flared in all oil fields and petroleum industry installations shall be assigned through public announcement to the people and the non-governmental sector by determining a fair rate for their consumption. This assignment will be valid for a maximum period of three months from the date of the enforcement of this law, ensuring that by the end of the program, a minimum of 90% of flared gases is contained and controlled.

The 2017 Guidelines for Dealing and Contracting with Flare Gas Buyers were issued with the aim of facilitating the attraction of more domestic and foreign investment for the purpose of collecting flare gases.

The 2022 Budget Act created an obligation for the NIOC and its relevant government subsidiary under the Ministry of Oil to utilize private sector investment, employing domestic resources of their affiliated companies, to carry out the upstream projects of utilizing valuable associated gas. The process allowed implementation and repayment of the investment made from the proceeds of the project.[38]

The same Note allowed implementation of projects for the collection, recovery, and processing of flare gases, aiming to produce a minimum of three hundred thousand tons per year of ethane and nitrogenous rock products from flare gases, prioritizing the regions of Pars Jonubi and Masjed Soleyman.[39]

Despite all government efforts, the ambitious goals set in the 6th Economic Development Plan were not met and there was no significant or consistent decrease in gas flares. This has enticed much public debate. The approach currently being discussed emphasizes not only affirmative methods but also setting penalties for responsible organs in case of failure to meet the pre-determined goals.

The new Economic Development Plan (7th Plan enacted in 2024) provides that Energy-intensive industries and petrochemicals are prioritized for flare gas collection projects and new gas fields, with the Ministry of Oil ensuring they receive natural gas from these sources. The produced gas belongs to these industries, which must settle accounts with the government as per the specified mechanisms.[40]

The Seventh Economic Development Plan Act also sets out to rectify the deficiencies in the existing framework by emboldening the consequences of the failure to reduce gas flares. In so doing, it sets primarily monetary penalties for failing to

38. Budget Act of 2022, Note 1 (Petroleum and its Financial Relations to the Government/National Development Fund).
39. *Ibid.*
40. Seventh Economic Development Plan Act (2024-2029), Art. 15, Note 3.

achieve the required reduction.[41] The penalties for non-compliance with energy consumption laws are based on natural gas export prices, increasing from 5% to 75% by the end of the program. Flaring gases that "cannot be technically collected (up to 3 billion cubic meters annually) are exempt. The Ministry of Oil must report progress biannually to the Parliament's Energy Commission."

According to Article 46 (D) of the Seventh Economic Development Plan Act, "Penalties ... are based on export prices, and the flaring gas charges burned in oil and gas facilities are calculated for each cubic meter of gas based on the monthly announcement by the Secretariat of the Supreme Supervisory Council on Oil Resources (Organization)." For the first year, this rate is set at 5% and will gradually increase to 75% by the end of the program, calculated based on the weighted average export price of natural gas. These charges are deposited from the internal resources of the subsidiaries of the Ministry of Oil into the energy consumption optimization account mentioned in Clause (2) of Part (a) of this Article.

Flaring gases that cannot technically be collected, as determined by the Secretariat of the Supreme Supervisory Council on Oil Resources (Organization), and up to a maximum volume of 3 billion cubic meters per year, are exempt from this provision ... .

"The Ministry of Oil and the Organization are required to submit a report of the actions taken every six months to the Energy Commission of the Parliament."

The introduction of this article basically means that failure to collect associated gas, resulting in flares, would result in monetary penalties. This approach appears to present what has always been considered the missing link in a comprehensive system aiming to fight gas flares. It appears to be economically motivated as the country is faced with an energy shortage and aims to increase the availability of natural gas for domestic consumption.

Regarding flared gases collected through contracts executed before the enforcement of this law, fees are calculated from the completion date of the contracts. In case subsidiary companies of the Ministry of Oil refuse to pay fees for non-collection of flared gases, the amount of these fees would be deducted from the internal resources of the mentioned companies in the annual budget laws, and after depositing it into the treasury, it is considered for optimizing energy consumption. The executive regulations of this paragraph are prepared by the Ministries of Oil and Energy and are approved by the Council of Ministers. This has been faced with serious criticism and has been dubbed too ambitious.[42]

3 CONCLUSION

In summary, Iran does not seem to have achieved much success in reducing gas flares and it continues to rank high, both in terms of the volume of gas flared and gas flaring

41. Seventh Economic Development Plan Act (2024-2029), Art. 46, para. D.
42. Radio Farhang, October 10, 2023, Islamic Assembly Parliament Discussions Coverage.

intensity. Momentary reduction from 2018 to 2020 was more a result of decreasing production than a telltale sign of any success in diminishing flares.

Even though there have been intense discussions and new regulations introduced to curb flaring in Iran, it does not appear to have been top on the government agenda as the oil and gas industry is faced with challenges resulting from international and U.S. sanctions. Contractors are unable to employ best industry practices as the sanctions imposed restrict the government's ability to attract foreign investment from giant multinationals. Existing operators, predominantly Iranian or Russian, do not seem to have enough incentive to prioritize environmentally friendly practices. International marketing of oil and gas products is the main challenge on which operators are focused.

From an environmental point of view, increasing gas flares have led to many serious issues in Iran. Environmental deterioration is turning into a potentially significant security concern and is thus prioritized.

Having said this, the energy crisis, i.e., the rising domestic gas consumption curve, has pushed the government to place collection of associated gas high on its agenda. The government is aware of the billions of dollars of lost profit and the wasted capacity which could be used for gas imports. It is because of these economic concerns, heightened as a result of sanctions, that new legislation appears to be more stringent and expected to be more effective.

From a technical perspective, the application of flare gas recovery technologies in Iran faces several challenges and problems, as outlined by the Ministry of Science Research & Technology in 2016. One significant obstacle is geographical limitations, with dispersed locations of associated and flare gas resources, both offshore and onshore. This dispersion poses difficulties in gathering and utilizing flare gas, leading to increased capital costs, especially when gas production fields are situated more than 80 km away from nearby islands. The long distances and associated high transmission costs, as seen in the Iranian Offshore Oil Company (IOOC) regions, can make the recovery technologies economically unfeasible, particularly in the compression/ liquefaction and transport category.

Additionally, there are obstacles related to the lack of access to essential transmission infrastructures such as gas, electricity, and steam, which can adversely impact the affordability of flare recovery processes. The absence of required infrastructures either altogether or with limited private sector access necessitates significant investments in infrastructure development. Technical and technological limitations further hinder the collection and utilization of flare gases, involving factors like gas composition, technology maturity, and economic justifiability. Economic constraints, including capital and operating costs associated with gathering, preprocessing, building utilization plants, and transmitting products to the market, contribute to limiting the application of flare recovery technologies. Moreover, structural and institutional problems, such as the absence of a long-term pricing policy for associated and flare gas, economic dependency on oil revenues, and the unavailability of essential data for associated and flare gas, pose additional hurdles to the development of flare gas recovery processes in Iran.

All in all, while laws and regulations have repeatedly emphasized the importance of collecting associated gas and several mechanisms have thus far been tried and tested, no consequences for non-fulfillment of such goals have ever been envisaged. This has led to ambitious goals being set every few years without any being even slightly realized. The new Economic Development Plan Act in force from March 2024 takes an unprecedentedly harsh position and punishes gas flares. This approach is expected to ameliorate the situation within the next few years.

CHAPTER 17

The Regulation of Gas Flaring in Kazakhstan

Reg Fowler

1 INTRODUCTION

The Republic of Kazakhstan is the 10th largest country on the planet by area and is entirely landlocked.[1] Population densities are extremely low, with significant concentrations of population and energy use around its political and economic capitals, Astana and Almaty.[2] As a former republic of the Soviet Union, it acted as a transit zone for the shipment of natural gas between Turkmenistan and Western Russia, and the development of the domestic gas distribution network was not a priority for the centralised Soviet government. Since independence in 1991, lack of investment in gas distribution networks led to significant regional disparities in domestic and industrial gas prices, particularly in the north-east and south-east sectors of the country, far away from the key hydrocarbon provinces of Atyrau and Mangistau in the Caspian region.[3] The desire to 'gasify' industrial and consumer energy sectors emerged from 2009 onwards and culminated in the Law 'on Gas and Gas Supply' in 2012. Its overall objective was to 'kickstart' a domestic gas market, relying on national production and enabling the emergence of interregional price competition and investment in interregional gas transportation. To reach that objective, the law increased central control of

1. US Central Intelligence Agency, 'The World Fact Book', https://www.cia.gov/the-world-factbook/countries/kazakhstan/ accessed 30 April 2024.
2. 7 per km^2, 234th in Global ranking. 'List of Countries and Dependencies by Population Density', Wikipedia https://en.wikipedia.org/wiki/List_of_countries_and_dependencies_by_population_density accessed 30 April 2024.
3. The full suite of documentation (in Russian and Kazakh) which accompanied the legislation in its passage through government and the Majilis (Досье на проект Закона Республики Казахстан 'О газе и газоснабжении' (23 мая 2011 года)) is available at the following address https://online.zakon.kz/lawyer accessed 7 July 2024.

gas transportation by appointing a 'national operator' to manage, if not own, all downstream gas pipelines, established a national gas specification, and limited or controlled natural gas and LPG prices. Upstream gas producers were also affected – the Law asserted the State's ownership of associated natural gas not already in production unless the pre-existing applicable production sharing agreement or concession granted the subsoil user the right to lift and monetise such gas for its own account. Furthermore, the Law provided a mandatory pricing mechanism for wholesale sales of natural gas by subsoil users, based on a 'cost plus profit margin' formula. For the upstream industry, a key component of the Law was the introduction of the requirement to present to the State a 'gas utilisation' program, a monitoring tool enabling the State to encourage maximum natural gas production into the domestic market, and routinely to discourage gas reinjection.[4] The provisions of the law dealing with the pricing of LPG have been particularly controversial as the State has sought progressively to lift the price ceiling, reducing state subsidisation of the national operator. Such an increase in LPG prices was the ostensible trigger for civil unrest in Kazakhstan in February 2022.[5]

The drive to increase natural gas supply and fix upstream wholesale prices naturally brought the State into conflict with foreign oil companies dominant in the Caspian region whose investments are protected under the terms of long-term concession agreements and production sharing agreements negotiated in the mid-1990s.[6] Such agreements not only established the investors' right to lift, export and monetise natural gas but also granted them the option to reinject the natural gas into the reservoir in order to sustain reservoir pressure and enhance crude oil production. The option to flare natural gas routinely as an alternative to reinjection or sale has been prohibited in Kazakhstan since 1999.[7] Furthermore, the long-term agreements governing such investments also provide for the investors to be able to export natural gas and to sell it at international gas market prices. As a result of lobbying by the industry, the Law on Gas and Gas Supply was amended in 2012[8] to disapply the pricing provisions of that law from production sharing agreements which contained alternative gas pricing terms and had been entered into prior to, and approved under, the terms of the Tax Code.

The key characteristic of Caspian region hydrocarbons is the significant presence of sulphur dissolved in the hydrocarbon resource. Indeed, the largest resource, the

4. The Law in its 2024 form is available at adilet.zan.kz/eng/docs/Z1200000532/ accessed 7 July 2024.
5. *See* Long, 'From a Birkin Bag to Bitcoin; Kazakhstan's Protests in Six Objects' Economist 12 January 2022 https://www.economist.com/1843/2022/01/12/from-a-birkin-bag-to-bitcoin-kazakhstans-protests-in-six-objects.
6. For a comprehensive perspective on foreign investment in Kazakhstan's oil industry since 1990, *see* Luong and Weinthal, 'Revisiting the Obsolescent Bargain: Foreign Private Ownership in Kazakhstan' in 'Oil Is Not a Curse: Ownership Structure and Institutions in Soviet Successor States'. Cambridge University Press 2010.
7. The Law on Petroleum 1995 (issued 28 June 1995, # 2350) was supplemented with Art. 30 – 5 in 1999 to include a prohibition on gas flaring save for emergency situations and threats to public health and the environment. Available in Russian at https://adilet.zan.kz/rus/docs/U950002350_.
8. Article 20(9)(4) was added to the law in 2012 and further amended in 2017, so as to refer to the current Tax Code Art. 722.

offshore Kashagan field, has probably the highest sulphur content by volume of any hydrocarbon reservoir presently in production.[9] This has three immediately relevant consequences – first, natural gas dissolved in hydrocarbon column is likely to contain dangerous levels of hydrogen sulphide and any venting of such gas is extremely hazardous. Second, the infrastructure required to handle and process raw hydrocarbons, particularly natural gas in order to reach international and Kazakhstan domestic gas sales specifications, is necessarily more expensive and sophisticated in order to address the corrosive nature of the raw hydrocarbons and to monitor processing and production in order to ensure full and safe containment. Lastly, and most importantly, any natural gas which needs to be released in the course of production and processing must be efficiently flared in order to burn hydrogen sulphide and oxidise it to the less dangerous but nonetheless pollutant sulphur dioxide.

These factors bring into sharp relief the State's desire to ensure efficient gasification and the maximisation of domestic gas supply, and its objective to reduce gas flaring as well as air pollution. Utilisation of highly sulphurous gas requires very significant investment in sophisticated equipment, and particularly results in the need to handle store and ultimately sell solid sulphur created as a byproduct of gas processing. This makes it prohibitively expensive for smaller reservoirs of high sulphur content hydrocarbons to process raw sulphurous gas to downstream market specifications; given the prohibition on routine gas flaring, this compels domestic upstream producers to reinject 100% of raw associated gas into the source reservoir.

The expense of handling raw sulphurous gas is compounded by the structure of the downstream gas market discussed above; even if an upstream producer can afford the facilities required to process raw gas to the required specification, it is unlikely that the relevant reservoir is conveniently located close to a trunk gas pipeline available to ship the resource to the domestic or international marketplace.

In the specific context of Kazakhstan, 'Gasification' is part of a wider process of 'diversification' as the State has sought to reduce its reliance on oil and gas revenues and foment the development of small- and medium-sized industry, releasing the State's grip on economic activity.[10] It has also become a key component in the drive to increase energy efficiency, reducing reliance on ageing and inefficient coal-fired power stations for heat and power generation, and meeting Kazakhstan's Nationally Determined Commitments to combat climate change under the 2016 Paris Agreement. A joint report prepared by the Partnership for Action on Green Economy and the Ministry of Ecology, Geology and Natural Resources of Kazakhstan in 2020 stated:

9. Nurbekov and van der Putte illustrate this point in figure 4 of their paper Nurbekov and van der Putte, 'An Ambitious But Realistic Roadmap to Virtually Eliminate Gas Flaring and Venting in Kazakhstan'. Journal of World Energy Law and Business 2014 vol. 7 no. 6 https://doi.org/10.1093/jwelb/jwu021. The figure illustrates that the Kashagan and Tengiz fields are characterised by extremely high levels of reservoir pressure and sulphur, exceeded only by one operating field in North Carolina.

10. *See*, for example, 'Privatisation and the Role of the State in the Economy of Kazakhstan' in OECD Development Pathways 'Multi-dimensional Review of Kazakhstan Volume II in Depth Analysis and Recommendations' OECD 2017. Available at https://www.oecd-ilibrary.org/development/multi-dimensional-review-of-kazakhstan_9789264269200-en accessed 7 July 2024.

> Kazakhstan's economy is still [sic] highly energy intensive one. The country's GDP-energy intensity with 0.42 TOE/$ (2010) is 3.5 times the OECD average and is on 119th place out of 147 countries.[11]

The same report points out that 80% of Kazakhstan's electricity is generated by coal. In 2024, Agora Energiewende, a think-tank based in Germany reported that:

> Kazakhstan is one of the few countries in the world where building new coal power plants is still being discussed.[12]

The same report notes that Kazakhstan is currently at a crossroads, as Soviet-era coal-fired power stations reach the end of their service life, and the State is forced to choose between a range of options, including the construction of new coal-fired power stations, with or without carbon capture and sequestration facilities, rapid investment in renewable resources, and potentially, forcing upstream gas producers to sell production into the domestic market at lower prices than they would obtain on international markets. Twelve years after the law 'on Gas and Gas Supply' was enacted, 'gasification' is still part of the mix of solutions the State is struggling to choose between.

The next section of this chapter discusses the mechanisms of gas flaring approval operated by Kazakhstan in the period to 2017. In particular, it summarises the different roles of the flaring permit, which was the Ministry of Energy's instrument for controlling efficient gas production, and the emissions permit, issued by the Ministry of Ecology and focussed on the regulation of air pollution. It also analyses the penalties imposed for exceeding either permit and assesses the State's regulatory strategy against OECD norms and recommendations. Section 3 considers two phases of reform to that legislation; the Subsoil Code in 2017 and the Ecological Code in 2021. Section 4 reviews some statistical evidence to consider if these reforms are on track to achieve lasting results. The conclusion considers what lessons can be drawn from Kazakhstan's experience in reducing gas flaring in the wider context of meeting its energy needs.

2 GAS FLARING REGULATION PRIOR TO 2017

As mentioned above, gas flaring without State prior approval was prohibited under the Law on Petroleum in 1999. It is a feature of Kazakhstan legislation that gas flaring falls to be regulated by two Ministries delivering against somewhat competing government objectives. The Ministry of Energy (formerly the Ministry of Oil and Gas) was responsible for awarding flaring permits under the Law on the Subsoil and Subsoil Use

11. PAGE and the Ministry of Ecology, Geology and Natural Resources 'Kazakhstan's Transition to Green Economy: A Stocktaking Report' 2020. Available at https://archive.un-page.org/files/public/ge_stocktaking_report_eng_final.pdf accessed 7 July 2024.
12. Agora Energiewende, 'Modernising Kazakhstan's Coal-Dependent Power Sector Through Renewables. Challenges, Solutions and Scenarios Up to 2030 and Beyond' 2024. Available at https://www.agora-energiewende.org/publications/modernising-kazakhstans-coal-dependent-power-sector-through-renewables accessed 7 July 2024.

2010[13] and Regulations 1174 (permit awards)[14] and 1319 (calculation of flared volumes).[15] The objective of the flaring permit was to limit the subsoil user's inefficient combustion of hydrocarbon resources. By contrast, the Ministry of Ecology, Geology and Natural Resources granted an emissions permit which set limits on the amounts of airborne pollutants which a subsoil user may emit into the atmosphere, in terms of tonnes per year and in terms of a specific salvo rate in grams per second.[16] The objective of the emissions permit was to restrict air pollution to levels below the maximum permissible concentration of each pollutant in the vicinity of the emission source. Infringement of one permit did not necessarily imply infringement of the other; efficient gas flaring might exceed the flaring permit in volume terms, but the resultant pollutants might not exceed emissions permit ceilings.

2.1 The Flaring Permit

The flaring permit was developed in accordance with the 'DPGP' or gas emissions project for the relevant field, which in turn should be consistent with the gas utilisation proposals set out in the field's environmental impact assessment. The permit was awarded in terms of a permitted volume of million cubic metres of flared gas per annum. This permit was arrived at through a complex process of negotiation during which the subsoil user was required to justify the need to flare gas in terms of three permitted purposes – testing of exploration wells, commissioning of new facilities and 'technologically unavoidable gas flaring'. Operationally, planning flaring in accordance with specific volumes, and specific timings is unrealistic, especially when handling high levels of sulphur content – with the result that subsoil users have frequently breached the specific conditions of their flaring permit simply because operational circumstances disrupted the flaring strategy on which the case for the flaring permit had been constructed, often without resulting in any exceedance of the overall permissible volume of flared gas per year.

Over the last decade, both State and subsoil users explored options for revising the details of Regulation 1174 governing the award of flaring permits. In some measure, the two sides were aligned in pursuing 'normalisation', the process of setting flaring limits objectively according to recognised industrial standards. The State has sought to normalise the permitted quantities of gas flaring by setting permitted levels of flaring for the purpose of commissioning and 'technologically unavoidable gas flaring' in

13. Law of the Republic of Kazakhstan dated 24 June 2010 'On Subsoil and Subsoil Use,' 24 June 2010 No. 291-IV Available at https://online.zakon.kz/.
14. 'Rules for the Issuing of Permits for the Flaring of Associated and(or) Natural Gas' approved by Government Resolution 8 November 2010. No,. 1174. Available at https://online.zakon.kz/.
15. 'Methodology for Calculations of Standards and Volumes of Associated Combustion and (or) Natural Gas During Oil Operations' approved by Government Resolution 8 December 2010 No. 1319 available at https://online.zakon.kz/.
16. Ecological Code of the Republic of Kazakhstan 2007 Art. 69(2). The latest set of rules applicable to the issue of emissions permits before the Code was repealed were 'Regulations for the provision of permits for emissions to the environment for objects in categories II, III & IV'. Approved by the order of the Ministry of Ecology, Geology and Natural Resources of 2 June 2020 No. 130.

accordance with operational data reported by the industry. This strategy aligned with the Ministry's policy on the introduction of best available technologies and enabled it to set permit terms premised upon high levels of production uptime and equipment availability. This development should have been positive for subsoil users, in so far as it would result in a more flexible flaring permit, based on industry experience and expectations, rather than the artificial process of approving specific gas flaring operations and their associated flared volumes a year in advance as a means of arriving at an annual permitted total volume.

However, subsoil users have also campaigned for the gas flaring permit to allow for an additional category of flaring – unplanned maintenance and the resolution of equipment failures. The State's interpretation of 'technologically unavoidable gas flaring' has been and remains limited to planned maintenance and controlled, expected flaring events. Unpredicted gas flaring was treated as an emergency and denoted a loss, or potential loss, of containment for which the subsoil user was automatically in breach of its permit. The industry contended that, in accordance with good industry practice, gas flaring may be incorporated into the gas safety management plan of facilities designed to handle sulphurous gas, as an automated response to unacceptable conditions registered by the remote control systems which monitor plant operations. Gas flaring may be necessary to depressurise the section of the facility where the relevant alarm has been triggered, for the cause to be investigated in safe conditions. In practice, the relevant instrumentation and monitoring devices are intentionally sensitive and false alarms are a regular event. Accordingly, unplanned gas flaring is a feature of gas processing facilities, particularly for sulphurous raw gas and is built into gas safety management cases which are routinely approved by the State.

Another point of debate concerned the challenge of ensuring that sulphurous raw gas is properly and safely combusted with the result that no hydrogen sulphide is vented. Sulphurous raw gas does not burn efficiently and often must be mixed with processed gas and/or enriched with oxygen to ensure complete combustion. This only adds to the quantity of gas that must be flared for safety reasons.

2.2 The Emissions Permit

In a separate process to obtain an emissions permit from the Ministry of Ecology, the subsoil user must contract with a recognised expert environmental consultancy to prepare an application for an emissions permit describing its expected flaring from each flare point in terms of each regulated air pollutant. As with the flaring permit, the subsoil user is expected only to conduct planned flaring, justifying a final permitted level of emissions of controlled pollutants in tonnes per year and grams per second.[17]

Unlike the flaring permit which is set in accordance with the State's assessment of a subsoil user's approved expected flaring, the level of permitted emissions was calculated 'backwards' – the State used approved emission standards which set a maximum permitted concentration of each pollutant for the purposes of human health

17. Ecological Code 2007 Art. 75.

and well-being.[18] Using dispersion models around the relevant flare source and monitoring stations, and taking into account existing pollution sources, the expert would propose, and the Ministry approve, a level of maximum permitted emissions for each pollutant, with the objective of constraining flaring within limits so as not to cause the maximum permitted concentration to be exceeded during subsoil operations. The permit also set a limit in terms of 'salvo' emissions in grams per second to ensure that intermittent flaring did not cause maximum permissible concentrations to be exceeded briefly, in the course of the year when the overall tonnes per year limit was not exceeded.[19]

Again, the process of arriving at a workable emissions permit was lengthy and complex. The Ministry's priority was to ensure that approved emissions would not exceed maximum permissible concentrations, with the result of the subsoil user had no guarantee that the permit approved would permit planned operations necessitating flaring to proceed – particularly if other sources of air pollution increased their output and overall levels of air pollution in the vicinity of its operations.

As with the flaring permit, there was no concept of emergency flaring or any excuse from liability arising by reason of force majeure; liability arising from exceeding an emissions permit was strict. This was a common characteristic of both the flaring permit and emissions permit; the motivation or cause behind any gas flaring event was immaterial if the volume and/or rate of flaring exceeded the levels set out in one or other of the permits. The purpose of planned gas flaring was only relevant to decide whether or not it could be taken into account in assessing the level of flaring permit granted.

Flare stacks were routinely provided with automatic remote monitoring stations, the readings from which were to be provided continuously and promptly to the Ministry. Ultimately the only defence might be that another emission source was responsible for the exceedance which the relevant monitoring station recorded. This naturally resulted in the proliferation of such stations.

Remarkably, the subsoil user was held in breach of its emissions permit if its emissions were recorded in excess of the maximum permissible emissions for the relevant pollutants set out in its permit. This would be the case even if the same monitoring station recorded that the maximum permissible concentrations of such pollutants (the levels below which harm to human health and the environment is not expected) were not exceeded. This might have arisen, for example, where the subsoil user conducted its operations close to other air pollution sources, and was granted low maximum permissible emissions in order to ensure that its emissions, when combined with the other sources, together did not exceed the safe level set by the maximum permissible concentrations. If those other sources of air pollution were not operating when the subsoil user exceeded the maximum permissible emissions in its permit, it was treated as having breached its permit, with the consequences described in section

18. Ecological Code 2007 Art. 25. 'Rules for developing environmental quality targets' approved by Order of the Minister of Energy 26 February 2015 No. 145. Available at ww.online.zakon.kz.
19. The format of emissions permit application including integrated environmental permits was set by Order of the Minister of Energy of 20 February 2015 No. 115. Available at online.zakon.kz.

2.3 below, even though the maximum permissible concentrations had not been exceeded and, in accordance with the State emission standards, no harm to human life or the environment was deemed to have occurred. This is an important point when considering how the State used the 'indirect method' for calculating environmental damages which is discussed in the next section.

The Environmental Code 2007 included the concept of 'integrated environmental permits' or complex environmental permits.[20] This enabled the subsoil user to negotiate potentially a more realistic emissions permit on condition that it committed to implementing an approved programme of modernisation introducing 'best available technologies' into its operations with the overall mid-term objective of reducing regulated emissions. As discussed in section 3, the 2017 Tax Code increased the relevance of such permits by granting a conditional exemption from the levy for nature use for subsoil users whose emissions performance remained 'on target'.[21] This concept has been grandfathered into the Ecological Code 2021.

2.3 'The Polluter Pays'; But How Much?

The debates between subsoil user and regulator about the level of permitted flaring and their pollutants were a smokescreen for the real controversy which regularly gave rise to disputes in the last decade – what penalties should a subsoil user pay for exceeding a flaring or emissions permit? Suffice it to say that the Republic of Kazakhstan imposed penalties and strict liability for civil damages for exceeding permitted levels of flaring to a degree that was not closely matched by any other hydrocarbon state. Applying the legislation in force as of 2013 to an example known to the author, a gas flaring event releasing approximately 1 million m^3 of gas incurred liability to an administrative fine of approximately USD 22 million, an excess tax penalty of USD 22 million and a liability to civil damages in the region of USD 345 million. The same event would have incurred a total liability of USD 600,000 under Russian law (the next most severe level of penalty),[22] USD 200,000 under Nigerian law and USD 265,000 under Norwegian law. Simply put, the subsoil user that exceeded its permitted emissions levels could face penalties and civil damages in Kazakhstan which exceeded the level of penalties and civil damages payable in Russia by a factor of 575.

Such extraordinary levels of penalty brought the regulatory regime into some disrepute. As the last section of this chapter will discuss, that disrepute was accentuated by the lack of expenditure by the state on remediation, with the bulk of the payments simply being allocated to the central budget. The following analysis seeks to explain how such exorbitant levels of penalty were calculated until reforms in 2017.

20. Ecological Code 2007 Art. 79.
21. 'On Taxes and other obligatory payments to the Budget' (the Tax Code) Code of the Republic of Kazakhstan of 25 December 2017 No. 120-VI. Articles 575 and following.
22. The Russian online legal information service 'Konsultantplus' provides a useful summary of relevant legislation and indexation of payable penalties which can be accessed at https://www.consultant.ru/document/cons_doc_LAW_154375/.

As is commonplace in former Soviet jurisdictions, the subsoil user and other users of natural resources pay a tax for the impact caused by their activities on the natural environment. Thus, under the 2008 Tax Code,[23] the emission of some 15 air pollutants was the subject of taxation in terms of a coefficient of monthly calculation indices[24] per tonne of projected emissions. The levy for burning methane or hydrocarbons in the course of natural or associated gas flaring was 4 times and 13.5 times higher respectively compared to the same emissions from another different stationary source. Any levy could be doubled on the authority of the local government to address particularly sensitive environments, but the higher levels charged for associated gas combustion could be increased by up to 20-fold by the relevant Akimat. Significantly, the public sector energy generation enterprises such as coal-fired power stations were entitled to a levy discount of up to 70%. This discriminatory feature was also a characteristic of environmental damages for pollution discussed below.

Any exceedance of the flaring permit level incurred a penalty tax of 1,000% of the tax for permitted emissions. In addition to the penalty tax, the subsoil user would also be subject to an administrative fine of the same amount as the penalty tax.[25]

If the subsoil user exceeded its emissions permit, it was exposed to a claim for environmental damages which the Ministry of Environment was exclusively entitled to enforce and collect. Uniquely, the Environmental Code 2007 provided for damages to be assessed on a direct or indirect basis. Strictly the Code set up an expectation that the direct basis would be applied – involving the assessment of the actual damage caused and the cost of adequate remediation.[26] On its face, the Code gave priority to practical measures for remediation where possible instead of recovering monetary penalties. If remediation was not possible, but there was still evidence of physical environmental damage, financial damages could be assessed on an indirect basis – which were calculated in accordance with Regulation 535.[27] In practice, this legislation was not followed by the Ministry or by the courts; damage was presumed where an emissions permit had been exceeded, regardless of whether the relevant maximum permissible concentrations had been exceeded and/or any physical evidence of harm identified, and a claim was routinely presented in terms of the indirect method.

In brief, the indirect method involved calculating the exceedance per controlled pollutant above the relevant emission standard in grams per second over the timeframe of the emission incident and applying a series of coefficients to arrive at a financial liability. Those coefficients had a very significant impact:

- The maximum permissible concentration of each pollutant was taken into account to arrive at a conventional tonne for each pollutant, having the effect of increasing the amount payable per unit mass of particularly toxic gases.

23. 'On Taxes and other obligatory payments to the Budget' (the Tax Code) Code of the Republic of Kazakhstan of 10 December 2008 No. 99. Articles 495 and following.
24. This statutory annual indexation factor can be obtained at https://www.gov.kz/article/17157?lang=en.
25. Administrative Offences Code 30 January 2001 No. 155 Article 243.
26. Ecological Code 2007 Art. 108(3). 'Regulations for the economic assessment of damage from environmental pollution' approved by Government resolution dated 27 June 2007 No. 535.
27. *See* Regulations 535 paras 4-6.

- The formula applied a factor increasing the damages by up to 200% according to the sensitivity of the affected ecosystem, increasing the damages for emissions into greenfield or protected environments.
- The level of damages could be increased by up to 100% in the event of recidivism by the subsoil user.
- A different factor was applied depending on whether the emission source was stationary, mobile (e.g., a vehicle) or arose from natural gas flaring. This last factor was particularly controversial insofar as it discriminated against natural gas flaring; the factor applicable to emissions from stationary sources such as coal-fired power stations was a multiplier of 2.2 and for hydrocarbon emissions, 52. Thus the liability which a hydrocarbon subsoil user might incur exceeding its emissions permit could be more than 23 times greater than the liability incurred by a power station for exactly the same quantities of air pollutants in equivalent circumstances. No explanation for this disparity was provided in the legislation.
- A further 10-fold multiplier was also applied in the formula.[28]

A state-owned gas-fired power station emitting methane in the same volumes as a subsoil user would incur an administrative fine and penalty tax equivalent to 0.5% of the fine and tax payable by the subsoil user, and environmental damages equivalent to 4.5% of the sum payable by the subsoil user.[29]

Such discriminatory treatment of the hydrocarbon sector (or alternatively protection of the state utility sector) undermined the legitimacy of the legislation. Many of the production sharing agreements and concessions negotiated in the 1990s for upstream hydrocarbon projects contained a form of legislative stability, which allowed the State to introduce legislative changes to the detriment of the subsoil users' commercial interests if such legislation was introduced in the interests of health, security or environmental protection, and such legislation was applied in a non-discriminatory basis.[30] The State was exposed to accusations that the environmental legislation constituted a form of disguised taxation targeting subsoil users, designed to exploit a loophole in the legislative stability regime, or worse, was a form of indirect expropriation, having the effect of shifting the commercial benefit of the contract substantially in the State's favour. Importantly, the administrative fines were collectable by the regional administration or Akimat, with the penalty taxes and environmental damages being payable to the central budget. The prevailing legislation provided no guidance as to how such monies should be deployed.

Another immediate point of contention was whether the relevant fines, penalty taxes and environmental damages paid by the subsoil user could be recovered by it as an operational cost from subsequent production revenues under the terms of the

28. *See* Appendix III of Regulations 535.
29. *See* Appendix III of Regulations 535.
30. The contract stabilisation regimes in both Azerbaijan and Kazakhstan oil sector production sharing agreements are discussed in Sahin, 'Production Sharing Agreements in the Caucasus and Central Asia: A Contextual Study of Azerbaijan and Kazakhstan'. Transnational Dispute Management vol. 17 no. 1 January 2020.

relevant production sharing agreements; arguably they could, in circumstances where the flaring was triggered automatically and as a matter of routine by an approved feature of the subsoil user's operational safety design, without any human interference, still less any negligence on the part of the subsoil user.

The terms on which these disputes were settled are confidential, but the following sections discuss the legislative changes which, to some degree, were driven by the desire to narrow the scope for controversy that significantly complicated relations between the State and international oil investors.

Before discussing the significant reforms to Kazakhstan's gas flaring legislation from 2017 onwards, the next section puts Kazakhstan's legislation before 2017 in the context of contemporary international practice, particularly with respect to environmental taxation.

2.4 The OECD Perspective

It is helpful to review Kazakh legislation on gas flaring and environmental pollution in the context of the OECD paper 'Liability for Environmental Damage in Eastern Europe, Caucasus and Central Asia (EECCA): Implementation of Good International Practices' published in 2012.[31]

The paper comments that EECCA countries routinely apply a fault-based approach to environmental liability, in line with Soviet legislation, but the authors select Kazakhstan as an exception where the authors observe that enterprises engaged in hazardous activities such as hydrocarbon extraction are strictly liable for environmental damage unless the polluter can show the incident arose by reason of force majeure, in accordance with the Ecological Code 2007 Articles 321(5). Ironically, as this chapter has sought to illustrate, the legislation implementing liability for exceeding flaring permits and emissions permits is not consistent with that proposition, because liability is incurred even in circumstances where the subsoil user flares gas in an emergency, including in circumstances where such flaring is necessary to eliminate the greater danger of venting hydrogen sulphide gas.

Regardless of the Environmental Code 2007s intentions, liability for breach of any gas flaring permit or emissions permit by a hydrocarbon subsoil user is practically strict. Indeed, the enforcing authorities have no need to prove that the maximum permitted concentrations of air pollutants were exceeded by any particular flaring event, evidencing a potential or actual threat to human health and environmental conditions, as long as the relevant emissions permit limits were exceeded.[32]

The OECD paper further recommends that EECCA countries amend their legislation in accordance with the 'polluter pays' principle; as section 4 argues, Kazakhstan is clearly an example of a state which has applied that principle to a fault, without feeling

31. Available at https://one.oecd.org/document/ENV/EPOC/EAP/REPIN(2011)6/en/pdf.
32. It is also helpful to consider Arts 40 and 41 of the Administrative Penal Code which address harm caused in the context of an emergency or the taking of a reasonable risk for a socially useful purpose.

constrained by a need to identify and compensate affected victims and impaired ecosystems.

The OECD's objective goes further in explaining 'the polluter pays' principle:

> Its objective is to encourage and prepare reforms of environmental liability provisions which are necessary to re-orient them toward the ultimate goal of restoring the damaged environment.

By contrast, Kazakhstan's legislation had the objective of punishing the polluter but provided no mechanism by which the penalty reflected the harm caused or the cost of remediation. The OECD paper concludes:

> One major avenue for reform is to re-orient EECCA environmental liability systems toward the restoration of the environment. Contrary to the EECCA region, environmental liability in OECD countries is not a penal regime designed to punish the party responsible for the damage (or simply non-compliance) but a system that is focused on remediating the damage done. Consequently, compensation of environmental damage is understood not as a monetary penalty payable by the responsible party to the government but either as remediation measures undertaken by the responsible party or as the reimbursement by the responsible party of clean-up costs borne by the government.

Section 3 will discuss how the relevant legislation has been reformed in the last five years and section 4 considers whether, following such reforms, Kazakhstan is now on track to meet the expectations of the OECD as well as to achieve significant reductions in gas flaring both to meet Paris Agreement and environmental targets.

3 ENVIRONMENTAL LAW REFORM IN KAZAKHSTAN

3.1 Reforms in 2017

Kazakhstan has responded to pressure to reform its gas flaring legislation. First, in 2017, it introduced the first Subsoil Code which consolidated a wide range of legislation affecting the hydrocarbon industry under the aegis of the Ministry of Energy.[33] Specifically, Article 146 legalised gas flaring in the event of emergencies which threaten public health, individuals and the environment. This has avoided the need to extend the concept of technologically unavoidable gas flaring to include flaring in emergencies or for unplanned maintenance; such remains subject to prior approval under the terms of the applicable flaring permit. This is not an attractive result for the oil and gas industry; unplanned gas flaring triggered by predictable and unavoidable equipment failures and false alarms may be supported by industry standards and availability statistics but may be rejected by the regulator simply because they are unplanned, but fall short of being classed as emergencies.

Second, the 2008 Tax Code which included the rates of levy for the emission of controlled pollutants both within and exceeding the relevant flaring permit, was

33. The Code 'On the Subsoil and Subsoil Use' dated 27 December 2017 No. 126-VI, available at https://adilet.zan.kz/eng/docs/K1700000125.

replaced by the 2017 Tax Code.[34] The latter provided a new basis for such calculations. Under the 2008 Tax Code, key air pollutants such as sulphur dioxide were subject to the same rates of levy (10 monthly calculation indices per tonne) whether the emission source was stationary or arose from the combustion of hydrocarbons; higher rates were imposed only for emissions of methane, hydrocarbons and oxides of carbon. In the 2017 Tax Code, the list of pollutants chargeable at a higher rate of levy as a result of associated gas flaring was extended from 3 to 8, such a higher rate being at least 20 times greater than the rate of levy incurred by other fixed sources of air pollution. This has perpetuated the discrimination observed in section 2.3 in relation to the enhanced level of environmental damages for hydrocarbon combustion imposed by the Environmental Code 2007 and Regulations 535.

However, such increased level of levy for hydrocarbon flaring is more than offset by the abolition of the administrative penalty and penalty tax for over-limit emissions achieved by the repeal of the Tax Code 2008. They were replaced by a fixed penalty for environmental infractions by subsoil users was introduced by a law of 2017 into the Administrative Procedural Code 2014 (Article 356). The fine for unauthorised gas flaring by larger enterprises amounted to 2,000 monthly calculation indices or KZT 7.38 million or just less than USD 17,000, applying an Monthly Calculation Index or MCI of KZT 3,692.

More significantly, the next section discusses how the Tax Code 2017 was further amended in 2021 (in alignment with the new Ecological Code) to exempt the subsoil user from paying such levy altogether in the event that it negotiated, obtained and complied with, an integrated environmental permit for gas flaring.

3.2 The Ecological Code 2021

The Ecological Code 2021 represents a step change in Kazakhstan's environmental legislation, not only in relation to environmental protection generally but also in relation to gas flaring specifically. It is difficult to summarise the scope of the changes adequately, but this section will try to analyse the Code where it impacts the issues discussed above.

The Code helpfully rehearses the key principles upon which it is founded – including 'the polluter pays' which it interprets as:

> a person whose activity causes or may cause pollution of the environment, degradation of the natural environment, causing environmental damage in any form or harm to life and (or) health of people, bears all costs for implementation of requirements of the environmental legislation of the Republic of Kazakhstan for prevention and control of the negative consequences of their activities, including the elimination of environmental damage caused in accordance with the principle of correction.[35]

34. Code 'On Taxes and other obligatory payments to the Budget' dated 25 December 2017 No. 120 VI, available at https://adilet.zan.kz/eng/docs/K1700000120.
35. Article 5(5).

The liability is expressed under Article 136(1) as follows:

> In accordance with the 'polluter pays' principle, a person whose actions or activity caused environmental damage is obliged to fully and at his own expense remediate the components of the natural environment that suffered environmental damage.

Article 13 provides that everyone has a right to a favourable environment, and specifically allows individuals to bring complaints with respect to environmental violations to the attention of the environmental authorities. The vestiges of the old regime remain; no individual may bring a claim for compensation arising from environmental damage and the State retains its exclusive right to pursue compensation from environmental damage under Article 136(2).

Under Article 175 of the Code, larger businesses are subject to a daily fine of 10 monthly calculation indices for every day that an emissions permit is exceeded, a far more lenient measure than the administrative fine and penalty tax under the 2008 Tax Code. A fundamental change is the elimination of damages for environmental harm caused by gas flaring in excess of emission permit limits under the Environmental Code 2007 and Regulations 535. It is replaced with the liability to remediate harm caused to the environment under Article 138. Environmental harm is no longer deemed to have arisen where an environmental emissions permit has been exceeded; the test for harm involves:

> a directly or indirectly measurable negative change in the state of the components of the natural environment or a measurable deterioration in their consumer properties or useful qualities.[36]

While Article 131(2) clarifies that air pollution may constitute environmental harm, the burden of proof of harm seems to lie fully with the State. This brings Kazakhstan legislation far closer to OECD practice as exemplified by the EU Environmental Liability Directive,[37] but it remains to be seen how these principles will be operationalised by the Ministry of Ecology and the courts in practice. While the 'indirect method' of calculating environmental damages resulted in extreme levels of liability, it had the advantage of predictability and transparency and avoided the need for Ministry officials to make administrative decisions at their discretion, for which they could be held accountable.

The drive to achieve 'normalisation' in terms of setting expectations which define and constrain gas flaring operations within a certain range of acceptable performance measures has continued. The emissions permit will be set using so-called technological standards mandating the progressive reduction in emissions of marker pollutants used to measure the licence holder's environmental performance.[38] The Code brings back into focus the concept of the integrated environmental permit first introduced in the

36. Article 131(1).
37. (2004/35/EC).
38. Article 40.

Ecological Code 2007. As discussed in section 3.1, compliance with that permit programme of emissions reduction may lead to the elimination or significant reduction of the levy for the use of environmental resources under the 2017 Tax Code.

Nonetheless, the oil and gas industry did not succeed in making the case for a wider definition scope of 'technologically unavoidable gas flaring'; Article 202(9) re-states that the State's previously held position that unplanned gas flaring may be permissible provided that emissions remain within the limits of the relevant permits nonetheless. Emissions arising outside such definition of technologically unavoidable gas flaring caused by equipment failure or other deviation from normal performance will be treated as excessive, but the Code does not make it clear whether a permit is treated as exceeded in such circumstances even if the relevant gas concentration limits are not breached. Article 202(10) also closed the door to providing norms for emergency gas flaring; no permit will include an allowance for accidental emissions.

4 RETROSPECTIVE: WHAT HAS REGULATION ACHIEVED?

In May 2022, the World Bank Global Gas Flaring Reduction Partnership issued a report,[39] lamenting slow progress in the reduction of global gas flaring, but highlighting Kazakhstan as an outlying success story, recording that it had reduced flaring from 4 bcm in 2012 to 1.5 bcm in 2021 *'thanks to strictly enforced regulations, coupled with a domestic gas market that incentivises associated gas recovery'*.

One headline can be offset with another; in February 2024, the BBC reported a methane leak of approximately 127,000 tonnes from a Buzachi Neft well in the Mangistau province of Kazakhstan. The leak had apparently begun in June 2023 and was brought under control in December. Apparently, this leak ranks second in the severity of recorded methane losses to the methane leak caused by the sabotage to the Nordstream 1 & 2 gas pipelines in the Baltic in September 2022.[40]

In the context of climate change, there is an understandable focus on methane and carbon dioxide leakage, but the overall picture with respect to the release into the atmosphere of all air pollutants in Kazakhstan remains less positive. The Ministry of Ecology issues an annual national report providing extensive data on environmental indicators with respect to air, water and land pollution, and the steps taken by the Ministry to mitigate or alleviate such effects.[41] The first graph below shows the quantity in thousand tonnes of air pollutants emitted in Kazakhstan from stationary sources since 2012 according to the National Reports, reflecting very little significant progress in the recent decade.

39. World Bank, 'Global Flaring and Venting Regulations: A Comparative Review of Policies' (English). Washington, D.C., World Bank Group. http://documents.worldbank.org/curated/en/099040224142534541/P1596901b39a4f0fe19cd4177dc016327e4.
40. BBC, 'Kazakhstan: Methane mega-Leak Went on for Months' 16 February 2024. Available at https://www.bbc.com/news/world-asia-68166298.
41. The National Reports are available at https://ecogosfond.kz/ltty-bajandama/.

The second graph below is drawn from data contained in a report by Kazakhstan's Economic Research Institute dated 28 April 2022.[42,43] It focuses on greenhouse gases and suggests that some recent progress in reducing greenhouse gas emissions is underway in the energy generation sector at least, but it hardly aligns with the overall picture of consistent and substantial flaring reduction asserted by the World Bank report mentioned above.

The discrepancy between these results can be attributed to three factors. First, the World Bank report focuses on the flaring of associated natural gas by subsoil users. It does not include gas flaring from stationary sources such as power generation and industrial processes, which is the subject of the second graph. There is in any case some controversy around the reliability of the relevant data; the World Bank data is consistent with the Ministry of Energy's data for 2012, which relies upon subsoil users' reported flaring. Satellite data reported by Nurbekov and van der Putte suggest that associated gas flaring may be as low as 0.9 bcm per annum for 2013, and the result may have been achieved possibly by the subsoil users diverting such gas to fuel internal production needs such as boilers.[44]

However, the World Bank report is consistent with the reported success of Kazakhstan's main upstream reservoirs, Kashagan, Karachaganak and Tengiz, in achieving extremely high levels of gas utilisation. The Ministry of Energy reports that Kazakhstan has 3,800 billion m^3 of gas reserves of which 60 % is associated natural gas, and 75 % of which is attributed to those three fields.[45] In its sustainability report for 2022, the Karachaganak project reports a gas utilisation factor of 99.93 %,[46] the Tengiz project also reports gas utilisation of 99.3 % in 1H2024 and a reduction in gas flaring of 96 % since 2000,[47] and the Kashagan project reports flaring 48.5 million m^3 of hydrocarbons in 2022, and produced 7.8 billion m^3 of gas in the same period, an effective gas utilisation factor of approximately 99.4 %.[48] These results have been achieved not only by gas reinjection but also more recently by the separation and sale of liquid petroleum gas for domestic and industrial use.

The reality may be that Kazakhstan has focused its attention on achieving high levels of gas utilisation from these megaprojects, not only by incentivising greater

42. Kazakhstan's Nationally Determined Commitments under the Paris Agreement include a pledge to achieve a 25 % reduction in carbon emissions by 2030 against a 1990 baseline.
43. 'National Greenhouse Gas Emissions in the Republic of Kazakhstan' Economic Research Institute Qazaqstan. Available in Russian at https://economy.kz/ru/Novosti_instituta/id=4512.
44. Nurbekov and van der Putte 'An Ambitious But Realistic Roadmap to Virtually Eliminate Gas Flaring and Venting in Kazakhstan'. Journal of World Energy Law and Business 2014 vol. 7 no. 6 https://doi.org/10.1093/jwelb/jwu021.
45. From https://www.gov.kz/memleket/entities/energo/activities/4905?lang=en and Nurbekov and van der Putte.
46. Available at https://www.kpo.kz/docs/sustainability_report_2023/en/024-vybrosy_v_atmosferu.php.
47. 'Tengizchevroil Fact Sheet 2 2024', https://www.tengizchevroil.com/docs/default-source/default-document-library/facts-and-figures/2024/tco-fact-sheet-2q-2024_e_final.pdf?sfvrsn=e50fcc5c_2. 'Tengizchevroil: Overview of 2023 Environmental Activities and Performance'. Available at https://www.tengizchevroil.com/sustainability.
48. NCOC Sustainability Report 2022 available at https://www.ncoc.kz/en/sustainability/2022/reports.

levels of gas utilisation but also by penalising excess gas flaring regulated by integrated environmental permits which set targets for lower gas flaring by the implementation of best available technologies. It has not set about incentivising lower levels of air emissions and gas flaring by power generation and heavy industry; reported emission levels remain high and as this chapter has argued, opportunities have been missed to apply the same penalty measures to such industries, in order to encourage the same behaviours. Accordingly, it is unlikely that the trend of reduced gas flaring reported by the World Bank with respect to associated gas will extend to downstream gas flaring and air emissions over the next decade.

There is one respect in which Kazakhstan may have turned the corner with respect to matters which this chapter has addressed. The last graph below is drawn from data provided by the Ministry of Ecology's national reports since 2017 and provides the Ministry's annual receipts in terms of air pollution emission payments and the Ministry's expenditure on related remediation activity. Up until 2022, the Ministry routinely did not spend more than 50% of such receipts on remediation and mitigatory activity. In 2022, for the first time, it spent more than it received in such emission-related payments, on remediation activities described in its 2022 report. In a significant departure from the practice of the last decade, the Ministry is apparently no longer collecting emissions payments as a stealth tax on behalf of the State but is genuinely focusing its resources upon the enforcement and implementation of 'the polluter pays' principle in terms of the Ecological Code 2021, and remediation of air pollution. This is a trend which one hopes will extend well into the future:

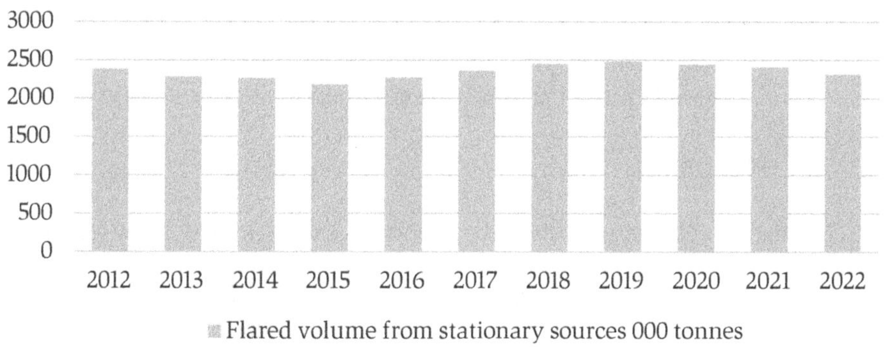

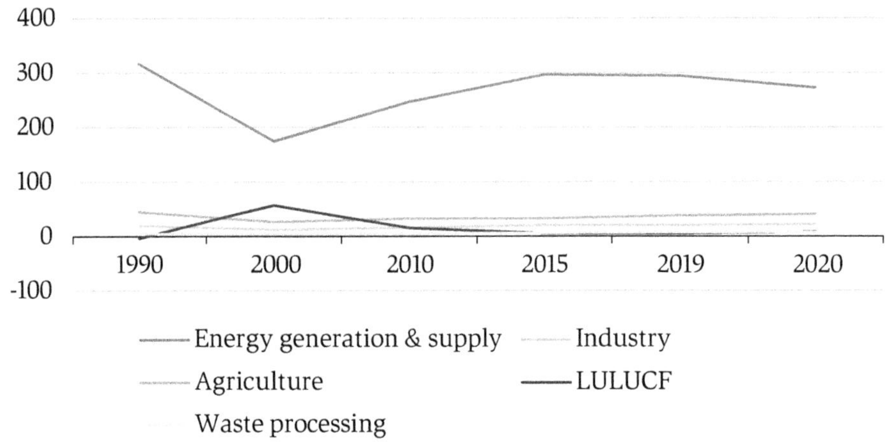

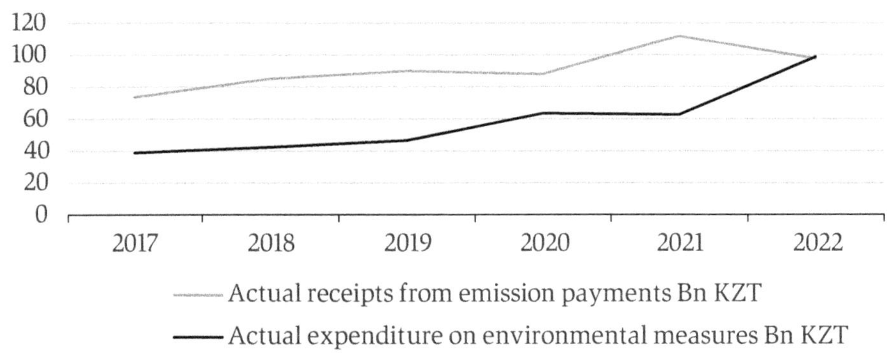

5 CONCLUSION

In 2019, Chatham House published the report 'Kazakhstan: Tested by Transition' which, *inter alia*, discussed the Republic's drive to use the oil and gas mega projects, Kashagan, Karachaganak and Tengiz, as both models for economic development as well as a source of rent to finance diversification away from reliance on oil and gas revenues.[49] The report also emphasised the potentially dead hand of state ownership of industry beyond such foreign-owned assets:

> The state's presence in the economy beyond formal asset ownership also remains significant, with widespread subsidies and price controls creating inefficiencies and distorted incentives. Significant tax incentives and exemptions, subsidized lending and implicit debt guarantees disproportionately benefit large state companies.

49. Chatham House, 'Kazakhstan: Tested by Transition' 2019. Available at https://www.chathamhouse.org/2019/11/kazakhstan-tested-transition accessed 8 July 2024.

This chapter has described how Kazakhstan's environmental legislation has imposed severe penalties on subsoil users for uncontrolled and excessive air pollution, while not penalising other industrial sources for equivalent emissions. This has contributed to the successful elimination of air pollution, investment in the best available technologies and very high levels of gas utilisation by foreign-funded large upstream assets. In statistical terms, results have been obtained and institutions such as the World Bank duly impressed. However, the question needs to be asked whether such a regulatory strategy was only going to work when applied to relatively well-funded and technologically advanced projects in private and foreign ownership, which could be incentivised to reduce emissions without significant impact on State revenues. The environmental rules pertaining prior to the Ecological Code 2021 could be interpreted as trying to meet several purposes at once – encouraging best practices, maximising state revenue and avoiding burdening inefficient state enterprises with new requirements to make capital investments in improved technology. The result was uneven at best, and discriminatory at worst. It is perhaps an example of the phenomenon which Chatham House describes as follows:

> In other ways, too, state-led initiatives reproduce the problems they are intended to solve. Top-down demands to fulfil directives and meet targets encourage a 'storming' approach to achieving outcomes – or the appearance of doing so – among officials. This premium on demonstrating quick results encourages short-cuts and quick fixes, in particular through imported technology or physical capacity rather than the slower, less tangible but essential work of building enabling systems and institutions.

The question arises whether the Ecological Code marks a departure from this practice, part of a new strategy which has the prospect of reproducing the progress made in reducing gas flaring, by extending its scope to include state-owned coal-fired power stations and state-owned oil and gas projects. On the one hand, as discussed the Ecological Code brings Kazakhstan's regulatory practice closer to OECD recommendations, following the principle of 'the polluter pays' as OECD intended it to mean. As of 2022, the Ministry of Ecology appears to be spending its revenues on environmental rehabilitation in line with those recommendations.

On the other hand, the Ecological Code has introduced a degree of flexibility, enabling the Ministry and the courts to define a polluter's responsibility on the basis of actual evidence of incurred harm. This then begs the question of whether the legislation will be implemented objectively in accordance with the rule of law, making no distinction between State-owned and privately-owned enterprises. As explained in the introduction, Kazakhstan is in the middle, not the end, of the process of 'Gasification', assessing potential costs of various options for replacing existing power generation assets and meeting objectives for reduced carbon emissions as well as improved energy efficiency and reduced air pollution. It remains to be seen whether the State's implementation of the Ecological Code will be influenced by the State's needs to accommodate such a transition, smoothing the pathway for state enterprises, after a period of more robust regulation for private and foreign investors.

CHAPTER 18

Jurisdictional Focus: Libya

Waniss Almashri Otman

1 INTRODUCTION

Within the framework of the energy transition and the amelioration of its national economy, Libya, like many other oil and gas-producing countries, seeks to eliminate the flaring of natural gas, thereby enhancing its energy security by making available additional quantities of gas to the local market or for export. Against this background, this chapter will attempt to provide a critical overview and provide a sound understanding of the legal framework relating to this issue. Key challenges and opportunities will also be assessed in order to identify barriers and benefits resulting from the reduction or elimination of gas flaring.

2 OVERVIEW OF THE UPSTREAM OIL AND GAS SECTOR

According to the OPEC Annual Statistical Bulletin, 2023, Libya's global rank is 23rd in terms of proven gas reserves, with 1,505 billion cubic meters (bcm) or 0.72 % of world reserves at the end of 2022.[1] In terms of gas production in Libya is derived from both associated and free gas, according to Energy Institute's statistical review for the year 2023, it was recorded at 14.8 billion cubic meters at the end of 2022.[2]

Libya's oil reserves are the largest in Africa and among the ten largest countries in the world (ranked 8th), at 48.363 billion barrels as of 2022.[3] Oil production was 1.088 million barrels per day as of 2022,[4] giving Libya about 122 years of reserves at current production rates if no new reserves were to be found.

1. OPEC Annual Statistical Bulletin, 58th edition 2023. Available at: www.opec.org.
2. Energy Institute Statistical Review of World Energy, 2023, 72nd edition.
3. OPEC, *supra* n. 1.
4. Energy Institute, *supra* n. 2.

3 THE LIBYAN POLICY VACUUM FOR GAS FLARING

Globally, nine countries are responsible for the vast majority of gas flaring: Russia, Iraq, Iran, Algeria, Venezuela, the United States, Mexico, Libya and Nigeria which account for nearly three-quarters of gas flaring and just under half of global oil production.[5]

According to World Bank estimates, Libya is one of the world's largest top nine flaring countries (responsible for 74% of gas flare volumes), in 2022, it ranked 8th highest in the world. It has always been ranked among the top three countries in Africa in terms of gas flaring, a position has maintained for many years.[6] In 2022, Libya's share of flaring natural gas in Africa was recorded at 18.4% of the total.[7] In the period from 2012 to 2022, an amount of 43.5 bcm of natural gas was flared in Libya. In the period under review, it registered the highest levels of natural gas flaring in 2021 and 2022 at 5.9 and 5.4 bcm respectively, and the flaring intensity for the last decade has remained high. There were 86 flare sites in Libya conducted in 2019.[8]

Table 18.1 covering the previous decade (2012-2022) illustrates that Libya was the third top gas flaring in Africa with an average annual flared gas quantity of about 3.954 bcm,[9] or the equivalent of almost half of its domestic gas consumption the same period.[10] Table 18.2 provides details of Libyan natural gas flaring when compared to oil production.

The LNOC owns the vast majority of the country's oil and gas production (about 80% of the country's total), mostly from older oil fields, and as a result, is responsible for most of the gas flaring. It completely owns most of the country's major oil fields that produce oil and flare-associated gas, and in partnership with foreign companies such as Eni, also operates fields that produce free gas and condensate, where the flaring process is very limited.[11]

It's worth mentioning that, as can be seen from the following table gas flaring in 2020 decreased to 2.5 bcm due to associated gas production which was shut in along with almost all of the onshore oil fields during most of 2020.[12]

5. The World Bank, Global Gas Flaring Tracker Report, 29 March 2023. Available at: https://www.worldbank.org/en/topic/extractiveindustries/publication/2023-global-gas-flaring-tracker-report.
6. The World Bank, Global Gas Reduction Partnership (GGRP), Global Gas Flaring Tracker Report, March 2023. Available at: https://thedocs.worldbank.org/en/doc/5d5c5c8b0f451b472e858ceb97624a18-0400072023/original/2023-Global-Gas-Flaring-Tracker-Report.pdf.
7. Energy Institute Statistical Review of World Energy, 2023, 72nd edition.
8. The World Bank, Global Gas Reduction Partnership (GGRP), Global Flaring and Venting Regulations: Libya Policy and Target, September 2021. Available at: https://flaringventingregulations.worldbank.org/libya.
9. Energy Institute, *supra* n. 2.
10. OPEC, *supra* n. 1.
11. U.S. Energy Information Administration (EIA), Libya: Executive Summary, 9 March 2022. Available at: https://www.eia.gov/international/analysis/country/LBY.
12. *Ibid.*

Table 18.1 Natural Gas Flaring in Libya Compared to Oil-producing African Countries, 2012-2022 (bcm)

Country	*2012*	*2013*	*2014*	*2015*	*2016*	*2017*	*2018*	*2019*	*2020*	*2021*	*2022*	*Total*
Algeria	3.4	8.8	9.2	9.6	9.7	9.2	9.4	9.7	9.3	8.1	8.5	94.9
Nigeria	12.9	9.2	8.3	7.5	7.2	7.5	7.3	7.8	7.0	6.5	5.3	86.5
Libya	3.8	4.1	2.9	2.7	2.4	4.0	4.7	5.1	2.5	5.9	5.4	43.5
Egypt	0.4	2.6	3.0	3.0	3.0	2.5	2.4	2.5	2.5	2.3	2.2	26.4
Other Africa	12.1	9.3	9.7	10.4	10.4	9.4	8.5	8.2	7.8	7.4	7.9	101.1

Source: Data gathered from Energy Institute Statistical Review of World Energy, 2023, 72nd edition.

Table 18.2 Libya Natural Gas Flaring Compared to Oil Production

Libya	*2012*	*2013*	*2014*	*2015*	*2016*	*2017*	*2018*	*2019*	*2020*	*2021*	*2022*
Oil Production (mm b/d)	1.539	1.048	0.518	0.437	0.412	0.929	1.165	1.228	0.425	1.269	1.088
Gas Flaring (bcm)	3.8	4.1	2.9	2.7	2.4	4.0	4.7	5.1	2.5	5.9	5.4

Source: Data gathered from Energy Institute Statistical Review of World Energy, 2023, 72nd edition.

Regrettably, due to the LNOC's historical focus on the Sirte Basin, Libya lacks sufficient natural gas infrastructure, especially processing plants and pipelines, required to capture natural gas from fields associated with oil production and transport it to demand centres or power plants.[13]

One of the main reasons for the continued flaring of gas in certain producing countries is the lack or inadequacy of policies and strategies to reduce gas flaring. This arises from a lack of coordination or integration between energy policies and environmental policies addressing gas emissions, and more specifically, gas flaring. This may explain why some nationally determined contributions (NDCs)[14] submitted by Arab producers include general measures to reduce gas flaring or do not include any measures at all. It must be emphasized that this problem also exists in other oil and gas-producing countries.[15]

13. *Ibid.*
14. NDCs embody efforts by each country to reduce national emissions and adapt to the impacts of climate change. The Paris Agreement (Art. 4, para. 2) requires each Party to prepare, communicate and maintain successive NDCs that it intends to achieve.
15. UN-ESCWA 2019, Reducing Gas Flaring in Arab Countries A Sustainable Development Necessity. United Nations publication issued by ESCWA, United Nations House, Beirut, Lebanon, p. 12. Available at: https://www.unescwa.org/sites/default/files/pubs/pdf/reducing-gas-flaring-arab-countries-english.pdf.

Thus, the lack of suitable policies and strategies translates into the absence of effective frameworks to regulate gas flaring. A very limited number of Arab oil and gas producers have regulations that adequately cover the reduction/elimination of gas flaring. If a regulatory framework is in place but it is not properly implemented, or if too many exceptions allow gas flaring to continue, the framework becomes ineffective. It should, however, be noted that some Arab producers who do not have clear regulations to limit gas flaring have been able to significantly reduce gas flaring through financial grants, government commitments and initiatives.[16]

4 NATURAL GAS FLARING REGULATIONS AND THE LEGISLATIVE FRAMEWORK

This section will first address the main Libyan Oil and Gas legislation related to the process of flaring natural gas and concurrent environmental pollution, after which the key environmental legislation in force in the country will be critically appraised to address these problems. It will also briefly review international agreements and treaties related to the environment that Libya has ratified and transposed into Libyan law.

The legal framework for the Libyan petroleum industry consists of legislative and contractual sources. The main legislative sources are the Petroleum Law No. 25 of 1955, as amended, and the Petroleum Regulations promulgated thereunder. As for the contractual sources, these comprise concession contracts and joint venture agreements, and the four iterations of the production sharing contracts,[17] generally known as Exploration and Production Sharing Agreements (EPSAs).[18] EPSA-IV is currently the only contractual model offered by the Libyan government to IOCs wishing to invest in the oil and gas E&P sector unless they take the route of acquiring existing assets through the takeover or direct equity participation of companies which own them.

- The Petroleum Law

The Petroleum Law No. 25 of 1955 remains today the most comprehensive piece of legislation regulating the petroleum industry in Libya. Since its promulgation, it has undergone several changes and amendments.

- Petroleum Regulations

Under Article 24 of the Petroleum Law, several petroleum regulations have been issued to implement the law. From 1955 to the early 1970s, the Libyan Ministry of Petroleum issued nine regulations relating to petroleum operations. Six of these regulations have

16. *Ibid.*
17. Otman A. Waniss, Libya Oil and Gas Resources: Key Players, Hydrocarbon Laws, Exploration and Production Records, Past Lessons, Future Potential, and Evaluating E and P Challenges, March 2008. Dar Al Rwad for Publication and Distribution, Tripoli, Libya.
18. For the last five decades, Libyan hydrocarbon sector has witnessed four successive generations of EPSAs. The first known as EPSA-I, was introduced in 1974; EPSA-II dated from early 1980; EPSA-III was introduced in the late 1988 and the final EPSA-IV was introduced in 2004. The first three generations of EPSAs were concluded on the basis of direct negotiations between the LNOC and IOCs. However, the EPSA-IV model was based on an open bidding system.

been incorporated within the amended Petroleum Law. Three remaining regulations are still in force: Petroleum Regulations 1, 8 and 9.[19]

Petroleum Regulation No. 1 was issued in August 1955 and dealt with Libyan geography – the country was divided into four zones, each with a different status with regard to upstream exploitation. Regulation No. 8 was issued in 1968 and dealt with petroleum operations, aiming to regulate oil and gas production levels and is considered to be one of the most important practical steps taken for the reformation of the Libyan petroleum industry. Finally, Petroleum Regulation No. 9, issued in July 1973, provided a comprehensive financial, administrative and technical framework for the implementation, for its time, of a comprehensive and sophisticated t structure to manage the country's oil wealth.

- EPSA-IV

The Government developed a gas fiscal policy to respond to the lifting of the sanctions in 2004 and sought to boost production capacity to increase both exports and domestic utilization. LNOC then outlined a formal framework incorporating clauses for gas exploitation in the new licensing round utilizing EPSA IV in September 2004.[20] These were announced as part of the modified EPSA-III that had already existed for oil E&P.[21] This restriction on gas development in previous EPSA's had in the past been cited as a deterrent for IOCs wishing to participate in Libya's gas future. However, the new EPSA IV terms are much more encouraging than those previously introduced.[22]

It's worth emphasizing that the Petroleum Law and Regulations remain an essential piece of legislation since the governing law of EPSAs expressly includes the Petroleum Law as amended, and the regulations issued thereunder, except as otherwise provided in the EPSA-IV itself. Article (21) of the EPSA-IV model thus states that: '*This Agreement shall be governed by and interpreted in accordance with the laws and regulations of Libya, including, without limitation, the Petroleum Law*'.

4.1 Gas Flaring under EPSA-IV: Fiscal Policy Concerns

Undoubtedly, due to a variety of reasons, the gas sector in Libya has been historically regarded as the poor sister of oil,[23] but now global trends leading to the increased usage

19. On 1 July 1973, Petroleum Regulation No. (9) was issued regarding 'Financial, Administrative and Technical Control to Preserve Oil Wealth' and was published in the Official Gazette of the Libyan Arab Republic, Issue No. 38, on 4 September 1973. Pursuant to Art. (2) Petroleum Regulation Nos 2, 3, 4, 5, 6 and 7 have been repealed, as well as any other provisions mentioned in Petroleum Regulation No. (1) or in periodic letters from the Ministry or in any agreements that are inconsistent with the provisions of this regulation.
20. Otman A. Waniss. Evaluating the Libyan Gas Sector: Fiscal Policy and Contractual Terms. Oil, Gas & Energy Law Intelligence (OGEL), Vol. 13, Issue 1: January 2015.
21. Otman A. Waniss. The Libyan Policy Vacuum for Gas Developments: Addressing the Key Issues. Oil, Gas & Energy Law Intelligence (OGEL), Vol. 4, Issue 3: September 2006.
22. Prof Alexander Kemp and Otman A. Waniss, The Petroleum Development Investment Risks and Return in Libya: a Monte Carlo Study of the Current Contractual Terms (EPSA IV), April 2004. North Sear Occasional Paper, Aberdeen, Scotland.
23. Otman A. Waniss, OGEL, Vol. 4, Issue 3: September 2006, *supra* n. 21.

of natural gas, because of its superior environmental credentials, as well as rapidly growing domestic demand in Libya itself, mean that policy, especially relating to any new discovery and the development of free or non-associated gas, is well due for a major overhaul.

In the thirty years spanning the use of the first three generations of the Libyan EPSAs, the failure of the LNOC to seriously address natural gas exploitation and development is very conspicuous. This has often been cited by analysts as one of the major reasons why the IOCs were reluctant to participate in Libya's gas industry.[24] This is in stark contrast to how the Qatar government, for example, has successfully developed its massive gas resources.[25]

As has been postulated by many gas industry researchers, it would be logical to assume that most governments in the world would have more favourable fiscal terms for gas than for oil in order to stimulate gas development.[26] This is due to a variety of factors leading to the view that the cost of developing and marketing gas is less economically attractive than that for oil. From the risk analysis approach, investors are concerned about political and economic risks because of the considerable capital expenditure that is required for the gas project cycle, including exploration, field development, gathering, processing and finally distribution and marketing, whether by pipeline for domestic or translational usage, LNG facilities or more recently, GTL (Gas to Liquids) technology. Under these conditions, exposure to a project cycle period of 25 years including exploration and production may be considered the norm, but in more demanding environmental situations, even this period is not enough to get a reasonable ROI. Despite these considerations, the fact is that, as revealed in the Van Meurs touched on earlier, the vast majority of countries still do not have separate fiscal terms for gas developments.[27]

In the following section, we will analyse those sections in EPSA-1V which relate specifically to gas flaring.

Fundamentally the terms of EPSA IV are in many ways similar to those of EPSA-III, but designed to be more attractive. In summary, they provided for exploration, appraisal, development and production costs to be recovered very quickly from a proportion of output, development costs to be equally shared between the investor and LNOC, and profit production share to be split on a sliding scale. The new EPSA IV covers all sizes of discoveries, with small discoveries still able to secure an acceptable return to the Second Party (IOC), as well as giving it a good return in the case of major or giant discoveries. Management committee (MC) rules are similar to EPSA III, with the only changes made as to their composition, which is now four members, two each from LNOC and the Second Party. Additionally, no income taxes, royalties, rents or fees are levied on the Second Party's share of production.

24. *Ibid.*
25. *Ibid.*
26. Dr Meurs H. van Pedro, World Fiscal Systems for Gas, Van Meurs & Associates Limited for Barrows, New York, 1997.
27. Otman A. Waniss, OGEL, Vol. 4, Issue 3: September 2006, *supra* n. 21.

Unlike the previous EPSA-III, exploitation of gas, whether associated or non-associated, is covered fairly extensively in Article 13, 'Natural Gas'. Again, on account of the generally poor accessibility to the EPSA-IV model contract, the author quotes below Article 13 in full, which requires the MC to approve the Development Plan[28] for any excess associated gas deemed commercial.

- Flaring or venting without prior approval

EPSA-IV does not expressly prohibit or permit flaring or venting of associated gas. Article 13 of the Model requires the disposal of non-commercial associated gas in accordance with good oilfield practices. The MC decides whether excess associated gas is classified as commercial or non-commercial.

- Permitting and processing approval for gas flaring/Development Plans

> 13.1 General
> The provisions of this Agreement applicable to Crude Oil shall apply (mutatis mutandis) to Natural Gas unless otherwise specified herein.
>
> 13.2 Excess Associated Gas
>
> 13.2.1 If the Proposed Development plan submitted to the Management Committee (MC) provides for the commercialization of Excess Associated Gas, then upon approval of such Development Plan:
> a. The parties (as sellers) shall endeavour to conclude with buyers a long-term gas sales agreement(s) incorporating the principles set forth in Article (13.4).
> b. When such gas sales agreement(s) is concluded, the Operator shall commence implementation of the Development Plan and construct the necessary facilities, such as, but not limited to, the gathering, treating, compressing, transporting and processing facilities required for the production and delivery to the delivery point of Excess Associated Gas as specified in the Development Plan or as may be otherwise agreed to in the gas sales agreement(s).
>
> 13.2.2 If the Management Committee does not declare a Commercial Discovery for a Discovery of Crude Oil containing Excess Associated Gas due to lack of a utilization scheme, then First party shall have the option to take the Excess Associated Gas, free of charge, at the delivery point which is immediately after the gas oil separation plant(s). If the Management Committee then declares a Commercial Discovery:
> a. Operator shall operate the separation facilities which will permit the delivery as aforesaid.
> b. Costs of such operation shall be considered Exploitation Operations Expenditures.

28. Development Plan (Art. 1.19 of EPSA-IV): Means a time scheduled program specifying Development Operations required developing an increment of producing capacity in a particular Field, such as initial, intermediate or complete Field Development, a Field extension, or a secondary or other subsequent recovery project.

c. First Party shall be responsible for the gathering at the delivery point specified in this Article (13.2.2), compressing and transporting of said Excess Associated Gas and shall bear all costs related thereto.

Any receipt and disposition of such Excess Associated Gas by First Party shall be carried out in accordance with Good Oil field Practices in a manner which will not unreasonably interfere with the Petroleum Operations regarding the said Commercial Discovery.

If First Party does not exercise the aforesaid option, the Parties shall meet to discuss an appropriate alternative.

4.2 Gas Flaring under the Libyan Petroleum Law and Regulations

Pursuant to Petroleum Law No. 25 of 1955 (and its amendments), the Ministry of Oil and Gas is responsible for implementing government policies and regulations related to oil and gas, such as managing production, export operations, proper exploitation, preserving the environment, developing oil wealth, and proposing the necessary legislation in this regard. As well as proposing and implementing organizational and executive policies for everything related to the Ministry, approving and following up on the transformation plan projects and plans related to increasing production capacity, studying them with the relevant authorities, and following up on their implementation after their approval. This is in addition to a number of related tasks and specializations. The Ministry includes three main departments concerned with the issue of environmental concern: the General Dept. for Technical Affairs and the Environment, the General Dept. for Planning and Follow-up, and the General Dept. for Inspection and Measurement.

According to Article (24), Petroleum Law No. 25 of 1955 stipulates the following: 'The Minister may issue the following regulations and any other regulations necessary for the implementation of this Law;

(a) Administrative and financial regulations.

(b) Petroleum regulations for safety precautions and the conservation of the petroleum resources in Libya, provided that said regulations or any amendment thereof shall not be contrary to the provisions of this Law or adversely affect the contractual rights expressly granted under any permit or concession and in existence at the time the regulation is made or amended.'

- Petroleum Regulation No. 8

Petroleum Regulation No. 8 for the Conservation of Petroleum Resources briefly addressed the environmental aspects related to burning gas and how to treat it, and the following items were as follows:

Article (35) The Concession Holder shall take every reasonable measure, that if economically justified for the utilization of associated gas for any of the following purposes:

(a) Pressure maintenance inside the reservoir in accordance with technical procedures recognized in the petroleum industry.
(b) Any domestic, commercial or industrial use, including use as fuel in the Concession Holder's own installations.
(c) Injection into the oil-bearing or other suitable strata, or underground storage in accordance with technical procedures recognized in the petroleum industry.
(d) Extraction of the natural gasoline and other lighter liquids contained in the wet gas.

Article (36) If the gas is not utilized by the Concession Holder under the conditions referred to in Article 35 above, the Ministry shall have the option to take delivery of it free of charge at the separator.

Article (37) Any associated gas which cannot be utilized in accordance with the two preceding Articles, shall be disposed of in a safe manner.

Article (38) The Concession Holder shall not produce any non-associated gas unless all the associated gas produced by him is totally utilized or unless such production is permitted by the Ministry in the light of special circumstances.

Article (45) Any violation of the provisions of this Regulation shall be considered a violation of oil industry practice based on appropriate scientific methods, according to Article 11 of the Petroleum Law.

Article (5) The Concession Holder shall submit to the Secretariat periodic programs, reports, data and information relevant to his operations, as specified herein.

5 CAPITALIZING ON LIBYA'S GAS FLARING: MAXIMIZING THE REAL POTENTIAL

In 2021, Libya joined the Paris Agreement on climate change. This accession not only reflects the international commitment to preserving the ecosystem but also indicates Libya's readiness to actively participate in preserving the environment and combating climate change. In this regard, in 2022, LNOC launched the '2030 Initiative' with the aim of eliminating gas emissions within the Libyan oil sector and achieving zero flaring emissions by 2030.

Since then, LNOC has joined the broader global oil and gas industry in committing to near-zero gas flaring by 2030, as part of the broader efforts of this state-owned energy producer to reduce greenhouse gas (GHG) emissions. In this regard, the LNOC chairman Farhat Bengdara recently stated in an interview with *the Arabian Gulf Business Insight* at the UN COP28 climate conference in Dubai, that LNOC is embracing sustainable development and diversified energy sources. He said that ... 'It is our stated policy to move beyond traditional oil-centric operations, towards realigning our services with the global shift toward sustainable practice. 'We are firmly committed to 83 percent reduction in gas flaring by 2030.'[29]

29. AGBI, 7 December 2023. Libyan Oil Company commits to cut gas flaring. Available at: https://www.agbi.com/articles/libyan-oil-company-commits-to-cut-gas-flaring/.

Field data collected by LNOC in 2023 reveals that approximately 391 million cubic feet of gas are burned daily in the Libyan oil sector, reflecting economic waste equivalent to USD 1.9 billion annually.[30]

In this connection, Eni has signed a memorandum of understanding (MoU) with Libya to identify opportunities to reduce the country's GHG emissions and develop sustainable energy. The company will work on limiting CO_2 emissions through the reduction of routine gas flaring, fugitive emissions and venting, and assess other avenues for lowering hard-to-abate sector emissions. Eni was responsible for producing 80% of Libya's gas in the year 2022 (1.6 Bcf/d) and jointly develops the country's largest offshore oil and gas fields with state-owned LNOC via Mellitah Oil and Gas.[31]

Figure 18.1 Percentage of Emissions for Each Company

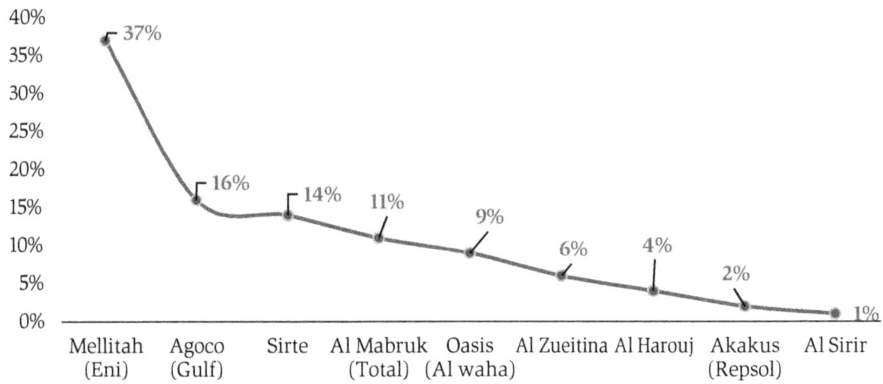

Source: LNOC 2024.

LNOC has categorically expressed its intention to decarbonize its activities in the upstream oil and gas sector. By concentrating on reducing gas flaring, the country aims to achieve net-zero emissions by 2030, supported by several initiatives led by Libya's leading oil and gas operators. By creating economic pathways to monetize gas, especially in marginal fields where gas flaring is a common practice, producers can extract greater value from their resources, while at the same time eliminating an important source of GHG emissions.

Field data collected by LNOC in 2023 from operating companies reveals that approximately 391 million cubic feet of gas are burned daily in this sector, which reflects an economic waste equivalent to USD 1.939 billion annually. It is worth noting

30. LNOC 2024, 2030 Initiative for Zero Routine Gas Flaring & Emission Reduction, LNOC, Tripoli, Libya.
31. Offshore, 9 June 2023. Eni, Libya sign GHG emissions MoU. Available at: https://www.offshore-mag.com/regional-reports/africa/article/14295012/eni-libya-sign-ghg-emissions-mou.

that the projects targeted by this initiative are expected to reduce flammable gas emissions by 68 % by 2028.[32]

Figure 18.2 The Quantity of Flare Gas by Companies and the Reduction Target According to the 2030 Initiative

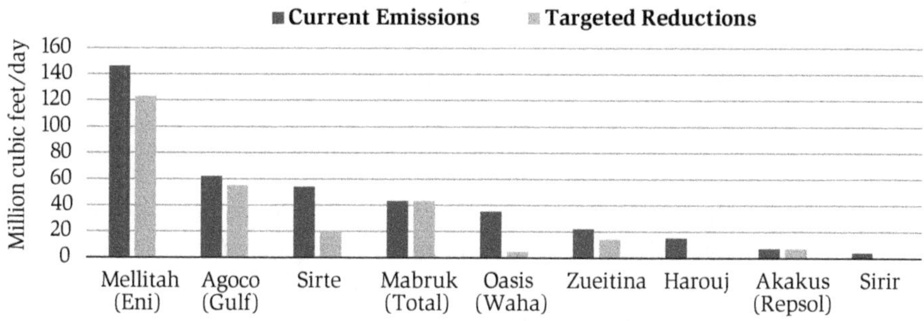

Source: LNOC 2024.

Figure 18.3 The Economic Value of the Burned Flare Gas and the Target Savings Value

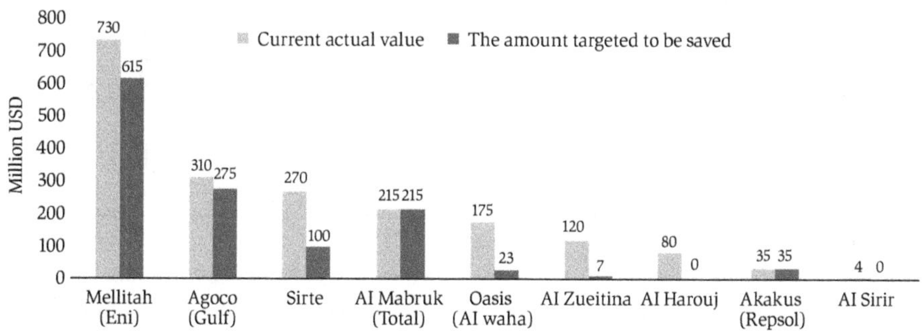

Source: LNOC 2024.

All approved projects focus on the desired environmental, social and economic value of the initiative. These projects have been classified based on the time frames required for implementation: short-term, medium-term, and long-term. All of these projects are approved based on their expected environmental, social and economic benefits. These projects aim to convert combustion gas into sources of electricity, or cooking gas for urban and residential areas, or re-inject it into oil reservoirs, or transform it into economically viable marketable products.

32. LNOC 2024, 2030 Initiative for Zero Routine Gas Flaring & Emission Reduction, LNOC, Tripoli, Libya.

To illustrate these very real Libyan targets, we present in Table 18.3 several noteworthy gas flaring reduction projects.[33]

Table 18.3 Ongoing Significant Projects in Libya to Reduce Gas Flaring

1 Table Projects Implemented 2022-2023	
Project No. 1	Restarting the Gas Processing Plant (GUP)
Company	Serir Company
Project Description	- The plant processes gas into condensates and pumps it to the Sidra Port for export. - The factory has been out of operation since 2013 due to the security situation in Libya. - The plant was restarted to process 25 million cubic feet of gas daily in Contract Area 91 near the Ejkhara area in 2023. - This in addition to the production of 1,800 barrels of condensates daily, equivalent to USD 49.5 million in annual exports.
Project No. 2	Carbon Emissions Reduction at Mesla Field
Company	Gulf Company
Project Description	- The sabotage of gas compressors in 2011 led to the emission of approximately 2.7 million tons of carbon from 2011 to 2022. Intensive gas flaring also resulted in the burning of approximately 1.9 million barrels. - In 2022, compressor maintenance reduced gas flaring by 100%, converting it to 500 barrels per day, equivalent to USD 13.7 million annually at a price of USD 75 per barrel.
Project No. 3	Natural gas transfer from the Lahib and Raqouba fields to the coastal network
Company	Sirt Company
Project Description	- In the third quarter of this year, the connection and gas transfer between Lahib and Raqouba fields were successfully completed. - Approximately 40 million cubic feet of gas per day, which was previously flared, is now being transferred to the Brega gas compression station. - The gas is compressed to the required pressure and then transmitted through the (36B) transmission line to the coastal network. - This project aims to supply power plants and industrial facilities, including the steel factory. - The annual financial benefit from utilizing this gas is estimated at approximately USD 138.7 million.

33. *Ibid.*

2 *Short-Term Projects 2023–2024*	
Project No. 1	Gas Transportation from Block 186 to Alfeel Field barrels
Company	Akakus Company
Project Description	- The project is 90% complete. - It aims to utilize flare gas from Block 186 and send it to Block 115, and transport it to Alfeel field for electricity generation located in the Sharara field for electricity generation, replacing crude oil as a fuel source. - The project targets 6 million cubic feet of gas and an annual economic benefit of USD 20.8 million at USD 9.5 per thousand cubic feet. - Expected to finish by the second quarter of 2024.
Project No. 2	Utilizing Associated Gas in KK Block
Company	Melita (Eni) Company
Project Description	- The project is in the engineering study phase. - A 12" pipeline, 39 km long, will transport flare gas from the KK Block to the Abu Al-Tufal field for processing and economic utilization. - Current flare gas emissions, estimated at a quantity of 13 million cubic feet per day, will be reduced by sending the flare gas to the Abu Al-Tufal field for processing and economic utilization. - Efforts are underway to identify the required materials and engage contractors for implementation. - The expected economic value from utilizing the flare gas is estimated at USD 45 million annually, based on a price of USD 9.5 per thousand cubic feet. - The project will be completed by the second quarter of 2024.
Project No. 3	Achieving Zero Emissions in Mesla and Serir Fields
Company	Gulf Company
Project Description	- Project J-22, 95% complete, aims to halt gas flaring in Mesla and Serir fields and send the gas to the Man-Made River Project for electricity generation. - The project will be completed by the first quarter of 2024. - Reducing emissions by 27 million cubic feet of gas daily and yielding USD 93.6 million annually at USD 9.5 per thousand cubic feet of gas.
Project No. 4	Gas Utilization for Cooking and Fuel in the South (KK Block)
Company	Akakus (Repsol) Company

2 Short-Term Projects 2023–2024	
Project Description	- The project has significant social objectives, as it will alleviate the suffering of the people in the southern regions by providing access to cooking gas, gasoline, and diesel, which are currently transported over a distance of 750 kilometres from the Misurata depot to the Sabha depot. - The project will achieve economic returns for the country by reducing transportation expenses, employing residents of the project's surrounding area, and fostering economic development. - Efforts are underway to identify the required materials and engage contractors for implementation. - The targeted quantity to be stopped from emissions is estimated at around 2.3 million cubic feet of gas per day. - The expected economic value from utilizing flare gas is estimated at USD 7.9 million annually, based on a price of USD 9.5 per thousand cubic feet. - It is expected to be completed by the end of 2026.
Project No. 5	Emissions Reduction at the Intisar Oil Gathering Tank
Company	Zueitina Company
Project Description	- The concern is being raised by the United Nations Development Programme (UNDP) in interim meetings with the initiative committee. - The issue concerns gas leakage from an oil-gathering tank at the Intisar 103-D field. - The tank has been scheduled for maintenance for several years without a decision. - Urgent actions have been recommended, including installing nitrogen units instead of gas in 2023 and replacing the tank due to its deterioration. - The project is expected to be finished during the year 2024, reducing the emission of 10 million cubic feet of gas per day, and yielding USD 13.5 million annually
Project No. 6	Reducing Gas Flaring in Field 103-A
Company	Zueitina Company
Project Description	- The project is 94% complete. - It aims to utilize 14 million cubic feet of gas daily and convert it into condensates. - The project will yield environmental and economic benefits amounting to USD 18 million annually. - Expected to be completed in the fourth quarter of 2023.

3 Medium-Term Projects 2023-2026	
Project No. 1	Achieving Zero Flaring at Al-Mabrook Field
Company	Al-Mabruk (Total Energy) Company
Project Description	- The project is in the engineering studies phase. - Utilization of the product from the Early Production Facility (EPF) is expected to commence in December 2023. - The Thermal Oxidizer technology is being used to minimize gas emissions except for security and safety reasons, thus achieving Zero Flaring in the field. - The targeted quantity is 0.6 million cubic feet per day. - The project is expected to be completed by 2026.
Project No. 2	Reduction of Flaring at Al-Raqubah Field
Company	Sirt Company
Project Description	- The project is in the engineering studies phase. - The project aims to utilize 20 million cubic feet of gas daily and inject it into production lines. - The project will yield environmental and economic returns equivalent to USD 69 million annually at a price of USD 9.5 per thousand cubic feet. - It is expected to be completed in the last quarter of 2026.

4 Long-Term Projects 2023-2030	
Project No. 1	Gas Flaring Treatment at Al-Bouri Offshore Field
Company	Mellita (Eni) Company
Project Description	- The project is in the engineering studies phase. - The project aims to utilize 110 million cubic feet of gas daily and reduce flaring at the Al-Bouri Offshore Field. - The project targets gas exports, thus achieving environmental and economic returns equivalent to USD 200.75 million annually at a price of USD 5 per thousand cubic feet. - It is expected to be completed in the last quarter of 2028.
Project No. 2	Gas Flaring Treatment at Al-Jurf Offshore Field
Company	Mabruk (Total Energy) Company
Project Description	- The project is in the engineering studies phase. - The project aims to treat 50 million cubic feet of gas daily. - The company is still considering several options for gas utilization: injection into reservoirs, conversion to liquid, or export through maritime facilities to Melita Company. - Technical study is expected to be completed in December 2023, with project execution in 2028.

4 Long-Term Projects 2023-2030	
Project No. 3	Gas Gathering at Al-Samah Field
Company	Oasis Company
Project Description	- The project is in the engineering studies phase. - Gas flaring at the field will be collected and used for operational purposes. - The targeted emission reduction is 4.5 million cubic feet of gas daily. - It is expected to be completed in the last quarter of 2025.
Project No. 4	Upgrading the Flaring System at Al-Nafoura Field
Company	Arabian Gulf Oil Company (AGOCO)
Project Description	- The project is in the engineering studies phase. - It aims to upgrade the condensate recovery system and reduce the flaring of 28 million cubic feet of gas daily. - The project is expected to yield environmental and economic returns equivalent to USD 97 million annually at a price of USD 9.5 per thousand cubic feet. - It is expected to be completed in the last quarter of 2025.

5.1 The Way Forward for Libya's Gas Sector

- Dedicated Fiscal Terms to End Gas Flaring

Libyan gas flaring, as the thrust of this chapter has appraised, stands at a very high figure when compared with the experience in other gas provinces, be they in the African countries, or elsewhere.

It is imperative that new and distinct fiscal terms, separate from those of EPSA-IV, need to be designed for the upstream gas sector to encourage investment. Stated plainly, new legislation for upstream gas developments needs to be drafted. In such drafting, existing perceived barriers to IOC's investing in Libyan gas projects should be addressed, and incentives offered. Is there a case, for example, for decreasing royalty on gas production from the 16.67% presently paid on crude oil production?

Although under EPSA-IV all royalty and taxes are paid by LNOC on behalf of the Second Party (Article 19.1.2), the cost to LNOC of paying this is still factored into the agreed production split, for both oil and gas. Again, is there a case for extending the period of the EPSA beyond 25 years in the case of gas, in view of higher perceived investment costs and slower return? Should the conditions and timing for declaring gas commerciality for gas discoveries be changed from those currently in force in EPSA-IV, to offer greater flexibility with respect to both of these key issues?

It is therefore long overdue that the Libyan energy policy makers must take some radical steps to end the flagrant waste of what is an increasingly valuable natural resource.

– Need for a Libyan Master Gas Plan (LMGP)

It is axiomatic that the upstream gas sector is focused on discovering and producing gas, while the downstream sector commercializes it.

As touched on earlier in this chapter, confronted with an existing governance and policy-making deficit for gas production, domestic energy security, and monetization of currently flared gas, is difficult to envisage the rejuvenation of the Libyan Gas Sector without the introduction of a LMGP. However, the design and implementation of this plan need to be considered and structured very carefully, even conservatively.

The LMGP must link proven reserves with production, and allocate these between the demands of the Libyan domestic, North African regional, and export markets within the context of a long-term horizon, potentially 50 years. Critics may say this is too long, but as the Saudi Arabian,[34] Indonesian and Malaysian experiences show,[35] early emphasis on securing foreign exchange through gas exports through downstream gas projects such as LNG or petrochemical plants using gas as feedstock, has frequently led to gas shortages in the local market, and at a point much sooner than anticipated. As reiterated throughout this chapter, a window of opportunity demonstrably exists for Libyan policymakers to formulate and implement an LMGP. In view of the relatively unexplored status of Libya's gas sector, there exists considerable potential for its expansion. The writer's view is insistent that a dedicated fiscal package for gas utilization, encapsulated within the framework of an LMGP, must be delivered by Libya's policymakers.

6 FINAL REMARKS

To conclude, there is no doubt in the author's mind that at some point in the near future, the Libyan gas sector is set to undergo comprehensive reform, whether in terms of legislation designed to stop flaring or to encourage its volume and monetization. In this regard, the Norwegian, Qatari and Saudi Arabian[36] gas experience over the past three decades can provide many ideas and guidelines for Libyan policymakers. It is crucial, in our view, that any gas sector reform should include the establishment of a

34. Bloomberg, 2 October 2023. Saudi Arabia Finally Joins the Natural Gas Wave. Available at: https://www.bloomberg.com/news/newsletters/2023-10-02/saudi-arabia-finally-joins-the-natural-gas-wave.

    Also *See*: Otman A. Waniss and Hesham Bin-Dehaish, Unrealised Potential in the Saudi Gas Industry: Fiscal and Economic Considerations. Oil and Gas & Energy Law Intelligence Journal OGEL. Vol. 4, Issue 4: November 2006.
35. Energy Monitor, Indonesia and Malaysia Want to Become CCS Hubs. What Does It Mean for the Energy Transition?, 12 December 2023. Available at: https://www.energymonitor.ai/carbon-removal/indonesia-and-malaysia-want-to-become-ccs-hubs-what-does-it-mean-for-the-energy-transition/.

    Also *See*: Wood Mackenzie, Comparative Energy Framework in Malaysia, Indonesia and Thailand. Wood Mackenzie Paper Prepared Presented for the 4th National Energy Forum in Malaysia, September 2012. Available at: https://www.st.gov.my/contents/K2/Presentation_slides/comparative%20energy%20framework%20in%20malaysia%20indonesia%20and%20thailand.pdf.
36. Otman A. Waniss and Hesham Bin-Dehaish, Unrealised Potential in the Saudi Gas Industry: Fiscal and Economic Considerations OGEL, June 2006.

separate and independent Libyan Gas Corporation (LGC), separate from LNOC, with the ability to structure a LMGP. This comprehensive approach must align gas reserves, domestic demand, and gas exports, whether as LNG or by pipeline, in a well-conceived ratio, to safeguard and achieve long-term Libyan macro-economic and climate change-related objectives.

The potential for Libyan gas, in a North African regional context, where there are already plans for its export via pipelines to Tunisia, for example, as part of the Western Libya Gas Project (WLGP)[37] project, is truly enormous. For many years, the Libyan government has also been in dialogue with Egypt configuring plans to construct and utilize cross-border pipelines, which could theoretically transport Libyan gas to foreign markets. Likewise, the success of the 2005 WLGP project, which made Libya a major exporter of gas via pipeline to Europe, will undoubtedly be emulated in the coming years as Libyan gas is discovered and developed as a result of earlier and projected EPSA-IV rounds.

Thus, when security and political conditions in the country eventually stabilize and exploratory activity returns to its previous level, this will dramatically position Libya as an important supplier of pipeline gas, both domestically and abroad, as well as a major supplier of liquefied natural gas.

37. Otman A. Waniss, OGEL, Vol. 13, Issue 1: January 2015, *supra* n. 20.

CHAPTER 19

Mexico

María Serna

1 INTRODUCTION

Over the past decade, Mexico has consistently ranked among the top 10 flaring countries, according to the World Bank. Despite a decline in oil production, the country has experienced a significant increase in gas flaring, with a more than 50% rise since 2018.[1] Flaring volumes surged from 3.8 billion cubic meters (bcm) in 2018 to 6.5 bcm in 2021.[2] This trend indicates that oil production is increasingly taking place at wells with higher gas-to-oil ratios (GOR). Without adequate infrastructure to capture and utilize the gas, the excess is being flared. In the marine region, where flaring volumes are highest, the use of nitrogen for artificial lift results in gas with high nitrogen content, which the domestic gas network cannot accommodate. Consequently, large amounts of this gas are flared both offshore and at onshore processing plants.

While Mexico has prioritized energy security in recent years, the rise in gas flaring has coincided with a steady increase in natural gas imports. This situation underscores the potential role that flare gas recovery could play in enhancing Mexico's energy independence. The inefficiency of flaring not only represents a waste of valuable natural resources but also poses significant environmental and economic challenges that necessitate urgent attention and action.[3]

1. World Bank, "Global Gas Flaring Reduction Partnership: 2022 Global Gas Flaring Tracker Report" (World Bank, 2022) https://www.worldbank.org/en/topic/extractiveindustries/brief/gas-flaring accessed September 30, 2024.
2. World Bank, *2022 Global Gas Flaring Tracker Report* (World Bank, 2022) https://thedocs.worldbank.org/en/doc/1692f2ba2bd6408db82db9eb3894a789-0400072022/original/2022-Global-Gas-Flaring-Tracker-Report.pdf accessed February 3, 2025.
3. World Bank, "Global Gas Flaring Reduction Partnership: 2022 Global Gas Flaring Tracker Report" (World Bank, 2022) https://www.worldbank.org/en/topic/extractiveindustries/brief/gas-flaring.

Addressing natural gas flaring aligns with global best practices and regulatory trends. As Mexico continues to integrate into global energy markets and attract foreign investment, demonstrating a commitment to reducing flaring is vital. Effective management of natural gas resources can improve the country's standing in the international community and attract investment by showcasing Mexico's commitment to sustainable and responsible energy practices. Additionally, reducing natural gas flaring contributes to several United Nations Sustainable Development Goals (SDGs), including SDG 7 (Affordable and Clean Energy), SDG 13 (Climate Action), and SDG 3 (Good Health and Well-being). By tackling flaring, Mexico can advance its progress toward these goals and promote sustainable development for its population.

This chapter aims to present a thorough analysis of natural gas flaring in Mexico, structured into several key sections. First, the contextual background of natural gas flaring will be explored, outlining its significance within the energy sector. This is followed by an examination of the regulatory evolution, particularly in relation to Petróleos Mexicanos's (PEMEX's) role and its legal framework. The chapter will then address the current challenges associated with natural gas flaring, including recent shifts in presidential policies and their implications for regulatory enforcement. Each section aims to provide a holistic understanding of the complexities surrounding natural gas flaring in Mexico.

2 CONTEXT

The origins of flaring in Mexico can be traced back to the major geological discoveries in the Campeche Sound and the subsequent commencement of production in these areas. Approximately 81.5% of the flaring recorded originates from the southeast marine region, located off the coasts of Campeche, Yucatán, and Quintana Roo. This area is also the largest contributor to Mexico's oil production, with approximately 797,617 thousand barrels per day in 2022.[4]

Following Cantarell, the northern region, which extends from the northern border with the United States to the Papaloapan River and consists mostly of onshore fields, accounts for 8.2% of the flaring. Next is the southern zone, encompassing all onshore and offshore fields in the states of Guerrero, Oaxaca, southern Veracruz, Tabasco, Campeche, Chiapas, Yucatán, and Quintana Roo, with 5.5% of national flaring. Finally, the northeast marine region, covering the entire continental shelf of the Gulf of Mexico and representing the coasts of Tamaulipas and northern Veracruz, accounts for the remaining 5% of national flaring.

Mexico saw a notable reduction in gas flaring of approximately 0.8 billion cubic meters (bcm), a 13% decrease from 2021 levels. This reduction primarily occurred in the offshore fields of Ku-Maloob-Zaap (KMZ) and Akal (part of the Cantarell complex), which together accounted for a 0.45 bcm reduction, and in the onshore Cactus

4. Salinas Díaz, Abraham. *La Quema y Venteo de Gas Natural: ¿Una Necesidad Estratégica o un Daño al Medioambiente?* (2023) https://www.cfenergia.com/wp-content/uploads/2023/10/La-Quema-y-Venteo-de-Gas-Natural-%C2%BFUna-Necesidad-Estrategica-o-un-Dano-al-Medioambiente.pdf accessed May 28, 2024, p. 113.

conventional oil field, which saw a 0.3 bcm reduction. These decreases are attributed to the shutting-in of wells with high GOR. In fact, flaring in these fields alone has reduced by over 1 bcm during 2021 and 2022 due to this policy shift in GOR control. Despite overall oil production levels remaining stable in Mexico during 2022, this decrease in flaring resulted in an improvement in Mexico's flaring intensity, from 10.3 m^3 per barrel in 2021 to 9.0 m^3 per barrel in 2022.[5]

Between 2012 and 2022, Mexico witnessed a significant transformation in its oil and gas sector, marked by notable shifts in production dynamics and environmental commitments. During this period, oil production in Mexico experienced a substantial decline, dropping by one-third. In contrast, the volume of gas flared increased by one-third, with a parallel doubling of flaring intensity, highlighting a critical environmental challenge.

Despite these trends, recent data shows a positive shift with a downward trend in gas flaring since 2021, coupled with stable oil production. This shift has led to a corresponding decrease in flaring intensity, indicating progress in addressing environmental concerns related to gas flaring activities. Notably, a comprehensive assessment in 2022 identified 152 individual flare sites, emphasizing the scope of the challenge and the need for targeted interventions.

In line with global environmental initiatives, Mexico took significant steps in 2016 by endorsing the Zero Routine Flaring by 2030 initiative and actively participating in the Global Methane Initiative and the Climate and Clean Air Coalition. These commitments were further solidified through an updated Nationally Determined Contribution (NDC) submitted to the United Nations Framework Convention on Climate Change in November 2022. Mexico committed to ambitious targets, including a 35% reduction in greenhouse gas (GHG) emissions compared to previous submissions.

The oil and gas sector, a significant contributor to emissions, outlined its goals for emission reduction, focusing on increasing cogeneration in processing plants, reducing fugitive emissions, and implementing energy efficiency programs. However, challenges in implementation were evident, especially concerning the guidelines set by the National Hydrocarbons Commission (CNH) for PEMEX to reduce flaring. Despite expectations for enforcement, limitations in financial resources and investment priorities hindered major projects' implementation, underscoring the complexities in translating commitments into actionable measures.

Mexico's collaborative approach with the United States and Canada in calling for a substantial reduction in methane emissions by 2025 demonstrated its commitment to regional environmental initiatives. In support of these efforts, Mexico's Agency for Safety, Energy and Environment (*Agencia de Seguridad, Energía y Ambiente*, ASEA) released comprehensive guidelines in 2018 for methane emission control in the hydrocarbons sector, emphasizing the importance of facility-wide emission limits.

5. World Bank, "2023 Global Gas Flaring Tracker Report" (2023) https://thedocs.worldbank.org/en/doc/5d5c5c8b0f451b472e858ceb97624a18-0400072023/original/2023-Global-Gas-Flaring-Tracker-Report.pdf accessed September 30, 2024.

3 ROLE OF PEMEX AND REGULATORY EVOLUTION

Mexico's regulatory landscape for natural gas flaring has evolved significantly, particularly in response to the considerable environmental impact attributed to PEMEX. Historically, PEMEX held a monopoly over the Mexican hydrocarbon sector, positioning it as the primary contributor to national flaring and venting activities. The legacy of PEMEX's dominance is intertwined with regulatory challenges and the need for robust policies to mitigate these practices.

PEMEX's historical position as the sole player in the oil and gas sector meant that its operational practices, including extensive flaring and venting of natural gas, went largely unchecked for decades. The environmental repercussions of these practices have become a focal point of regulatory reforms, particularly as Mexico seeks to align its energy sector with global sustainability standards.

In 2008, Mexico reached a record high in natural gas flaring, coinciding with sustained oil production growth that peaked at 3.165 million barrels per day. This surge was notably visible off the coast of Campeche, Mexico's leading oil-producing state, where numerous oil platforms engaged in gas flaring, evidenced by visible flares and smoke trails. Highlighting the magnitude of the problem, flaring was observable even from space. The National Hydrocarbons Commission, established by the 2008 Energy Reform, has been pivotal in Mexico's efforts to address this issue. At that time, gas flaring accounted for 17% of the country's total annual gas production. To combat this, the CNH mandated that PEMEX reduce flaring to 2% of production by 2012 and to 0.6% by 2024.

Alongside this dramatic increase in flaring and oil production, Mexico also faced a decline in Cantarell field reserves, which had been compromised by rapid production. Proven reserves fell from 1,743.6 million barrels in 2005 to 1,630.1 million in 2008.

Since 2009, gas flaring management has been regulated by CNH. The Commission, with the most significant responsibilities, was tasked with technical oversight, regulation, and enforcement, including controlling, supervising, and mitigating flaring. In 2009, it issued technical provisions to prevent gas flaring and venting during hydrocarbon exploration and extraction.[6]

The technical provisions aimed to regulate the extraction processes of natural gas from PEMEX's associated fields, planning techniques to preserve the economic value of associated gas, and designating it as a national asset to be produced and utilized economically. The provisions outlined six key principles for gradually reducing flaring.[7]

First, PEMEX and its subsidiaries had to adhere to the regulatory framework established by the CNH to avoid operational flaring, except in emergencies or external incidents. Second, the established provisions would create technical and technological methodologies for PEMEX to follow in designing exploration and extraction projects,

---

6. Franco Hernández, Gaspar and Samuel Isaí, *Cinco años de la reforma constitucional en materia energética: en camino a un manejo eficiente del gas natural asociado a la extracción de hidrocarburos* (2019) Boletín Mexicano de Derecho Comparado, p. 1192.
7. *Ibid.*

evaluating, installing, and selecting technical alternatives such as compression centers, turbo-compressors, vapor recovery units, and gas pipelines to maximize the use, conservation, and transportation of natural gas, preventing its destruction through flaring.

The third principle emphasized immediate priority for investments in techniques and technology to avoid and reduce gas flaring and venting in the Mexican oil industry. Investments in technical industrial safety to mitigate risks associated with the sector's activities, such as maintaining natural gas transport systems, analyzing the presence of radioactive materials or heavy metals, and supervising leak detection systems, are also prioritized.

The fourth principle mandated the CNH to oversee the implementation and supervision of investment programs for constructing, maintaining, and operating facilities designed to minimize gas flaring volumes at extraction wells selected by PEMEX, aligning with the third principle.

The fifth principle established the methods for verifying compliance with all provisions and future progress within development plans for maximum natural gas utilization. Finally, the processes PEMEX had to follow when presenting a compliance program to the CNH, ensuring the proposed technological flaring or venting reduction measures are technically and economically viable without interrupting oil extraction activities.

These provisions subjected the volume of national gas flaring and venting to an annual maximum limit calculation, conducted by PEMEX, based on an integrated planning of all active, new, and abandoned associated hydrocarbon fields. The annual maximum limits fluctuated between 400 and 450 million cubic feet per day. Since the publication of these mechanisms, PEMEX committed to reducing flaring and venting indices, with significant investments in the Campeche Sound production areas, including Cantarell and the new KMZ prospect, amounting to approximately USD 3 billion. Subsequent investments flowed into other productive areas, such as the northern region, Poza Rica-Altamira, and the southern region, Bellota-Junco, Cinco Presidentes, and Samaria. These efforts led to a significant national reduction in flaring, reaching a minimum level of 1.4 billion cubic meters in 2012, far below the levels seen in 2008.[8]

The enactment of these regulations was seen as a crucial test of CNH's authority, amidst concerns that PEMEX might prioritize production over environmental regulations. Contrary to these doubts, PEMEX launched a strategy to reduce flaring. To address the issue comprehensively, PEMEX announced a USD 2.4 billion investment program to reduce emissions. By 2010, Pemex had successfully cut its flaring by over 50% compared to 2008, a significant achievement highlighted at the COP16 conference

8. Salinas Díaz, Abraham, *La Quema y Venteo de Gas Natural: ¿Una Necesidad Estratégica o un Daño al Medioambiente?* (2023) https://www.cfenergia.com/wp-content/uploads/2023/10/La-Quema-y-Venteo-de-Gas-Natural-%C2%BFUna-Necesidad-Estrategica-o-un-Dano-al-Medioambiente.pdf accessed May 28, 2024, p. 124.

in Cancun. The plan included updating facilities and reinjecting gas into fields to cap flaring at 2% of output by 2012.[9]

In 2010, Mexico hosted the United Nations Climate Change Conference, bringing global attention to the issue of gas flaring, especially in light of the record-high flaring levels in 2008. This international scrutiny propelled gas flaring reduction to the forefront of Mexico's national priorities, leading to its formal inclusion in national hydrocarbon policies.

3.1 Climate Change Law and Policy Obligations

In 2012, Mexico enacted the General Law on Climate Change (*Ley General de Cambio Climático*, LGCC). This landmark legislation established comprehensive obligations for public policies aimed at mitigating climate change, explicitly targeting the reduction of natural gas flaring and venting.

Article 33. The objectives of public policies for mitigation are:

> VIII. Reduce *gas flaring and venting* to decrease losses in extraction processes and distribution systems and ensure maximum utilization of gas in industrial, oil, gas, and refining installations;

Article 34. To reduce emissions, federal public administration agencies and entities, Federal Entities, and Municipalities, within the scope of their competence, shall promote the design and development of mitigation policies and actions associated with the corresponding sectors, considering the following provisions:

> I. Reduction of emissions in the generation and use of energy:
> f) Promote technology transfer and financing to *reduce gas flaring and venting*, decrease its losses in extraction processes and distribution systems, and promote its sustainable utilization.

The LGCC mandates the formulation of a National Climate Change Strategy (*Estrategia Nacional de Cambio Climático*, ENCC), which outlines opportunities for mitigating GHG emissions across various sectors, including hydrocarbons.

Article 64. The National Strategy must reflect the objectives of mitigation and adaptation policies to climate change established in this Law and shall contain, among other elements, the following:

> VI. Opportunities for emission mitigation in energy generation and use, natural gas *flaring and venting*, land use and land use change, transportation, industrial processes, waste management, and other sectors or activities;

In 2013, the ENCC was published delineating a roadmap to guide the Nation's actions over a 40-year period. Within its strategic framework, specifically in line of action M5 aimed at reducing short-lived climate pollutant emissions and promoting

9. Mexico Business News, *Green PEMEX: The Challenge of Reducing Gas Flaring* (January 25, 2012) https://mexicobusiness.news/oilandgas/news/green-pemex-challenge-reducing-gas-flaring accessed May 5, 2024.

co-benefits of health and well-being, item number 17 emphasizes the need to "*establish [Measurement, Reporting, and Verification] (MRV) mechanisms in methane flaring and venting operations during gas and oil production; as well as strengthen surveillance.*"[10]

The LGCC also stipulates the creation of a six-year Climate Change Program, which must incorporate specific goals and priorities for reducing flaring and venting. This program is a critical instrument in operationalizing the National Strategy, ensuring that tangible targets are set and progress is monitored.

Article 67. The Program must contain, among other elements, the following:

> II. Six-year mitigation targets, prioritizing those related to energy generation and use, *gas flaring and venting*, transportation, agriculture, forests, other land uses, industrial processes, and waste management;

Article 102. In terms of climate change mitigation, the evaluation shall be carried out regarding the following objectives:

> XI. *Reduce gas flaring and venting* to decrease losses in extraction processes and distribution systems and ensure maximum utilization of gas in industrial, oil, gas, and refining installations;

3.2 New Regulators, Laws, and Regulations Regarding Flaring Since the Energy Reform

In 2013, President Enrique Peña Nieto presented the energy reform constitutional amendment initiative. It was approved by the Senate of the Republic on October 11, 2013, and by the Chamber of Deputies a day later. On December 18, 2013, the reform was declared constitutional by the Federal Legislative Power; it was promulgated by the Executive on December 20, 2013, and published in the evening edition of the Official Gazette of the Federation on that same day.

A year later, the secondary legislation package was published including, among other legislative changes, the Hydrocarbons Law, and two laws that created the energy regulators: (a) the Organic Law of the Coordinated Regulatory Bodies in Energy Matters (*Ley Orgánica de los Órganos Reguladores Coordinados en Materia Energética*), which transformed the CNH; and (b) the Law of the National Agency of Industrial Safety and Environmental Protection in the Hydrocarbons Sector (*Ley de la Agencia Nacional de Seguridad Industrial y de Protección al Medio Ambiente del Sector Hidrocarburos*) that created said agency, which in short is referred to as ASEA).

The energy reform in Mexico not only transformed the competitive landscape of the hydrocarbon sector but also ushered in new regulators, laws, and regulations, including those aimed at addressing the pressing issue of flaring in the oil and gas industry.

10. Gobierno de la República, *ENCC 2013. Estrategia Nacional de Cambio Climático. Visión 10-20-40* (2013) https://www.gob.mx/cms/uploads/attachment/file/41978/Estrategia-Nacional-Cambio-Climatico-2013.pdf accessed May 28, 2024, p. 53.

Until the energy reform, CNH had no independency from the Secretariat of Energy. As part of the institutional changes, the National Hydrocarbons Commission transformed into a key autonomous regulatory body, overseeing the hydrocarbons exploration and production activities, including PEMEX and new players. The CNH plays a pivotal role in setting guidelines and enforcing regulations related to flaring reduction, particularly for national oil company PEMEX and other operators.

The reform created a specialized office for overseeing health, safety and environment in the hydrocarbons sector, including measures to control and minimize flaring activities. The Agency for Safety, Energy and Environment (*Agencia de Seguridad, Energía y Ambiente*, ASEA). Unlike the National Hydrocarbons Commission, ASEA is not an autonomous body but depends on the Secretariat of Environment and Natural Resources (*Secretaría de Medio Ambiente y Recursos Naturales*).

3.3 First Climate Change Program

In 2014 the first Climate Change Program (Program 2014) was published. Within Objective 4, Indicator 6th, Annually mitigated methane emissions, it mentioned natural gas flaring. At the time, it stated a 2013 baseline of 0, with a 2018 goal of 161,724 metric tons of methane per year:

> The mitigation of methane emissions includes action lines on urban solid waste, wastewater treatment plants, biodigesters, and natural gas *flaring and venting* from the hydrocarbons sector. In addition to having a significant impact on global warming as a greenhouse gas, methane is one of the precursors of tropospheric ozone, another Short-Lived Climate Pollutant. Methane has an atmospheric lifetime of approximately 12 years, so its mitigation has short-term effects. Among SLCPs, methane is the gas that occurs in the largest quantity, and it is the one for which there is the most experience in making estimations and measurements.[11]

3.4 New Commitments for Current Regulatory Landscape

In 2016, during the North American Leaders' Summit held in Ottawa, President Enrique Peña Nieto, along with leaders from the United States and Canada, committed to a series of climate change initiatives. This trilateral agreement emphasized cooperation on reducing methane emissions, a potent GHG with significant implications for climate change. During this year, Mexico pledged support for the Zero Routine Flaring by 2030 campaign and is actively engaged in initiatives like the Global Methane Initiative and the Climate and Clean Air Coalition.

As part of this commitment, Mexico pledged to cut methane emissions from the oil and gas sector by 40%-45% by 2025. This ambitious target aligned with the broader North American goal of mitigating climate impacts and underscores Mexico's dedication to environmental sustainability.

11. Secretaría de Medio Ambiente and Recursos Naturales, *Programa Especial de Cambio Climático 2014-2018* (April 28, 2014) https://dof.gob.mx/nota_detalle.php?codigo=5342492&fecha=28/04/2014#gsc.tab=0 accessed May 28, 2024, p. 56.

Consequently, in 2016, the regulatory landscape for gas flaring in Mexico shifted its focus from merely minimizing flaring production to maximizing the utilization of associated hydrocarbons, while also placing environmental protection at the forefront of rule and guideline formulation. CNH continued to play a central role in this matter. However, the 2013 Energy Reform empowered additional agencies to support the CNH, notably the National Agency for Industrial Safety and Environmental Protection in the Hydrocarbons Sector (ASEA). ASEA is tasked with overseeing the compliance of safety standards, operating conditions, and environmental protection norms by oil operators regarding gas flaring and venting.

In this context, ASEA published the Guidelines for the Prevention and Comprehensive Control of Methane Emissions in the Hydrocarbons Sector in 2018, shortly before President Peña Nieto, who promoted the energy reform, left office. These guidelines set forth technical and technological requirements, such as compressors and pipelines, that both existing and new facilities in the hydrocarbons value chain need to meet to comply with GHG emission limits and gas flaring regulations.[12]

The National Hydrocarbons Commission, within its regulatory and technical supervisory duties to combat flaring, reestablished guidelines and processes outlining its responsibilities and those of oil operators. This new approach centers on setting natural gas utilization targets for each extraction well in a reservoir. Instead of directly mitigating flaring production, the focus is now on the mandated use of certain quantities of gas present in the reservoir. Theoretically, over time, this obligation would gradually reduce flaring.

The National Hydrocarbons Commission, as part of its updated objectives to counteract flaring, aims to fulfill three central goals that encompass the utilization of gas as a key tool. These objectives include establishing the procedures, criteria, and requirements for evaluating compliance with the associated gas utilization target and gas utilization programs, issuing administrative procedures for monitoring compliance with the target and defining the technical and operational elements that will determine the target level. This data will be used to structure associated natural gas utilization programs. According to certain bases and criteria, the target is defined as the percentage of natural gas present in a reservoir that must be utilized, typically set around 98 % annually.[13]

These provisions aim to define how oil operators should plan and execute their investment actions to have the technological and technical capacity to maximize the utilization of associated gas in each of their reservoirs. From the development of the exploration and extraction plan for a reservoir, operators must create an annexed plan that projects the required installed capacity throughout the extraction cycle for managing the anticipated natural gas. Based on this gas management capacity,

12. World Bank, "2023 Global Gas Flaring Tracker Report" (2023) https://thedocs.worldbank.org/en/doc/5d5c5c8b0f451b472e858ceb97624a18-0400072023/original/2023-Global-Gas-Flaring-Tracker-Report.pdf accessed September 30, 2024.
13. Salinas Díaz, Abraham, *La Quema y Venteo de Gas Natural: ¿Una Necesidad Estratégica o un Daño al Medioambiente?* (2023) https://www.cfenergia.com/wp-content/uploads/2023/10/La-Quema-y-Venteo-de-Gas-Natural-%C2%BFUna-Necesidad-Estrategica-o-un-Dano-al-Medioambiente.pdf accessed September 30, 2024.

operators will determine the actions and investments needed to maintain a continuous improvement policy in optimizing gas utilization and reducing non-utilized volumes.

Additionally, based on the CNH's established target, each oil operator must present their respective associated natural gas utilization programs to the CNH. These projects must align with the exploration and exploitation plans of the reservoir, evaluating alternatives to achieve the proposed utilization target. Operators must make necessary investments throughout the project's life cycle to increase or maintain compliance with the established target and to prevent or reduce any destruction of natural gas. Finally, operators should promote technological efforts to develop projects that increase associated natural gas utilization capacity and prioritize using gas in turbines for energy generation, reserving flaring for safety purposes only. Properly designing gas utilization programs and adhering to each of these stages will help operators achieve the highest potential for natural gas utilization, thereby defining the increase or decrease in flaring.

4 FLARING REDUCTION REGULATIONS

The Flaring Reduction framework in Mexico represents a comprehensive approach that intertwines the National Hydrocarbons Commission's regulations for the use of associated natural gas and ASEA's regulations for methane emissions. This dual regulatory framework ensures that environmental protection and resource optimization go hand in hand.

4.1 CNH's Regulations for the Use of Associated Natural Gas

CNH has played a pivotal role in establishing regulations aimed at maximizing the utilization of associated natural gas. These regulations focus on setting specific gas utilization targets for each extraction well in a reservoir. By doing so, CNH aims to ensure that the natural gas produced during oil extraction is used productively rather than flared. The regulations require oil operators to: (i) Develop and implement programs for the maximum utilization of associated natural gas; (ii) Establish technical and operational measures to meet the utilization targets; (iii) Invest in the necessary infrastructure and technology, such as compressors and pipelines, to handle and utilize the gas effectively; and (iv) Report and verify their gas utilization performance regularly, ensuring compliance with the set targets.[14]

CNH's regulations mandate oil operators to present an associated natural gas utilization program within the development plan for every contract or entitlement area, seeking approval. This program[15] encompasses various components, such as the routine flaring and temporary or intermittent venting program, the *Controlled Destruction for Maintenance program*, and the *Controlled Destruction for Operational*

14. *Disposiciones Técnicas para el aprovechamiento del gas natural asociado, en la exploración y extracción de hidrocarburos* (Technical Provisions for the utilization of associated natural gas in the exploration and extraction of hydrocarbons) (Mexico) 2016, Art. 1.
15. *Ibid.*, Annex I—Associated Natural Gas Utilization Program, e).

Clearances and Movements program. The overarching aim is to ensure adherence to the gas utilization target within hydrocarbon exploration and extraction activities.

4.2 ASEA's Regulations for Methane Emissions

Complementing CNH's focus on gas utilization, one of Mexico's key actions to reduce methane emissions and flaring was the implementation of the "Guidelines for the Prevention and Integral Control of Methane Emissions from the Hydrocarbon Sector" (ASEA Guidelines) which took effect on November 7, 2018, just before President Peña Nieto left office. Issued by ASEA, these legally binding guidelines are the result of extensive collaboration with international expert non-government organizations (NGO) and a public consultation process that garnered over 500 comments. Based on international regulations and best practices, the guidelines aim to significantly reduce methane emissions and flaring worldwide. According to the International Energy Agency, applying such best practices globally can potentially cut methane emissions from the hydrocarbon sector by up to 75%, with a 50% reduction achievable at no net cost. The guidelines also allow for the introduction of new and improved practices for both new and existing oil and gas facilities, positioning Mexico's hydrocarbon sector as a leader in environmental sustainability.

These guidelines outline technical and technological requirements that both existing and new facilities in the hydrocarbons value chain must meet to comply with GHG emission limits and gas flaring regulations. The guidelines mandate:[16] (i) Implementation of advanced technologies to capture and utilize methane, including compressors and gas pipelines; (ii) Regular monitoring and reporting of methane emissions to ensure compliance with environmental standards; (iii) Adoption of best practices in operations to minimize methane leaks and flaring; and (iv) Investment in infrastructure to support methane capture and utilization, reducing the environmental impact of oil and gas operations.

The guidelines set forth steps for annual improvements in methane emissions prevention, control, and flaring reduction.[17] These include defining new and existing facilities, diagnosing potential emission sources, classifying emissions, and setting reduction goals. Each existing facility must establish a long-term "integral goal" for emission reduction, to be achieved within six years, along with annual percentage reduction targets. New facilities must maintain baseline emission rates established during their diagnosis, adhering to best practices.

The guidelines require each facility to develop a Program for the Prevention and Integral Control of Methane Emissions in the Hydrocarbon Sector (PPCIEM),[18] which

16. *Disposiciones Administrativas de carácter general que establecen los Lineamientos para la prevención y el control integral de las emisiones de metano del Sector Hidrocarburos* (Guidelines for the Prevention and Integral Control of Methane Emissions from the Hydrocarbon Sector) (Mexico) 2018.
17. *Ibid.*, Art. 93.
18. *Ibid.*, Art. 19.

includes a quarterly leak detection and repair (LDAR) program and specific plans for reducing routine flaring and intermittent venting. All applicable best practices must be implemented, with specific actions drawn from international initiatives and regulations.

Continuous improvement is mandated, with annual internal evaluations and compliance reports verified by an authorized third party.[19] Deadlines are set for both existing and new facilities to complete and submit their PPCIEM and compliance reports, with penalties for non-compliance. ASEA emphasizes a "corrective enforcement" approach, encouraging facilities to find solutions and meet established reduction goals, particularly in flaring reduction.

ASEA oversees the Guidelines regulating methane emissions from three main sources: destruction of equipment, leaks during well operations, and hydrocarbons venting. Unlike Canada and the U.S., where companies comply with emission limits through the standardized practice of a LDAR Program, ASEA's Guidelines are applied on a case-by-case basis and introduce three additional requirements:

(1) Measurement of total emissions from a base year, documented in the Methane Emission Baseline (MEBL).
(2) A six-year planning document called the Integral Program for Preventing and Controlling Methane Emissions (PPCIEM), detailing all activities to reduce emissions and achieve a self-defined goal with respect to the MEBL.
(3) A favorable technical opinion from a third party for both the PPCIEM and the MEBL.

These additional requirements impose a significant bureaucratic burden without apparent benefits. If the LDAR mechanism is well-regulated, implemented, and reported, there would be no need for both the PPCIEM and MEBL, as the emissions detection and reduction report would suffice for determining total emissions and the activities to lower them. Furthermore, implementing both the PPCIEM and MEBL requires robust third-party capacity, which is currently lacking. This shortage is partly due to ASEA's delay in publishing the call for third-party registration and the stringent requirements for becoming an authorized third-party emission expert, including financial, material, and human capacity, facilities, equipment, and sufficient technology.

In response to these challenges, ASEA granted a 19-month extension for submitting the PPCIEM and MEBL. However, there is still a high risk of not having sufficient third-party capacity. The development of third-party capacity should be closely monitored by both the government and the oil and gas industry. Without adequate third-party capacity, the regulation's implementation is at high risk of failure.

19. *Ibid.*, Art. 89.

4.3 Intertwining CNH and ASEA Regulations

The integration of CNH's and ASEA's regulations creates a robust framework for reducing flaring and methane emissions in Mexico's oil and gas sector. This synergy ensures that: (i) operators are held accountable for both the efficient use of natural gas and the minimization of methane emissions; (ii) there is a cohesive strategy that addresses both the economic and environmental aspects of gas utilization and flaring reduction; and (iii) encourage continuous improvement and innovation in gas management practices, promoting sustainable development in the hydrocarbons sector.

By intertwining CNH's regulations for the use of associated natural gas and ASEA's regulations for methane emissions, Mexico's regulatory framework aims to significantly reduce flaring, enhance resource utilization, and mitigate the environmental impact of its oil and gas industry.

5 2018 PRESIDENTIAL ENERGY POLICY SHIFT

In 2018, Mexico changed president to Andrés Manuel López Obrador who has an approach to achieve energy sovereignty by strengthening PEMEX, advocating for increased investment and support for the national oil company. This stance has often led to a more permissive approach towards PEMEX's operations, including its practices related to flaring and venting of natural gas. In line with this public policy approach, the 2021 Climate Change Program[20] did not specifically address flaring, reflecting a prioritization of other aspects of energy policy over environmental concerns. This omission has raised concerns among environmental advocates and stakeholders, highlighting the challenges of balancing economic priorities with environmental sustainability in Mexico's energy landscape under López Obrador's administration.[21]

The issue of regulatory capture further complicates the landscape of Mexican flaring regulations and their alignment with PEMEX's goals. Addressing regulatory capture requires robust mechanisms to ensure regulatory agencies maintain their independence and prioritize public welfare over industry interests. Transparency, accountability, and periodic reviews of regulatory performance are vital to detect and mitigate instances of capture.

In practice, the autonomy of regulatory bodies like CNH in Mexico has been compromised by political appointments and influence. The administration of President López Obrador has appointed commissioners who align with his political views, potentially affecting the impartiality and independence of regulatory decisions. For its part, ASEA is not an autonomous entity, the influence of political agendas and interests

20. Secretaría de Medio Ambiente y Recursos Naturales, *Programa Especial de Cambio Climático 2021-2024* (November 8, 2021) https://www.gob.mx/cms/uploads/attachment/file/685848/SEMARNAT_081121_EV.PDF accessed May 28, 2024.
21. Juárez, *Solo 7% de las empresas cumple con regulación para reducir emisiones de metano* (Energía a Debate, January 25, 2023) https://energiaadebate.com/solo-7-de-las-empresas-cumple-con-regulacion-para-reducir-emisiones-de-metano/ accessed May 28, 2024.

can extend into ASEA's operations, potentially affecting its ability to act autonomously and enforce regulations without bias.

6 CONCLUSIONS

International agreements and initiatives have played a crucial role in pressuring Mexico to take regulatory action to combat gas flaring. The country's endorsement of the Zero Routine Flaring by 2030 initiative, along with its participation in the Global Methane Initiative and the Climate and Clean Air Coalition, has driven significant policy changes and regulatory measures. These international commitments have underscored the importance of reducing flaring and methane emissions, encouraging Mexico to align its domestic regulations with global best practices. Despite challenges related to regulatory capture and political influences, these international frameworks have been instrumental in pushing Mexico towards more stringent and effective flaring regulations. This external pressure has highlighted the need for robust regulatory enforcement and the development of infrastructure to manage associated gas, ultimately contributing to Mexico's efforts to reduce its environmental impact and promote sustainable energy practices.

The 2013 energy reform and its subsidiary legislation, which included the creation and empowerment of energy regulators, were crucial steps toward achieving flaring reduction goals in Mexico. These reforms established a regulatory framework designed to promote transparency, accountability, and efficiency within the energy sector. CNH and ASEA are key to implementing measures to control and reduce flaring. Additionally, the reform meant that PEMEX would no longer be the only regulated operator, compelling PEMEX to improve its practices to compete effectively.

Policy shifts under President Andrés Manuel López Obrador may have halted the implementation of flaring reduction regulations. These shifts have undermined the initial momentum towards achieving flaring reduction goals, highlighting the challenges of balancing political priorities with environmental commitments.

It is important to note that the impetus for reducing flaring originated primarily from external pressures rather than a proactive decision by Mexican authorities. Consequently, the legal measures taken to address flaring have lacked long-term robustness, highlighting a reactive rather than a proactive approach to environmental regulation in Mexico.

CHAPTER 20

Natural Gas Flaring and the Energy Transition: Laws, Policies and Regulations in Nigeria

Opeyemi Y. Omotuyi

1 INTRODUCTION

The flaring of associated gas that is, the gas produced alongside oil, constitutes one of the most significant challenges posed by the Nigerian petroleum industry since the inception of oil production in the country. Although the level of gas flaring has reduced in recent years, the practice is still prevalent in the industry, and Nigeria is currently the 9th country responsible for most of the gas flared globally.[1] Copious volumes of natural gas are flared annually at different oil fields resulting in environmental pollution with significant adverse effects on the host communities. With over 178 flare sites nationwide, gas flaring contributed 12 million tonnes of carbon emissions in Nigeria in 2022 alone, thus constituting a continuing source of environmental and health hazards to the inhabitants of the oil-producing communities.[2] Beyond the adverse environmental effects, gas flaring also poses multifaceted adverse effects to other aspects of sustainable development in the country including, social and economic aspects. For instance, the Nigerian government was estimated to have lost USD 16 trillion in economic revenue to gas flaring between 2012 to 2022.[3] In the same vein, various empirical studies on the impact of gas flaring in Nigeria indicate that gas flaring impacts the

1. The World Bank, *Global Gas Flaring Tracker Report* (International Bank for Reconstruction and Development/The World Bank, 2023).
2. Emmanuel Addeh, '10 Billion SCF of Gas Flared in December Despite Nigeria's Net Zero Commitments' This Day (Nig.) 7 February 2023.
3. OpeOluwani Akintayo, 'FG Lost $16tn to Gas Flare in 10 Years: Report' Punch (Nig.) 21 November 2023 https://punchng.com/fg-lost-16tn-to-gas-flare-in-10-years-report/ [accessed 13 January 2025].

social, economic and environmental quality of the communities studied.[4] This highlights the necessity of eradicating this menace through effective regulatory and other relevant mechanisms in Nigeria.

Against this background, this chapter analyses the legal and regulatory framework relevant to combating gas flaring in Nigeria. Subsequent sections of the chapter are structured as follows: While section 2 explores the context for the regulation of gas flaring in Nigeria, section 3 highlights the legal framework relevant to combating gas flaring in Nigeria. Section 4 presents the current issues and challenges with gas flaring in Nigeria. In response to the identified issues and challenges, section 5 proposes relevant recommendations. Section 6 concludes the chapter with a summary of the relevant findings and lessons.

2 CONTEXT OF NATURAL GAS FLARING REGULATION IN NIGERIA

The Nigerian government started implementing several attempts at curbing the incidence of gas flaring in the country in 1969. However, various impediments have hindered the success of these attempts. The first of such attempts was the introduction of the requirement for submission of a feasibility study, programme or proposals for the utilization of any natural gas discovered in a licensed area within five years of the commencement of production from such area.[5] This was followed by the enactment of the Associated Gas Reinjection Act in 1979 and the Associated Gas Re-injection (Continued Flaring of Gas) Regulations in 1984, both of which implemented a ban system on gas flaring in Nigeria. The Associated Gas Reinjection Act prohibits the flaring of associated natural gas in Nigeria except with the written permission of the Minister for Petroleum Resources, who is empowered to grant such permission upon satisfaction that utilization or reinjection of such gas is not feasible or appropriate. The Minister may permit the continued flaring of gas in such instances pursuant to such terms and conditions as deemed fit and pursuant to the payment of such sum as may be prescribed periodically for the volume of gas flared.[6] Hence, the Act mandates every oil and gas producer in Nigeria to implement programmes and plans for the re-injection of all associated gas or put in place schemes for the viable utilization of all associated gas in industrial projects.[7] The Associated Gas Re-injection Regulations specify some of the circumstances under which the Minister may grant permission for continued flaring including:

4. Gabriel C. Ndinwa, Solomon A. Akpafun & Charity O. Chukumah, 'Perceived Environmental and Health Impacts of Gas Flaring on Residents in Kwale Communities, Southern Nigeria' (2020) 4(1) *Asian Journal of Energy Transformation and Conservation* 1-21; Adewale Omoniyi Omotayo & Mustapha Ubale, 'The Impact of Gas Flaring in Nigeria' (2015) 5(2) *International Journal of Science, Technology and Society* 40-50 https://doi.org/10.11648/j.ijsts.20150302.12; Nwanya S. Chinwe, 'Climate Change and Energy Implications of Gas Flaring for Nigeria' (2011) 6(5) *International Journal of Low-Carbon Technologies* 195-199 https://doi.org/10.1093/ijlct/ctr007.
5. The Petroleum (Drilling and Production) Regulations 1969, regulation 43.
6. Associated Gas Re-injection Act 1979, section 3.
7. *Ibid.*, sections 1 & 2.

- where more than 75% of the associated gas had been effectively utilized or conserved;
- where the associated gas contains more than 15% impurities rendering the gas unsuitable for industrial purposes;
- where an ongoing utilization programme is frequently interrupted by equipment failure and the period of any one interruption is more than three months; and
- where utilization of the associated gas is not commercially viable and it is not technically advisable to re-inject such associated gas.[8]

These regulatory frameworks support gas commercialization and utilization, or re-injection as strategies for minimizing the incidence of gas flaring in Nigeria. However, there has been a failure in meeting up with the repeatedly extended deadlines set for ending gas flaring in the country pursuant to these frameworks. This failure has been attributed to various impediments including a lack of gas infrastructure, under-developed domestic gas market, capital-intensive gas technologies, and inadequate penalty for non-compliance, among others.[9]

Since 2002, the Nigerian government has consistently indicated a renewed significant commitment towards the eradication of gas flaring in the country. For instance, in 2002, Nigeria joined the Global Gas Flaring Reduction Initiative and in 2016, endorsed the World Bank's Zero Routine Flaring Initiative thereby committing to eliminating routine flaring in the country by 2030. By this endorsement, Nigeria further commits to the provision of a '*legal, regulatory, investment and operating environment that is conducive to upstream investments and to the development of viable markets for utilization of gas and the infrastructure necessary to deliver gas to gas markets*'.[10] It is apparent that Nigeria's commitments under the Zero Routine Flaring Initiative are capable of addressing some of the challenges impeding the utilization of natural gas thereby encouraging gas flaring in the country.

Furthermore, Nigeria participates in various international climate initiatives that target reduced emissions. For instance, Nigeria has participated in the Climate & Clean Air Coalition since 2012 with a commitment to scaling rapid reductions in short-lived climate pollutants.[11] Pursuant to this commitment, Nigeria issued the National Action Plan to Reduce Short-Lived Climate Pollutants in 2018, targeting a reduction in fugitive

8. Associated Gas Re-injection (Continued Flaring of Gas) Regulations 1984, regulation 1.
9. Robin Abu, Kumar Patchigolla & Nigel Simms, 'A Review on Qualitative Assessment of Natural Gas Utilisation Options for Eliminating Routine Nigerian Gas Flaring' (2023) 3 *Gases* 1-24 https://doi.org/10.3390/gases3010001. *See also* Samuel C. Dike & Sandra E. Osinachi-Nwandem, 'Regulatory Framework Governing Gas Operations and Utilization in the Nigerian Petroleum Industry' (2023) 7 *African Journal of International Energy & Environmental Law* 29-40.
10. The World Bank Global Initiative to Reduce Gas Flaring: Zero Routine Flaring by 2030, https://thedocs.worldbank.org/en/doc/984231518029901708-0110022018/original/ZRFInitiative.pdf [accessed 2 March 2024].
11. The Climate & Clean Air Coalition to Reduce Short-lived Climate Pollutants, https://www.ccacoalition.org/content/climate-and-clean-air-coalition [accessed 2 March 2024].

methane emissions and leakage in the oil and gas industry by 50% by 2030.[12] Nigeria is also a participant in the Global Methane Initiative and Global Methane Pledge, an international public-private partnership aimed at the reduction of methane gas emissions and advancement of methane recovery and use as a clean source of energy.[13]

Moreover, Nigeria announced her commitment to the achievement of carbon neutrality by 2060 during COP26 in 2021, further to which an updated Nationally Determined Contribution (NDC) was submitted to the United Nations Framework Convention on Climate Change. The updated NDC included reduced gas flaring as one of the measures to be adopted for the mitigation of climate change in Nigeria. As part of the specified 47% conditional reduction target, Nigeria targets zero routine flaring by 2030, and a 60% reduction in fugitive methane emissions by 2031.[14] This formed the premise of the Energy Transition Plan (ETP) which was developed thereafter as a pathway to meet up with the climate commitments, particularly in terms of energy consumption in the country. Some of the core objectives of the ETP include availability of modern energy services, and promotion of gas as a transition fuel, especially in the power and cooking sectors.[15] Thus, the ETP identifies the need for a reduction in flaring and fugitive emissions as some of the strategies required to ensure a just transition.[16] In fact, the then President of Nigeria, Muhammadu Buhari, proclaimed the period covering 2020-2030 as the 'decade of gas' in Nigeria, signalling a compelling commitment on the part of the government towards natural gas as a transition fuel to further the country's ETP and its ambitious climate targets.[17]

An examination of these various commitments reveals that the Nigerian government has shown consistent political willingness to completely eradicate routine gas flaring in the country. To this end, the Nigerian government is significantly exploring natural gas commercialization and utilization as a strategy for the eradication of flaring in the country. Arguably, this strategy is poised to achieve substantial success in the surge towards eradication of gas flaring in Nigeria. In its 2023 flaring report, the World Bank reports a 3% decrease in the global gas flaring volume in 2022 compared to 2021.[18] The report identifies Nigeria as one of the countries that accounted for most of the decline in global gas flaring in 2022. In fact, Nigeria contributed the most to the overall global flaring reduction having reduced its flare volume by 1.3 billion cubic meters in 2022, representing a 20% reduction from 2021 levels.[19] Even though this reduction is largely attributable to the 14% decline in oil production within this period,

12. Nigeria's National Action Plan (NAP) to Reduce Short-Lived Climate Pollutants (SLCPs) 2018, https://climatechange.gov.ng/wp-content/uploads/2020/09/nigeria-s-national-action-plan-nap-to-reduce-short-lived-climate-pollutants-slcps-.pdf [accessed 2 March 2024].
13. Global Methane Initiative, https://www.globalmethane.org [accessed 2 March 2024].
14. Nigeria's First Nationally Determined Contribution – 2021 Update, https://climatechange.gov.ng/wp-content/uploads/2021/08/NDC_File-Amended-_11222.pdf [accessed 5 March 2024].
15. The Energy Transition Plan, https://energytransition.gov.ng [accessed 5 March 2024].
16. *Ibid.*
17. Uchechukwu Okoro, *Assessing the First Years of Nigeria's Decade of Gas* (Energy & Utilities, 14 September 2023).
18. The World Bank, *Global Gas Flaring Tracker Report*, *supra* n. 1.
19. *Ibid.*

it is noteworthy that the country also had an improvement in its flaring intensity with a reduction from 11.8 cubic meters per barrel of oil produced in 2021 to 11.1 cubic meter per barrel of oil produced in 2022.[20] This indicates that even though Nigeria is still one of the top flaring countries globally, some level of progress is being made at reducing gas flaring in the country. The reduction in the flaring intensity suggests that oil and gas companies are implementing some level of material improvement in their operational performance thereby, reducing the incidence of flaring of the associated gas from their oil fields. In addition, the attribution of the flaring reduction to a decline in oil production indicates that the high incidence of gas flaring in Nigeria is primarily a result of the production of associated natural gas from oil production. Therefore, a total move away from oil production to the exploitation of the non-associated gas reserves could compel the eradication of gas flaring in Nigeria. This is more so since the contribution of the oil sector to the national gross domestic product (GDP) has been declining since 2020.[21] The decline in the revenue generation from the oil sector in addition to the increasing volatility of international oil markets due to the global climate and energy transition agendas among others, further affirms the need to completely shift focus from oil production with its attendant associated gas flaring to natural gas development. This however requires the development of the domestic gas market to ensure viable commercialization and utilization of natural gas in the country.

3 NATURAL GAS FLARING: THE LEGAL FRAMEWORK IN NIGERIA

The legal framework for natural gas flaring in Nigeria derives its basis from the Nigerian Constitution (hereafter referred to as 'the Constitution').[22] The Constitution provides the socio-economic objectives necessary to be achieved by the Nigerian government. Some of these constitutionally recognized socio-economic objectives include harnessing national resources and promoting national prosperity and an efficient, dynamic and self-reliant national economy. This is in addition to the prevention of the exploitation of natural resources in any form or for any reason other than the good of the society.[23] Moreover, the Constitution vests the entire property in and control of all minerals, mineral oils and natural gas within the Nigerian jurisdiction on the government which is required to manage such in any manner as may be prescribed by legislations.[24] Hence, the Nigerian legislature has implemented a comprehensive legal framework to discourage gas flaring and promote the commercialization and utilization of Nigeria's enormous gas resources.

20. *Ibid.*
21. The contribution of the oil sector to the national GDP declined from 9% pre-2020 to 5.9% in 2020, and 5.34% in the second quarter of 2023; Doris Dokua Sasu, *Contribution of Oil Sector to GDP in Nigeria 2018-2023* (Statista, 27 September 2023), https://www.statista.com/statistics/1165865/contribution-of-oil-sector-to-gdp-in-nigeria/ [accessed 5 March 2024].
22. The Constitution of the Federal Republic of Nigeria 1999 (as amended).
23. *Ibid.*, sections 16(1)(a) & 17(2)(d).
24. *Ibid.*, section 44(3).

3.1 Flare Gas (Prevention of Waste and Pollution) Regulations 2018

These regulations were enacted to provide legal support for the implementation of the NGFCP and the NGP particularly, creating social and economic benefits from natural gas.[25] Pursuant to the regulations, the Nigerian government is vested with the right to take associated gas free of cost and without payment of royalty.[26] To this end, the government is empowered to conduct competitive bid processes whereby a qualified bidder is granted a permit to access and take associated gas from designated flare sites, and utilize such gas or dispose of same in any manner authorized by the government.[27] Likewise, oil and gas licensees or lessees may apply to the government for a permit to utilize the associated gas from their oilfields for commercialization, and upon such permit being granted, such licensee or lessee may utilize associated gas for its own purposes.[28] To encourage associated gas capturing and prevent flaring, such applicants for permit to take flare gas are not liable to pay any royalties to any person or the government in respect of any gas taken.[29] Therefore, with these provisions in place, the regulations prohibit gas flaring and permit the flaring of gas only upon the issuance of a certificate by the Minister of Petroleum Resources pursuant to the Associated Gas Re-injection Act. The regulations prescribe new penalty for flaring including; USD 2 per one thousand standard cubic feet of gas flared from an oilfield that produces 10,000 barrels or more of oil per day, and USD 0.50 per one thousand standard cubic feet of gas flared from an oilfield that produces less than 10,000 barrels of oil per day.[30]

Furthermore, to ensure adequate compliance monitoring and evaluation, an oil licensee or lessee is required to maintain a daily record of associated gas produced, as well as a daily log of associated gas flared on its oilfield and submit the same to the government on a monthly basis.[31] Likewise, licensees or lessees are required to install metering equipment on their facilities so as to ensure the accuracy of the data reported in the flare log. Hence, the flare log is required to be maintained based on data from the metering equipment, including the date, time, duration, rate, volume, and the gas type, with regard to each flaring reported.[32] In addition, a licensee or lessee is required to prepare and submit an annual report containing all flare gas data with respect to each license area including information on the volume of gas utilized, flared or vented on such area.[33] Where a licensee or lessee fails to comply with these obligations, such shall be liable to pay an additional sum of USD 2.50 per one thousand standard cubic feet of gas flared or vented for each day that the failure persists.[34]

---

25. Flare Gas (Prevention of Waste and Pollution) Regulations 2018, regulation 1.
26. *Ibid.*, regulation 2(1).
27. *Ibid.*, regulations 3(1) & 8(1).
28. *Ibid.*, regulation 3(2) & (3).
29. *Ibid.*, regulation 3(4).
30. *Ibid.*, regulation 13.
31. *Ibid.*, regulation 15(1) & 16.
32. *Ibid.*, regulation 15(3).
33. *Ibid.*, regulations 17 & 18.
34. *Ibid.*, regulation 21(1).

Thus, the regulations incentivize the commercialization and utilization of flare gas through the application of a zero-royalty regime to flare gas, while de-incentivizing flaring through the provision of the new penalty regime for flaring.

3.2 Petroleum Industry Act 2021

The Petroleum Industry Act (PIA) is currently the principal legal framework regulating all aspects of oil and gas operations in Nigeria. It is a legislative consolidation of all legal, governance, fiscal and regulatory aspects of oil and gas development in Nigeria. Notwithstanding, the PIA recognizes the continued validity of any other framework that is repealed or amended by its enactment in so far as such is not inconsistent with its provisions and until such is revoked or replaced.[35] In other words, although the PIA is the principal and consolidated law that currently regulates all aspects of oil and gas development in Nigeria, preceding laws and regulations are still relevant to the extent of their consistency with the provisions of the PIA. Such preceding laws and regulations are deemed to have been issued under the PIA.

In alignment with the NGMP and NGP, the PIA adopts gas-based industrialization, as well as domestic commercialization and utilization of natural gas as strategies for regulating flaring and promoting natural gas development in Nigeria. The PIA establishes the Nigerian Upstream Petroleum Regulatory Commission (NUPRC) with the objectives of ensuring that upstream petroleum operations are carried out in a manner that minimizes waste and achieves optimum government revenues, promoting an enabling environment for investment in upstream petroleum operations, and implementing national policies for upstream petroleum operations, among others.[36] Since gas flaring typically occurs during upstream petroleum operations, the regulation of gas flaring and recovery falls within the jurisdiction of the NUPRC. Thus, where a prospecting licensee makes a commercial discovery on an oilfield, such licensee is required to submit to the NUPRC a field development plan which shall only be approved where it results in the maximum economic recovery of natural gas, provides for the elimination of routine flaring, and does not conflict with the domestic gas delivery obligation of the licensee.[37] In addition to the field development plan, licensees are required to submit a natural gas flare elimination and monetization plan (FEMP) to the NUPRC.[38] Such FEMP is to further promote the commercialization of associated gas by licensees thereby eliminating the flaring option. Furthermore, to ensure minimum flaring and optimum gas recovery, the PIA grants the NUPRC the right to take associated gas that would otherwise be flared free of charge from the relevant flare site.[39] Additionally, the PIA prescribes some fiscal measures to further discourage flaring and encourage re-injection or commercialization of associated gas. For instance, the costs of gas re-injection wells which are reinjecting natural gas that

35. The Petroleum Industry Act 2021, section 311(1).
36. *Ibid.*, sections 4 & 6.
37. *Ibid.*, section 79.
38. *Ibid.*, section 108.
39. *Ibid.*, section 105(2).

would otherwise be flared are permitted as deductible allowances for tax purposes.[40] Likewise, expenses incurred by licensees as penalty for flaring, natural gas flare fees, or any other imposition relating to natural gas flare, are disallowed from being deductible for tax purposes.[41] Other fiscal incentives provided for natural gas commercialization include the exemption of companies engaged in the production of associated gas and natural gas liquids produced from non-associated gas from paying hydrocarbon tax.[42]

Aside from the various provisions that promote commercialization over flaring, the PIA places an express prohibition on gas flaring except in cases of emergency, for safety reasons, or pursuant to an exemption granted by the NUPRC. In furtherance of this, an offender is liable to the penalty for flaring as prescribed by the Flare Gas Regulations.[43] To ensure compliance with the flare ban and enable adequate monitoring of flare gas volumes, licensees are required to install metering equipment that conforms to prescribed specifications on their facilities before commencing operations. Failure to install such metering equipment is an offence that attracts a prescribed fine as penalty.[44]

Addressing the infrastructural challenges plaguing the domestic gas sector, the PIA establishes a Midstream and Downstream Gas Infrastructure Fund, which is to be funded by the wholesale price of petroleum products and natural gas sold, funds and grants accruing from international institutions, money accrued from gas flaring penalties, and donations received for such infrastructural development. The fund is applicable to equity investments in infrastructural development in midstream and downstream gas operations targeting increased domestic gas consumption. Through the fund, the Nigerian government aims at encouraging private investment in midstream and downstream gas operations through risk-sharing by participating in selected high-risk midstream and downstream gas projects and equity investments that target midstream and downstream gas infrastructure.[45] Such infrastructural development contributes significantly to the development of natural gas thereby, reducing or eliminating flaring.

3.3 Gas Flaring, Venting and Methane Emissions (Prevention of Waste and Pollution) Regulations 2023

The PIA vested the NUPRC with the responsibility of setting, defining and enforcing standards and regulations for the elimination of natural gas flaring and venting.[46] In furtherance of this responsibility, the NUPRC issued these regulations with the objectives of reducing the adverse impact of flaring, preventing waste of natural

40. *Ibid.*, section 263(1).
41. *Ibid.*, section 264.
42. *Ibid.*, section 260.
43. *Ibid.*, sections 104 & 105(1).
44. *Ibid.*, section 106.
45. *Ibid.*, section 52.
46. *Ibid.*, section 7(e).

resources, and creating social and economic benefits from gas flaring and venting.[47] In other words, the regulations also seek a reduction in gas flaring while promoting commercialization of natural gas as a viable alternative. Hence, the regulations affirm the requirement for licensees to develop a FEMP where a commercial discovery is made on an oilfield. The FEMP is required to contain the methods for the elimination and monetization of gas flaring from a requisite oilfield, including an implementation plan for the stated methods, as well as a timeline for the execution of the implementation plan.[48] Upon the approval of a FEMP, a licensee is required to enter into a Milestone Development Agreement with the NUPRC for the implementation of the FEMP, and also execute a milestone bond in favour of the NUPRC.[49] While the milestone development agreement seeks to support the continuous monitoring and evaluation of licensees' performance in respect of the FEMP, the milestone bond serves the purpose of a financial guarantee that a licensee will implement the FEMP as approved.

The regulations empower the NUPRC to establish a gas flaring threshold for licensees biannually. Thus, except in cases of emergency, gas flaring is allowed within the approved threshold upon the payment of a flaring fee as charged by the NUPRC.[50] Any licensee who flares, vents or wastes gas without authorization is therefore liable to a fine of USD 3.50 per one thousand standard cubic feet of gas flared.[51] Hence, licensees are required to keep and maintain a record of daily fugitive methane emissions data from their licensed areas, and the NUPRC is empowered to request the submission of gas data from licensees including gas volumes, flare site data, routine and non-routine flaring data, etc.[52] Likewise, licensees are required to keep and maintain daily records of natural gas produced from an oilfield and submit a monthly report of natural gas produced, as well as the volume of the produced natural gas that was utilized or disposed.[53] A failure to submit the requisite gas data within the prescribed time, the submission of inaccurate data, and the failure to install the prescribed metering equipment on an oilfield attract a fine of USD 10,000.[54]

The regulations only prohibit gas flaring in respect of flare sites that have been awarded to a permitholder and commissioned pursuant to a gas flare commercialization programme.[55] Hence, petroleum licensees and flare gas permitholders are required to maintain a daily log of gas flaring and venting from a flare site and submit the same to the NUPRC monthly, as well as an annual report which includes gas data in respect of each flare site. To ensure accuracy, the log is required to be maintained based on data retrieved from the installed metering equipment on a petroleum facility including the date, time, duration, and volumes of each flare.[56]

47. Gas Flaring, Venting and Methane Emissions (Prevention of Waste and Pollution) Regulations 2023, regulation 1.
48. *Ibid.*, regulation 3(4).
49. *Ibid.*, regulation 3(5) & (6).
50. *Ibid.*, regulations 12 & 17.
51. *Ibid.*, regulation 21.
52. *Ibid.*, regulation 4.
53. *Ibid.*, regulation 18.
54. *Ibid.*, regulation 21.
55. *Ibid.*, regulation 14(1) & (2).
56. *Ibid.*, regulation 15 & 19.

3.4 Domestic Gas Delivery Obligation Regulations 2022

To ensure adequate domestic gas supply therefore enhancing domestic commercialization and utilization of gas, the PIA empowers the NUPRC to issue and enforce a regulation or guideline prescribing and allocating a domestic gas delivery obligation among all licensees on the basis of a determined domestic gas demand requirement.[57] Thus, all licensees are required to submit a marketable natural gas production and supply plan consistent with the allocated domestic supply obligation.[58] Any licensee that fails to meet the domestic delivery obligation is liable to a penalty of USD 3.50 per MMBtu of gas not delivered.[59]

The domestic gas delivery obligation regulations were issued by NUPRC in furtherance of this responsibility. Pursuant to the regulations, the NUPRC is empowered to allocate domestic gas delivery obligations to licensees based on the volume of natural gas to be supplied by the licensees on a voluntary basis for a specified price level.[60]

3.5 Gas Pricing Regulations 2022

The PIA establishes the Nigerian Midstream and Downstream Regulatory Authority (NMDRA) and empowers it to make regulations in respect of midstream and downstream petroleum operations in Nigeria. Since the marketing and distribution of petroleum products fall within the purview of downstream operations, the issue of gas pricing falls within the jurisdiction of the NMDRA. Hence, the NMDRA issued the Gas Pricing Regulations in 2022, to provide a gas pricing regime for the domestic gas market, and to repeal the National Gas Supply and Pricing Regulations of 2008. In alignment with the NGMP, NGP, and the PIA, the regulations support domestic commercialization and utilization of natural gas as a strategy for promoting natural gas development over flaring in Nigeria.

In furtherance of this, the regulations empower the NMDRA to determine the annual domestic gas demand requirement for all domestic demand sectors, pursuant to which the NUPRC exercises its power to allocate domestic gas supply obligations to licensees.[61] This provision ensures the availability of adequate supply of gas to the domestic gas market. For pricing purposes, the regulations adopt the pricing system prescribed in the national domestic gas supply and pricing policy. In so doing, the regulations group the domestic demand sector into three; power sector, gas-based industries including those that utilize gas as feedstock or industrial raw material, and commercial sector including those that use gas as an energy source.[62] For the power and commercial sectors, the regulations prescribe a pricing regime consisting of a

57. The Petroleum Industry Act, *supra* n. 35, section 110(1).
58. *Ibid.*, section 110(12).
59. *Ibid.*, section 110(8).
60. Domestic Gas Delivery Obligation Regulations 2022, regulation 4(1) & (2).
61. Gas Pricing Regulations 2022.
62. *Ibid.*

domestic base price that is determined based on adjustments to export parity price in addition to gas transport and processing allowance, or the domestic gas supply price, whichever is lower. For the gas-based industries, the regulations prescribe a feed gas price regime determined based on the price of the product generated by a gas-based industry from gas utilization.[63] These pricing regimes ensure affordability of gas based on the capacity of the different demand sectors to pay gas prices, while also ensuring that suppliers earn an acceptable return for their domestic supply obligations.

The regulations also support a transitional pricing regime whereby a domestic gas aggregator is responsible for managing the domestic supply obligations and pricing regimes. In so doing, the aggregator is empowered to determine an aggregate gas price based on the aggregate volume of domestic supply obligations to the different demand sectors. Whenever a free-market status is however achieved, the regulated pricing regime ceases to apply and a free-market price on a voluntary buyer and voluntary seller basis becomes applicable.[64]

4 NATURAL GAS FLARING: ISSUES AND CHALLENGES IN NIGERIA

As already established, Nigeria is promoting natural gas development through commercialization and utilization as a strategy for eradicating gas flaring in the country. Even though some levels of success have been recorded in this regard, however, there are still some challenges affecting the commercialization and utilization of natural gas in Nigeria. First, the gas sector in Nigeria is still currently under-developed as the production-to-reserves ratio is very low, and natural gas production is substantially from associated gas even though Nigeria holds more volume of non-associated gas reserves. This has been attributed to a lack of significant investment in the exploration and production of non-associated gas sites in the country.[65] Second, there are inadequate gas infrastructures and the existing ones are old and inefficient thereby resulting in shortfalls in the volumes of gas supply to the domestic market in comparison with domestic gas demand requirements.[66] Also, petroleum infrastructures are typically built with a focus on oil production rather than gas capture and retrofitting gas technologies into such infrastructures may be capital-intensive. Likewise, the exploration and production of non-associated gas reserves may require new capital-intensive investments in gas infrastructures.

Further is the lack of adequate and flexible funding mechanisms for investments in gas infrastructural development, as well as the implementation of domestic gas utilization projects across the natural gas value chain. For instance, the 250 billion naira intervention fund established under the National Gas Expansion Programme (NGEP) to incentivize private investment in the gas sector has remained dormant since

63. *Ibid.*
64. *Ibid.*
65. PWC, 'Evaluating Nigeria's Gas Value Chain', https://www.pwc.com/ng/en/assets/pdf/evaluating-nigeria-gas-value-chain.pdf [accessed 13 January 2025].
66. *Ibid.*

its establishment since no investor has been able to access it because of the stringent conditions attached to it.[67] This is in addition to the lack of adequate budgetary allocation on the part of government for the effective execution of projects earmarked under the NGEP such as the conversion of substantial number of engines to CNG tanks, as well as the construction of CNG fueling stations across the country.[68]

Another major challenge is the lack of a market-driven pricing system in the Nigerian gas sector. Gas producers would typically prefer a gas market based on international market prices rather than a domestically regulated price. Thus, the regulation of the domestic pricing system occasions the focus of domestic gas production on LNG for exports with a multiplier effect of shortfalls in the domestic market supply. Also, inadequate penalty prescriptions may still continue to inhibit natural gas development while encouraging continued flaring in Nigeria. This is because IOCs may rather opt to pay cheaper penalties for flaring than invest in capital-intensive gas capture technologies. The current penalty rate is as prescribed in the flare gas regulations since 2018, and this may currently be grossly inadequate to deter flaring.

Moreover, there is the issue of regulatory inconsistencies in the legal framework on gas which may operate to impede the realization of the objectives of government on natural gas development. Although the government seeks to promote natural gas commercialization and utilization as a strategy for eradicating flaring in the country, some regulatory provisions are inhibitive of this. For instance, the PIA is enacted in a manner that makes it challenging for licensees to commercialize or utilize associated gas from their licensed areas. Specifically, the PIA requires licensees, who account for the incidence of gas flaring in Nigeria, to apply for a permit before they can take and utilize associated gas from their license areas. This connotes that licensees are only vested with the right to extract oil from their license areas with no corresponding right to exploit the associated gas produced from their operations. It is noteworthy that the conditions coupled with the bureaucracy of applying for the requisite permit may discourage licensees from taking and utilizing associated gas but resort to flaring instead. Likewise, the gas flaring, venting and methane emissions regulations contain provisions which appear inconsistent and conflicting with the PIA and the objective of the government to eradicate flaring. The regulations permit routine flaring within a prescribed threshold and upon payment of a fee for flaring thus, prohibiting and permitting flaring at the same time. Further, while the PIA in alignment with the various national gas policies seeks the prescription of domestic supply obligations on the basis of domestic demand requirements, the domestic gas delivery obligation regulations seek the allocation of the same on the basis of the volume of natural gas that licensees are willing to supply voluntarily. This may occasion shortfalls in meeting with domestic demand as licensees will typically prefer gas exports to domestic market

67. Abdullateef Aliyu, 'N250bn Gas Expansion Fund Dormant For 4 Yrs: FG' Daily Trust (Nig.) 29 August 2023.
68. Omono Okonkwo, 'National Gas Expansion Programme (NGEP) is Still Ongoing Despite Paltry N18.26 million Budget', Nairametrics, 14 October 2022, https://nairametrics.com/2022/10/14/national-gas-expansion-programme-ngep-is-still-ongoing-despite-paltry-n18-26-million-budget/ [accessed 13 January 2025].

supply, therefore, defeating the essence of implementing a domestic delivery obligation to wit, to encourage adequate domestic market supply and utilization.

5 RECOMMENDATIONS

The attribution of the flaring reduction to a decline in oil production indicates that the high incidence of gas flaring in Nigeria is primarily a result of the production of associated natural gas from oil production. Therefore, a gradual move away from oil production to the exploitation of the non-associated gas reserves may not only compel the eradication of gas flaring in Nigeria but also enhance the realization of her ETP. This however requires significant legal and policy reforms by the government. Presently, the NGFCP and the PIA primarily target the commercialization of associated gas from existing licensed oilfields in the country. This may be reviewed to include the implementation of bidding rounds and award of permits targeted specifically at the exploration and production of non-associated natural gas. This also calls for the implementation of regulatory provisions and incentives that encourage significant investments in the exploration and production of non-associated gas sites in the country. The relevance of sustainable finance cannot be over-emphasized in this regard. As a complement to government funding, the government must implement and promote sustainable finance policies in the energy sector. Such policies may particularly be relevant to provide fiscal support for the implementation of the gas infrastructure blueprint as highlighted in the NGP. To this end, the government must also ensure that incentives and disincentives are put in place so that investments in such natural gas development are financially attractive to investors.

Fuel subsidy reforms have been identified as a valuable tool for tackling the ongoing global energy transitions.[69] Therefore, rather than the current regulated pricing regime of gas in the domestic market, the Nigerian government may adopt a gas subsidy regime which ensures affordability of gas in the domestic market while gas producers still earn international parity prices for their domestic gas supply.

To ensure effective deterrence of gas flaring, the NUPRC should be empowered to periodically determine the penalty for flaring in alignment with prevailing socio-economic conditions per period rather than having a static legislative prescription. In addition, the rate of prescribed penalties should be a value that actually deters flaring since licensees may rather flare gas and pay cheaper penalties than invest in gas development.

It is noteworthy that eradication of flaring may require a synergy between the petroleum industry and different industries that utilize natural gas so as to enhance commercialization and utilization. For instance, even though the current energy transition is mainly driven by the global climate agenda, its implementation is largely dependent on the provision of energy security through availability of alternative energy sources. Natural gas is a globally accepted efficient and sustainable energy source

69. Victoria Bassetti & Kelsey Landau, *Seizing Opportunities for Fuel Subsidy Reform* (Brookings, 25 February 2021), https://www.brookings.edu/blog/up-front/2021/02/25/seizing-opportunities-for-fuel-subsidy-reform/ [accessed 18 March 2024].

capable of enhancing energy security. This may therefore call for a synergy between the petroleum industry and the power sector, for instance, so as to enhance energy security in Nigeria. This may involve an industry-wide collaboration in the development of a robust transportation network that connects gas supply from producers to thermal stations across the country.

To further the flare-out objectives of the government through commercialization and utilization, legal and regulatory reforms may also be necessary. For instance, the gas flaring, venting and emissions regulations may be reviewed so that flaring is only permitted for safety reasons and in cases of emergency. This is so that the provisions of the regulations may be aligned with the PIA and other flaring regulations. Likewise, the PIA may be reviewed to grant licensees a corresponding right to take, commercialize or utilize associated gas from licensed areas without necessarily having to apply for a separate permit.

6 CONCLUSION

Gas flaring constitutes one of the significant challenges that may adversely affect the realization of Nigeria's ETP. Although the level of gas flaring has reduced in recent years, the practice is nevertheless still prevalent in the country. Aside from the impact on the realization of the ETP, gas flaring poses significant adverse impacts to all aspects of sustainable development in Nigeria including, environmental sustainability, social well-being, and economic development. In response, the Nigerian government has implemented several policies, laws and regulations, etc., for the regulation of gas flaring in the country.

This chapter traces the evolution and highlights the context of the legal and regulatory framework on gas flaring in Nigeria. In so doing, the chapter identifies that the government has implemented substantial regulatory measures to eradicate gas flaring in the country. Through the relevant regulatory and legislative frameworks, the Nigerian government adopts the commercialization and utilization of natural gas as a strategy for eradicating gas flaring in the petroleum industry. It is noteworthy that this strategic approach to ensuring a flare-out is laudable as it not only contributes to the eradication of gas flaring but also enhances the realization of a just energy transition as well as sustainable development.

The chapter further identifies some persisting issues and challenges affecting the development as well as commercialization and utilization of natural gas in Nigeria. To further the flare-out objectives of the Nigerian government therefore, the chapter makes some plausible recommendations to address the issues and challenges identified.

CHAPTER 21

Norway: Regulation of Flaring and Venting of Natural Gas from Petroleum Activities in Norway

Catherine Banet

1 INTRODUCTION

This chapter reviews the regulatory approach applied in Norway to the flaring and venting of natural gas from petroleum exploitation activities. The national regime applies to both flaring (ignition of gas) and venting of gas (release of unignited gas). As in other jurisdictions, the flaring or venting of gas will happen when natural gas is produced as a byproduct of oil extraction or presents a safety problem for the operators.

Although Norway is a relatively small producer of crude oil and natural gas compared to other countries, it has Europe's largest hydrocarbon reserves and is an important supplier to the global market.[1] In 2022, production of oil liquids (crude, NGL and condensate) reached around 2 million barrels per day, and Norway supplied about 2% of global oil consumption.[2] This makes Norway the 11th largest oil producer.[3] In the same year, the Norwegian production of natural gas covered around 3% of global demand. Norway was in 2022 the third largest exporter of natural gas in the world behind Russia and Qatar.[4] Domestic consumption of gas in Norway is very low, and

1. "Exports of Norwegian Oil and Gas" (*Norwegianpetroleum.no*, October 7, 2024) https://www.norskpetroleum.no/en/production-and-exports/exports-of-oil-and-gas/ accessed November 13, 2024.
2. "Overview" (*Homepage—U.S. Energy Information Administration (EIA)*) https://www.eia.gov/international/content/analysis/countries_long/norway/ accessed November 13, 2024.
3. BP/Energy Institute, Statistical Review of World Energy, 2023.
4. "Exports of Norwegian Oil and Gas" (*Norwegianpetroleum.no*, October 7, 2024) https://www.norskpetroleum.no/en/production-and-exports/exports-of-oil-and-gas/ accessed November 13, 2024.

nearly all the gas produced on the Norwegian Continental Shelf (NCS) is exported. In recent years, Norway has supplied between 20% and 25% of the European Union (EU) and United Kingdom gas demand.[5] Combined, oil and gas account for more than half of the total value of Norwegian exports of goods. This makes oil and gas the most important export commodities in the Norwegian economy.

Norwegian authorities have introduced a series of measures on emissions reductions since the years 1970s that have directly and indirectly contributed to the reduction of flaring and venting.[6] Notably, flaring from oil and gas exploitation—for the whole part located offshore—has been prohibited since the very start of petroleum activities. Flaring and venting is only permitted for safety reasons and is subject to a permit. This restrictive regulatory approach to gas flaring and venting has resulted in low levels of flaring on the NCS compared to other countries. Indeed, Norway is consistently ranked as having the lowest flaring intensity within producing countries. For example, in 2021, Norway produced about the same amount of oil as Kazakhstan and Mexico, but these countries flared 7-42 times the volume flared in Norway.[7] In 2022, there were around 25-30 offshore individual flare sites in the country.[8]

The strict control of flaring and venting is in line with the international and national commitments taken by Norway under the United Nations Framework Convention on Climate Change (UNFCCC), the Paris Agreement and the Norwegian Climate Act. Norway's target under the Climate Act is to reduce greenhouse gas emissions by at least 55% by 2030 compared to 1990 levels, and that Norway will be a low emission Society by 2050.[9]

2 CONTEXT ABOUT NATURAL GAS FLARING IN NORWAY: EARLY PROHIBITION AND PERMITTING REGIME

Gas flaring and venting has been prohibited in Norway since the beginning of petroleum production from the NCS in the early 1970s.[10] In 1971, the Norwegian parliament endorsed the so-called 10 Oil Commandments as part of a Parliamentary Recommendation on Norwegian petroleum policy.[11] The fifth oil commandment provides that: "Flaring of unusable gas on the NCS must not be accepted, except during

5. Norwegian Offshore Directorate.
6. "Norway: Ieexi" (*Download the full reports.*) https://flaringventingregulations.worldbank.org/norway accessed November 13, 2024.
7. World Bank Global Gas Flaring Tracker, 2023. Available at: Global Gas Flaring Data (worldbank.org).
8. *Ibid.*
9. Sections 3 and 4, Norwegian Climate Act.
10. (*Regulation of associated gas flaring and venting*) https://www.esmap.org/sites/default/files/esmap-files/Rpt_GBL_RegOfGasFlaringandVenting.pdf accessed November 13, 2024.
11. The "10 oil commandments" refer to a statement of the main principles for national oil policy presented by the standing committee on industry of the Storting (parliament) in June 1971 (Innst. S. nr 294 (1970-71)). The recommendation from the committee was the Parliamentary response to the White Paper put forward by the Ministry for Industry (Stortingsmelding nr. 76 (1970-71), "*Undersøkelse etter og utvinning av undersjøiske naturforekomster på den norske kontinentalsokkel m.m.*").

brief periods of testing."[12] This declaration set an important principle that has ever since guided the national regime, according to which flaring (and venting) on the NCS are prohibited except during short periods of testing and for safety-related reasons.

The introduction of the prohibition was motivated by two main reasons. The first and original reason was to avoid wasting valuable energy resources and losing revenues from the sale of petroleum products.[13] The second reason was the limitation of greenhouse gases emissions into the air, although historically it appeared later on.

In addition, several additional measures have acted, directly and indirectly, in favor of the strict flaring and venting regime in the country. In terms of direct regulation, the Norwegian legislation contains several environmental measures that aim at controlling and reducing harmful emissions and discharges. These include economic instruments in the form of a CO_2 tax,[14] a NOx tax, and regulatory instruments in the form of permits with emissions thresholds. Indirect regulation, and notably emissions trading scheme, is playing an effective incentive role in decreasing emissions. Finally, strict emissions control from natural gas flaring and venting measures have played a role in developing specific technologies, such as carbon capture and storage and enhanced oil/gas recovery.

In recent times, there has been a very limited amount of flaring in Norway, which can be considered a successful result of legislation implementation and of the economic incentives created, which render investments in emissions reduction solutions economically attractive.

3 NATURAL GAS FLARING LEGAL FRAMEWORK

Emissions from gas flaring and venting in relation to petroleum activities are regulated under several acts. Their control aligns with a general duty to conduct prudent operations.

3.1 The Duty to Conduct Prudent Operations

The Petroleum Act defines a general obligation to conduct oil and gas operations in a prudent manner (section 4-1). This so-called "prudent operation principle" applies to both licensees and authorities.[15] It is referred to in several provisions of the Petroleum Act, focusing on safety, prudent technical and sound economic management of operations and reservoir. Environmental protection is also included in the scope of

12. Author's own translation. Original wording: "*brenning av unyttbar gass på den norske kontinentalsokkel ikke må aksepteres unntatt for kortere prøveperioder.*"
13. This comes clearly forward in the NOU 1979:43 Petroleumslov med forskrifter, section IV.
14. Under the regime of the CO_2 Tax Act, venting of natural gas is taxed at a rate determined in the national budget every year. The CO_2 tax on methane emissions from petroleum production activities was set at 1,689 NOK/Sm^3 for the budget year 2024, which is an increase by 23.6% compared with the year 2023. (*Stortingsvedtak om CO_2-avgift i petroleumsvirksomheten på kontinentalsokkelen for 2024.*).
15. Ot.prp. nr. 72 (1982-83) section 56.

prudent petroleum activities, and more explicitly in section 10-1 of the Petroleum Act which reads as follows:[16]

> Petroleum activities according to this Act shall be conducted in a prudent manner and in accordance with applicable legislation for such petroleum activities. The petroleum activities shall take due account of the safety of personnel, the environment and of the financial values which the facilities and vessels represent, including also operational availability.
>
> The petroleum activities must not unnecessarily or to an unreasonable extent impede or obstruct shipping, fishing, aviation or other activities, or cause damage or threat of damage to pipelines, cables or other subsea facilities. All reasonable precautions shall be taken to prevent damage to animal life and vegetation in the sea, relics of the past on the sea bed and to prevent pollution and littering of the seabed, its subsoil, the sea, the atmosphere or onshore.

One can conclude from the wording of section 10-1, that the reduction of emissions in relation to flaring and venting derives from the prudent operation principle, in addition to environmental control rules. Conversely, when a licensee applies for a production license, it must prevent flaring and cold-venting from happening under the conditions described below.

3.2 General Prohibition and Exemption Grounds

The Petroleum Act defines a general prohibition against flaring from petroleum activities in section 4-4,[17] which provides that: "Burning of petroleum in excess of the quantities needed for normal operational safety shall not be allowed unless approved by the Ministry." The Ministry in charge is the Ministry of Energy. The wording of this provision has evolved to a limited extent compared to the former version of the Petroleum Act.

In terms of scope, the prohibition covers both flaring and cold-venting. This is clarified in the Guidelines elaborated by the Norwegian Offshore Directorate (NOD) on the interpretation and implementation of the Petroleum Act in relation to the production permit application ("Guidelines for production permit application," hereafter the Guidelines).[18]

The wording of section 4-4 of the Petroleum Act is itself explicit as to the fact that the prohibition is not absolute. The burning of petroleum could be allowed within a certain threshold corresponding to normal safety operations. If natural gas flaring cannot be avoided beyond that threshold, operators are required to obtain an emission permit setting emission limits.

The first assessment of gas flaring from the field will be made as part of the Plan for Development and Operation (PDO). Pursuant to the Petroleum Act, the licensee is

16. Non official translation provided by the Offshore Directorate.
17. Act November 29, 1996 No. 72 relating to petroleum activities.
18. Last revised Spring 2023. Available at: https://www.sodir.no/globalassets/1-sodir/regelverk/veiledninger/guidelines-for-production-permit-applications.pdf.

required to submit the PDO to the Ministry for approval.[19] The PDO must cover all dimensions of the field development, including economic aspects, resource profile, technical solutions, safety and commercial aspects, as well as environmental and decommissioning aspects. As part of the technical solutions and environmental aspects, the plan must cover the list of measures envisaged to prevent and minimize environmentally harmful discharges and emissions, including flaring and venting. If authorizations have been applied for, including for flaring and venting, they must be included. The exact content of the PDO is detailed in the Petroleum Regulations.[20] No production permit will be issued before a PDO is approved or an exemption from such a plan is provided.

3.3 Gas Flaring and Venting Permit Application

If flaring and venting is expected to happen beyond what is considered necessary for safety reasons for normal operations, the licensee needs to apply for and obtain a dedicated permit. In practice, it is the operator of the fields and the facilities that applies, on behalf of the other licensees, for both the production permit and the flaring and venting permits. Flaring and cold-venting permits are issued for a period of one calendar year at a time. This means that the operator will put forward an application for each calendar year. The operator's strategy for flaring and cold-venting for the specific facility must be enclosed with the application. Following the application, the Ministry will specify, based on the recommendations from the Directorate, the volumes that can be flared and cold-vented for specific periods.[21] The volumes set in the permit are maximum quotas per quarter. These volumes cannot be exceeded, transferred or distributed within the calendar year. Land facilities and non-field installations which need flaring and/or cold-venting shall also apply for a permit. The application shall be submitted no later than six weeks prior to the earliest scheduled start of production. If the scheduled production start-up does not coincide with the start-up of flaring and cold-venting, two separate applications can be submitted; one for production and injection, and one for flaring and cold-venting, respectively.[22]

If it becomes obvious that the permitted quota for flare and cold-venting will not cover the emissions, a reasoned application for a revised permit shall be submitted without any delay to the Ministry, with a copy to the Directorate. Applications for an increased quota shall include an account/clarification of the factors listed in Appendix 2 to the Guidelines for production permit application of the Norwegian Offshore Directorate.[23]

19. Section 4-2, Petroleum Act.
20. Section 21 (content of the PDO) and section 22, 22(a) and 22(c) (environmental impact assessment of the PDO), Petroleum Regulations.
21. Guidelines for production permit application, Norwegian Offshore Directorate. The sources of cold-venting must be indicated in a table enclosed with the application, corresponding to the sources listed in the EEH (Fugitive Emission and Venting).
22. Guidelines for production permit application, Norwegian Offshore Directorate.
23. *Ibid.*, section 6.3.

Land facilities and non-field installations which need flaring and or cold-venting shall also apply for a permit. This only applies to volumes not already included in a field application.[24]

One can wonder who owns the gas that is vented and is responsible for its management. The starting point in the Petroleum Act is that The Norwegian State has the proprietary right to subsea petroleum deposits and the exclusive right to resource management.[25] However, the award of a production license provides the licensee with an exclusive right to survey, exploration drilling and production of petroleum deposits for the areas covered by the license.[26] As the licensee obtains title to all oil and gas produced, it also owns all gas that is flared or vented from these fields. This ownership allocation is also in line with the CO_2 Tax Act,[27] which requires the licensees to pay the CO_2 tax for the related emissions from the field.[28]

3.4 Measurement, Record Keeping and Reporting

Pursuant to the Petroleum Regulations,[29] the licensee must submit to the Norwegian Offshore Directorate information on the volume of petroleum produced and the composition of the petroleum, including burning of petroleum and cold venting. The information provided should be based on metering as far as possible.[30] The Measurement Regulations (last in 2023)[31] detail the manner to measure and report flare and gas volumes, including the measurement methods.[32] Separate Guidelines to the Measurement Regulations further precise that an uncertainty level of 5 % for measuring the flow of gas to the flare and cold-venting system is allowed.[33]

Operators have a general reporting obligation under the Petroleum Regulations.[34] An annual status report for fields in production must be submitted to the Norwegian Offshore Directorate every year, by October 15. The report must describe activities and measures to serve as the basis for the authorities' evaluation of, among other things, production strategy and environmental issues such as flaring and venting. The Measurement Regulation further precises that this annual report must, when necessary, contain information about measurement, measuring systems and allocation.[35]

24. *Ibid.*
25. Section 1-1, Petroleum Act.
26. Section 3-3, Petroleum Act.
27. Act December 21, 1990 No. 72 relating to tax on discharge of CO_2 in the petroleum activities on the continental shelf (CO_2 Tax Act).
28. Section 4, CO_2 Tax Act.
29. Section 48, Petroleum Regulations.
30. *Ibid.*
31. Regulations relating to fiscal measurement in the petroleum activities, issued by the Norwegian Offshore Directorate on April 21, 2023.
32. Section 12, Measurement Regulations.
33. Comment on section 28 (Instrumental measurement uncertainty), Guidelines for Regulations relating to the fiscal measurement in the petroleum activities, February 2024.
34. Section 47, Petroleum Regulations.
35. Section 95, Measurement Regulations.

In terms of record keeping, operators have also a general obligation to keep an emissions inventory. In addition, the Environmental Information Act and the petroleum legislation require the publication of relevant emissions data. The information is published on a public website and the Norwegian employer and industry organization for companies with activities related to the Norwegian Continental Shelf (Offshore Norge) has established a national database for reporting all releases from petroleum activities to air/soil/water in the so-called EPIM Environment Hub.

3.5 Monitoring and Enforcement

The Norwegian Offshore Directorate, in cooperation with the Ministry of Energy, is the main institution responsible for the regulatory oversight and enforcement of gas flaring and venting requirements in Norway, as regulated by the Petroleum Act, the Petroleum Regulations, and associated legislation.[36]

In addition, the Environment Directorate, under the Norwegian Ministry of Climate and Environment, is in charge of supervising the implementation of climate and environmental policies, and notably environmental permits and emissions reporting, as regulated among others by the Pollution Control Act. These responsibilities cover areas relevant to flaring and venting, such as the promotion of clean air and a toxic-free environment and the reduction of noise pollution.

To perform their tasks, representatives from the Ministry of Energy, the Norwegian Offshore Directorate or other authorities as decided by the Directorate are given access to vessels and petroleum facilities, as well as existing data and materials, that are necessary for them to perform their supervision tasks. They also have a right to take part in survey activities and to stay on vessels and facilities as long as necessary.[37]

The sanction regime foreseen by the petroleum and environmental legislation includes both financial and non-financial penalties, as reviewed thereafter. Violation of an order issued in accordance with the Petroleum Act may be sanctioned by a daily fine applied for each day that passes after the expiry of the time limit set for implementation of the order, and so on until it has been complied with.[38] This would for example apply to situations for submission of false information, or of excessive flaring beyond the limits for safe operations as set in the PDO and, if so provided, beyond the limits in the permit. In case of serious or repeated violations of the legislation and stipulated conditions or orders issued, the Ministry may impose a temporary suspension of the activities.[39] Violation of the CO_2 Tax Act obligations is subject to the payment of a fine.[40]

36. "Regulations" (*The Norwegian Offshore Directorate*) https://www.sodir.no/en/regulations/ accessed November 13, 2024.
37. Section 81, Petroleum Regulations.
38. Section 10-16, Petroleum Act.
39. *Ibid.*
40. Section 7, CO_2 Tax Act.

In addition to financial sanctions, the Petroleum Act foresees non-monetary penalties, including temporary suspension of activity, license revocation and improvement in situations of wilful or negligent violation of the Act or decisions issued pursuant to the Act.[41] The CO_2 Tax Act and the Environmental Protection Act foresee similar types of penalties.

4 CURRENT ISSUES

The combined application of the emissions control measures described above have resulted in very low flaring intensity and venting from petroleum activities on the Norwegian Continental Shelf. Nevertheless, new initiatives have been taken during the past few years to further limit these emissions.

From the technology side, the fiscal measures, and particularly the NOx tax regime, continue to contribute to technology innovation for methane emissions control, where payments made to, e.g., the NOx Fund are used to support technological innovation. For example, new offshore platforms do not operate with gas combustion engine like flare boom and/or, ensure the re-use of flared gas.

From the policy side, Norway is part of several initiatives that aim to foster international awareness and cooperation around flaring reduction.[42] The Norwegian government endorsed the World Bank Zero Routine Flaring by 2030 Initiative in 2016.[43] It was preceded by the endorsement of the Initiative by Equinor ASA the year before, in 2015. Norway participates in the Global Methane Pledge and the Climate and Clean Air Coalition, under which it submitted its National Methane Action Plan in November 2022. Norway has also joined international efforts to finance the cut of methane emissions from flaring and endorsed the Global Flaring and Methane Reduction (GFMR) Partnership launched by the World Bank at the UNFCCC COP28 in December 2023.[44] The GFMR Partnership is a multi-donor trust fund that aims to help developing countries cut carbon dioxide and methane emissions generated by the oil and gas industry.

In May 2024, the EU formally adopted a new regulation for curbing methane emissions in the energy sector.[45] The Regulation establishes a framework for monitoring and mitigating methane emissions within the EU. Among the main requirements of the Regulation are: improved measurement, reporting and verification of energy sector methane emissions; an immediate reduction in emissions through mandatory leak

41. Section 10-17, Petroleum Act.
42. "Norway" (*Climate & Clean Air Coalition*) https://www.ccacoalition.org/partners/norway accessed November 13, 2024.
43. "Zero Routine Flaring by 2030 (ZRF)" (*World Bank*) https://www.worldbank.org/en/programs/zero-routine-flaring-by-2030 accessed November 13, 2024.
44. "Global Flaring and Methane Reduction Partnership (GFMR)Homepage" (*World Bank*) https://www.worldbank.org/en/programs/gasflaringreduction accessed November 13, 2024.
45. Regulation of the European Parliament and of the Council on the reduction of methane emissions in the energy sector and amending Regulation (EU) 2019/942. The Regulation was not yet published at the time of writing this contribution. The analysis of the Regulation is based on the version published by the Council and the European Parliament on June 13, 2024.

detection and repair and a ban on venting and flaring practices; a methane transparency requirement on imports, collecting information on whether and how exporter countries/companies are measuring, reporting and abating methane emissions, with a view of establishing a methane intensity profile of those entities. As far as petroleum production activities are concerned, oil and gas companies will be subject to a series of new requirements, and notably a frequent check of their equipment to detect leaks, with an obligation to immediately repair them in case of default. The regulation also bans venting and routine flaring, allowing venting only in exceptional or unavoidable circumstances for safety reasons. It allows flaring only if re-injection, utilization on-site or transport of the methane to a market are not technically feasible, with more restrictive rules for how it can be carried out.

The relevance of the Regulation under the European Economic Area (EEA) Agreement will need to be assessed, notably in view of the geographical scope of application of the EEA Agreement.[46] Some of the requirements defined in the new Regulation are already in place in Norwegian legislation, without causing any challenge. For example, both venting and routine flaring are already prohibited.[47] However, for a few provisions, there will be a need for further interpretation as the measures defined may have an unprecise wording. For example, the Regulation provides for an exemption to the venting and flaring prohibition only in case of an emergency or malfunction and requires the use of "commercially available" devices[48] or specific inspection routines.[49]

5 RECOMMENDATIONS

The Norwegian strategy for regulating gas flaring and venting, which combines direct prohibition, permitting requirements, and economic mechanisms, teaches useful lessons to other oil and gas-producing countries.[50] The effectiveness of this multifaceted regulatory framework in obtaining extremely low flaring intensities on the Norwegian Continental Shelf serves as a compelling example for further investigation and possible adoption by other jurisdictions.[51]

A crucial takeaway from the Norwegian experience is the power of direct legislation, such as explicit restrictions on frequent flaring and venting, as an effective

46. "European Economic Area (EEA) Agreement" (*European Economic Area (EEA) Agreement | Access2Markets*) https://trade.ec.europa.eu/access-to-markets/en/content/european-economic-area-eea-agreement accessed November 13, 2024.
47. Draft Art. 15(1) of the Regulation provides that "Venting shall be prohibited except in the circumstances provided for in this Article. Routine flaring shall be prohibited."
48. *Ibid.*, draft Art. 16—Reporting of venting events and flaring events.
49. *Ibid.*, draft Art. 17—Flaring efficiency requirements.
50. "Norwegian Lesson in Gas Flare Elimination: Egypt Oil & Gas" (*Egypt Oil & Gas | Connecting The Pieces*, May 4, 2016) https://egyptoil-gas.com/features/norwegian-lesson-in-gas-flare-elimination/ accessed November 13, 2024.
51. (*Global flaring and venting regulations—a comparative …*) https://flaringventingregulations.worldbank.org/sites/ieexi/files/2022-04/Global%20Flaring%20and%20Venting%20Regulations%20-%20A%20Comparative%20Review%20of%20Policies.pdf accessed November 13, 2024.

tool to promote emissions reductions. Norway has set a high bar by imposing clear, explicit regulations from the start, forcing the industry to find alternative solutions rather than relying on flaring as a disposal option.[52] The permitting process for any residual safety-related flaring and venting acts as a crucial safety valve, although the default presumption is against such actions.

The employment of economic mechanisms, notably the CO_2 and NOx taxes, has added an extra layer of incentive to cut emissions. By making flaring and venting financially expensive, these fiscal policies have encouraged innovation and investment in technology and operating practices that reduce the need to dispose associated gas in this manner.[53] The tax regime's consistent metering and reporting rules have also been critical to guaranteeing the integrity and efficacy of these economic instruments.

While Norway's regulatory structure has been extremely effective, there is always an opportunity for more refining and development. Continued technical innovation should be a priority in addressing any remaining flaring and venting difficulties. Regulators should investigate new support mechanisms, such as increased R&D funding, technological demonstration programs, and targeted tax credits or subsidies, to encourage the development and implementation of cutting-edge technologies.[54]

Another significant objective is to align Norway's regulatory regime with growing international norms, such as the EU's new rule on methane emissions in the energy industry. While Norway's current framework is already in line with many of the new EU criteria, there may be chances to harmonize specific sections or include additional best practices.[55] This could include clarifying definitions of "commercially available" technologies, strengthening enforcement capacities, and increasing openness through more detailed public reporting on field-level performance.

Maintaining and improving enforcement procedures in general should be a priority. Regulators should regularly assess their ability to perform thorough inspections, analyze emissions data, and enforce effective penalties for noncompliance.[56] Increased public sharing of flaring and venting data at the plant or field level can also help to encourage accountability and further emissions reductions.

52. Aoun, Ala Eddine, Pu, Hui and Khetib, Youcef, *Natural Gas Flaring Status in the Bakken Shale Play and Potential Remedial Solutions*. Available at SSRN: https://ssrn.com/abstract=4313153 or http://dx.doi.org/10.2139/ssrn.4313153.
53. Bruvoll, Annegrete and Larsen, Bodil Merethe, *Greenhouse Gas Emissions in Norway Do Carbon Taxes Work?*, 2002, Discussion Papers, No. 337, Statistics Norway, Research Department, Oslo.
54. World Bank Group, "GFMR Progress Update: Transforming Oil and Gas Operations to Curb Emissions" (*World Bank*, November 12, 2024) https://www.worldbank.org/en/programs/gasflaringreduction/brief/gfmr-progress-update-transforming-oil-and-gas-operations-to-curb-emissions accessed November 13, 2024.
55. European Parliament, "Reducing Methane Emissions in the Energy Sector: Legislative Train Schedule" (*European Parliament*) https://www.europarl.europa.eu/legislative-train/theme-a-european-green-deal/file-reducing-methane-emissions-in-the-energy-sector accessed November 13, 2024.
56. Brandt, Adam R. et al., "Methane Leaks from Natural Gas Systems Follow Extreme Distributions," Environmental science & technology Vol. 50, 22 (2016): 12512-12520 https://doi.org/10.1021/acs.est.6b04303.

Norway can preserve its position as a global pioneer in responsible associated gas management by being committed to innovation, regulation refinement, and effective enforcement. Sharing these experiences and best practices with other oil and gas-producing countries, particularly those in the developing world, can help speed progress toward the common goal of eradicating routine flaring globally by 2030.[57] Norway's performance illustrates that a multifaceted regulatory approach, founded on explicit prohibitions and supplemented by economic incentives and enabling policies, may be extremely effective in reducing harmful flaring and venting behaviors.

6 CONCLUSION

Norway's comprehensive legislative strategy for managing gas flaring and venting from petroleum activities provides a persuasive model for other oil and gas-producing countries to follow. Norway has achieved one of the lowest levels of flaring intensity in the world by building a multifaceted structure based on strict prohibitions, permitting procedures, and economic incentives.[58] This accomplishment illustrates that a comprehensive regulatory framework, along with industry collaboration and technology innovation, may be extremely effective in reducing dangerous flaring and venting behaviors.

Norway's approach has been based on an uncompromising commitment to reducing routine flaring and venting. An outright ban, with restricted exceptions for safety concerns, has forced the industry to seek alternate solutions rather than relying on these emissions-intensive disposal technologies.[59] The comprehensive permitting mechanism ensures that any residual flaring and venting activities are thoroughly investigated and justified. Economic measures, such as the CO_2 and NOx taxes, supplement these direct prohibitions by making flaring and venting a financially costly proposition, encouraging innovation and investment in emissions-reduction technology.[60]

57. (*Electric mobility market assessment, business model and ...*) https://documents1.worldbank.org/curated/en/099651206172224743/pdf/IDU02131336d03f5c04f11093bd095d144caa38f.pdf accessed November 13, 2024; "Norway: Ieexi" (*Download the full reports*) https://flaringventingregulations.worldbank.org/norway accessed November 13, 2024.
58. (*Global flaring and venting regulations—a comparative ...*) https://flaringventingregulations.worldbank.org/sites/ieexi/files/2022-04/Global%20Flaring%20and%20Venting%20Regulations%20-%20A%20Comparative%20Review%20of%20Policies.pdf accessed November 13, 2024; (*Global Flaring and venting regulations: 28 case studies ...*) https://thedocs.worldbank.org/en/doc/fd5b55e045a373821f2e67d81e2c53b1-0400072022/related/Global-Flaring-and-Venting-Regulations-28-Case-Studies-from-Around-the-World.pdf accessed November 13, 2024.
59. "Norwegian Lesson in Gas Flare Elimination: Egypt Oil & Gas" (*Egypt Oil & Gas | Connecting The Pieces*, May 4, 2016) https://egyptoil-gas.com/features/norwegian-lesson-in-gas-flare-elimination/ accessed November 13, 2024.
60. "Tackling Flaring: Lessons from the North Sea" (*Flareintel*, October 8, 2020) https://flareintel.com/insights/tackling-flaring-lessons-from-the-north-sea accessed November 14, 2024.

The efficacy of Norway's architecture is underpinned by stringent metering, reporting, and transparency regulations.[61] These provide the reliable data required to support economic incentives and ensure effective enforcement.[62] Regulators have also shown a readiness to constantly improve the regulatory framework, matching it with growing worldwide standards and encouraging the development of innovative technical solutions.

While Norway's regulatory model is currently regarded as a global best practice, there is always potential for additional development and refining.[63] Norway's future priorities include further technical innovation, regulatory conformity with peers, and strengthened enforcement capabilities.[64] Equally essential is Norway's role as a thinking leader, sharing its lessons and insights with other oil and gas-producing countries to speed progress toward the common goal of eradicating routine flaring globally by 2030.[65]

By maintaining its unwavering commitment to responsible resource management and environmental stewardship, Norway can continue to serve as a leading example of how effective regulation, combined with industry collaboration and technological advancement, can dramatically reduce the oil and gas sector's climate and environmental impacts.[66] As the global energy market changes, Norway's regulatory regime for regulating gas flaring and venting is expected to become a more valuable reference point for policymakers worldwide.[67]

61. "Natural Resource Management in Norway" (*OECD iLibrary*) https://www.oecd-ilibrary.org/ accessed November 14, 2024.
62. *Ibid.*
63. OECD, *Shaping Norway's Digital Future*, OECD Publishing, Paris, 2024, https://doi.org/10.1787/d3af799c-en.
64. *Ibid.*
65. "Norwegian Lesson in Gas Flare Elimination: Egypt Oil & Gas" (*Egypt Oil & Gas | Connecting The Pieces*, May 4, 2016) https://egyptoil-gas.com/features/norwegian-lesson-in-gas-flare-elimination/ accessed November 14, 2024.
66. Wadsworth D, "Is Norway Ahead of Everyone Else?" (*Is Norway Ahead of Everyone Else?*, February 8, 2024) https://www.tunley-environmental.com/en/insights/why-norway-is-setting-the-standards-for-sustainability accessed November 14, 2024.
67. *Ibid.*

Chapter 22

Gas Flaring in Qatar

Eduardo G. Pereira & Mostapha Al-Masry

1 INTRODUCTION

Generally speaking, gas flaring[1] is a major global problem.[2] This is because gas contributes to air pollution and global warming, leading to different socio-economic and environmental consequences.[3] The most recent report by the World Bank has shown that "global gas flaring at upstream oil and gas facilities increased by 7 percent-9 billion cubic meters (bcm) from 139 bcm in 2022 to 148 bcm in 2023."[4] This report highlights the urgent need for countries to take stringent policy actions to get rid of gas flaring. The practice is common in the oil and gas industry and involves mainly burning

1. *Flaring* is a controlled combustion process in which unwanted or excess hydrocarbon gas during normal operation (e.g., off specification product streams) or abnormal operation (e.g., plant emergency shutdowns, system over pressurization) are sent to flare stack for complete combustion. Furthermore, *Gas flaring* refers to the burning of natural gas that is released during the extraction of crude oil. Crude oil production results in huge quantities of natural gas which needs to be disposed-off. Instead of recovering the gas or injecting it back into the oil formations, which would be a relatively safe and responsible choice, many oil-producing nations flare the gas. During flaring, the gas is burned off, reducing its pollution potential; yet, flaring can send up emissions like sulphur dioxide, carbon monoxide, and black carbon (soot), along with GHGs like CO_2 and CH_4. Basically, the gas is routed to a special flare stack head where it is ignited by a pilot flame. for further information about the technical Gas Flaring, *see*: S Sarkar, "Operational Risk Assessment of Routing Flare Gas to Boiler for Cogeneration" (Master Thesis at Texas A&M University 2019).
2. MR Rahimpour and others, "A Comparative Study of Three Different Methods for Flare Gas Recovery of Asalooye Gas Refinery" (2012) 4 Journal of Natural Gas Science and Engineering, 17-28 https://doi.org/10.1016/j.jngse.2011.10.001.
3. Y Liu and others, "Global Declines of gas Offshore Flaring Inadequate to Meet the 2030 Goal" (2023) 6 Nature Sustainability, 1095-1102 https://doi.org/10.1038/s41893-023-01125-5.
4. World Bank Group, "Global Gas Flaring Tracker Report" (2023) https://www.worldbank.org/en/topic/extractiveindustries/publication/2023-global-gas-flaring-tracker-report, accessed September 6, 2024.

off excess natural gas that is produced during oil extraction, especially in countries with large reserves of natural gas. This process releases harmful greenhouse gases (GHGs) into the atmosphere, contributing to climate change. This practice involves the burning of natural gas that is released during oil extraction and production processes.

Qatar, being a leading producer of natural gas, is no exception to this practice, and is regarded as the 23rd largest gas flaring in the world.[5] Based on this, the extensive flaring of gas in Qatar has raised concerns about its environmental impact and sustainability. There has been a growing emphasis on reducing gas flaring and finding alternative ways to utilize this valuable resource. Flaring and venting are two gas and hydrocarbon processing activities. Flaring is a combustible technique that is used to dispose of natural gas, for example, sweet, sour, acidic gas, or other hydrocarbon vapors through a vertical stack. Commonly, small volumes of natural gas that are technically impossible and uneconomic to save may be routinely flared in oil and gas facilities.

Flaring of gas connected with these businesses is estimated to be over 148 bcm in 2023, generating around 381 Million tonnes of carbon dioxide equivalent ($MMtCO_2e$) including 45 MMtCO2e in the form of unburned methane.[6] Flaring, which can be defined as either routine or non-routine operation, is a vital safety measure used to safely dispose of natural gas that might otherwise endanger personnel and facility equipment in the event of an emergency, process upset, or equipment and power failure. Routine flare sources are the product of facility pipe and process control design configurations and are regarded as normal under steady-state plant process and equipment operations. Non-routine flaring encompasses irregular and rare events, such as planned maintenance, process disruptions, and emergencies. It is defined as all flare events that occur outside of typical steady-state plant process and equipment operations.[7]

Local and global concerns have risen in recent years regarding exceeding the normal levels of GHG emissions.[8] The anticipated local impacts of this issue are related to agricultural production and food security, water stress and water insecurity, rising sea levels and exposure to climate disasters, ecosystems and biodiversity, and Human health. The issue of gas flaring in Qatar has become a major concern due to its contribution to these local impacts. The excessive GHG emissions from gas flaring can negatively affect agricultural production and food security by impairing soil quality and reducing crop yields. The World Resources Institute (WRI) has maintained that the Gulf region contributed for more than 15% of global carbon emissions since 1999.[9] By

5. The World Bank, "Global Gas Flaring Tracker Report" (2023) 7 https://thedocs.worldbank.org/en/doc/5d5c5c8b0f451b472e858ceb97624a18-0400072023/original/2023-Global-Gas-Flaring-Tracker-Report.pdf?_gl=1*1nz2qk8*_gcl_au*MTU3NDE3NTgwNy4xNzI1NjA4NjMw, accessed September 6, 2024.
6. The World Bank, " Global Gas Flaring Tracker Report" (2024) 13 https://thedocs.worldbank.org/en/doc/d01b4aebd8a10513c0e341de5e1f652e-0400072024/original/Global-Gas-Flaring-Tracker-Report-June-20-2024.pdf accessed January 14, 2025.
7. M John, "Encyclopedia of Chemical Processing and Design" (Marcel Dekker 1985) 144.
8. Sara A Al-Mohannadi and Dhabia M Al-Mohannadi, "Qatar in the Energy Transition: Low Carbon Economy Challenges and Opportunities" in L Cochrane and R Al-Hababi (eds), Sustainable Qatar. Gulf Series (vol. 9, Springer, 2023).
9. "The Green House Gas Effect: Climate Change." Retrieved from http://www.bom.gov.au/info/GreenhouseEffectAndClimateChange.pdf, accessed November 27, 2023.

assumption, it is possible for a higher percentage of carbon emissions in Qatar. The viability of this forecast stems from the Gulf region countries' massive expansion of oil and gas businesses, which are sources of GHG emissions. Qatar, in particular, has experienced a significant increase in its oil and gas production in recent years, leading to a rise in gas flaring activities. Efforts are being made to mitigate this issue in Qatar, such as implementing technologies to capture and utilize the flared gas, but more needs to be done to reduce carbon emissions and promote sustainable practices in the region.

The World Bank's Global Gas Flaring Reduction Partnership (GGFR) has also revealed that Qatar flares about 1.1 bcm each year, out of a total of 148 bcm flared Globally at upstream oil and gas facilities and liquefied natural gas (LNG) liquefaction plants in 2023.[10] By 2050, it is anticipated that Qatar will lead the world in emissions per person.[11] More so, a research carried out by the General Secretariat for Development Planning demonstrates that Qatar's contribution to global GHG emissions amounts to 0.2%. Qatar is rated first in per capita carbon emissions but 58th in total carbon emissions.[12] Losses from flaring include energy, raw material, and manufacturing losses. Therefore, it is necessary to research and recommend several options to the global industry. Against this background of gas flaring and its negative impacts, Qatar has taken significant steps to address this issue. The country has implemented strict regulations and invested in advanced technologies to minimize flaring and capture the gas for productive use.

This chapter aims to analyze Qatar's efforts to reduce gas flaring and its effectiveness in achieving sustainable development goals. The chapter is divided into five sections, starting with this introduction. Then, section 2 examines the major causes of gas flaring and related consequences in Qatar. The 3 section analyzes Qatar's major gas flaring policies, while section 4 presents a future outlook on gas flaring in Qatar and makes recommendations. Finally, section 5 summarizes the key points and lessons from the chapter.

2 CAUSES OF GAS FLARING IN QATAR

2.1 Key Causes of Gas Flaring

Gas flaring in Qatar is primarily caused by various factors including economic considerations, investment in advanced gas utilization technologies, regulatory policies aiming for industrial development, and the reliance on gas production as an

10. World Bank Group, "Global Flaring and Methane Reduction partnership" (n.d.) https://www.worldbank.org/en/programs/gasflaringreduction/global-flaring-data, accessed August 5, 2024.
11. Environmental Systems Research Institute. (1996). World Countries (1995). Redlands, CA: ESRI. 2. DOE (U.S. Department of Energy). (2001). International Energy Annual (1999). Washington, DC:DOE, Energy Information Administration. Available Online at: http://www.eia.doe.gov/emeu/iea, accessed August 5, 2024.
12. Qatar General Secretariat for Development Planning, "Qatar National Development Strategy 2011-2016: Towards Qatar National Vision 2030" (2011) https://www.un.org/development/desa/disabilities/wp-content/uploads/sites/15/2019/10/Qatar_Qatar-National-Development-Strategy.pdf, accessed September 6, 2024.

alternative to costly crude oil. As a major producer of natural gas, Qatar's strategy centers around utilizing gas as a cost-effective and easily accessible energy source. The economic gain from recovering gas is often overlooked, resulting in the wasteful practice of flaring it in open pits.

2.1.1 Technological Aspects

In Qatar, the oil and gas industry is crucial for the country's exports and revenue. However, concerns about global gas flaring persist, as significant amounts of valuable gas are wasted rather than utilized for commercial purposes. Qatar, with the third-largest proven natural gas reserves, has taken steps to address this issue through policy initiatives, technological advancements, and collaboration with oil and gas stakeholders. Before implementing policy changes, it's important to consider the specific context of the country.[13]

Technical issues or Equipment malfunctions in the oil and gas industry can result in the release of gas that needs to be burned off through flaring. These malfunctions can occur in various stages of production, transportation, or processing. Furthermore, routine maintenance and shutdowns during maintenance activities or plant shutdowns may be another cause of gas flaring, it may be necessary to flare excess gas for safety reasons. This is done to avoid the buildup of pressure or to ensure the safe handling of equipment.[14]

There could be occasions for emergency situations, in which cases unexpected events, such as equipment failures, leaks, or accidents can lead to the need for gas flaring as a safety measure because it can help prevent the release of potentially hazardous gases into the environment.[15] Equipment failures, maintenance, and operational constraints generally can result in flaring. Regular maintenance and upgrading of equipment can help minimize technical issues.

In addition, Flaring can be caused by technological barriers such as the absence and limits of combustion devices and flare gas recovery devices, malfunctioning of combustion devices, absence of alternative systems or fuels, absence and limits of systems for gas treatment or use prior to combustion (injured gas), technical limits and shutdowns of alternative facilities or systems, absence or limits of gas transmission pipelines and other transport systems/ facilities and excessive costs of onshore means of gas collection and transportation.[16] Such barriers are expected on oil and gas fields

13. *See*: Sarkar, *supra* n. 1; E Ojijiagwo, C Oduoza and E Nwabueze, "Development of a Framework for Reduction of Flare Gas in an Oil and Gas Processing Environment" (Petroleum and Coal 2017).
14. *See*: E Mahdi and A Esmaeili, "Failure Analysis of a Flare Tip Used in Offshore Production Platform in Qatar" (2020) 13 Materials 3426 https://doi.org/10.3390/ma13153426.
15. IEA, "Gas Flaring" (n.d.) https://www.iea.org/energy-system/fossil-fuels/gas-flaring, accessed August 6, 2024.
16. O Hafeez Rufai, R Oluwole Alademomi and E Tetteh Teye, "A Mixed Method Inquiry of Gas Flaring Consequences, Mitigation Strategies and Policy Implication for Environmental Sustainability in Nigeria" (2019) 9 Journal of Environment and Earth Science 48.

at the beginning of development but should be removed as field exploitation progresses.

2.1.2 Economic Factors

Gas flaring represents the burning of natural gas associated with crude oil production, whether as a result of operational combustion devices or fixtures used for burning off natural gas. With the commencement of oil drilling, gas production usually follows. There may be situations whereby gas pipelines are not available for transporting gas to sales like in developing nations and hence the flaring of gas is viewed as an economic decision, which is usually made by the companies.[17] This decision is mostly driven by the overall cost implications of providing gas processing facilities and prepaid facilities in regard to regulations and prices in the market perceptions to flare gas instead of incurring large costs for gas installation facilities. From an economic perspective, therefore flaring has a natural tendency to occur when consumption possibilities are rather poor, especially on local spot markets.[18]

Furthermore, Qatar's oil and gas fields produce more gas than can be processed or utilized domestically. This excess gas is often flared due to a lack of infrastructure or market demand. There is insufficient infrastructure for gas processing, transportation, and storage. Qatar needs to invest in building more gas processing plants, pipelines, and storage facilities or explore export options or develop new markets to utilize and handle the excess gas.[19] Flaring is often believed to be more cost-effective than investing in infrastructure or processing facilities. However, these short-term cost savings come at the expense of long-term environmental and economic benefits.

In addition, the availability of gas transportation fleets is influenced by onshore infrastructure and is expected to significantly affect gas price regulations. Lowering gas prices could lead to more stable and reasonable global energy markets and provide financial benefits for reducing gas flaring beyond taxation.[20] With the perspective of realized natural gas price control, also a business decision and economic concern abstraction are outlined whereby the price perceptions usually contain an unofficial consumption area. Due to a focus on economic factors rather than operational and technological aspects of flaring, the consideration of approaches that address the negative external impacts of flaring in a specific and intentional manner has been disregarded. This is because the benefit of producing saleable gas is not seen as sufficient to offset the harmful effects of flaring.[21] Over the past few decades, there have

17. Sarkar, *supra* n. 1, 15 et seq.
18. For further information, *see*: M Zhizhin and others, "Measuring Gas Flaring in Russia with Multispectral VIIRS Nightfire," 13 Remote Sens., 3078 https://doi.org/10.3390/rs13163078.
19. R Abu, K Patchitgolla and N Simms, "A Review on Qualitative Assessment of Natural Gas Utilisation Options for Eliminating Routine Nigerian Gas Flaring" (2023) 3(1) Gases, 1-24 https://doi.org/10.3390/gases3010001.
20. E Tok, M Koç and CD'Alessandro, "Entrepreneurship in a Transformative and Resource-Rich State: The Case of Qatar. The Extractive Industries and Societies," (2020) 6.
21. E Romsom and K McPhail, "Capturing Economic and Social Value from Hydrocarbon Gas Flaring and Venting: Evaluation of the Issues" (WIDER Working Paper 2021).

been changes in global LNG trading patterns. The transportation of LNG has shifted from the Pacific to the Atlantic, and Asian markets are becoming more cost-competitive, potentially impacting fueling corridors in Japan and South Korea.[22]

2.1.3 *Regulatory Frameworks*

Institutional development of regulatory agencies is absolutely essential and crucial if policy interventions on gas flaring in the region are to achieve resounding success. There are a plethora of regulatory frameworks and policies that meticulously dictate the profound effect of gas flaring in Qatar from a comprehensive perspective of policies and regulatory frameworks, basically Law N. 3 of 2007 on Natural Resources (and its amendments) and the Decree Law N. 10 of 1974 (and its amendments). However, Qatar has no specific gas flaring regulation, but the Environmental Protection Law (Decree Law N. 30 of 2002)[23] and its executive regulations apply to flaring and set flaring limits.[24]

Accordingly, these regulatory frameworks generally assess the rules, regulations, treaties, and principles of law of gas flaring in Qatar, ensuring a comprehensive and multifaceted approach. But more often than not, inadequate regulations or enforcement can contribute to excessive flaring.[25] This is perhaps a problem for Qatar, as in most other cases of countries flaring. Qatar needs to strengthen its regulations and enforcement mechanisms to prevent unnecessary flaring.[26] Given Qatar's quick expansion of oil and gas production, outpacing infrastructure development and leading to flaring, the country should prioritize infrastructure development to keep pace with production growth.[27] Domestic demand for gas may be limited, leading to flaring of excess production. Thus, it is important to channel part of the flare gas for domestic gas obligation to meet the energy needs of the citizens.

In conjunction with the legal dimensions, governance dimensions play a pivotal role in controlling this crisis. These dimensions meticulously detail the public institutions and agencies that bear the monumental responsibility for the comprehensive enforcement of flaring regulations, leaving no stone unturned. According to the Natural Resource Governance Institute (NRGI) report in 2021, Qatar scored 45 out of 100 points in the 2021 Resource Governance Index (RGI), moving from the "poor" performance

22. *See*: Q Zou and others, "Global LNG Market: Supply-Demand and Economic Analysis," *IOP Conference Series: Earth and Environmental Science* (IOP Publishing 2022).
23. *See* the Arts 28-39.
24. ESCWA, "Reducing Gas Flaring in Arab Countries: A Sustainable Development Necessity" (2019) 10 https://www.unescwa.org/sites/default/files/pubs/pdf/reducing-gas-flaring-arab-countries-english.pdf accessed August 12, 2024.
25. A Afe Babalola and D S Olawuyi, "Overcoming Regulatory Failure in the Design and Implementation of Gas Flaring Policies: The Potential and Promise of an Energy Justice Approach" (2022) 14(11) Sustainability, 6800 ttps://doi.org/10.3390/su14116800.
26. L Moller and JI Mohammed, "The Problem of Gas Flaring: A Review of Current Legal and Policy Efforts in the UK and Nigeria" (OGEL, 2021).
27. M Davoudi and others, "The Major Sources of Gas Flaring and Air Contamination in the Natural Gas Processing Plants: A Case Study" (2013) 13 Journal of Natural Gas Science and Engineering, 7-19 https://doi.org/10.1016/j.jngse.2013.03.002.

band to the lower end of the "weak" band.[28] Despite the 10-point progress achieved by QatarEnergy since 2017 RGI, significant areas of concern exist across the index's value realization and revenue management components, with scores on the licensing, local impact and sovereign wealth fund subcomponents classified as "failing."[29] Furthermore, the government of Qatar should establish laws compelling extractive companies to publicly disclose Environmental Impact Assessments, to allow citizens a better understanding of the impacts that the extractive sector has on Qatar's seas, coastline, biodiversity and economy.[30]

2.2 Consequences of Gas Flaring

2.2.1 Environmental Consequences

Climate Change: Flaring of natural gas adds to environmental pollution and climate change,[31] which has major consequences for both Qatar and the rest of the globe. The Intergovernmental Panel on Climate Change (IPCC) has revealed that the combustion of fossil fuels, primarily coal, oil, and gas has caused global warming and is expected to worsen over the course of the twenty-first century. Based on many research findings, climate change is particularly dangerous for developing countries,[32] and Africa as a continent is viewed as very vulnerable with low adaptability.[33] By emitting carbon dioxide, the major GHG, gas flaring contributes to climate change. Methane (CH_4), one of the most significant GHGs, is released when gas is vented without being burned, a practice for which flaring appears to be frequently used as a synonym. To date, these gases account for over 96% of global warming.[34]

Most times, drilling mud and oil seep into streams, surface waters, and the land, rendering them unfit for human or animal habitation or consumption. To a great extent, a number of multinational oil firms that have been in business for more than 40

28. Natural Resource Governance Institute (NRGI), "2021 Resource Governance Index: Qatar" (2021) 1.
29. *Ibid.*
30. *Ibid.*, 4.
31. The gas flaring is presently producing pronounced GHG emissions of CO_2, along with CH_4, Nitrous oxide (N_2O) and high concentration of soot, an agent of black carbon. The accumulation of these gases in the planet's atmosphere disturbs the Earth's natural heat regulating "greenhouse" effect.
32. J Rocha and others, "Climate Change and Its Impacts on Health, Environment and Economy," (2022) One Health, 253-279 https://doi.org/10.1016/b978-0-12-822794-7.00009-5; Kashif Abbass and others, "A Review of the Global Climate Change Impacts, Adaptation, and Sustainable Mitigation Measures" (2022) 29 Environ Sci Pollut Res, 42539-42559 https://doi.org/10.1007/s11356-022-19718-6.
33. A Ayanlade and others, "Extreme Climate Events in Sub-Saharan Africa: A Call for Improving Agricultural Technology Transfer to Enhance Adaptive Technology" (2022) 27 Climate Services, 100311 https://doi.org/10.1016/j.cliser.2022.100311.
34. National Oceanic and Administrative and Atmospheric Administration (NOAA), "NOAA Index Tracks How Greenhouse Gas Pollution Amplified Global Warming in 2020" (2021) https://research.noaa.gov/2021/05/24/noaa-index-tracks-how-greenhouse-gas-pollution-amplified-global-warming-in-2020/, accessed September 6, 2024.

years are to blame for this issue.[35] This high degree of petrol flaring has detrimental effects on the ecology and the economy because it wastes a lot of potential fuel and pollutes Qatar's soil, water, and air at the same time.

Acid Rain: Research has linked acid rain to gas-flaring activities.[36] The composition of the rain that falls as a result of flare has damaged corrugated roofs in the Delta region. Both sulfur dioxide (SO_2) and nitrogen oxides (NO) emissions are the principal drivers of acid rain, which interact with atmospheric moisture to generate sulfuric acid and nitric acid, respectively. The industry's size and environmental attitude have a significant positive impact on gas-flaring-related CO_2 emissions.[37] More so, acid rain degrades plants and acidifies lakes and streams. Furthermore, acid rain hastens the deterioration of building materials and paints. SO_2 and NO_2 gases, as well as their particulate matter derivatives, sulfates and nitrates, contribute to visibility degradation and impair public health before descending to the earth.

Agriculture: Flares related to gas flaring emit pollutants into the atmosphere. Major GHGs, such as CO_2, SO_2, etc., and also particulate matter, hydrocarbons and ash, photochemical oxidants, and hydrogen sulfide (H_2S) are among such pollutants.[38] These pollutants deplete soil nutrients by acidifying the soil. Previous research has indicated that crops in such areas have a lower nutritional value. In other circumstances, there is no plant in the areas surrounding the flare, owing to the immense heat generated and the acidic nature of the soil pH. The effects of temperature variations on crops included slowed growth, scotched plants, and withering immature crops. According to one study,[39] the soils of the research region are rapidly losing their fertility and capacity for sustainable agriculture due to acidity caused by different contaminants connected with gas flaring in the area.

2.2.2 Health Consequences

Adverse Effects: The effects of gas flaring on human health are all related to the exposure to hazardous air pollutants released during the incomplete combustion of a gas flare. These contaminants have been linked to a number of negative health effects, including cancer, and neurological, reproductive, and developmental disorders.[40]

35. GO Aigbe, M Cotton and LC Stringer, "Global Gas Flaring and Energy Justice: An Empirical Ethics Analysis of Stakeholder Perspectives" (2023) 99 Energy Research and Social Science, 103064 https://doi.org/10.1016/j.erss.2023.103064.
36. JK Nduka and others, "Impact of Oil and Gas Activities on Acidity of Rain and Surface Water of Niger Delta, Nigeria: An Environmental and Public Health Review" (2016) 7(4) Journal of Environmental Protection, 566-581 https://doi.org/10.4236/jep.2016.74051.
37. A Hassan and R Konhy, "Gas Flaring in Nigeria: Analysis of Changes in Its Consequent Carbon Emission and Reporting," (2013) 37(2) Accounting Forum, 124-134 https://doi.org/10.1016/j.accfor.2013.04.004.
38. WB Kindzierski, "Importance of Human Environmental Exposure to Hazardous Air Pollutants from Gas Flares," (2000) 8 Environmental Reviews, 41-62 https://doi.org/10.1139/a00-005.
39. OI Orimoogunje, et al., "Perception on the Effect of Gas Flaring on the Environment," (2010) 2(4) Research Journal of Environmental and Earth Sciences 188-193.
40. W Blundell and A Kokoza, "Natural Gas Flaring, Respiratory Health, and Distributional Effects" (2022) 208 Journal of Public Economics, 104601 https://doi.org/10.1016/j.jpubeco.2022.104601.

Children's deformities, lung damage, and skin disorders have also been recorded.[41] Further, hydrocarbon chemicals have been linked to several negative changes in hematological markers. These modifications have a deleterious impact on blood and blood-forming cells. And it has the potential to cause anemia (aplastic), pancytopenia, and leukemia.[42]

2.2.3 *Economic Consequences*

Financial Loss: Distant from the health and environmental repercussions of gas flaring, Qatar loses billions of dollars in gas that is physically burned off in the atmosphere every day. A large portion of this can be utilized for home usage and electrical generation. By doing so, the country's electrical generation capacity might be increased to satisfy national demand. This huge economic loss is typical in many other gas-flaring countries, for example, Nigeria has suffered a significant economic loss as a result of gas flaring and oil leakage.[43] Despite the fact that oil accounts for more than 65% of government revenue, it is estimated that gas flaring costs the government USD 2.5 billion each year.[44]

Hence, a critical need to implement gas flaring reduction initiatives will inevitably incur heavy costs upfront. These costs must be examined and juxtaposed with the benefits linked to gas flaring reduction in order to assess the economic feasibility of the suggested flaring reduction measures. Consequently, a rough estimation of the costs involved in the implementation of gas flaring reduction options, as well as the redirected revenues, attributable to mitigated gas flaring, can be calculated. Finally, it is of paramount importance to analyze the potential costs of not pursuing the flaring reduction measures.[45]

3 QATAR'S GAS FLARING POLICIES

The government of Qatar, with Petroleum, is committed to trying to achieve zero gas flaring. There have been important field changes to reduce it, which as a result tend to have significantly reduced gas flaring, recovered more hydrocarbons, protected the environment, and made financial gains by optimum utilization of the field's existing

41. SI Ovuakporaye, et al., "Effects of Gas Flaring on Lung Function Among Residents of IB Gas Flaring Community in Delta State, Nigeria," (2012) 4(5) Res. J. Env. Earth Sci. 525-528.
42. Warren B Kindzierski, "Importance of Human Environmental Exposure to Hazardous Air Pollutants from Gas Flares," (2000) 8 Environmental Reviews, 41-62 https://doi.org/10.1139/a00-005.
43. SA Effiong and UE Etowa, "Oil Spillage Cost, Gas Flaring Cost and Life Expectancy Rate of the Niger Delta People of Nigeria," (2012) 2(2) Advances in Management & Applied Economics, 211-228.
44. OS Ismail and GE Umukoro, "Global Impact of Gas Flaring" (2012) 4 Energy and Power Engineering 290, 292.
45. *See:* Ojijiagwo, Oduoza and Nwabueze, *supra* n. 13.

infrastructure.[46] There is evidence that Qatar's Flaring Policy is a significant step towards reducing carbon emissions and promoting environmental sustainability. The policy aims to minimize the burning of natural gas that is released during oil extraction, by imposing strict regulations on oil companies. By implementing this policy, Qatar is demonstrating its commitment to mitigating climate change and preserving its natural resources.

QatarEnergy, the national energy company responsible for the sustainable development of Qatar's energy sector, set out on a mission to devise solutions to accomplish the objective of Zero Routine Flaring by 2030.[47] The company confronted the dual task of delivering energy while also decreasing emissions: it was committed to both, but energy demand was increasing as Qatar's industrial sector expanded. Reduced gas flaring provides an efficient option for Qatar to help decarbonize its energy production.[48] Qatar flares approximately 1.1 bcm in 2023, according to satellite-based estimates provided by the World Bank's GGFR (out of a total of 148 bcm flared globally in 2023).[49]

Moving forward, a steering committee was formed with the backing of senior management, and QatarEnergy began its flare reduction journey, with the goal of reducing Scope 1 emissions from its operations. Thus far, QatarEnergy has embraced environmentally responsible and sustainable development. The reduction of gas flaring and CH_4 emissions is a primary focus of the organization's operations. QatarEnergy set two goals as part of this journey: to reduce gas flaring to the absolute lowest technically feasible level by 2025, and to eliminate routine flaring by 2030.[50] By 2012, QatarEnergy initiated a routine flaring mitigation program for non-operated plants in Ras Laffan Industrial City (RLC), one of the world's largest industrial cities. Since then, prominent activities have included a passing valve monitoring program to reduce fugitive losses, implementing projects to allow fuel gas to be recovered and reused during plant shutdowns or start-ups, and reducing fuel gas in flare purge applications.

Moreover, QatarEnergy launched the Jetty boil-off gas (JBOG) facility in 2014 to recover boil-off gas during LNG loading operations. The JBOG complex is the largest JBOG recovery facility in the world. The JBOG project involves around USD 1 billion in investments and recovers more than 90% of the boil-off gas that was flared previous to the facility's commissioning. The initiative will save around 1.6 million tonnes of CO_2 each year, which is the equivalent of taking 175,000 automobiles off the road in a year. The JBOG facility has collected approximately 4 million tonnes of gas since its

46. MS Al-bidaiwi, M Beg and MI Al-Muhannadi, "Gas Flaring Initiatives in Dukhan Oil and Gas Field" (SPE International Production and Operations Conference and Exhibition, Doha, Qatar, May 14-16, 2012).
47. "Zero Routine Flaring by 2030 (ZRF)" (*World Bank*) https://www.worldbank.org/en/programs/zero-routine-flaring-by-2030#1, accessed August 5, 2024.
48. World Bank Group, "Qatar's Journey to End Routine Gas Flaring" (*WBG*, 2023) https://www.worldbank.org/en/programs/gasflaringreduction/brief/qatar-s-journey-to-end-routine-gas-flaring#:~:text=Gas flaring and methane emissions,end routine flaring by 2030 accessed September 6, 2024.
49. World Bank Group, "Global Gas Flaring Data" (*WBG*, 2023) https://www.worldbank.org/en/programs/gasflaringreduction/global-flaring-data accessed September 6, 2024.
50. *Ibid.*

beginning. More so, it invested an additional USD 200 million in flaring reduction in addition to the JBOG project. Flaring in RLC operating firms has been reduced by around 70% for on-plot facilities and more than 90% for the LNG loading area as a result of the organization's flare reduction measures. These initiatives have had a major influence on Qatar's flaring per barrel of oil equivalent produced, with GGFR satellite estimates indicating that the country's flaring intensity from oil production facilities has decreased by more than a third since 2012. (In contrast, non-GGFR Partners' worldwide flaring intensity has increased during the same time span.) QatarEnergy has successfully reduced gas flaring while maintaining safety by investing in facility renovations and process and operational controls.[51]

QatarEnergy established a governance structure in which teams were charged with finding "flaring hotspots" in their operations, setting targets, and proposing gas flaring reduction solutions. Simultaneously, the steering committee analyzed the viability of the initiatives and got consent to implement them. Meanwhile, QatarEnergy assembled a team of gas flaring experts and launched a series of workshops aimed at decreasing the environmental impact of its operations. QatarEnergy's gas flaring reduction program is an ongoing and iterative process in which the business evaluates opportunities to minimize emissions in close partnership with industrial cities such as RLC. QatarEnergy's revised Sustainability Strategy, unveiled in March 2022, highlighted a number of actions aimed at reducing the carbon intensity of Qatar's LNG facilities by 35% and its upstream facilities by 25% by 2035.[52]

Future Outlook and Recommendations

The energy transformation, while beneficial to Qatar in the short term, exposes the country to long-term risks as a petroleum producer. There will be a great need to consider a holistic sustainable solution that considers not only local emissions or the next fuel but also a new market beyond responding to climate mitigation demands.[53] Expectedly, new markets are likely to emerge, bringing with them both opportunities and risks. Qatar must be adaptable and robust, depending on innovation and evidence-based policies rather than reacting to changes in climate policy and shifting demand. To do this, Qatar should invest in the development of system analysis methods and build knowledge for its own future.[54]

Finally, techniques would enhance government decision-making and regulation and should be implemented swiftly. Qatar must decide on an alternative to natural gas as soon as possible. The country is well positioned due to its access to experience and know-how accumulated over many years as an energy leader. With data transparency

51. Qatar Energy LNG, "Jetty Boil-Off Gas Recovery Project: Recovering 90% of Total Flared Gases at LNG Berths" (2014) 145 The Pioneer, 1-24.
52. *Ibid.*
53. B Sinha, S Roy and M Bhagat, "Sustainable Green Policy by Managing Flare Gas Recovery: A Case with Middle East Oil and Gas Industry" (2020) 24(1) Vision, 35-46 https://doi.org/10.1177/0972262919862410.
54. Al-Mohannadi SA and Al-Mohannadi DM, "Qatar in the Energy Transition: Low Carbon Economy Challenges and Opportunities" (*Gulf Studies*, November 24, 2022) https://doi.org/10.1007/978-981-19-7398-7_7, accessed August 5, 2024.

of emission sources and accounting, as well as providing the next product of the future, the reputation of being a reliable, stable, and trustworthy provider should be preserved. To create resilience and continue monetizing the lucrative resource, Qatar will need to diversify its hydrocarbon sector. Therefore, it is recommended that Qatar should:

(a) Move towards adopting and implementing carbon capture utilization and storage (CCUS) in its oil and gas industry. The need for the application of carbon utilization means to produce value-added products, as a utility or in enhanced hydrocarbon production.
(b) Transition to low-carbon economy and technologies. Transitioning to large-scale renewable energy and technologies has the potential to avoid producing emissions locally.
(c) Qatar should adopt the Near-Term Gains. This means it is easier and cheaper for Qatar to produce LNG than other places in the world.

4 CONCLUSION

This chapter focused on gas flaring in Qatar, to examine its causes and consequences and policies targeted at such a practice. The chapter takes a future at Qatar's gas flaring and makes some recommendations. Gas flaring in Qatar is a pressing socio-economic and environmental concern that requires immediate attention and action. The causes of gas flaring in Qatar are multifaceted, ranging from excess gas production and lack of infrastructure to economic factors and technical issues. The consequences of gas flaring are severe, including air and water pollution posing health risks to nearby communities, climate change contributing to global warming and associated impacts, and wasted resources depriving the country of potential revenue and energy security.

Qatar has taken steps to address gas flaring through policies and initiatives, such as setting flaring reduction targets, investing in gas processing infrastructure, and promoting research and development of new technologies. However, more needs to be done to effectively mitigate this issue. The future outlook for gas flaring in Qatar depends on the country's ability to adopt and implement effective solutions, including increasing investment in gas processing and transportation infrastructure, promoting the adoption of gas capture and utilization technologies, strengthening regulations and enforcement mechanisms, encouraging research and development of new technologies, and improving operational efficiency and safety.

These steps, if taken can help Qatar reduce gas flaring and associated environmental impacts, minimize waste and maximize the value of its natural resources, enhance its reputation as a responsible and sustainable energy producer, and contribute to global efforts to combat climate change. Qatar is well suited for the energy transition due to its abundance of natural gas—a widely acceptable transition fuel. Technological improvement in renewable energy as well as fast-moving competition in the hydrogen market, however, showcases Qatar's hydrocarbon export vulnerabilities.

But ultimately, addressing gas flaring in Qatar requires a collaborative effort from the government, industry, and civil society. By working together, Qatar can overcome the challenges of gas flaring and achieve a more sustainable energy future.

CHAPTER 23

Russia

Anna Ovcharova

Overview and Introduction

For many years already in the Russian economy, there have been discussions in relation to the reduction of greenhouse gas (GHG) emissions, including as a part of the transitional economy and replacement of fossil fuels by other, less carbon footprint burdensome types of energy resources. The discussions became even more active after the Russian Federation joined the Paris Agreement on April 22, 2016, and adopted the same by the Decree of the Government of the Russian Federation on September 21, 2019, No. 1228.[1] The Paris Agreement imposes on its parties obligations in relation to the reduction of GHG and reduction of the carbon footprint overall, and thus, Russia started to expand its activities in this regard.

These discussions are a priority on the agenda, but not easy for the Russian Government, as the Russian Federation is still one of the most significant producers and suppliers of fossil fuels worldwide.[2] At the same time, 87% of the energy generation in Russia is referred to low-carbon sources. Among them, 39% refer to atomic energy plants, hydropower generation plants and wind energy and 48% to gas power generation stations.[3] This already demonstrates that Russia is also well placed among green energy economies and the carbon footprint in Russia is relevantly insignificant.

To further improve its well placement among green energies, the Russian Federation continues to conduct other activities, including modernization of the existing gas power generation stations, and is constructing new gas power generation stations with gas turbines of purely Russian origin and contents. The efficiency and environmental friendliness of such energy production are increasing.

1. Постановление Правительства Российской Федерации от September 21, 2019 No. 1228 Официальное опубликование правовых актов (pravo.gov.ru).
2. International—U.S. Energy Information Administration (EIA).
3. *Source*: https://www.kommersant.ru/doc/5999149 Коммерсантъ (kommersant.ru).

On top of this, Russia, willing to demonstrate a progressive approach, also sets the trend toward a transitional economy and becomes compatible and competitive with the other developed economies in this aspect.

At the same time and despite Russia's well placement among green economies, Russia continues to flare the most associated natural gas, released from upstream oil and gas fields during oil production.[4] This situation certainly requires specific regulation and actions to reduce such flaring.

This chapter will elaborate on both aspects of the current Russian energy-specific regulations: historical heritage, related to gas flaring and its regulation and new trends, and developments in the energy transition area.

Legal Framework

In view of the green energy trend, the Russian Federation has already adopted and also plans to adopt certain legal acts, which are featured to formalize and support energy transition trends. At the same time, specific gas flaring regulations are also retained in the Russian legal framework and continue to function unless gas flaring exists.

The main legislation in Russia on the issue of gas flaring includes the following laws and Government regulations. Most of the below-mentioned documents have a general regulation nature, reflecting only a few specifics, related to the gas flaring. At the same time, all of them currently remain relevant and set up basic requirements for the gas flaring process:

- the Federal law on "Subsoil use" dated February 21, 1992 N 2395-1;[5]
- the Federal law "On gas supply" dd. March 31, 1999 #69-FZ in the current edition;[6]
- the Federal law "On environmental protection" dd. January 10, 2002 #7-FZ in the current edition;[7]
- the Federal law "On limitation of greenhouse gas emissions" on July 2, 2021 #296-FZ in the current edition;[8]
- the Government regulation dd. November 8, 2012 #1148 "On features counting of payment for negative influence on the environment during emissions in the atmospheric air of pollutants forming during oil associated gas flaring" in the current edition;
- the Government regulation dd. September 13, 2016 No. 913 "On rates of payment for negative environmental impact and additional coefficients";[9]

4. https://www.worldbank.org/en/programs/gasflaringreduction/global-flaring-data (GGFR), Global Gas Flaring Tracker (accessed February 2024).
5. О Недрах (pravo.gov.ru).
6. Законодательство России. Интеллектуальный поиск "Федеральный закон В«О газоснабжении в РФВ»" (pravo.gov.ru).
7. Об охране окружающей среды (pravo.gov.ru).
8. Федеральный закон от July 2, 2021 No. 296-ФЗ · Тестовый заголовок (pravo.gov.ru).
9. О ставках платы за негативное воздействие на окружающую среду и дополнительных коэффициентах (pravo.gov.ru).

- the Government regulation dd. March 14, 2022 #355 "On criteria of attribution of legal entities and individual entrepreneurs to regulated organizations" in the current edition.

While gas flaring remains a topic to be resolved and reduced, Russia continues to develop within the energy transition trend and creates a new legal framework to enable such development. As already mentioned, in 2019, Russia joined the Paris Agreement dated 2015. In view of the implementation of the Paris Agreement in 2020, the President of the Russian Federation has adopted the Presidential Decree #666 "On reduction of greenhouse gas emissions." Further to the Presidential Decree, the Russian Government has issued a more detailed document, which, in turn, is featured for practical implementation of the main principles established by the Presidential Decree. The Government regulation dd. October 29, 2021 #3052-r approved the "Strategy of social and economic development of Russian Federation with low level of reduction of greenhouse gas emissions until 2050 year." Also, the Government of the Russian Federation established the Low carbon print development policy.

In 2021, the Federal law dated July 2, 2021 N 296-FZ "On restriction of greenhouse emission" has been adopted, establishing the main principles and restrictions related to the GHG reduction process. In 2022, the Federal law dated March 6, 2022 N 34-FZ "On experiment on reduction of greenhouse gases emission in certain subjects of the Russian Federation" set up the specific program to be implemented in selected subjects of the Russian Federation. In view of the said document, the flagman project in Sakhalin has been already launched.

Russian Government and the Ministries also issued certain acts, featured to develop the energy transitional economy. The Order of the Russian Ministry of Economic Development dd. May 11, 2022 #248 "On establishment of criteria for the climate projects implemented by the legal entities and entrepreneurs and on the form of report on realization of climate projects."

The Russian Government also establishes the system of control in relation to the entities which have significant GHG emissions. Such entities in accordance with the Government regulation dd. March 14, 2022 #355 "On criteria of attribution of legal entities and individual entrepreneurs to regulated organizations" might refer to the regulated entities. Such regulated entities shall normally meet more administrative and legal requirements, including requirements for reporting.

There are also some recent sub-laws regulating the parameters of the climate projects, serving for the purposes of implementation of the energy transition program and establishing the industrial standards. Such documents include among others the following: GOST R ISO 14064-2007 "Greenhouse gases" in three parts[10] and GOST R ISO 14080-2021 "Management of greenhouse gases and activities connected with them."[11]

10. ГОСТ Р ИСО14064-1-2007 Газы парниковые. Часть 1. Требования и руководство по количественному определению и отчетности о выбросах и удалении парниковых газов на уровне организации—docs.cntd.ru.
11. ГОСТ Р ИСО14080-2021 Управление парниковыми газами и связанные виды деятельности. Система подходов и методическое обеспечение реализации климатических проектов—docs.cntd.ru.

The Presidential Decree dd. November 4, 2020 #666 "On reduction of greenhouse gas emissions" serves as the framework document issued further to the accession of the Russian Federation to the Paris Agreement related to climate matters. The Decree entrusts the Russian Government within the period of up to 2030 to take measures to reduce the amount of GHG emissions to the level of 70% emissions in comparison to the level of 1990. Also, the Russian Government shall elaborate and establish the Strategy for social and economic development of the Russian Federation with low level of reduction of GHG emissions by 2050 and shall procure the conditions for realization of measures for reduction and prevention of GHG emissions. Important documents approved by the Russian Government in 2021 to implement the instruction of the Russian President are the Policy of low carbon development and the "Strategy of social and economic development of Russian Federation with low level of greenhouse gas emissions until 2050 year."[12] The strategy comprises the following elements:

- The initial basic scenario prescribes the present economic model. The amount of gas emissions by 2030 year will increase by 8%. The industrial equipment will be renewed and the technologies with the reduced level of GHG emissions will be introduced.
- The target (intensive scenario) prescribes ensuring global competitiveness and sustained economic growth of the Russian Federation. The following instruments for quoting GHG emissions will be applied: "green projects" and certificates of energy origin. Technologies for the reduction of GHG emissions will be also in place. Realization of this scenario will cause a reduction of GHG emissions by 2050 by 60% in comparison to 2019 and 80% in comparison to 1990.

The Strategy prescribes different measures for Strategy implementation, including, general, energetic, constructional, industrial, transport, etc.

Specific Measures in Relation to Gas Flaring and Its Reduction

Figure 23.1 shows the structure of GHG emissions worldwide and a breakdown of the type of emissions and their portion in the overall GHG emissions.[13] Russia is certainly part of such an overall emissions process.

12. ADKkCzp3fWO32e2yA0BhtIpyzWfHaiUa.pdf (government.ru).
13. Oil and gas industry's GHG emissions structure in 2017 | Download Scientific Diagram (researchgate.net).

Figure 23.1 Global Oil and Gas GHG Emissions Structure in 2017

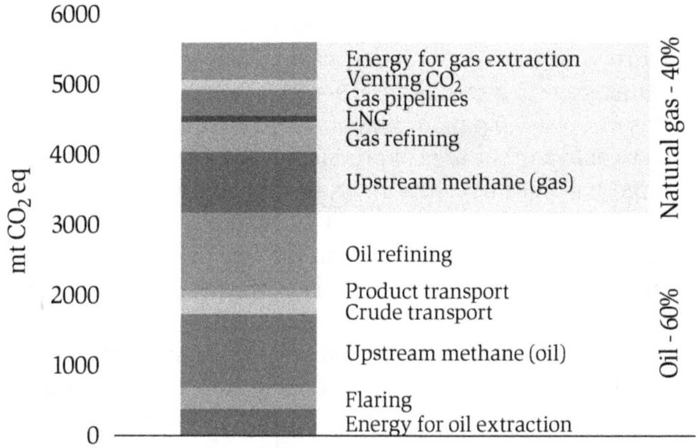

As could be seen in the structure of GHG emissions, one of the greenhouse emission sources is oil-associated gas flaring. Such emission is related to oil production process and is associated with 300 mt CO_2eqt per year of emissions worldwide. In Russia, such emission is also associated with oil production process. Russia flares the most natural gas, released from upstream oil and gas fields, of any country in the world. In 2022, 901 billion cubic feet (Bcf) of natural gas was flared, and 898 Bcf was flared in 2021 (about 5.5% of consumption).[14]

In Russia, under "gas," the law understands natural gas, oil-associated gas, topped dry gas, gas from gas condensate fields mined and collected by gas-producing and oil-producing organizations, and gas-producing by gas-producing and oil-producing organizations.[15]

Based on the fact that in Russia the oil-associated gas, which typically is burned by oil and gas producers, still falls into the definition of "gas," such activity also falls within the legal framework established by the Federal Law dated February 21, 1992 N 2395-1 "On Subsoil use" and the Code of Administrative violations. This constitutes the initial legal grounds for regulation of gas flaring. Further grounds are defined by the specific regulations, including those elaborating on emissions thresholds. There is no unified legislation in relation to the associated gas burning and the regulation is based on the separate legal acts by the Government as well as on the basis of specific industrial law. In 2000, there was an attempt to adopt the Federal Law "On regulation of oil-associated gas," which was supposed to serve as the unified act to regulate

14. https://www.worldbank.org/en/programs/gasflaringreduction/global-flaring-data (GGFR), Global Gas Flaring Tracker (accessed February 2024).
15. Article 2 of the Federal law "On gas supply" dd. March 31, 1999 #69-FZ in the current edition.

oil-associated gas, but such attempt failed in 2023 at the level of State Duma. Such draft law proposed important definitions of terms, such as "oil-associated gas," "usage of oil-associated gas," and "utilization of oil-associated gas,"; the threshold for utilization was established as well as some other important principles.[16]

In accordance with the annual report of the Ministry of Energy of the Russian Federation (Minenergo)—as a result of 2019—the average efficiency factor of the gas flaring in Russia is 81.5% (-3.5 p.p. in comparison to 2018). The increase in production as well as the enlargement of the area of production have a significant influence on this factor.[17] Minenergo has not published any new data about associated gas utilization recently, as we might assume due to the fact that currently, refineries are less eager to accept the volumes of associated gas based on the fact that export levels decreased.

In accordance with the law "On subsoil use," the license holder shall conduct the activities in compliance with the object, timeline and conditions, envisaged in the license. One of the conditions is the condition of compliance with the applicable laws and regulations in the area of subsoil use and environmental protection.

Under Article 22 of the law "On subsoil use," the license holder shall ensure compliance with the requirements of the technical projects, plans and development schemes. Also, the license holder shall not admit exceeding the norm losses, dilution and selective mining.

One of the main requirements for the rational usage and protection of subsoil is the requirement to ensure rational and complex usage of the subsoil (Article 23 of the law "On subsoil use").[18]

Selective and non-rational (including exceeding thresholds for losses) usage of the subsoil field, which leads to unreasonable losses of resources, and dilution are the grounds for imposition of administrative liability under Article 8.10 of the Code for Administrative Breaches.

The law provides with the obligation of the subsoil user to collect the oil-associated gas and take measures for prevention against negative impact on the environment, including certain payments.[19] There have been established certain thresholds for the gas flaring volumes as well as for the emissions. The additional coefficients are applied during calculation of the payment for emissions of pollutants forming during the burning and/or dispersion of oil-associated gas.[20]

The Russian legislation prescribes the following features of payment counting for negative influence on the environment during emissions of pollutants in the atmospheric air in the process of oil-associated gas burning:

16. *Source*: Нормативно-правовое регулирование в области использования и утилизации нефтяного попутного газа в Российской Федерации (cyberleninka.ru).
17. Коллегия Минэнерго России 2021 (minenergo.gov.ru).
18. О Недрах (pravo.gov.ru).
19. Clause 1 Art. 46 of the Federal law "On environmental protection" dd. January 10, 2022 #7-FZ in the current edition.
20. Clause 3 Art. 16.3. of the Federal law "On environmental protection" dd. January 10, 2022 #7-FZ in the current edition.

- The Russian Government establishes rules of counting and charging payment for negative influence on the environment during oil-associated gas burning.[21]
- The maximum permissible value of the index of the oil-associated gas burning is no more, than 5% of the volume of the produced oil-associated gas. The maximum permissible value in the amount of 5% does not apply in the following cases:
  - if the degree of depletion of reserves on oil plot is less or equal to 0.01;
  - during three years from the moment of exceeding the index in amount of 0.01; or
  - until the degree of depletion of reserves on oil plot becomes equal to 0.05 if such event comes into effect earlier.[22]

For comparison, there is a legislative prohibition in the U.S. to burn more than 3% of the associated gas. In Canada and Norway, it is prohibited to burn the associated gas at all.[23]

In case of exceeding 5% maximum permissible value of the index of the oil-associated gas burning, the amount of payment for negative impact on the environment is counted with special rates. Such special rates are established in a separate Government Regulation. Such rates can be applied only with the additional coefficient "K" in the amount of 25 since 2014. There are several exceptions to this rule.[24]

Apart from already mentioned measures on regulating the gas flaring activities the Rules "On exploitation of oil and gas fields" dd. October 15, 1984, prescribes that the introduction of the oil and gas fields into full-scale industrial production is not permitted without the system of collection and usage of the associated gas.[25]

Since gas burning is one type of activity, which can cause emission of GHGs,[26] the legal entity might become a regulated organization in case gas flaring exceeds a certain dimension. The Russian Government establishes the criteria for referring legal entities and individual entrepreneurs to regulated organizations. Such criteria refer to economic and other activities accompanied by GHG emissions in the weight of 150,000 tonnes or more of CO_2 in a year for the period until January 1, 2024, and in the weight of 50,000 tonnes or more of CO_2 in a year for the period since January 1, 2024. Regulated organizations shall bear additional obligations towards the Government.

21. Clause 2 of the Government regulation dd. November 8, 2012 #1148 "On features counting of payment for negative influence on the environment during emissions in the atmospheric air of pollutants forming during oil associated gas flaring" in the current edition.
22. Clause 3 of the Government regulation dd. November 8, 2012 #1148 "On features counting of payment for negative influence on the environment during emissions in the atmospheric air of pollutants forming during oil associated gas flaring" in the current edition.
23. st_17.pdf (nedra21.ru).
24. Clause 2 of the Regulation approved by the Government regulation dd. November 8, 2012 #1148 "On features counting of payment for negative influence on the environment during emissions in the atmospheric air of pollutants forming during oil associated gas flaring" in the current edition.
25. Правила разработки нефтяных и газонефтяных месторождений—docs.cntd.ru.
26. Article 2 of the Federal law "On limitation of greenhouse gas emissions" on July 2, 2021 #296-FZ in the current edition.

Among such obligations, such regulated entity shall provide to the authorized federal executive authority a report on emission of GHGs by July 1 of the year next for the reporting one.[27]

There are also some other criteria, allowing to refer the legal entities and individual entrepreneurs to regulated organizations, e.g., the activity responds to production processes and (or) types of economic and other activity according to the list and indicators from the annex to the Government Regulation. The annex, among others, includes the following types of activities: combustible natural gas, liquefied gas, oil-associated gas and burning of oil-associated gas and natural gas on flare systems.[28]

Criteria for the activity accompanied by GHG emissions in the lower weight of 50,000 tonnes or more of CO_2 in a year must be worked out by the Ministry of Economic Development by March 1, 2024.[29] Currently only the draft of the new version of Government regulation dd. March 14, 2022 #355 is available.

Russia demonstrates a positive trend in relation to the decrease in gas flaring. The Russian President noted that the amount of burning of oil-associated gas from 2010 to 2019 decreased from 25.7% to 18.5%.[30] Such a positive dynamic was seen in Russia at least until 2022.

Interesting fact is that many producing oil companies, which collect and transport for sale through pipelines gas which accompanies oil production, are currently unable to sell such gas due to the closure of export markets. It has been reported by some mass media sources in spring 2022 that certain oil companies requested the Russian Government to introduce the temporary measure, allowing an increase in the limit of permitted gas flaring up to 30% instead of the currently established 5%.[31] It seems that the government does not allow to increase such level. From a practical point of view, this means that oil producers exceeding the allowed dimension of gas flaring shall process payments to the Russian budget for negative impact on the environment or find other solutions to utilize natural gas, other than flaring. It might be also concluded that the positive dynamic of decreasing the burning level of associated gas has turned out to be negative, as many producers did not have any other choice than to continue burning associated gas in bigger volumes starting in 2022 again.

Significant Russian oil and gas companies continue to establish internal programs for reduction of gas burning:

- In 2020, PJSC "NK Rosneft" established a program "Carbon management: complex approach to reduction of methane emissions." The program prescribes the following reduction of GHG emissions to 2035: prevention of

27. Clauses 1 and 2 of the Art. 7 of the Federal law "On limitation of greenhouse gas emissions" on July 2, 2021 #296-FZ in the current edition.
28. Clause 1 of the criteria of attribution of legal entities and individual entrepreneurs to regulated organizations approved by the Government regulation dd. March 14, 2022 #355 "On criteria of attribution of legal entities and individual entrepreneurs to regulated organizations" in the current edition.
29. Clause 2 of the Government regulation dd. March 14, 2022 #355 "On criteria of attribution of legal entities and individual entrepreneurs to regulated organizations" in the current edition.
30. https://tass.ru/ekonomika/10142785.
31. https://lenta.ru/news/2022/05/19/fire/.

emissions (-20 m tonnes CO_2), reduction of intense of emissions (- 30%), reduction of intense of methane emissions (less, than 0.25%), emission of associated petroleum gas in 0 amount.
- Since 2017 PJSC "Lukoil" has been a participant in an initiative of the International Bank "Zero routine burning of associated petroleum gas until 2030. The company took an obligation to reduce flare burning of associated petroleum gas."[32]

The Russian fiscal legislation prescribes that associated petroleum gas directed for sale is taxed at the rate of 0%.[33] The present Russian fiscal regulation does not prescribe general taxes or any special taxes on gas emissions or gas flaring. This issue on introduction of such special tax is only in the stage of discussion.[34]

Case Law Associated with the Gas Flaring

Case law of the Russian Arbitrazh courts on gas flaring is mainly focused on: (1) rational usage of subsoil and established thresholds for flaring, emission and pollutions; (2) correctness of application of payments and relevant coefficients, including specific coefficient "K" in case the company exceeds the maximum permissible value of the index of the oil associated gas burning. The coefficient "K" applied not to all fields. It applied only to those areas of field, on which the company exceeded the 5% maximum permissible value of the index of the oil-associated gas burning.[35]

In typical cases, the Russian arbitrazh courts confirm the applicability of additional payments for non-rational usage and in case of exceeding the thresholds. The main dispute goes about the correctness of application of coefficients and the amounts.[36]

Also, the arbitrazh courts, while considering the disputes about oil-associated gas flaring normally take into account the principle of rational usage of the subsoil and analyze the rules, established by: (1) the license; (2) project documentation, including development plan.[37]

Russian Transitional Energy and Actions to Reduce Carbon Footprint and Implement Green Energy Strategy

As earlier mentioned, in 2021, the Russian Government established the policy of low carbon development by the Government regulation dd. October 29, 2021 #3052-r, the

32. https://fs.moex.com/f/13105/angl.pdf.
33. Subclause 2 cl. 1 Art. 342 of the Russian Tax Code.
34. Углеродный налог 2023: с какой целью вводится, что под него попадает, как реализуется в России и Европе (kp.ru).
35. The Ruling of State Arbitrazh court of West Siberian district dd. January 21, 2021 on case #A45-41221/2019, The Ruling of State Arbitrazh court of West Siberian district dd. February 5, 2019 on case #A67-941/2018.
36. Incl, the ruling of the Arbitrazh court of the West-Siberian district dated May 20, 2021 N Ф04-1992/2021 on case N 70-15557/2020.
37. Decision of the Arbitrazh Court of West-Siberian district dated April 22, 2021 N Ф04-1030/2021 on case N A70-11853/2020; Decision of the Arbitrazh court of Wes-Siberian District dated May 20, 2021 N Ф04-1992/2021 on case N A70-15557/2020; Decision of the Arbitrazh Court of Povolzhskiy District dated June 29, 2021 N Ф06-5470/2021 on case N A65-23294/2020.

"Strategy of social and economic development of Russian Federation with low level of reduction of greenhouse gas emissions until 2050 year." This is one of many documents, formalizing the transitional framework for the transitional energy.

Such policy comprises of three main elements:

(1) Establishment of the national system of monitoring of the GHG emissions.
(2) Formation of regulatory framework in the area of reporting, monitoring and incentivizing the reduction of GHG emissions.
(3) International cooperation in the sphere of climate.[38]

There have already been multiple steps taken in each of the three mentioned areas. Thus, within the establishment of the national system of monitoring of the GHG emissions, the register of GHG emissions has been set up as well as the register of issued carbon units. Some legal entities have been confirmed as the verificators of the climate projects, several carbon polygons have been set up, etc. The operator for registering and maintaining the carbon units register has been appointed.

Within the second element of the state program, the Russian Parliament has adopted some laws, including the Federal law dated July 2, 2021 N 296-FZ "On restriction of greenhouse emission" and the Federal law dated March 6, 2022 N 34-FZ "On experiment on reduction of greenhouse gases emission in certain subjects of the Russian Federation." In the course of implementation of the provisions of the Federal law dated March 6, 2022 N 34-FZ, the Sakhalin region was identified as the region for such experiment.

The purpose of such experiment is to make the level of GHG emissions lower or equal to absorption capacity of local ecosystems and approbation of carbon regulation until the end of 2028.[39] This program was approved by the Government of the Sakhalin region.[40]

Formally, the experiment started in September 2022. At the same time, the preparation steps and regulatory framework establishment have taken some time and were initiated before.

Within the course of the implementation of the experiment for the first time in the modern history of the Russian Federation in Sakhalin, the quotes for GHG emissions have been established. The quotes in Sakhalin have been established for 35 companies, which verified their climate projects. As a result of 2025, these companies shall cumulatively reduce 160 mt CO_2eqt, which equals the amount lower than 2% of the level of emissions of 2022, taking into consideration the plans to increase industry production.[41]

38. *Source*: DoFhF6zbaji5mAKgkefAjTssLofyUOyS.pdf (government.ru).
39. https://ecosphere.press/2022/10/31/sahalinskij-eksperiment-kak-sozdaetsya-pervyj-v-mire-region-nulevyh-vybrosov/.
40. The Regulation of the Sakhalin region dd. November 28, 2022 #551.
41. *Source*: https://tass.ru/obschestvo/18860767.

The Russian Ministries have adopted by-laws for the implementation of the Policy of low carbon development, as well as several specific industry standards (GOSTs) have been introduced.

Probably, the major challenge in the implementation of the Policy of low carbon development lies currently in the third area: the area of international cooperation. Due to the challenging geopolitical situation, the Russian Federation is experiencing difficulties in international cooperation with certain Western countries now. However, it is unlikely that such difficulty will prevent the Russian Federation from a full-fledged implementation of the state policy and relevant state programs.

In order to take further steps in the transition energy development, Russia takes specific measures in different areas. Below we will elaborate on the different groups of methods and their result.

1 CORPORATE METHODS

Corporate methods might range from divestment of carbon-rich assets, which are typically mature or small-scale upstream assets as well as the sale of excess capacity infrastructure to carbon credits and nature-based solutions.

In terms of divestment of upstream mature/small-scale assets for the Russian market, it might be noted that the buyers for such assets currently will be solely Russian entities and investors and such divestments will not change the picture of the Russian energy market as the structure and amount of emissions will not change due to such sales. Such divestments will only have an impact on the assets portfolio of particular Russian energy companies, either improving them or the opposite.

Corporate-wise more impact will be the introduction of a system of registering and monitoring climate projects and carbon units created as a result of realization of climate projects.

The carbon unit is a verified result of realization of a climatic project in weight of GHGs equal to 1 tonne of CO_2. Issuance of the carbon units will be limited to the quota execution unit, which is a verified result of an execution of an established quota expressed in the difference between an established quota and an actual mass of GHG emissions equivalent to 1 tonne of CO_2.[42] Carbon units will be issued on the account of the company realizing a climatic project. Carbon units are issued in a number, mentioned in a report on a climatic project, and in a number corresponding to a reduction in the amount of GHG emissions equivalent to 1 tonne of CO_2.[43] The legislation does not include other limitations to the number of issued carbon units, other than carbon quotas for the particular regions and the entities, having operations there.

In order to receive carbon units, the company shall verify and confirm the climate project. The company files an application to the operator for registration of the climatic project. The application must have the following annexes: a document, which proves

42. **Реестр углеродных единиц** (carbonreg.ru).
43. The Regulation of the Russian Government dd. April 30, 2022 #790.

the powers of the signatory, and a positive conclusion of an accredited person, that the project meets the following criteria altogether:

- Activities of the project do not contradict the requirements of the Russian legislation and are realized in accordance with the documents of the national standardization system, including documents in the sphere of limitation of GHG emissions.
- The implementation of the project shall lead to the reduction of GHG emissions and/or an increase in their absorption.
- Activities of the project do not cause a total increase in GHG emissions or reduction in the level of their absorption outside the area of influence of activities of the project.
- The reduction of GHG emissions and/or increase in their absorption during the period of realization of the project is not the result of the influence of factors not connected with the activities of the project.
- Activities of the project are realizing in addition to activities aimed at realization of mandatory requirements of Russian legislation acting on the stage at the beginning of the project.[44]

The abovementioned list of requirements includes the necessity of compliance of climatic projects to Russian Government Standards (GOST).[45]

Among all GOSTs, we should mention two main GOSTs in Russia regulating GHG emissions: (i) GOST R ISO 14064-2007 "Greenhouse gases" in three parts and (ii) GOST R ISO 14080-2021 "Management of greenhouse gases and activities connected with them." These GOSTs include requirements on quantitative determination and reports on GHG emissions in organizations and projects on reduction of GHG emissions, validation and verification of statements re GHG emissions, management of GHGs and activities connected with them.[46]

The procedure of evaluation of the project by an accredited company includes the following stages:

- Stage 1. On the stage of filing an application to the operator for registration of the climatic project, an accredited company gives a positive conclusion, that the project requires the following all criteria prescribed by law. This is the process of validation of a project. An accredited company, which validates the project, must be accredited in a national system of accreditation and must be not affiliated to the company, which prepared the project. A validation is done on the basis of a contract concluded between an accredited company and a company, which prepared the project. An accredited company must use a

44. The Order of the Russian Ministry of economic development dd. May 11, 2022 #248.
45. Article 26 of the Federal law dd. June 29, 2015 #162-FZ "On Standardisation in Russian Federation."
46. GOST R ISO 14064-2007 "Greenhouse gases" in three parts and GOST R ISO 14080-2021 "Management of greenhouse gases and activities connected with them."

special method for counting the volume of greenhouse emissions and absorption of greenhouse emissions. The result of such validation must be the following documents: (1) a report on validation of a project; (2) a positive or a negative conclusion on validation of a project. The accredited company gives a positive conclusion if a project meets the requirements prescribed in an appropriate Regulation of the Russian Government.[47]
- Stage 2. On the stage of verification of results of realization of a climatic project, an accredited company checks and approves information on reduction of GHG emissions or on an increase in the absorption of GHG emissions upon results of realization of a climatic project. The accredited company prepares a report on realization of a climatic project. An accredited company, which verifies the project, must be accredited in a national system of accreditation and must be not affiliated to the company, which realized the project. A verification is done on the basis of a contract concluded between an accredited company and a company, which realized the project. The result of such verification must be the following documents: (1) a report on verification of a project; (2) a positive or a negative conclusion on verification of a project.[48]

One of the steps of realization GHG reduction program was establishment of the Russian Register of carbon units. The register has started functioning since September 1, 2022.[49] The operator of this register is AO "Kontur."[50] The register and the market of carbon units will be valid until September 1, 2028.

The company, which realizes the climatic project can receive carbon units by making the application to an operator with the following annexes: a document, which proves the powers of the signatory, and a report on results of realization of a climatic project verified by a company accredited for verification of climatic projects by the Russian Ministry of Economic Development. In case the application with annexes meets the legal requirements, the operator issues carbon units for the company, which successfully realized a climatic project. These carbon units can be sold by the owner of the climatic project to other companies with GHG emissions exceeding their quota.[51]

The examples of climatic projects, which received a positive conclusion of an accredited company on stage 1 (validation of a project) and an interim positive verification conclusion of an accredited company (part of stage 2) are the following:

- A climatic project #64-2022-00000001 of LLC "Dalenergoinvest." It is the first registered climatic project in Russia. The period of realization of a project is

47. The Order of the Russian Ministry of economic development dd. May 11, 2022 #248.
48. The Regulation of the Russian Government dd. March 22, 2022 #455.
49. **Реестр углеродных единиц** (carbonreg.ru).
50. The Order of the Russian Government dd. March 1, 2022 #367-r.
51. The Regulation of the Russian Government dd. April 30, 2022 #790 "On approvement of the Rules of establishment and maintaining a register of carbon units and maintaining operations with carbon units in a register of carbon units"; the Regulation of the Russian Government dd. March 22, 2022 #455.

2022-2031. The project received a positive conclusion of an accredited company on a validation of a project (stage 1) and an interim positive verification conclusion of an accredited company for the first period of realization of the project (stage 2). The company now has 96 carbon units.[52]

- A climatic project #05-2023-00000001 of PJSC "Rushydro." The period of realization of a project is 2022-2027. The project received a positive conclusion of an accredited company on a validation of a project (stage 1) and an interim positive verification conclusion of an accredited company dd. July 12, 2023, for the first period of realization of the project (stage 2). The company can receive 381820 carbon units.[53]

PJSC Gazprom and Wintershalldea AG Russian Joint venture JSC Achimgaz has begun implementation of a *pilot climate project*. "Installation of an innovative high-pressure heat exchanger at UKPG-31 is necessary to reduce the heating time of gas gathering manifolds when well clusters are put into operation. This project will make it possible *to prevent the emission of about 28,000 tonnes of CO_2 annually for 10 years*, reducing the load on the atmosphere, and to produce carbon units in the same volume, improving the economic performance of the enterprise."[54]

2 OPERATIONAL METHODS

Role of Natural Gas in the Process of Reduction of GHG Emissions

Fewer GHG emissions come from gas production and processing than do from oil. Sixty percent of total O&G GHG emissions come from the oil industry, and only 40% come from gas. On top of this, natural gas is recognized as more cleaner fossil fuel, leaving less carbon footprint. Natural gas serves perfectly for the energy transition period and implementation of different GHG reduction strategies.

Currently, Russia's energy balance is one of the greenest in the world, as Russia uses multiple carbon footprint-free energy sources, such as natural gas, hydro energy, nuclear energy and other green sources of energy.

Russian Deputy Prime Minister Novak announced that the level of gasification in Russia reached 72% in 2021 and will continue to rise with the aim to raise it up to 83% level in 2030. PJSC Gazprom, as the major gas producer, which has been assigned the task of increasing the gasification, continues the realization of the development of gas supply and gasification program.

Currently, the following measures for gasification development are being realized: (a) bring gas services to more than 3,600 population centers; (b) convert more than 3,200 boiler houses to gas; and (c) build more than 24,000 km of inter-settlement gas pipelines. All the above mentioned measures allow lifting the level of gasification in the country to 75%.

52. Реестр углеродных единиц (carbonreg.ru).
53. Реестр углеродных единиц (carbonreg.ru).
54. https://neftegas.info/magazines/gas-industry/36/811.

Additionally, the president of Russia has given instructions to expand the gasification program in the updated Energy Strategy to 2050. Particular attention here will be devoted to the gasification of industrial consumers and population centers along the Power of Siberia and Sakhalin-Khabarovsk-Vladivostok gas pipelines, which will reduce consumption of fuel oil and diesel fuel and as a result of such reduction, will reduce GHG emissions.[55]

On top of some operational regulatory measures, multiple purely technical measures have been traditionally implemented in Russia. Among them are: reinjection of drilling cutting—largely used in Russia since 2004—cuts rig time by 50%, requires minimum maintenance in the presence of safe operations, in addition, usage of interchangeable skids (could be placed apart from each other), and leaks control solution.

Methane emissions reduction is one of the major challenges in GHG reduction strategy. Methane emissions are a significant problem; they account for 45% of aggregate emissions.

Despite different approaches to reducing methane emissions in gas production and transportation, concentration of efforts of technological, operational and scientific nature, for example, in the upstream sector can bring greater benefits.

Deep Decarbonization, CCUS and Hydrogen

For Russia's transition to diversified low-carbon economic development, entering new emerging "green" product markets is naturally required. It is essential to maintain and expand existing niches by ensuring the global competitiveness of Russian goods and produced energy in terms of their carbon intensity. The achievement of synergistic effects from implementing the measures stated in the Strategy concerning the goals of Russian economy sustainable development has also to be considered.

The development of carbon capture, utilization and storage (CCUS) is one of the main instruments to achieve stated goals. The total potential CO_2 volume available to CCUS technologies in Russia is estimated as:

- in the fuel and energy sector, 1.2 Gtpa (oil and gas 355 Mtpa);
- in the industry, 270 Mtpa;
- with the development of technologies, producing "blue" hydrogen (by 2030), 20 Mtpa.

The potential capacity of CCUS technologies is close to 50 Mtpa by 2030 and > 400 Mtpa by 2050.[56]

Currently, the CCUS projects are not widely spread in Russia. The closest to implementation is probably the CCUS project realized by Gazprom Neft in the Orenburg region with the announced value of investments of circa RUB 30 billion. In the initial phase, Gazprom Neft expects to gradually increase the capacity to store up to

55. Gasification level in Russia far exceeds EU countries—Novak (interfax.com).
56. *Source*: https://www.sciencedirect.com/science/article/abs/pii/S2214993722000665.

1 million tonnes of carbon dioxide in depleted oil and condensate reservoirs at a depth of about 2,500 meters.

The project is to be located at the Orenburg oil and condensate field which is operated by the company's regional subsidiary Gazprom Neft Orenburg and lies near the Russia-Kazakhstan border. According to a company presentation, the project is described as a commercial undertaking aimed at capturing carbon dioxide at the gas-fired Kargalinskaya thermal and electric power plant and the Orenburg gas and condensate processing facility.

Gazprom Neft estimates the power plant and processing facility—operated by parent company Gazprom—produce about 800,000 tonnes per annum of CO_2. The captured CO_2 will be transported by pipeline to the Orenburg field to be injected into the reservoir.[57]

In terms of *hydrogen production* and its usage as a source of clean energy, Russia is currently at the development stage, elaborating the legal framework, identifying projects and setting the preparatory stage.

In August 2021, the Russian Government approved the Concept of Hydrogen Development establishing three stages for its implementation:

(1) Stage 1 (2021-2024)—export target of 0.2 million tonnes. During this period Russia plans to:
  - Establish four hydrogen clusters: (i) Eastern—to export hydrogen to Asia and develop hydrogen transportation and power infrastructure—primarily to be located in Sakhalin island, north of Japan; (ii) North-Western—to export hydrogen to the European Union (EU) and reduce Russian exporters' carbon footprint—primarily to be located in St. Petersburg and Leningrad region, located on Russia's Baltic shore; (iii) Arctic—to ensure the low-carbon energy supply of Russia's Artic Zone and export hydrogen (potentially via Northern Sea Route); (iv) Southern—that may be set up in Russia's south having developed infrastructure, high natural gas availability, renewables potential and proximity to major export cities.
  - Implement pilot hydrogen projects, including those based on electrolysis power by low-carbon power and those based on fossil fuels coupled with CCUS.
  - Develop technologies and industrial technologies, including those to produce hydrogen via water electrolysis and out of fossil fuels, its energy mixes, utility-scale storage and transportation, fuel cells, turbines and hydrogen power stations, fuelling installations, vehicles and robotics (hydrogen tech and products).
  - Conduct relevant R&D activities.
  - Develop relevant regulations and incentives.

57. Ambitious: Gazprom Neft gets serious on its first CCS pilot | Upstream Online.

(2) Stage 2 (2025-2035) envisages some export targets as well as set and development of internal Russian consumption market, including implementation of hydrogen technologies in petrochemicals, electric power, transportation etc.
(3) Stage 3 (2036-2050) with enlargement of the export target as well as further development of industry hydrogen consumption.[58]

All three stages apart from the development of Russian internal market consumption envisage hydrogen export, mainly to the Asia-Pacific region as well as the development of international cooperation with a focus on the Asia-Pacific area. It should be noted that provided that Russia is currently in challenging geo-political circumstances, the Asia-Pacific region will remain the main focus with the view to developing international cooperation and establishing and increasing hydrogen export volumes.

As it has been already mentioned above on October 6, 2021, the Russian Government approved a series of Russia's strategic development initiatives until 2030, including the one titled "Clean energy (renewables and hydrogen)"—being a part of the "Technological Breakthrough" section of the said initiatives. The authorities are now developing a federal project to detail the "Clean Energy" initiative.[59]

On October 15, 2021, the Ministry of Industry and Trade of the Russian Federation released the Russian Atlas listing more than 40 low-carbon hydrogen and ammonia projects across Russia prepared in cooperation with businesses. The Atlas aims to be a reference point for investors.[60]

LNG Projects

Among the measures related to reduction of GHG emissions, Russian Liquefied Natural Gas (LNG) projects also play a significant role in the Strategy for the socio-economic development of the Russian Federation with low GHG emissions until 2050. Apart from supporting LNG production plants, the government is also subsidizing the construction of compressed natural gas fueling infrastructure and conversion of transport to gas, a program to support construction of LNG filling stations is in the works, and subsidies are being considered for construction of mini LNG plants, foremost along international transport corridors.[61]

Some industry standards have been introduced to standardize and develop LNG production: *State standard specification (GOST) 34894-2022; Interstate standard; and Liquefied natural gas. Technical conditions*[62] is the document which defines the requirements for the physical and chemical indicators of LNG, the correct terms, safety requirements, environmental protection requirements, and basic rules for storage, transportation and acceptance.

58. 5JFns1CDAKqYKzZ0mnRADAw2NqcVsexl.pdf (government.ru).
59. http://static.government.ru/media/files/jwsYsyJKWGQQAaCSMGrd7q82RQ5xECo3.pdf.
60. https://minpromtorg.gov.ru/common/upload/docVersions/6169d30a61364/actual/atlas_en.pdf.
61. Gasification level in Russia far exceeds EU countries—Novak (interfax.com).
62. 78878.pdf (meganorm.ru).

Order of Rostechnadzor dated December 11, 2020 N 521 "On approval of federal norms and regulations in the field of industrial safety 'Safety Rules for Liquefied Natural Gas Facilities'"[63] is the set of rules and requirements aimed at ensuring the industrial safety of hazardous production facilities of LNG, at which technological processes of production, storage, reception/dispatch, and regasification of LNG are carried out. The rules are intended for application in the design, construction, operation, reconstruction, technical re-equipment, repair, conservation and liquidation of LNG hazardous production facilities. The rules also describe how maintenance and repair of process equipment and pipelines should be carried out, and rules about the analysis of the risk of accidents.

Russia's first *LNG* plant was built by Sakhalin Energy and began operation in 2009. The shareholders of Sakhalin Energy were Gazprom (50% plus one share), Shell (27.5% minus one share), as well as Mitsui & Co (12.5%) and Mitsubishi (10%).

At the end of February 2022, Shell announced its withdrawal from joint projects with Gazprom, including the Sakhalin 2 project. The Japanese government decided not to withdraw from the project. In August 2022, the Government of the Russian Federation decided to create a new operator of Sakhalin 2—Sakhalinskaya Energia LLC with registration in Yuzhno-Sakhalinsk:

- Gazprom Sakhalin Holding received a 50% stake in the authorized capital of Sakhalinskaya Energia.
- Mitsui agreed to take ownership of a 12.5% stake in Sakhalinskaya Energia. The owner of the share was MIT SEL Investment Ltd (registered in Dubai, UAE), which is 100% owned by Mitsui.
- Japanese Mitsubishi also decided to maintain a 10% stake in the new operator of Sakhalin 2, with the share being owned by a subsidiary of DGS Japan.

The Japanese energy company JERA also agreed to continue the contract with Sakhalinskaya Energia, concluding a contract for the long-term supply of LNG on the same terms as in the previous agreement.

In 2022, the new operator of the LNG plant within the Sakhalin 2 project produced 11.5 million tonnes of LNG and 3.7 million tonnes of oil.

In April 2023, the Government of the Russian Federation approved the sale of Shell's share of 27.5% to Novatek. The acquirer of the share in Sakhalinskaya Energia was Novatek's subsidiary, Novatek Moscovskaya Oblast. The design capacity of the plant is 9.6 million tonnes of LNG per year.

LNG production at the first production line of the second Russian LNG plant—Yamal LNG—began in 2017. In 2018, two more production lines of the plant were launched. In November 2018, Yamal LNG produced LNG on the third production line. The fourth line of the Yamal LNG project with a capacity of 0.9 million tonnes of LNG per year was launched in May 2021. A complex of engineering structures designed to receive raw gas, prepare gas for liquefaction, liquefy natural gas, store LNG and load

63. https://rulaws.ru/acts/Prikaz-Rostehnadzora-ot-11.12.2020-N-521/.

LNG onto gas carriers with further transportation to the LNG receiving terminal located on the coast of the Baltic Sea near Kaliningrad.

In 2021, Yamal LNG received approval from technical expertise that phases 1 to 3 of the project are capable of operating at 120% of design capacity in subzero temperatures. In 2021, Yamal LNG produced 19.64 million tonnes of LNG. In 2022, Yamal LNG shipped 20.6 million tonnes of LNG for export.

In 2022, TotalEnergies announced the termination of purchases of Russian LNG on the spot market and the continuation of purchases under a long-term contract with Yamal LNG and did not plan to leave the project.

Second Novatek's significant project is Arctic LNG 2. The project involves the construction of three technological lines for the production of LNG with a capacity of 6.6 million tonnes per year. The total capacity of the three lines will be 19.8 million tonnes of LNG and up to 1.6 million tonnes of stable gas condensate per year.

The resource base of the Arctic LNG 2 project is the Utrenneye field, located on the Gydan Peninsula in the Yamalo-Nenets Autonomny Okrug, approximately 70 km from the Yamal LNG project across the Gulf of Ob.

In 2018, the main technical solutions and design documentation (FEED) were completed, engineering preparation of the territory, construction of priority energy supply facilities and drilling of production wells, and construction of a quay began.

Arctic LNG 2 participants made the final investment decision on the project in September 2019. At the end of 2021, the project readiness was estimated at 59%, and the readiness of the first line at 78%.

The project is based on an innovative construction concept using gravity-based foundations (GBF). The application of the technological concept of construction at the GBF, as well as the extensive localization of the production of equipment and materials in Russia, will significantly reduce capital costs per ton of LNG produced within the project. This will ensure low production costs and maximum competitiveness in all LNG markets.

Unfortunately, for the time being and due to geopolitical hurdles, the project was halted and might not restart too shortly.[64]

Novatek uses renewable energy sources based on solar panels and wind generators for its LNG projects, which power telemechanics system points to control line valve stations of main pipelines and multi-well pads of gas condensate fields.

In addition, Novatek and Baker Hughes signed a cooperation agreement in 2021 to convert gas turbines to hydrogen-containing fuel gas mixtures to reduce carbon dioxide emissions from LNG facilities. At that time, Baker Hughes was one of the suppliers of major equipment for the Yamal LNG and Arctic LNG 2 projects.

Similarly, a memorandum of understanding on LNG supply and decarbonization in 2021 was signed with RWE Supply & Trading GmbH, as well as an agreement on decarbonization of LNG production in 2020 with Siemens Energetika.

64. https://oilprice.com/Latest-Energy-News/World-News/Russias-Arctic-LNG-2-Project-Put-on-Ice-With-No-Restart-Plans.html#: ~ :text = Russia%27s%20Novatek%20recently%20halted%20operations%20at%20its%20Arctic,a%20significant%20setback%20for%20the%20country%27s%20gas%20ambitions.

Another LNG project is Gazprom LNG Portovaia, which is located in the Vyborg district of the Leningrad region of the Russian Federation, on the northeastern coast of the Gulf of Finland, between Portovaya and Dalnyaya bays on Cape Konek.

The project was commissioned in 2022 by Gazprom without the participation of the licensor of the natural gas liquefaction technology, Linde, which announced its withdrawal from Russian projects.

The design capacity of the plant's two technological lines is 1.5 million tonnes of LNG per year. The complex is connected to the unified gas supply system of Russia.

In February 2023, the general director of Gazprom LNG Portovaya reported that the complex had produced 500 thousand tonnes of LNG since its launch.

Tax Aspect for LNG Projects

For companies that carry out LNG production activities and have exported at least one batch of LNG before December 31, 2022, in the tax periods 2023-2025 the corporate income tax rate is set at 34% (clause 1.17 of Article 284 Tax Code). However, if the company carries out LNG production activities, but does not have the exclusive right to export LNG, the grounds for such organization to apply the tax rate in the amount of 34% is not available (Letter of the Ministry of Finance dated March 17, 2023 No. 03-03-06/1/22853).

Conclusion

Despite multiple geopolitical challenges Russia continues to be focused on reduction of gas flaring and development within the transitional energy concept.

It is not easy under the circumstances when the gas export drops and the western technologies are limited or not available at all. At the same time, the Russian Government maintains its position to reduce gas flaring and did not agree to lower the requirement for appropriate associated gas utilization from 95%. Oil and gas producers are forced to find other technological, operational and corporate solutions to keep the legally required level of utilization or otherwise shall pay for a threshold-exceeding level.

As mentioned, Russia is already well placed among green energy countries as most of its energy generation operates in the area of low carbon footprint sources, such as gas sources, atomic, hydro, thermal and other low carbon energy sources. At the same time, Russia looks further and having already good ground to say that it is at the top level among green energies worldwide, it continues to implement steps to further decrease the carbon footprint. Russia introduces green projects, trading of carbon units and many other measures to further stimulate the development of green energy.

CHAPTER 24

Trinidad and Tobago

Shereece Smith

1 INTRODUCTION

There is significant discourse amongst oil and gas practitioners that human-induced greenhouse gas emissions are beginning to affect the Earth's climate, necessitating substantial reductions to mitigate the negative consequences of climate change. The primary contributor to these emissions on a global scale is the combustion of fossil fuels, which are extensively used for generating electricity, heating, and powering transportation. These fossil fuels include coal, oil, and natural gas.

The Paris Climate Agreement, established under the United Nations Framework Convention on Climate Change (UNFCCC), became effective on November 4, 2016. This agreement obligates nations to outline specific strategies and targets aimed at reducing greenhouse gas emissions. These commitments are classified as Nationally Determined Contributions (NDCs), which can be either unconditional—meaning they are pursued without expecting external financial or technical support—or conditional—indicating that reductions depend on receiving such assistance.

The World Bank highlights that effective collaboration between public and private sectors is essential for minimizing flaring volumes, advocating for comprehensive regulations to address this issue. Recent shifts in global demand for natural gas have further complicated the situation in Trinidad and Tobago ("T&T"). Post-pandemic changes have led to volatility in natural gas prices, raising concerns about economic sustainability within the sector.[1] While the petrochemical industry significantly benefits from utilizing natural gas over electricity generation due to cost

1. Elvidge (2024), "Post-Pandemic Natural Gas Utilization in Trinidad and … ." Retrieved from https://www.ej-energy.org/index.php/ejenergy/article/view/134.

efficiency, reliance on this single resource renders the economy vulnerable to external shocks. Thus, strategic investments in renewable energy sources are imperative for fostering resilience against market fluctuations.

Moreover, reducing flaring can play a crucial role in meeting climate commitments outlined by international agreements such as the Paris Agreement. Although Trinidad and Tobago's contribution to global flaring may seem minor compared to larger nations, localized efforts could yield substantial environmental benefits while enhancing compliance with NDCs.[2] Therefore, integrating these practices into national policies is essential for achieving both economic stability and environmental sustainability.

One strategy for achieving NDCs targets involves minimizing natural gas flaring. Flaring is a common method for disposing of excess natural gas in situations where local infrastructure is inadequate for its use or transport. In addition, flaring is predicted to waste up to 5% of worldwide natural gas production each year. Natural gas flaring is occasionally required during the initial commissioning of a well or for safety reasons.

The legitimacy of using flaring reductions to meet emission goals traces back to provisions in the Kyoto Protocol's Clean Development Mechanism. Gas flares can be found at various sites including oil exploration facilities and refineries. A recent study indicated that approximately 90% of globally flared gas originates from upstream production facilities. This associated gas often escapes due to technical or economic barriers despite efforts by governments and companies to capture it effectively.

Currently, thousands of flares worldwide combust roughly 140 billion cubic meters of natural gas annually, releasing nearly 300 million tons of carbon dioxide into the atmosphere. Notably, methane—a potent greenhouse gas—is released alongside this process; it has a warming potential significantly higher than that of carbon dioxide (Herring, 2023).[3] This practice not only contributes to greenhouse gas emissions but also exacerbates climate change due to the simultaneous release of methane, a potent greenhouse gas with a warming potential far exceeding that of carbon dioxide. The inefficiencies associated with flaring practices underscore the need for improved management strategies to mitigate these harmful emissions.

Consequently, while flaring reduces atmospheric impacts compared to venting directly into the air, it remains an area requiring urgent attention in climate mitigation efforts. Natural gas flaring is a significant environmental issue, particularly in oil-rich countries like Trinidad and Tobago. The regulation of this practice has gained increasing attention over the years due to its detrimental effects on air quality and

2. UNDP (2017). "Webinar: Implementing Trinidad and Tobago's Nationally Determined Contribution (NDC)." Available at: https://www.undp.org/content/dam/LECB/events/2017/20170807-webinartrinidad-tobago-implementation-plan-ndcs/undp-lecb-trinidad-tobago-NDC-ImplementationPlan-Fact-Sheet-2017.pdf.
3. Herring (2023), "IPCC Climate Change Reports: Why They Matter to Everyone on the Planted." Retrieved from https://www.nrdc.org/stories/ipcc-climate-change-reports-why-they-matter-everyone-planet.

climate change. In Trinidad and Tobago, where the energy sector plays a crucial role in the economy, effective management of associated gas flaring has become imperative.

Aging oil fields in T&T have led to decreased efficiency in production processes, resulting in increased volumes of associated natural gas being flared (International Monetary Fund, 2024). While international best practices exist for managing flare volumes—such as those outlined by the World Bank Group—implementation at the national level remains inconsistent (World Bank Group, 2019). This gap highlights the need for stronger policy measures that align with global standards while considering local contexts.

Trinidad and Tobago's rate of flaring is a critical concern in the context of global oil production, particularly when compared to other oil-producing nations. According to Siu and Perseval (2016),[4] Trinidad and Tobago experiences significant natural gas flaring, which leads to considerable economic and environmental losses. The country's flaring rates have been attributed to inefficiencies in flare management, highlighting the need for more robust strategies aimed at recapturing and utilizing hydrocarbons effectively. This situation is exacerbated by the absence of stringent regulations that govern flaring practices compared to countries like Norway.

The regulatory landscape for natural gas flaring in Trinidad and Tobago has evolved through various legislative frameworks aimed at minimizing environmental impacts while maximizing economic benefits from hydrocarbon extraction. Historically, regulations were lax, allowing companies considerable leeway regarding flaring practices. However, as global awareness of climate issues intensified and international pressure mounted for more sustainable practices, Trinidad and Tobago began to adopt stricter regulations.[5] These measures align with broader initiatives supported by organizations such as the World Bank's Global Gas Flaring Reduction Public-Private Partnership (GGFR), which provides guidance on reducing flaring through best practices and technological innovations.

Despite these advancements, challenges remain in enforcing regulations effectively. The need for comprehensive policies that integrate environmental considerations with economic incentives is critical for achieving sustainable development within the energy sector. As Trinidad and Tobago continues to address its energy infrastructure challenges amidst global shifts towards cleaner energy sources, robust regulation of natural gas flaring will be essential not only for environmental protection but also for ensuring long-term socio-economic viability. This paper examines the current legislation governing natural gas flaring in Trinidad and Tobago, identifies its shortcomings, and offers recommendations for improvement.

4. Siu, Perseval & Group (2024), "Effective Flare and Vent Management." Paper presented at the SPE Trinidad and Tobago Section Energy Resources Conference, Port of Spain, Trinidad and Tobago, June 2016 https://doi.org/10.2118/180835-MS.
5. World Bank (2019), "Trinidad and Tobago. CO_2 Emissions (Metric Tons Per Capita)." Available at: https://data.worldbank.org/indicator/EN.ATM.CO2E.PC?locations=TT&year_high_desc=true.

2 CONTEXT OF NATURAL GAS FLARING REGULATION IN TRINIDAD AND TOBAGO

Trinidad and Tobago is an industrialized economy heavily reliant on fossil fuels and is the leading producer of oil and gas in the Caribbean region. The country also plays a key role in supplying manufactured goods such as food products, beverages, and cement, as well as ammonia, methanol, iron, and steel. However, the petroleum sector remains the dominant economic sector, contributing 35% to the Gross Domestic Product (GDP) and making up 80%[6] of exports. As climate change impacts such as more intense tropical storms, rising sea levels, increased temperatures, and loss of coastal habitats loom, T&T's economic development, citizen livelihoods, and health are at risk.

Being a Small Island Developing State (SIDS), T&T faces challenges hindering its sustainable socio-economic growth, particularly environmental concerns. The National Development Strategy, known as VISION 2030,[7] acknowledges these challenges and places environmental issues at the forefront of social and economic development. By aligning with international environmental agreements, T&T aims to reduce its national carbon footprint and enhance its resilience to climate change in the short, medium, and long term.

Although T&T's contribution to global greenhouse gas emissions is minimal, its high emissions per capita due to its reliance on fossil fuels necessitate the implementation of domestic climate change mitigation policies. Through frameworks like the National Environmental Policy and the National Climate Change Policy, T&T seeks to transition to a low-carbon economy, reduce emissions, and build resilience using cleaner and energy-efficient technologies. The country's Carbon Reduction Strategy outlines a plan to decrease emissions until 2040, with specific measures for the power generation, transport, and industry sectors.

Efforts are underway to update the National Climate Change Policy to align with the Paris Agreement and emerging scientific findings. Four Nationally Appropriate Mitigation Actions (NAMAs) have been developed for high-emission sectors, including promoting renewable energy, improving public transportation, reducing flaring and venting in the oil and gas industry, and providing incentives for emission reductions in the petrochemical and heavy industry sectors. These actions have the potential to reduce greenhouse gas emissions by 42 $MtCO_2e$[8] from 2017 to 2030.

6. Ministry of Energy and Energy Industries (2016), "Oil and Gas Industry Overview." Available at: http://www.energy.gov.tt/our-business/oil-and-gas-industry/.
7. Government of Trinidad and Tobago (2015b), "Strategy for Reduction of Carbon Emissions in Trinidad and Tobago, 2040." Available at: https://www.planning.gov.tt/sites/default/files/CRS%20_ Strategy_Final.pdf.
8. UNDP (2016a), "Nationally Appropriate Mitigation Action (NAMA) in Trinidad and Tobago: Power Sector." UNDP Low Emission Capacity Building (LECB) Programme. Version 1.0. August 12, 2016.

   UNDP (2016b), "Nationally Appropriate Mitigation Action (NAMA) in Trinidad and Tobago: Industry Sector—Heavy and Petrochemical Industry." UNDP Low Emission Capacity Building (LECB) Programme. Version 1.0. August 12, 2016.

Natural gas flaring, the process of burning off excess natural gas during oil extraction, poses significant environmental and economic challenges. In Trinidad and Tobago, a country heavily reliant on its hydrocarbon industry, the regulation of gas flaring is crucial to balancing economic benefits with environmental responsibility. While flaring is necessary for safety reasons and to prevent the release of harmful gases into the atmosphere, excessive and unregulated, flaring can have negative impacts on the environment, public health, and the economy of a country. Trinidad and Tobago, a major producer of natural gas, has been grappling with the issue of deregulated flaring and its implications for the nation.

The burning of natural gas releases greenhouse gases such as carbon dioxide and methane, contributing to global warming and climate change. Deregulated flaring can also lead to air pollution and the release of harmful chemicals into the atmosphere, affecting the health of nearby communities and ecosystems. According to the World Bank,[9] Trinidad and Tobago is one of the top 10 gas-flaring countries in the world, with an estimated 21.2 billion cubic feet of natural gas being flared annually.

A direct economic impact of flaring natural gas results in the wastage of a valuable resource that could have been used for power generation or industrial purposes. Trinidad and Tobago relies heavily on natural gas for its energy needs and as a source of revenue through exports. The country is losing millions of dollars in potential revenue due to flaring, as well as incurring costs associated with environmental cleanup and healthcare expenses for affected communities.

Despite the significant challenges the country faces with managing natural gas flaring, there have been notable positive developments in the country's approach:

(1) Initiatives for Reduction: The government of T&T has launched initiatives focused on reducing gas flaring, including the Gas to Liquids (GTL) project. This project is designed to convert flared gas into usable products, with the goal of minimizing waste. However, the implementation of these initiatives has faced challenges, leading to slow progress and limited impact on reducing flaring rates.

(2) Collaboration with International Bodies: Trinidad and Tobago has actively collaborated with international organizations such as the World Bank to develop strategies for reducing gas flaring. Through partnerships like the GGFR, T&T has gained access to frameworks and resources to improve its regulatory approach. While these collaborations offer valuable opportunities for advancement, the full integration of these international frameworks into effective local practices is yet to be fully realized.

UNDP (2016c), "Nationally Appropriate Mitigation Action (NAMA) in Trinidad and Tobago: Industry Sector—Oil and Gas Production." UNDP Low Emission Capacity Building (LECB) Programme. Version 1.0. August 12, 2016.

UNDP (2016d), "Nationally Appropriate Mitigation Action (NAMA) in Trinidad and Tobago: Industry Sector—Transport."

9. *Ibid.*, 5.

3 NATURAL GAS FLARING: THE LEGAL FRAMEWORK IN TRINIDAD AND TOBAGO

The legal framework governing natural gas flaring in Trinidad and Tobago is primarily established through the Petroleum Act ("The Act"),[10] and the accompanying Petroleum Regulations ("The Regulations").[11] Together, these legal instruments create a comprehensive regulatory framework that governs the issuance of Exploration and Production Licenses (E&P Licenses)[12] and Production Sharing Contracts (PSCs). This framework is essential for overseeing upstream exploration and production activities both on land and in submarine areas within Trinidad and Tobago's territorial waters and continental shelf and outlines the regulatory obligations for companies engaged in hydrocarbon extraction. This legislative framework mandates that operators must minimize environmental impacts associated with oil and gas production, including flaring. The act emphasizes compliance with specific conditions set forth in exploration and production licenses, which require licensees to implement best practices for resource management and to adhere to local and international environmental standards.

The Ministry of Energy and Energy Industries (MEEI) is primarily responsible for overseeing the regulatory framework that manages flaring in Trinidad and Tobago. The MEEI enforces guidelines aimed at reducing flaring and promoting resource efficiency in petroleum operations, ensuring that regulatory approval is required for a wide range of activities. This regulatory approach is consistent with global efforts to reduce greenhouse gas emissions and comply with international agreements such as the Paris Agreement.[13]

Additionally, the government has engaged with global initiatives aimed at reducing gas flaring. The World Bank's Global Gas Flaring Reduction initiative serves as a crucial reference point for Trinidad and Tobago's regulatory approach.[14] This initiative provides a platform for knowledge sharing among countries striving to mitigate flaring through innovative technologies and regulatory frameworks. By aligning its policies with successful international practices, Trinidad and Tobago aims to enhance its domestic regulations while also contributing to global climate goals.

In Trinidad's oil and gas sector, licenses are used as a regulatory tool to control flaring. These licenses typically include provisions for monitoring, reporting, and reducing flaring, as well as penalties for non-compliance. Sector Operators are required to obtain licenses from the government that outline specific conditions and limits for flaring activities. The Act encompasses a broad definition of "petroleum operations," ensuring that no such activities can be undertaken without proper regulatory approval.

10. The Petroleum Act, Chapter 62:01.
11. The Petroleum Regulations, Chapter 62:01.
12. Exploration and Production (Private Petroleum Rights) License (2018). [PDF] The Republic of Trinidad and Tobago. Retrieved from https://www.energy.gov.tt/wp-content/uploads/2018/08/Exploration-and-Production-Public-Petroleum-Rights-Licence-Offshore.pdf.
13. Government of the Republic of Trinidad and Tobago (2019), "Government Ratifies Paris Agreement." Available at: https://www.planning.gov.tt/content/government-ratifies-paris-agreement.
14. Gerner and others, "Regulation of Associated Gas Flaring and Venting: A Global Overview and Lessons from International Experience" (World Bank 2003) Report 3.

For example, the Minister permits the flaring of gas in instances where if the Licensee does not need associated Natural Gas for Petroleum Operations or sales, they must return it to the subsurface structure. If it is not economically viable to use, sell, or return the gas, the Licensee must provide the Minister with explanations supported by engineering and economic justifications.

Operators are mandated to submit annual reports detailing their flaring activities, which are then evaluated by regulatory bodies. The MEEI employs satellite technology and other monitoring tools to assess compliance levels and identify potential violations. Furthermore, Trinidad has adopted best practices from international experiences, emphasizing collaboration between governmental agencies and industry stakeholders to develop effective strategies aimed at reducing flare volumes.

Sections 17 and 32 of the Act and Regulation 94 in essence, delineate that adherence to specific legislative frameworks is not merely advisable but mandatory for those operating under such licenses. The implications of non-compliance are significant, as they can lead to liabilities that are explicitly outlined within relevant statutes. A license must include sanctions such as license revocation for failure to fulfill obligations by the licensee. Reasons for license revocation may include failure to meet work obligations, breach of terms, non-payment of stipulated amounts, bankruptcy, or misrepresentation. The Minister may[15] require the licensee to remedy breaches and pay compensation within a specified time period if the breach is deemed capable of remedy. Upon license revocation, all rights and privileges conferred by the license shall cease, except in cases where advance notice of noncompliance was given. License revocation does not absolve the licensee of any pre-existing obligations or liabilities. The President may order temporary discontinuation of operations for serious and repeated violations of license terms or laws. Authorized persons may inspect and report on operations carried out under the license as per the Minister's authorization.

Effective regulation of natural gas flaring in Trinidad and Tobago is essential for aligning national interests with global sustainability objectives. By adopting lessons from comprehensive reports like those produced by the Global Gas Flaring Reduction initiative,[16] policymakers can craft more robust regulations that not only address local challenges but also contribute positively to global climate goals. Thus, prioritizing efforts to reduce gas flaring should be seen as an urgent imperative for both environmental stewardship and economic development.

This intricate web of regulations underscores not only the importance of compliance but also highlights various stakeholders involved in managing Trinidad and Tobago's petroleum resources. The effectiveness of these regulations ultimately influences both economic stability and sustainable development within this vital sector.

However, despite having legislation in place, such as the Environmental Management Act and the Petroleum Act, flaring continues at unacceptably high levels and the effectiveness of these regulations remains questionable. The potential for Trinidad

15. *Ibid.*, 1, section 17.
16. Elvidge et al. (2018), "The Potential Role of Natural Gas Flaring in Meeting Greenhouse Gas Mitigation Targets" Volume 20 Energy Strategy Reviews 156 https://repository.library.noaa.gov/view/noaa/21009/noaa_21009_DS1.pdf https://doi.org/10.1016/j.esr.2017.12.012.

and Tobago to meet its NDCs under the Paris Agreement hinges on substantial reductions in flaring volumes. The analysis provided by recent studies[17] indicates that while global flaring constitutes less than 2 % of total NDCs targets, specific nations could leverage reductions in flaring to achieve significant environmental goals. For Trinidad and Tobago, which has historically engaged in extensive oil extraction activities, addressing natural gas flaring could not only mitigate environmental concerns but also enhance energy efficiency within its economy.

4 NATURAL GAS FLARING: ISSUES AND CHALLENGES IN TRINIDAD AND TOBAGO

Trinidad and Tobago is striving to decrease overall emissions by 15 % by 2030 from the Business As Usual baseline as outlined in the UN Framework Convention on Climate Change. The country has committed to reducing flaring through various policies, including the National Energy Policy, which emphasizes sustainable energy practices. However, implementation has been inconsistent, and flaring rates remain significant. According to Elvidge,[18] various countries have implemented regulatory frameworks aimed at reducing flaring by promoting the utilization of associated gas. Trinidad and Tobago's current regulatory landscape, however, appears fragmented, lacking comprehensive policies that align with global best practices as outlined by international partners such as Shell and BP. Despite these regulations, the enforcement and compliance mechanisms are often inadequate.

This lack of stringent enforcement and adequate monitoring mechanisms often leads to non-compliance by oil companies, undermining national efforts to meet international climate agreements. Moreover, the absence of comprehensive data collection and reporting further exacerbates the challenge, as it hinders transparency and accountability in flaring activities. Whilst the regulation of natural gas flaring in Trinidad requires stringent monitoring and reporting requirements for oil companies there is little to no enforcement.

Despite these regulatory measures, challenges remain in achieving substantial reductions in flaring rates. Economic pressures often compel companies to prioritize immediate financial returns over long-term environmental considerations. Nevertheless, ongoing efforts by the GGFR highlight the importance of fostering cooperation between governments and private entities in addressing this issue. Ultimately, a comprehensive approach combining regulation, technology adoption, and stakeholder engagement will be essential for effectively mitigating natural gas flaring in Trinidad.

To address these issues, it is imperative that Trinidad strengthens its regulatory framework by adopting best practices from countries with successful flaring reduction initiatives. Incorporating advanced technologies for real-time monitoring and reporting could significantly enhance the enforcement of flaring regulations, ensuring compliance and facilitating Trinidad's alignment with its climate objectives. Furthermore,

17. *Ibid.*, 16.
18. *Ibid.*

fostering collaboration with international organizations such as the GGFR could provide Trinidad with technical expertise and financial resources to enhance its regulatory capabilities.

Moreover, successful regulation of associated gas flaring requires comprehensive strategies that incorporate lessons learned from global practices. Trinidad's regulatory approach could benefit from adopting best practices observed in other countries with more effective flaring management systems. For instance, integrating stricter penalties for non-compliance and incentivizing companies to invest in technologies that utilize or transport excess gas could enhance compliance rates. However, the effectiveness of these penalties remains a subject of debate. Research indicates that while financial penalties can deter some non-compliance behaviors, they often fall short without robust enforcement mechanisms. This suggests that merely imposing fines is insufficient to eliminate gas flaring; rather, a multifaceted approach is essential.

The International Energy Agency (IEA)[19] argues that addressing gas flaring and methane emissions can enhance energy security by making additional natural gas available to markets. Their analysis reveals that eliminating unnecessary flaring could yield nearly 210 billion cubic meters of natural gas annually. Thus, it becomes clear that regulatory frameworks must evolve beyond punitive measures to include proactive strategies aimed at improving compliance through technological advancements and market incentives. Countries like Norway have successfully reduced their flare volumes by integrating stricter enforcement alongside innovative solutions.

Additionally, while Trinidad's NDCs under the Paris Agreement outline ambitious sustainability goals, the potential role of reducing gas flaring is not fully realized. The country possesses significant opportunities for improvement; reducing flared gas could substantially contribute to its NDCs targets. As such, a reevaluation of current regulations alongside increased collaboration between governmental bodies and private sector stakeholders is crucial for enhancing environmental outcomes and aligning with global climate objectives.

Gas flaring poses a considerable obstacle to Trinidad and Tobago's energy transition strategy, which targets a 30% decrease in carbon emissions by 2030. The practice of gas flaring involves the combustion of natural gas that cannot be processed or is uneconomical to transport. Unfortunately, this results in substantial greenhouse gas emissions, estimated at approximately 3.8 million tCO_2e annually.[20] Such emissions not only contribute to climate change but also undermine the nation's commitment to a more sustainable energy future.

Moreover, gas flaring leads to significant economic losses for Trinidad and Tobago. The unutilized natural gas could otherwise be harnessed for power generation or other downstream processing activities that could contribute positively to the

19. IEA (2022), "The Energy Security Case for Tackling Gas Flaring and Methane Leaks." OECD Publishing, Paris, https://doi.org/10.1787/251cc7bc-en.
20. Siu & Perseval. "Effective Flare and Vent Management." Paper presented at the SPE Trinidad and Tobago Section Energy Resources Conference, Port of Spain, Trinidad and Tobago, June 2016 https://doi.org/10.2118/180835-MS.

country's economy. Findings highlight that in 2015 alone, Trinidad flared approximately 10 million standard cubic feet per day of associated gas, resulting in an estimated loss of USD 7.3 million in potential revenue and the emission of around 1.5 million tons of CO_2 equivalent.[21] These figures underscore the urgent need for effective management strategies that address both economic inefficiencies and environmental concerns.

By continuing to flare large quantities of gas, Trinidad and Tobago fails to capitalize on valuable resources that could support energy diversification and economic growth. Addressing these inefficiencies is essential for achieving both environmental sustainability and economic resilience.

The implications of gas flaring extend beyond immediate financial losses; they also hinder progress toward sustainable energy practices essential for achieving Trinidad's long-term goals. The unmonetized value of even a small percentage (10%) of the difference between natural gas production and utilization amounted to over USD 18 million annually.[22] This wasted potential not only reflects poorly on operational efficiency but also contributes significantly to greenhouse gas emissions that contradict the objectives outlined in the energy transition plan.

5 RECOMMENDATIONS

To address the challenge of gas flaring in Trinidad and Tobago, it is essential to prioritize the strengthening of enforcement and compliance measures. As Trinidad grapples with increasing pressure to reduce its carbon footprint, optimizing the management of flared gas emerges as both an ecological imperative and an economic opportunity. The potential for capturing this gas could facilitate power generation, ammonia production, methanol synthesis, and refinery operations, thereby fostering sustainable development.[23] This involves empowering regulatory bodies to enforce existing laws more effectively, with a particular focus on establishing clear and significant penalties for non-compliance to serve as a deterrent.

In examining the prospects for reducing gas flaring in Trinidad, it is instructive to consider parallels with Nigeria's experience as the challenges faced are similar challenges and not unique to Trinidad. As it relates to excessive gas flaring, in Nigeria—approximately 800 million standard cubic feet per day—prompting initiatives like the Nigerian Gas Flare Commercialization Programme aimed at monetizing flared gas (Perseval, 2020). This initiative highlights not only the feasibility of capturing waste gases but also underscores the significant economic benefits that can accrue from effective utilization strategies. Such examples suggest that Trinidad could adopt innovative approaches modeled after successful international practices to mitigate its own flare-related issues.

To mitigate these challenges, Trinidad must implement effective flare management practices that prioritize capturing and re-utilizing hydrocarbons rather than

21. *Ibid.*, 7.
22. *Ibid.*
23. *Ibid.*, 18.

allowing them to be wasted through flaring. By adopting such measures, Trinidad can enhance its revenue generation while simultaneously reducing its carbon footprint, thereby facilitating a more successful realization of its energy transition goals.[24] Without addressing gas flaring comprehensively, the nation risks undermining its commitment to sustainable development and climate change mitigation.

Research indicates that upstream flaring dominates global emissions, with over 90%[25] occurring in just twenty countries including Trinidad and Tobago. The continued reliance on gas flaring undermines potential contributions to national climate targets outlined under international agreements such as the Paris Accord. The country's NDCs could significantly benefit from enhanced regulations aimed at reducing gas flaring practices. Moreover, other nations have successfully implemented more stringent regulations that have led to notable reductions in associated emissions.

While the legal framework sets out requirements for companies to minimize flaring and submit reports on flaring activities, there are significant gaps that need to be addressed. The Petroleum Act of Trinidad and Tobago serves as a critical framework for regulating the exploration and production of petroleum resources However, a significant critique arises regarding its approach to gas flaring, an environmentally detrimental practice prevalent in oil extraction operations. One of the main issues with the legal framework in Trinidad and Tobago is the lack of strict enforcement measures. Whilst sector operators are required to pay a fee for flaring above certain thresholds, it is often seen as a cost of doing business rather than a deterrent to flaring. In addition, there is limited monitoring and reporting on flaring activities, making it difficult to hold companies accountable for their flaring practices. Increasing penalties for Non-Compliance can reinforce compliance with flaring regulations. It is essential to strengthen penalties for violations. By increasing the consequences of non-compliance, a stronger deterrent effect can be created, encouraging companies to invest in measures to reduce flaring. One effective strategy could involve imposing penalties in a globally recognized currency, such as USD, GBP, CAD, or AUD, to underscore the seriousness of the violations.

The fiscal implications of fuel subsidies in Trinidad and Tobago exacerbate the problem by perpetuating a cycle of inefficient resource use and environmental degradation. These subsidies disproportionately favor higher-income earners while contributing to increased fossil fuel dependency and pollution. Reforming these subsidies could create an opportunity for better regulation of gas flaring practices, allowing for more sustainable energy consumption patterns while aligning with global emission reduction targets.

Furthermore, the current regulations do not address the cumulative impacts of flaring on the environment and public health. Studies have shown that flaring can release harmful pollutants such as sulfur dioxide and nitrogen oxides, which can

24. Nickie (2015), "A Deepwater Gas Field Development Strategy for T&T." Paper presented at the SPE Latin American and Caribbean Petroleum Engineering Conference, Quito, Ecuador, November 2015 https://doi.org/10.2118/177102-MS.
25. Elvidge (2018), "The Potential Role of Natural Gas Flaring in Meeting Greenhouse Gas Mitigation Targets." 20 Energy Strategy Reviews 152 https://doi.org/10.1016/j.esr.2017.12.012.

contribute to respiratory problems and other health issues. The legal framework should include more stringent requirements for monitoring and mitigating these impacts to protect the well-being of communities living near flaring sites.

The current legal framework falls short in addressing key issues such as enforcement, monitoring, and mitigating the impacts of flaring. It is essential for the government to review and strengthen the regulations to ensure that companies are held accountable for their flaring practices and that the environment and public health are protected. Implementing robust regulatory frameworks that limit gas flaring could position Trinidad and Tobago as a leader in sustainable energy management, setting a precedent for other nations grappling with similar challenges. By adopting such measures, Trinidad and Tobago could not only mitigate environmental harm but also enhance its economic resilience by fostering innovation in cleaner energy technologies and attracting investments aligned with sustainable development goals.

There is a need to implement specific flaring limits to address the issue of gas flaring effectively, it is crucial to establish clear and enforceable limits on flaring volumes and durations. These limits should be in line with international best practices and should take into account technological advancements in gas capture and utilization. By setting such specific limits, the industry can work towards reducing wasteful practices and improving environmental sustainability. Various jurisdictions have implemented specific legislation to regulate this practice, reflecting their commitment to mitigating its adverse effects. For instance, in Norway,[26] the Petroleum Act mandates that all gas produced during oil extraction must be utilized or reinjected unless it is technically infeasible. This stringent regulation aims to minimize flaring and underscores the country's focus on sustainable energy practices. The lack of specific quantitative limits on flaring in T&T's legislation further exacerbates this issue and highlights the need for reform. The comparison with countries like Norway reveals that robust regulatory frameworks can lead to significant reductions in gas flaring when combined with proper enforcement strategies. Thus, adopting effective measures from successful jurisdictions could enhance T&T's approach to managing gas flaring.

Norway exemplifies successful mitigation of gas flaring through its "zero flare" policy,[27] which has resulted in industry-leading low flaring intensity (Chivers 2020)[28] The Norwegian government has invested heavily in an expansive gas pipeline network and implemented strong governance frameworks that incentivize reduced emissions from oil production activities. This proactive approach not only minimizes environmental impact but also positions Norway competitively in an evolving energy market increasingly focused on sustainability. In contrast, Trinidad and Tobago's policies lag behind such initiatives, resulting in higher emissions that could jeopardize its attractiveness as a destination for investment as global energy transitions accelerate.

26. Act No. 72 Relating to Petroleum Activities, 1996, or the Norwegian Petroleum Act, 1996, prohibits gas flaring in excess of the quantities needed for operational safety unless approved by the Norwegian Petroleum Directorate (NPD).
27. Zero Flare policy, "Means That Oil and Gas Developers Are Required to Make Gas Utilisation Plans Before Carrying Out Any Field Developments."
28. Chivers (2020), Retrieved from https://capterio.com/wp-content/uploads/2020/10/20201008-Tackling-flaring-Lessons-from-the-North-Sea-final.pdf.

By investing in advanced monitoring technologies, such as satellite and drone surveillance, there can be enhanced monitoring capabilities which can significantly enhance the oversight of flaring activities. Real-time data on flaring can improve regulatory monitoring and compliance enforcement. By leveraging these monitoring capabilities, authorities can ensure that operators adhere to the established limits and minimize the environmental impact of gas flaring.

As Trinidad and Tobago navigates its energy future amidst climate change pressures and a global shift towards renewable sources, addressing natural gas flaring becomes even more critical. The economic implications are significant; reducing flare can enhance revenue from captured natural gas while mitigating environmental impacts. Therefore, concerted efforts involving government regulation, industry collaboration, and public-private partnerships will be essential to tackle this pressing challenge effectively.

Additionally, the implementation of a comprehensive monitoring system for gas flaring is crucial for providing accurate data to inform policymaking decisions. Addressing these challenges requires a concerted effort from both governmental bodies and industry players. Enhanced monitoring systems should be established to ensure that all flare activities are properly permitted and managed according to best practices outlined in contemporary literature.[29] Developing a real-time monitoring system that is transparent and accessible to the public can enhance accountability and ensure that progress toward reducing flaring is tracked and monitored effectively.

A key strategy to combat gas flaring is to foster public-private partnerships that incentivize investment in technologies for capturing and utilizing natural gas. By encouraging collaboration between the government and private companies, financial incentives such as tax breaks or subsidies can be offered to companies that invest in gas recovery systems, promoting environmentally friendly practices.

Drawing lessons from international best practices, Trinidad and Tobago can leverage successful strategies from countries like Nigeria, particularly through initiatives such as the Nigerian Gas Flare Commercialization Program (NGFCP). By adopting proven approaches, such as offering tax incentives for gas utilization projects, T&T can strengthen its efforts to reduce gas flaring.

Lastly, promoting awareness and education about the environmental impacts of gas flaring is essential to mobilize civil society and hold companies accountable for their actions. Through educational campaigns and public outreach, individuals can be empowered to advocate for better practices and push for greater accountability in the management of gas flaring in Trinidad and Tobago.

6 CONCLUSION

The context of natural gas flaring regulation in Trinidad and Tobago reveals a complex landscape marked by regulatory frameworks that are often inadequately enforced. The

29. Ramgarib-Mosadee, "Exploitation of Cased Hole Reserves in a Mature Oil Field on Land in South Trinidad." Paper presented at the SPE Trinidad and Tobago Section Energy Resources Conference, Port of Spain, Trinidad and Tobago, June 2016 https://doi.org/10.2118/180863-MS.

regulatory landscape governing oil and gas flaring in Trinidad is characterized by a mix of national policies and international commitments aimed at reducing greenhouse gas emissions. The government has implemented several initiatives aimed at curbing flaring; however, enforcement remains weak. This is particularly concerning given that Trinidad's economy heavily relies on hydrocarbon production. As such, balancing economic growth with environmental sustainability presents an ongoing challenge for policymakers.

Real-life examples illustrate the ongoing challenges, including insufficient data transparency and the negative impact on local communities. However, with targeted reforms—strengthening enforcement, improving data management, engaging communities, and learning from global best practices—T&T can make significant strides in reducing natural gas flaring and protecting both its environment and its citizens.

Additionally, whilst penalties for non-compliance in Trinidad's oil and gas sector serve as a deterrent to some extent, however, they are insufficient on their own. Effective reduction of gas flaring requires comprehensive reforms encompassing enhanced regulatory frameworks, technological innovation, and fiscal incentives tailored to encourage compliance. The experience from other nations such as Norway and Nigeria demonstrates that a collaborative approach—combining regulation with industry engagement—can significantly reduce flare volumes while simultaneously addressing broader environmental concerns.

Moreover, the potential for natural gas flaring reduction to contribute to national climate targets is significant. Research indicates that while flaring accounts for a minor percentage of global NDCs, specific countries can achieve substantial progress through targeted reductions. For Trinidad and Tobago, aligning its flaring regulations with NDCs commitments could enhance its credibility on the international stage while simultaneously addressing local environmental issues. However, achieving this requires not only governmental commitment but also collaboration with industry stakeholders to develop sustainable practices.

The deregulation of natural gas flaring in Trinidad and Tobago has become a pressing environmental and economic issue. As a major producer of liquefied natural gas (LNG), the country faces significant challenges regarding the management of associated gas flaring, which occurs when excess natural gas is burned off during oil extraction. This practice not only contributes to greenhouse gas emissions but also represents a waste of valuable energy resources. The World Bank[30] highlights that effective collaboration between public and private sectors is essential for minimizing flaring volumes, advocating for comprehensive regulations to address this issue.

Recent shifts in global demand for natural gas have further complicated the situation in Trinidad and Tobago. Post-pandemic changes have led to volatility in natural gas prices, raising concerns about economic sustainability within the sector. While the petrochemical industry significantly benefits from utilizing natural gas over electricity generation due to cost efficiency, reliance on this single resource renders the

30. *Ibid.*, 3.

economy vulnerable to external shocks. Thus, strategic investments in renewable energy sources are imperative for fostering resilience against market fluctuations.

Moreover, reducing flaring can play a crucial role in meeting climate commitments outlined by international agreements such as the Paris Agreement. Although Trinidad and Tobago's contribution to global flaring may seem minor compared to larger nations, localized efforts could yield substantial environmental benefits while enhancing compliance with NDCs.[31] Therefore, integrating these practices into national policies is essential for achieving both economic stability and environmental sustainability.

Deregulated natural gas flaring in Trinidad and Tobago is having far-reaching impacts on the environment, public health, and economy of the country. It is imperative for the government to strengthen regulation and enforcement mechanisms to reduce flaring levels and promote sustainable energy practices in the oil and gas industry. Collaboration between industry stakeholders, regulatory bodies, and local communities is essential to address the challenges posed by flaring and ensure the long-term sustainability of Trinidad and Tobago's natural resources.

In examining the circumstances under which a minister may grant permission for continued flaring, it is crucial to consider regulatory frameworks that govern this practice. The World Bank's Global Gas Flaring Reduction initiative underscores the necessity for stringent regulations and public-private partnerships to mitigate the adverse effects of gas flaring. Such collaborations involve stakeholders from various sectors, including government bodies and major oil companies like Shell and BP, highlighting a collective responsibility to address this issue effectively.

The existing framework presents several barriers and wider institutional challenges that hinder investment in sustainable alternatives. A minister's decision to permit continued flaring should therefore be informed by a commitment to reforming these regulatory structures while prioritizing environmental sustainability and community welfare.

While Trinidad and Tobago has made strides in addressing natural gas flaring, significant challenges remain. T&T can identify critical gaps in its legislation and enforcement mechanisms. Implementing robust monitoring systems, strengthening regulatory frameworks, and fostering collaboration between stakeholders will be essential in reducing flaring and mitigating its environmental impact. It is imperative for T&T to take decisive action to ensure that its natural resources are utilized sustainably, benefiting both the environment and the economy.

For Trinidad and Tobago to effectively reduce gas flaring rates, investment in infrastructure will be crucial for facilitating these technologies' implementation. Overall, there exists a compelling argument for reducing gas flaring in Trinidad through strategic policy measures that prioritize both environmental sustainability and economic viability.

The implications of Trinidad and Tobago's high flaring rates extend beyond environmental concerns; they also represent unmonetized economic potential. By

31. Global Gas Flaring Reduction Public-Private Partnership.

adopting effective flare management strategies akin to those employed by leading countries like Norway, Trinidad and Tobago could significantly enhance its energy sector's efficiency while simultaneously contributing to global efforts aimed at reducing methane emissions. Such changes would not only bolster the local economy but also position Trinidad and Tobago favorably within the competitive landscape of international oil production and energy transition.

In conclusion, reducing gas flaring in Trinidad represents an essential step toward enhancing both economic viability and environmental sustainability within its energy sector. By adopting effective monitoring strategies along with innovative utilization methods for associated gases, Trinidad can mitigate the adverse effects of flaring practices while capitalizing on newly created revenue streams. This multifaceted approach promises not only improved resource management but also aligns with global efforts to combat climate change through reduced carbon emissions.

CHAPTER 25

Natural Gas Flaring in the United Arab Emirates*

Felipe Villasuso

1 INTRODUCTION

Natural gas flaring is the process of burning off the excess gas that is produced during oil extraction or processing. Flaring is a common practice in the oil and gas industry, but it has significant environmental and economic impacts.

Flaring contributes to greenhouse gas emissions, air pollution, noise, and waste of valuable resources. According to the World Bank,[1] in 2019, the world flared about 150 billion cubic meters of natural gas, equivalent to the annual gas consumption of Sub-Saharan Africa. In the report, it is also noted that gas flaring has significantly increased despite only a modest increase in underlying oil production.

This should be of grave global concern because there is no net zero without dramatically reducing flaring. The global oil industry must collaborate more to make good on much-publicized initiatives such as the World Bank's 'Zero Routine Flaring' initiative and the COP28-brokered 'Oil and Gas Decarbonisation Charter'.[2]

The Middle East and North Africa (MENA) region accounts for 40% of the world's flaring. In the region, flaring has increased year-on-year – apart from 2018 – to almost 6 billion cubic feet of gas per day, generating up to 300-500 million tonnes of CO_2-equivalent emissions per year. These emissions result not only from the

* This chapter reflects the personal research and opinion of its author and not necessarily the opinion of its employees.

1. *World Bank. GGFR to evolve to the Global Flaring & Methane Reduction Partnership*. https://www.worldbank.org/en/programs/gasflaringreduction/brief/ggfr-to-evolve-to-the-global-flaring-methane-reduction-partnership.
2. *Gas Flaring Is Heading in the Wrong Direction, But It's Not Too Late to Act Differently*. Available from: https://flareintel.com/insights/gas-flaring-is-heading-in-the-wrong-direction-but-its-not-too-late-to-act-differently.

combustion of gas but also from the venting, from inefficient flares, of un-combusted methane, a more potent greenhouse gas. Yet much of this is avoidable. There are many commercially attractive options to reduce flaring in MENA. The key is to use the right proven technology and to be agile in commercial structuring. And the prize could be a boost to MENA's annual revenues by up to USD 200 per second (up to USD 6.4 billion per year) by delivering wasted gas to the market by pipeline, as power or in liquid form.[3]

The benefits of reducing and eventually eliminating all gas flaring are important steps to sustain the achievement of the United Nations Sustainable Development Goals ('SDG'). As highlighted by the United Nations there are different goals that can be achieved and mapped based on the SDG framework. One common aspect of gas flaring mitigation under some of the SDGs is how local communities are affected by it. In some Arab hydrocarbon-producing countries, gas flaring occurs in remote desert areas far from human settlements, but this is not the case for all Arab producers. Furthermore, gas flaring affects not only human beings but also the whole ecosystem.

In this regard, the following SDGs are relevant to gas flaring and due to the following reasons:[4]

(1) *SDG 3 (Good health and well-being)*: Gas flaring has been proven to affect the health and well-being of communities located near flaring sites, so flaring mitigation will meet SDG 3.
(2) *SDG 7 (Affordable and clean energy)*: The recovery of flared gas and its use as a cleaner fuel (compared with other polluting fuels) to generate electricity will ensure or improve access to energy, especially for local communities and/or regions not linked to an electrical grid.
(3) *SDG 8 (Decent work and economic growth)*: The monetization of recovered gas to create projects that consume natural gas and/or liquefied petroleum gas ('LPG') extracted from associated gas will create economic growth and employment opportunities.
(4) *SDG 9 (Industry, innovation and infrastructure)*: Gas flaring reduction and elimination actions involve investment in infrastructure development. The availability of gas-fired electricity generation also facilitates the development or sustainability of small industries.
(5) *SDG 11 (Sustainable cities and communities)*: The continuous flaring of gas near communities has significantly affected them. Reducing this flaring and preferably eliminating it altogether will result in a clear improvement in these communities' environment and health.
(6) *SDG 12 (Responsible consumption and production)*: Stopping or adequately reducing the wasteful and environmentally harmful burning of gas associated

3. Hamaizia A. & Davis M., *Flaring in MENA: The Multibillion Dollar Decarbonization Lever.* Available from: https://www.chathamhouse.org/2020/07/flaring-mena-multibillion-dollar-decarbonization-lever.
4. United Nations Economic and Social Commission for Western Asia. Reducing Gas Flaring in Arab Countries A Sustainable Development Necessity. https://www.unescwa.org/sites/default/files/pubs/pdf/reducing-gas-flaring-arab-countries-english.pdf.

with crude oil production is consistent with the responsible production of hydrocarbon resources.

(7) *SDG 13 (Climate action)*: The reduction and eventual elimination of gas flaring has a direct link to climate change action, as it reduces carbon dioxide emissions. It is consistent with all climate change mitigation agreements, especially the Paris Agreement.

(8) *SDG 14 (Life below water)*: Gas flaring produces greenhouse gas emissions that lead to acid rain, which water and its marine environment.

(9) *SDG 15 (Life on land)*: The flaring of gas produces atmospheric contaminants, including nitrogen, carbon and sulphur particulate matter, hydrocarbons and ash, photochemical oxidants, and hydrogen sulphide that acidify the soil and deplete soil nutrients. b Reducing or stopping gas flaring will therefore have a significant impact on land and ecosystems close to flaring sites. This could also be relevant to SDG 6, as gas flaring could affect water supplies through acid rains.

Therefore, the structure of the chapter encompasses the context of Gas Flaring in the UAE, a review of the legal framework and relevant regulations in place, a review of the current issues, policy recommendations and conclusion.

2 CONTEXT ABOUT NATURAL GAS FLARING IN THE COUNTRY

The contribution of the MENA region is essential in order to have a decisive global impact on flaring reduction and associated gas utilization over the long run. Gas flaring in the MENA region is about 50 billion cubic meters annually, which makes it the second flaring region in the world after Russia and the Caspian region which is almost about 60 bcm. Sub-Saharan Africa flares about 35 bcm. The amount of gas flared in the Middle East alone, almost 30 bcm, could feed a 20 million-ton liquefied natural gas plant and substantially reduce environmental pollution in the region.[5]

According to Envirotech, global investigations have identified millions of tons of undeclared emissions from gas flaring in oil fields operated by giants like BP, Eni, ExxonMobil, Chevron, and Shell. These emissions significantly contribute to greenhouse gas levels, yet often go unreported due to loopholes and lax regulations in reporting standards. These practices are particularly prevalent in Iraq, Iran, and Kuwait and there have been allegations about the UAE.

Envirotech defends that while the UAE banned routine flaring two decades ago, satellite images and data analysis reveal continued flaring activities. These findings highlight a disconnect between the public environmental commitments of Gulf nations and their actual practices on the ground. Oil companies, when confronted with these

5. Mani I., *Gas Flaring and Venting in MENA: Need for Urgent Action.* Available from: https://www.ecomena.org/gas-flaring-and-venting-in-mena/.

findings, often point to industry-standard reporting methods, which only account for emissions from sites they directly operate.[6]

In the view of Afanasiev, the UAE has a long history of natural gas flaring, a practice that involves burning excess natural gas released during oil extraction, and is undertaking several efforts to achieve a green economy with the aim of achieving zero flaring of oil and gas, to include, without limitation:

(1) An offshore exploration and production company has already achieved zero flaring at its Zakum oilfields for the first time.
(2) Onshore, a gas E&P company developed a flare management strategy for its Shah Gas Development Project, with the aim of minimizing flaring from well-testing and clean-up operations.
(3) Abu Dhabi Future Energy Company ('Masdar') has accumulated knowledge on formulating policies and projects to reduce flaring and has been serving as a partner of the World Bank's Global Gas Flaring Reduction Partnership (GGFR) since 2009.
(4) To share its advanced experiences of flaring reduction, Abu Dhabi has been hosting the annual Flare Management and Reduction Summit since 2012.[7]

According to the World Bank, the Global Flaring and Methane Reduction ('GFMR') Partnership was launched as a new multi-donor trust fund focused on helping developing countries cut carbon dioxide and methane emissions generated by the oil and gas industry which was announced At COP28.[8]

According to the GFMR, the support to long-term emissions reduction projects and initiatives to access project development and financing support would be subject to the following commitments:

(1) measure and report emissions through the Oil and Gas Methane Partnership 2.0 framework;
(2) achieve near-zero absolute methane emissions by 2030 by reducing methane intensity to below 0.2%; and
(3) achieve zero routine flaring by 2030.

Such Partnership is composed of governments, companies, and multilateral organizations committed to ending routine flaring at oil production sites across the world and reducing methane emissions to the greatest extent possible along the entire oil and gas value chain.

6. *Unreported Gas Flaring Endangering Public Health in Gulf, Claims BBC.* Available from: https://www.envirotech-online.com/news/industrial-emissions/160/international-environmental-technology/unreported-gas-flaring-endangering-public-health-in-gulf-claims-bbc/61637.
7. *Efforts to Achieve Green Economy.* Available from: https://u.ae/en/information-and-services/environment-and-energy/the-green-economy-initiative/efforts-to-achieve-green-economy-.
8. *World Bank. GGFR to evolve to the Global Flaring & Methane Reduction Partnership.* https://www.worldbank.org/en/programs/gasflaringreduction/brief/ggfr-to-evolve-to-the-global-flaring-methane-reduction-partnership.

The Partnership has secured funding commitments from several governments, including Germany, Norway, the United States, and the UAE; and several international oil companies, including BP, Eni, Equinor, Oxy, Shell, and TotalEnergies.

For the last two decades, 'GGFR' provided technical advice and support to help developing countries end routine gas flaring, which is a significant source of carbon dioxide emissions. The new GFMR Partnership will build on this legacy and expand the World Bank's efforts to decarbonize the global energy system.

Building on the above-mentioned World Bank findings on gas flaring, and the International Energy Agency's 2023 assessments of global methane emissions, Vladimir Afanasiev[9] provided its own estimates for gas venting and leaking as it turned the spotlight once again on the increase in wasted volumes from the global oil and gas sector.

In the report, Vladimir reinforces that the total volume of gas flared, vented and leaked represents about 6.6% of all gas production in the world last year. It is about 1.7 times higher than the annual European imports of Russian pipeline gas before the country's invasion of Ukraine in 2022 and capturing and using the lost gas presents a 'revenue opportunity of up to USD 48 billion per year' at a conservative USD 5 per million British thermal units, and emissions reduction of between 2.6 billion and 6.8 billion tonnes of carbon dioxide equivalent. He concludes that countries with enduring policies enforced by credible and independent regulators – including Saudi Arabia, the United Arab Emirates and Norway – have done 'particularly well on reducing the flaring intensity' of their oil and gas industries.

According to research from JP Morgan,[10] the management of Gas Flaring reflects significant reduction of methane emissions which is attributed to 40% of human activity (second only to agriculture). Together, these methane emissions sources account for around 55% of operational emissions (Scope 1 and 2) from the Oil & Gas sector, which is an extremely relevant figure for the energy transition.

More recently, following the COP28 and as part of the 'Oil and Gas Decarbonisation Charter'[11] signed by 50 fossil-fuel companies, it was pledged to end gas flaring by 2030, 'zero-out' methane emissions and 'align' with net-zero by 2050.[12]

Finally, according to a commitment from the UAE First Long-Term Strategy (LTS),[13] the oil and gas, fugitive emissions and unintentional flaring will be reduced by capturing leaking and flared natural gas with clear action from national players and the

9. Afanasiev V., *Global Gas Flaring Could Be $48 Billion Opportunity, Says New Report.* https://www.upstreamonline.com/environment/global-gas-flaring-could-be-48-billion-opportunity-says-new-report/2-1-1678294.
10. *The Methane Emissions Opportunity: Our Perspective on Leveraging Technology in Continuous Improvement in the Oil & Gas Sector.* Available from: https://www.jpmorgan.com/content/dam/jpm/cib/complex/content/redesign-custom-builds/carbon-compass/JPMC_methane.pdf.
11. *COP28. Oil and Gas Decarbonization Charter.* https://www.ipieca.org/news/the-oil-gas-decarbonization-charter-publishes-its-first-report.
12. *COP28: Key Outcomes Agreed at the UN Climate Talks in Dubai.* Available from: https://www.carbonbrief.org/cop28-key-outcomes-agreed-at-the-un-climate-talks-in-dubai/.
13. The United Arab Emirates Ministry of Climate Change and Environment. The United Arab Emirates' First Long-Term Strategy (LTS). Demonstrating Commitment to Net Zero by 2050. Available from https://unfccc.int/sites/default/files/resource/UAE_LTLEDS.pdf.

UAE is well advanced in reducing fugitive emissions. The UAE already implemented a zero routine flaring policy in the early 2000s, resulting in an 89% reduction in gas flaring since the company's inception. Measures to minimize flaring include the installation of flare gas recovery systems, regular leak detection and repair (LDAR) programmes, and green completions during drilling. Furthermore, the UAE is committed to an upstream methane intensity target of 0.15% by 2025, one of the lowest targets in the Middle East.

As a result, any additional measures in this area will be expensive and are expected to be delayed until the mid-2040s. Climate action in the oil and gas industry will contribute to the UAE's advanced goal of becoming a diversified, net zero emissions energy company by 2045 (Scope 1 and Scope 2 emissions), in support of UAE's Net Zero by 2050 Strategic Initiative.

3 NATURAL GAS FLARING LEGAL FRAMEWORK

In 1978, the UAE's founding father, Sheikh Zayed, passed Law No. 8 to regulate oil and gas operations, banning routine flaring and preventing air and water pollution. The law requires the industry to use the most reliable technological methods, equipment, and materials that adhere to international standards, both in safety and efficiency.

At COP28 in 2023, the UAE launched the Oil & Gas Decarbonization Charter (OGDC) with a focus on eliminating methane emissions by 2030. Over 50 oil and gas companies, representing 40% of global oil production, committed to the OGDC.[14]

The legal framework of natural gas flaring in the UAE consists of a hierarchy of laws and regulations that are issued by different levels of government and authority. The following are the main sources of law and regulation that are relevant to natural gas flaring in the UAE:

- The Constitution of the UAE, which is the supreme law of the land and establishes the federal system of government, the distribution of powers and competencies between the federal and the emirate levels, and the principles and objectives of the state, including the protection and preservation of the environment and natural resources.
- The Federal Law No. 1 of 1972 on the Jurisdiction of the Ministries and the Powers of the Ministers, which defines the roles and responsibilities of the federal ministries and the ministers, including the Ministry of Energy and Infrastructure, the Ministry of Climate Change and Environment, and the Ministry of Industry and Advanced Technology, which are the main federal ministries that are involved in natural gas flaring regulation and management.
- The Federal Law No. 8 of 1980 on the Regulation of Labor Relations, which regulates the labour relations and conditions in the UAE, including the health

14. UAE Ministry of Foreign Affairs. *UAE Strengthens Support for Global Flaring and Methane Reduction Partnership*. Available from: https://www.mofa.gov.ae/en/mediahub/news/2024/6/7/7-6-2024-uae-global.

and safety standards and measures for the workers in the oil and gas sector, which are exposed to the risks and hazards of natural gas flaring.

- The Federal Law No. 14 of 1999 on the Civil Transactions Law, which governs the civil transactions and obligations in the UAE, including the contracts and agreements between the parties involved in natural gas flaring, such as the state, the oil and gas companies, and the gas consumers and suppliers.
- The Federal Law No. 24 of 1999 on the Protection and Development of the Environment, which is the main environmental law in the UAE, and sets the general framework and principles for environmental protection and management, including the prevention and control of environmental pollution, the conservation and rational use of natural resources, the assessment and mitigation of environmental impacts, and the imposition of environmental fees and fines.
- The Cabinet Resolution No. 37 of 2006 on the Executive Regulations of the Federal Law No. 24 of 1999, which provides the detailed rules and procedures for implementing and enforcing the provisions of the Federal Law No. 24 of 1999, including the standards and limits for air emissions, the requirements and conditions for environmental permits and licenses, the obligations and responsibilities of the environmental inspectors and violators, and the methods and techniques for environmental monitoring and measurement.
- The Ministerial Resolution No. 495 of 2009 on the Regulation of Gas Flaring and Venting, which is the specific regulation that deals with natural gas flaring and venting in the UAE, and defines the terms and concepts related to natural gas flaring and venting, the objectives and targets for reducing and eliminating natural gas flaring and venting, the roles and duties of the competent authorities and the oil and gas companies, the procedures and mechanisms for reporting and verifying natural gas flaring and venting data, and the sanctions and penalties for non-compliance with the regulation.
- Federal Decree-Law No. 11 of 2024, on the Reduction of Climate Change Effects, which sets out requirements for the competent authorities to determine annual targets for emission reduction for all sectors at the national level in accordance with the national pathway to climate neutrality[15]
- The Emirate-level laws and regulations, which are issued by the individual emirates, and supplement and complement the federal laws and regulations, especially in the areas that are under the exclusive or shared jurisdiction of the emirates, such as the ownership and management of natural resources, the regulation and supervision of the oil and gas activities, and the protection and development of the local environment.

By way of illustration, Abu Dhabi, which is the largest oil and gas producer in the UAE, has issued several laws and regulations that are relevant to natural gas flaring, such as the Law No. 23 of 1999 on the Establishment of the Environment Agency – Abu

15. Government of the UAE. *Federal Decree-Law No. 11 of 2024, on the Reduction of Climate Change Effects.* Available from: https://uaelegislation.gov.ae/en/legislations/2558.

Dhabi (EAD), the Law No. 11 of 2006 on the Regulation of the Oil and Gas Sector in the Emirate of Abu Dhabi, and the Regulation No. 42 of 2009 on the Control of Air Pollution.

In a similar vein, the United Nations Economic and Social Commission for Western Asia highlights the importance of Articles 44 to 46 of the Petroleum Resource Conservation Law, whereby a government authorization is required for associated gas flaring and the Environmental Protection Law requires that the burning of any type of fuel, including in the production of crude oil, be minimized and kept within prescribed limits.[16]

Regardless of having enacted relevant legislation, there are still challenges in developing a clear and comprehensive legal framework on gas flaring given that creating the right institutional set-up for practical coordination and cooperation of the diverse stakeholders and institutions involved in gas flaring reduction programs is another complex challenge.

The need for a comprehensive legal framework on gas flaring has its importance emphasized by the literature.[17] National visions and ultimatums on gas flaring without comprehensive laws that set out specific and measurable steps that must be taken by stakeholders across the various stages of project planning and implementation will only result in missed deadlines and eventual policy failure. It is essential for national authorities and energy regulators to support existing national gas flaring strategies and programs with clear, comprehensive, and legally binding legislative frameworks that address all the potential energy justice impacts of gas flaring across the entire project value chain.

The lack of institutional coordination and coherence between supervisory bodies and regulatory institutions leads to piecemeal approaches to addressing the different energy justice concerns associated with gas flaring, which ultimately results in regulatory failure in the overall implementation of gas flaring reduction programs. Fragmentation problems arise when different legislation delegates oversight functions to various competing agencies and ministries, without clearly delineating their scope and spheres of operations or providing a framework for their effective coordination.[18]

Based on the above description of the UAE legal framework and respective literature, it is also important to compare such legal framework with other Gas Flaring

16. United Nations Economic and Social Commission for Western Asia. *Reducing Gas Flaring in Arab Countries A Sustainable Development Necessity*. Available from: https://www.unescwa.org/sites/default/files/pubs/pdf/reducing-gas-flaring-arab-countries-english.pdf.
17. Olawuyi D., *Overcoming Regulatory Failure in the Design and Implementation of Gas Flaring Policies: The Potential and Promise of an Energy Justice Approach*. Sustainability. June 2022. Available from https://www.researchgate.net/publication/361735474_Overcoming_Regulatory_Failure_in_the_Design_and_Implementation_of_Gas_Flaring_Policies_The_Potential_and_Promise_of_an_Energy_Justice_Approach.
18. Olawuyi D., *Overcoming Regulatory Failure in the Design and Implementation of Gas Flaring Policies: The Potential and Promise of an Energy Justice Approach*. Sustainability. June 2022. Available from https://www.researchgate.net/publication/361735474_Overcoming_Regulatory_Failure_in_the_Design_and_Implementation_of_Gas_Flaring_Policies_The_Potential_and_Promise_of_an_Energy_Justice_Approach.

regulations. Hence the below paragraphs will explore the regulations and literature with respect to the United Kingdom (*'UK')* and the Kingdom of Saudi Arabia (*'KSA'*) which are developed markets in such fields for benchmarking.

In the UK, the main legislation regulating oil and gas is the Energy Act 1976 and the Petroleum Act 1998 (as amended). These are the environmental statutes regulating onshore hydrocarbon companies. The UK's Petroleum Act 1998 requires that each production facility has to preserve gas and avoid needless depletion of the ozone layer during oil exploration activities. The license to flare gas is for a long term of three years and flaring of less than 40 tons per day (Scottish Carbon Capture and Storage, 2014). The Flare Transfer Pilot Trading Scheme is another mechanism put in place to combat gas flaring in the UK through trading of gas flaring volumes.[19]

In KSA, there are currently no specific regulations for eliminating gas flaring and venting in exploration and production. Regulations and standards to monitor and impose a limit on gas vapours do exist, but they are more focused on the downstream (refining and oil storage) aspect of the oil and gas industry. Saudi Aramco and its subsidiary, the Aramco Gulf Operations Company, have taken air-quality-improvement measures seriously in the partitioned zone between Saudi Arabia and Kuwait as part of their health, safety, and environmental guidelines and best practices.

During the past two decades, Saudi Aramco has been implementing corporate wide programmes to further mitigate routine gas flaring across its oil and gas value chain. This has included revisions to its standards and the use of innovative technologies in well-cleanup operations before placing them onstream, as well as the deployment of flare-gas-recovery systems in its GOSPs and crude and gas processing complexes. Flaring at wellheads gradually has been eliminated in Saudi Aramco's upstream operations by ensuring that oil wells do not go online until gas takeaway is in place.[20]

In the UK, the principle of 'Polluter pays' is strictly applied by the court in all flaring and environmental law provisions infringement cases in the sector while in KSA there are other economic benefits such as extraction of ethane and natural gas liquids from the associated gases were derived from midstream sector to raise revenues for the government.[21]

19. Olujobi O. & Olujobi T., *Comparative Appraisals of Legal and Institutional Framework Governing Gas Flaring in Nigeria's Upstream Petroleum Sector: How Satisfactory?*. Available from: https://www.researchgate.net/publication/342663758_Comparative_Appraisals_of_Legal_and_Institutional_Framework_Governing_Gas_Flaring_in_Nigeria%27s_Upstream_Petroleum_Sector_How_satisfactory.
20. *Saudi Arabia Case Study Illustrates Road to Zero Routine Gas Flaring*. Journal of Petroleum Technology, April 2023. Available from: https://jpt.spe.org/saudi-arabia-case-study-illustrates-road-to-zero-routine-gas-flaring.
21. Olujobi O. & Olujobi T., *Comparative Appraisals of Legal and Institutional Framework Governing Gas Flaring in Nigeria's Upstream Petroleum Sector: How Satisfactory?*. Available from: https://www.researchgate.net/publication/342663758_Comparative_Appraisals_of_Legal_and_Institutional_Framework_Governing_Gas_Flaring_in_Nigeria%27s_Upstream_Petroleum_Sector_How_satisfactory.

4 CURRENT ISSUES

Despite these legal and policy measures, flaring remains a significant issue in the UAE and globally. A 2023 analysis assessed flaring in 32 oil and gas fields and found that four fields flared on at least 97% of days, with an average of just 14 days unavailable due to cloud cover. The field appears to be constantly emitting and burning polluting methane. Flaring is also costing the UAE a fortune. The country flared, vented, and leaked gas worth USD 800 million in 2022, according to a company that tracks flaring worldwide.[22]

With respect to the costs, Plant et al.,[23] defends that because flaring has long been treated as effective, there is little to no assessment of repair and maintenance costs, particularly for the issue of unlit flares. In principle, addressing unlit flares presents a simple and cost-effective CH_4 mitigation opportunity.

Further investigation into the cause of flare malfunction could further inform mitigation measures and costs. Therefore, this highlights the need for more measurements of flare performance around the globe and represents a heretofore unrealized – or at least greatly underestimated – large source of methane emissions with known mitigation options. He also stresses the lack of transparent guidelines on how such waivers and approvals are to be granted, a lack of information on how many such applications have been made and subsequently granted or denied, and a failure to align the minimum standards on permissible flaring, as well as the fines and penalties in cases of default, with international best practices, have all created a culture of approvals in which politically sensitive projects have been able to escape regulatory scrutiny.

The need for further investigation is also emphasized by the United Nations Environment Programme.[24] According to them, additional scientific work is needed to assess flaring efficiency and the prevalence of unlit flares in regions outside the United States of America. Considering the direct measurements of flares in US onshore production, regions found that both unlit flares and inefficient combustion contribute comparably to ineffective methane removal – with flares effectively destroying on average only 91% of methane. This means that nearly five times more methane is released to the atmosphere from flares than is presently assumed (i.e., based on current assumptions from the oil and gas industry that the flare is always lit and that the destruction efficiency is above 98%).

Another important issue to note is the lack of consistency and transparency in the design and implementation of energy policies which result in eventual failure. To ensure stringency and consistency, prescribed penalties and fines must be aligned with

22. *UAE Oil Fields Constantly Flaring Despite 20-Year-Old Commitment To Stop, Analysis Shows.* Available from: https://www.desmog.com/2023/11/17/uae-oil-fields-constantly-flaring-despite-20-year-old-commitment-to-stop-analysis-shows/.
23. Plant G. et al. *Inefficient and Unlit Natural Gas Flares Both Emit Large Quantities of Methane.* Science 377, 1566-1571 (2022) 30 September 2022.
24. United Nations Programme – An eye on methane The road to radical transparency. Available from: https://www.unep.org/resources/report/eye-methane-international-methane-emissions-observatory-2023-report.

benchmarks in comparative jurisdictions, while discretionary decision-making by regulators should be eliminated as much as possible or kept at the barest minimum, with reasons adduced for each decision.[25]

Insurance providers like Chubb have introduced underwriting criteria for oil & gas projects requiring methane and flaring emission reductions. The hub will assist Chubb-insured clients in navigating the introduction of underwriting criteria for oil and gas extraction projects, which require them to reduce methane emissions, a byproduct of oil and gas production that are among the most damaging greenhouse gases. The standards – the first of their kind in the insurance industry – require implementation of evidence-based plans to manage methane emissions including, at a minimum, having in place programs for LDAR and the elimination of non-emergency venting. Clients must also adopt one or more measures that have been demonstrated to reduce emissions from flaring.[26]

Finally, the United Nations Economic and Social Commission for Western Asia reinforced the same issues to the UAE. This report indicated that according to Articles 44 to 46 of the Petroleum Resource Conservation Law, government authorization is required for associated gas flaring. The Environmental Protection Law requires that the burning of any type of fuel, including in the production of crude oil, be minimized and kept within prescribed limits.[27]

5 RECOMMENDATIONS

To address the issue of natural gas flaring and accelerate the energy transition, the following initiatives can be considered best practice for the UAE:

(1) Strictly enforce existing laws and regulations prohibiting routine flaring, with penalties for non-compliance.
(2) Invest in infrastructure and technology to capture and utilize the gas that is currently flared, generating electricity or heat.
(3) Increase transparency by requiring oil and gas companies to report all flaring activities and associated emissions.
(4) Collaborate with regional partners to address cross-border air pollution caused by flaring.
(5) Diversify its economy away from fossil fuels and towards renewable energy sources.
(6) Incorporate the issue of gas flaring reduction/elimination in an integrated national energy and environmental policy, with clearly defined targets and timeframes.

25. Olawuyi D., *Overcoming Regulatory Failure in the Design and Implementation of Gas Flaring Policies: The Potential and Promise of an Energy Justice Approach*. Sustainability. June 2022.
26. *Chubb Launches Client Methane Resource Hub*. Available from: https://news.chubb.com/2023-11-15-Chubb-Launches-Client-Methane-Resource-Center.
27. United Nations Economic and Social Commission for Western Asia. *Reducing Gas Flaring in Arab Countries a Sustainable Development Necessity*. https://www.unescwa.org/sites/default/files/pubs/pdf/reducing-gas-flaring-arab-countries-english.pdf.

(7) Conduct the process of reporting and verification of associated gas flaring in full transparency and involve all stakeholders.
(8) Encourage the use of technologies that minimize associated gas flaring and improve flaring efficiency.
(9) Promulgate and/or strengthen relevant regulatory frameworks to provide incentives to mitigate gas flaring, following consultations with all relevant private and public stakeholders.
(10) Growing awareness and engagement from investors, policymakers, and insurance providers are creating momentum and opportunities for collaboration and action on flaring reduction.
(11) Identify and legally empower implementing institutions, and clearly define their roles and responsibilities.
(12) Avoid the multiplication and duplication of roles among government and regulatory agencies.
(13) Revisit upstream agreements regarding production of associated gas with crude oil to assess how gas flaring mitigation is addressed in these contracts and their consistency with policies and regulations.
(14) Draw on best international and regional practices to implement gas flaring mitigation measures.

On recommendations Nos 6 and 14 above, it should be noted that in 2022, the United Nations Programme[28] kicked off a global measurement campaign to cover all material methane emission sources of our operated assets. Non-operated assets to follow during 2023. They strongly engage with our partners to reduce methane emissions through 'LDAR' programmes, reduce flaring and optimize energy efficiency. Offsetting:

They intend to invest in nature-based solutions to compensate for unavoidable emissions. Technology: investment is being made in projects like carbon capture and storage ('CCS') and hydrogen. By accelerating hydrogen and CCS projects, we are delivering our goal to control and reduce our net carbon intensity from initial production to the final consumption of energy and the reduction of Scope 1, 2 and 3 emissions.

6 CONCLUSION

Natural gas flaring is a significant environmental and economic issue in the UAE, as well as in the global oil and gas industry which has been noted with the establishment of the Oil and Gas Decarbonization Charter as part of COP28.

Flaring contributes to greenhouse gas emissions, air pollution, noise, and waste of valuable resources and its appropriate management is key for the effective achievement of the SDGs and achievement of the commitments under the Paris Agreement.

28. United Nations Programme – An eye on methane The road to radical transparency. Available from: https://www.unep.org/resources/report/eye-methane-international-methane-emissions-observatory-2023-report.

The UAE has a legal framework that regulates natural gas flaring, but it has some limitations and gaps that need to be addressed.

The UAE has also taken some initiatives and actions to reduce natural gas flaring and utilize the associated gas, but it still faces some challenges and obstacles that hinder its progress. The UAE should adopt a comprehensive and coordinated strategy to overcome these challenges and obstacles and achieve its flaring reduction and gas utilization objectives.

The UAE is already aligning its strategy with the international best practices and standards and cooperating with regional and global partners to enhance its natural gas flaring management and has enacted new regulations, such as Law No. 11 for the Reduction of Climate Change Effects, with the goal to control and reduce the net carbon intensity from initial production to the final consumption of energy and the reduction of Scope 1, 2 and 3 emissions.

In comparison with the UK and KSA, the UAE has the potential and the opportunity to become a leader in the energy transition and the green economy, by harnessing its natural gas resources and reducing its flaring emissions.

CHAPTER 26

United Kingdom

Magnus C. Abraham-Dukuma

1 INTRODUCTION

This chapter discusses the regulatory regime relating to gas flaring in the United Kingdom (UK), with a particular focus on the applicable laws, policies, and best practices while exploring current challenges and recommendations for the future. Natural gas flaring is a significant environmental and economic issue in the oil and gas production industry, particularly in countries like the UK where offshore oil and gas extraction is critical to the energy sector. Flaring refers to the combustion of excess natural gas that cannot be processed or sold during oil extraction. While flaring can serve as a safety measure to prevent the accumulation of hazardous gases,[1] it also represents a loss of potentially marketable resources and contributes to greenhouse gas (GHG) emissions.[2]

The UK's commitment to reducing carbon emissions in alignment with its international climate obligations, such as the Paris Agreement, has placed increased pressure on the oil and gas sector to minimize flaring. Regulatory frameworks and technological advancements have improved the industry's ability to limit flaring; however, several challenges remain, particularly as the UK transitions to net-zero emissions by 2050. This ambitious binding target was set under the country's climate change legislation.[3] To guide this long-term goal, the Act mandates the establishment of legally binding carbon budgets, which are five-year caps on the total GHGs the UK can emit. As of October 2024, the UK has set its sixth carbon budget, covering the period from 2033 to 2037, which targets a 78% reduction in emissions by 2035

1. Liane Smith and Dragan Zivko Milanovic, *The Total Control of Well Integrity Management* (SPE-117121-MS) Abu Dhabi International Petroleum Exhibition and Conference, 3-6 November 2008, Abu Dhabi, UAE.
2. David T. Allen and Others, 'Carbon Dioxide, Methane and Black Carbon Emissions from Upstream Oil and Gas Flaring in the United States' (2016) 13 Current Opinion in Chemical Engineering 119, 121 https://doi.org/10.1016/j.coche.2016.08.014.
3. Climate Change Act 2008, Cap 27 2008, section 5.

compared to 1990 levels.[4] The enactment of the climate change legislation in 2008 was a landmark legislative development which marked the UK as one of the countries that have directly legislated on climate change mitigation with legally binding emissions reduction targets.[5] This ambitious target has placed pressure on all sectors of the economy, including oil and gas, to minimize their carbon footprint, making the reduction of gas flaring a priority.

Natural gas flaring in the UK is primarily associated with offshore oil production in the North Sea, which has been a key contributor to the country's energy supply since the 1960s. The extraction of oil often results in the co-production of natural gas, a valuable resource. However, in instances where infrastructure for gas capture or transport is not in place, flaring is employed as a method to dispose of the gas safely. Flaring volumes in the UK have fluctuated over the decades, with a sharp increase during periods of intense oil production followed by a decline as regulations became more stringent and technological solutions were implemented,[6] as illustrated in *Figure 26.1*.

Figure 26.1 UK Flared and Vented Gas Volumes and Value, 2012-21[7]

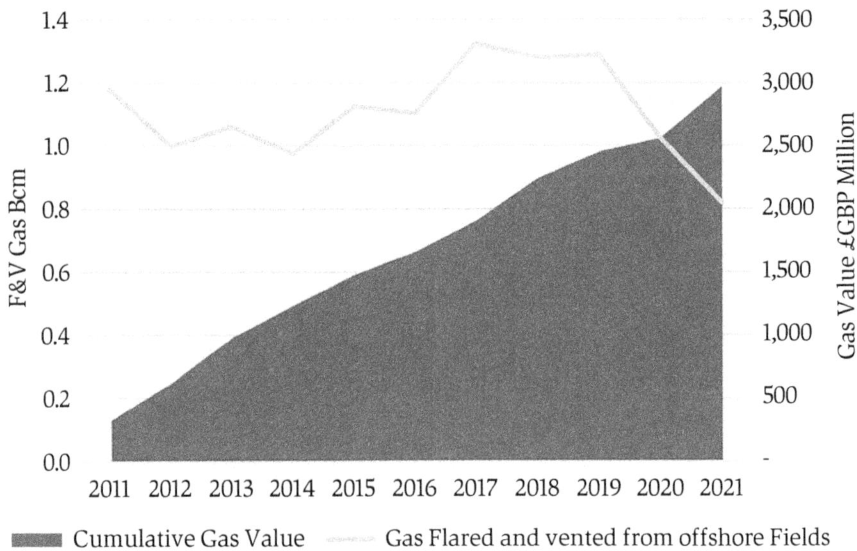

4. Committee on Climate Change The Sixth Carbon Budget (December 2020) Presented to the Secretary of State pursuant to section 34 of the Climate Change Act 2008 https://www.theccc.org.uk/wp-content/uploads/2020/12/The-Sixth-Carbon-Budget-The-UKs-path-to-Net-Zero.pdf accessed 26 October 2024.
5. Suzie Cave, *Climate Change Legislation and Targets* (Northern Ireland Assembly Research and Information Service Research Paper 135/13, 19 June 2013) at 4.
6. Andrew Reid and Arjun Flora, *UK Offshore Flaring and Venting* (March 2023, Institute for Energy Economics and Financial Analysis) available at https://ieefa.org/sites/default/files/2023-03/UK%20Offshore%20Flaring%20and%20Venting_March%202023_0.pdf accessed on 12 October 2024.
7. *Ibid.*

Historically, flaring was seen as a necessary byproduct of oil extraction. However, its environmental impacts – especially methane release and carbon dioxide emissions – have increasingly drawn public and governmental scrutiny. In recent years, the focus has shifted to minimizing routine flaring and seeking alternatives, such as gas reinjection, improved gas capture, and storage technologies. The UK's energy transition trajectory has placed a strong emphasis on reducing carbon emissions from the oil and gas sector, making the reduction of gas flaring an integral part of national climate change policy, as will be discussed in this chapter. The next sections of the chapter will consider the legal and policy frameworks for regulating gas flaring in the UK (section 2), discuss relevant best practices which other jurisdictions could learn from the UK (section 3), and examine the current challenges stymying the effective regulation of gas flaring in the UK (section 4). Concluding remarks and some recommendations are presented in section 5.

2 LEGAL AND POLICY FRAMEWORKS ON GAS FLARING IN THE UK

2.1 Petroleum and Energy Law Dimension

Broadly speaking, the regulation of gas flaring in the UK is governed by a combination of domestic laws, European Union (EU) directives (pre-Brexit), and international agreements. Particularly, speaking, the principal piece of legislation governing gas flaring in the UK is the Petroleum Act 1998,[8] which outlines the licensing regime for oil and gas exploration and extraction on the UK Continental Shelf (UKCS). The UKCS refers to the area of the continental shelf surrounding the UK, where the UK has exclusive rights to explore and exploit natural resources, such as oil, gas, and minerals. The UKCS extends into the North Sea, the North Atlantic, the Irish Sea, and other parts of the surrounding waters. These waters generally encompass the seabed and subsoil beyond the UK's territorial waters up to 200 nautical miles from the coast or to agreed boundaries with neighbouring countries. The UKCS is divided into regions such as the Northern North Sea, Central North Sea, Southern North Sea, and West of Shetland areas, each of which plays a crucial role in the UK's offshore energy sector.[9]

Meanwhile, the Energy Act of 1976[10] provides for the Oil and Gas Authority (the OGA) and its functions. There are several bodies that regulate different aspects of onshore and offshore oil and gas activities.[11] It should be noted that on 21 March 2022, the OGA adopted the 'North Sea Transition Authority (NSTA)' as its new trading

8. Petroleum Act 1998 Chapter 17.
9. Marshall Hall, *Gas Production from the UK Continental Shelf: An Assessment of Resources, Economics and Regulatory Reform* (Oxford Institute for Energy Studies Working Paper: NG 148, July 2019) at 35-40.
10. Energy Act 1976 (As amended by the Energy Act 2016) Chapter 20, Part 6 – Final provisions.
11. United Kingdom Onshore Oil and Gas Regulation (UKOOG 2017) www.ukoog.org.uk accessed 17 September 2024.

name.[12] References to NSTA in the subsequent sections of this chapter also relate to any pre-existing policy and regulatory frameworks established by the OGA.

The Petroleum Act requires petroleum operators to ensure appropriate arrangements for emissions monitoring (especially methane) and waste management plans as part of the environmental impact assessment (EIA) prior to issuance of licenses.[13] Under the Energy Act,[14] flaring is strictly controlled, and operators are required to obtain consent before undertaking flaring activities. This consent is regulated by the OGA, which oversees the licensing, development, and environmental impact of oil and gas operations.[15]

2.2 Subsidiary Legislation: Consolidated Flaring and Venting Guidance

As noted above, the Energy Act requires the consent of the OGA (now NSTA) for flaring and venting.[16] In line with these, the OGA (before its metamorphosis to NSTA) expressed its commitment to eliminating unnecessary emissions from oil and gas operations, whether onshore or offshore. Its Flaring and Venting Guidance outlines best practices for operators to follow in managing flaring and venting. Prior to 2021, the OGA had policy documents for onshore[17] and offshore[18] activities-related flaring, which stipulate strict conditions for flaring and venting consents, and only necessary as a safety mechanism or where it is impracticable to re-inject gas. In addition, it requires operators to execute their operations using customary good oilfield practices.[19] There is a theory that this common requirement is a form of transnational law.[20]

In June 2021, the OGA/NSTA consolidated and updated its Flaring and Venting Guidance,[21] which now provides a comprehensive regulatory framework to control and reduce gas flaring and venting on the UKCS. The key provisions relevant to gas flaring and venting are distilled and summarized below.

Principles and Approach

- Reduction mandate: The Guidance emphasizes the principle of minimizing flaring and venting to the lowest feasible level, with a goal of zero routine flaring and venting by 2030.[22]

12. North Sea Transition Authority, *Oil and Gas Authority changes name to North Sea Transition Authority* (North Sea Transition Authority 21 March 2022) https://www.nstauthority.co.uk/news-publications/oil-and-gas-authority-changes-name-to-north-sea-transition-authority/ accessed 15 September 2024.
13. *Ibid.*, section 4, columns 1 and 2.
14. *Ibid.*
15. Energy Act, *supra* n. 10, section 12A.
16. *Ibid.*
17. UK Oil and Gas Authority Policy on Flaring and Venting during the Production Phase, October 2016.
18. UK Oil and Gas Authority Policy Position on Offshore Flaring and Venting, 2018.
19. *Ibid.*, at 2.
20. Terence Daintith, 'Against "*Lex Petrolea*"' (2017) 10 Journal of World Energy Law and Business 1-13 https://doi.org/10.1093/jwelb/jww036.
21. Flaring and Venting Guidance, North Sea Transition Authority June 2021.
22. *Ibid.*, section 3(2).

- New developments: All new oil and gas developments must be designed with zero routine flaring and venting as a standard.[23]
- Continuous reduction requirement: Operators are expected to implement Flaring and Venting Management Plans, which should be part of broader GHG Emissions Reduction Action Plans.[24]

Regulatory Approach

- Consent regime: The NSTA requires operators to obtain consents for any flaring and venting activities. These consents are given based on specific quantity and time-bound limits, which operators must strictly adhere to. Consent variations are discouraged and permitted only under exceptional circumstances.[25]
- Decision-making criteria: In assessing consent applications, the NSTA considers factors like emissions, flare combustion efficiency, equipment maintenance, and historical flaring/venting performance.[26]

Operational Phases and Guidelines

- Extended well tests (EWT): Flaring and venting are regulated during EWTs, with operators required to minimize emissions by optimizing well test durations.[27]
- Commissioning phase requirements: During commissioning, flaring and venting are limited to between one and three months with capped gas volumes. Operators must submit commissioning plans detailing efforts to minimize emissions.[28]
- Production phase requirements: Annual consents are generally issued for stable operations, though shorter terms may apply for operations with elevated or fluctuating flaring and venting levels.[29]
- Late-life operations: Flaring and venting must be minimized through the asset lifecycle, particularly in late-life operations, and managed through lifecycle planning to reduce emissions.[30]

Technical Parameters and Source Categorization

- Source categories:[31] Flaring and venting emissions are classified into three categories, aligning with the World Bank's Zero Routine Flaring Initiative:

23. *Ibid.*, section 3(3).
24. *Ibid.*, section 3(1).
25. *Ibid.*, sections 3(2) and 4(1).
26. *Ibid.*, section 3.
27. *Ibid.*, section 4(2).
28. *Ibid.*, section 4(3).
29. *Ibid.*, section 4(4).
30. *Ibid.*, section 4(5).
31. *Ibid.*, section 5(3).

  - Category A: Routine flaring for asset operation, which generally requires facility modifications for reduction.
  - Category B: Non-routine operational flaring that can be reduced through optimization and operational changes.
  - Category C: Emergency flaring for safety-critical operations, where reduction efforts are limited to maintaining operational safety.
- Reporting requirements: Operators must submit monthly flaring and venting data through the Petroleum Production Reporting System, and the data is disclosed publicly with a time delay.[32]

Consent Variations

- Operators are discouraged from exceeding approved consent levels. In case of potential breaches, operators must inform NSTA promptly and provide a robust justification, including remediation plans or curtailment options if necessary.[33]

These provisions aim to drive continuous reduction in GHG emissions associated with flaring and venting, supporting the UK's net-zero targets while ensuring operational safety and efficiency.

2.3 Subsidiary Legislation: Offshore Petroleum Production and Pipelines

The Offshore Petroleum Production and Pipelines Regulation 1999[34] specifically regulates emissions from offshore petroleum activities. Pursuant to this regulation, the Offshore Petroleum Regulator for Environment and Decommissioning (OPRED) – a section of the UK Department for Business, Energy and Industrial Strategy (BEIS) – promulgates regulatory notices touching on emissions and discharges. One such notice relevant to the present discussion is the 2017 Guidance Note,[35] which requires offshore operators to obtain a permit from OPRED for any emissions to air or discharges to sea in the course of offshore exploration and production activities.[36] This is in addition to the requirement of an Environmental Statement (ES) prior to the commencement of operations, which, among other things, must describe proposed measures to eliminate or mitigate potential adverse environmental concerns such as emissions.[37] The key provisions relevant to gas flaring and venting in the Offshore Petroleum Production and Pipelines Regulation 1999 are distilled and summarized below.

32. *Ibid.*, section 5(2).
33. *Ibid.*, section 6.
34. Offshore Petroleum Production and Pipelines (Assessment of Environmental Effects) Regulations 1999 (As Amended), Petroleum Operations Notice No. 16.
35. Department for Business, Energy and Industrial Strategy, BEIS OPRED: The Offshore Petroleum Production and Pipelines (Assessment of Environmental Effects) Regulations 1999 (As Amended) – A Guide, September 2017.
36. *Ibid.*, at 22.
37. *Ibid.*, at 42.

EIA Requirements: Before granting consent for activities like gas flaring and venting, operators must submit an ES outlining potential environmental impacts.[38] The EIA process requires identifying, describing, and assessing significant effects on factors such as air quality and climate.

Consent Requirements for Flaring and Venting: Operators are mandated to obtain prior consent from the OGA for operations involving the extraction of petroleum, including activities related to flaring and venting. Consent is also needed for any changes to existing facilities that may influence emissions.

Operational Limits and Variations: Operators must not exceed certain thresholds for extraction, such as gas extraction exceeding 500,000 cubic meters per day, without prior consent.[39] Operators must ensure flaring and venting volumes align with these limits, and any adjustments require OGA approval.

Habitat and Biodiversity Considerations: If flaring and venting activities might impact protected habitats or species, operators must complete a Habitats Regulations Assessment in addition to the EIA.[40]

Public Disclosure and Transparency: Consent applications must be publicly accessible, and ESs are required to include non-technical summaries for public understanding. Moreover, the Secretary of State may mandate additional disclosures if the project affects transboundary areas with environmental sensitivity.[41]

Conditions for Minimizing Environmental Impact: The Regulations empower the Secretary of State to impose conditions on consents to mitigate adverse environmental effects, such as stipulating technology use or operational practices to reduce emissions.[42]

These provisions establish a regulatory framework to monitor and control gas flaring and venting, ensuring compliance with environmental standards and supporting the UK's climate and environmental objectives.

2.4 Subsidiary Legislation: Offshore Combustion Installations Regulations

The OPRED also implements the UK Offshore Combustion Regulations,[43] which is originally a transposition of the EU Industrial Emissions Directive (IED)[44] for the control of industrial atmospheric emissions. The Offshore Combustion Installations Regulations established several key provisions relevant to gas flaring and venting, particularly through pollution prevention and control measures. The key provisions

38. Offshore Petroleum Production and Pipelines Regulations, *supra* n. 34, section 3A.
39. *Ibid.*, section 4.
40. *Ibid.*, section 3A.
41. *Ibid.*, section 5.
42. *Ibid.*, section 5(7).
43. The Offshore Combustion Installations (Pollution Prevention and Control) Regulations, Statutory Instrument No. 971 of 2013.
44. Directive 2010/75/EU of the European Parliament and of the Council on Industrial Emissions (IPPC).

relevant to gas flaring and venting in the Regulations are distilled and summarized below.

Permit requirement for combustion installations: Operators must obtain a permit from the Secretary of State to operate any offshore combustion installation.[45] This permit includes conditions specific to emissions and waste management, emphasizing that operations must minimize pollution, including from gas flaring and venting.

Best available techniques (BAT) requirements: Permits require the use of the BAT to prevent or reduce emissions.[46] This ensures that operators apply the most effective methods to control emissions from flaring and venting, aligning with environmental standards and minimizing environmental impact.

Emission limit values (ELVs): For pollutants likely to be emitted in significant quantities, such as those from flaring, the regulations enforce ELVs within permits.[47] ELVs aim to control the total mass of emissions, considering factors like the pollutant's nature and potential to cause pollution across mediums (e.g., air and water).

Monitoring and reporting requirements: The regulations mandate continuous monitoring of emissions, including those resulting from flaring and venting, with detailed documentation to verify compliance with ELVs.[48] Operators must report these emissions to the Secretary of State regularly, ensuring transparency and accountability.

Accident and incident management: In cases of significant environmental impact from incidents or accidents (including emergency flaring events), operators are required to inform the Secretary of State immediately.[49] Measures must be taken to mitigate any environmental damage and prevent recurrence.

Conditions for operational phases: Specific requirements are imposed on start-up and shutdown phases, with controls to minimize flaring and venting emissions during these times.[50] This includes minimizing start-up and shut-down durations to reduce the environmental impact.

Public access to permit information: Permit applications, EIAs, and related documents are made publicly accessible.[51] This provision enhances transparency and enables public oversight of gas flaring and venting activities in offshore installations.

These regulations collectively support the reduction of environmental impacts from gas flaring and venting, reinforcing the UK's commitment to environmental protection in offshore oil and gas operations.

2.5 Complementary Environmental Law Position

The Environmental Protection Act 1990 (EPA 1990)[52] also plays a role in the regulation of gas flaring, particularly through its provisions on pollution control. Operators must

45. The Offshore Combustion Installations Regulations, *supra* n. 43, sections 3 and 4.
46. *Ibid.*, sections 7(3)(a), 9(1)(b) and (d), 3(2) (a) and (b) and Schedule 1 to the Regulations.
47. *Ibid.*, sections 9(2)(b) and (d), 9A(2)(d)-(e), and (g), 9B and 10.
48. *Ibid.*, sections 4(2), 9(2)(c)-(e), 9A(2)(b), (d) and (g).
49. *Ibid.*, sections 7(3)(f), 23, 28 and Schedule 1.
50. *Ibid.*, sections 9A and 13.
51. *Ibid.*, sections 5(2)(b), 20(2)(b) and (c), (4)(b), 21(2), 23(4), 39.
52. Environmental Protection Act 1990, United Kingdom Public Genera Acts c. 43.

ensure that flaring does not result in emissions that exceed statutory limits or cause harm to the environment. There are specific ways through which the EPA 1990 influences gas flaring regulation, including the following:

Integrated Pollution Control (IPC): One of the key provisions of the EPA 1990 was the introduction of IPC, which required operators to use the 'best available techniques not entailing excessive costs' (BATNEEC) to minimize environmental impacts. For the oil and gas sector, this means companies must implement feasible measures to reduce gas flaring. Although this framework was later replaced by Integrated Pollution Prevention and Control (IPPC)[53] in the early 2000s, it laid the groundwork for subsequent regulations.

Environmental Permits: Under the EPA 1990, companies must obtain environmental permits for activities with pollution potential, such as gas flaring.[54] These permits specify conditions for operation, including limits on emissions, requirements for monitoring, and obligations to reduce waste. In cases where flaring is necessary, operators are required to report emissions data, ensuring transparency and accountability for the environmental impacts.

Pollution Control Standards: The EPA 1990 also enabled the setting of pollution control standards, allowing the government to establish specific thresholds for emissions, including those from flaring.[55] This regulatory authority provides a legal basis for imposing fines or other penalties if operators exceed the allowed limits.

EIA Requirements: The Act laid a foundation for EIAs, which became more prominent in later legislation. Before undertaking projects with potential environmental impacts, such as drilling operations that may involve flaring, companies must assess and mitigate negative effects. This practice, established in part by the EPA 1990, requires consideration of alternatives to flaring, such as gas reinjection or capture.

Public Health Protection Requirements: The EPA 1990 emphasizes protecting human health from pollution. Gas flaring releases not only GHGs but also pollutants that can harm local communities. The Act supports monitoring and reporting mechanisms to ensure that flaring activities comply with health-based standards, thus indirectly controlling the frequency and intensity of flaring in populated areas.

Since the EPA 1990, regulations on gas flaring in the UK have been further tightened under the IPPC Directive, the Environmental Permitting Regulations, and the UK's Climate Change Act. These frameworks, building on the EPA's foundations, now enforce more stringent rules on gas flaring, prioritizing emissions reduction, climate goals, and health protections.

3 BEST PRACTICES AND LESSONS FROM THE UK

From the foregoing discussion, certain best practices could be distilled from the UK's approach to regulating gas flaring and venting.

53. *Ibid.*, Part I Integrated Pollution Control and Air Pollution Control by Local Authorities.
54. *Ibid.*, section 28.
55. *Ibid.*

3.1 Permit System with Strict Emission Limits

As evinced in the discussion, the UK requires operators to obtain permits for flaring and venting, which come with specific conditions tailored to each facility's emissions profile. This ensures that every flaring activity is controlled and monitored under legally enforceable limits, driving accountability. For other regions, implementing a similar permit system can enable more tailored regulatory oversight and prevent excessive emissions. A complementary approach to the permit system is the enforcement of ELVs on pollutants from flaring, which are determined based on the environmental and health impacts of emissions. Establishing strict ELVs encourages operators to adopt emission-reducing practices and technologies to meet the set limits. Replicating ELV standards can help other countries drive emission reductions systematically and consistently.

3.2 Integration with Climate Targets and Zero Flaring Goal

The UK integrates its flaring policies with national and international climate commitments, such as the net-zero 2050 goal discussed as part of the country's climate governance architecture. This holistic approach ensures that flaring regulations contribute to broader sustainability targets. Aligning flaring policies with climate goals can help other countries achieve emissions reductions in line with global environmental targets, adding coherence to policy frameworks. Similarly, the UK is a signatory to the World Bank's initiative to eliminate routine flaring by 2030.[56] This initiative was launched in 2015 and commits member oil companies and governments to end routine flaring no later than 2030. The Initiative aims to support cooperation between all relevant stakeholders so that solutions to gas flaring can be found through appropriate regulation, application of technologies, and financial arrangements.[57] As part of its commitment to this initiative, the UK aims for zero routine flaring by 2030, aligning with international climate goals. Setting a definitive target timeline provides a clear pathway for gradual reduction and allows operators to plan accordingly. A clear phase-out timeline helps drive investment in flaring alternatives, such as gas capture and reinjection and makes the transition more manageable for operators.

3.3 Emphasis on BAT and Technologies

Requiring the use of BAT forces operators to adopt the latest and most effective methods to control flaring emissions. This requirement promotes technological innovation and environmental responsibility. For other jurisdictions, mandating BAT can drive continuous improvement, as operators must regularly review and upgrade

56. World Bank, *Zero Routine Flaring by 2030*, https://www.worldbank.org/en/programs/zero-routine-flaring-by-2030.
57. *Ibid.*

technology to reduce their environmental footprint. Additionally, technological advancements, such as flare gas recovery units (FGRUs) and vapour recovery systems, have enabled operators to capture more gas for sale or reinjection, reducing the need for flaring. One of the most effective methods for reducing flaring is re-injection into oil reservoirs (gas capture and reinjection). This technique not only minimizes emissions but also helps maintain reservoir pressure, enhancing oil recovery. As part of its commitment under the Zero Routine Faring by 2030 initiative,[58] the UK is requiring operators to implement technologies that capture or utilize associated gas rather than flaring it as waste.

3.4 Monitoring, Reporting, and Transparent Public Disclosure

As demonstrated above, the UK regulations mandate continuous monitoring of flaring emissions, along with frequent reporting to authorities. This practice improves transparency and helps regulators track compliance over time. Other countries can adopt robust monitoring and reporting protocols to ensure real-time compliance, enabling rapid responses to any issues or non-compliance. Similarly, the regulatory system mandates that permit applications, environmental data, and compliance reports be publicly available. This level of transparency enhances public trust, encourages operators to maintain high standards, and enables third-party scrutiny. Making environmental data accessible to the public can foster an atmosphere of shared responsibility and motivate companies to perform better.

3.5 EIA and Emergency Response

The UK regulatory system requires EIAs for new projects involving flaring. EIAs help to identify and mitigate potential environmental impacts before a project begins, reducing harm from the outset. Implementing mandatory EIAs for new developments elsewhere could similarly protect the environment by anticipating and mitigating flaring impacts. Additionally, operators are required to notify authorities immediately following any incident or accident involving significant flaring emissions. Operators are also required to implement measures to mitigate environmental impact and prevent recurrence. Establishing clear emergency protocols and accountability can ensure that flaring incidents are managed efficiently, reducing long-term environmental harm.

4 CURRENT CHALLENGES RELATED TO GAS FLARING IN THE UK

Despite the progress made in reducing gas flaring, multiple challenges remain, cutting across infrastructure, technological, economic, and regulatory constraints. These are discussed considerably below.

58. *Ibid.*

4.1 Infrastructure Constraints

Managing gas flaring in the UK, particularly on the UKCS, faces significant infrastructure constraints that impact the ability to minimize or eliminate flaring. These constraints include limitations in gas capture, processing, transportation, and storage infrastructure, which are crucial for sustainable management of associated gas.[59] So, first, there is the challenge of limited gas capture and storage infrastructure. For oil fields with associated gas, reinjecting gas into the reservoir is an effective way to avoid flaring. However, many older facilities on the UKCS lack reinjection capabilities, which limits the operators' ability to store the gas. Retrofitting these facilities is costly and technically challenging, especially for ageing platforms. Gas storage infrastructure, both offshore and onshore, is equally limited in the UK. This restricts the ability to temporarily store gas during periods of low demand or when transport facilities are unavailable, which often results in flaring as a temporary solution.

Second, there is the challenge of ageing and unsuitable infrastructure. Many offshore platforms in the North Sea were constructed decades ago without gas capture and transport in mind, as flaring was more acceptable at the time. Retrofitting these platforms to capture and transport associated gas is often technically and economically unfeasible, especially in late-life assets. As North Sea fields near the end of their productive life, the high cost of upgrading old infrastructure to meet current environmental standards discourages operators from investing in flaring reduction technologies. With limited economic incentives, operators may prioritize short-term solutions, such as controlled flaring, over costly retrofits.

Third, there are insufficient processing facilities. Offshore processing facilities are often limited in their ability to handle the full volume of gas produced, particularly if there is a high concentration of contaminants. This lack of processing capacity contributes to flaring since unprocessed gas cannot be safely or economically transported to shore. Efficient transportation of gas to onshore facilities requires compression to maintain pipeline pressure. Many older offshore installations lack adequate compression facilities, making it difficult to transport gas over long distances or integrate it into existing pipelines, leading to flaring when production exceeds processing and compression capabilities.

Fourth, there are pipeline capacity and connectivity issues. Pipeline networks for gas transportation in the North Sea are limited, especially in more remote fields or those far from existing pipeline routes. Without sufficient pipeline connections, capturing and transporting associated gas becomes a logistical and financial challenge, leading operators to flare the gas instead. Even when pipeline connections exist, capacity constraints can hinder operators' ability to transport gas. Pipelines may already be operating near capacity, especially during high-demand periods, leaving no room for the additional gas produced as a byproduct of oil extraction. This issue is exacerbated when multiple operators share pipeline access, leading to bottlenecks.

59. R. Jamie Stewart, *A Review of Flaring and Venting at UK Offshore Oilfields* (Scottish Carbon Capture & Storage Working Paper 11, November 2014) at 4 and 11.

4.2 Technological Limitations

There are several technological limitations that hinder efforts to capture, process, and utilize associated gas efficiently. This is one area that has received considerable attention in literature for regulatory attention in the UK.[60] As highlighted above, the North Sea's complex and ageing infrastructure, along with the unique challenges of offshore operations, creates barriers to implementing the latest technologies in gas flaring reduction. One of such challenges is gas compression technology limitation. Compressing gas for transport or reinjection requires specialized equipment capable of withstanding offshore environmental conditions. High compression demands and the need for robust, corrosion-resistant materials make compression units for offshore use more costly and complex to install. Gas compression requires substantial energy, and offshore facilities often rely on gas-fired power, which can increase emissions and necessitate flaring. Alternative power sources like electrification from renewable sources are still in the early stages offshore, limiting the viability of widespread gas compression without increasing emissions.

Second, and to add to the above discussion regarding gas re-injection, reinjecting gas back into reservoirs is a feasible alternative to flaring, but it requires advanced technology and equipment for pressurization, injection, and monitoring. High-pressure injection equipment must be carefully managed to avoid damaging the reservoir, and many existing facilities lack the space or design for this equipment. Reinjection relies on the presence of suitable reservoir formations, which may not be available or geologically feasible at every location. Additionally, accurately maintaining reservoir pressure and avoiding operational hazards can be technically challenging, especially for fields with irregular pressure requirements.

More so, there is room for improving the availability and use of monitoring and emissions quantification technologies. Monitoring gas flaring emissions accurately requires advanced sensing and measurement technologies, such as infrared cameras or specialized gas flow meters, which can be difficult to deploy on offshore platforms. Limited space and challenging environmental conditions impact the performance of these technologies, reducing accuracy. Advanced emissions data integration technologies, which provide real-time analysis and feedback, are not widely adopted offshore due to high costs, connectivity issues, and installation challenges. This limits operators' ability to monitor flaring effectively and adjust operations in real time to reduce emissions.

Furthermore, there are energy-efficient technology and power constraints. Offshore installations typically use gas turbines powered by associated gas, which leads to a paradox: reducing flaring can sometimes increase the use of gas-fired power to generate energy for flaring reduction technologies, such as compression and reinjection. Until offshore renewable integration or electrification solutions are widely implemented, operators face limitations in adopting energy-intensive flare reduction technologies. Electrifying offshore installations with renewable power would reduce

60. Hall, *supra* n. 9, at 8 and 14.

dependency on gas-fired power, indirectly reducing flaring. However, connecting installations to renewable power sources like offshore wind is technically challenging and costly, especially for ageing facilities not originally designed for electrical power infrastructure.

4.3 Economic and Technology Scalability Constraints

The economics of oil and gas production play a significant role in determining the extent of flaring. In periods of low oil prices, operators may be less willing to invest in costly flaring reduction technologies. Additionally, the decommissioning of North Sea platforms presents its own challenges, as operators may prioritize short-term cost savings over long-term environmental goals.

Amidst the economic realities, there is the possibility of scaling emerging technologies such as hydrogen conversion and utilization technologies, and carbon capture and storage (CCS). Converting associated gas into hydrogen for onsite use or transport is a promising area of innovation. However, the technology to produce and store hydrogen offshore is in the early stages and faces scalability issues, particularly in terms of safety and cost. It requires specialized infrastructure, which is often infeasible on existing platforms. Similarly, while CCS is a valuable technology to mitigate emissions, offshore CCS are still under development and face significant technological and logistical barriers. Injecting CO_2 into suitable reservoirs is complex, requiring monitoring and management technologies that are not yet broadly available or financially viable for many operators.

Other advanced technologies for reducing flaring, such as gas-to-liquid (GTL) systems, and compression, demand significant upfront investment. Operators, especially smaller firms, may not have the capital resources required to implement these technologies, and the high cost can deter investments in flaring reduction. The cost of advanced technology implementation often outweighs the potential revenue from captured associated gas, particularly in marginal or late-life fields, coupled with a lack of viable gas markets.[61] This creates a financial disincentive to adopt flaring-reducing technologies, limiting their widespread adoption across the industry.

4.4 Regulatory Constraints

Although the regulatory framework for flaring in the UK is robust, enforcement remains a challenge. Limited resources and personnel can hamper the ability of regulators to monitor flaring activities comprehensively. Moreover, operators may seek exemptions or extensions to flaring permits, particularly in cases where infrastructure upgrades are deemed economically unfeasible. There are several specific regulatory constraints to consider. First, there is economic incentive misalignment. The costs associated with implementing gas capture, reinjection, or processing technologies can be prohibitive, especially for smaller operators or those nearing end-of-life asset stages.

61. Reid and Flora, *supra* n. 6, at 4.

This economic burden creates a misalignment with regulatory goals, as operators may prioritize cost-cutting over compliance when enforcement is less likely or costly penalties are minimal. Financial penalties for non-compliance may be insufficient to deter flaring, especially when the cost of compliance significantly outweighs potential fines. Without sufficiently robust penalties, operators may opt to accept penalties as a cost of doing business rather than invest in costly upgrades to reduce flaring.

Regulatory fragmentation is also evident in the UK regulatory ecosystem for managing flaring. Flaring regulation in the UK involves several entities, including the NSTA, the Department for Energy Security and Net Zero, and local environmental agencies. Overlapping jurisdictions can create regulatory confusion, making it challenging for operators to navigate compliance requirements and for authorities to coordinate enforcement effectively. These different regulatory bodies may have varying priorities (e.g., environmental conservation, energy production, or economic development), leading to conflicting enforcement strategies. For example, while the NSTA focuses on emissions reduction, other departments might prioritize energy security, resulting in inconsistent approaches to enforcement that can weaken flaring regulation.

Third, there are resource constraints within regulatory bodies. Enforcing advanced flaring regulations requires specialized technical expertise in emissions measurement, gas handling, and environmental compliance. Regulatory agencies may face challenges in retaining or acquiring the expertise needed to assess compliance with complex flaring reduction technologies, which can hinder enforcement efficacy. Regulatory bodies, such as the NSTA may face staffing and budget constraints that limit their capacity for conducting regular inspections and thorough assessments. This constraint can lead to less frequent monitoring, particularly on smaller or more remote installations, increasing the risk of undetected non-compliance.

Fourth, there seems to be a challenge of policy conflicts with economic and energy goals in the UK, as there could be in many other countries. Two key themes come to sharp focus – balancing flaring reduction with energy security, and regulatory concessions for marginal or late-life fields. Regulatory bodies face the challenge of balancing flaring reduction targets with the UK's energy security and economic stability, especially given the fluctuating demand for oil and gas. In some cases, regulators may grant flaring exemptions to ensure production continuity, which can undermine the integrity of flaring regulations. For smaller fields or assets nearing the end of their operational life, strict enforcement of flaring regulations may lead to premature decommissioning, affecting the economic viability of these fields. Regulators may therefore grant concessions to avoid field shutdowns, which can conflict with environmental targets and create a precedent for exceptions that weaken overall enforcement.

5 CONCLUSION

In conclusion, the UK's efforts to regulate gas flaring underscore its commitment to reducing environmental impacts and aligning with ambitious climate targets, including achieving net-zero emissions by 2050. The regulatory framework established through laws such as the Petroleum Act 1998, Energy Act 1976, and the EPA 1990, along with recent updates in the NSTA's guidance, provide a comprehensive basis for managing and mitigating flaring. By mandating the integration of BAT, ELVs, and robust monitoring and reporting requirements, the UK has cultivated a proactive approach that could serve as a model for other oil-producing nations.

However, the UK still faces considerable obstacles in fully achieving its zero-flaring goals. The existing infrastructure constraints in older offshore fields and the high costs associated with technological retrofits pose a major challenge to reducing flaring. Technological limitations, particularly regarding gas compression and reinjection, continue to hinder the efficient utilization of associated gas. Economic and regulatory constraints further complicate these efforts, as the costs of implementing advanced flaring reduction technologies can be prohibitive, particularly for smaller operators or those in late-life asset stages. The fragmentation within the regulatory framework and limited resources for enforcement weaken the otherwise stringent regulatory mandates.

To advance toward a zero-flaring future, the UK should consider adopting a multifaceted approach. Increased government investment in infrastructure, especially in gas capture and transportation facilities, would alleviate some of the physical limitations impeding emissions reductions. Economic incentives, like tax breaks or carbon credits, could encourage operators to adopt flaring reduction technologies even in economically challenging fields. Strengthening regulatory oversight with adequate resources and staff to monitor and enforce compliance would reinforce adherence to flaring limitations. Additionally, continued technological innovation will be essential, with ongoing research into enhanced reinjection methods and offshore hydrogen and carbon capture technologies providing longer-term solutions. Collaborating internationally through initiatives like the World Bank's Zero Routine Flaring by 2030 initiative can help the UK share insights and access global best practices, positioning it as a leader in sustainable oil and gas production.

By addressing these challenges comprehensively, the UK cannot only contribute significantly to reducing global GHG emissions but also ensure that its energy production sector remains both economically viable and environmentally responsible, supporting broader national and global climate commitments.

CHAPTER 27

United States

Keith B. Hall

1 INTRODUCTION

Oil wells produce oil, but along with the oil, many oil wells also produce "associated" natural gas, or water, or associated gas and water.[1] In such cases, the operator will separate the oil from other substances by density—much in the same way that, in a bottle of oil and vinegar salad dressing, the vinegar (which is mostly water) will rest on the bottom, the vegetable oil will float on the water, and a layer of air will be located above the liquid layers.[2]

In some cases, if an oil well produces natural gas, the operator of the oil well will routinely vent the natural gas to the atmosphere or send it to a flare, rather than using the gas or selling it. As between venting and flaring, flaring will often be preferable because it can be safer than venting gas and because natural gas has a higher greenhouse gas potential than the carbon dioxide that would result from the combustion of the natural gas.[3] But natural gas can be a valuable commodity and neither venting nor flaring makes use of that value. So why do operators sometimes flare gas?

Often, an operator will drill a well that is capable of producing marketable quantities of oil, along with associated natural gas.[4] There are multiple practical options for transporting oil. It can be transported by tanker truck, railcar, or barge, as

1. Norman J. Hyne, *Nontechnical Guide to Petroleum Geology, Exploration, Drilling & Production* (3rd edn PennWell 2012) 375.
2. *Ibid.*, at 375-378.
3. U.S. Environmental Protection Agency, "Basic Information about Oil and Natural Gas Air Pollution Standards" (stating that methane, the main component of natural gas, is "a potent greenhouse gas with a global warming potential more than 25 times that of carbon dioxide." https://www.epa.gov/controlling-air-pollution-oil-and-natural-gas-operations/basic-informatio n-about-oil-and-natural accessed September 16, 2024).
4. Norman J. Hyne, *Nontechnical Guide to Petroleum Geology, Exploration, Drilling & Production* (3rd edn PennWell 2012) 375.

well as by pipeline or ocean-going tanker. Further, oil is relatively easy to store. If the operator is going to periodically transport oil via truck, rail, or barge, the operator can build storage tanks at the site of the well to store oil between shipments.[5] However, natural gas is difficult to store. It is also more difficult to transport. Typically, it can only be economically transported in significant quantities by pipeline or by liquefied natural gas tankers, but the facilities to liquefy natural gas are extremely expensive.

Thus, the operator may be able to economically deliver the oil that the well can produce to a willing buyer, but the operator may not be able to deliver the natural gas to a willing buyer. Thus, the operator has a choice when a well will produce both oil and associated natural gas—shut in the well until the natural gas can be marketed (which may not be possible for many years to come) or produce and sell the oil, while simultaneously producing and flaring the gas.

Often, from the operator's perspective, it will make economic sense to produce and sell oil from a well that will produce oil and associated gas, while flaring the gas. Thus, most routine flaring of natural gas involves the flaring of associated gas that is co-produced with oil. Certainly, there are occasions when an operator drills a well that is capable of producing gas only, or mostly gas, and there is no way to get the gas to a market, the operator has little or no incentive to operate the well because the well will be producing little or no liquid hydrocarbons. Therefore, the operator will just shut-in the well until (if ever) it is economically feasible to market the gas that the well can produce.

Around the world, "routine flaring" of natural gas has become a concern. Here, "routine flaring" typically means the ongoing flaring of associated natural gas from an oil well during the production of oil, as opposed to flaring of gas during the initial drilling and completion of the well, testing of the well, while performing maintenance on the well, or in emergency situations. There are two main objections to routine flaring—first, it wastes a valuable natural resource, and second, it can have adverse environmental impacts, including climate change impacts. The World Bank, various nongovernmental organizations, and others have campaigned to stop routine flaring of associated natural gas.[6]

2 CONTEXT FOR NATURAL GAS FLARING IN THE U.S.

The United States has a mature oil and gas industry. It is the largest producer of petroleum[7] and the largest producer of natural gas in the world[8] and also is one of the

5. *Ibid.*, at 382, 385.
6. *See, e.g.*, World Bank, "Zero Routine Flaring by 2030" https://www.worldbank.org/en/programs/zero-routine-flaring-by-2030 accessed September 16, 2024.
7. U.S. Energy Information Administration, "Today in Energy: United States Produces More Crude Oil Than Any Country, Ever" (*Today in Energy*, March 11, 2024) (U.S. has been world's largest crude oil producer since 2018) https://www.eia.gov/todayinenergy/detail.php?id=61545 accessed September 16, 2024.
8. International Energy Agency, "North America: Energy systems of North America" (U.S. is world's largest producer of natural gas) https://www.iea.org/regions/north-america accessed September 16, 2024.

largest consumers of hydrocarbons. The country has well-developed markets for the sale of natural gas and an extensive network of natural gas pipelines, though there are some parts of the country where pipeline capacity at times is insufficient to meet market demand for gas. Further, although the parts of the country with oil and gas activity tend to have well-developed pipeline networks, there nevertheless are occasions when an operator drills a well that is capable of producing oil, along with associated gas, and there is not a nearby natural gas pipeline. Moreover, in the last couple of decades, there have been examples of oilfields that have seen rapid increases in crude oil production, along with associated gas. In some cases, there was some natural gas pipeline capacity available, but not sufficient capacity to handle the surge in production. Additional natural gas pipeline capacity was eventually constructed, but for a time there was a significant increase in flaring in such fields as the Bakken in North Dakota, the Permian in West Texas and the eastern portion of New Mexico.

As will be discussed in more detail in the next section, the law relating to natural gas flaring in the U.S. has some unique features and complexities. There are a few reasons for this. First, in the U.S., the general rule is that the right to explore for and produce minerals is privately owned, rather than being owned by the sovereign. Second, the "conservation" laws that govern the oil and gas industry—that is, the laws that seek to encourage efficiency and discourage or prohibit wasteful exploration and production practices—tend to be state law, rather than federal law, and can be different as between the different states.

Third, the environmental laws that regulate oil and gas activity in order to minimize adverse environmental impacts have been evolving and changing. Many of the environmental laws are federal laws and therefore are generally uniform across the country, but in recent years these have been changing from one Presidential administration to the next.

3 NATURAL GAS FLARING LEGAL FRAMEWORK IN THE U.S.

In the United States, there are various types of laws that discourage or restrict flaring of natural gas. These include: (1) private law; (2) state conservation laws; (3) federal lands law; and (4) environmental law.

3.1 Private Law

In the United States, unlike much of the rest of the world, the right to explore for and produce minerals generally does not belong to the sovereign, but instead is privately owned, as one of the benefits that comes with ownership of land.[9] Thus, the right to explore for and produce minerals is governed by the private law portion of oil and gas law, which is a specialized branch of property law. This law typically is a matter of state law (rather than federal law) in the U.S.

9. Keith B. Hall and Hannah J. Wiseman, *Hydraulic Fracturing: A Guide to Environmental and Real Property Issues* (American Bar Assn. 2017) 11.

The person who has a right to explore for and produce minerals will not necessarily be the landowner, however, because state law generally allows the owner of land to permanently sever mineral rights from landownership by conveying the mineral rights to another person or by conveying the land to someone else while reserving the mineral rights to the transferor.[10] This creates a "split estate," with one person owning the "mineral estate" and another person owning the land (sometimes called the "surface estate," even though the surface estate also encompasses ownership of the subsurface, excepting the minerals or the right to extract minerals).[11] An exception is Louisiana, which does not allow the creation of a mineral estate.[12] However, Louisiana allows the creation of a mineral servitude in favor of a person other than the landowner, and the person holding the servitude will have a right to explore for, extract, and own minerals.[13]

Without regard to whether the person who has exploration and production rights is the landowner, a mineral estate owner, or a mineral servitude owner, the right to explore and produce generally will be governed by the private law portion of state oil and gas law. For convenience, this Chapter will refer to the person who owns the right to explore for and produce minerals as the "landowner," even though this person sometimes will be some other person to whom the right has been transferred.

In locations where the federal, a state, or local government owns the land, the government typically owns the mineral rights, but in the role of landowner, rather than as sovereign. In such locations, the same private law that governs oil and gas development on privately owned land will apply, but federal and state and local governments often have special laws that also apply to mineral development on those government-owned lands.

There is a notable exception to the rule that the right to explore for and produce minerals is a matter of private ownership, rather than the prerogative of the sovereign. It applies offshore. For inland waters—as opposed to offshore—the bottoms of a navigable water body within the U.S. is owned by the state in which the water body is found, rather than by private individuals or the national (federal) government.[14] Prior to 1947, many legal scholars in the U.S. believed that a similar rule applied offshore and that the bottoms of offshore waters were owned by the nearest state, rather than the federal government. This became a matter of dispute between certain states and the federal government when offshore oil and gas activity began to become more common. The federal government brought the states to court, seeking a ruling that the federal government owned the bottoms of offshore waters. The United States Supreme Court declined to declare that the federal government owned that area, but the Court nevertheless ruled in favor of the federal government, holding that the federal government has "paramount" authority offshore. This meant that the federal government would control offshore oil and gas development, though it would do so in its

10. *See, e.g., Barker v. Campbell-Ratcliff Land, Co.*, 167 P. 468 [Okla. 1917].
11. *Ibid.*, at 23.
12. *Wemple v. Nabors Oil & Gas Co.*, 97 So. 666 [La. 1923]; *Frost Johnson Lumber Co. v. Salling's Heirs*, 91 So. 207 [La. 1922].
13. La. Rev. Stat. 31:21.
14. *Pollard v. Hagan*, 44 U.S. 212 [1845].

sovereign capacity, rather than as landowner or mineral owner. The effect of the Court's judgment was to prohibit any offshore oil and gas activity unless it was authorized by the federal government.[15]

Leases and Lease Provisions That May Discourage Flaring

Most landowners do not drill for oil and gas (or attempt to develop other minerals on their own). They do not have the expertise, the capital, or the risk tolerance. It is much more common for landowners to grant a mineral lease to an oil and gas company. The typical oil and gas lease authorizes the leaseholder to explore for oil and gas at its own risk and expense. If the leaseholder produces oil and gas, the leaseholder will pay the lessor who granted the lease a royalty that typically is defined as a specified fraction of the value of the oil or natural gas extracted.

There are at least two possible ways that a leaseholder's contractual obligations under the lease may discourage flaring of natural gas. First, there is the possibility that the leaseholder will have to pay a royalty on flared gas. This is not always the case, though. Under many leases, the leaseholder will only owe a royalty on natural gas if the gas is either sold by the leaseholder or used by the leaseholder at a location other than the leased premises. Thus, the leaseholder will not owe a royalty on flared gas (or gas that the leaseholder reinjects for pressure maintenance, or gas that the leaseholder uses to operate equipment used to facilitate the production of hydrocarbons from the leased premises). However, this will depend on the language of the individual lease. Some leases may require the payment of a royalty on any natural gas extracted, even if it is flared. If the lease requires payment of a royalty on flared gas, that will be a disincentive to flaring.

Second, courts in the United States have concluded that oil and gas leaseholders are bound by several implied covenants.[16] One of these is an implied covenant to diligently market hydrocarbons that are discovered on the leased premises.[17] This implied covenant historically was applied to require oil and gas leaseholders to diligently seek a market for natural gas that could be produced from a natural gas well. This often became an issue when a natural gas deposit was found during the drilling of a wildcat well or other well that was not located near an existing natural gas pipeline network. In such situations, leaseholders typically would shut-in the natural gas well until they found a buyer and until there was access to a pipeline that could carry the gas.

Sometimes a natural gas well might be shut-in for years, much to the frustration of lessors who would be hoping for the leaseholder to sell the natural gas and pay a royalty to the lessor. To ensure that the leaseholder at lease makes reasonable efforts to find a buyer and secure a pipeline connection, the implied covenant of diligent

15. *See United States v. California*, 333 U.S. 19 [1947]; *see also United States v. Louisiana*, 339 U.S. 699 [1950]; *United States v. Texas*, 339 U.S. 707 [1950].
16. Keith B. Hall, "The Continuing Role of Implied Covenants in Developing Leased Lands" [2010] 49 Washburn L.J. 313 https://doi.org/10.2139/ssrn.2281490.
17. *See, e.g., Robbins v. Chevron U.S.A., Inc.* 785 P.2d 1010 [Kan. 1990]; *Risinger v. Arkansas-Louisiana Gas Co.*, 3 So. 2d 289 [1941]. *See also* Keith B. Hall, "Implied Covenants and the Drafting of Oil and Gas Leases" [2019] 7 LSU J. Energy L. & Resources 401, 418-419.

marketing requires leaseholders to do whatever a reasonably prudent operator would do to find a buyer for the gas and to find a pipeline to carry the gas.

Although the implied covenant of diligent marketing historically has most often been used when a leaseholder shuts-in natural gas wells because of the lack of a buyer or lack of pipeline access, this implied covenant could be applied to require a leaseholder to do whatever a reasonably prudent operator would do to find a buyer and a pipeline that could be used to transport associated gas that is produced from an oil well, instead of flaring the natural gas.

3.2 State Conservation Laws

Most of the laws that govern oil and gas activity in the United States are not federal laws of national government, but instead or state laws of the state in which the oil and gas activity takes place (the main subnational units within the United States are called "states," and the country has fifty states, several of which have oil and gas activity within their borders). Starting in the early 1900s, the various states with oil and gas activity began to enact "conservation" laws that were designed to conserve natural resources by prohibiting or discouraging activities that would waste such resources.[18] This often includes limitations on the flaring of associated gas. There has been a trend in recent years toward stricter limitations on flaring of associated gas. Because conservation laws are typically state laws, these laws will vary from one state to another.

For example, in early 2024, Louisiana put into effect new regulations to restrict flaring. Louisiana regulations have long distinguished between an "oil well" and a "gas well." If the regulator has classified a well as an oil well, and the ratio of natural gas production to oil production exceeds 2,000 cubic feet per barrel of oil, regulations generally require that the maximum allowable rate of oil production be reduced if "the operator cannot use or sell the gas."[19] This encourages operators to use or sell associated gas produced from an oil well.

In addition, under Louisiana's new regulations, for any well whose gas-to-oil ratio exceeds 2,000 cubic feet of gas to barrel of oil, Louisiana's regulations prohibit the "routine flaring of natural gas ... except in those instances where the Office of Conservation finds, upon written application, that such prohibition would result in an economic hardship on the operator of the well."[20] "Routine flaring" is defined as "flaring during normal oil production operations in the absence of sufficient facilities or amenable geology to re-inject the produced gas, utilize it on-site, or dispatch it to a market."[21]

18. *See* Keith B. Hall, "Single Well Spacing and Pooling: State Spacing and Jurisdiction Over Conservation," [2014] Rocky Mt. Min. L. Fdn. Special Institute on Federal Onshore Oil & Gas Pooling & Unitization.
19. La. Admin. Code tit. 43, pt. XIX, §3505(A).
20. La. Admin. Code tit. 43, pt. XIX, §3507(B).
21. *See* La. Admin. Code tit. 43, pt. XIX, §3503.

Further, the Office is prohibited from making a finding of such hardship "where the current market value, at the point of delivery, of the gas proposed to be flared exceeds the cost involved in making such gas available to a market, or where revenue or economic benefit from a beneficial use identified in [section 103 of the Office of Conservation regulations] exceeds the cost involved in implementing same."

Also, a new provision in Louisiana's regulations requires that the use of natural gas be considered when an operator submits an application for a permit to drill for oil or gas. The regulations require that, when an operator submits an application, it must certify that:

(a) it will be able to connect the well to a natural gas gathering system in the general area with sufficient capacity to transport 100% of the volume of natural gas the operator anticipates the well will produce; or

(b) it will not be able to connect to a natural gas gathering system in the general area with sufficient capacity to transport 100% of the volume of natural gas the operator anticipates the well will produce. The operator shall state that they will either:

 (i) shut-in the well until the operator can comply with [paragraph (a) above]; or

 (ii) evaluate if well is a candidate for flaring based on economic hardship per [Louisiana's regulations that generally prohibit routine flaring]; or

 (iii) provide a gas capture plan that evaluates and selects one or more beneficial uses until a natural gas gathering system is available, including:

  (a) field use;

  (b) power generation for alternative use;

  (c) enhanced recovery operations; and

  (d) other alternative beneficial use that does not result in venting or flaring.[22]

In Colorado, regulations went into effect in early 2021[23] that restrict the flaring of natural gas during the flowback period for a well that has been hydraulically fractured.[24] In addition, the regulations generally prohibit flaring of natural gas from a well after the commencement of production.[25] The regulations make limited exceptions for gas flared during upset conditions, maintenance or repair work, and liquids unloading at a well.[26] In addition, the regulation authorizes the regulatory agency to authorize flaring during a production test, for a period not exceeding 60 days, provided that the operator has submitted a plan for connecting the well to a natural gas gathering

22. La. Admin. Code tit. 43, pt. XIX, §103.
23. Colorado Register, Volume 43, No. 24 [December 25, 2020] (publication of final regulations, with an effective date of January 15, 2021).
24. 2 Colo. Code Reg. 404-1-903.c.
25. 2 Colo. Code Reg. 404-1-903.d.
26. *Ibid.*

system.[27] The Colorado rules also require operators to measure and report to the mineral owners the volume of gas flared after the well has gone into production.[28]

New Mexico also put stricter flaring regulations into effect in 2021.[29] The new regulations generally prohibit flaring of natural gas during production operations.[30] The regulations make exceptions for emergency situations and malfunctions, liquid unloading, and maintenance.[31] If the regulator approves a well as an exploratory well, the operator may flare natural gas for up to 12 months, provided that the operator submits a gas capture plan to the regulator, showing a timeline and plan to connect the well to a gas gathering system.[32]

In Texas, the state with the largest production of oil and gas, flaring is governed by "Rule 32," which is found in 16 Texas Administrative Code §3.32. This rule is not as new as the flaring rules found in some other states, but the rule does place restrictions on flaring. Subsection (c) establishes the general rule, stating, "All gas from any oil [or] gas well ... shall be utilized for purposes and uses authorized by law, except as provided in this section." If natural gas is not going to be utilized, a release lasting more than 24 hours generally should be flared, rather than vented.[33]

There are exceptions to the general rule that gas should be utilized.[34] For example, natural gas "may be released for a period not to exceed ten producing days after initial completion, recompletion in another field, or workover operations in the same field, including but not limited to perforating, stimulating, deepening, cleanout, well maintenance or repair operations." Further, the state's oil and gas regulator (the Texas Railroad Commission) may grant an administrative exception, but the exception generally cannot exceed 180 days[35] unless the volumes of gas equal to or less than 50,000 cubic feet per day "for each gas well, ... oil lease, or commingled vent or flare point."[36] These "administrative exception[s]" can be granted by the professional staff of the regulator.

An operator can request an administrative exception that exceeds 180 days, but such an exception must be approved by a final order signed by at least two of the three elected "Commissioners" who oversee the regulator.[37] The regulator often grants exceptions, but the exceptions account for a relatively small fraction of Texas oil and gas wells. For example, as of August 31, 2019, the state had 264,877 producing oil and

27. 2 Colo. Code Reg. 404-1-903.d.1.C & 404-1-903.e.
28. 2 Colo. Code Reg. 404-1-903.d.4.
29. New Mexico Register [May 25, 2021] (publication of final regulations, with an effective date of May 25, 2021).
30. N.M. Admin. Code 19.15.27.8(D).
31. *Ibid.*
32. *Ibid.*
33. *See* 16 Tex. Admin. Code §3.32(e); *but see* 16 Tex. Admin. Code §3.32(d)(1)(G) (exceptions to general rule).
34. *See, e.g.,* 16 Tex. Admin. Code §3.32(e), (f), & (h).
35. 16 Tex. Admin. Code §3.32(h)(2).
36. 16 Tex. Admin. Code §3.32(h)(3).
37. *See* 16 Tex. Admin. Code §3.32(h)(4).

gas wells.[38] During its 2019 fiscal year, the regulator 6,972 exceptions.[39] In 2022, the regulator granted 3,667 exceptions.[40]

Many other states have rules that restrict flaring of associated gas.

3.3 Federal Lands

The U.S. federal government owns a large portion of the land in the United States, particularly in the western states. The federal government has granted oil and gas leases that cover much of its land. In addition, the U.S. helps manage "Indians lands" (areas that have been set aside for North American indigenous tribes) that cover a significant amount of land, and oil and gas leases have been granted over some Indian lands. The conduct of these federal and Indians lands leaseholders is regulated by a combination of the lease terms, state laws that govern oil and gas activity, and federal laws that govern oil and gas leases on federal and Indian lands. The federal laws governing leases are primarily administered by the Bureau of Land Management (BLM), which is part of the U.S. Department of Interior (DOI).

The DOI has the authority to prevent waste of natural gas from federal and Indian lands under various statutes. For example, 30 U.S.C. §225, a portion of the Mineral Leasing Act, requires lessees to "use all reasonable precautions to prevent waste of oil or gas" produced from federal leases. Further, 30 U.S.C. §187 provides that federal leases shall contain "a provision that such rules for the ... prevention of undue waste as may be prescribed by said Secretary [of Interior] shall be observed." This is also part of the Mineral Leasing Act. In addition, 30 U.S.C. §1756, part of the Federal Oil and Gas Royalty Management Act of 1982 (FOGRMA), provides: "Any lessee is liable for royalty payments on oil or gas lost or wasted from a lease site when such loss or waste is due to negligence on the part of the operator of the lease, or due to the failure to comply with any rule or regulation, order or citation issued under this chapter or any mineral leasing law."

To some extent, these regulations can be compared to private law, in the sense that the federal government uses regulations, in addition to contractual terms, to protect its interest under federal oil and gas leases. But even more, these regulations are comparable to the state conservation laws that are designed to prevent waste, particularly undue waste.

3.3.1 NTL-4 and NTL-4A

Of course, persons can disagree about the circumstances in which flared gas constitutes "undue waste" and what precautions to prevent waste are reasonable. For years, the

38. *See* Texas Railroad Commission, "Flaring Regulation: How Many Exceptions Authorizing Flaring or Venting Permits Have Been Issued in Texas?" https://www.rrc.texas.gov/about-us/faqs/oil-gas-faq/flaring-regulation/ accessed September 16, 2024.
39. *Ibid.*
40. *Ibid.*

federal government had a practice of exempting from royalty obligations any oil or gas unavoidably lost or used in lease operations. Then, in 1974, the Conservation Division of the U.S. Geological Survey (which at that time oversaw federal oil and gas leases), part of the DOI, issued NTL-4 (on occasion, the federal regulator occasionally publishes a "Notice to Lessees and Operators of Onshore Federal and Indian Oil and Gas Leases," which is written guidance to lessees under federal leases, and specific Notices are identified by the letters "NTL" followed by a dash and a numeral). NTL-4 would have required that a royalty be paid, even on all flared gas, even in circumstances in which, in the past, the gas would have been considered "unavoidably lost" and not subject to a royalty. This and certain other portions of NTL-4 were challenged in court, and courts held that those portions of NTL-4 were invalid. The court reasoned that the DOI had acted in an arbitrary and capricious manner in reversing the Department's longstanding interpretation of royalty obligations under the Mineral Leasing Act, and under the Administrative Procedures Act, this was grounds to invalidate the Department's action.[41]

The DOI issued NTL-4A, regarding "Royalty or Compensation for Oil and Gas Lost," which was printed in the Federal Register in late 1979, with an effective date of January 1, 1980.[42] NTL-4A, which superseded NTL-4, sought to restrict flaring by requiring lessees under federal and Indian lands leases to pay a royalty on flared or vented natural gas in certain circumstances. NTL-4A remained in effect until late 2018 and then came back into effect in late 2020 with respect to venting and flaring. It remained in effect until June 2024, the effective date of a final rule entitled "Waste Prevention, Production Subject to Royalties, and Resource Conservation," which was published by DOI's BLM in the Federal Register on April 10, 2024.[43]

NTL-4A distinguished between "avoidably lost" natural gas and "unavoidably lost" gas and generally required that a royalty be paid on all gas, other than gas used in lease operations unless the gas was unavoidably lost or the DOI had given its prior authorization for venting or flaring. The Notice defined "Avoidably lost" natural gas as follows:

> "Avoidably lost" production shall mean the venting or flaring of produced gas without the prior authorization, approval, ratification, or acceptance of the Supervisor [meaning the federal regulator's "Area Oil and Gas Supervisor"] and the loss of produced oil or gas when the Supervisor determines that such loss occurred as a result of (1) negligence on the part of the lessee or operator, or (2) the failure of the lessee or operator to take all reasonable measures to prevent and/or to control the loss, or (3) the failure of the lessee or operator to comply fully with the applicable lease terms and regulations, appropriate provisions of the approved

41. *Marathon Oil Co. v. Andrus*, 452 F. Supp. 548, 553 [D. Wyo. 1978]; *see also Gulf Oil Corp. v. Andrus*, 460 F. Supp. 15, 18 [C.D. Cal. 1978]. *Cf. Amoco Production Co. v. Andrus* [E.D. La. 1981] (federal offshore royalties); *Placid Oil Co. v. Department of Interior*, 491 F. Supp. 895 [N.D. Tex. 1980] (same).
42. 44 Fed. Reg. 76600 [December 27, 1979].
43. 89 Fed. Reg. 25378 [April 10, 2024].

operating plan, or the prior written orders of the Supervisor, or (4) any combination of the foregoing.

In contrast, NTL-4A defined "Unavoidably lost" natural gas as follows:

> "Unavoidably lost" production shall mean (1) those gas vapors which are released from storage tanks or other low-pressure production vessels unless the Supervisor determines that the recovery of such vapors would be warranted, (2) that oil or gas which is lost because of line failures, equipment malfunctions, blowouts, fires, or otherwise except where the Supervisor determines that said loss resulted from the negligence or the failure of the lessee or operator to take all reasonable measures to prevent and/or control the loss, and (3) the venting or flaring of gas in accordance with Section III [of NTL-4A, which authorized venting or flaring during emergencies, well purging, evaluation tests, initial production tests, and other tests, if approved in advance by the regulator].

This definition of "unavoidably lost" would not apply to most associated gas flared during normal operations. Thus, to avoid a royalty obligation on flared gas, an operator generally would need to secure the DOI's consent to flaring. The grounds for consent were provided in section IV of NTL-4A, which is entitled "Other Venting or Flaring." Subsection B of section IV provides that the DOI may approve an application for flaring or venting if the applicant demonstrates that such flaring or venting is justified by submitting "an evaluation report supported by engineering, geologic, and economic data which demonstrates to the satisfaction of the Supervisor that the expenditures necessary to market or beneficially use such gas are not economically justified and that conservation of the gas, if required, would lead to the premature abandonment of recoverable oil reserves and ultimately to a greater loss of equivalent energy than would be recovered if the venting or flaring were permitted." Thus, the authority to flare associated gas generally comes down in large part to an evaluation of whether the costs necessary to market or use the gas can be economically justified, though, as an alternative, an application to permit flaring or venting can be approved if the applicant submitted "an action plan that will eliminate venting or flaring of the gas within 1 year from the date of application."

NTL-4A generally required the operator to pay a royalty on avoidably lost gas, assuming the DOI had not approved an application for flaring or venting. In addition, NTL-4A generally prohibited the venting or flaring of associated gas, except for unavoidably lost gas and gas vented or flared pursuant to section III of NTL-4A, unless the DOI had approved venting or flaring under section IV of NTL-4A.[44] Also, NTL-4A required operators of oil and gas leases on federal and Indian lands to measure and report the volumes of vented and flared gas, even if the gas qualified was "unavoidably lost" or other gas on which a royalty was not owed.[45]

---

44. *See* NTL-4A, section IV.B.
45. *See* NTL-4A, section V.

3.3.2 *The Obama Administration's Actions, Trump Administration's Responses, and Related Litigation*

NTL-4A remained in effect for well over 30 years after its effective date in 1980. But in November 2016, late during President Barack Obama's administration, BLM published its "Waste Prevention Rule" in the Federal Register.[46] The Rule sought to place stricter limits on the venting and flaring of natural gas.

The Rule purported to be effective January 17, 2017, though most of the rules were to be phased in over time.[47] A complex series of events then ensued. These events included court challenges to the Waste Prevention Rule. In addition, after Donald Trump became President in January 2017, his administration sought to delay enforcement of the new Waste Prevention Rule, while the new administration evaluated the Rule and decided whether to promulgate new regulations to undo the Rule. But supporters of the Waste Prevention Rule brought a successful challenge to the delayed implementation of the Waste Prevention Rule. The Trump administration then began a rulemaking process to undo the Waste Prevention Rule, and all the while the court challenge to the 2016 Waste Prevention Rule itself was pending.

Eventually, in 2018, the 2016 Waste Prevention Rule went into effect after a federal court in California vacated a 2018 rule from the DOI that rescinded the 2016 Waste Prevention Rule.[48] In the meantime, a legal challenge to the Waste Prevention Rule itself was pending in the United States District Court for the District of Wyoming. In October 2020, however, that court entered a judgment that critical portions of the Rule were invalid.[49] The court's reasoning was that DOI's BLM had justified its Rule primarily on grounds that it would improve air quality, though BLM had also noted that the Rule would decrease the waste of natural gas. The court noted that BLM has the authority, on behalf of DOI, to promulgate rules to minimize waste, but BLM does not have the authority to issue rules to promote air quality. Given that BLM's primary justification for the Rule was to promote air quality, the rule was invalid. The fact that BLM had noted that the rule would have ancillary effects of minimizing waste was not sufficient to give BLM authority to issue the Rule. With this ruling, NTL-4A came back into effect with respect to venting and flaring of associated natural gas.

3.3.3 *The 2024 Waste Prevention Rule*

Joe Biden became President of the United States in January 2021, and his administration almost immediately sought to place more stringer regulations on the oil and gas industry. This included several initiatives, two of which sought to place stricter rules on the venting and flaring of associated natural gas. One of these involves rules promulgated by the U.S. Environmental Protection Agency. These EPA rules address oil and gas activity generally, not just oil and gas activity on federal and Indian lands, and are

46. 81 Fed. Reg. 83,008 [November 18, 2016].
47. *Ibid.*
48. *California v. Bernhardt*, 472 F. Supp. 3d 573 [N.D. Cal. 2020].
49. *Wyoming v. Dept. of Interior*, 493 F. Supp. 3d 1046 [D. Wyo. 2020].

justified on grounds of protecting air quality—a matter which is generally outside of BLM's authority, but over which EPA has some authority. These are discussed in the next section of this Chapter.

The other Biden administration effort addressed toward venting and flaring of natural gas has involved BLM and has been justified as a waste reduction initiative. BLM published proposed rules in November 2022[50] and then accepted public comments regarding the proposed rules (under the Administrative Procedures Act, a public comment period generally is required as part of administrative agencies' development and promulgation of regulations). BLM published its final rule on April 10, 2024, with the Rule scheduled to go into effect on June 10, 2024, though certain provisions regarding the measurement of flared gas will be phased in over time.[51] The new Rule, which addresses venting and flaring of associated gas, as well as other forms of loss of gas, is primarily codified at 43 Code of Federal Regulations Part 3170 (43 C.F.R. §§3171.1 through 3179.200), though the Rule also amends 43 C.F.R. 3162.3-1, dealing with applications for a permit to drill.

The amendments to 43 C.F.R. §3162.3-1 (Drilling applications and plans) revised paragraph (d) and adds new paragraphs (j) and (k), in addition to a new paragraph (l). The new paragraph (l) merely referred to BLM's authority to act on applications, but the other changes and additions were more significant. The revision to paragraph (d) adds a requirement that an application for a permit to drill a well on federal or Indian lands must include, "[f]or an oil well, a Waste Minimization Plan (WMP), as required by paragraph (j) or a self-certification statement, as required by paragraph (k)." A WMP is designed to show that the operator has plans to avoid the waste of gas. Paragraph (j) of §3162.3-1 requires a WMP to include:

(1) The anticipated initial oil production rate from the oil well and the anticipated production decline over the first three years of production.
(2) The anticipated initial oil-well gas production rate from the oil well and the anticipated production decline over the first three years of production.
(3) Certification that the operator has a valid, executed gas sales contract to sell to a purchaser 100% of the produced oil-well gas, less gas anticipated for use on-lease pursuant to 43 CFR subpart 3178.
(4) Any other information demonstrating the operator's plans to avoid the waste of gas production from any source, including, as appropriate, from pneumatic equipment, storage tanks, and leaks.

Section 3162.3-1 allows an applicant for a permit to drill to forego a WMP if the applicant instead makes a "self-certification" pursuant to paragraph (k). This self-certification is a representation by the applicant that it can contain all the associated gas produced by the well and that the operator will owe a royalty on all the gas, except for any gas lost during an emergency situation. Paragraph (k) states:

50. *See* 87 Fed. Reg. 73,588 [November 30, 2022].
51. 89 Fed. Reg. 25,378 [April 10, 2024].

> A self-certification is a written statement that the operator will be able to capture, as defined in 43 CFR 3179.10, 100 percent of the oil-well gas that the oil well produces. An approved Application for Permit to Drill with a self-certification statement is not subject to 43 CFR 3179.70(a), and all flared gas is an avoidable loss with a royalty obligation, except for emergencies as identified in 43 CFR 3179.83. A self-certification statement applies and is enforceable from the date of first production until the well is plugged and abandoned.

"Capture" is defined as follows: "Capture means the physical containment of natural gas for transportation to market or productive use of natural gas and includes reinjection and royalty-free on-site uses pursuant to subpart 3178."[52] In turn, 43 C.F.R. §3179.83 states in part, "an 'emergency situation' is a temporary, infrequent, and unavoidable situation in which the loss of gas is necessary to avoid a danger to human health, safety, or the environment." The section also specifies certain circumstances that do not qualify as an emergency. Specifically, 43 C.F.R. 3179.83(b) states:

> The following examples do not constitute emergency situations for the purposes of royalty assessment:
> (1) Recurring failures of a single piece of equipment;
> (2) The operator's failure to install appropriate equipment of a sufficient capacity to accommodate the production conditions;
> (3) Failure to limit production when the production rate exceeds the capacity of the related equipment, pipeline, or gas plant, or exceeds sales contract volumes of oil or gas;
> (4) Scheduled maintenance; or
> (5) A situation caused by operator negligence.

The 2024 Waste Prevention Rule makes several notable changes from NTL-4A regarding the venting and flaring of associated natural gas. For example, the 2024 Rule eliminates the economic feasibility analysis that had been in effect for decades under NTL-4A's section IV, in which the DOI typically would grant the authority to flare associated gas without a royalty obligation if the operator demonstrated, with evidence, that the actions necessary to market the gas or put it to beneficial use were not cost-effective.

Instead, 43 C.F.R. §3179.70 establishes an amount of gas that may be flared and considered "unavoidably lost" if it is "flared due to pipeline capacity constraints, midstream processing failures, or other similar events that prevent produced gas from being transported through the connected pipeline." The amount of gas that may be flared under this section is based on a gas-to-oil ratio. Starting on July 1, 2024, the maximum amount of gas that may be flared under this section is 0.08 Mcf (an "Mcf" is thousand standard cubic feet at standard conditions)[53] per barrel of oil produced. This limit decreases to 0.07 Mcf per barrel in July 2025, to 0.06 Mcf per barrel in July 2026, and then to 0.05 Mcf per barrel in 2027, then the allowed ratio will remain at 0.05 Mcf per barrel.

Federal regulations expressly provide that a royalty is due on all avoidably lost gas, but that no royalty is due on unavoidably lost gas. Up to the allowed gas-to-oil

52. 43 C.F.R. § 3179.10.
53. *See* 89 Fed. Reg. 25,378 [April 10, 2024].

ratio, any gas flared because of midstream constraints would be considered "unavoidably lost." Thus, for the flaring of that amount of gas, no royalty would be owed. Any gas flared in excess of the allowed ratios will be considered "avoidably lost," and a royalty will be owed pursuant to 43 C.F.R. §3179.42.

The new regulations state that any previously granted approvals to flare associated gas royalty-free (e.g., approvals based on an economic analysis under section IV of NTL-4A) from a well will remain in effect until November 1, 2024. After that, the flaring of gas from such a well will be governed by the 2024 Waste Prevention Rule.

3.4 Environmental Laws

Historically, most of the restrictions on the venting or flaring of associated gas in the United States have been justified on conservation grounds—to avoid or limit the waste of natural resources, including natural gas. However, there has been increasing concern about the environmental impacts of venting or flaring of associated natural gas. The primary compound in natural gas is methane, and methane is a greenhouse gas that, in the short term, can have a much stronger greenhouse gas impact for a given quantity of molecules. For example, BLM cited studies stating that methane has roughly 28 to 36 times the climate impact of carbon dioxide when measured over a 100-year period, and about 84 times the climate impact when measured over a 20-year period.[54]

Thus, the venting of natural gas can have adverse climate impacts. Further, flaring natural gas can also have adverse climate impacts because combustion of methane in the flare will produce carbon dioxide, and some portion of the methane that is sent to the flare will exit without being converted to carbon dioxide. Of course, the most beneficial uses of natural gas involve combustion of natural gas into carbon dioxide that is emitted, but at least in those circumstances energy needed by society is recovered in the process. But no energy is recovered in flaring.

The BLM's 2016 Waste Prevention Rule promulgated near the end of the Obama administration was, in large part, a response to these environmental concerns. Indeed, because environmental concerns such as mitigating climate change—a matter outside BLM's regulatory authority—appeared to be the primary motivation for BLM's 2016 Rule, a federal district court held that the 2016 Rule was invalid. As noted above, the BLM stated that its 2024 Waste Prevention Rule was based on a desire to minimize waste, not protect the environment.

However, the U.S. Environmental Protection Agency published a new rule on March 8, 2024, that is expressly designed to limit emissions from upstream oil and gas sources, including releases from the venting or flaring of natural gas.[55] These rules went into effect on May 7, 2024.[56] These rules were promulgated under the authority of the Clean Air Act.

54. 89 Fed. Reg. 25,379 at 25,382 [April 10, 2024].
55. 89 Fed. Reg. 16,820 [March 8, 2024].
56. *Ibid.*

The EPA's new rules seek to prohibit the venting of associated gas in almost all circumstances. The new rules also seek to phase out the routine flaring of associated gas from oil wells that are drilled after the effective date of the rule. For new oil wells that produce associated natural gas, the operator generally will be required to do one of four things with the natural gas: (1) route the gas to a sales line; (2) use the gas as a source of fuel on the lease site; (3) use gas for some other beneficial purpose; or (4) reinject the gas into the formation.[57]

Existing wells that produce more than 40 tons per year of methane generally will be required to do one of the four things with associated gas as is required for new wells.[58] However, the operator may still be allowed to route the gas to a flare if the operator demonstrates to EPA that none of these four options is technically feasible, and if the flare combusts at least 95% of the methane sent to it.[59] For wells that produce 40 tons of methane per year or less, EPA's rules would allow the associated gas to be routed to a flare, provided that the flare achieves a 95% reduction in methane.[60]

4 CURRENT ISSUES

As noted in the prior section, the laws relating to flaring of natural gas have been changing rapidly. One of the current issues in the U.S. is whether the BLM's 2024 Waste Prevention Rule will remain in effect. If there is a change from a Democrat administration to a Republic administration after the 2024 U.S. Presidential election, there could be a change in BLM policy.

Further, even if there is no change in BLM policy, it is possible that the 2024 Waste Prevention Rule could be overturned in court. In its written explanation for the 2024 Waste Prevention Rule, BLM stated: "Finally, the BLM is expressly excluding the social cost of greenhouse gases from its decisions on any of the proposed waste prevention requirements, thereby addressing the Wyoming court's concern (discussed in the prior section of this Chapter) that the 2016 Rule was inappropriately supported by 'climate change benefits,'" rather than conservation or waste minimization. This is referring to the court decision discussed above, in which a federal district court based in Wyoming held that the Obama Administration's 2016 Waste Prevention Rule was invalid because BLM's primary justification for that rule was that the 2016 Rule would produce environmental benefits—particularly, climate change mitigation—a matter which is beyond BLM's regulatory authority, with the minimization of waste (a matter which is properly within BLM's regulatory authority) being only an ancillary benefit.

In developing the 2024 Waste Prevention Rule, BLM tried to keep the focus on avoiding the waste of natural gas, rather than on climate change. The opening sentence of the second paragraph of the Executive Summary states: "This final rule aims to reduce the waste of natural gas from oil and gas leases administered by the BLM. This gas is lost during oil and gas exploration and production activities through venting,

57. *See* 40 C.F.R. § 60.5391c.
58. 89 Fed. Reg. 16,820 at 16,889 [March 8, 2024].
59. *Ibid.*
60. *Ibid.*

flaring, and leaks."[61] The BLM's discussion notes that its 2024 Waste Prevention Rule could have ancillary climate change benefits, but the BLM contends that this was not the motivation for the Rule.[62]

Nevertheless, certain parties have filed suit in federal court in North Dakota, arguing that BLM's 2024 Waste Prevention Rule is invalid. They suggest that, notwithstanding the BLM's statement that its 2024 Waste Prevention Rule is not motivated by environmental concerns, the Rule really is just an environmental initiative disguised as a waste prevention rule. Essentially, the litigants are claiming that BLM's real goal is the same as before—to address climate change—and the agency is simply claiming that the real goal is waste minimization this time around in hopes that this claim will prevent a court from holding that the new rule is invalid. It is too early to know how this litigation will fare.

5 RECOMMENDATIONS

Federal rules have been changing rapidly. They have changed from one Presidential administration to the next and also have changed when courts have struck down regulations. Why is this occurring? One reason is that there is not a consensus in the country for enacting environmental laws that are much stricter than those that have been in place. For this reason, the U.S. Congress has not passed significant new environmental statutes for the most part. However, many members of one of the two major political parties are strongly in favor of significantly more stringent environmental laws. Those individuals are frustrated that the Congress has not enacted more stringent environmental statutes, and when their party controls the Presidency, they are tempted to use that executive power to have regulatory agencies draft more stringent regulations, even though some of those regulations are difficult to justify under the existing statutes.

This, in turn, leads to court challenges to the new regulations, and several of those challenges have been successful. Further, when the other party gains the Presidency, it is tempted to use the executive power to undo regulations promulgated by the other party, to the extent that the regulations promulgated by the other party have survived court challenges. This has led to rapid changes in regulations and significant uncertainty that is not good for anyone, except perhaps lawyers who earn fees on the litigation challenging the validity of regulations. There is no easy solution to this, but perhaps the problem could be somewhat lessened by a legislative compromise between those who want more stringent environmental protection and those who do not. That might somewhat lessen the incentive of those who want more stringent environmental protection, and who exist in significant numbers, though not in sufficient numbers to have yet convinced the U.S. Congress to enact more protective statutes, to promulgate regulations (when their party controls the Presidency) that stretch and sometimes surpass what can be justified under the existing environmental

61. 89 Fed. Reg. 25,378 [April 10, 2024].
62. 89 Fed. Reg. 25,379 at 25,382 [April 10, 2024].

statutes. Although such legislative compromise is difficult, it is not impossible. The misnamed Inflation Reduction Act contains significant compromises relating to energy and protecting the environment.

Further, the ability to reach compromises might be improved if those who want more environmental protection would avoid demonizing the extractive industries. There is no doubt that extractive industries have externalities that include some adverse impacts on the environment, but some of those who seek more environmental protections exaggerate the impact. Further, some of them go beyond pointing out those externalities to cast the extractive industries as evil. Some of them do this even though virtually all of them use the products produced by the extractive industries. This demonization creates a counterreaction that may include ignoring or underestimating the impact of extractive industries. Together, the demonization and counterreaction make it more difficult to reach a compromise. Further, it ignores the fact that the alternative energy sources promoted by opponents of the extractive industries also have externalities that include some adverse impacts on the environment. The solution to this is to have a more civil, reasonable, and rational discussion of energy issues, environmental protections, and the tradeoffs between affordable secure supplies of energy and environmental protection.

6 CONCLUSION

The regulation of natural gas flaring in the United States is complex and changing. It includes private laws that sometimes discourage flaring by requiring oil and gas operators to make reasonable efforts to market whatever hydrocarbons they find, including associated gas. They include state conservation laws that regulate oil and gas activity in a particular state in order to minimize the waste of natural resources. These laws will vary from one state to the next, but they often put some limitations on the flaring of associated gas. Some of these regulations put significant restrictions in place, while others are not very strict.

Also, because the federal government is a major landowner in the U.S., particularly in the western portion of the U.S., the federal government often is the lessor under oil and gas leases, and federal rules seek to restrict flaring in order to maximize royalty revenue to the federal government (royalties are owed on product that is sold or used by the lessee, but may not be owned on flared gas—hence, the flaring of gas, rather than the recovery and selling of it, can decrease revenues to the U.S. government under oil and gas leases covering federal land). These regulations have been changing as the federal government, at least under certain Presidential administrations, has attempted to significantly restrict the flaring or venting of associated natural gas.

Finally, there are federal environmental regulations that seek to minimize flaring to lessen adverse environmental impacts. The Biden administration has made these regulations stricter in recent years.

CHAPTER 28

A Framework to Address Gas Flaring in Eastern Venezuela*

Roland Pettersson

1 AN INTRODUCTION TO VENEZUELA'S GAS INDUSTRY

Venezuela has vast natural gas reserves estimated at 6,300 billion cubic meters (bcm), the seventh largest in the world and several orders of magnitude above its peers in Latin America, which is enough natural gas—at its current production rate—to last over 300 years. For comparison, the United States has just under 14 years' worth of proven reserves. If Venezuela were to produce at the same rate as the U.S., its annual production would be about 450 bcm (compared to its paltry current production of almost 19 bcm per annum).[1] These massive gas reserves are overwhelmingly associated gas, notwithstanding the existence of important offshore and onshore non-associated gas reservoirs.

Surprisingly to some, the country has already in place an extensive infrastructure to collect, compress, process, treat, transport, store, extract, fractionate, and market natural gas liquids (NGLs) obtained from gas. In addition, the gas pipeline system connects all major fields from east to west, including an export pipeline to Punta Ballenas in Colombia. Despite this, Venezuela has yet to export the first molecule of methane extracted from the country's sizeable deposits. This is because the nation's policymakers have historically prioritized oil and liquid hydrocarbons production as export product, leaving gas as a second-tier byproduct and subsidized local fuel for the basic industry.

* The views expressed in this chapter are those of the author, and they do not in any way express nor reflect those of any company, firm or organization with which the author is or might be affiliated.

1. U.S. Congressional Research Service (CRS), *Venezuela's Natural Gas: Questions Endure* (July 7, 2023) https://crsreports.congress.gov/product/pdf/IF/IF12448/2 (accessed on June 23, 2024).

The twenty-first century has posed a long stretch of socioeconomic and political challenges which have ultimately weighed over the country's oil & gas industry, leading first to an oil production plateau which was then followed by a rapid dwindling of crude oil output and exports. Unable to sustain major maintenance operating expenditures (OPEX) and capital expenditures (CAPEX), along with a substantial brain-drain in the industry, it has ultimately resulted in aging infrastructure currently at the heart of a gas-flaring problem. Complicating matters further, Venezuela and the national oil company have been subject to broad blocking economic sanctions imposed by the United States of America, beginning in 2017, making it virtually impossible to repair the infrastructure needed to reduce the flared gas as all major compressor components used in the country are of U.S. making.

All these circumstances—in conjunction with multiple others—have triggered and compounded a myriad of other direct and indirect ripple effects, one of which is a significant increase in carbon dioxide emissions deriving from the flaring and venting of excessive methane gas produced, thus wasting this precious natural resource and contributing to climate change.

Figure 28.1 Flaring Volumes

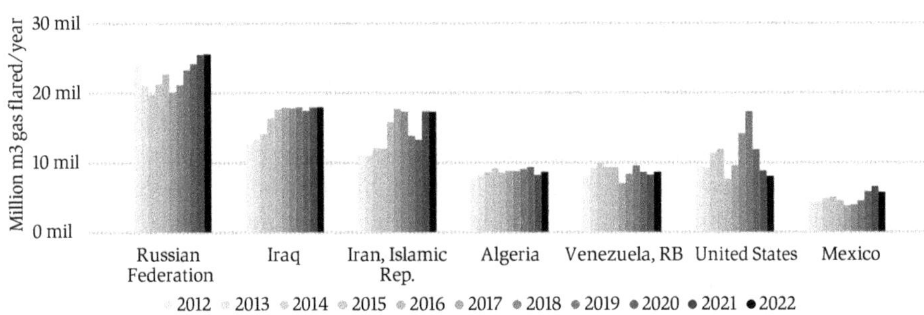

Source: World Bank https://www.worldbank.org/en/programs/gasflaringreduction/global-flaring-data accessed on July 1, 2024.

Although the country has stated its intent to reduce emissions by at least 20% by 2030, as submitted to the UN Framework Convention on Climate Change, and substantial work has been done to understand the causes and solutions for the problem, no final plan has been put into action thus far. Relative to 2020, flared gas has somewhat decreased recently but mainly due to lowering oil production; a general reactivation of the oilfields will foreseeably lead to a substantial uptick in flared gas. Within the context of the Paris Agreement, in an inertial scenario where Venezuela does nothing to combat climate change, around 381 million metric tons of carbon dioxide equivalents ($MMTCO_2Eq$) would be emitted in 2030.

Given the scale, magnitude and complexity of the problem, we intend to present in this short chapter a brief snapshot of the technical issues, the legal and regulatory context, and financial and operational challenges and opportunities, aiming to provide a practical framework to address feasible solutions to mitigate the increasingly global problem posed by excessive gas flaring in Venezuela. In doing so we will do our best to remain grounded on the general context prevailing in Venezuela, as of July 2024.

The first part of the chapter will give a brief description of the current flaring woes in eastern Venezuela. The second part will provide a summary description of relevant regulations and laws governing gas activities in the country. A third part will introduce and analyze aspects relevant to carrying out a project aiming to reduce gas flaring in eastern Venezuela. And, finally, the last part will set out general recommendations to approach such project.

2 GAS FLARING IN VENEZUELA: THE SITUATION IN THE NORTH OF MONAGAS

While Venezuela and the U.S. burn through similar volumes of gas, the former produces around 1/12th of oil as the latter. In fact, Venezuela—a country of about 25 million inhabitants—flares as much gas yearly as Colombia consumes in a year (a country with about double the population and a relatively industrialized economy, for regional standards).[2]

According to The World Bank, in 2022 Venezuela's flaring intensity was 33.53 m^3 per barrel of crude oil produced, the highest of all countries studied—by a wide margin.

Figure 28.2 Flaring Intensity

Source: World Bank https://www.worldbank.org/en/programs/gasflaringreduction/global-flaring-data accessed on July 1, 2024.

Years of under maintenance, underinvestment, the impact of sanctions on strategic suppliers and key operators, the normal deterioration of equipment, investment-deterrent internal policies, and other concurrent elements have severely deteriorated the physical condition of Venezuela's vast and complex gas compression system, producing at times severe shortages of liquefied petroleum gas (LPG) and the

2. E. Ferrer, "*Europe To Drop Over-Compliance In Venezuela Over Natural Gas?*" (Forbes, September 21, 2023) https://www.forbes.com/sites/eliasferrerbreda/2023/09/21/europe-to-drop-over-compliance-in-venezuela-over-natural-gas/?sh=2369548d70ba (accessed on July 1, 2024).

serious environmental threat of flaring and venting,[3] whose epicenter is located in the northeastern part of the country, in Punta de Mata and the north of the State of Monagas.

It is in the compression system where one of the main problems lies, leading to Venezuela's current excess flaring and venting of methane.

The processing system that collects the associated gas resulting from crude oil production in the east of the country is vast, very complex and of superlative importance for the transportation and distribution of natural gas and LPG in the country. It covers the states of Monagas and Anzoátegui, which have estimated reserves of 90 trillion cubic feet (TCF), placing them—on their own—high atop the world in terms of reserves. The system begins with the separation of gas from the crude oil, which is then compressed using a set of compressors.

After being compressed, the gas is transported in its gaseous state to a distribution center to be destined for three extraction plants of enormous size and capacity created in the 1980s and 1990s: Jusepín, Santa Bárbara, and San Joaquín. The objective of these extraction plants is to separate the liquids containing rich gas (NGL) from methane gas (or dry gas), through a process that includes dehydration (using separators, glycol and molecular sieves), cooling (using a cryogenic exchanger and a turbo expander), stabilization/rectification (using a deethanizer tower) and compression.

Once the separation process is completed, two ostensible products remain: (i) the NGLs, and (ii) the dry gas or lean methane gas. From this extraction, the NGL (which is already in a liquid state) goes by pipeline to the state-of-the-art José Antonio Anzoátegui Fractionation and Dispatch Plant (Jose) in the Anzoátegui coastline. The Jose plant features four remarkable fractionation trains (unfortunately not all in the same state of maintenance) with a significant installed capacity of 200,000 barrels per day. The Jose Fractionation and Dispatch Plant also has a dedicated dock that has all the necessary facilities to export these LPGs. As for the dry gas or methane, when it leaves the extraction plants, it has mainly two possible uses and destinations: (a) reinjection into reservoirs for the production of more hydrocarbons; and (b) its distribution from Anaco to various parts of the country for use in thermoelectric plants, basic industries, petrochemical, as vehicle fuel, and residential.

Overall, this system of more than 150 compressors, kilometers of gas pipelines and fittings, three world-class extraction plants and fractionation trains with their system of docks and storage is known as the Eastern Cryogenic Complex of Venezuela; a system of essential importance for the nation, holding potential for economic growth, and perhaps at some in the future also even relevant for the energy security of the region.

More than 50% of the compressor park of the Eastern Cryogenic Complex needs urgent repairs or replacement and start-up of new compression, making it by far the most affected infrastructure within the system. Without compression, the rest of the system cannot properly function as designed, and the only remaining solution to

3. While flaring results mainly in carbon dioxide ("CO_2") emissions, venting is basically the release of methane into the atmosphere, a process with the equivalent "global warming potential" of about twenty-one times (per kilogram) of CO_2 over a 100-year period (*see* International Association of Oil & Gas Producers (OGP), *Flaring & Venting in the Oil & Gas Exploration & Production Industry* (Report No: 2.79/288, January 2000) 3).

palliate these inefficiencies is to flare and vent the gas that cannot be otherwise properly processed.

3 RELEVANT LEGAL AND REGULATORY FRAMEWORK

Gas Regulations

The regulatory framework for Venezuela's oil & gas industry—and the role played by the State within that context—has been subject to several structural shifts and changes throughout the last hundred years. For multiple decades, since 1975, the Venezuelan State has been playing the starring role in the country's oil & gas industry. On the one hand, it legislates, regulates and taxes the sector, and on the other, it is in charge of Venezuela's upstream and midstream operations, as well as international marketing.

As the gas industry has remained largely in the shadow of crude oil production, taking a back seat to it in terms of overall development, its regulatory framework allows for a wider private participation across the value chain, even allowing total private ownership of upstream operations.

The cornerstone of oil & gas regulations in Venezuela is Article 12 of the Constitution, pursuant to which hydrocarbon deposits are of public domain and State ownership.

Free gas activities are further expanded in: (i) the Organic Gaseous Hydrocarbons Law, passed in 1999 (the "*Gas Law*"); and (ii) the Regulations to the Gas Law, enacted in 2000 (the "*Gas Law Regulations*"). Petroleum activities are governed mainly by the 2001 Organic Hydrocarbons Law, partially reformed in 2006 (the "*Oil Law*"), in addition to multiple other laws and regulations.

Transportation and distribution of gas destined for general consumption is considered a public utility in Venezuela.[4]

As gas flaring in Venezuela is mostly correlated with upstream oil production, an interplay between the oil and gas regulations exists, depending mostly on extraction activities up to the wellhead separation and from there onwards.

Pursuant to Article 2 of the Oil Law, activities related to gaseous hydrocarbons fall outside the scope of oil activities and are governed by the Gas Law, except for the extraction of associated gas which is governed by the Oil Law.

Any activity other than extraction is governed by the Gas Law. According to Article 2 of the Gas Law, the activities of collection, storage and use of gas produced associated with oil or other fossils, as well as the processing, industrialization, transportation, distribution, domestic and export of such associated gas, are governed by the Gas Law—as opposed to the Oil Law and the legal framework applicable to crude oil—and, as such, can be undertaken even by private foreign investors. As for "processing" of gas, it refers to the processes of separation, extraction, fractionation, storage and marketing of NGLs and other substances associated with natural gas.[5]

4. Gas Law, Art. 5.
5. Gas Law Regulations, Art. 75.

Oversight powers over both oil and gas activities in Venezuela fall to the Ministry of Oil, which has ample discretionary powers to regulate both industries, including by exercising its direct control over the national oil company (and, indirectly, its affiliates). Additional oversight powers specifically for the gas industry are conferred upon the Ente Nacional del Gas ("*ENAGAS*"), which functions as an industry watchdog and development-promoting entity, although in practice the relevance of ENAGAS has been rather limited.

There is a restriction on vertical integration of gas-related activities covering production, transportation and distribution within a single region within Venezuela, limiting private licenses and permits to one single activity, unless otherwise waived by the Ministry of Oil (which may do so to ensure the financial viability of a project, for instance).[6]

Licensing and Permitting of Gas Operations

An operator of non-associated gas upstream activities requires a license issued by the Ministry of Oil. Midstream activities, including the transportation, distribution and processing of associated or non-associated gas, require a permit issued by the Ministry of Oil.[7]

Standard provisions included in licenses and permits are: (i) requirements on national sourcing of procurement and subcontracting; (ii) a term of usually 20 to 35 years; (iii) a special contribution in addition to the applicable royalty; (iv) broad causes for unilateral revoking and termination by the Ministry of Oil; (v) force majeure; (vi) restriction on transfer of operational assets and reversion of said assets to Venezuela upon expiration of the license/permit, without compensation; (vii) decommissioning duties (to upstream activities); (viii) transfer restrictions (including, generally, those effected through changes of control over the operator); and (ix) submission to Venezuelan courts.

Basic Environmental, Venting and Flaring Regulations

The Venezuelan Government may allow the development of industrial projects and activities that potentially have an adverse impact and degrade the environment, as long as: they are conducted in adherence to a broad nation-wide territorial planning, their effects are tolerable, socio-economic benefits arise as trade-offs, and a minimum threshold on procedures and standards is met.

Specific regulatory approvals—in the form of authorizations, permits, licenses and concessions, among others—may be needed from the Ministry for Ecosocialism. Pursuant to Articles 23, 24, and 25 of the Environment Organic Law of 2006, these approvals must adhere to an underlying environmental planning, in which a sustainable socioeconomic development balance should be achieved between economic growth and

6. Gas Law, Art. 9.
7. *See* Gas Law, Arts. 22, 24 and 27.

environmental and ecosystems' sustainability. The specific terms, conditions, limitations and restrictions, applicable to a specific project or activity are determined and established on a case-by-case basis, in the specific authorization.[8]

A business operating in an industry potentially affecting the environment (such as oil & gas) is required to register before the Ministry for Ecosocialism's Registry of Activities Capable of Degrading the Environment (*RACDA*).

Upstream oil & gas operators must also follow the guidelines enacted by the Ministry for Ecosocialism for drilling and wellhead operations, in the specific administrative authorization, which should address conditions for injection, mud and wastewater management, etc. Additionally, the following permits are also typically required for upstream operators: (i) an authorization for the affectation of natural resources; (ii) hazardous waste handling authorization; and (iii) an area-occupation permit.

Pursuant to Article 80(2) of the 2015 Water and Air Quality Law, the Ministry for Ecosocialism may also order the drilling of wells at the groundwater level, as a monitoring and control measure for permanent injection operations, in addition to requiring the use of techniques such as electrical, flow, pressure and temperature recording, cementing tests and any other mechanism that allows the monitoring and control of the advance of the fluid injected into the aquifer or receiving reservoir.

Provided that most gas deposits in Venezuela are of associated gas and that venting and flaring is largely correlated to upstream oil activities, of particular relevance is the Regulation for the Conservation of Hydrocarbons enacted in 1969, which requires operators to take reasonable measures to use associated gas for maintenance of reservoir pressure, or internal, commercial, and industrial use, or its reinjection. The Regulation for the Conservation of Hydrocarbons further calls for the disposal of unused gas "in a manner that does not cause harm."[9]

The Ministry for Ecosocialism regulates emissions from oil & gas operations and is responsible for authorizing flaring and venting. Permits are granted on a case-by-case basis, pursuant to the 1995 Norms on Air Quality and Control of Atmospheric Pollution,[10] which sets air and emission standards for controlling gas emissions. Applications to such permit must be filed in advance of the commencement of operations and must include an environmental impact assessment,[11] as well as a monitoring plan.[12]

8. Environment Organic Law, Art. 83.
9. Regulation for the Conservation of Hydrocarbons, Art. 22.
10. Presidential Decree No. 638, published in Official Gazette Extraordinary No. 4,899 of May 19, 1995.
11. *See* Art. 20, Norms on the Environmental Assessment of Activities Potentially Degrading of the Environment, enacted by Presidential Decree No. 1,257, published in Official Gazette No. 35,946 of April 25, 1996.
12. Norms on the Environmental Assessment of Activities Potentially Degrading of the Environment, Art. 28.

Standard of Environmental Liability

The obligation to take reasonable measures as required in terms of the duty of care is on a no-fault basis (i.e., negligence or intention is not a requirement to establish liability to comply with the duty of care), with strict liability of the wrongdoer for criminal environmental offenses.

Under Venezuelan law, shareholders and administrators (a category which includes both directors and managers) of corporations may be personally liable for environmental crimes committed in the course of business,[13] provided that the personal liability of the shareholders and administrators is fault-based, however.[14] Although not entirely clear in the law, shareholders and administrators could also be liable for torts and damages.

Joint and several liability exists between the contractual counterparties under joint operating agreements, for environmental damages and hazards.

Tax Framework and the Potential of Tax Incentives

Natural gas production pays a 20% fixed royalty and a standard income tax at the corporate rate of 34%.

In addition to the specific taxes and contributions applicable to the oil & gas industry—including a 16% value-added tax—operators may be subject to the following special contributions: (i) science and technology contribution (1% of gross profits); (ii) anti-drugs trafficking contribution (1% of net profits); and (iii) sports contribution (1% of net profits). Oil & gas companies are not subject to municipal business taxes.

Notably, certain tax breaks and incentives may be subject to direct negotiation between the investors, operators and the Venezuelan government. The President of the Republic has the authority—relying upon the advice of the environmental and tax authorities—to provide specific tax breaks and exonerations to investors in environmental conservancy initiatives by decree.[15]

4 THE POTENTIAL FOR PRIVATELY-LED GAS FLARING REDUCTION PROJECTS

Potentials and Opportunities for Investment

As we have already commented, perhaps the single largest factor contributing to Venezuela's increase in flaring and venting of gas is the state of its gas compression assets and facilities. For instance, the current state of the Eastern Cryogenic Complex of Venezuela (the "*ECC*") which is in urgent need of either extensive repairs or replacement, has derived a significant portion of the flaring-related CO_2 emissions from the past decade.

13. Environmental Law, Art. 130 and Environment Criminal Law, Art. 11(2).
14. Environment Criminal Law, Art. 11(2).
15. Environment Organic Law, Arts. 102, 104 and 105.

The silver lining to the above is that flaring can be significantly curbed simply by addressing the shortcomings in the ECC's compression system, a relatively straightforward undertaking with a relatively low CAPEX requirement (at least within the context of such a capital-intensive industry).[16] Thus, addressing Venezuela's gas flaring woes by investing the gas compression facilities in eastern Venezuela may likely yield the highest possible marginal utility for every single penny invested.

Relevant Legal Aspects of the Compression System

As gas-flaring reduction projects can be foreseeably linked to investment and operations over the ECC's gas compression system, then it can be anticipated that for any private operator to undertake such project, it would require granting of a permit by the Ministry of Oil, as the operations would essentially cover midstream activities of associated gas, produced in eastern Venezuela's different geological oil reservoirs.

The ECC assets and facilities are owned by the national oil company's gas arm. There are specific laws and regulations governing State-owned assets in Venezuela, pursuant to which the transfer of title and ownership over the national gas company's operating assets (or even their lease to a private operator, holding a permit) might require in certain cases the approval of the Public Assets Commission of the Superintendence of Public Assets,[17] which is an agency under the purview of the Ministry of Finance.[18]

However, simply assigning control over these assets in an operating agreement or similar contractual arrangement would be excluded from the requirements established under the Public Assets Law for the sale of public assets, as it would not entail transfer of title over public property. It would also be possible for the national gas company to grant a free right to use and bailment (*comodato*) over compression and gas transportation assets if a particular project qualifies as a "public interest program" (although the Public Assets Law does not indicate what does this term actually mean).[19] The Public Assets Law also allows the transfer of public assets "through other types of legally permitted transactions,"[20] which may cover any valid contractual type, not expressly prohibited under Venezuelan law.

---

16. Examples abroad can be found on initiatives curbing CO_2 emissions by reducing gas flaring via investing in compression infrastructure, such as the experience of Vankor oil field in Russia, where the addition of compressor stations and connections to Gazprom's national gas transport network reportedly achieved a 77% reduction in gas flaring (at nearby oilfields) from 2012 to 2017 (*see* R. Calel and P. Mahdavi, "*The Unintended Consequences of Antiflaring Policies: And Measures for Mitigation*" (May 2020) 117(23) Proceedings of the National Academy of Sciences of the United States of America (PNAS) https://doi.org/10.1073/pnas.2006774117 PL 12506).
17. Just for the sake of illustrating the potential issues which may arise and ways forward to address them, for instance in the widely-publicized Basrah midstream gas project in southern Iraq, the South Gas Co. (a State-owned gas company) contributed existing gas processing and transportation infrastructure to the project's incorporated JV—Basrah Gas Co.—at an agreed valuation determined by an independent appraiser, while the underlying real estate was leased under long-term agreements (*see* C.B. Strong, "*A Template for Infrastructure Investment in Iraq*" (E&P Magazine, Hart Energy, October 2013).
18. *See* the Public Assets Organic Law, published in Official Gazette Extraordinary No. 6,155 of November 19, 2014 (the "*Public Assets Law*").
19. Public Assets Law, Art. 73.
20. *See* Public Assets Law, Art. 87(6).

Note that the operation of gas compressors used specifically for reinjection in oil production is an activity reserved to the Venezuelan state under local law.[21]

Challenges of Project Finance Structures

There are multiple challenges to the bankability of a project-finance type of structure designed to carry out investments and operations of midstream gas assets with the final aim to increase efficiencies of the compressing system and, ultimately, reduce carbon dioxide emissions resulting from venting and flaring of otherwise unusable gas.

Operationally, it might be very complex to segregate and cherry-pick specific assets from a gas processing system and fractionation train and keep them ringfenced within the boundaries of a project's scope. In practice, this means that shared facilities between multiple players and operators—including the national oil company and its affiliates and subsidiaries—might be unavoidable to some extent.

From the revenue and cash flows perspective, there exists the commercial risk of having a limited set of potential buyers of the additional volumes of gas which would be added into the system, most—if not all—of which would be either the Venezuelan state or State-owned entities, making for a one-sided commercial interaction where the buy-side will hold significant leverage to: (a) set the pricing, and (b) default on the payments for the delivered volumes of gas. The national gas company is usually the sole off-taker of the gas produced by both onshore and offshore upstream gas producers, and the gas market is still to this day in its infancy in terms of depth and public policy development. For instance, it was only recently that the Ministry of Oil issued a new resolution setting a three-tiered gas pricing system (one for public enterprises, one for the private commercial industry, and the remaining one for residential), with an overall average price of 1.4 metric million British thermal units (MMBTU)—likely below the threshold of a reasonable long-term price to incentivize new developments.

Furthermore, Venezuela lacks both liquefied natural gas (LNG) and pipeline exporting facilities (other than the Ricaurte pipeline connecting Lake Maracaibo—and ideally at some point, up to the Perla offshore blocks comprising the Rafael Urdaneta project in western Venezuela, such as Cardon IV—to the northeastern Colombian Guajira). No exporting facilities exist in eastern Venezuela, which could be of use to the ECC. Although multiple plans are—and have been for decades—in the works for laying out pipelines from the Venezuelan mainland and offshore producing platforms to Trinidad and Tobago, no such facilities exist today.

Finally, from a financial perspective, there are very limited sources of capital available for long-term investments in Venezuela nowadays. Not even multilateral and development banks' financing has been forthcoming to potentially sensitive environmental endeavors, such as those aimed at reducing the venting and flaring of

21. *See* Art. 2 of the Organic Law that Reserves to the State Assets and Services Related to Upstream Hydrocarbon Activities, published in Official Gazette Extraordinary No. 5,908 of February 19, 2009.

associated petroleum gas.[22] This, despite a current global context where significant capital is flowing towards efficiency-driven upstream, midstream, and downstream oil and gas projects[23] (notwithstanding the adoption/implementation trend of increasingly restrictive financing policies for the oil & gas sector, such as the Equator Principles).

One aspect notably blocking availability of financing alternatives in the country is the existence of the already mentioned broad sanctions program imposed by the U.S. over Venezuela's oil & gas industry. The United States sanctions program on Venezuela indeed casts a long shadow over the country's natural resources and has materially reduced foreign participation in the country's oil & gas industry, with few international oil companies (IOCs) still active in the country (and those who are, are mostly doing so in very restrained basis).

Note that Caribbean and Andean countries are currently suffering a shortage of gas supply. Notably Trinidad and Tobago had to shut down Train 1 of Atlantic LNG and several industry plants at Point Lisa are at risk of shutting down. Colombia itself is now dependent on balancing its energy supply with costly LNG, far too burdensome for its fiscal capacity. Dominican Republic's growing gas demand is in need of a long-term, fairly priced gas supply. Brazil—the region's largest economy—will need evermore gas to keep its gargantuan industry humming. The U.S. and many G7 countries have recognized that the easiest win for climate change is methane reduction initiatives.

Combining these factors and a need to revise U.S. sanction policy with respect to the gas industry in Venezuela becomes self-evident. Perhaps some first steps in that regard have already been taken, as the government of Trinidad and Tobago has been granted specific licenses from the Office of Foreign Assets Control (OFAC) of the Department of Treasury of the U.S., covering the planning, financing, development, execution and management of two offshore gas fields in Venezuela: (i) Dragon,[24] as well as (ii) the Cocuina-Manakin field.[25]

All things considered, the circumstances and externalities above-described would need to be accounted for and incorporated into the assumptions of any contemplated gas flaring-reduction project regarding the ECC's processing infrastructure.

22. Multilateral development banks and public strategic investment funds should probably be a natural source of financing for cost-effective methane abatement projects, especially in circumstances where de-risking of investment is required (*see* International Energy Agency (IEA), *Financing Reductions in Oil and Gas Methane Emissions* (2022) 18).
23. J.P. Sweny, Rachel Croft and Andrew Jerjian, "*Financing Oil and Gas through the Energy Transition*" (2021) 36(7) J.I.B.L.R., p. 274.
24. *See* press release by the Ministry of Energy and Energy Industries of Trinidad and Tobago (October 19, 2023) https://www.energy.gov.tt/ofac-license-amendment-information/ (accessed on July 16, 2024).
25. Press release by the Ministry of Energy and Energy Industries of Trinidad and Tobago (May 29, 2024) https://www.energy.gov.tt/ministry-of-energy-and-energy-industries-media-conference-on-specific-ofac-licence/ (accessed on July 16, 2024).

5 FINAL THOUGHTS: A HOLISTIC VIEW

Gas flaring not only contributes to climate change but also ultimately wastes a valuable energy-intensive resource that could be otherwise used to advance sustainable development and low-carbon transition in oil-producing countries.[26] From a financial and economic standpoint, the flaring problem in eastern Venezuela represents a massive lost opportunity—the flip side of which is that it holds also a huge potential for upside—in terms both of the domestic use of such resources at an industrial and household level within the country, as well as the chance to develop an international market to export and monetize it abroad.[27]

Although it is true that compression is the most obvious issue to address to solve the current problem posed by flaring and venting of methane gas in Venezuela, it is a problem which ultimately has broad and deep roots and as such depends on structural, holistic solutions, which adequately take into consideration the integral operation of the gas processing system.

The need for a holistic approach is, indeed, quite evident. Sporadic and episodic repairs and interventions "here and there," inconsistent with an integral, well-coordinated, and high-level vision, may lead to some quick gains, but is unlikely to yield long-term achievements which are necessary if Venezuela intends to realize the full potential of its gas industry.

Already a first stepstone has been set in place over a quarter of a century ago, in the form of an adequate legal and regulatory framework (at least regarding the fundamentals of private investors' participation, as well as other potentially relevant aspects, such as the possibility of adopting tax incentives), but further structural challenges remain ahead, such as operational predictability and stability, and a much-needed synergy between the private and public sector in terms consistent with rule of law and long-term respect of private investment—as investors and lenders' bankability assessment tends to focus on expropriation risks, change in law protections and tax incentives afforded by the host government agreements and general legal framework.[28]

Having a fair and scalable commercialization scheme is also essential. From a purely commercial standpoint, however, the value chain involved in producing, processing and marketing gas is simply too expensive and complex to be built upon a subsidized domestic gas market.[29] On the other hand, the gas that is currently flared

26. OECD, *Equitable Framework and Finance for Extractive-based Countries in Transition (EFFECT)* (OECD Development Policy Tools, OECD Publishing, Paris, 2022) https://doi.org/10.1787/7871c0ad-en 37.
27. P.D. Pitts, "*Venezuela's Burning Through Gas and Cash*" (Hart Energy, August 11, 2023) https://www.hartenergy.com/exclusives/venezuelas-burning-through-gas-and-cash-206128 (accessed on July 1, 2024).
28. S. Szczetnikowicz and J. Dewar, *Financing Options in the Oil and Gas Industry* (2018) Thomson Reuters Practical Law UK https://www.milbank.com/a/web/97930/Financing-options-in-the-oil-and-gas-industry.pdf 19 (accessed on July 1, 2024).
29. Fixed gas pricing linked to a subsidies-heavy internal policy was indeed perceived as a major barrier to a commercially viable use of associated petroleum gas in Iraq, leading to the development of the Basrah gas project (as pointed out by S. Banerjee and P. Toledano, *A Policy*

and vented in eastern Venezuela—as well as the rest of the associated and non-associated gas produced in the country—can easily fit into and find its place within international gas markets, such as Trinidad and Tobago, a producer of ammonia and methanol, with demands of over 3 BCF of gas per day at full operation. Indeed, excess gas produced from Venezuela is very much needed in Trinidad, where it can be transported relatively easily.[30] Venezuelan gas processed in Trinidad could then be made available to international markets looking for products. From a climate change point of view, the ability to process volumes of gas that are currently being flared and bring it into productive use can be a significant win-win, especially if it then displaces other carbon-intensive means of power generation, such as coal-fueled thermoelectric plants.[31]

Without the serious committal of considerable volumes of gas to export, it will be difficult to untie the Gordian knot and obtain the necessary financing to build the infrastructure currently needed to export gas from eastern Venezuela to Trinidad and Tobago (as well as from the Lake Maracaibo basin in western Venezuela to Colombia).

Project finance-type of structures can be useful to tackle any undertaking aiming to increase efficiencies in upstream oil & gas operations, the associated petroleum gas processing and compression system, and the development of APG exporting infrastructure, as—from a credit perspective—it relies on limited recourse[32] over the project's assets and eventual cash flows, without assuming direct credit exposure vis-à-vis the country's national oil and gas company. Risks should be separately assessed for each "tranche" of the project, as there are clear-cut, distinct capital requirements, timeframes and inherent complexities for each: (a) ECC's gas compression park overhaul; and (b) the pipeline project consisting of connecting sources of Venezuelan gas to Trinidad.

Multiple iterations on the actual scope of the definitive project(s) are evidently possible. It is conceivable that connecting sources of currently flared APG might be deliberately left outside the direct scope of a gas flaring-reduction project (limiting, effectively, such a project to the ECC's processing infrastructure), setting aside the Trinidad pipeline as a separate stand-alone endeavor. For instance, connecting offshore non-associated gas production gas platforms to Trinidad and Tobago (which could be undertaken by IOCs currently operating offshore blocks—such as the Dragon field—[33] together with both countries' governments, in public-private partnerships, or

---

Framework to Approach the Use of Associated Petroleum Gas (Columbia Center on Sustainable Investment Staff Publications, 2016) https://scholarship.law.columbia.edu/sustainable_investment_staffpubs/19 39 (accessed on July 1, 2024)).

30. *See* P. Garip, "*Venezuela Gas Flaring in Spotlight as Nation Gradually Re-opens*" (Gas Outlook, September 2, 2023) https://gasoutlook.com/analysis/venezuela-gas-flaring-in-spotlight-as-nation-gradually-re-opens/ (accessed on July 1, 2024).
31. Energy Chamber of Trinidad and Tobago, *Enlightened self-interest: Trinidad & Tobago, Venezuela and Global Gas Markets* (January 11, 2023) https://energynow.tt/blog/enlightened-selfinterest-trinidad-amp-tobago-venezuela-and-global-gas-markets (accessed on July 1, 2024).
32. *Limited recourse* means that the lenders' primary source of repayment consists mainly of property, assets and revenues of the project (*see* N. Cuthbert, "*Project Risks*" (Dentons, 2018) 5).
33. F. Zerpa, "*Trinidad and Tobago Eyes More Natural Gas from Venezuela Fields*" (Bloomberg, January 23, 2024) https://www.bloomberg.com/news/articles/2024-01-23/trinidad-tobago-eyes-more-natural-gas-from-venezuela-fields (accessed on July 19, 2024).

even downstream buyers in Trinidad), and offsetting the exported volumes of non-associated gas from such fields against the increased volumes of non-flared APGs which would be made available domestically in Venezuela, might make economic and environmental sense for all parties involved.

Although standard factors would need to be factored in when performing the risk analysis and bankability of a project, the ultimate financing structure would need to be tailored in a risk mitigation effort, with bankers, lawyers and advisors playing a potentially key role in unlocking value by using their creativity to develop innovative—yet feasible—structures,[34] which can ultimately be negotiated and come to life upon dealing with policymakers, regulators and project sponsors, both in Venezuela as well as abroad.

34. R.J. Clews, *Project Finance for the International Petroleum Industry* (Elsevier 2016) 285.

Part III Looking Ahead and Conclusions

CHAPTER 29

Contentious Aspects of Natural Gas Flaring and Venting

Aaron E. Koenck

1 INTRODUCTION

Global gas flaring increased by 9 billion cubic meters in 2023 for a total of 148 billion cubic meters—the highest level in nearly half a decade.[1] To put this number into perspective the amount of gas flared—if produced by a country—would make it equivalent to the 8th largest producer of gas in the world.[2] From an economic perspective, the value of the gas has a potential market value of the overall amount of gas flared in 2023 could have been between USD 9 billion and USD 48 billion.[3] The latter of which, is the equivalent of the 88th largest gross domestic product of a country in 2023.[4] From an environmental perspective, this is the equivalent of 381 million tons of carbon dioxide equivalent emissions being released into the atmosphere each year.[5] From a humanitarian perspective, if used to produce electricity, it would have

1. "2024 Global Gas Flaring Tracker Report" (*World Bank*) https://www.worldbank.org/en/programs/gasflaringreduction/publication/2024-global-gas-flaring-tracker-report#:~:text=Highlights%201%20Global%20gas%20flaring%20increased%20by%209,%28CO2e%29%2C%20including%20a%20substantial%20amount%20of%20methane.%20 accessed September 28, 2024.
2. Pistilli M and Williams G, "Top 10 Countries for Natural Gas Production (Updated 2024)" (*INN*, August 16, 2024) https://investingnews.com/top-natural-gas-producers/ accessed September 28, 2024.
3. "Global Gas Flaring Tracker Report," (*World Bank*, June 20, 2024) p. 11 https://thedocs.worldbank.org/en/doc/d01b4aebd8a10513c0e341de5e1f652e-0400072024/original/Global-Gas-Flaring-Tracker-Report-June-20-2024.pdf accessed September 28, 2024.
4. "GDP by Country" (*Worldometer*) https://www.worldometers.info/gdp/gdp-by-country/ accessed September 28, 2024.
5. *Ibid.*, p. 11.

generated enough electricity to double the amount currently provided in Sub-Saharan Africa—a region struggling with significant energy poverty concerns.[6] Accordingly, it is not a surprise that disputes arise from flaring and venting when many stakeholders consider these economic, environmental, and humanitarian concerns as significant. Notably, The Russian Federation, the Islamic Republic of Iran, Iraq, the United States, República Bolivariana de Venezuela, Algeria, Libya, Nigeria, and Mexico remain the top nine flaring countries in 2023 producing 75% of the world's flared gas.[7] However, as discussed below, disputes regarding flaring certainly still exist in countries producing the remaining 20% of flared gas. Aside from the United States, the big nine seem to have few reported disputes—whether formal or otherwise—regarding flared gas. This may be due to immediate energy production being prioritized for short-term political, economic, environmental, and humanitarian concerns over their long-term counterparts.

Moreover, when someone mentions natural gas flaring, the first image to come to people's mind is often a tall candle-like structure at a refinery reaching into the heavens steadily burning as if it is in Prometheus's torch. However, natural gas is flared and vented at many points throughout its travel from the wellhead until its final use. On the upstream side, flaring occurs at various points at the well pad and for various reasons. In some cases, natural gas production is an unusable byproduct of crude oil production due to economic and infrastructure limitations.[8] Other times flaring is simply a way to relieve unwanted pressure in lines and tanks which may lead to safety issues during completion or production. As for midstream activities, flaring is generally for safety purposes. While upstream flare points are generally limited, midstream flare points can be vast. For example, flaring can take place in transportation pipelines, and compressed tanks on trucks, rail, and ships to maintain safe operating pressures.[9] As with upstream activities, downstream activities and flaring generally center around safety and unwanted process byproducts.

From these activities disputes of various forms can arise. Some are commercial in nature and others center around health safety and the environment. This chapter will examine each in detail with sample disputes around the globe. It should also be noted that while the term disputes may conjure formal dispute resolution practices such as through a jurisdiction's courts and alternative dispute resolution, this chapter discusses disputes in a broader sense, hence the name of the contentious aspects of natural gas flaring. In addition to formal dispute resolution, the contentious aspects of flaring issues may be resolved through regulation, policy, and even in the court of public opinion.

6. "2024 Global Gas Flaring Tracker Report" (*World Bank*).
7. *Supra* n. 4, p. 11.
8. "Our Estimated Rate of U.S. Natural Gas Vented or Flared Declined in 2023: U.S. Energy Information Administration (EIA)" (*Today in Energy*, June 20, 2024) https://www.eia.gov/todayinenergy/detail.php?id=62383 accessed September 28, 2024.
9. *Ibid.*

2 CONTENTIOUS COMMERCIAL ASPECTS OF NATURAL GAS FLARING

Whether selling natural gas is commercially viable depends on various continuously changing factors. These include the quantity and quality of gas, available infrastructure, market pricing, regulatory hurdles, and the terms of the production agreement. Whether it is a private landowner in the United States or a government entity, the owner of the mineral *in situ* wants the gas to be sold and not simply flared into the atmosphere where the value of the natural gas will literally and figuratively go up in smoke. However, the party developing the oil and gas resources is not necessarily incentivized to maximize the development of gas where it can be commercially successful through the production of crude oil alone. In gas wells, the developer of the resource may not always take care to prevent waste of the resource for various commercial reasons. As a consequence, tensions can rise between the various stakeholders.

Commercial disputes almost always require the review of a contract. As such, these disputes will largely be governed by the same. These contracts will have a royalty clause or other mechanism that determines payment. In the United States, royalty clauses typically require payment of royalty for oil and gas "produced from the Leased Premises and sold or used on or off the Leased Premises." Disputes have arisen about whether flaring qualifies as "produced" or "used."[10] In the United States, state regulators have taken various positions on the issue. For example, Texas charges royalties for flared gas on state leases while Utah does not.[11] In newly developed areas such as the Bakken Formation, where infrastructure for gas lagged behind oil production, significant litigation spawned from landowners alleging they were underpaid in royalties due to excessive flaring periods.

Because oil and gas assets are owned by solely the government in the remainder of the world, there are additional commercial contentious aspects to consider that are not present in purely private oil and gas transactions as it relates to flaring and venting. These include the desire to collect revenue from the production of the gas whether through royalties, sales, taxes, or all three.

For example, in the United Kingdom's North Sea Transition Authority's flaring guidance it is noted that the regulator has the right to consent to flaring to prevent waste.[12] Accordingly, it has stated it has the right to consent to flaring and venting according to the set out in the Energy Act 1976[13] and the applicable offshore production license granted under the Petroleum Act 1984. It should be noted that The Energy Act 2016 transferred certain powers from the secretary of state, including the issuance of consents for flaring and venting, to the Oil and Gas Authority (OGA which is now the

10. Kelly A. Williams and Joshua B. Cannon, Frontier Flaring: Science & Economics, Politics & Regulation: The Future of Flaring, 60 RMMLF-INST 5 at 3-4 (2014).
11. Frontier Flaring, 60 RMMLF-INST at 10.
12. North Sea Transition Authority, Flaring and Venting Guidance 2021, p. 4.
13. "[T]he Secretary of State's consent is required for natural gas to be disposed of (whether at source or elsewhere) by flaring or by releasing it unignited into the atmosphere."

North Sea Transition Authority).[14] Initially, the main objective of the North Sea Transition Authority has been maximizing the economic recovery of oil and gas resources on the UK continental shelf.[15] Accordingly, the "Maximizing Economic Recovery of UK Petroleum" (MER UK), was established as a government priority in 2015 and was the driver for creating the OGA.[16] The Energy Act 2016 charged the OGA with pursuing MER UK.[17] Since then, the objective has been expanded to include the reduction of greenhouse gas emissions from the production of oil and gas.[18] The latter point is discussed in more detail below section regarding contentious environmental aspects of flaring. Nonetheless, in 2021, around 1 billion cubic meters of natural gas was either flared or vented in the United Kingdom—equivalent to 3% of production. Moreover, over the past decade, the economic value of this gas has increased significantly, totaling some GBP 2.6 billion in lost gas sales from the United Kingdom. As such, in addition to greenhouse gas emission concerns, the lost gas sales have spurred regulators to issue fines where gas is flared or vented without its consent. As such, tension can rise between the UK regulators and those seeking to produce oil in the North Sea and have led to operators being fined.[19]

Over the last decade in the United States, federal regulators have attempted to enact waste prevention rules that would reduce flaring and venting.[20] These typically are in the form of Notices to Lessees which update the oil and gas lease terms and are typically phased in to allow operators to comply. In 2022, the Bureau of Land Management, the U.S. federal agency responsible for managing public lands and mineral resources, provided new flaring and venting requirements for federal and Indian leases. The final rule aimed to reduce the waste of natural gas from flaring, venting, and leaks during oil and gas operations and to collect royalties on "avoidably lost" gas.[21] As a basis for this new rule, the regulators rely on the Mineral Leasing Act which requires that operators "use all reasonable precautions to prevent waste of oil or gas developed in" federal lands.[22] In addition, the Federal Oil and Gas Royalty Management Act, states that oil and gas lessees are "liable for royalty payments on oil or gas lost or wasted from a lease site when such loss or waste is due to negligence on the part of the operator of the lease, or due to the failure to comply with any rule or

14. "Global Flaring and Venting Regulations: United Kingdom" (*World Bank*, December 2023) https://flaringventingregulations.worldbank.org/united-kingdom accessed September 28, 2024.
15. *Ibid.*
16. *Ibid.*
17. *Ibid.*
18. *Ibid.*
19. "Operators Fined Total of £265,000 as NSTA Moves to Enforce Net Zero and Security of Supply Requirements" (*North Sea Transition Authority*, December 19, 2022) https://www.nstauthority.co.uk/news-publications/operators-fined-total-of-gbp265000-as-nsta-moves-to-enforce-net-zero-and-security-of-supply-requirements/ accessed September 29, 2024.
20. "BLM Proposes Rule to Reduce Methane Emissions on Public Lands" (*Practical Law Finance*, November 30, 2022) https://uk.practicallaw.thomsonreuters.com/w-037-7510?transitionType=Default&contextData=%28sc.Default%29&firstPage=true accessed September 29, 2024.
21. "Waste Prevention, Production Subject to Royalties, and Resource Conservation" (*Federal Register*, Vol. 87, No. 229, p. 73588, 2022) https://www.govinfo.gov/content/pkg/FR-2022-11-30/pdf/2022-25345.pdf.
22. 30 U.S.C. §225.

regulation, order or citation issued under this chapter or any mineral leasing law."[23] The agency alleges that the new rule will allow it to recover an additional USD 39 million in royalty revenues from the recovered and flared gas per year.[24] However, the agency has also stated that the new rule would cost lessees an additional USD 122 million a year.[25] While this would be offset by the additional gas sells from the saved gas, the agency states that this will only amount to USD 55 million per year.[26] Accordingly, it is suspect that this Rule is actually a rule designed to recover lost royalties as it appears that it makes it uneconomic to recover oil and gas on these federal lands.

Based on this it is no surprise that the new rule, which was set to take effect on December 10, 2024, has been met with legal challenges which are working its way through the United States' judicial system. The industry appears to be successfully challenging these new flaring and venting rule.[27] For example, in October 2020, a federal court vacated the 2016 rule concluding that the Bureau of Land Management exceeded its statutory authority and acted arbitrarily and capriciously in adopting the rule.[28] Both of these are grounds for successfully challenging a Federal Rule in the United States.[29] In September 2024, a federal judge in North Dakota temporarily stayed the 2022 Rule from going into effect.[30] The court ruling makes it clear that this new Rule will cause states to be economically harmed due to decreased revenue from royalties and extraction on adjacent nonfederal lands.[31]

3 CONTENTIOUS HEALTH, SAFETY, AND ENVIRONMENTAL ASPECTS OF NATURAL GAS FLARING

Non-commercial continuous aspects of natural gas flaring around the world center around health, safety, and the environment. These disputes may be a collective action by a group of individuals or groups such as indigenous tribes while others focus on the effect on an individual. The causes of action asserted in the disputes range from nuisance to human rights violations. Moreover, the forum, person, or entity bringing these claims can vary and is ever-evolving. Lastly, claims have seen various levels of success depending on the claim brought and the forum. Each of these points will be discussed in greater detail below with the help of cases brought around the world.

23. 30 U.S.C. §1756.
24. *Supra* n. 22, at p. 73589.
25. *Ibid.*
26. *Ibid.*
27. In July 2020, a court vacated the Bureau of Land Management's rescission of the 2016 rule. *See California v. Bernhardt*, 472 F. Supp. 3d 573 (N.D. Cal. 2020).
28. *See Wyoming v. U.S. Dep't of Interior*, 493 F.Supp.3d 1046 (D. Wyo. 2020).
29. *Ibid.*
30. Boxerman S, "District of North Dakota Halts Bureau of Land Management's Venting and Flaring Rule" (*Environmental and Energy Brief*, September 18, 2024) https://environmentalenergybrief.sidley.com/2024/09/19/district-of-north-dakota-halts-bureau-of-land-managements-venting-and-flaring-rule/ accessed September 29, 2024.
31. *Ibid.*

3.1 Private Suits

Private suits by individuals have been brought seeking to enforce various individual rights. These suits have taken place in various continents, but all generally center around concerns of air quality resulting from flaring operations.

For example, in Nigeria in 2005 a representative of the Niger Delta Iwherekan community, on behalf of himself and his community instituted an action against the Nigerian government and Shell regarding flaring related to their exploration and production activities in the area.[32] The representative alleged harms such as chronic bronchitis and lower crop yields.[33] He claimed that the gas flaring activities and alleged harms resulting therefrom violated his and the community's rights to life and human dignity as constitutionally guaranteed by sections 33 and 34 of the 1999 Nigerian Constitution, and reinforced by Articles 4, 16, and 24 of the African Charter on Human and Peoples Rights. The latter was ratified and domesticated by Nigeria as Cap. A9, Laws of the Federation of Nigeria, 2004. Ultimately, judgment was entered in favor of the representative and Shell and the Nigerian government to stop the flaring and take steps to amend the Nigerian law affecting flaring to be in line with the Nigerian constitution.[34]

An example from the South American country can be seen in Ecuador where a group of girls in 2020 brought suit against the government and oil companies flaring gas at hundreds of sites in the Amazon claiming violations of their constitutional rights.[35] After a lengthy factual finding noting the poor quality of the flares, the Court ordered the flares to be shut down and reparations made to the people in the affected communities by the government.[36]

In April 2024, an Iraqi national, on behalf of his deceased son, began legal proceedings in England against a British oil and gas company claiming that a subsidiary of the company's flaring activity in Rumaila caused cancer in the deceased.[37] The firm stated that it believes that Iraqi law will govern the dispute and the penal code prohibits deliberately or negligently releasing emissions that cause harm to others.[38] This suit, like the one above, could be an interesting test case for bringing actions against oil and

---

32. *See* generally, *Gbemre v. Shell Petroleum Development Company of Nigeria Ltd. and Others.* https://climatecasechart.com/wp-content/uploads/non-us-casedocuments/2005/20051130_FHCBCS5305_judgment.pdf.
33. *Ibid.*, at pp. 2, 4, and 5.
34. "Sabin Center for Climate Change Law" (January 27, 2022). *Gbemre v. Shell Petroleum Development Company of Nigeria Ltd. and others.* Climate Change Litigation. https://climatecasechart.com/non-us-case/gbemre-v-shell-petroleum-development-company-of-nigeria-ltd-et-al/.
35. *See* Ecuador Provincial Court of Justice of Sucumbíos, *Herrera Carrion et al. v. Ministry of the Environment et al. (Caso Mecheros*, 2020), at pp. 21-22 https://www.derechosdelanaturaleza.org.ec/wp-content/uploads/2021/05/3.-CASO-MECHEROS-SENTENCIA-PRIMERA-INSTANCIA-1.pdf.
36. *Ibid.*
37. Hausfeld (n.d.), "BP Hit by Legal Action Alleging That Its Excessive Gas Flaring Caused Death of Young Iraqi" (Hausfeld, LLP) https://www.hausfeld.com/en-gb/news/bp-hit-by-legal-action-alleging-that-its-excessive-gas-flaring-caused-death-of-young-iraqi/.
38. *Ibid.*

gas companies in developed nations as a result of actions taken in distant parts of the world.

In other cases, private suits may be brought to enforce national legislation where the government has primacy of enforcement. While the enforcement arms of national regulators are the stakeholders that bring legal action to enforce national legislation, some national and local governments have authorized these suits to be brought by private citizens. As it relates to gas flaring, these private litigation mechanisms have been particularly useful to those seeking to change flaring practices.

For example, in 2021, utilizing the "citizen suit" provision of the United States' Clean Air Act, several environmental activist groups filed suit alleging that the natural gas processing plant in West Texas flaring of "sour" gas, resulting in the emission of sulfur dioxide and hydrogen sulfide into the air.[39] This matter was ultimately resolved through a consent decree in which the company agreed to make improvements that reduce gas flaring, pay USD 500,000, and pay certain penalties if hydrogen sulfide emissions exceeded certain thresholds.[40] This suit is not unique. In the years before the suit, a similar one was brought in the same area against another gas plant complaining of the flaring practices.[41] However, in that case, in addition to changing flaring practices, the plaintiffs also required air filters to be bought for local classrooms.[42]

Environmental groups have stated that these private rights of action are critical in enforcing certain environmental regulations where they believe the government has otherwise failed to do so.[43]

3.2 Governmental

National and local governments do in fact bring actions to address health, safety, and environmental concerns related to gas flaring. However, governments and their enforcement of arms do not have unlimited resources to address every instance of flaring that may affect health, safety, and the environment.

For example, in June of 2023, the United States Environmental Protection Agency brought an administrative enforcement action pursuant to the Clean Air Act against an oil and gas operator in the Permian Basin of Texas after observing tanks, flares, and other equipment using a helicopter equipped with a special infrared camera that detects hydrocarbon leaks.[44] The matter was resolved through a consent decree which

39. *See* generally, *Texas Campaign for The Environment, Environment America, Inc. D/B/A Environment Texas et al., v. DCP Operating Company, L.P.*, Cause No. 7:21-cv-00048-DC in The United States District Court For The Western District of Texas—Midland Division.
40. Environmental Integrity Project, "Environmental Groups Reach Settlement That Reduces Gas Flaring at Permian Basin Gas Plant" (May 27, 2022). Environmental Integrity Project. https://environmentalintegrity.org/news/environmental-groups-reach-settlement-that-reduces-gas-flaring-at-permian-basin-gas-plant/.
41. *Ibid.*
42. *Ibid.*
43. *Ibid.*
44. Environmental Protection Agency, "EPA Announces $1.3 Million Settlement for Permian Basin Company" (*EPA*, July 13, 2023). https://www.epa.gov/newsreleases/epa-announces-13-million-settlement-permian-basin-company.

required the operator to pay a penalty in the amount of USD 1.3 million.[45] Like the private actions discussed above, these disputes regarding flaring are all designed to protect the environment as many of the constituents of flared gases are considered pollutants.

In a similar fashion, the United Kingdom's North Sea Transition Authority formerly known as the OGA, views the flared gas not just as pollutants but also as climate-changing greenhouse gases that must be reduced to meet its Net-Zero goals.[46] This includes reducing "routine flaring" by 2030 to zero.[47] To ensure that companies are in compliance with this goal, the North Sea Transition Authority, as the regulator of flaring can and has issued penalties for unauthorized flaring in the North Sea. For example, recently fined an operator GBP 160,000 (USD 202,164) for alleged flaring and venting breaches amounting to more than 73 tons of gas from its Auk North, Fulmar, and Halley fields in the North Sea.[48]

In some cases, environmental cases there have been attempts to rebrand environmental litigation as anti-waste commercial litigation. For example, and as noted above, in the North Sea Transition Authority's flaring guidance it is noted that the regulator has the right to consent to flaring to prevent waste.[49] But looking at the document as a whole, it is clear that the North Sea Transition Authority is using this authority for another goal—greenhouse gas reduction.[50] Moreover, in *Wyoming v. U.S. Department of the Interior*,[51] several states challenged the United States Bureau of Land Management's new rule purportedly aimed at reducing waste of natural gas in flaring and venting known as *Waste Prevention, Production Subject to Royalties, and Resource Conservation*. The government argued that the rationale for the rule was waste prevention which would allow it to recover additional royalties. It further noted that the ancillary benefit would be better air quality. However, the court noted that "significant aspects of the Rule evidence its primary purpose being driven by an effort to regulate air emissions, particularly greenhouse gases."[52] One such example noted by the Court was the preference for the rule for flaring over venting, which it noted led to the same amount of waste but different environmental outcomes. Ultimately, the Court ruled against the Bureau of Land Management's new rule for exceeding the statutory grant of power. This, however, is not the point of this chapter. The point is that governments will likely continue to find creative methods for reducing greenhouse emissions even under challenging statutory frameworks.

45. United States Environmental Protection Agency. (n.d.), "EPA Administrative Enforcement Dockets" (*EPA*) https://yosemite.epa.gov/oa/rhc/epaadmin.nsf/All + Dockets + by + Case + Number/CAA-06-2023-3339.
46. North Sea Transition Authority, Flaring and Venting Guidance 2021, p. 3.
47. *Ibid.*
48. Battersby A, "Repsol Hit by Largest-Ever Fine Imposed by UK Regulator" (*Upstream*, December 14, 2023). https://www.upstreamonline.com/finance/repsol-hit-by-largest-ever-fine-imposed-by-uk-regulator/2-1-1571039.
49. North Sea Transition Authority, Flaring and Venting Guidance 2021, p. 4.
50. *Ibid.*, at 3.
51. 493 F. Supp. 3d 1046 (D. Wyo. 2020).
52. *Ibid.*

3.3 International

International law, like national law, provides a basis for disputes relating to flaring because of greenhouse concerns whether burned (CO_2) or vented (methane). Moreover, International law related to greenhouse gases includes agreements and advisory opinions that outline governments' legal obligations to reduce emissions. These include the United Nations Framework Convention on Climate Change (UNFCCC) which includes the Kyoto Protocol. Adopted in 1997, this agreement is the only legally binding treaty to reduce greenhouse gas emissions.[53] It requires 41 countries and the European Union to reduce emissions of six greenhouse gases by 5.2% below 1990 levels.[54] These include methane and carbon dioxide. Accordingly, nations who are parties to these agreements may face actions relating to flaring if they have not adhered to their 2030 flare reduction pledges common in the oil and gas industry.

Because large amounts of oil and gas are produced offshore, it is also important to discuss a recent advisory opinion from The International Tribunal For The Law of The Sea.[55] The tribunal is responsible for interpreting and upholding the 1982 United Nations Convention On The Law of The Sea, an international treaty representing 169 countries. In its advisory opinion, the tribunal specifically noted that aside from vessels, greenhouse gas emissions originate from seabed activities such as venting and flaring.[56] The tribunal reiterated that section 5 of Part XII of the Convention addresses the obligations to adopt national laws and regulations and establish international rules and standards to prevent, reduce, and control marine pollution from six different sources including pollution from seabed activities subject to national jurisdiction.[57] As a result of this advisory opinion, it is expected that a flurry of disputes may arise in jurisdictions that are part of the treaty but have not adopted national legislation to prevent reduce, and control marine pollution from the seabed. Moreover, it is expected that additional disputes will center on whether the legislation has taken into account "internationally agreed rules, standards and recommended practices and procedures."[58]

4 FORMS OF DISPUTE RESOLUTION

The form of the dispute resolution method varies depending on the underlying dispute type, the parties, and oil and gas operations location.

53. Britannica T, Editors of Encyclopedia, "Kyoto Protocol" (*Encyclopedia Britannica*, March 7, 2024) https://www.britannica.com/event/Kyoto-Protocol.
54. *Ibid.*
55. Advisory Opinion for the *Request for An Advisory Opinion Submitted by The Commission of Small Island States on Climate Change and International Law,* The International Tribunal For The Law Of The Sea. https://www.itlos.org/fileadmin/itlos/documents/cases/31/Advisory_Opinion/C31_Adv_Op_21.05.2024_orig.pdf May 21, 2024.
56. *Ibid.*, at ¶ 263.
57. *Ibid.*, at ¶ 260. (citing Art. 208).
58. *Ibid.*, at ¶ 270.

Regulatory action disputes can often occur outside the national courts, at least initially. Instead, these disputes will go through the administrative dispute process. Examples of this include the United States Environmental Protection Agency's administrative docket and the North Sea Transition Authority's administrative action. As seen above, while these disputes are outside the national courts, the stakes are high. For example, breaches in the regulations surrounding flaring can and do lead to serious fines on companies that are millions of dollars.[59] Moreover, particularly egregious offenders may lose the right to operate the oil and gas assets or be disqualified from operating other assets.[60] Accordingly, operators should be well versed in the regulatory framework surrounding gas flaring in addition to how they can navigate the administrative dispute resolution system. Lastly, because one of the parties to the suit will effectively be a sovereign or agent in the administrative process, oil and gas operators will likely face various degrees of bias against them.[61] This is not necessarily dependent on how developed the nation is, as there may be economic interests at play that ultimately favor the company in the administrative dispute process. In other words, the government may be willing to resolve the dispute amicably in order to ensure that oil and gas are produced at acceptable levels.

The national court system can also be a method for resolution of flaring disputes. This form of dispute resolution is particularly important for private flaring disputes between individuals as it is often the only means of dispute resolution available to these stakeholders. As seen in the Amazon flaring disputes matter discussed in this chapter, impoverished individuals do that have the means to resolve their disputes at regional and international levels. Moreover, these individuals do not have standing to resolve their dispute with the party flaring—whether a governmental entity or private company—in international courts and arbitration. Moreover, these individuals often do not have the requested power to resolve their disputes through negotiation with government entities and large multinational companies. Accordingly, in order to resolve the dispute, individuals need a robust, independent national court system to vindicate their rights where appropriate. This includes the ability of the national court to ensure compliance with its decisions. Moreover, national court systems are often used to resolve disputes between oil and gas companies that did not enter into an arbitration agreement or disputes which are not covered by the arbitration agreement. How utility of the national courts can vary depending on the system. Judicial systems that welcome expert resolution of matters may be better than systems where judges or

59. Battersby A, "Repsol Hit by Largest-Ever Fine Imposed by UK Regulator" (*Upstream*, December 14, 2023) https://www.upstreamonline.com/finance/repsol-hit-by-largest-ever-fine-imposed-by-uk-regulator/2-1-1571039.

60. *See*, for example, section 23(a) of the United States' "Oil And Gas Lease of Submerged Lands Under The Outer Continental Shelf Lands Act" which states "[w]henever the Lessee fails to comply with any of the provisions of the Act, the regulations issued pursuant to the Act, or the terms of this lease, the lease shall be subject to cancellation ..." (Form BOEM-2005).

61. *See*, for example, in Federal Arbitrazh Court of the Volgo-Vyatsky Region, Case No. A43-10716/02-27-10, February 17, 2003 (Russian Federation) where the court's refusal to enforce an arbitral award went beyond the legal issues and considered the factual consequences of the award, social, and economic damage to the city.

tribunals are generalists.[62] Finally, many of the same issues raised in the administrative dispute resolution process are implicated when the government or its agents are a party to the suit. This is likely why some host government agreements will require the dispute to be heard in national courts.[63] Whether the arbitration is commercial arbitration or centers around an investment treaty, the New York Convention with more than 150 parties, is a particularly useful method of dispute resolution because of the reduced risk that an award will not enforced in various jurisdictions.[64] The same cannot be said of national courts enforcing awards of other national courts.

Arbitration is often a commonly used form of dispute resolution. Agreements between commercial parties, such as Joint Operating Agreements, require the dispute to be resolved through arbitration. Moreover, investment treaties also provide a basis for the parties to have their dispute resolved by arbitration. Arbitration does not necessarily favor either party because of the strict neutrality rules in a dispute. Moreover, because arbitration rules allow the parties to choose the arbitrator or the arbitrators, the parties are afforded expert arbitrators who will likely be able to more effectively understand the issues and resolve the issues presented better than generalist judges and tribunals.

Where the parties wish to preserve their commercial relationship, negotiation and mediation may be utilized to resolve the dispute. Moreover, some contractual agreements and court systems require good faith negotiation or mediation before either party can enter into a formal dispute resolution process such as arbitration or the national court system. This has the advantage of the parties quietly resolving the dispute without the publicity associated with arbitration and national courts. In addition, like arbitration, for commercial flaring disputes, the Singapore Convention on Mediation, which helps promote cross-border enforcement of mediation agreements may be available to the parties. However, with over fifty signatories and a limited scope, it is not as useful as the New York Convention for arbitral award enforcement at this time.

As shown above there are many forms of dispute resolution methods potentially implicated when disputes arise as a result of flaring, whether commercial or environmental.

5 IMPACTS OF FLARING DISPUTES

Flaring disputes, particularly those centered around environmental concerns, are likely to force innovations regarding flaring practices. In some cases, these disputes may cause less productive areas, such as mature fields, to no longer be produced because

62. Issues, "Science in the Courtroom" (*Issues in Science and Technology*, July 1, 2022) https://issues.org/breyer-science-courtroom/ accessed September 20, 2024.
63. Baker M, "The Future of Oil and Gas Arbitration: The Impact of ESG Policies on Oil and Gas Disputes" (*Thought Leadership*, May 2023) https://www.nortonrosefulbright.com/en-us/knowledge/publications/d4daa555/the-future-of-oil-and-gas-arbitration accessed September 29, 2024.
64. United Nations Convention on the Recognition and Enforcement of Foreign Arbitral Awards (New York, June 10, 1958).

they will no longer be economically viable or competitive. Moreover, because gas and oil are generally found together, where there is not sufficient infrastructure to produce the oil and not flare gas outside of concerns of safety, these areas may not be produced, or their production delayed until technology or economic conditions permit their production. In other cases, flaring will continue, just in a more efficient and environmentally friendly way.

Nonetheless, as long as these disputes do not cause the production of natural gas and oil to cease, the impact should be positive as captured gas which would otherwise be a waste product of production, would be transformed into an economic resource. For example, in 2019 Angola, the petroleum minister noted that most of the 3 billion cubic feet per day of associated natural gas Angola produced was flared.[65] The minister noted aside from the environmental concerns, Angola was missing out on significant economic benefits due to the flaring.[66] As of 2022, Angola had one liquified natural gas facility to monetize the natural gas being produced during oil extraction. While this facility has a 1.1 billion cubic feet daily capacity, this still falls short of the 3 billion produced per day. Nonetheless, it shows a commitment to monetizing what would otherwise be flare gas in various natural gas project announcements.

Moreover, the additional gas may supplant more carbon-intensive forms of power generation such as coal. In addition, less developed areas with populations which rely on wood, coal, dung, and other pollutant-heavy sources for heat and cooking may positively benefit from the use of the captured gas. For example, the World Economic Forum has stated that nearly 4 million people a year die from illnesses linked to cooking with polluting fuels and women are the most affected.[67] Along the same lines, the Darfur Sudan Cookstove Project helps replace traditional biomass stoves with liquified petroleum gas (a product of wet natural gas processing) to lower carbon emissions and improve air quality in homes.[68] According to participants in the projects, the replacement reduced illnesses such as chest infections.[69]

6 FUTURE OF FLARING DISPUTES

As noted herein, 2030 has become an important date in natural gas flaring. This is because, in 2015, The World Bank launched the Zero Routine Flaring initiative.[70] This initiative aims to end routine flaring—i.e., non-emergency or safety-related—by 2030. Both industry and government bodies have made the zero routine flaring commitment

65. Angola seeks to reduce gas flaring to capture revenue. Reuters. (October 9, 2019). https://www.reuters.com/article/idUSKBN1WO114/.
66. *Ibid.*
67. Whiting K, "Cooking with Polluting Fuels Is a Silent Killer: Here's What Can Be Done" (*World Economic Forum*, October 27, 2021) https://www.weforum.org/agenda/2021/10/polluting-cooking-fuels-deaths-women-climate/.
68. *Ibid.*
69. *Ibid.*
70. World Bank, "About the ZRF" (n.d.) https://www.worldbank.org/en/programs/zero-routine-flaring-by-2030/about.

by 2030. However, the commitment itself is not legally binding.[71] Instead, it is up to private parties to hold themselves or their partners accountable and for government regulators who have made the commitment to impose legally binding measures to ensure their partners are in compliance with their 2030 commitments. Examples of this can be seen across the world.

For example, the English regulator, the North Sea Transition Authority in 2021 made it clear that it expects its industry partners to be part of its zero routine flaring goal by 2030 aspirations and will (and has) issued fines for failing to comply with its flaring consent process designed to reduce this routine flaring.[72] Another example is the Ecuador decision discussed above which required flares near populated areas to cease operations immediately and others to cease by 2030.[73]

Accordingly, flaring disputes between now and 2030 may continue to center around defining legal obligations—nationally and internationally—until 2030. An example is the advisory opinion discussed above. After 2030 it is expected various disputes will arise regarding these obligations for those who have not achieved the zero routine flaring goal. It is also expected that these disputes will rely on the currently developing law on issues of human rights and climate change obligations.

Moreover, between stakeholders participating in the oil and gas development, it is expected that future disputes will focus on ensuring their partners are participating in a way which ensures that one or more of the parties is meeting their publicly stated goals and international commitments. As noted above this could include disputes around joint operating agreements and investment treaties.

7 CONCLUSION

As seen in this chapter there are generally two types of disputes as it relates to natural gas flaring and venting: commercial and environmental. Commercial disputes largely revolve around the language of the granting instrument and the calculation (and collection) of royalties or taxes. However, as shown herein, the environmental side of natural gas flaring can take many forms and is regularly brought by both government and private citizens. Moreover and more recently, due to the fact that natural gas largely consists of methane and when burned is transformed into carbon dioxide, the world's attitude toward these two greenhouse gases is a source for disputes from the local to international levels.

Litigation in the United regarding the new flaring and venting rules highlights that there are issues with using existing statutory language in order to creatively create

71. *Ibid.*
72. North Sea Transition Authority, "Flaring and venting" (n.d.) https://www.nstauthority.co.uk/regulatory-information/licensing-and-consents/consents/flaring-and-venting/#: ~ :text = flarin g%20and%20venting%20and%20associated,zero%20routine%20flaring%20and%20venting.
73. Guardian News and Media, "'Just By Breathing We Are Contaminated': Schoolgirls Fight to Extinguish Ecuador's Gas Flares" (*The Guardian*, May 16, 2024) https://www.theguardian.com/global-development/article/2024/may/16/breathing-contaminated-ecuador-schoolgirls-fight-fossil-gas-flaring.

new venting and flaring rules. As such, until there is sufficient political will to create new statutes to serve as a basis for the new flaring and venting rules, courts will have little choice but to strike them down. The English experience, however, appears to be very different. Parliament has provided the necessary statutes for regulators to regulate and fine oil and gas flaring.

Finally, while a survey of flaring and venting disputes appears to show there are well-developed legal remedies surrounding flaring and venting on the local and national level, future flaring disputes will undoubtedly develop additional remedies on the international stage which will trickle down to the local and national level. Two such examples given in this chapter include the cases in Ecuador and Nigeria.

CHAPTER 30

ESG Agenda

Timothy Affonso

1 INTRODUCTION

Environment, society and governance (ESG) is collectively defined as a firm's obligation to improve social welfare; and equitable and sustainable long-term wealth for stakeholders.[1] The ESG Agenda is a framework within which organizations can operate so as to ensure that they do not negatively impact the wider human and social environment in which they operate. For the purposes of this chapter, the ESG Agenda will be used as a framework within which the Oil and Gas Industry (O&GI) utilizes natural gas flaring. With a specific focus on the risks associated with the practice of natural gas flaring in the O&GI, the ESG Agenda has the potential to serve as a true panacea. When one considers how natural gas flaring functions, the justification and dangers of the practice become clearer. In essence, gas flaring is the burning of excess methane gas and carbon dioxide (CO_2) which are released when drilling for crude oil. The natural consequences of flaring are increases in emissions of CO_2, carbon monoxide and methane resulting in a direct impact on global boiling[2] which consequently facilitates significant wastage of marketable products which could be sold. The simplicity of this explanation of flaring provides the necessary linkages to the environmental, social and governance (ESG) threads which guide the ESG Agenda. To this end,

1. Dima Jamali, Charlotte Karam, Juelin Yin & Vivek Soundararajan, "CSR Logics in Developing Countries: Translation, Adaptation and Stalled Development" [2017] Journal of World Business, 52 (3) 343 https://doi.org/10.1016/j.jwb.2017.02.001 cited in Wan Masliza Wan Mohammed & Shaista Wasiuzzaman, "Environmental, Social and Governance (ESG) Disclosure, Competitive Advantage and Performance of Firms in Malaysia" [2021] Cleaner Environmental Systems, 2 https://doi.org/10.1016/j.cesys.2021.100015.
2. Teerachai Amnuaylojaroen, "Perspective on the Era of Global Boiling: A Future Beyond Global Warming" [2023] Advances in Meteorology, 12 https://doi.org/10.1155/2023/5580606.

this chapter will seek to use the ESG Agenda as a lens through which natural gas flaring is examined.

First, the practice of natural gas flaring will be discussed. This part of the paper will allow for a brief discussion of the process of oil extraction and where flaring fits in the macro process. The second part of the paper will examine the ESG elements in three separate sections. Initially, there will be a careful analysis of how flaring impacts the environmental element of the ESG Agenda. There will then be a discussion of the effects of flaring on the social dimension of the ESG Agenda. Finally, there will be an interrogation of the way in which flaring can impact the governance of states. Layered over the entire discussion will be an examination of whether flaring can ever be compatible with an ESG Agenda. The importance of examining each element of the ESG Agenda as it relates to flaring is that it will demonstrate how the ESG Agenda can be used by companies and industries to ensure compliance. There will then be a separate section on recommendations on how an ESG Agenda can help minimize or eradicate the risks associated with flaring.

2 THE PROCESS OF NATURAL GAS FLARING EXPLAINED

Flaring is the burning of natural gas byproducts during the crude oil extraction process.[3] Flaring lights the released gas and burns the methane.[4] This is a common feature of many oil fields. The commonness of this feature of oil extraction stems from the oil extraction process itself. At a practical level, when oil forms underground, generally some amount of natural gas forms with it, and together the two are trapped inside an oil and gas reservoir.[5] It is this natural phenomenon that creates the birth of the challenge in oil extraction. Being less dense than oil, natural gas settles above the oil in a pocket of gas.[6] As such, any oil extraction activity will result in a corollary and unintended extraction of natural gas. When companies drill for this oil in an attempt to extract it, this natural gas now has a place to escape the reservoir and accompany the oil to the surface.[7] In some reservoirs, enough natural gas exists that it is economical to extract it along with the oil.[8] In such a situation, a natural gas industry develops alongside an oil extractive industry. In this scenario, there will be no flaring but instead, there will be a need for infrastructure to extract and store the natural gas. However in other cases, the gas exists in such small quantities that it is essentially of no use or of low quality, and thus flaring is utilized.[9] Additionally, when there is maintenance needed on facilities, flaring is used to reduce the levels of natural gas in

3. Wesley Blundell & Anatolii Kokoza, "Natural Gas Flaring, Respiratory Health and Distributional Effects" [2022] Journal of Public Economics 208 https://doi.org/10.1016/j.jpubeco.2022.104601.
4. Genevieve Plant et al., "Inefficient and Unlit Natural Gas Flares Both Emit Large Quantities of Methane" [2022] Science, 377 (6614), pp. 1566-1571 https://doi.org/10.1126/science.abq0385.
5. Energy Education, "Flaring," University of Calgary https://energyeducation.ca/encyclopedia/Flaring accessed August 27, 2024.
6. *Ibid.*
7. Energy Education, *supra* n. 5.
8. *Ibid.*
9. Canadian Association of Petroleum Producers, "Guide for Estimation of Flaring and Venting Volumes," (Clearstone Engineering Ltd., 2014).

order to create a safer environment for workers.[10] These two scenarios tend to be where the practice of flaring finds its popularity. It is this cheaper way of dealing with the unwanted gas that makes the flaring process desirable in the O&GI and also why it is so difficult to stop. Another takeaway from the foregoing is that flaring finds its genesis in the need to both protect workers from ignition and the economical disposal of gas. In essence, the practice of flaring is not, at its heart, sinister in nature but linked to the health and safety of workers and workplace.

While it can be shown that flaring has its utility, another side to the practice is that it is done by many oil producers because it is not profitable to capture, transport and process the methane.[11] As has already been established, this is in part because sometimes the methane gas is either low quality or insufficient to justify expenditure on alternate treatment options besides flaring. It must be noted that flaring is not better justified if it seeks to protect workers versus save money for O&G companies. The real threat of natural gas flaring is the extent of its implementation both from a numerical perspective and duration and also the serious side-effects of its usage.

Based on gas-flaring satellite data from 2020, Russia, Iraq, Iran, the United States, Algeria, Venezuela and Nigeria remain the top seven gas-flaring countries and account for two-thirds of global gas flaring.[12] According to the World Bank in 2021, the widespread use of gas flaring by the aforementioned countries is not necessarily linked to irresponsible extractive policies but resource challenges. For example, the United States and Russia have flaring oil fields that are remote and lack the infrastructure to capture and transport the associated gas.[13] This introduces the reality of the O&GI relative to flaring. Flaring takes place due, principally, to market and economic constraints as identified previously and also due to a lack of appropriate regulation and political will.[14] It is not being advanced that there is any form of opposition to the fact that gas flaring is environmentally deleterious. Therefore, with acceptance of the ill effects of flaring, the question that must be asked is why the practice persists. This question becomes that much more relevant when one considers the extensive dangers associated with flaring. These dangers will now briefly be discussed.

One facet of the danger of flaring is the immediate environmental impact of the practice. First, since flaring has been a feature of the O&GI for over 160 years, its negative consequences have far-reaching impacts. When one considers the almost two-century practice of flaring, one can better understand the scary reality for the global community if it is discovered that there are negative environmental consequences of flaring.

10. Canadian Association of Petroleum Producers, "Emergency Air Monitoring Best Management Practices," (August 5, 2014).
11. Blundell et al., *supra* n. 3.
12. The World Bank, "Seven Countries Account for Two-Thirds of Global Gas Flaring," (Press Release, April 28, 2021) https://www.worldbank.org/en/news/press-release/2021/04/28/seven-countries-account-for-two-thirds-of-global-gas-flaring accessed August 27, 2024.
13. *Ibid.*
14. *Ibid.*

The truth is that flaring can be considered a major contributor to methane emission, a greenhouse gas (GHG), which is 80 times more powerful than CO_2 as a warming gas in a 20-year timeframe.[15] The impact of this comparison is that methane emissions hasten the global warming phenomenon exponentially faster than CO_2 emissions would. Putting this in the context of a practice that has been ongoing for almost two hundred years, the devastating reality of flaring on generations comes to light.

Further, there is an estimation that gas flaring has resulted in approximately 400 million tonnes of CO_2 being released into the atmosphere.[16] While this number may sound significant, research has shown that the emissions from flaring account for less than 1 % of the total CO_2 released into the atmosphere.[17] That is not to say that the issue of flaring and the deleterious consequences of engaging in the practice are insignificant. On the contrary, through the lens of the ESG Agenda, the full threat posed by flaring can be appreciated. When one considers that one activity in one industry has the capacity to affect global temperatures so substantially and has been allowed to continue for decades, one can realize the true gravity and effect of flaring on the world's population and environment. It is this extensive background to flaring and the intersectionality of its effects that each of the dimensions of the ESG Agenda will now be addressed in turn as it relates to the continued practice of natural gas flaring in the O&GI.

3 ESG AGENDA

Before embarking on the ESG elements, it is first necessary to highlight that the various dimensions of the ESG Agenda are not hermetically sealed off from one another. These three elements have formed key features of the Agenda because of the natural linkages among them. It should also be noted that satisfying an ESG Agenda is not seeking to achieve as many of the targets as possible but to modify activities to ensure that there is consistency and compliance with the ESG Agenda which is being used. To this end, it is impossible to discuss flaring under each category of the ESG Agenda without seeing the connection of each issue with another element. All activities have multiple dimensions to their effects. This is why an ESG Agenda can be so useful because it is multi-sectoral in its approach.

Some academics argue that ESG investing suffers from a well-documented problem of defining exactly what it is.[18] The combination of definitional ambiguity and enormous market impact is accompanied by burgeoning risks of different types.[19]

15. DTE Staff, "Global Warming: 400 Million Tonnes CO2 Pumped to Atmosphere a Year from This Source the World Is Blind to," (Down to Earth, 2022) https://www.downtoearth.org.in/news/environment/global-warming-400-million-tonnes-co2-pumped-to-atmosphere-a-year-from-this-source-the-world-is-blind-to-82726 accessed August 27, 2024.
16. *Ibid.*
17. Energy Education, "Flaring," University of Calgary, https://energyeducation.ca/encyclopedia/Flaring accessed August 27, 2024.
18. Ryan Thomas Trahan & Brad Jantz, "What Is ESG? Rethinking the 'E' Pillar" [2023] Business Strategy and the Environment, 32 (7) https://doi.org/10.1002/bse.3371.
19. *Ibid.*

However, the meaning, scope and application of an ESG Agenda is self-determined. If there is definitional ambiguity, it is because the ESG Agenda has been misunderstood and/or not properly adapted to the needs of the particular situation. Turning the attention now to each limb of the ESG Agenda, it will be clear what each pillar covers and how it can be used in the extractive industry, specifically flaring.

The environmental aspect of ESG, the "E" pillar, employs quasi-private governance investing principles and tools to address the impacts of commercial and industrial activities on shared air, land, and water resources.[20] This means that the environmental pillar of the ESG Agenda looks at how the environment is affected by activities which are engaged in by companies. To apply the environmental pillar to a given activity, one must first identify the ways in which the commercial activity interacts with the natural environment. When the attention is turned to flaring later in this Chapter, it will become clear how this dimension of the ESG Agenda is used. An important aspect of "G" (governance) that is sometimes forgotten, is that most companies are already inherently familiar with it, a major benefit when it comes to rolling out a wider ESG framework.[21] What is meant by this is that governance in the ESG Agenda refers to both internal corporate governance frameworks as well as the national governmental laws, policies and regulations which operate in a specific industry or sphere of commercial activity. While environmental reporting affects the "S" pillar (social relationships), there may be new territory for compliance teams in respect of human rights and United Nations Sustainable Development Goals (UNSDGs) which can be closely intertwined with existing compliance functions such as legal affairs, internal audits, and human resources.[22] It is perhaps the social pillar of the ESG Agenda that best demonstrates the interconnectedness of the limbs of the Agenda more than any other limb. The relationship between law, human rights, and the environment is naturally synergistic and it helps show the linkages which undergird the three pillars of the ESG Agenda.

While it has been stated that the role of each limb of the ESG Agenda has historical roots and collectively may suffer from a challenge of definitional clarity, it is much easier to see the ESG Agenda in the O&GI when it is actively applied. For example, a company with poor environmental practices may be subject to increasingly strict regulation, which could hurt profits and a company with poor social practices may also face reputational damage, leading to lost customers and revenue.[23] Similarly, a company with weak governance practices may be more likely to experience fraud or other financial problems.[24]

20. Pedros Matos, "ESG And Responsible Institutional Investing Around The World: A Critical Review," (CFA Institute Research Foundation, 2020).
21. Niall McCarthy, "Making Sense of ESG's Governance Pillar," [2022] EQS Group https://doi.org/10.4324/9781315866765-1.
22. *Ibid.*
23. Jo Ellis, "What Are the Three Pillars of ESG?," (Lexicon, Corporate Governance Institute) https://www.thecorporategovernanceinstitute.com/insights/lexicon/three-pillars-of-esg-ultimate-guide-to-esg/ accessed September 2, 2023.
24. *Ibid.*

These foregoing examples demonstrate the close relationship the actors in the O&GI have with both their economic strength and ESG compliance. Ultimately, ESG impacts company success and has the potential to preserve the ESG systems. It is to this end that ESG initiatives can significantly impact how consumers perceive a brand, so it is essential to ensure that ESG efforts are consistent with the image the company wants to project.[25] That is why it is important to highlight ESG as a tool for financial success within the O&GI. While ESG is perceived by some to be difficult to implement, and it may seem like a profit-killer, the irony is that for most companies that implement ESG programs, including those within the O&GI, it has the opposite effect.[26] When one considers the growing role of corporate social responsibility and corporate reputation, one may appreciate how a company is seen can also directly impact a company's market share. If a company is able to meaningfully operate within an ESG Agenda it may benefit from customer loyalty, increased revenue, reduced penalties for regulatory infractions and even goodwill. This means that the investment in ESG compliance has real and direct benefits to a company. Furthermore, according to the International Energy Association's (IEA's) 2021 Global Energy Review, renewable energy grew 3% in 2020, inclusive of a 7% increase in electricity generation from renewable sources.[27] This means that clean energy is on the increase and when one considers the move to sustainability and the UNSDGs, an ESG Agenda can only help support a company's growth and economic success.

Widespread support of ESG policies, matrices and the overall energy transition is no doubt rooted in some critical and likely accurate assumptions.[28] Climate change poses a serious threat to the destabilization of global economies in decades to come; large tracts of farmland could become unproductive due to shifts in temperatures and major coastal cities could become uninhabitable due to rising ocean tides.[29] This reinforces the basic argument that there is a need to urgently address climatological deterioration in an attempt to prosper: both in economic and social terms at national and international levels. As will be discussed in the following part of this Chapter, flaring causes serious harm to the environment and to society, and as such the relevance of an ESG Agenda is that much more relevant. Further, the lack of national legislative frameworks in many countries relative to flaring is yet an additional layer to the immediacy of action required to curb this activity in the O&GI. After establishing the importance of the ESG Agenda to the overarching theme of climate change in the O&GI, it is now necessary to interrogate each of the three limbs of the ESG Agenda and

25. *Ibid.*
26. Lisa Rushton, "ESG: How It Applies to the Oil & Gas Industry and Why It Matters," (Womble Bond Dickinson, September 22, 2021) https://www.womblebonddickinson.com/us/insights/articles-and-briefings/esg-how-it-applies-oil-gas-industry-and-why-it-matters accessed September 2, 2023.
27. *Ibid.*
28. *Ibid.*
29. *Ibid.*

critically examine how the ESG Agenda can be used to curb the implementation of natural gas flaring.

3.1 Environmental Dimension

As has already been mentioned, there is a correlation between flaring and global warming due to the increase in CO_2 emissions. However, beyond these emissions, there are also methane emissions, black soot and nitrous oxide which are injurious to health.[30] In fact, in a study conducted in 2022, it was revealed that flaring is five times more pollutive than was previously thought.[31] While there have been assertions that flaring has a 98% efficiency rate at combusting unwanted gas, contemporary research shows that it has an actual efficiency rate that is closer to 91%.[32] This inefficiency results in dangers associated with more gas being released into the atmosphere than initially thought accompanied by increased levels of soot. Based on research done in the Niger Delta, flaring is a significant factor responsible for unfavorable water quality, high-temperature variation and the rapid decline in the health of natural vegetation.[33] These consequences on the environment impact national populations and will, necessarily, require a discussion under the social pillar as well as the ESG Agenda. This is stated because a clean environment, biological diversity and potable water are obligations which fall squarely in the framework of international environmental law and human rights. Without delving too deeply into the social dimension of Nigerian research, it is necessary to further interrogate the impact of flaring on the physical environment and the resultant massive environmental degradation.

The nature of the environmental impact caused by flaring is linked to the chemical composition of the natural gas which is being flared.[34] The effects posed on the environment by the emission include, but are not limited to, global warming as a result of the release of GHGs, acidification of rain or acid rain, and close heating of surrounding vegetation, and surrounding air.[35] It is pellucid that flaring has a negative impact on the environment and would be incompatible with an ESG Agenda. That is not, however, the end of the complexity of the current discussion.

There is also a relationship between the ESG Agenda and the UNSDGs. As sustainable energy continues to be an important driving force for economies, states can try to implement their ESG Agenda within the guidance provided by Sustainable

30. IEA, "Gas Flaring," https://www.iea.org/energy-system/fossil-fuels/gas-flaring accessed August 27, 2024.
31. Jon Goldstein, "New Study Finds Flaring Source of Five Times More Pollution Than Previously Thought" [2022] Environmental Defense Fund.
32. *Ibid.*
33. N.A. Akeem & A.Y.B. Anifowose, "Effect of Gas Flaring on the Environment: A Case Study. Of a Part of Niger Delta, Nigeria" [2016] American Geophysical Union.
34. A. Kwame Sekyi, "The Impact of Gas Flaring on Man and His Environment and the Way Out" [2017] International Journal of Engineering and Management Sciences (I) EMS 2 (3) https://doi.org/10.21791/ijems.2017.3.8.
35. *Ibid.*

Development Goal (SDG) 1,[36] 3,[37] 4,[38] 8,[39] 9,[40] 11,[41] 12,[42] 13,[43] 15.[44] It must be noted at this juncture that UNSDGs will be an example of a consideration that affects all three elements of the ESG Agenda. With a global effort to guide states to achieve developmental goals, practices which are inimical to the advancement of those goals should be stopped. In a similar fashion to the UNSDGs, where commercial activities cause harm to the environment, of such a nature as that of flaring, it would similarly require immediate action to halt the activity. Recognizing that the joint application of the UNSDGs and the ESG Agenda in the context of flaring in the O&GI are incompatible, there will be a need to either manage the reduction in flaring and/or guide the stoppage of the practice. However, the continued utilization of flaring in the O&GI despite the harmful effects on the environment reveal a realistic side of the discussion that will best be addressed in the next section of this chapter. Attention will now be turned to the social dimension of the ESG Agenda.

3.2 Social Dimension

There is a cross-cutting effect of natural gas flaring on the environment and society. This is because "social" in the ESG Agenda speaks to human rights and equity; an organization's relationship with people as well as its policies and actions that impact individuals, groups and society.[45] One such example is the causal link between natural gas flaring and human health.[46] The effects of flaring on the society in which the O&GI operates are devastating. Based on the research of Blundell and Kokoza, it was discovered that a 1% increase in the amount of flared natural gas in North Dakota would increase the respiratory-related hospital visitation rate by 0.73%.[47] This may not seem like a significant rise but it does show that there is a link between flaring and hospitalization. Taking this to a more meaningful level, if there is a 10% increase in flared natural gas, there will be a 7% increase in respiratory-related hospitalizations in North Dakota only. Taking this to its natural conclusion on the impact of flared gas globally, it becomes easy to see the extent of the human impact caused by the continuation of this activity. When one considers that there is a rising trend in flaring in Russia, it becomes even more plausible that any negative health impacts will also increase.

36. No poverty.
37. Good Health and Well-being.
38. Quality Education.
39. Decent work and economic growth.
40. Industry, Innovation and infrastructure.
41. Sustainable cities and communities.
42. Responsible consumption and production.
43. Climate Action.
44. Life on land.
45. Jamie Molnar, "ESG 101: What Does Social in ESG Mean?," (OneTrust, 2023) https://www.onetrust.com/blog/esg-101-what-does-social-in-esg-mean/#:~:text=At%20its%20core%2C%20ESG%20social,justice%2C%20and%20care%20for%20wellbeing accessed August 27, 2024.
46. Blundell et al., *supra* n. 3.
47. *Ibid.*

Also, it must be noted that carbon monoxide is just one of the gases that is released during flaring. Another dangerous gas which is released during flaring is carbon monoxide. Research has shown that persons exposed to carbon monoxide have gender-specific sexually-related impacts. In respect of men, carbon monoxide can cause reproductive toxicity which includes altered sexual behavior; altered fertility and problems with sperm shape and count.[48] In women it can cause menstrual problems; altered sexual behavior; infertility; altered puberty onset; altered length of pregnancy; lactation problems; altered menopause onset and spontaneous abortion.[49]

There are also a number of additional adverse health impacts derived from flaring which are non-gender specific.[50] First, flaring is a significant source of nitrogen oxides (NOx) as volatile organic compounds (VOCs) including formaldehyde, acetaldehyde and ethene, and can contribute to the development and exacerbation of asthma as well as the formation of ground-level ozone, which in turn is linked with effects on the respiratory, cardiovascular, and nervous systems and with reproductive effects and mortality.[51] Second, flaring also emits hazardous air pollutants—including benzene and polycyclic aromatic hydrocarbons (PAHs)—as well as particulate matter in the form of black carbon which are carcinogens and have also been linked to birth defects, while exposure to black carbon is associated with higher rates of mortality as well as cardiopulmonary hospital admissions.[52] With the specific example of Iraq, research has specifically shown that flaring releases toxic pollutants known to harm human health including benzene which is a known human carcinogen that causes leukemia.[53] It is therefore unsurprising that there has been a 20% rise in cancer in Iraq between 2015 and 2018 with an acknowledgement by Iraqi officials that there is a link between oil pollution from flaring and cancer.[54]

With the foregoing dangerous impacts of flaring on societies, it can be said with little opposition, that an ESG Agenda will be inconsistent with any activity that causes this kind of human harm. Moreover, taking a human rights lens to this discussion it is clear that states which knowingly engage in practices that cause harm will be in breach of several international environmental obligations not to cause harm. However, that discussion requires a more in-depth analysis of treaty ratification. Furthermore, for a state-owned oil company establishing state liability may not be overly troublesome. It is a very different situation when it relates to privately owned companies for which treaty obligations will not necessarily apply. Therefore, beyond calling for judicial intervention in the O&GI because of flaring, a robust ESG Agenda which seeks to curtail activities that negatively affect a society, is a more efficient tool to achieve meaningful change. Additionally, when one considers the lack of targeted anti-flaring legislation, policy or regulation, the continued spread of these kinds of medical consequences will

48. Sekyi, *supra* n. 34.
49. *Ibid.*
50. Blundell et al., *supra* n. 3.
51. *Ibid.*
52. *Ibid.*
53. Antonia Juhasz, "Iraq Gas Flaring Tied to Cancer Surge" [2023] Human Rights Watch.
54. *Ibid.*

be left unabated. This leads naturally to a discussion of the governance pillar of the ESG Agenda.

3.3 Governance Dimension

The impact of flaring on the governance element of the ESG Agenda is profound. At the heart of the governance dimension is the sustainable harvesting and use of energy. The world in 2021, burnt 144 billion cubic meters (bcm) of gas at oil and gas facilities.[55] This burnt gas had the potential to generate 1800 terawatt hours of energy or nearly two-thirds of the European Union's (EU's) net domestic electricity generation.[56] The effect of this is that in a world where energy facilitates modern living, the practice of flaring in the O&GI is resulting in significant wasted energy. Energy wastage was also assessed by the United States in its Energy Information Administration data which revealed that the United States wastes roughly 1 billion dollars of gas each year by flaring.[57] Meanwhile, on public lands, over USD 400 million dollars of gas was vented or flared in 2019 alone.[58] That translates to roughly USD 50 million in lost revenue and taxpayer resources.[59]

Pervasive flaring can also erode operators' social license to operate and has spurred campaigns to regulate such emissions through oversight, penalties, and taxes on flaring.[60] Methane emissions have also emerged as a concern among some energy customers, as seen in the abandonment of plans by France's Engie to import U.S. liquefied natural gas, due to its climate footprint.[61] It can therefore be seen that flaring impacts a company's corporate social responsibility which may in turn affect its reputation and resultant revenue.

Beyond the internal corporate governance perspective of the ESG Agenda, is the governmental feature. Globally there has been the intervention of legislation and/or regulations to guide ESG.

In April 2022, the UK enacted two mandatory ESG disclosure laws. These are the Companies (Strategic Report) (Climate-related Financial Disclosure) Regulations 2022 and the Limited Liability Partnerships (Climate-related Financial Disclosure) Regulations 2022.[62]

These Regulations require certain companies to provide climate-related financial disclosures in their strategic report.[63]

In 2023, the Non-Financial Reporting Directive (NFDR) was replaced by a new ESG reporting directive—the Corporate Sustainability Reporting Directive (CSRD).[64]

55. DTE Staff, *supra* n. 15.
56. *Ibid.*
57. Goldstein, *supra* n. 31.
58. *Ibid.*
59. *Ibid.*
60. Blundell et al., *supra* n. 3.
61. *Ibid.*
62. Countries affected by mandatory ESG Reporting, Worldfavor, September 2, 2023.
63. *Ibid.*
64. *Ibid.*

The CSRD will significantly extend the scope of companies obliged to comply with approximately 50,000 companies in the EU, corresponding to 75% of the EU's companies' turnover.

There are currently no mandatory ESG disclosure requirements on the federal level in the U.S. However, in May 2022, the U.S. Securities and Exchange Commission (SEC) proposed "amendments to rules and reporting forms to promote consistent, comparable, and reliable information for investors concerning funds' and advisers' incorporation of environmental, social and governance (ESG) factors."[65] If the proposal is adopted, it will establish disclosure requirements for funds and advisers that market themselves as having an ESG focus and be a large win against ESG greenwashing.[66]

In April 2022, the Canadian federal government released its 2022 budget, where they promised to bring mandatory climate-related reporting requirements to federally regulated banks and insurance companies.[67] The financial institutions in scope will be required to publish their climate disclosures in alignment with the Task Force on Climate-related Financial Disclosures (TCFD) framework starting in 2024.[68] Although the regulation focuses on federally regulated financial institutions, the government expects it to have an impact on Canada's entire economy.[69]

In Malaysia, ESG reporting has been mandatory for all publicly listed companies since 2016, making it one of the first countries to introduce this kind of disclosure requirement.[70]

There is currently no mandatory ESG reporting legislation in China. However, with effect from June 1, 2022, China's first set of (voluntary) guidelines for Chinese companies to report on ESG metrics came into effect—the Guidance for Enterprise ESG Disclosure.[71]

The New Zealand government has adopted legislation making climate-related disclosure mandatory for large publicly listed companies, insurers, banks, non-bank deposit takers, and investment managers from the 2023 financial year and forward.[72]

It is therefore possible to see the role governance plays in the achievement of an ESG Agenda. In the context of the ESG Agenda, there are two sides to the governance element. There is first the corporate governance aspect of the actors in the O&GI and there is also the state governance which can lead to both statute and regulations to give the ESG Agenda the necessary teeth. The foregoing discussion reveals that there is still far to go in respect of regulating and/or eradicating the use of flaring in the O&GI. Therefore, recognizing that the ESG Agenda can be used to guide companies in their extractive process, leaving the regulation up to individual companies may only result in the maintenance of the status quo.

65. *Ibid.*
66. *Ibid.*
67. *Ibid.*
68. Worldfavor, *supra* n. 62.
69. *Ibid.*
70. *Ibid.*
71. *Ibid.*
72. *Ibid.*

4 RECOMMENDATIONS TO ACHIEVE THE ESG AGENDA IN O&GI (FLARING)

The immediate solution to the harm caused by flaring would be a global ban on the practice. However, that may be a solution that is theoretically sound but practically impossible in the short term. To this end, there are ways in which the effects of flaring can be slowed or halted. Global policies on a gradual reduction of flaring are possible with the support of global organizations such as the United Nations, the World Bank, the EU, the Organization of American States and the African Union. A globally orchestrated approach to reducing flaring in the O&GI could promulgate alternatives to flaring. This is reflected in the 2015 World Bank-initiated Zero Routine Flaring initiative which sought to end flaring by 2030.[73] Based on its assessment in 2022, the result of the initiative appears to be reaping fruit as the current levels are consistent with commitments made. However, as global economies face diverse challenges, only time will tell if current trends continue, particularly as Russia is increasing its output and has not reduced its flaring activities in any significant way.[74]

Another possible solution is the establishment of feasible flare utilization in light of the safety element of flaring in circumstances where the amount of gas is too small. This solution relates to process safety and a flaring management guide that can assist the industry in regulating the way in which flaring, when done for safety, is carried out. This is the rationale for the joint Guide established by the International Association of Oil and Gas Producers and the Global Gas Flaring Reduction Partnership.[75] It must be noted that this recommendation should only be a short-term objective in a broader ESG Agenda as the ultimate goal should be the eradication of the practice in its entirety.

At a more practical level, flaring can better fit within the ESG Agenda if the total amount of flaring is reduced and, where it continues, its efficiency is increased.[76] Also, the reduction in the amount of unlit flares can also prove significantly beneficial.[77]

While it is important to address flaring as a practice that is inimical to the environment, there is also a need to have a robust ESG policy. In this vein, aside from the monetary pressure on companies to implement ESG programs, there also is increasing pressure on companies to properly manage ESG issues.[78]

In a U.S. context, the Biden Administration has made both the fight against climate change and environmental justice foundational to its Agenda.[79] Upon his inauguration, President Biden quickly rejoined the Paris Agreement and set a 2030 target to cut GHG emissions by 50% from 2005 levels. Getting there will require stepped-up federal regulation and enforcement of environmental protection across a

73. DTE Staff, *supra* n. 15.
74. Vladimir Afanasiev, "Russian Flaring Spooks European Markets But Also Shows the Environmental Costs of War" Upstream: Energy Explained https://www.upstreamonline.com/environment/russian-flaring-spooks-european-markets-but-also-shows-the-environmental-costs-of-war/2-1-1287194 accessed August 27, 2024.
75. "Flaring Management Guidance: For the Oil and Gas Industry" [2021] IPIECA, IOGP, GGFR.
76. Goldstein, *supra* n. 31.
77. *Ibid.*
78. Rushton, *supra* n. 26.
79. *Ibid.*

wide range of industries.[80] Additionally, within days of his inauguration, President Biden signed Executive Order 14008 entitled *Tackling the Climate Crisis at Home and Abroad*, further making clear his intent to establish a government-wide approach to address the "climate crisis" and ensuring environmental and economic justice issues are key considerations in how the Administration governs.[81] This approach to central government taking an active role in the formalization of an ESG Agenda serves as a template of how to effectively engage the "G" facet of any ESG Agenda. The reality is that any policy framework requires governmental support and where the government is willing to establish national policies, legislation and regulations, the ESG Agenda is given fertile ground on which it can operate. However, where the extent of governance is self-regulatory in nature, it operates in a place of voluntariness and inconsistency within the industry.

5 CONCLUSION

Natural gas flaring is both a historical and modern feature of the O&GI. It represents a necessary step in the extraction of oil. From a health and safety perspective, flaring allowed for a safer working environment for oil workers. There are, however, deleterious effects of flaring on the environment and these cannot be understated. It is for this reason that flaring, as part of the oil extractive process, has been reviewed through a sustainable analysis. In particular, the ESG Agenda has been used to critique the flaring practice.

As has been seen, the ESG Agenda serves as guidance on how to engage in commercial activities which are supportive of ESG factors. While at first blush it may be difficult to fully articulate what each facet of the ESG Agenda entails, in a careful and deliberate exercise of exploring gas flaring's causes and effects, the ESG Agenda can be very useful.

The ESG Agenda seeks to refocus a company's attention on core stakeholders within its sphere of operations paying particular attention to the environment, the society and governance structures. To thrive, a company/industry must ensure that it can operate within an ESG Agenda because it has the potential to increase a company's success, and commercial viability, protect a company's goodwill and reputation; and ultimately increase revenue. Each element of the ESG Agenda creates a dimension which demands state attention. While it is obvious to see the environmental impact of flaring, the situation is one that is more complex because of the industrial utility of the practice set against the unwanted gases released when flaring occurs. To this end, it presents a double-edged sword in the context of the broader industry. Furthermore, the social and governmental dimensions of the Agenda recognize that the environmental effect of flaring creates a duty on states to safeguard the rights of society as it relates to the negative effects on the environment. As has been highlighted, the impact of flaring has the potential to further destroy the lived experiences of vulnerable groups in

80. *Ibid.*
81. *Ibid.*

society. Perhaps, it is this delicate interplay among the different dimensions of the Agenda that highlights the complexity of flaring.

Moreover, it should be noted that the heart of the issue is not whether an ESG Agenda is applicable but how compatible ongoing activities are with an ESG Agenda. While numerous examples have been given in this chapter relating to each limb of the ESG Agenda and flaring, the harsh reality is that flaring has utility in the industry. This utility makes an immediate stoppage of the practice impossible. This is why steps have been taken globally to gradually reduce flaring in an attempt to achieve a realistic realization of the ESG Agenda.

This incremental strategy to reduce flaring is set in the context of the ESG Agenda's incompatibility with natural gas flaring. However, the incompatibility must be balanced with the practicality and utility of flaring in a safety context and resource availability reality. It is advanced that investing in ESG can help organizations reduce their environmental impact, improve social outcomes, and build better governance structures.[82] This is why it would be an act of futility to abandon the ESG Agenda for the sole reason that flaring cannot be stopped immediately. On the contrary, the agreement by states to even embark on a flaring reduction agreement demonstrates the importance of the ESG Agenda. It becomes that much more necessary in situations which pose high risks to the environment and people.

Flaring, which causes significant harm to the environment and has the potential to cause cancer, infertility, and premature childbirth, just to name a few, cannot satisfy an ESG Agenda. This is even more poignant when one considers the direct effect flaring has on global warming. It is to this end that regulation and proper corporate and state governance are essential to the survival of the planet. As has been discussed, there are two main recommendations on how to move forward in the O&GI. They are the gradual elimination of flaring or a managed sustainable engagement of flaring. In either situation, it becomes necessary to realize that the status quo ought not to continue because of the damage which unregulated flaring can cause. As such, in a situation where the stakes are literally life and death, an ESG Agenda can serve as the last bastion of hope, if it is managed actively and responsibly.

82. Ellis, *supra* n. 23.

CHAPTER 31

Natural Gas Commercialization: Alternative Uses of Associated Gas and the Place of Law, Regulation, and Policy

Tara Righetti, Scarlett Forrest & Colton Edwards

1 INTRODUCTION

Flaring and venting of natural gas contributes significantly to greenhouse gas emissions. Although it may be necessary in emergency situations, most flaring or venting results from a lack of infrastructure or economically feasible options for gas marketing or utilization.[1] In these cases, the gas that is produced with oil—called associated gas—is vented or flared. During the flaring process, the methane is only partially combusted, resulting in a release of unburnt methane and carbon dioxide (CO_2).[2] This significantly contributes to greenhouse gas emissions.[3] The World Bank estimated that in 2023 approximately 148 billion cubic meters of gas was burned, resulting in 381 million tonnes of CO_2 emissions, 45 million tonnes of unburnt methane, and soot.[4]

1. The World Bank, "Global Gas Flaring Reduction Partnership (GGFR)" www.worldbank.org/en/programs/gasflaringreduction/gas-flaring-explained#: ~ :text = Safety%20reasons&text = Although%20rare%2C%20industrial%20accidents%20involving,by%20burning%20any%20excess%20gas accessed September 6, 2024.
2. U.S. Department of Energy, "Natural Gas Flaring and Venting: State and Federal Regulatory Overview, Trends, and Impact" (2021).
3. The World Bank, "Global Gas Flaring Reduction Partnership (GGFR)" www.worldbank.org/en/programs/gasflaringreduction/gas-flaring-explained#: ~ :text = Safety%20reasons&text = Although%20rare%2C%20industrial%20accidents%20involving,by%20burning%20any%20excess%20gas accessed September 6, 2024.
4. The World Bank, "Global Gas Flaring Tracker Report" (2024) https://thedocs.worldbank.org/en/doc/d01b4aebd8a10513c0e341de5e1f652e-0400072024/original/Global-Gas-Flaring-Tracker-Report-June-20-2024.pdf?_gl = 1*1jogaeb*_gcl_au*MjQ4MDM1MTI5LjE3MjU2MzYxNzU accessed September 11, 2024.

In addition to the climate and air quality impacts, releases of associated gas also result in significant resource and economic loss. According to the 2024 Global Gas Flaring Tracker Report, 2023 global flaring increased by 7% from 2022 flaring levels, even though oil production only increased by 1%.[5] This increase in flaring intensity more than offset the flaring reductions in areas with success such as the United States, and, according to the World Bank analysis, also indicates that prior efforts to reduce flaring have not been sustainable.[6] The report estimates the lost value at between USD 9 and USD 48 billion.[7]

To address these impacts, governments, NGOs, and oil companies globally have enacted policies that aim to eliminate routine flaring and reduce the impacts and frequency of emergency flaring. While this portends an end to most flaring, as long as production continues the challenge of associated gas will remain: The gas will need to be reinjected, transported and marketed, or put to beneficial use at the place of production.

This chapter explores potential options for commercialization of associated gas. It begins by describing existing policies worldwide that are intended to reduce or disincentivize venting or flaring. Adhering to these policies will require significant investment, potentially leading to the early abandonment of some production areas. The chapter then examines currently available technologies for the reinjection and use of associated gas. It notes that many of these technologies are vulnerable to the same challenges that currently preclude the sale of associated gas into natural gas markets, such as issues with capture and transportation. These challenges suggest the need for significant public sector support for technology and infrastructure development. The chapter concludes by suggesting policies that could support greater utilization and commercialization of associated gas, finding that coordinated efforts in both the public and private sectors are needed to enable the phase out of associated gas flaring.

2 FLARING REDUCTION POLICIES

At COP26 in Glasgow, the European Union (EU) and the United States launched the global methane pledge, promising to reduce methane emissions by 30% from 2020 levels by 2030.[8] Today, 159 countries plus the European Commission have joined the pledge, representing more than 50% of global anthropogenic methane emissions.[9] Participating countries are expected to enact policies to reduce emissions from the food and agriculture, waste, and energy sectors. The proposed measures for the energy sector "include upstream and downstream leak detection and repair, recovery and

5. *Ibid.*
6. *Ibid.*
7. *Ibid.*
8. Global Methane Pledge, "Homepage" www.globalmethanepledge.org/ accessed January 28, 2025.
9. *Ibid.*

utilization of vented gas and improved control of unintended fugitive emissions from the production of oil and natural gas."[10] This pledge builds on anti-flaring policy efforts in numerous countries and suggests that similar lawmaking efforts are likely to continue. As of 2022, prior to the methane pledge, several countries had already enacted new laws, regulations, financing programs, and voluntary agreements aimed at limiting venting and flaring, including embedded flaring emissions from oil and gas imports.[11] Collectively, these laws and those likely to be enacted this decade preview an end to all but emergency flaring and venting.

2.1 Prohibitions on Flaring and Venting

2.1.1 The European Union

The EU has had a methane emissions strategy since 1996.[12] While emissions have halved since then, methane emissions remain a significant challenge.[13] In the EU methane strategy released in 2020, the Commission identified the need to improve monitoring and reporting, potentially revise aspects of the EU Emissions Trading System, impose an obligation on upstream gas companies to improve and expedite leak detection and repair (LDAR), and through the LDAR obligations, address flaring efficiency as a priority.[14] It found that "[v]enting and routine flaring should be restricted to unavoidable circumstances, for example for safety reasons, and recorded for verification purposes."[15] In response, the Commission suggested legislation to improve LDAR, monitoring, reporting, and verification, along with more stringent non-financial reporting requirements.[16]

Consistent with these suggestions, in June of 2024, the EU Parliament and Council adopted new and amended regulations related to the reduction of methane emissions from the energy sector.[17] The new regulation provides that "[r]e-injection or utilisation on-site of methane, or dispatch of methane to a market should always be preferable to venting or flaring" and requires operators who vent and/or flare to prove

10. Global Methane Pledge, "Energy Pathway" www.globalmethanepledge.org/annual-report/energy-pathway January 28, 2025.
11. According to a comparative study compiled by The World Bank, 21 oil and gas producing countries have enacted regulations that limit or prohibit non-emergency flaring, many of these associated with countries NDC plans pursuant to the Paris agreement, I. The World Bank, "Global Flaring and Venting Regulations: A Comparative Review of Policies" (Summary Report, 2022) 11-15.
12. Commission, "Strategy Paper for Reducing Methane Emissions" (Communication) COM (96) 557 final.
13. Commission, "EU Strategy to Reduce Methane Emissions" (Communication) COM (2020) 663 final.
14. *Ibid.*
15. *Ibid.*
16. *Ibid.*
17. Commission, "Commission Welcomes Deal on First-ever EU Law to Curb Methane Emissions in the EU and Globally" (Press Release) IP/23/5776, November 15, 2023.

to the applicable authority that these measures were not possible.[18] Additionally, Article 17 of this regulation compels operators to install an auto-igniter or continuous pilot burner with a "destruction and removal efficiency by design level of at least 99 % " on any new, replaced, or refurbished flare stacks or combustion devices by February 5, 2026.[19] The new regulation also bans venting and flaring methane from drainage stations by 2025 and from ventilation shafts by 2027.[20]

The new regulations also addressed the energy intensity of oil and gas imports. Since oil and gas imports make up 80% of the oil and gas consumed in the EU, the law requires importers to demonstrate "equivalent monitoring, reporting, and verification requirements at production level" by January 2027.[21] Lastly, the new regulations tasked the European Commission with setting methane intensity classes for crude oil, natural gas, and coal entering the EU market within the next three years.[22]

2.1.2 The USA

The United States has also acted to reduce venting and flaring. The Inflation Reduction Act (IRA) provided new authority under the Clean Air Act to create a Methane Emissions Reduction Program focused on reducing methane emissions from the oil and gas sector.[23] This included three parts: financial and technical assistance, a waste emissions charge, and revision of Environmental Protection Agency's (EPA's) regulations under the Greenhouse Gas Reporting Program (GHGRP).[24] Financing from the program will support state efforts to identify leaks, remediate abandoned and leaking wells, and provide operators with technical assistance.[25] So far, approximately USD 350 million in funding has been provisionally designated to 14 states.[26] In addition, USD 850 million of federal funds were made available to the private sector for projects "that will help monitor, measure, quantify and reduce methane emissions from the oil and gas sectors."[27] Revisions to the GHGRP, proposed in August 2023 and finalized in May 2024, would update reporting requirements to provide greater accuracy and

18. Parliament and Council Regulation (EU) 2024/1787 of June 13, 2024 on the reduction of methane emissions in the energy sector and amending Regulation (EU) 2019/942 [2024] OJ L, 15.7.2024 ¶ 44.
19. *Ibid.*, Art. 17.
20. *Ibid.*, Art. 22; European Parliament, "Fit for 55: Deal to Boost Methane Emission Reductions from the Energy Sector" (Press Release) November 15, 2023.
21. *Ibid.*
22. *Ibid.*
23. Inflation Reduction Act of 2022 §60105(e) (US).
24. *Ibid.*, §60113.
25. Press Release, White House, Biden-Harris Administration Announces USD 350 Million to 14 States to Reduce Methane Emissions from Oil and Gas Sector as Part of Investing in America Agenda (December 15, 2023).
26. *Ibid.*
27. Press Release, DOE Announces USD 850 Million to Reduce Methane Pollution from the Oil and Gas Sector (June 21, 2024).

transparency in calculation, monitoring, and reporting.[28] Finally, while the United States does not have a general carbon tax, the newly created Methane Emissions Charge would assess a progressively increasing fee on facilities exceeding congressionally established waste emissions thresholds of 25,000 metric tons of CO_2 equivalent per year.[29]

The IRA's Methane Emissions Reduction Program complements methane emissions reduction rules enacted by the United States Environmental Protection Agency (USEPA) under its authority in the Clean Air Act. In 2023, the USEPA updated its performance standards for oil and natural gas operations.[30] The rule requires extensive new monitoring and leak detection efforts and, like the EU law, eliminates routine flaring.[31] The rule permits flaring only where it would be "technically infeasible or unsafe" to comply with the rule.[32] In these situations, flaring must be limited in duration and comply with specific performance standards. For example, in the event of a pipeline interruption, the rule permits an operator to flare for a maximum of 30 days.[33] Collectively, these actions are anticipated to have a significant impact on reducing CO_2 and methane emissions from the oil and gas sector.[34]

U.S. flaring reduction policies, however, may change. Following the inauguration in January of 2025, the Trump administration issued three executive orders rescinding many of the climate policies of the previous Biden administration and announcing a new energy policy that emphasizes removing regulatory restrictions from the oil and gas sector.[35] Among these changes, the administration withdrew the U.S. from the Paris Agreement.[36] The full effects of the new administration's policies on methane reduction requirements will not be realized until after this chapter is published. These policies highlight the tensions between the directives in the Bipartisan Infrastructure Law and the IRA (which can only be altered by Congressional action) and the Executive's role in administering these laws.[37]

---

28. Greenhouse Gas Reporting Rule: Revisions and Confidentiality Determinations for Petroleum and Natural Gas Systems, 89 Fed. Reg. 42062 (May 14, 2024) (to be codified at 40 C.F.R. pt. 98) (US).
29. Waste Emissions Charge for Petroleum and Natural Gas Systems, 89 Fed. Reg. 5,318, (January 26, 2024) (to be codified at 40 C.F.R. pt. 99) (US).
30. Standards of Performance for New, Reconstructed, and Modified Sources and Emissions Guidelines for Existing Sources, 42 C.F.R. §7401 (2024) (US).
31. *Ibid.*
32. *Ibid.*
33. *Ibid.*, Table 17.
34. The Methane Emissions Charge is expected to result in "Cumulative Emissions Reductions of 960 Thousand Metric Tons of Methane Over the 2024 to 2035 Period." *See*, U.S. Environmental Protection Agency, PA-430/R-23-005, Regulatory Impact Analysis of the Proposed Waste Emissions Charge 1-3 (2024) (US).
35. *See* Exec. Order No. 14154, "Unleashing American Energy" (2025) (U.S.); Exec. Order No. pending, "Putting America First in International Environmental Agreements" (2025) (U.S.); Exec. Order No. pending, "Declaring a National Energy Emergency" (2025) (U.S.).
36. Please note the global methane pledge website still lists the U.S. as a participant as of January 28, 2025. Exec. Order No. pending, "Putting America First in International Environmental Agreements" (2025) (U.S.).
37. *See* Exec. Order No. 14154, "Unleashing American Energy" (2025) (U.S.) ("Sec. 7. Terminating the Green New Deal. (a) All agencies shall immediately pause the disbursement of funds

2.1.3 Canada

Canada's methane strategy, released in 2022, parallels those of the EU and the United States.[38] In 2018, pursuant to authority granted by the Canadian Environmental Protection Act, the Minister of the Environment, through the Department of Environment and Climate Change Canada (ECCC), published *Regulations Respecting Reduction in the Release of Methane and Certain Volatile Organic Compounds*.[39] These regulations limited methane emissions from onshore upstream and midstream sources.[40] In September 2023, the ECCC announced an update to its methane strategy to achieve net zero emissions and achieve at least a 75% reduction in oil and gas methane emissions by 2030.[41] The strategy proposed amending the 2018 methane regulations to "eliminate exclusions, and drive as many individual sources as possible toward zero emissions."[42] The ECCC also announced its intention to develop requirements to actively control venting and flaring (outside of safety purposes and emergency situations). Draft regulations consistent with this strategy were published by the ECCC in December 2023.[43]

Three Canadian provinces also adopted regulations eliminating routine flaring, requiring operators to limit non-routine flaring, and imposing performance requirements on unavoidable flaring. These include Directive 060: Upstream Petroleum Industry Flaring, Incinerating, and Venting in Alberta,[44] Directive S-20: Saskatchewan Upstream Flaring and Incineration Requirements in Saskatchewan,[45] and the Flaring and Venting Reduction Guideline in British Columbia.[46] Alberta's Directive 060 sets out

appropriated through the Inflation Reduction Act of 2022 (Public Law 117-169) or the Infrastructure Investment and Jobs Act (Public Law 117-58) ... and shall review their processes, policies, and programs for issuing grants, loans, contracts, or any other financial disbursements of such appropriated funds for consistency with the law and the policy outlined in section 2 of this order."); *see also*, Jennifer Scholtes & Nicholas Wu, "Trump Administration Orders Sweeping Freeze of Federal Aid" (Politico, January 27, 2025) ("[A] two-page memo obtained by POLITICO ... broadly orders federal agencies to 'temporarily' stop sending federal financial assistance that could be affected by Trump's executive actions. That includes the president's orders to freeze all funding from the Democrats' signature climate and spending law—the Inflation Reduction Act and the bipartisan infrastructure package enacted in 2021.") https://www.politico.com/news/2025/01/27/trump-freezes-federal-aid-omb-00200891 accessed January 27, 2025.

38. Env't & Climate Change Can., Faster and Further: Canada's Methane Strategy (2022) (CA).
39. *Regulations Respecting Reduction in the Release of Methane and Certain Volatile Organic Compounds (Upstream Oil and Gas Sector), SOR/2018-66* (CA).
40. *Ibid.*
41. Press Release, Department of Environment and Climate Change Canada, Update on Path Forward for Oil and Gas Sector Methane Mitigation (September 20, 2023).
42. *Ibid.*
43. Press Release, Department of Environment and Climate Change Canada, Minister Guilbeault Announces Canada's Draft Methane Regulations to Support Cleaner Energy and Climate Action (December 4, 2023).
44. Directive 060: Upstream Petroleum Industry Flaring, Incinerating, and Venting, Alta. Reg. 076/2022 (CA).
45. Directive S-20: Saskatchewan Upstream Flaring and Incineration Requirements, The Oil and Gas Conservation Act, MRO 120/2022 (CA).
46. Flaring and Venting Reduction Guideline, *B.C.-ER.CA v. 5.4* (2022) (CA).

the requirements for venting and flaring for all upstream petroleum industry wells and facilities.[47] This Directive addresses venting and flaring activities through Alberta's waste management regulations and requires upstream petroleum operations to assess public safety and environmental concerns before venting and flaring associated gas.[48] Saskatchewan's Directive S-20 requires wells or facilities licensed under the Saskatchewan Oil and Gas Conservation Act to update or design their flaring systems to meet the standards in the Directive.[49] British Columbia's Flaring and Venting Reduction Guideline is similar to Alberta's Directive 060 in that it requires assessing public safety and environmental concerns before allowing operators to vent and flare.[50] However, British Columbia's Guideline also factors in the economics of associated gas conservation as part of the assessment, and defines "conservation" as recovering gas "and using it as a fuel for production facilities and other useful purposes (e.g., power generation), sales, or beneficial injection into an oil or gas pool."[51]

2.2 Market Mechanisms

In addition to prohibitions on flaring, governments have implemented market mechanisms to prevent or discourage methane waste and to encourage natural gas commercialization and utilization. While these policies do not prohibit or limit flaring outright, they impose a cost on emitting that may encourage emitters to make greater investments in capture infrastructure. For example, The EU's regulation passed in response to the methane strategy allows for Member States to develop their own system of fees and charges to facilitate investing in methane emissions reductions.[52] The regulation also emphasizes that Member State systems could "incentivise investments into methane capture and injection to the grid and the reduction of methane emissions from ventilation shafts and from flaring."[53]

Methane emissions may also be discouraged through the use of carbon taxes and cap-and-trade systems. Between 2026 and 2030, Canada plans to implement a national emissions cap-and-trade system through new regulations under the Canadian Environmental Protection Act.[54] This emissions cap-and-trade system will apply to all Liquified Natural Gas (LNG) facilities and upstream oil and gas facilities, and the greenhouse

47. Directive 060: Upstream Petroleum Industry Flaring, Incinerating, and Venting, Alta. Reg. 076/2022 (CA).
48. *Ibid.*
49. Directive S-20: Saskatchewan Upstream Flaring and Incineration Requirements, The Oil and Gas Conservation Act, MRO 120/2022 (CA).
50. Flaring And Venting Reduction Guideline, *B.C.-ER.CA v. 5.4* (2022) (CA).
51. *Ibid.*
52. Parliament and Council Regulation (EU) 2024/1787 of June 13, 2024 on the reduction of methane emissions in the energy sector and amending Regulation (EU) 2019/942 [2024] OJ L, 15.7.2024 ¶ 61.
53. *Ibid.*
54. The Canadian government intends to publish the final regulations in 2025. Environment and Climate Change Canada, "A Regulatory Framework to Cap Oil and Gas Sector Greenhouse Gas Emissions" (2023) ECCC Public Information Centre 1, 11.

gasses covered include CO_2 and methane.[55] Calculations for the cap level include the assumption that reduced flaring and carbon capture and storage (CCS) technologies will be deployed at that time.[56]

Governments may also increase gas flaring costs by requiring royalty payments for flared gas from sovereign-owned resources. These requirements may arise through regulation or as a term of exploration agreements. For example, the United States Bureau of Land Management (BLM) recently proposed new regulations that would assess royalties on gas flared from federal and Indian lands.[57] In both Brazil and Queensland, Australia, the standard terms of oil and gas exploration agreements require payment of royalties on flared gas.[58] This creates an avoided cost to flaring which, like carbon taxes, may help justify investments in new marketing or utilization infrastructure.

These market-driven disincentives to flaring may also extend to production in third countries. Oil-importing countries may have more stringent environmental regulations than the countries from which they import oil. As a result, the carbon intensity of imports may exceed domestic production.[59] This results in carbon leakage, as well as undermining demand for locally produced goods, which may have a higher cost. To address these concerns, the EU recently enacted a Carbon Border Adjustment Mechanism (CBAM) which imposes tariffs with greater emissions than those produced in the EU.[60] While the CBAM only applies to imports of electricity and not directly to oil imports, if extended to those sectors it could have a substantial impact on oil exporters and producers exporting products that use oil as a feedstock. Other oil-importing countries with stringent domestic emissions regulations may also consider similar trade-based mechanisms to adjust for emissions intensity.[61] The Methane Agreement

55. *Ibid.*, 3.
56. *Ibid.*, 13.
57. A prior version of the rule was overturned, *see* Waste Prevention, Production Subject to Royalties, and Resource Conservation ("Proposed Rule"), 87 FR 73588 (November 30, 2022) at 6; *Wyoming v. Dep't of the Interior*, 493 F. Supp. 3d 1046, 1065 (D. Wyo. 2020); Cong. Research Serv., LSB10882, The Debate over Flaring and Venting on Federal Lands (2022) (US).
58. Federal Republic of Brazil Ministry of Mines and Energy, ANP Draft Concession Agreement for the Exploration, Development and Production of Oil and Natural Gas (2017) (BR); Queensland Government, *Production, Reserve and Royalty Notices and Reports* (AU).
59. Mark Davis, "Comment: Europe's Ban on Dirty Methane Imports will Be Good for Oil and Gas Producers as Well as the Planet" (Reuters, November 22, 2023) www.reuters.com/sustainability/climate-energy/comment-europes-ban-dirty-methane-imports-will-be-good-oil-gas-producers-well-2023-11-22 accessed September 10, 2024; Yash Dixit et al., "Carbon Intensity of Global Crude Oil Trading and Market Policy Implications" (2023), 14(5975) Nature Communications https://doi.org/10.1038/s41467-023-41701-z accessed September 10, 2024. NAT COMMUN. 5975 (2023); The same may be true in the UK, *see*, Chris Hilson, "Emissions Intensity: Do We Need a CBAM for Oil and Gas Imports?," (2023) 17 The Journal of World Energy Law & Business 136, (2023) https://doi.org/10.1093/jwelb/jwad036.
60. Commission, Guidance Document on "CBAM Implementation for Importers of Goods into the EU" (Guidance Document) (December 13, 2023); Technology Innovation and Emissions Reduction Regulation, Alta. Reg. 251/2022 (CA).
61. Chris Hilson, "Emissions Intensity: Do We Need a CBAM for Oil and Gas Imports?" (2023) 17 The Journal of World Energy Law & Business 136 https://doi.org/10.1093/jwelb/jwad036.

would impose the same monitoring, verification, and reporting obligations on all exporters as of 2027.[62]

Finally, flaring may be discouraged by non-financial reporting obligations in climate disclosure rules that require companies to track and report emissions. In the United States, the Securities and Exchange Commission (SEC) promulgated a final rule requiring all companies to report Scope 1 and 2 emissions and financially material climate risks.[63] While the rule does not require a company to lower its emissions, it is expected to increase transparency and accountability and provide greater comparability between firms, potentially driving Environmental, Social, and Governance (ESG) investment.[64] In the EU, the Corporate Sustainability Reporting Directive expands the climate reporting obligations of firms and adopts the European Sustainable Reporting Standards.[65] The directive expands these rules and could have a significant impact on capital markets for oil and gas projects.

2.3 Voluntary Programs

Lawmaking efforts in oil-producing and importing countries align with almost a decade of voluntary programs to reduce flaring. For example, in 2015, the World Bank launched the Zero Routine Flaring Initiative.[66] As part of the initiative, companies, governments, and development institutions representing 62% of global flaring committed to improving infrastructure for gas capture, delivery, and utilization and to reporting flaring emissions to the World Bank for data aggregation.[67] Numerous large oil and gas companies have also committed to voluntarily reduce or eliminate flaring. During COP28, under the UAE Presidency, more than 50 oil and gas companies announced their commitment to join the Oil and Gas Decarbonization Charter.[68] The pledge includes a commitment to "reach net-zero CO_2eq emissions (Scope 1 and 2) for

62. Strategy Paper, *supra* n. 12.
63. The Enhancement and Standardization of Climate-Related Disclosures for Investors, 89 FR 21,670, (March 28, 2024) (to be codified at 17 C.F.R. pts. 210 et seq.) (US).
64. Victor Flatt, "SEC Climate Change Rules Will Have Most Impact on Energy Markets" (Bloomberg Law, January 5, 2023) https://news.bloomberglaw.com/us-law-week/sec-climate-change-rules-will-have-most-impact-on-energy-markets-1 accessed September 10, 2024; Some U.S. states have expanded these rules. While the SECs rule would only apply to public companies, new climate disclosure laws enacted in California could apply to large private firms doing business in the state S.B. 253, Ch. 382, 2023-2024 Reg. Sess. (Cal., 2023) (US).
65. Council Directive (EU) 2022/2464 of the European Parliament and of the Council of December 14, 2022, amending Regulation (EU) No 537/2014, Directive 2004/109/EC, Directive 2006/43/EC and Directive 2013/34/EU, as regards corporate sustainability [2022] OJ L322/15.
66. The World Bank, "Global Initiative to Reduce Gas Flaring: Zero Routine Flaring by 2030" (2015) https://thedocs.worldbank.org/en/doc/a903b5e6456991faf3b5e079bba0391a-0400072021/related/ZRF-Initiative-text-list-map-104.pdf accessed September 10, 2024.
67. *Ibid.*
68. Signatories included national oil companies as well as multi-national companies such as Exxon, BP, and Shell. COP28, "Oil and Gas Decarbonization Charter" (U.N. Climate Change Conference, Dubai, December 2023) https://prod-cd-cdn.azureedge.net/-/media/Project/COP28/COP28-OG-Decarbonization-Charter.pdf?rev=f7f76056724e4caebf7aaa803e53e18e accessed September 10, 2024; Press Release, COP28 UAE, Oil & Gas Decarbonization Charter Launched to Accelerate Climate Action (December 2, 2023).

operations under our control … by or before 2050" to "eliminate routine flaring by 2030," and to achieve "net zero upstream methane emissions by 2030."[69] While the commitments are voluntary, the pledge is supported by third-party tracking by the Environmental Defense Fund, the UN Environment Programme, the International Energy Agency, and RMI to provide additional transparency and accountability.[70] If implemented, these voluntary corporate commitments will contribute to flaring reductions even in countries that have not enacted stringent methane regulations.

Market mechanisms, command and control regulations, and voluntary programs represent a substantial step toward ending flaring. However, gaps remain. The charter signatories do not cover the full sector[71] and not all countries have enacted regulations. Trade policies—though extend the reach of flaring regulations to third countries—affect only exporters. Small operators who do not sell into global markets and operate in countries without regulations or carbon penalties are likely to continue flaring.

3 IMPROVING CAPTURE, TRANSPORT, AND UTILIZATION

Flaring has become more prominent over the last five years as unconventional, tight oil and shale resources have been developed.[72] Expansion of crude oil production has outpaced the ability to bring the associated natural gas production to the market.[73] Eliminating routine flaring therefore requires the capture of the associated gas and development of infrastructure so that the gas can be transported to market, reinjected, or utilized at the wellhead.[74] While technologies for capturing and monetizing flared gas exist, these technologies are not used if their cost exceeds the market value of the associated gas.[75]

Many of the commercially available alternatives to flaring are combustive uses. Natural gas can be compressed and as fuel at the oilfields or utilized to produce

69. COP28, "Oil and Gas Decarbonization Charter" (U.N. Climate Change Conference, Dubai, December 2023) https://prod-cd-cdn.azureedge.net/-/media/Project/COP28/COP28-OG-Decarbonization-Charter.pdf?rev = f7f76056724e4caebf7aaa803e53e18e accessed September 10, 2024.
70. Bloomberg Philanthropies, "Bloomberg Philanthropies, UN Environment Programme, Environmental Defense Fund, International Energy Agency, and RMI Launch Groundbreaking Transparency and Accountability Measure for Methane Emissions" (December 2, 2023) www.bloomberg.org/press/groundbreaking-transparency-and-accountability-measure-for-methane-emissions/ accessed September 10, 2024.
71. Oil Change International, "Open Letter: The World Needs a Transformational Outcome, Not More Voluntary Pledges" (December 1, 2023), https://priceofoil.org/2023/12/01/ogda/ accessed September 10, 2024.
72. U.S. Dep't of Energy, Flaring and Venting Reduction Research & Development Activities Report to Congress 1 (2021) [hereinafter *R&D Activities Report*] (US).
73. *Ibid.*, 5. North Dakota and Texas have accounted for 85% of the vented and flared gas reported in the U.S.
74. This aligns with requirements in many regulations, *see, e.g.*, Standards of Performance for New, Reconstructed, and Modified Sources and Emissions Guidelines for Existing Sources: Oil and Natural Gas Sector Climate Review, 86 Fed. Reg. 63110 (November 15, 2021) (to be codified at 40 C.F.R. pt. 60) (US); Mohammad Reza Rahimpour et al., "A Comparative Study of Three Different Methods for Flare Gas Recovery of Asalooye Gas Refinery" (2012) 4 J. of Nat. Gas Sci. & Eng. 17 https://doi.org/10.1016/j.jngse.2011.10.001.
75. *See* R&D Activities Report, *supra* n. 72, 8.

electricity in in small-scale generators to power oil and gas operations or for high-energy uses such as bitcoin mining.[76] These alternatives decrease resource waste and may provide economically viable options for commercialization of associated gas. However, utilizing the associated gas still requires burning it, and therefore, unless paired with Carbon capture, utilization and storage (CCUS), these methods could be inconsistent with pledges to eliminate upstream methane emissions.

The following section evaluates four technologies with the potential to address upstream methane emissions by either reducing flaring through reinjection or allowing on-site conversion of associated gas into higher-value, more transportable products.

3.1 Reinjection of Pre-combustion Gas

Where associated gas cannot be commercialized, flaring can be reduced by capturing gas that would otherwise be flared or vented and reinjecting it into subsurface formations.[77] This gas can be utilized for enhanced recovery[78] or pressure maintenance,[79] stored for later use,[80] or disposed of as production waste. Which of these options is viable will depend on site-specific hydrogen properties and production rates as well as subsurface conditions such as depth, permeability, and faults and fractures.[81] For example, a case study conducted in Nigeria concluded that the Niger Delta basin reservoir was suitable for injection of natural gas for storage but would not support injections to maintain reservoir pressure or enhanced oil recovery (EOR).[82]

76. Pavel Snytnikov & Dmitry Potemkin, "Flare Gas Monetization and Greener Hydrogen Production via Combination with Cryptocurrency Mining and Carbon Dioxide Capture" (2022) 25 iScience 1 https://doi.org/10.1016/j.isci.2022.103769 (Considering use of associated gas onsite as a feedstock for blue hydrogen production, which could generate electricity for cryptocurrency mining, on-site food production, and data processing centers).
77. *See* U.S. Gov't Accountability Office, GAO-04-809, Natural Gas Venting and Flaring: Opportunities to Improve Data and Emissions 2, 18 (2004) (US).
78. *See Enhanced Oil Recovery*, Dep't of Energy Office of Fossil Energy & Carbon Mgmt, https://www.energy.gov/fecm/enhanced-oil-recovery#:~:text=Gas%20injection%20%2C%20which%20uses%20gases,and%20improves%20its%20flow%20rate (last visited December 21, 2023) (US); Enoc Basilio & Tayfun Babadagli, "Use of Air with Methane in Cyclic Solvent Injection Applications for Improved Foam Stability and Cost Effective Heavy Oil Recovery" (2020) 34 Energy & Fuels 278 https://doi.org/10.1021/acs.energyfuels.9b03677; Charles Ohalekwu, "Modeling the Effect of Methane vs. Carbon Dioxide Injection on Oil Recovery: A Case Study: The East Vacuum Grayburg-San Andres Unit, Lea County, New Mexico" (2017) (Master's thesis, Montana Tech of the University of Montana).
79. J.S Archer & C.G Wall, "Secondary Recovery and Pressure Maintenance" in Springer, Dordrecht (ed.), *Petroleum Engineering* (1986); Jaime Eduardo Moreno et al., "Flaring, Gas Injection and Reservoir Management Optimization: Preserving Reservoir Energy Maximizes Recovery and Prolong the Life of an Ageing Brown Field" (Asia Pacific Oil and Gas Conference & Exhibition, 2009) https://doi.org/10.2118/122339-MS.
80. *See e.g.*, Odigie Eghon & Koso I. Idigbe, "Injection of Natural Gas into Reservoirs: A Feasible Solution to Gas Flaring in Nigeria" (2013) 4 Acad. Research Int'l 90.
81. Gbubemi H. Harrison & A. Sahel, "Optimal Profitable Allocation of Associated Natural Gas Resource on a Countrywide Basis to Mitigate Flaring" (2023) 10 Energy Reports 2551, 2552-53 https://doi.org/10.1016/j.egyr.2023.09.015; Moreno et al., *supra* n. 79; Sara Thomas, "Enhanced Oil Recovery: An Overview" (2008) 63 Oil & Gas Sci. & Tech. 9 https://doi.org/10.2516/ogst:2007060.
82. Eghon & Idigbe, *supra* n. 80, 94.

While reinjection of gas may reduce flaring and related emissions, regulation is necessary to prevent damage to the environment and ensure that reinjected gasses are not later released into the atmosphere through containment losses. For example, in the United States, injections associated with oil and gas production are regulated pursuant to Class II of the Underground Injection Control Program of the Safe Drinking Water Act. This law includes standards to assure the mechanical integrity of wells and to prevent migration of gas into underground sources of drinking water.[83] The EPA also monitors and regulates reinjection facilities under its authority in the Clean Air Act. Operators must report any losses of gas pursuant to subsection W of the greenhouse gas reporting program.[84]

The use of flare gas as an injectate is appealing because it can be done at the well site and results in both emissions reduction and resource conservation. Because the gas would remain in the subsurface, reinjection prevents the un-combusted methane and carbon dioxide bioproducts from contributing to climate and air quality issues. Where flare gas can be used in lieu of other injectates such as water, it may also result in diminished use of those resources. However, while reinjection would prevent methane losses and therefore be compatible with ambitions for net-zero upstream emissions, reinjection of flare gas alone is not commercialization. In many cases, the operator will not only bear the cost of injection but also lose the value of the injected gas. However, this may still be a preferable option where commercial utilization technologies are unavailable or where costs are lower than alternatives.

3.2 Utilization

Associated gas can also be used as a feedstock to produce value-added products such as hydrogen, graphene, and fertilizer or for electricity or heat generation. These products can support local use or development of new manufacturing facilities. While these utilization methods are proven and provide alternative markets for natural gas, currently most of them require high volumes and access to transport infrastructure to markets—the same challenges that have made the capture and transport of associated gas uneconomic. As noted by the DOE's strategy, commercialization of natural gas in the production area requires scaling technology to be transportable.

3.2.1 Hydrogen & Ammonia

Policymakers around the globe are considering hydrogen as part of the strategy to utilize decarbonized energy sources.[85] Hydrogen production has long provided a

83. United States Environmental Protection Agency, "Class II Oil and Gas Related Injection Wells" (*Underground Injection Control* (UIC), July 10, 2024) www.epa.gov/uic/class-ii-oil-and-gas-related-injection-wells accessed September 13, 2024.
84. 40 C.F.R. § 98.236 (2024) (US).
85. Commission, "A Hydrogen Strategy for a Climate-Neutral Europe" (Communication) COM (2020) 301 final; Osama Massarweh et al., "Blue Hydrogen Production from Natural Gas Reservoirs: A Review of Hydrogen Production from Natural Gas Reservoirs: A Review of

commercialization opportunity for natural gas. Most hydrogen is currently created using steam methane reforming.[86] This process involves converting natural gas into hydrogen and by-product CO_2.[87] To create blue hydrogen, the CO_2 is captured and geologically sequestered or used in EOR.[88]

Commercially developing blue hydrogen is projected to be the most successful where natural gas is low-cost and readily available, making flare gas a potentially valuable and suitable feedstock for hydrogen production.[89] However, feasibility studies examining of use of flare gas for hydrogen production thus far have focused on flares from industrial facilities and not associated gas from oil production.[90] For example, one study found that use of recovered flare gas from natural gas refineries could produce hydrogen with economically reasonable costs if the gas was both low cost and available at a high flow rate.[91] A project underway in Oman illustrates this model.[92] If developed the project will use flare gas from an ARA Petroleum refinery as a feedstock for the production of blue hydrogen which will then be used to fuel ARA Petroleum's H_2-powered field vehicles with the captured CO_2 sold to Omani industries.[93] While this project focuses on gas from refineries, it may be transferable to some oil and gas production locations. According to ARA's CEO: "One of the most robust design elements of this hybrid project is the ease to replicate the concept in other ARA Petroleum fields and any [energy and production] operation in Oman where associated gas is currently being flared."[94] Oil and gas production fields may include several attributes conducive to hydrogen production including a feedstock for natural gas, and availability of depleted formations or secondary recovery reservoirs for CO_2 sequestration.[95] Building these projects, however, will require significant new infrastructure and technology. Successfully developed blue hydrogen projects currently tend to be regional, large-scale, and based around an industrial hub, with existing pipeline-based

Application and Feasibility" (2023) 70 J. of CO_2 Utilization 2, https://doi.org/10.1016/j.jcou.2023.102438 accessed September 17, 2024.

86. Massarweh et al., *supra* n. 85, 5.
87. *Ibid.*, 2, 5. Hydrogen can also be created from autothermal reforming—a slightly different process than steam methane reforming—where a portion of the natural gas is burned to create the heat necessary for the reaction that creates hydrogen, *see*, Mohammad Moosazadeh et al., "Flare-to-Hydrogen in Oil and Gas Industries: Techno-Economic Feasibility of a Net-Negative Alternative" (2023) 300 Energy Conversion & Mgmt https://doi.org/10.1016/j.enconman.2023.117926 accessed September 17, 2024.
88. *Ibid.*
89. Kaveh Zayer Kabeh et al., "A Realistic Analysis of Hydrogen Production Based on Flare Gas Considering Life Cycle Assessment" (2023) 57 Sustainable Energy Tech. and Assessments https://doi.org/10.1016/j.seta.2023.103174 accessed September 17, 2024.
90. *Ibid.*; ARA Petroleum, "A Unique H2 Project in Oman by ARA Petroleum & Sumitomo Corporation" (May 3, 2021) https://arapetroleum.com/corporate-presentation/ accessed September 17, 2024; Sumitomo Corporation, "Commencement of Feasibility Study on Hydrogen Hybrid Project Based on Local Production and Consumption in Oman" (January 22, 2021), https://www.sumitomocorp.com/en/jp/news/release/2021/group/ accessed September 17, 2024.
91. Zayer Kabeh et al., *supra* n. 89.
92. ARA Petroleum, *supra* n. 90; Sumitomo Corporation, *supra* n. 90.
93. *Ibid.*
94. ARA Petroleum, *supra* n. 90.
95. Moosazadeh et al., *supra* n. 87, 18-19.

gas transportation infrastructure and nearby carbon sequestration facilities.[96] Because routine flaring associated with oil and gas production most often results from lack of transportation infrastructure, most oil and gas fields where associated gas is flared are unlikely to have these facilities. Gas will need to be gathered, hydrogen production facilities constructed, and storage capacity developed. Moreover, if fields were not close to industrial facilities with hydrogen demand, hydrogen transport or facilities for onsite utilization would be needed.[97] The cost of these investments may exceed that of gathering and transporting the gas to more central areas to access conventional natural gas markets as well as those for hydrogen production.

The U.S. has provided public support for research and demonstration projects and hydrogen-production tax credits to address some of these obstacles. The Bipartisan Infrastructure Law dedicated USD 8 billion to the development of regional clean hydrogen hubs.[98] Thus far, the U.S. DOE awarded funding to seven hydrogen hub projects across the U.S., four of which plan to utilize natural gas as feedstock.[99] Additionally, § 45V of the Inflation Reduction Act of 2022 supplies a tax credit of up to USD 3 per kilogram of hydrogen.[100] While these projects are not specifically oriented toward the use of associated or flare gas, financial support from these programs may help to offset the incremental costs associated with the capture and utilization of associated gas for hydrogen production. The U.S. DOE has developed additional programs authorized by the Bipartisan Infrastructure Law and IRA to support hydrogen and CO_2 transportation and the development of sequestration facilities.[101] These programs may help fill core infrastructure gaps that will ultimately improve the feasibility of associated gas utilization for hydrogen or other combustive uses.

---

96. *Ibid.*
97. Snytnikov & Potemkin, *supra* n. 76.
98. Infrastructure Investment and Jobs Act (Bipartisan Infrastructure Act), Pub. L. No. 117-58, § 813(d), 135 Stat. 429 (2021) (US).
99. The four hubs are Appalachian Hydrogen Hub, Gulf Coast Hydrogen Hub, Heartland Hydrogen Hub, and the Midwest Hydrogen Hub, however, it is unclear whether these hydrogen hubs will contribute to reducing flaring or whether associated gas would be used as feedstock. U.S. Department of Energy, "Biden-Harris Administration Announces Awards for Up to $2.2 Billion for Two Regional Clean Hydrogen Hubs to Bolster America's Global Clean Energy Competitiveness and Strengthen Our National Energy Security" (November 20, 2024) https://www.energy.gov/articles/biden-harris-administration-announces-awards-22-billion-two-regional-clean-hyd rogen-hubs accessed February 12, 2025; U.S. Department of Energy, "Appalachian Hydrogen Hub" (December 2012) https://www.energy.gov/sites/default/files/2024-12/scoping-eis-0569 -app-hub_description.pdf accessed February 12, 2025; U.S. Department of Energy, "Heartland Regional Report: Building A Clean Energy and Industrial Economy and the Supporting Role of the U.S. Department of Energy's Office of Fossil Energy and Carbon Management" (August 2024) https://www.energy.gov/sites/default/files/2024-09/Heartland%20Regional%20Repo rt.pdf accessed February 12, 2025.
100. U.S. Department of Energy, "Clean Hydrogen Production Tax Credit (45V) Resources" (January 3, 2025) https://www.energy.gov/articles/clean-hydrogen-production-tax-credit-45v-reso urces accessed January 21, 2025.
101. United States Department of Energy, "Hydrogen Program" https://www.hydrogen.energy.gov/ accessed January 29, 2024; United States Department of Energy, "DOE Announces $45 Million for Carbon Capture, Transport, and Storage to Reduce Carbon Pollution, Office of Fossil Energy and Carbon Management" (May 22, 2023) www.energy.gov/fecm/articles/doe-announces-45-million-carbon-capture-transport-and-storage-reduce-carbon-pollution accessed January 29, 2024.

Advances in technology can also address challenges associated with using associated gas for hydrogen production. In 2022, H2 Industries announced technology using pyrolysis that can convert flare gas into solid, zero-emission carbon black and clean hydrogen at the site.[102] During the same year, Levidian announced a separate deal with the UAE, whereby flare gas could be used in its loop system to create hydrogen and graphene.[103] These technologies reduce the need for carbon sequestration by utilizing the byproduct CO_2 from steam methane reforming to create value-added products. Other innovations in hydrogen production may reduce the CO_2 produced or improve capture. In March 2024, energy and petrochemical conglomerate, Shell, announced its newly developed blue hydrogen process is "[t]he most cost-effective technology for avoiding CO_2 emissions[.]"[104] According to Shell, the technologies generate blue hydrogen using partial oxidation technology instead of steam methane reforming, allowing for the capture of CO_2 "at higher pressures and at larger scales."[105] Expansion of low-carbon hydrogen availability will present additional opportunities for decarbonization of the power production and agricultural sectors as well as providing opportunities for energy storage and manufacturing. For example, hydrogen is used in the production of ammonia, which is a core component of manufacturing nitrogen fertilizers for the agricultural industry,[106] and can also be used as a low/no carbon fuel and as a medium to store and transport energy.[107] While early efforts to use associated gas as a feedstock for ammonia production stagnated,[108] new research and project announcements indicate progress. One promising study modelled the integration of flare gas feedstock to produce nitrogen fertilizer, among other things, in an algal bioproduct system.[109] Oman Shell recently initiated "Blue Horizons," a large-scale blue hydrogen and ammonia project that "aims to supply low-carbon blue

102. Michael Stusch, "Technology Company Plans to Transform Flaring Gas to Clean Hydrogen" (2022) J. of Petroleum Tech. https://jpt.spe.org/technology-company-plans-to-transform-flaring-gas-to-clean-hydrogen accessed January 29, 2024.
103. Ed Reed, *Turning Flare Gas into Hydrogen and Graphene, Levidian Seals UAE Deal,* Energy Voice, May 16, 2022, https://www.energyvoice.com/oilandgas/middle-east/411701/uae-levidian-hydrogen-flaring/.
104. Chris Egby, "The Shell Blue Hydrogen Process: The Most Cost-Effective Technology for Avoiding CO_2 Emissions" (Shell Global, March 21, 2024), www.shell.com/business-customers/catalysts-technologies/resources-library/shell-blue-hydrogen-process-cost-effective-technology-avoiding-CO2-emissions.html accessed September 11, 2024.
105. *Ibid.*
106. Hanh Nguyen, "Decarbonizing the World's Fertilizer Supply" (OCI *Global,* November 24, 2023), https://oci-global.com/news-stories/opinion/the-need-to-continue-producing-nitrogen-fertilizers-while-at-the-same-time-decarbonizing-them-is-paramount/ accessed January 29, 2024.
107. *Ibid.*
108. North Dakota—one of the U.S. states with the highest amount of flaring—found that use of associated gas as feedstock for nitrogen fertilizers was economically infeasible. Thein Maung et al., "Economics of Using Flared vs. Conventional Natural Gas to Produce Nitrogen Fertilizer: A Feasibility Analysis" (2012) N. Dakota State Univ. Dept. of Agribusiness and Applied Econ.
109. The algal bioproduct system modelled in this study was intended to produce algae meal, a protein product, and biocrude a liquid biofuel. Colin M. Beal et al., "Flare Gas Recovery for Algal Protein Production" (2016) 20 Algal Res. 142, 143 https://doi.org/10.1016/j.algal.2016.09.022.

hydrogen to local and international markets, enabled by capturing and storing carbon dioxide associated with the production process."[110]

3.3 Electricity & Heat Generation

Associated gas can also be burned for power generation. Rather than combusting the gas as a form of waste disposal, it can be burned as an alternative to more carbon-intensive fuel sources and the electricity can be sold or used on site.[111] While this process has historically been done at a large scale in natural gas power plants, new technologies may allow the electricity to be generated at the flaring site, providing more flexibility and reducing infrastructure requirements to bring the gas to market.[112] While combustion for power generation will still generate emissions, depending on the type of turbine used, converting natural gas to power may reduce some types of emissions as compared to flaring.[113] While, without sequestration, CO_2 emissions from the flare site do not decrease, the produced energy may also partially or completely negate the need to buy electricity from other sources, thereby helping to reduce overall emissions.[114]

Utilizing flare-to-power technology can be especially beneficial in countries with high quantities of associated gas and growing electric needs. For example, one study suggests that Iran could generate close to 60 billion kWh of power annually, almost enough to meet 30% of the country's power consumption.[115] Flare-to-power systems may also provide more opportunities for access where large, distributed grids are not available. For example, small communities in rural regions could use flare-to-power generation in microgrids and small local power systems that are tailored to the specific community's load and storage demands.[116] These projects can quickly become profitable, as one study projected the possibility of turning profits within five years.[117] While this may provide opportunities for local utilization, bringing excess power to other

110. Conrad Prabhu, "Oman Shell Appoints pre-FEED contractor for Blue Horizons Project" (Oman Daily Observer, July 15, 2024).
111. Paolo Iora et al., "Flare Gas Reduction Through Electricity Production" (2016) 38(21) Energy Sources, Part A: Recovery Utilization, and Environmental Effects 3116, 3123 https://doi.org/10.1080/15567036.2015.1129471.
112. *Ibid.*
113. Mahya Nezhadfard & Amirhossein Khalili-Garakani, "Power Generation as a Useful Option for Flare Gas Recovery: Enviro-Economic Evaluation of Different Scenarios" (2020) Energy 12 https://doi.org/10.1016/j.energy.2020.117940.
114. Matthias Bauer et. al., "Flare-Gas Recovery in Tunisia: From Liability to Value" (2012) 1(3) Oil and Gas Facilities, 50 https://doi.org/10.2118/155946-pa.
115. Ahmad K. Sleiti et al., "Flare Gas-to-Power by Direct Intercooled Oxy-Combustion Supercritical CO2 Power Cycles" (2021) 308 Fuel 1 https://doi.org/10.1016/j.fuel.2021.121808.
116. Oludamilare Bode Adewuyi et al., "Techno-Economic Analysis of Robust Gas-to-Power Distributed Generation Planning for Grid Stability and Environmental Sustainability in Nigeria" (2022) 55 Sustainable Energy Techn. and Assessments 3 https://doi.org/10.1016/j.seta.2022.102943.
117. Iora et al., n. 108, 3123.

markets from the oil field can be difficult.[118] Flare sites are often located in remote locations, away from electricity consumers, or in regions lacking necessary transmission infrastructure.[119] This may require the development of new energy-intensive uses that can consume excess electricity generated from associated gas power systems onsite.

Cryptocurrency production may provide one option for on-site utilization of electricity generated in flare-to-power systems. Cryptomining does not require the same grid availability or access as the production of electricity for delivery to consumers. A 2019 study estimated global energy consumption for bitcoin mining to be 87.1 TWh, equivalent to the entire electricity consumption of Chile or Belgium, resulting in significant carbon emissions annually.[120] Companies mining cryptocurrency may reduce costs by placing their facilities at oil and gas sites, negating the need for either pipeline transport or transmission.[121] One U.S.-based company, Crusoe Energy, estimates that powering its cryptomining system with flare gas onsite can reduce an oil and gas operation's CO_2 emissions by 63%.[122] Claims of emissions reductions, however, have been critiqued based on concerns regarding additionality. Some critics have argued that using flared gas encourages more CO_2 emissions by providing more incentives to continue combustion of associated gas rather than finding alternative low-carbon solutions.[123]

4 ENABLING POLICIES FOR A NO-FLARE FUTURE

Unless oil and gas production is shut-in, eliminating flaring will require policies and financing to support the technology and infrastructure necessary for natural gas capture and utilization. This requires the support of research to develop new opportunities for commercialization and infrastructure.

4.1 Support for Research and Development

Public investment in research and development will be necessary to commercialize economic technologies and processes for natural gas utilization.[124] These efforts are currently underway with public sector support. In 2019, the U.S. DOE prepared a report

118. Amirhossein Khalili-Garakani et al., "A Review on the Potentials of Flare Gas Recovery Applications in Iran" (2020) 279 J. Cleaner Production 24 https://doi.org/10.1016/j.jclepro.2020.123345.
119. *Ibid.*
120. Snytnikov & Potemkin, *supra* n. 76, 1.
121. Jennifer Vazquez & Donald Larry Crumbley, "Flare Gas Can Reduce Some Risks in Crypto Mining as Well as Oil and Gas Operations" (2022) 10 Risks 6 https://doi.org/10.3390/risks10060127.
122. *Ibid.*, 4.
123. Andrew R. Chow, "Fact-Checking 8 Claims About Crypto's Climate Impact" (Time, July 1, 2022).
124. R&D Activities Report, *supra* n. 72.

on its research and development activities for natural gas flaring and venting reduction.[125] It emphasized development of small-scale, modular systems that could be transported to the flare site and technologies that could use natural gas which would otherwise be flared as a feedstock to produce "transportable, value-added products like carbon-free fuels (e.g., hydrogen), chemicals (ammonia), and carbon materials (e.g., solid carbon)."[126] To successfully implement no-flare rules, the efforts must not only focus on innovation but also assure technology transfer to developing countries.[127] The U.S. DOE is also investing in research and development related to the transportation of CO_2 and carbon capture and sequestration, both of which will be necessary for the decarbonization of natural gas commercialization technologies.

4.2 Public Education and Outreach

Public opposition to new decarbonization technologies may make development of new infrastructure difficult. Whether associated gas is transported to market or utilized on site, new infrastructure will be needed. This includes pipelines for natural gas, CO_2, and hydrogen, powerlines, natural gas and hydrogen storage facilities, and reservoirs for geologic sequestration. Lack of local economic benefit and transparent dialogue may present challenges to projects even where there is political support.[128]

Communities have opposed pipelines due to concerns about their safety, environmental impacts, and damage to arable land, tourism impacts, and opposition to expropriation.[129] This is true even for pipelines that are intended to support decarbonization efforts. For example, following public opposition, the North Dakota Public Service Commission denied Summit Carbon Solutions' request for a route permit to build a CO_2 pipeline that would have supported decarbonization of many ethanol facilities in the midwestern United States.[130] Legal challenges to permitting and environmental assessments may be another significant obstacle.[131]

Public engagement and outreach can support increased social acceptance of decarbonization projects. In France, for example, Total led the Lacq pilot project in

125. *Ibid.*
126. *Ibid.*
127. Barbara Olfe-Kräutlein, "Advancing CCU Technologies Pursuant to the SDGs: A Challenge for Policy Making" (2020) 8 Front. Energy. Res. 198 https://doi.org/10.3389/fenrg.2020.00198; Miria Pigato, et al., "Technology Transfer and Innovation for Low-Carbon Development" (2020) The World Bank.
128. Carola Braun, "Not in My Backyard: CCS Sites and Public Perception of CCS" (2017) 37(12) Risk Analysis 22 https://doi.org/10.1111/risa.12793; Terry L. Jones, "Public Outcry Against Carbon Capture in Louisiana Growing" (New Orleans Public Radio, January 2, 2024).
129. Allessandra Bergamin, "A Pipeline Brings Gas and Revolt to Southern Italy" (In These Times, February 10, 2023); *Puntenney v. Iowa Utilities Board*, 928 N.W.2d 829 (Iowa 2019) (US).
130. State of North Dakota Public Service Commission, SCS Carbon Transport LLC, Findings of Fact, Conclusions of Law, and Order, Case No. PU-22-391 (August 4, 2023) (US).
131. Madison Hinkle and Jesse Richardson, "How Environmental Litigation has Turned Pipelines into Pipe Dreams" (2022) 52 Environmental L. Reporter 10558; Congressional Research Services, *Siting Challenges for Carbon Dioxide (CO_2) Pipelines*, IN12269 (November 30, 2023) (US).

Chapelle-de-Rousse between 2007 and 2013.[132] During that time they engaged in a dialogue with the public and stakeholders.[133] Among the topics discussed were security, land value, and image risk for agricultural products like wine.[134] During the pilot, some citizens formed an opposition group to raise their concerns about leaks, damage to clean water aquifers, seismicity, and contamination resulting from CO_2 transport.[135] Total reported that these debates ultimately improved governance of the project.[136]

Building decarbonization infrastructure like pipelines and storage resources will require reexamining the way that projects are developed, the opportunities for local participation,[137] and how the benefits of the project are equitably shared among stakeholders. Policies can help support these efforts by providing local residents with incentives to host carbon removal infrastructure, thereby assuring that communities participate in the economic benefits of the project.[138] Investments in public education about technologies and environmental safeguards may also help improve social acceptability.[139]

4.3 Management of Subsurface Resources

Requiring natural gas reinjection or carbon storage will increase competition for subsurface resources, potentially resulting in a scarcity of suitable locations for CCUS, hydrogen and natural gas storage, produced water injection, and other subsurface uses. Strategic efforts to identify and designate or regulate uses of the subsurface may therefore be necessary. This could include public investments in geologic characterization and front-end engineering design (FEED) feasibility studies related to infrastructure development to identify possible outcomes. These could then be implemented into regulations that would "zone" the subsurface based on its highest and best use.[140] Drawing from land use regulations, this could assure efficient use of the subsurface property to best achieve the common good around numerous decarbonization initiatives competing for limited resources.

132. Global CCS Institute, "Carbon Capture and Storage, The Lacq Pilot: Project and Injection Period 2006-2013" https://totalenergies.com/sites/g/files/nytnzq121/files/atoms/file/Captage-Carbon-capture-and-storage-the-Lacq-pilot.pdf accessed January 29, 2024.
133. *Ibid.*
134. Minh Ha-Duong, et al., "Social Aspects of Total's Lacq CCS Pilot Project" (Hal Open Science, 2013).
135. Sébastien Chailleux1 et Xavier Arnauld de Sartre, "L'acceptabilité au prisme du stockage géologique de CO2: retour sur un débat non émergé" (2021) 29 Natures Sciences Sociétés S12-S24.
136. Global CCS Institute, *supra* n. 132, 238.
137. EU CCUS Projects Network, "Public Perception of CCS: A review of Public Engagement for CCS Projects" (May 2020).
138. *See, e.g.*, Ashleigh Ross and Anna Littlefield, "Aligning Value with Communities: Conceptualizing a 'Carbon Steward' Federal Tax Credit" (2022) The Payne Institute for Public Policy.
139. Charli Sitinjak, et. al, "Exploring Public Attitudes and Acceptance of CCUS Technologies in JABODETABEK: A Cross-Sectional Study" (2023) 16(10) Energies 4026 https://doi.org/10.3390/en16104026.
140. Hannah Wiseman, et al., "Zoning the Subsurface" 72 UCLA L. Rev. (forthcoming 2025).

4.4 Facilitating Grid Access

Policy changes can also help encourage operators to use methane which would otherwise be flared for heat and power that can be delivered into the grid system. This could accelerate decarbonization both by eliminating flaring or venting and by offsetting other more polluting sources of generation. Policies can support this by making it easier for these projects to access electricity markets. For example, the Public Utility Regulatory Policy Act in the United States requires public utilities to purchase electricity generated from small facilities using renewable sources or waste at their avoided cost of generation.[141] However, in most situations, associated gas is not considered waste generation, and therefore a flare-to-power project would not constitute a qualified facility.[142] Enacting or revising laws to facilitate grid access for flare-to-power generators could help accelerate the use of associated gas for generation. This may have benefits in terms of reliability as well. If temporary on-site storage could be developed, it is possible that flare gas could be used as a demand-responsive, dispatchable energy resource.

4.5 Curbing Carbon Leakage

Eliminating routine flaring may increase the cost of production in remote areas without transportation infrastructure and in the time between when oil and gas is discovered and when it can be brought into production. Some projects may not be viable at current commodity prices when the additional cost of gas capture and transportation is included. This could contribute toward the non-development or early abandonment of some petroleum resources. For example, the Independent Petroleum Association of America (IPAA) estimated that the United States new methane rules will lead to the shutdown of approximately half of the nations "low production" wells.[143] To offset these impacts, policies at the national level could examine the feasibility of providing oil and gas producers with tax offsets or other incentives to cover some of the cost of reinjection.

Carbon leakage can also result between sectors, with gas utilization moving from regulated sectors to unregulated sectors. For example, the newly enacted Methane Emissions Charge imposes a fine on high-emitting oil and gas facilities within 10 segments of "petroleum and natural gas systems."[144] Utilization and power production

141. 16 U.S.C. §2601 et seq. (US).
142. John Wyeth Griggs, "Competitive Bidding and Independent Power Producers: Is Deregulation Coming to the Electric Utility Industry?" (1988) 9 Energy L. J. 415, 423.
143. Independent Petroleum Association of America, "IPAA Statement on Negative Impact of EPA Regulations Ahead of Energy and Commerce Hearing" (January 9, 2024) https://www.ipaa.org/ipaa-statement-on-negative-impact-of-epa-regulations-ahead-of-energy-and-commerce-hearing/ accessed January 29, 2024.
144. U.S. Envt'l Protection Agency, Waste Emissions Charge for Petroleum and Natural Gas Systems, Draft Proposed Rule, 27 (January 12, 2024) (US).

facilities are not covered by the emissions charge.[145] A facility that transferred the associated or flare gas for use in cryptomining or other applications could therefore potentially avoid the methane emissions charge without an actual reduction in CO_2 emissions. Addressing these gaps will require expanding emissions regulations beyond the oil and gas sectors.

Without efforts to close policy gaps in zero-routine flaring regulations, these policies may contribute towards greater carbon leakage by driving production into countries and sectors without methane regulations. While other oil-importing countries could consider implementing trade rules like those adopted in the EU, even these leave a gap for carbon leakage for non-exporters producing in unregulated countries. Accordingly, efforts to support policy development, implementation, and enforcement should be expanded. Many of these policy options can be implemented through mechanisms envisioned by the Paris Agreement. For example, adopting zero flare policies could be established as a condition to finance or foreign investment whereas technology transfer and capacity-building efforts would support feasible policy implementation.

4.6 Methane Reinjection Policies

Currently, policies in the U.S. and Canada provide incentives for the injection of CO_2, however, no equivalent policies exist for the injection of methane. The 45Q tax credit pays USD 85 per ton of CO_2 sequestered into geologic formations and USD 60 per ton of CO_2 used for EOR.[146] In some cases, the capture and re-injection of naturally occurring, pre-combustion waste CO_2 will qualify for the higher credit.[147] This credit, however, is limited only to "qualified carbon oxides" thereby excluding methane. A producer therefore could only claim the credit for disposal of associated gas if it first combusted the methane, captured the CO_2, and reinjected it. In state tax policies, similar disparities exist. For example, in Texas, an oil and gas enhanced recovery project is eligible for reduced severance taxes where it uses anthropogenic CO_2, but would not get the same benefit if it used associated methane that would otherwise have been flared or vented.[148] Harmonizing policies that encourage CO_2 injection so that they apply equally to methane reinjection may encourage investments in methane-based EOR or infrastructure to reinject associated gas that would otherwise be flared. Like the 45Q policy, these incentives could require that reinjected methane be put into permanent storage and would not be available for later use.

145. *Ibid.*
146. The 45Q tax credit was increased with the passage of the Inflation Reduction Act. I.R.C. § 45Q(a); Inflation Reduction Act of 2022, Pub. L. No. 117-169, 136 Stat. 1819 (2022) §13104 (US).
147. Tara Righetti, "Capturing All the (Tax) Credit: Carbon Capture & Storage" (2023) Envtl. L. Inst.: Vibrant Env't Blog https://www.eli.org/vibrant-environment-blog/capturing-all-tax-credit-carbon-capture-storage accessed January 29, 2024.
148. Tex. Tax Code § 202.0545 (2024) (US). In Wyoming, natural gas is exempted from production (severance) taxes whether it is flared or utilized on site, Wyo. Stat. §35-14-205 (US).

4.7 Public Investments and Incentives

Policymakers can also support natural gas commercialization through direct investment in infrastructure and creation of investment incentives. While the use of flare gas can displace current uses of natural gas as a feedstock for chemical and fuel production, developers will still need to confront issues of transportation for any products developed from flare gas and emissions either from utilization or electricity generation. Many of these projects are currently uneconomic. Public investments in physical infrastructure and the creation of investment tax incentives may encourage project development.

5 CONCLUSION

Policies enacted worldwide have targeted methane-emitting sources to disincentivize resource waste and carbon emissions caused by flaring. These efforts in response to climate change suggest an end to flaring in all but emergency circumstances. Compliance with these requirements will require new infrastructure and opportunities for natural gas commercialization, specifically in the oil field. Regulatory efforts to prohibit flaring must therefore be paired with policies to support infrastructure and the development of low-carbon opportunities for the utilization of associated gas.

Achieving this will require extensive public investments in research, infrastructure, and public education and outreach. Addressing methane emissions from the oil and gas sector, alone, however, will be insufficient. Policymakers must pair these efforts with regulations that limit carbon leakage, improve grid access, manage resource conflicts, encourage private investments, and support just siting procedures. These efforts must not only be extensive but also coordinated through capacity building and technology transfer mechanisms to assure congruent policies and capabilities.

CHAPTER 32

Reflections and Conclusions

Magnus C. Abraham-Dukuma, Opeyemi Y. Omotuyi & Eduardo G. Pereira

1 OVERVIEW

The role of natural gas in the global energy landscape is at the crossroads of climate change mitigation, energy security, and sustainable development. Throughout the chapters of this book, the complex relationship between natural gas, environmental sustainability, economic imperatives, and social impacts is examined, highlighting the urgency of addressing the ongoing issues of gas flaring, the transition to cleaner energy sources, and the need for a just and equitable energy transition. As we come to the end of the text, we would like to put the pieces together distill the key themes and provide some reflections on a path forward. This concluding chapter, therefore, integrates the key findings from the chapters, providing a comprehensive overview of the role of natural gas in the context of climate change, energy security, and sustainable development. In the next sections, we summarize some of the key observations gleaned from the jurisdictional chapters, offer some insights, and briefly discuss a path forward for abating gas flaring.

2 OBSERVATIONS FROM THE JURISDICTIONAL CHAPTERS

(1) Common Themes: Countries across the board are recognizing the environmental and economic downsides of gas flaring. International initiatives like the Zero Routine Flaring by 2030 initiative play a crucial role in guiding national policies. Most countries considered in this text are signatories to this initiative and are taking steps to reduce flaring by adopting new regulations or strengthening existing ones.

(2) Technological and Policy Solutions: Advances in technology, such as methane recovery systems, gas reinjection, and liquefied natural gas (LNG)

production, are common solutions employed by countries like Angola, Brazil, and China. Countries that can effectively combine regulatory measures with technological innovations tend to see more success in reducing flaring, as evidenced by Brazil's 45% reduction in flaring over a decade.

(3) Challenges: Countries like Iran struggle with enforcement due to economic sanctions and internal challenges, highlighting the importance of strong governance and international cooperation in reducing gas flaring. In contrast, countries like the UK and Norway, with robust governance structures, have been more successful in curbing gas flaring through stringent regulations and enforcement mechanisms. More conceptually, almost all countries are struggling with building the relevant infrastructure and establishing suitable regulatory regimes to incentivize large-scale commercialization of gas to reduce flaring. This is an area deserving further exploration and legal intervention.

(4) Economic and Environmental Trade-offs: While environmental concerns drive flaring reduction policies, economic factors—such as the cost of infrastructure for gas recovery and utilization—often influence how strictly these policies are enforced. Developing nations like Angola and Iran, which rely heavily on oil revenues, face significant trade-offs between economic growth and environmental sustainability.

3 KEY INSIGHTS

Natural Gas and Climate Change Mitigation

Natural gas occupies a unique position in the broader context of the energy transition.[1] As discussed in Chapter 2, the world faces a dual challenge: reducing greenhouse gas (GHG) emissions to mitigate the impacts of climate change while ensuring that energy remains accessible and affordable. The continuous rise in global temperatures has driven nations to adopt international frameworks such as the Paris Agreement, which sets out ambitious targets for reducing GHG emissions.

Despite the global push towards renewable energy, natural gas remains a vital component of energy strategies, particularly in developing economies where the infrastructure and financial resources for large-scale renewable energy deployment remain limited.[2] As countries like Nigeria, India, and China move towards achieving their net-zero targets by 2050 or 2060, natural gas serves as a crucial bridge fuel, providing a less carbon-intensive alternative to coal while renewable energy systems are scaled up. A lot of other countries have set climate targets, with major international

1. C. Gürsan and V. de Gooyert, "The Systemic Impact of a Transition Fuel: Does Natural Gas Help or Hinder the Energy Transition?" (2021) 138 Renewable and Sustainable Energy Reviews 110552 https://doi.org/10.1016/j.rser.2020.110552.
2. A.B. Bugaje and others, "Rethinking the Position of Natural Gas in a Low-Carbon Energy Transition" (2022) 90 Energy Research & Social Science 102604 https://doi.org/10.1016/j.erss.2022.102604.

oil and gas players gravitating towards integrated energy companies and setting ambitious net-zero targets.[3]

However, as highlighted in the discussion of gas flaring (Chapter 2 and Chapter 19), the environmental damage caused by methane emissions during natural gas extraction and flaring activities is significant. Methane, a potent GHG, contributes significantly to global warming, and thus, reducing flaring and methane leakage is critical for achieving climate goals.

Energy Security and the Energy Transition

The energy trilemma, as discussed in Chapter 3, presents a significant challenge in the global energy transition. Striking a balance between energy security, affordability, and sustainability is particularly difficult in countries with large natural gas reserves.[4] The dependence on natural gas for energy security is evident in countries like Nigeria, where the economic reliance on fossil fuels is entrenched. The recent geopolitical shifts, such as the Russia-Ukraine conflict, have further underscored the importance of natural gas as a buffer against energy crises, especially for European countries diversifying their gas sources.

Natural gas remains an essential energy source for ensuring stable electricity grids, particularly during periods of high demand or when renewable energy sources such as solar and wind are not available. This intermittent nature of renewable energy makes natural gas an indispensable element of many nations' energy security strategies, at least in the short-to-medium term.

However, as the global energy landscape continues to evolve, there is a growing recognition of the need to diversify energy sources and reduce reliance on natural gas. Technological innovations, such as carbon capture, utilization, and storage (CCUS), offer a way to mitigate the environmental impacts of natural gas while maintaining its role in energy security.

Addressing Gas Flaring: Technological, Legal and Policy Solutions

Gas flaring, the practice of burning off excess natural gas during oil extraction, is a significant contributor to GHG emissions and a major environmental concern. As described in Chapters 2, 3, and 5, this practice not only wastes valuable energy resources but also exacerbates the climate crisis by releasing large quantities of methane and carbon dioxide into the atmosphere. As discussed in Chapter 6, emissions occur in the three primary streams of the oil and gas industry: upstream (exploration and production), midstream (transportation and processing), and downstream (refining and distribution). All these streams contribute to significant GHG emissions, including carbon, methane, and other volatile organic compounds. Upstream gas flaring looms large amongst these various streams and accounts for about 75% of the

3. M.C. Abraham-Dukuma, "Dirty to Clean Energy: Exploring 'Oil and Gas Majors Transitioning'" (2021) 8:1 The Extractive Industries and Society https://doi.org/10.1016/j.exis.2021.100936.
4. I. Khan and others, "World Energy Trilemma and Transformative Energy Developments as Determinants of Economic Growth Amid Environmental Sustainability" (2022) 108 Energy Economics 105884 https://doi.org/10.1016/j.eneco.2022.105884.

emissions intensity of upstream GHG emissions. Besides flaring, fugitive emissions from leaks in infrastructure, aging oil fields, and decommissioned wells also contribute significantly to GHG emissions. Ensuring asset integrity and reducing leaks is crucial.

Reducing gas flaring is not only an environmental imperative but also an economic opportunity. The flared gas could be captured, processed, and monetized, providing a cleaner alternative to other fossil fuels and boosting local economies. However, the primary challenges to addressing gas flaring include technical, economic, and infrastructural constraints. For example, inadequate pipeline networks, high capital costs for mitigation technologies, and regulatory uncertainty make large-scale reductions in flaring difficult. These factors continue to hinder progress in this area.

Several countries have introduced policies aimed at curbing gas flaring, as seen in Nigeria's Petroleum Industry Act (2021), which seeks to replace outdated regulatory frameworks that allowed flaring under certain conditions. In addition, global initiatives such as the World Bank's Zero Routine Flaring by 2030 initiative aim to eliminate routine flaring, setting a clear path for governments and industry to follow.

Chapters 4 and 6 and several other chapters in the text clearly showcase technological advancements which offer solutions to the problem of gas flaring. Some mitigation techniques considered in these chapters are worth recapitulating. Through Advanced Process Control (APC), it is possible to improve energy efficiency and reduce flaring through software and algorithmic control. By deploying gas re-injection and carbon capture (CCUS), gas could be injected back into wells or underground formations to prevent flaring. Leak Detection and Repair (LDAR) technologies like infrared cameras and smart sensors could be used to detect and repair gas leaks, while captured gas could be commercialized and used for industrial applications, enhancing oil recovery, or manufacturing materials like petrochemicals. While these technologies are still in the early stages of development and deployment, they represent a critical tool in reducing the environmental impact of natural gas production.

In it all, law serves as a social control mechanism, dictating behavior through prescriptive or descriptive rules.[5] In the context of gas flaring, laws establish norms, backed by sanctions for non-compliance, to ensure operators follow standards that reduce emissions. From the discussion in Chapter 8, it is evident that there is a good place for robust legal frameworks and policies that encourage investment in emissions reduction technologies and incentivize best practices. Regulatory bodies need to push for more stringent enforcement to curb the prevalence of gas flaring.

While prescriptive and principles-based regulatory approaches have their place, there is a growing trend toward hybrid regulatory frameworks, which combine government oversight with self-regulation, voluntary industry actions, and market mechanisms. Decentralized regulation allows non-state actors, such as industry organizations or private companies, to play a role in setting and enforcing standards for emissions reduction. These could all be deployed thoughtfully towards addressing gas flaring and other petroleum industry-related emissions.

5. M.C. Abraham-Dukuma and others, "Improving the Climate Change Mitigation Regime of Major Emitting Countries: The Case of South Africa, China, Germany and the United States of America" (2022) Environmental Policy and Governance https://doi.org/10.1002/eet.1961.

However, effectively regulating gas flaring also requires robust systems for monitoring emissions, collecting data, and ensuring compliance. Examples include metering systems, LDAR programs and strict penalties for non-compliance. Overall, laws and regulations are critical to mitigate gas flaring, but their effectiveness depends on proper enforcement, strong legal frameworks, and cooperation between governments, industries, and international organizations.

Energy Justice and Equity

A significant theme across the chapters is the concept of energy justice, which seeks to ensure that the benefits of the energy transition are distributed equitably and that vulnerable communities are not disproportionately affected by the negative impacts of energy production. This is particularly important in the context of natural gas, where the environmental damage caused by flaring and other extraction processes often impacts marginalized communities living near oil and gas fields.

As discussed in Chapter 17, lawsuits and public opposition to gas flaring in countries like Nigeria and Ecuador have highlighted the need for stronger regulatory frameworks to protect the rights of these communities. Energy justice also intersects with broader social and environmental issues, such as health risks from air pollution, loss of agricultural productivity, and displacement caused by environmental degradation.

The transition away from fossil fuels, including natural gas, must therefore be managed in a way that is socially just. This means ensuring that workers in the fossil fuel industry are retrained for jobs in the renewable energy sector, that communities dependent on fossil fuel revenues are supported during the transition, and that the benefits of clean energy are accessible to all.

ESG Agenda, Disputes and Future Scenarios for Natural Gas

The environmental, social, and governance (ESG) agenda has become an increasingly important consideration for natural gas companies as they seek to align their operations with global sustainability goals.[6] As explored in Chapter 29, ESG principles require companies to address not only their environmental impacts but also their social responsibilities and governance structures.

For natural gas producers, this means investing in cleaner technologies, such as CCUS and renewable energy projects, as well as ensuring that their operations do not harm local communities. Transparent reporting, stakeholder engagement, and adherence to international best practices are essential for maintaining a social license to operate in a rapidly changing energy landscape.

From the discussion in Chapter 30, we understand that there are potential disputes surrounding natural gas flaring. These disputes could be multi-faceted and multi-dimensional. Commercial disputes often arise due to royalty and contractual

6. H. Ahmad, M. Yaqub, and S. Hwan Lee, "Environmental-, Social-, and Governance-Related Factors for Business Investment and Sustainability: A Scientometric Review of Global Trends" (2023) 26 Environ Dev Sustain 2965-2987 https://doi.org/10.1007/s10668-023-02921-x.

conflicts and waste of resources. Disputes often arise between landowners or governments and oil and gas operators regarding the value and royalties of flared gas. Discrepancies in interpreting contractual terms like "produced" and "used" have led to litigation. For example, disputes in areas like Texas and Utah have centered on whether royalties are owed for flared gas. Commercial disagreements also stem from operators prioritizing oil production over the utilization of natural gas, often leading to excessive flaring, which stakeholders view as wasteful.

Health, safety, and environmental disputes arise broadly due to health impacts and environmental concerns. Many disputes revolve around health hazards caused by flaring, such as respiratory problems and lower crop yields. Cases in Nigeria, Ecuador, and Iraq highlight communities or individuals seeking justice for the health impacts of prolonged flaring activities. Additionally, flaring contributes to air pollution and global warming, as it releases carbon and methane. Several environmental groups have filed lawsuits against oil and gas operators, citing environmental regulations, such as the Clean Air Act in the United States, to push for stricter control over flaring practices.

Governmental and regulatory actions are also often the subject matter of disputes. Governments and regulatory bodies, like the U.S. Environmental Protection Agency (EPA) and the North Sea Transition Authority (UK), act against operators who violate flaring regulations. These actions often result in penalties or mandates to reduce flaring in line with environmental goals, such as the UK's push to eliminate routine flaring by 2030.

Furthermore, international legal disputes could arise from climate agreements and international conventions. International agreements, such as the Kyoto Protocol and the United Nations Framework Convention on Climate Change (UNFCCC), create legal frameworks for reducing GHG emissions, including those from flaring. Countries failing to meet these obligations could face international disputes. Also, the 1982 United Nations Convention on the Law of the Sea, obliges nations to regulate pollution from seabed activities, including flaring, leading to potential international disputes over marine pollution and flaring.

Disputes can lead to improvements in flaring practices, pushing companies to adopt more efficient technologies or methods to capture and utilize gas. For instance, Angola's efforts to capture flared gas for economic benefit show how disputes can drive innovation and infrastructure development. However, flaring disputes may affect the economic viability of oil fields, especially in areas with poor infrastructure, leading to delayed production or the abandonment of mature fields.

Looking to the future, Chapter 31 provides an overview of possible scenarios for natural gas commercialization. As the world transitions to cleaner energy sources, natural gas will likely play a diminishing role in the global energy mix. However, its role as a transitional fuel, combined with innovations in carbon capture and hydrogen production, suggests that natural gas could continue to be a significant part of the energy landscape for decades to come,[7] particularly in countries that lack the financial and technological capacity to rapidly scale up renewable energy production.

7. McKinsey & Company, Global Energy Perspective 2024 (McKinsey & Company September 2024), available online at https://www.mckinsey.com, at 9, 26-28.

4 A PATH FORWARD

In conclusion, natural gas occupies a pivotal position in the global energy transition, serving as both a critical energy source and a significant environmental challenge. The chapters in this book demonstrate the complexity of managing natural gas resources in a way that balances economic development, energy security, and environmental sustainability.

Managing gas flaring is a complex issue that requires a combination of strong legal frameworks, technological innovation, and economic incentives. While many countries have implemented regulatory frameworks to reduce gas flaring, success varies based on enforcement, economic incentives, and infrastructure investment. Countries like Norway and Qatar have made significant progress by combining strict regulations with economic instruments and technological investments. Others, like Venezuela and Iran, face structural challenges that hinder their ability to fully control flaring. The United States and Nigeria have made progress through state-level regulations and market-driven approaches, but both still face regional challenges. Moving forward, greater international cooperation and alignment with global initiatives like the Zero Routine Flaring by 2030 will be crucial to achieving significant reductions in gas flaring worldwide.

While natural gas will continue to play an important role in the global energy mix in the near term, the long-term goal must be to transition to cleaner energy sources. This will require significant investments in renewable energy infrastructure, as well as the development and deployment of technologies like CCUS to mitigate the environmental impact of natural gas production.

Governments, industry, and civil society must work together to ensure that the energy transition is not only environmentally sustainable but also socially just, providing opportunities for all communities to benefit from the clean energy future. By addressing the challenges of gas flaring, methane emissions, and energy justice, the natural gas sector can contribute to a more sustainable and equitable energy system for the future.

ENERGY AND ENVIRONMENTAL LAW & POLICY SERIES

1. Stephen J. Turner, *A Substantive Environmental Right: An Examination of the Legal Obligations of Decision-makers towards the Environment*, 2009 (ISBN 978-90-411-2815-7).
2. Helle Tegner Anker, Birgitte Egelund Olsen & Anita Rønne (eds), *Legal Systems and Wind Energy: A Comparative Perspective*, 2009 (ISBN 978-90-411-2831-7).
3. David Langlet, *Prior Informed Consent and Hazardous Trade: Regulating Trade in Hazardous Goods at the Intersection of Sovereignty, Free Trade and Environmental Protection*, 2009 (ISBN 978-90-411-2821-8).
4. Louis J. Kotzé and Alexander R. Paterson (eds), *The Role of the Judiciary in Environmental Governance: Comparative Perspectives*, 2009 (ISBN 978-90-411-2708-2).
5. Tuula Honkonen, *The Common but Differentiated Responsibility Principle in Multilateral Environmental Agreement's: Regulatory and Policy Aspects*, 2009 (ISBN 978-90-411-3153-9).
6. Barbara Pozzo (ed.), *The Implementation of the Seveso Directives in an Enlarged Europe: A Look into the Past and a challenge for the Future*, 2009 (ISBN 978-90-411-2854-6).
7. Henrik M. Inadomi, *Independent Power Projects in Developing Countries: Legal Investment Protection and Consequences for Development*, 2010 (ISBN 978-90-411-3178-2).
8. Nahid Islam, *The Law of Non-Navigational Uses of International Watercourses: Options for Regional Regime-Building in Asia*, 2010 (ISBN 978-90-411-3196-6).
9. Yasuhiro Shigeta, *International Judicial Control of Environmental Protection: Standard Setting, Compliance Control and the Development of International Environmental Law by the International Judiciary*, 2010 (ISBN 978-90-411-3151-5).
10. Katleen Janssen, *The Availability of Spatial and Environmental Data in the European Union: At the Crossroads between Public and Economic Interests*, 2010 (ISBN 978-90-411-3287-1).
11. Henrik Bjørnebye, *Investing in EU Energy Security: Exploring the Regulatory Approach to Tomorrow's Electricity Production*, 2010 (ISBN 978-90-411-3118-8).
12. Véronique Bruggeman, *Compensating catastrophe victims: A Comparative Law and Economics Approach*, 2010 (ISBN 978-90-411-3263-5).
13. Michael G. Faure, Han Lixin & Shan Hongjun, *Maritime Pollution Liability and Policy: China, Europe and the US*, 2010 (ISBN 978-90-411-2869-0).

14. Anton Ming-Zhi Gao, *Regulating Gas Liberalization: A Comparative Study on Unbundling and Open Access Regimes in the US, Europe, Japan, South Korea and Taiwan*, 2010 (ISBN 978-90-411-3347-2).
15. Mustafa Erkan, *International Energy Investment Law: Stability through Contractual Clauses*, 2011 (ISBN 978-90-411-3411-0).
16. Levente Borzsa´k, *The Impact of Environmental Concerns on the Public Enforcement Mechanism under EU law: Environmental protection in the 25th hour*, 2011 (ISBN 978-90-411-3408-0).
17. Tarcísio Hardman Reis, *Compensation for Environmental Damages under International Law: The Role of the International Judge*, 2011 (ISBN 978-90-411-3437-0).
18. Kim Talus, *Vertical Natural Gas Transportation Capacity, Upstream Commodity Contracts and EU Competition Law*, 2011 (ISBN 978-90-411-3407-3).
19. WangHui, *Civil Liability for Marine Oil Pollution Damage: A Comparative and Economic Study of the International, US and Chinese Compensation Regime*, 2011 (ISBN 978-90-411-3672-5).
20. Chowdhury Ishrak Ahmed Siddiky, *Cross-Border Pipeline Arrangements: What Would a Single Regulatory Framework Look Like?*, 2012 (ISBN 978-90-411-3844-6).
21. Rozeta Karova, *Liberalization of Electricity Markets and Public Service Obligations in the Energy Community*, 2012 (ISBN 978-90-411-3849-1).
22. Sandra Cassotta, *Environmental Damage and Liability Problems in a Multilevel Context: The Case of the Environmental Liability Directive*, 2012 (ISBN 978-90-411-3830-9).
23. Mark Wilde, *Civil Liability for Environmental Damage: Comparative Analysis of Law and Policy in Europe and US*, 2013 (ISBN 978-90-411-3233-8).
24. Bernard Taverne, *Petroleum, Industry and Governments: A Study of the Involvement of Industry and Governments in Exploring for and Producing Petroleum*, Fourth Edition, 2022 (ISBN 978-94-035-3230-1).
25. Anton Ming-Zhi Gao & Chien Te Fan (eds), *Legal Issues of Renewable Energy in the Asia Region: Recent Developments in a Post-Fukushima and Post-Kyoto Protocol Era*, 2014 (ISBN 978-90-411-4856-8).
26. Sabina Manea, *The Instrumentalization of Property: Legal Interests in the EU Emissions Trading System*, 2014 (ISBN 978-90-411-5420-0).
27. Joseph A. Tolorunse, *Protection of Property Rights in Discovered Petroleum Reservoirs*, 2014 (ISBN 978-90-411-5604-4).
28. Katelijn Van Hende, *Offshore Wind in the European Union: Towards Integrated Management of Our Marine Waters*, 2015 (ISBN 978-90-411-5613-6).
29. Ken'ichi Matsumoto & Anton Ming-Zhi Gao (eds), *Economic Instruments to Combat Climate Change in Asian Countries*, 2015 (ISBN 978-90-411-5408-8).

30. Eduardo G. Pereira & Damilola S. Olawuyi (eds), *Practical Considerations to Negotiate an Enforceable Joint Operating Agreement under Civil Law Jurisdictions*, Second Edition, 2020 (ISBN 978-94-035-0664-7).
31. Ying Shen, *China's Way to Carbon Emissions Reduction: The Choice of Regulatory Instruments and Its Legal Challenges*, 2015 (ISBN 978-90-411-6049-2).
32. Roy Andrew Partain, *Environmental Hazards from Offshore Methane Hydrate Operations: Civil Liability and Regulations for Efficient Governance*, 2017 (ISBN 978-90-411-8730-7).
33. Anton Ming-Zhi Gao & Chien-Te Fan (eds), *The Development of a Comprehensive Legal Framework for the Promotion of Offshore Wind Power: The Lessons from Europe and Pacific Asia*, 2017 (ISBN 978-90-411-8397-2).
34. Tade Oyewunmi, *Regulating Gas Supply to Power Markets: Transnational Approaches to Competitiveness and Security of Supply*, 2018 (ISBN 978-90-411-9869-3).
35. Huseyin Cagri Corlu, *Application of Anti-manipulation Law to EU Wholesale Energy Markets and Its Interplay with EU Competition Law*, 2018 (ISBN 978-90-411-9603-3).
36. Kaisa Huhta, *Capacity Mechanisms in EU Energy Law: Ensuring Security of Supply in the Energy Transition*, 2019 (ISBN 978-94-035-1451-2).
37. Maria João C. Pereira Rolim, *Reconciling Energy, the Environment and Sustainable Development: The Role of Law and Regulation*, 2019 (ISBN 978-94-035-1461-1).
38. Eduardo G. Pereira, Alexandra Wawryk, Heike Trischmann, Catherine Banet & Keith B. Hall (eds), *The Regulation of Decommissioning, Abandonment and Reuse Initiatives in the Oil and Gas Industry: From Obligation to Opportunities*, 2020 (ISBN 978-94-035-0693-7).
39. Rasa Engstedt, *Handbook on European Nuclear Law: Competences of the Euratom Community under the Euratom Treaty*, 2021 (ISBN 978-94-035-2830-4).
40. Cinzia Caporale, Ilja Richard Pavone & Maria Pia Ragionieri (eds), *International Food Law: How Food Law can Balance Health, Environment and Animal Welfare*, 2021 (ISBN 978-94-035-1761-2).
41. Rafael Leal-Arcas, *Climate Clubs for a Sustainable Future: The Role of International Trade and Investment Law*, 2021 (ISBN 978-94-035-3715-3).
42. Wang Xi & Richard Ottinger, *A Tale of Two Cities: A Comparison of Air Pollution Governance in the Los Angeles Area of the USA and the Beijing-Tianjin-Hebei Area of China*, 2024 (ISBN 978-94-035-4237-9).
43. Nina Claudia Miron & Liam Cashman, *European Union Case Law on the Birds and Habitats Directives*, 2024 (ISBN 978-94-035-2557-0).
44. Eduardo G. Pereira, Magnus C. Abraham-Dukuma & Opeyemi Y. Omotuyi (eds), *Natural Gas Flaring & Energy Transition: Laws, Policies and Regulations*, 2025 (ISBN 978-94-035-2617-1).

www.ingramcontent.com/pod-product-compliance
Lightning Source LLC
Chambersburg PA
CBHW071235230926
51849CB00001B/111
* 9 7 8 9 4 0 3 5 2 6 1 7 1 *